ATTACK on TITAN JUNIOR HIGH

4

SAKI NAKAGAWA

Based on "Attack on Titan" by
HAJIME ISAYAMA

Contents

SCHEDULE FOR TUESDAY, DECEMBER 25

PETRA

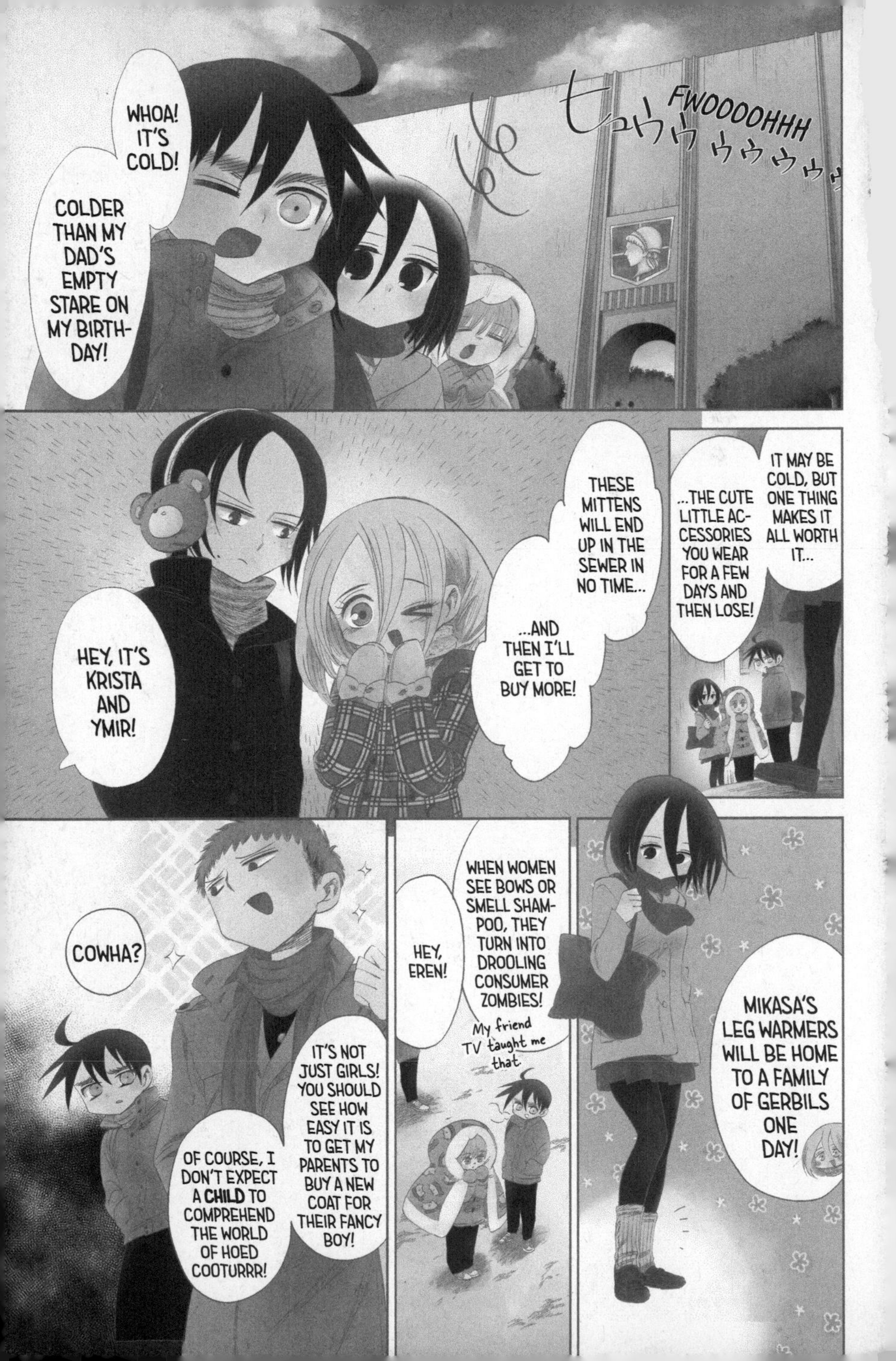
FWOOOOHHH
WHOA! IT'S COLD!
COLDER THAN MY DAD'S EMPTY STARE ON MY BIRTH-DAY!
IT MAY BE COLD, BUT ONE THING MAKES IT ALL WORTH IT...
...THE CUTE LITTLE AC-CESSORIES YOU WEAR FOR A FEW DAYS AND THEN LOSE!
THESE MITTENS WILL END UP IN THE SEWER IN NO TIME...
...AND THEN I'LL GET TO BUY MORE!
HEY, IT'S KRISTA AND YMIR!
MIKASA'S LEG WARMERS WILL BE HOME TO A FAMILY OF GERBILS ONE DAY!
WHEN WOMEN SEE BOWS OR SMELL SHAM-POO, THEY TURN INTO DROOLING CONSUMER ZOMBIES!
HEY, EREN!
My friend TV taught me that.
COWHA?
IT'S NOT JUST GIRLS! YOU SHOULD SEE HOW EASY IT IS TO GET MY PARENTS TO BUY A NEW COAT FOR THEIR FANCY BOY!
OF COURSE, I DON'T EXPECT A **CHILD** TO COMPREHEND THE WORLD OF HOED COOTURRR!

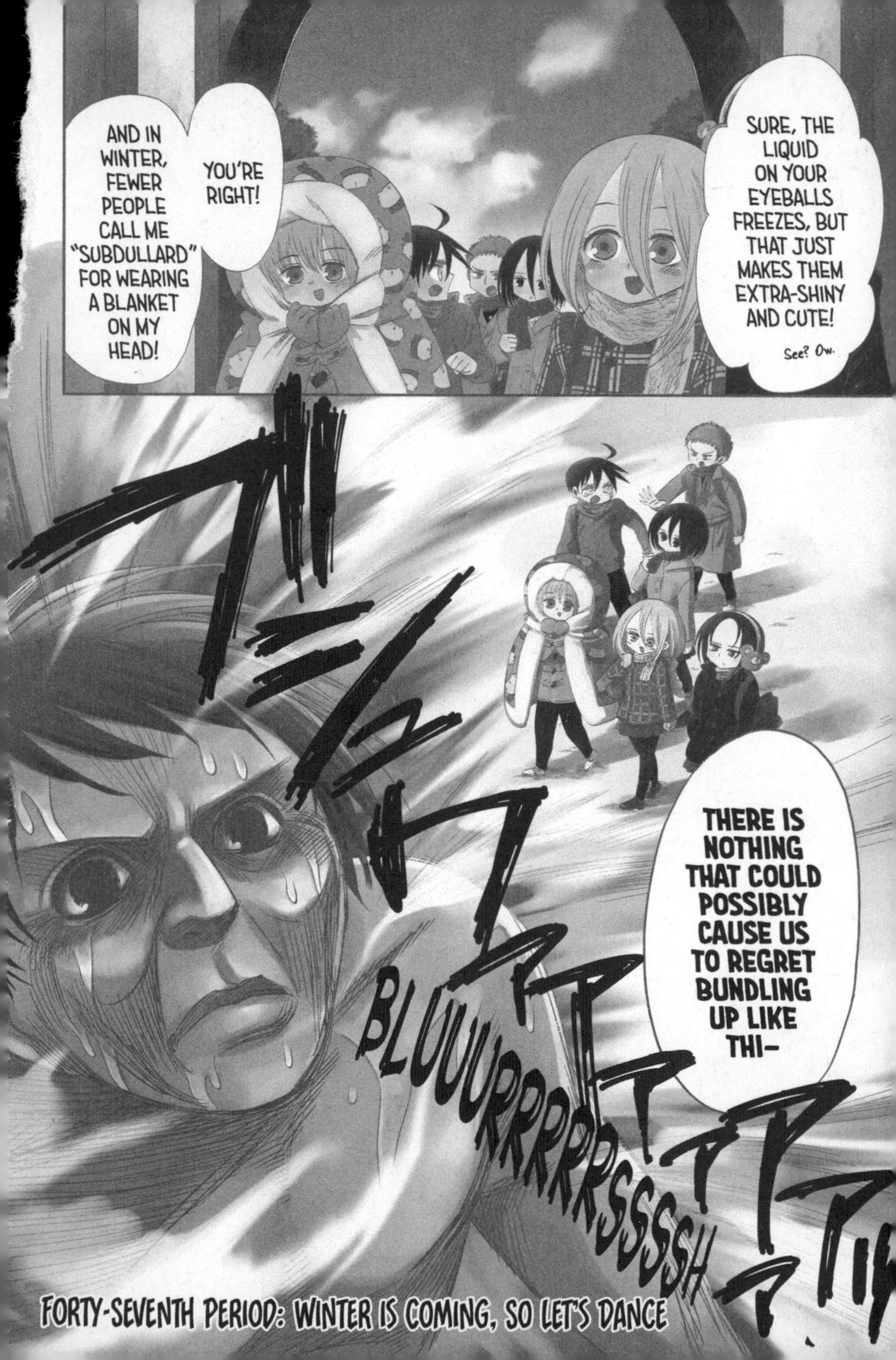
SURE, THE LIQUID ON YOUR EYEBALLS FREEZES, BUT THAT JUST MAKES THEM EXTRA-SHINY AND CUTE!
See? Ow.
YOU'RE RIGHT!
AND IN WINTER, FEWER PEOPLE CALL ME "SUBDULLARD" FOR WEARING A BLANKET ON MY HEAD!
THERE IS NOTHING THAT COULD POSSIBLY CAUSE US TO REGRET BUNDLING UP LIKE THI–
BLUUURRRRRSSSSSH

FORTY-SEVENTH PERIOD: WINTER IS COMING, SO LET'S DANCE

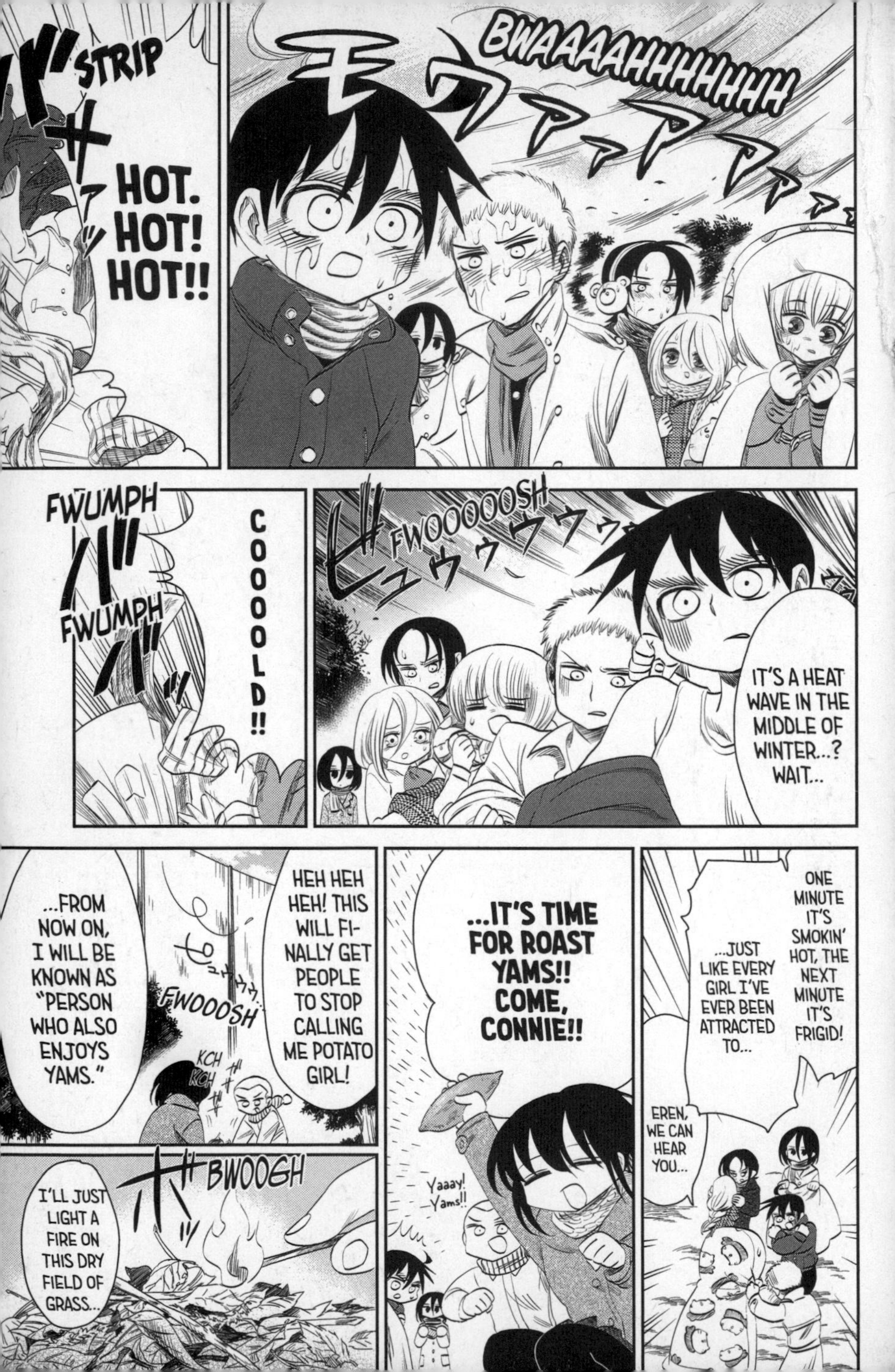
BWAAAAHHHHHHH
STRIP
HOT. HOT! HOT!!
FWOOOOOSH
IT'S A HEAT WAVE IN THE MIDDLE OF WINTER...? WAIT...
FWUMPH
FWUMPH
COOOOOLD!!
ONE MINUTE IT'S SMOKIN' HOT, THE NEXT MINUTE IT'S FRIGID!
...JUST LIKE EVERY GIRL I'VE EVER BEEN ATTRACTED TO...
EREN, WE CAN HEAR YOU...
...IT'S TIME FOR ROAST YAMS!! COME, CONNIE!!
Yaaay! Yams!!
HEH HEH HEH! THIS WILL FI-NALLY GET PEOPLE TO STOP CALLING ME POTATO GIRL!
...FROM NOW ON, I WILL BE KNOWN AS "PERSON WHO ALSO ENJOYS YAMS."
FWOOOSH
KCH KCH
BWOOGH
I'LL JUST LIGHT A FIRE ON THIS DRY FIELD OF GRASS...

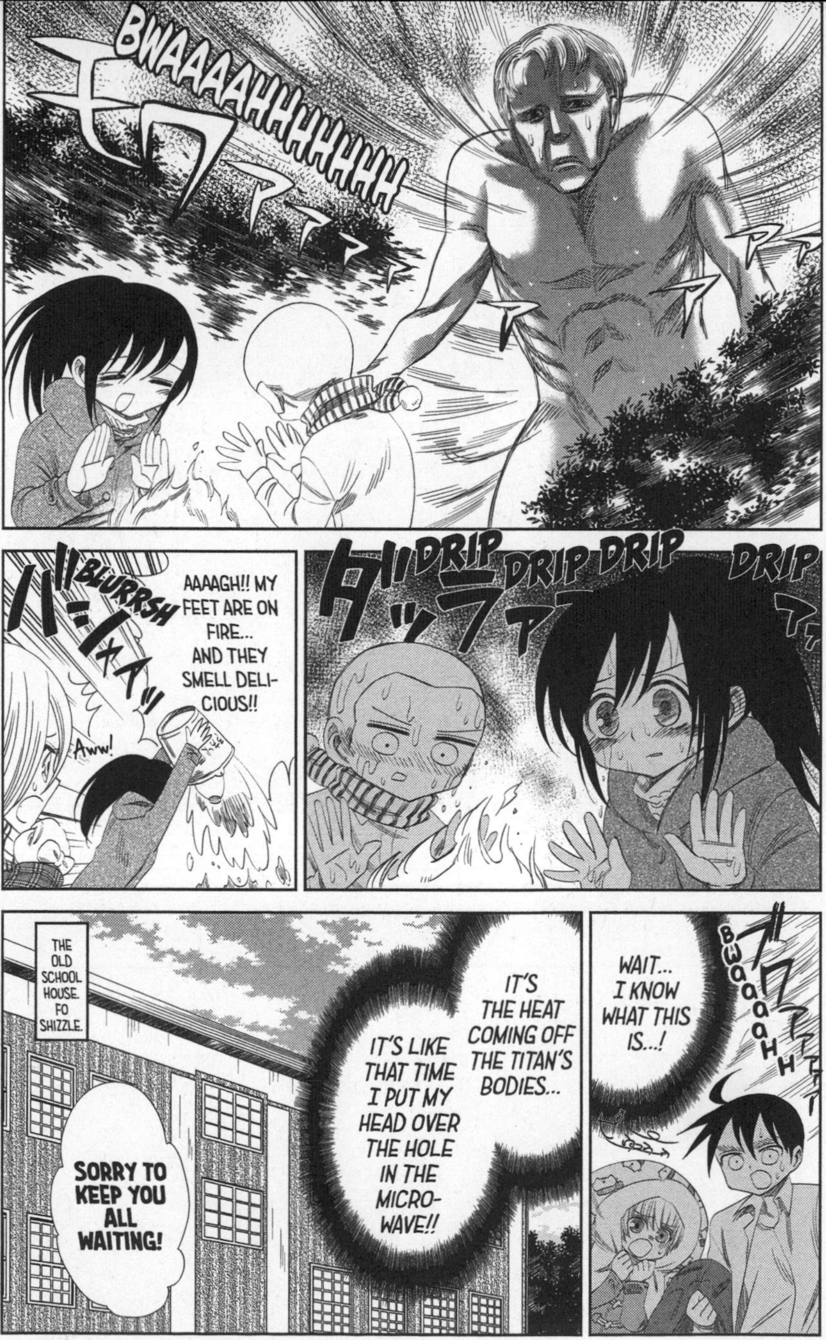
BWAAAAAHHHHHHHH
DRIP
DRIP
DRIP
DRIP
BLURRSH
AAAAGH!! MY FEET ARE ON FIRE... AND THEY SMELL DELI-CIOUS!!
Aww!
BWaaaaAHH
WAIT... I KNOW WHAT THIS IS...!
IT'S THE HEAT COMING OFF THE TITAN'S BODIES...
IT'S LIKE THAT TIME I PUT MY HEAD OVER THE HOLE IN THE MICRO-WAVE!!
THE OLD SCHOOL HOUSE. FO SHIZZLE.
SORRY TO KEEP YOU ALL WAITING!

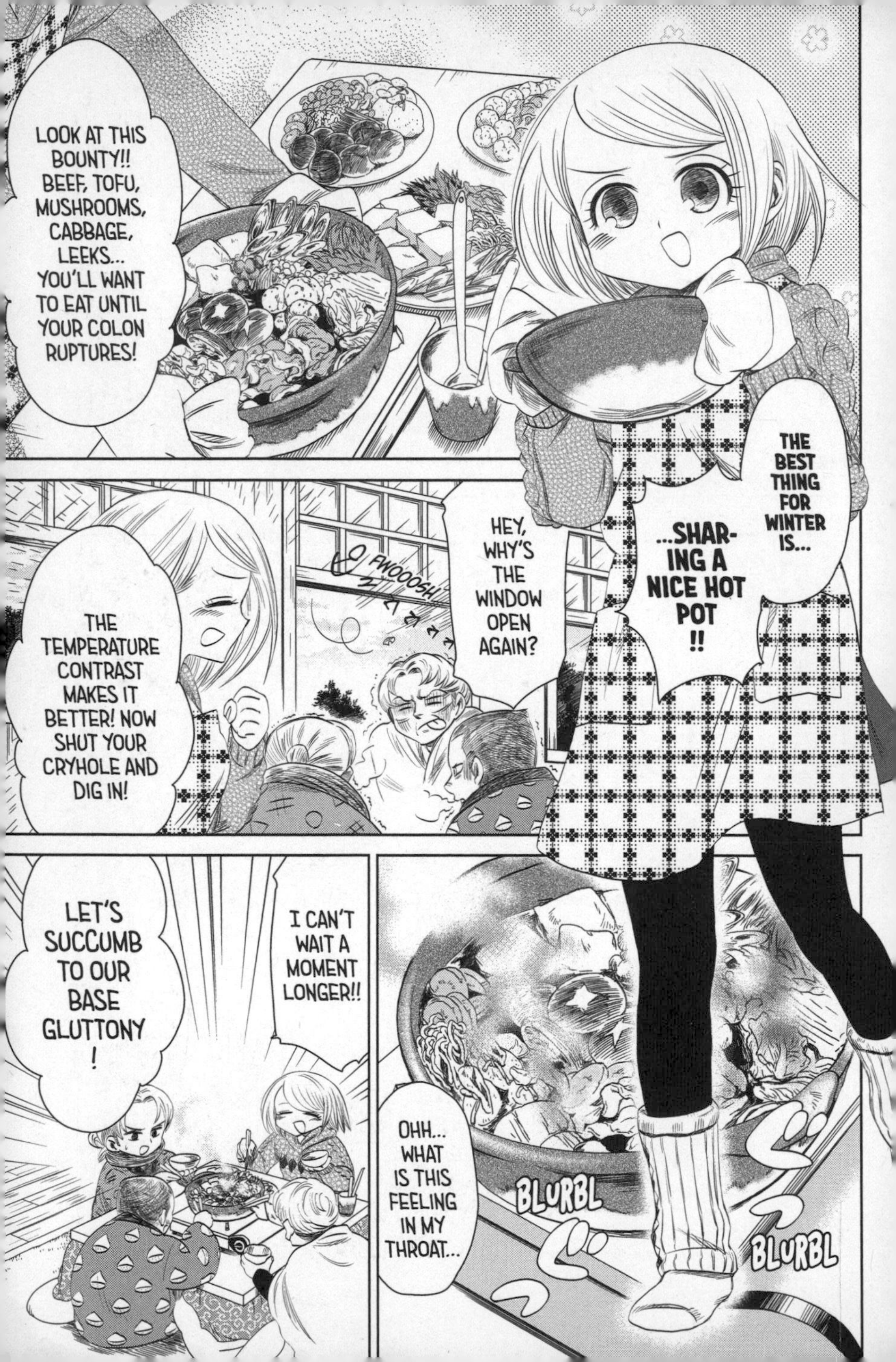
THE BEST THING FOR WINTER IS...
...SHAR-ING A NICE HOT POT !!
LOOK AT THIS BOUNTY!! BEEF, TOFU, MUSHROOMS, CABBAGE, LEEKS... YOU'LL WANT TO EAT UNTIL YOUR COLON RUPTURES!
HEY, WHY'S THE WINDOW OPEN AGAIN?
FWOOOSH
THE TEMPERATURE CONTRAST MAKES IT BETTER! NOW SHUT YOUR CRYHOLE AND DIG IN!
BLURBL
BLURBL
OHH... WHAT IS THIS FEELING IN MY THROAT...
I CAN'T WAIT A MOMENT LONGER!!
LET'S SUCCUMB TO OUR BASE GLUTTONY !

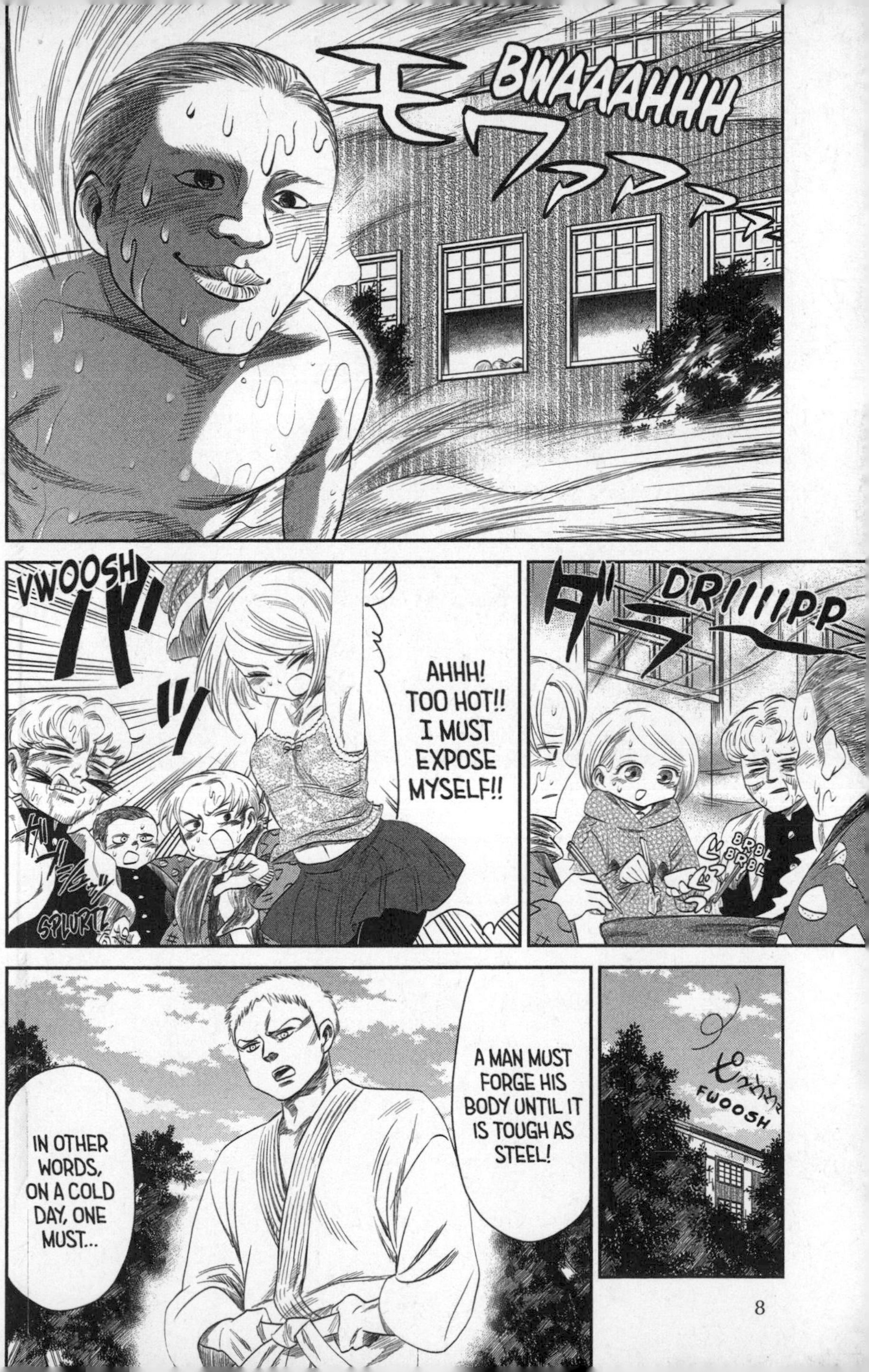
BWAAAHHH
DRIIIIPP
BRBL BRBL
VWOOSH
AHHH! TOO HOT!! I MUST EXPOSE MYSELF!!
SPLURT
FWOOSH
A MAN MUST FORGE HIS BODY UNTIL IT IS TOUGH AS STEEL!
IN OTHER WORDS, ON A COLD DAY, ONE MUST...

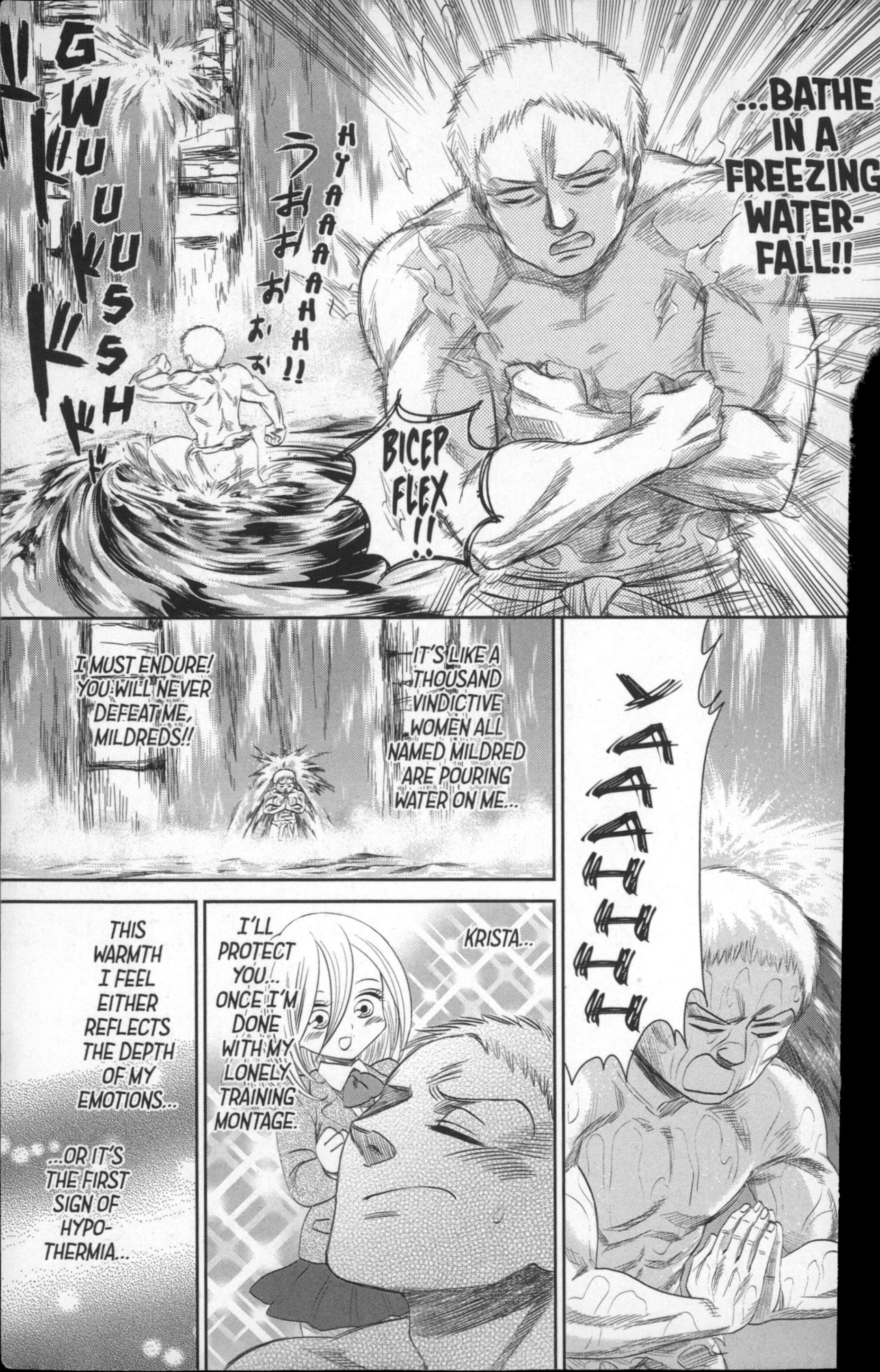

...BATHE IN A FREEZING WATER-FALL!!
BICEP FLEX!!
HYAAAAAHH!!
うおおおお
GWUUUUSSHH
ドドドドド
YAAAIIII
IT'S LIKE A THOUSAND VINDICTIVE WOMEN ALL NAMED MILDRED ARE POURING WATER ON ME...
I MUST ENDURE! YOU WILL NEVER DEFEAT ME, MILDREDS!!
KRISTA...
I'LL PROTECT YOU... ONCE I'M DONE WITH MY LONELY TRAINING MONTAGE.
THIS WARMTH I FEEL EITHER REFLECTS THE DEPTH OF MY EMOTIONS...
...OR IT'S THE FIRST SIGN OF HYPO-THERMIA...

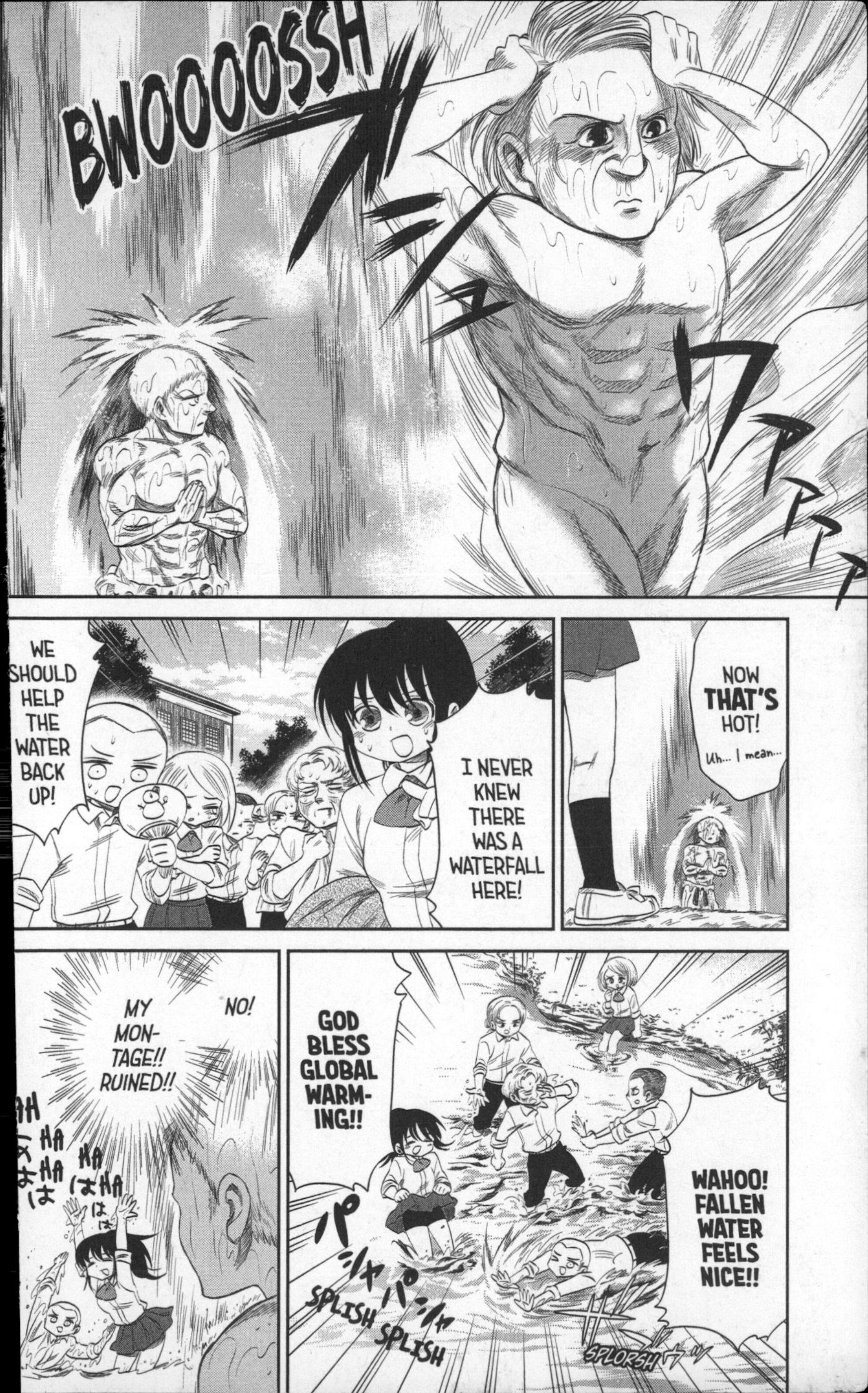
BWOOOOSSH
NOW THAT'S HOT!
Uh... I mean...
I NEVER KNEW THERE WAS A WATERFALL HERE!
WE SHOULD HELP THE WATER BACK UP!
WAHOO! FALLEN WATER FEELS NICE!!
GOD BLESS GLOBAL WARMING!!
SPLISH SPLISH
SPLORSH
NO!
MY MON-TAGE!! RUINED!!
HA HA HA HA

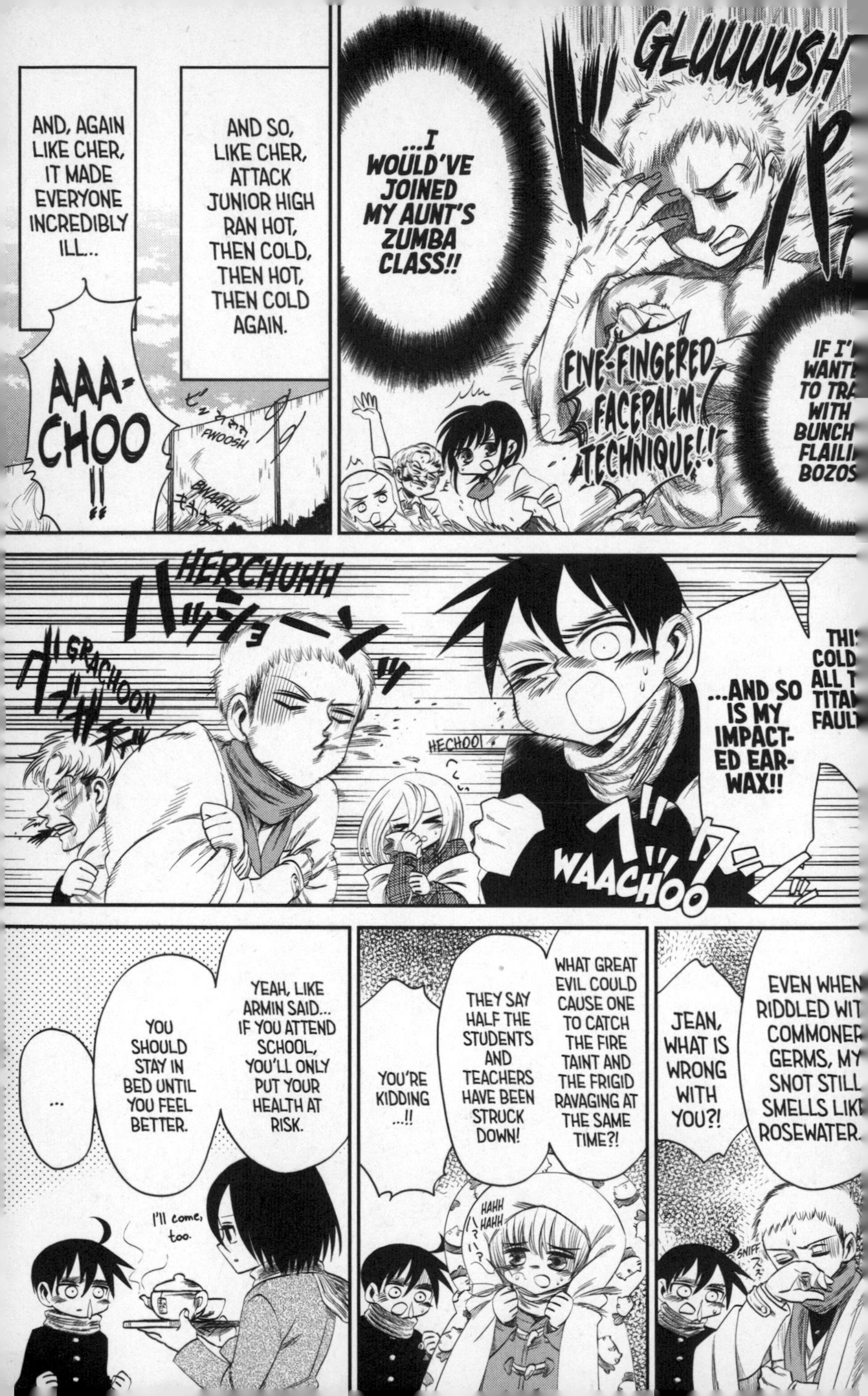
GLUUUUSH
IF I' WANTE TO TRA WITH BUNCH FLAILI BOZOS
...I WOULD'VE JOINED MY AUNT'S ZUMBA CLASS!!
FIVE-FINGERED FACEPALM TECHNIQUE!!
AND SO, LIKE CHER, ATTACK JUNIOR HIGH RAN HOT, THEN COLD, THEN HOT, THEN COLD AGAIN.
AND, AGAIN LIKE CHER, IT MADE EVERYONE INCREDIBLY ILL...
FWOOSH
AAA-CHOO!!
THIS COLD ALL T TITA FAULT
...AND SO IS MY IMPACTED EARWAX!!
WAACHOO
HECHOO!
HERCHUHH
GRACHOON
EVEN WHEN RIDDLED WIT COMMONER GERMS, MY SNOT STILL SMELLS LIK ROSEWATER.
JEAN, WHAT IS WRONG WITH YOU?!
SNIFF
WHAT GREAT EVIL COULD CAUSE ONE TO CATCH THE FIRE TAINT AND THE FRIGID RAVAGING AT THE SAME TIME?!
THEY SAY HALF THE STUDENTS AND TEACHERS HAVE BEEN STRUCK DOWN!
YOU'RE KIDDING ...!!
HAHH HAHH
YEAH, LIKE ARMIN SAID... IF YOU ATTEND SCHOOL, YOU'LL ONLY PUT YOUR HEALTH AT RISK.
YOU SHOULD STAY IN BED UNTIL YOU FEEL BETTER.
...
I'll come, too.

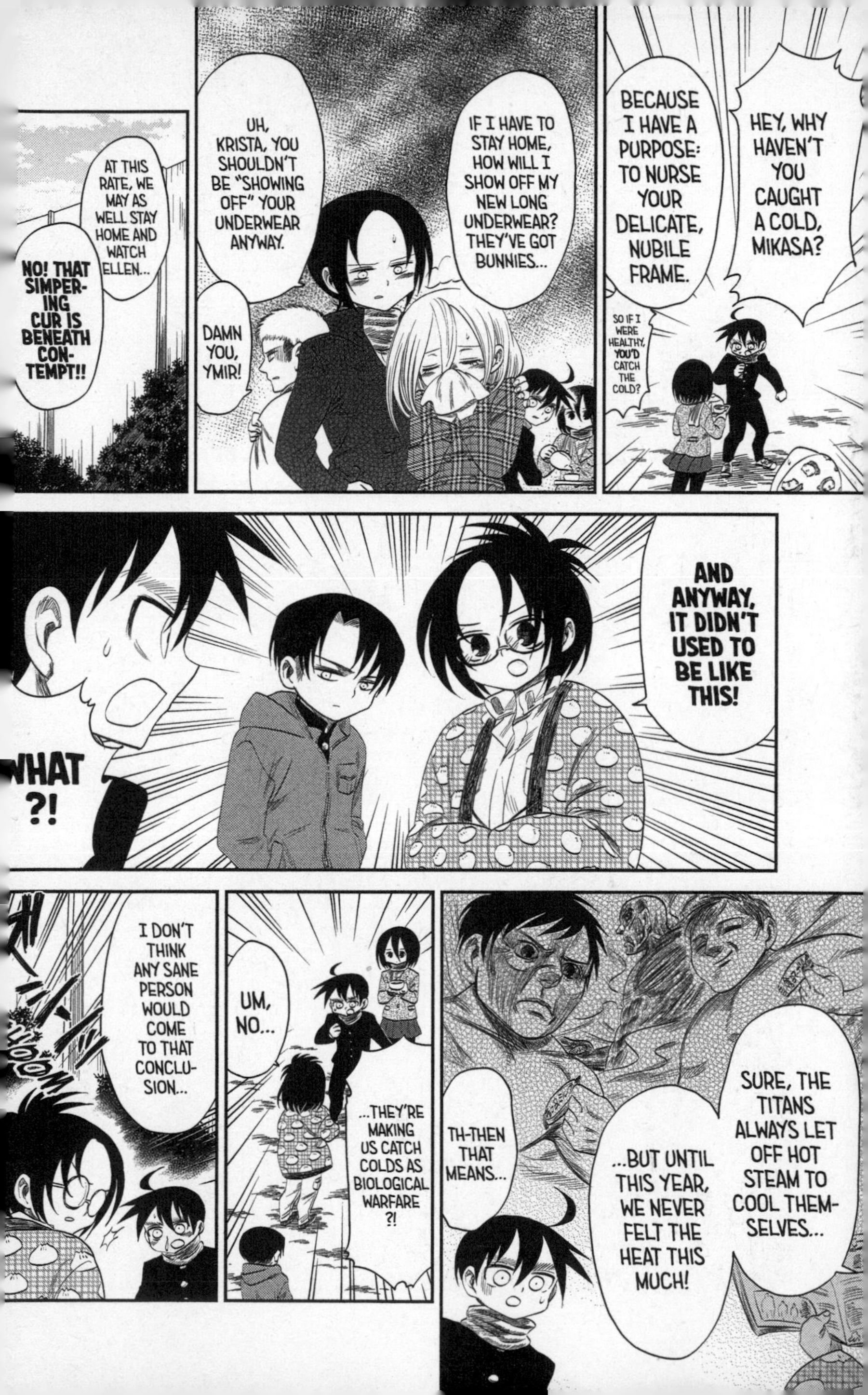
HEY, WHY HAVEN'T YOU CAUGHT A COLD, MIKASA?
BECAUSE I HAVE A PURPOSE: TO NURSE YOUR DELICATE, NUBILE FRAME.
SO IF I WERE HEALTHY, YOU'D CATCH THE COLD?
IF I HAVE TO STAY HOME, HOW WILL I SHOW OFF MY NEW LONG UNDERWEAR? THEY'VE GOT BUNNIES...
UH, KRISTA, YOU SHOULDN'T BE "SHOWING OFF" YOUR UNDERWEAR ANYWAY.
DAMN YOU, YMIR!
AT THIS RATE, WE MAY AS WELL STAY HOME AND WATCH ELLEN...
NO! THAT SIMPERING CUR IS BENEATH CONTEMPT!!
AND ANYWAY, IT DIDN'T USED TO BE LIKE THIS!
WHAT ?!
SURE, THE TITANS ALWAYS LET OFF HOT STEAM TO COOL THEMSELVES...
...BUT UNTIL THIS YEAR, WE NEVER FELT THE HEAT THIS MUCH!
TH-THEN THAT MEANS...
...THEY'RE MAKING US CATCH COLDS AS BIOLOGICAL WARFARE ?!
UM, NO...
I DON'T THINK ANY SANE PERSON WOULD COME TO THAT CONCLUSION...

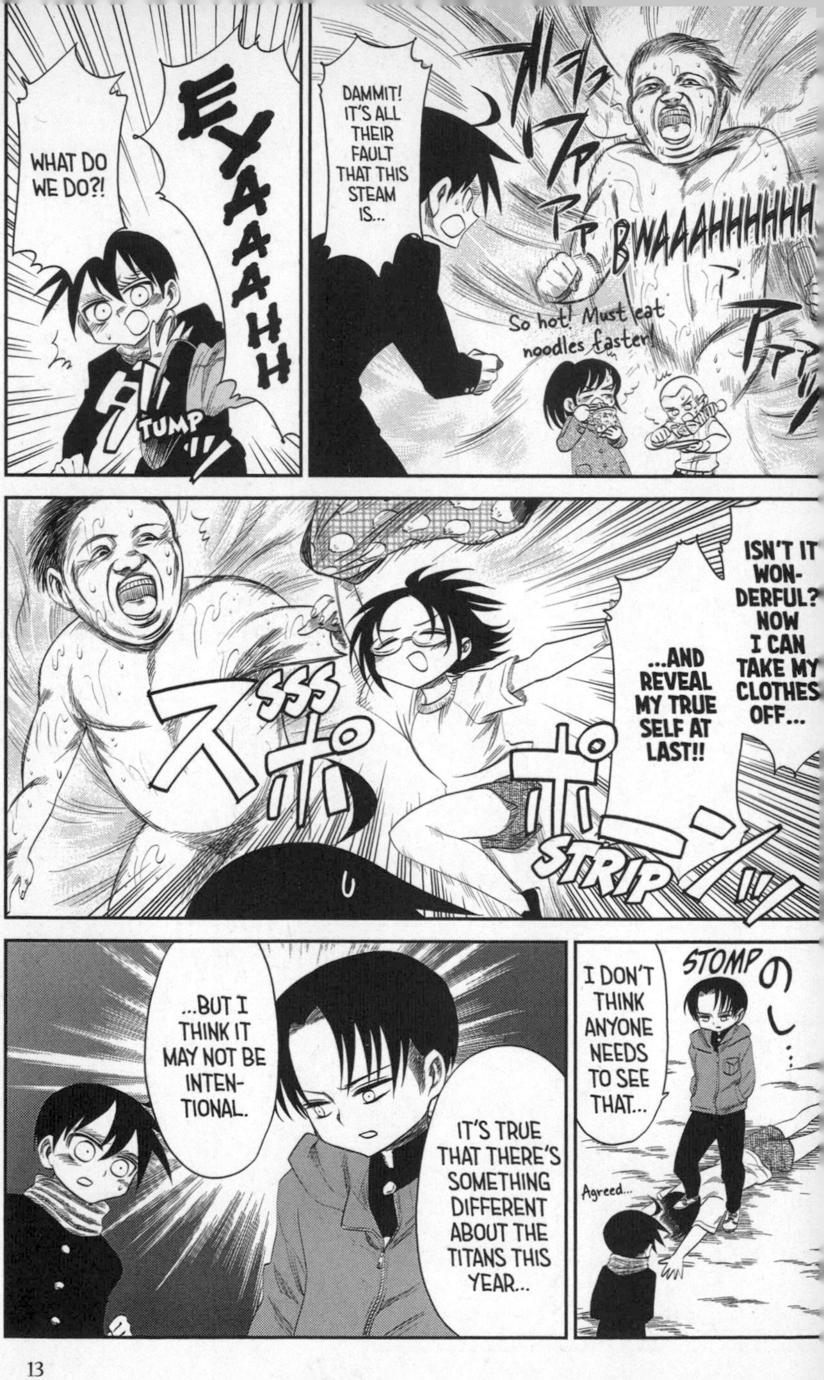
DAMMIT! IT'S ALL THEIR FAULT THAT THIS STEAM IS...
BWAAAHHHHHH
So hot! Must eat noodles faster!
EYAAAAHH
WHAT DO WE DO?!
TUMP
ISN'T IT WONDERFUL? NOW I CAN TAKE MY CLOTHES OFF...
...AND REVEAL MY TRUE SELF AT LAST!!
SSS
STRIP
STOMP
I DON'T THINK ANYONE NEEDS TO SEE THAT...
Agreed...
IT'S TRUE THAT THERE'S SOMETHING DIFFERENT ABOUT THE TITANS THIS YEAR...
...BUT I THINK IT MAY NOT BE INTENTIONAL.

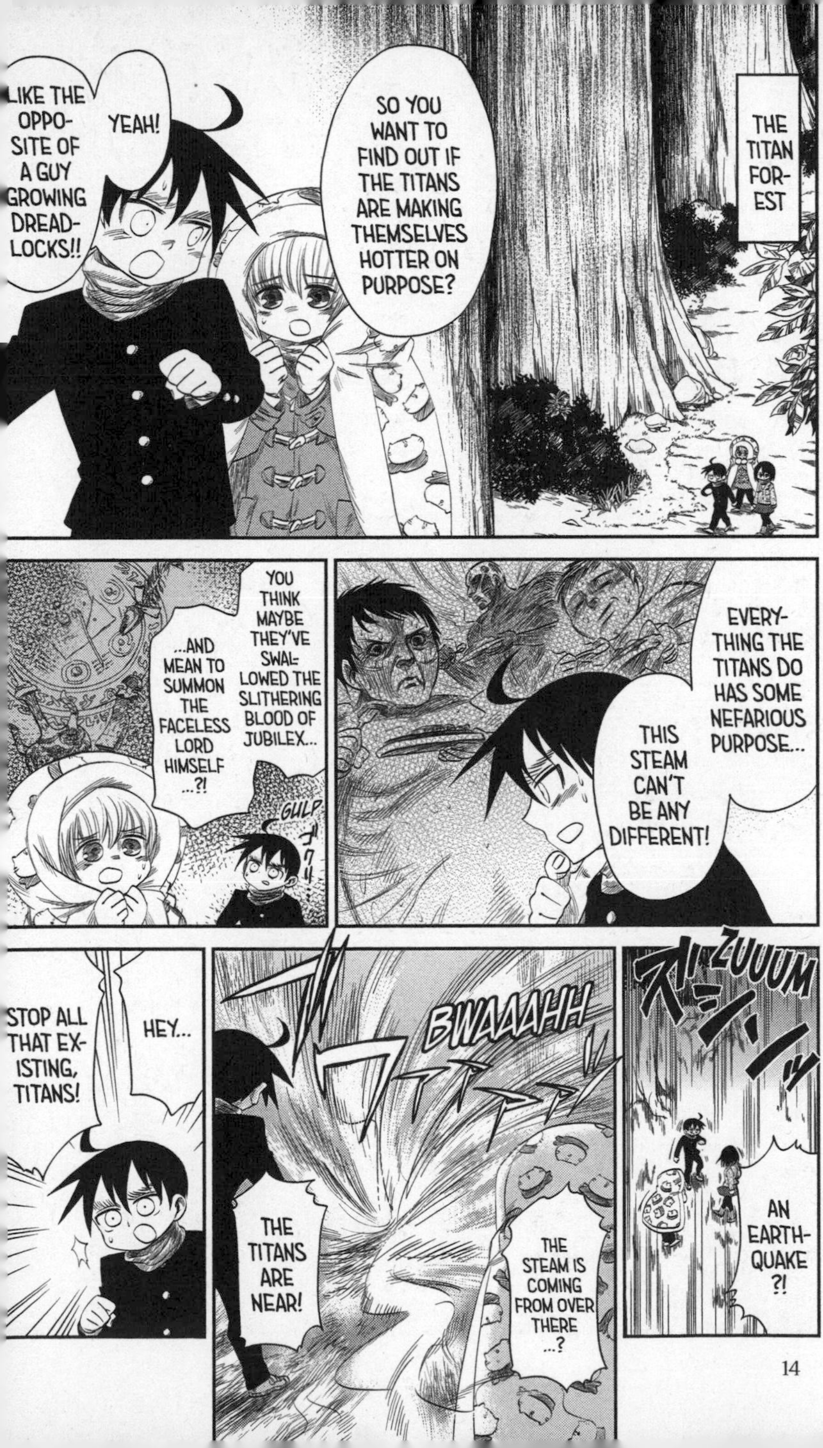
THE TITAN FOR-EST
SO YOU WANT TO FIND OUT IF THE TITANS ARE MAKING THEMSELVES HOTTER ON PURPOSE?
YEAH!
LIKE THE OPPO-SITE OF A GUY GROWING DREAD-LOCKS!!
EVERY-THING THE TITANS DO HAS SOME NEFARIOUS PURPOSE...
THIS STEAM CAN'T BE ANY DIFFERENT!
YOU THINK MAYBE THEY'VE SWAL-LOWED THE SLITHERING BLOOD OF JUBILEX...
...AND MEAN TO SUMMON THE FACELESS LORD HIMSELF ...?!
GULP
ZUUUM
AN EARTH-QUAKE ?!
BWAAAHH
THE STEAM IS COMING FROM OVER THERE ...?
THE TITANS ARE NEAR!
HEY...
STOP ALL THAT EX-ISTING, TITANS!

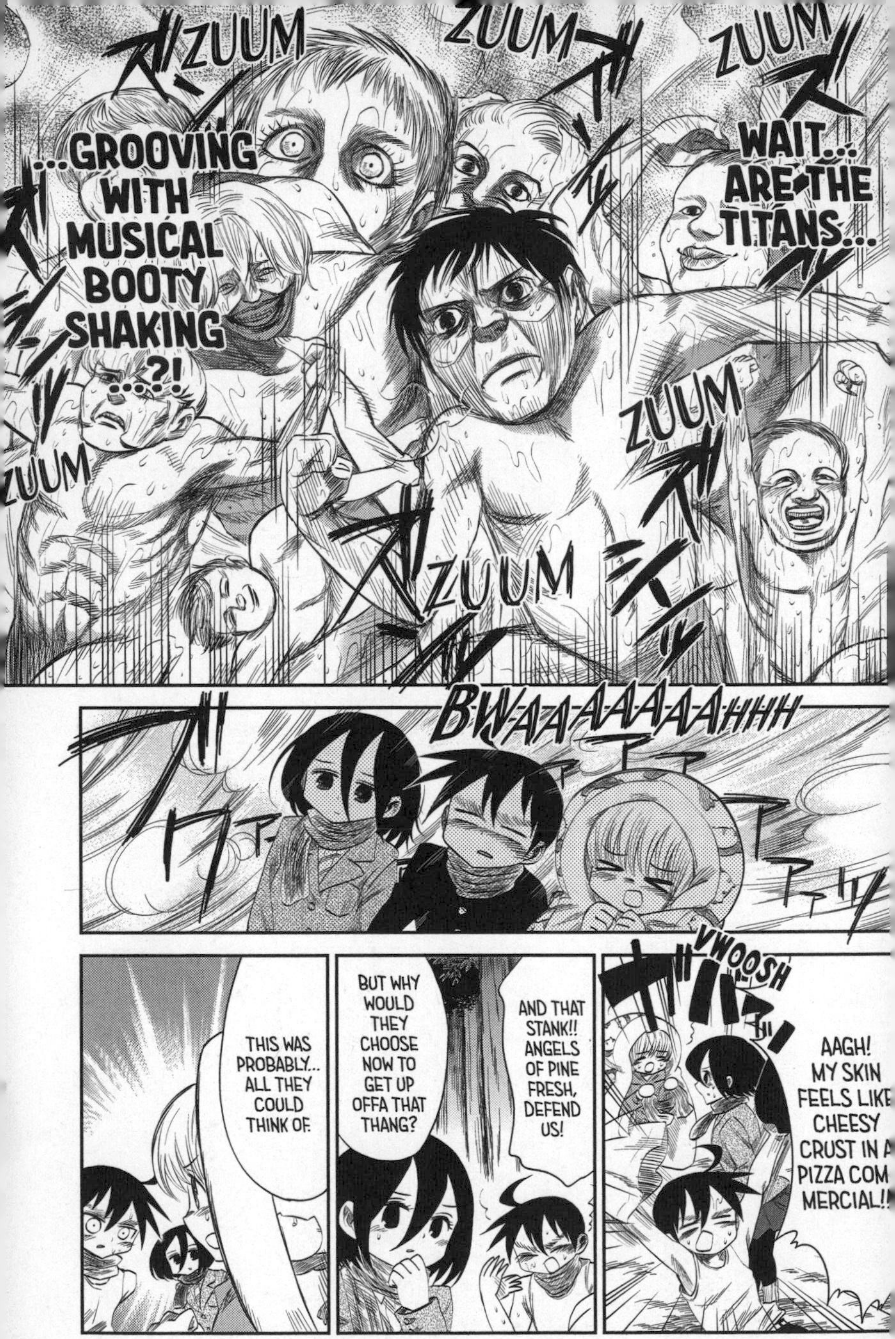
ZUUM
WAIT... ARE THE TITANS...
ZUUM
ZUUM
...GROOVING WITH MUSICAL BOOTY SHAKING ...?!
ZUUM
ZUUM
ZUUM
BWAAAAAAAAHHH
VWOOSH
AAGH! MY SKIN FEELS LIKE CHEESY CRUST IN A PIZZA COMMERCIAL!!
AND THAT STANK!! ANGELS OF PINE FRESH, DEFEND US!
BUT WHY WOULD THEY CHOOSE NOW TO GET UP OFFA THAT THANG?
THIS WAS PROBABLY... ALL THEY COULD THINK OF.

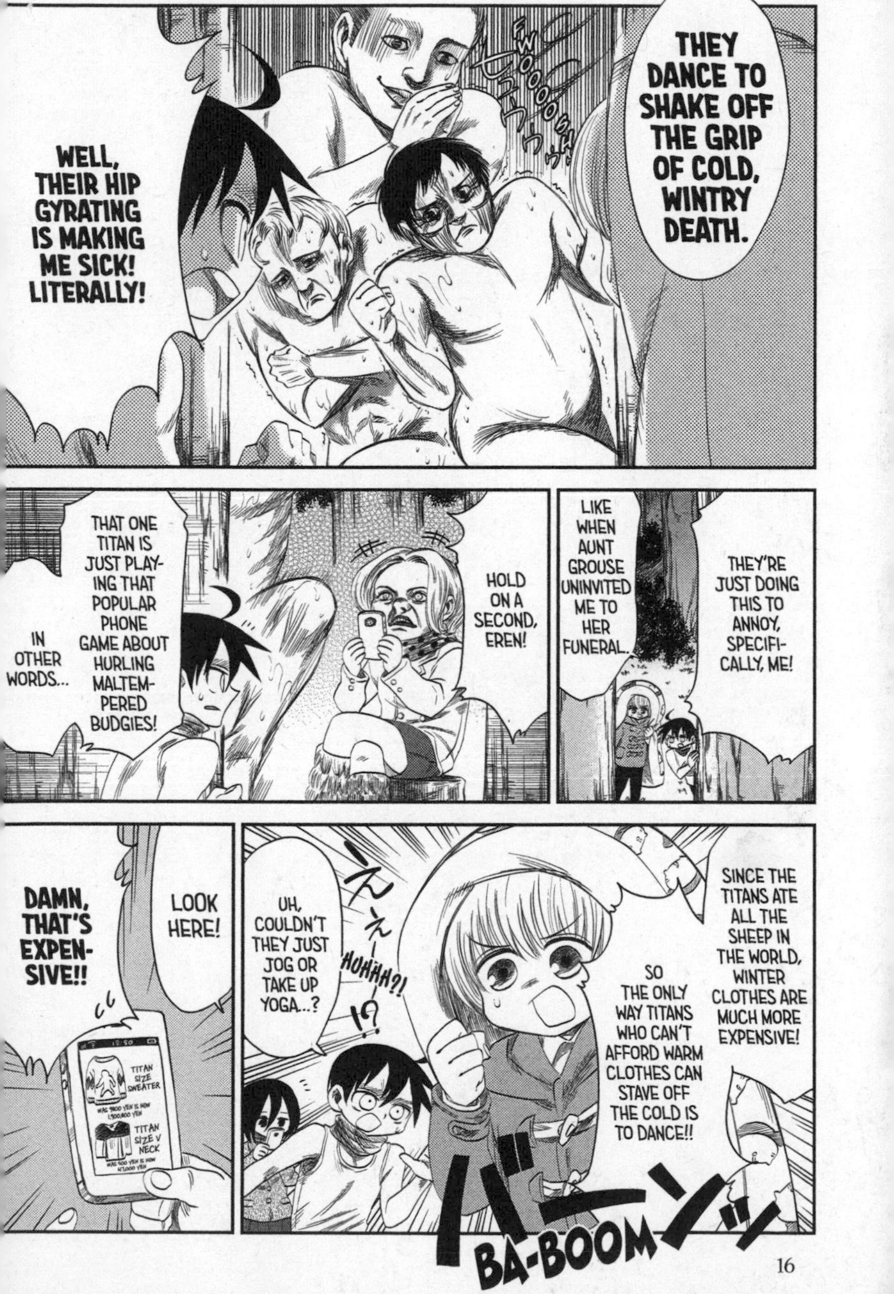
THEY DANCE TO SHAKE OFF THE GRIP OF COLD, WINTRY DEATH.
FWOOOOOSH
WELL, THEIR HIP GYRATING IS MAKING ME SICK! LITERALLY!
THEY'RE JUST DOING THIS TO ANNOY, SPECIFI-CALLY, ME!
LIKE WHEN AUNT GROUSE UNINVITED ME TO HER FUNERAL.
HOLD ON A SECOND, EREN!
THAT ONE TITAN IS JUST PLAY-ING THAT POPULAR PHONE GAME ABOUT HURLING MALTEM-PERED BUDGIES!
IN OTHER WORDS...
SINCE THE TITANS ATE ALL THE SHEEP IN THE WORLD, WINTER CLOTHES ARE MUCH MORE EXPENSIVE!
SO THE ONLY WAY TITANS WHO CAN'T AFFORD WARM CLOTHES CAN STAVE OFF THE COLD IS TO DANCE!!
UH, COULDN'T THEY JUST JOG OR TAKE UP YOGA...?
HUHHH?!
BA-BOOM
LOOK HERE!
DAMN, THAT'S EXPEN-SIVE!!
12:50
TITAN SIZE SWEATER
TITAN SIZE V NECK

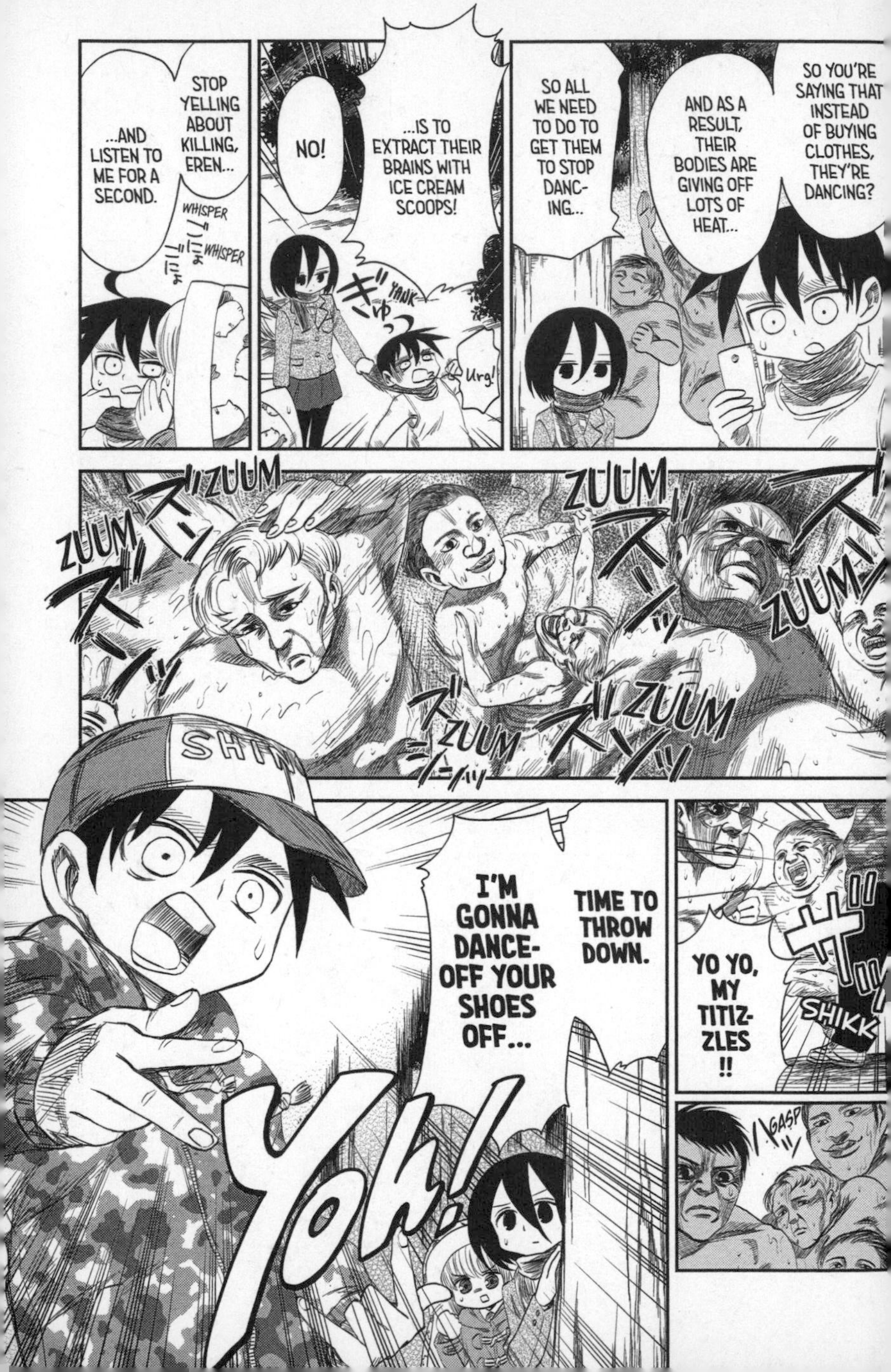
SO YOU'RE SAYING THAT INSTEAD OF BUYING CLOTHES, THEY'RE DANCING?
AND AS A RESULT, THEIR BODIES ARE GIVING OFF LOTS OF HEAT...
SO ALL WE NEED TO DO TO GET THEM TO STOP DANC-ING...
...IS TO EXTRACT THEIR BRAINS WITH ICE CREAM SCOOPS!
NO!
YANK
Urg!
STOP YELLING ABOUT KILLING, EREN...
...AND LISTEN TO ME FOR A SECOND.
WHISPER
WHISPER
ZUUM
ZUUM
ZUUM
ZUUM
ZUUM
ZUUM
YO YO, MY TITIZ-ZLES !!
SHIKK
GASP
TIME TO THROW DOWN.
I'M GONNA DANCE-OFF YOUR SHOES OFF...
Yoh!

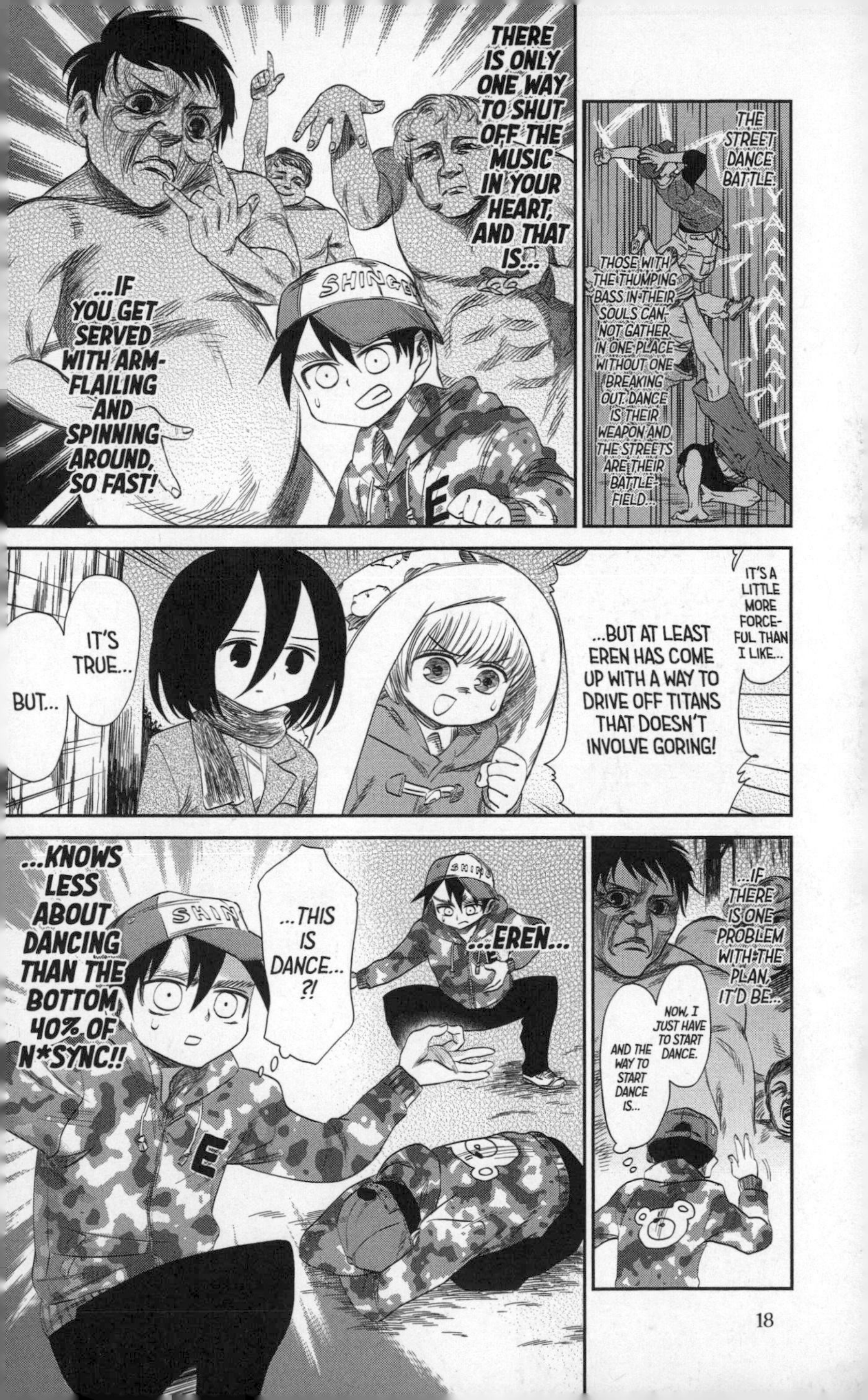
THE STREET DANCE BATTLE.
THOSE WITH THE THUMPING BASS IN THEIR SOULS CANNOT GATHER IN ONE PLACE WITHOUT ONE BREAKING OUT. DANCE IS THEIR WEAPON AND THE STREETS ARE THEIR BATTLEFIELD...
THERE IS ONLY ONE WAY TO SHUT OFF THE MUSIC IN YOUR HEART, AND THAT IS...
...IF YOU GET SERVED WITH ARM-FLAILING AND SPINNING AROUND, SO FAST!
IT'S A LITTLE MORE FORCEFUL THAN I LIKE...
...BUT AT LEAST EREN HAS COME UP WITH A WAY TO DRIVE OFF TITANS THAT DOESN'T INVOLVE GORING!
IT'S TRUE... BUT...
...IF THERE IS ONE PROBLEM WITH THE PLAN, IT'D BE...
NOW, I JUST HAVE TO START DANCE.
AND THE WAY TO START DANCE IS...
...EREN...
...THIS IS DANCE...?!
...KNOWS LESS ABOUT DANCING THAN THE BOTTOM 40% OF N*SYNC!!

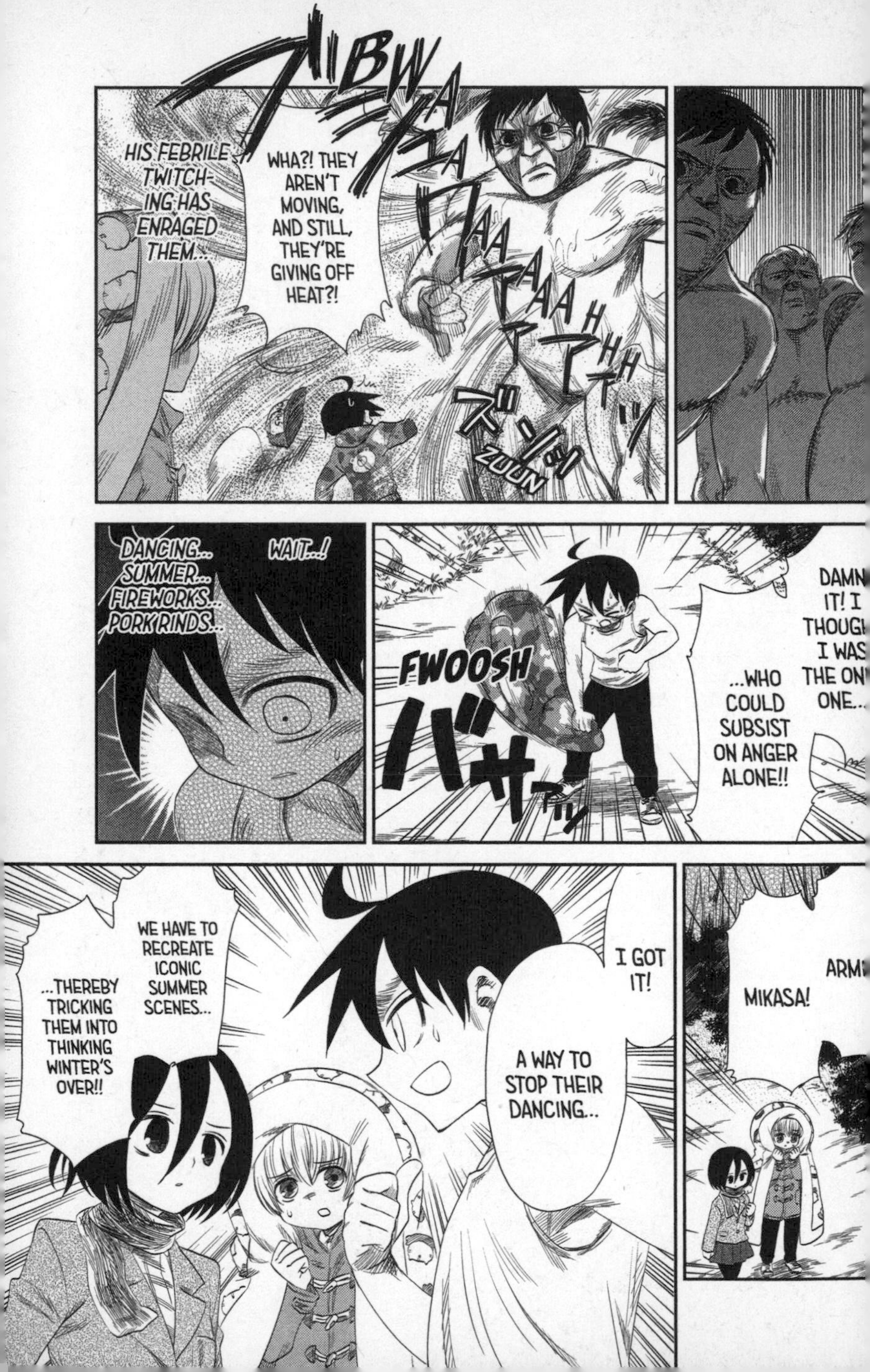
BWA
AAAAAAAHHH
ZUUN
WHA?! THEY AREN'T MOVING, AND STILL, THEY'RE GIVING OFF HEAT?!
HIS FEBRILE TWITCHING HAS ENRAGED THEM...
DAMN IT! I THOUG I WAS THE ON ONE...
...WHO COULD SUBSIST ON ANGER ALONE!!
FWOOSH
WAIT...!
DANCING... SUMMER... FIREWORKS... PORK RINDS...
ARM
MIKASA!
I GOT IT!
A WAY TO STOP THEIR DANCING...
WE HAVE TO RECREATE ICONIC SUMMER SCENES...
...THEREBY TRICKING THEM INTO THINKING WINTER'S OVER!!

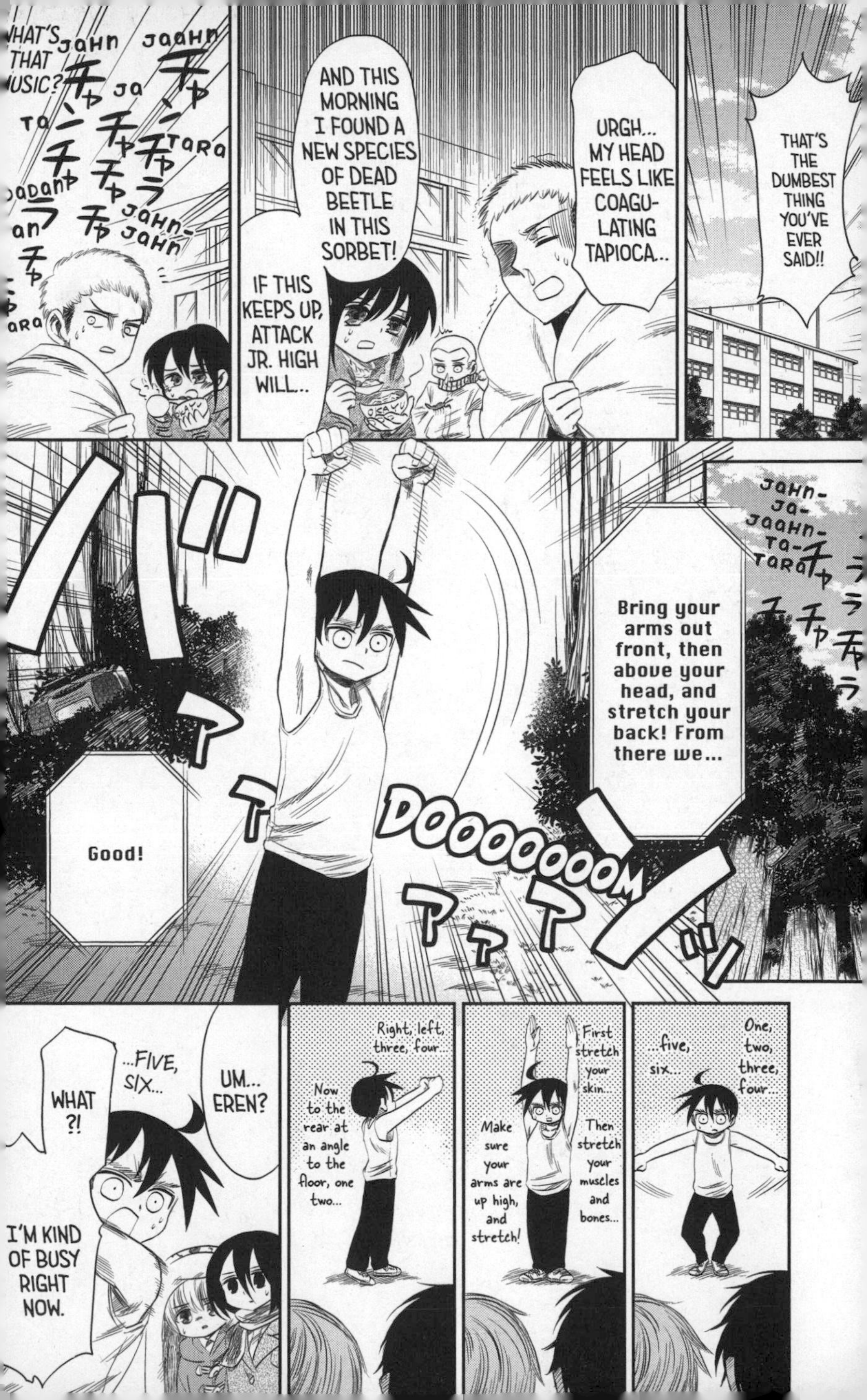

THAT'S THE DUMBEST THING YOU'VE EVER SAID!!
URGH... MY HEAD FEELS LIKE COAGU-LATING TAPIOCA...
AND THIS MORNING I FOUND A NEW SPECIES OF DEAD BEETLE IN THIS SORBET!
IF THIS KEEPS UP, ATTACK JR. HIGH WILL...
jaahn
jahn
WHAT'S THAT MUSIC?
ja
ta
tara
jahn-jahn
JAHN-JA-JAAHN-TA-TARA
Bring your arms out front, then above your head, and stretch your back! From there we...
DOOOOOOOOM
Good!
One, two, three, four...
...five, six...
First stretch your skin...
Then stretch your muscles and bones...
Make sure your arms are up high, and stretch!
Right, left, three, four...
Now to the rear at an angle to the floor, one two...
UM... EREN?
...FIVE, SIX...
WHAT?!
I'M KIND OF BUSY RIGHT NOW.

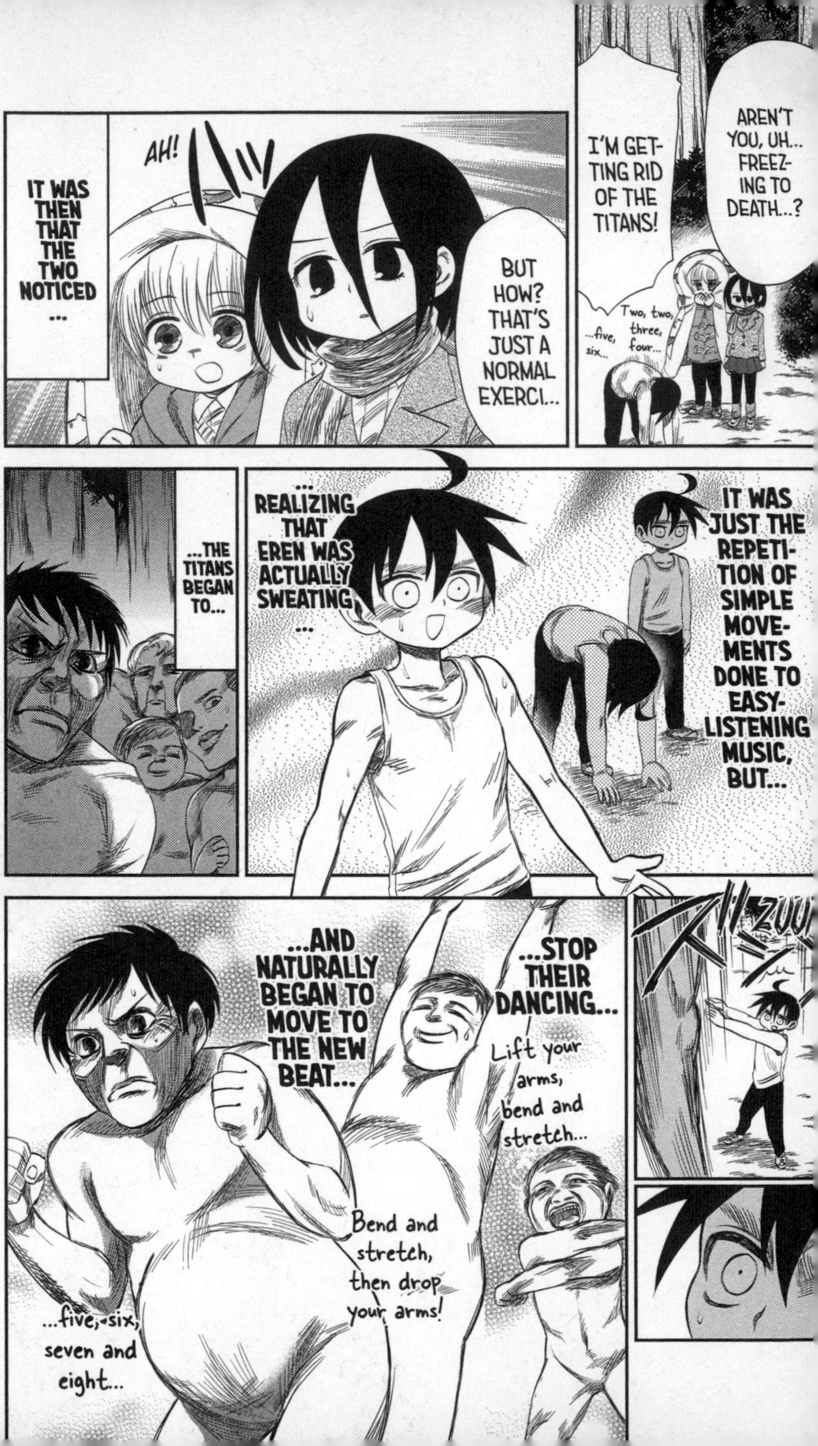
AREN'T YOU, UH... FREEZ-ING TO DEATH...?
I'M GET-TING RID OF THE TITANS!
Two, two, three, four...
...five, six...
AH!
BUT HOW? THAT'S JUST A NORMAL EXERCI...
IT WAS THEN THAT THE TWO NOTICED...
IT WAS JUST THE REPETI-TION OF SIMPLE MOVE-MENTS DONE TO EASY-LISTENING MUSIC, BUT...
...REALIZING THAT EREN WAS ACTUALLY SWEATING...
...THE TITANS BEGAN TO...
ZUU
...STOP THEIR DANCING...
...AND NATURALLY BEGAN TO MOVE TO THE NEW BEAT...
Lift your arms, bend and stretch...
Bend and stretch, then drop your arms!
...five, six, seven and eight...

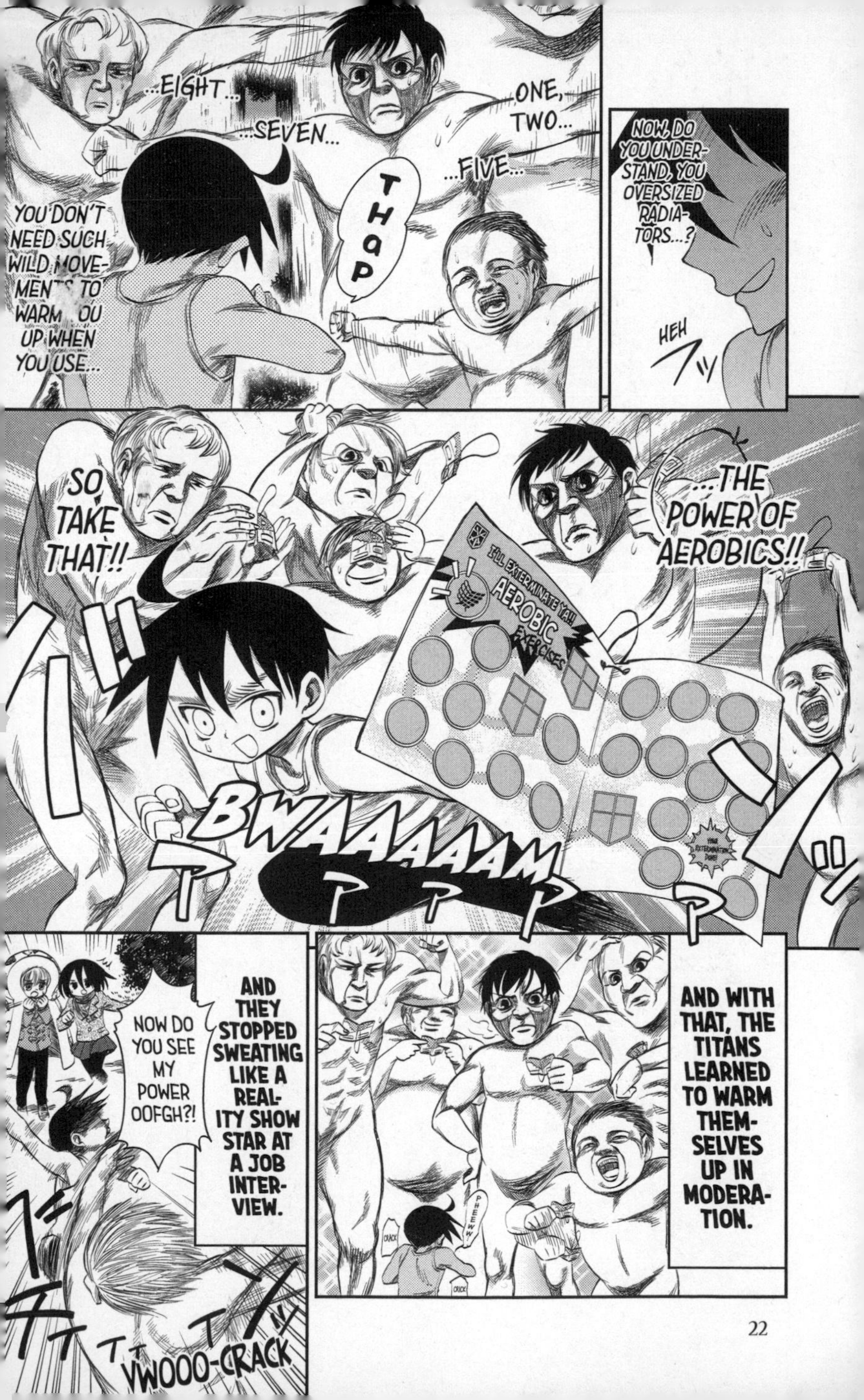
NOW, DO YOU UNDER-STAND, YOU OVERSIZED RADIA-TORS...?
HEH
ONE, TWO...
...FIVE...
THAP
...SEVEN...
...EIGHT...
YOU DON'T NEED SUCH WILD MOVE-MEN... TO WARM ...OU UP WHEN YOU USE...
...THE POWER OF AEROBICS!!
SO, TAKE THAT!!
I'LL EXTERMINATE YA!! AEROBIC EXERCISES
BWAAAAAAM
AND WITH THAT, THE TITANS LEARNED TO WARM THEM-SELVES UP IN MODERA-TION.
PHEEW!
CRACK
CRACK
AND THEY STOPPED SWEATING LIKE A REAL-ITY SHOW STAR AT A JOB INTER-VIEW.
NOW DO YOU SEE MY POWER OOFGH?!
VWOOO-CRACK

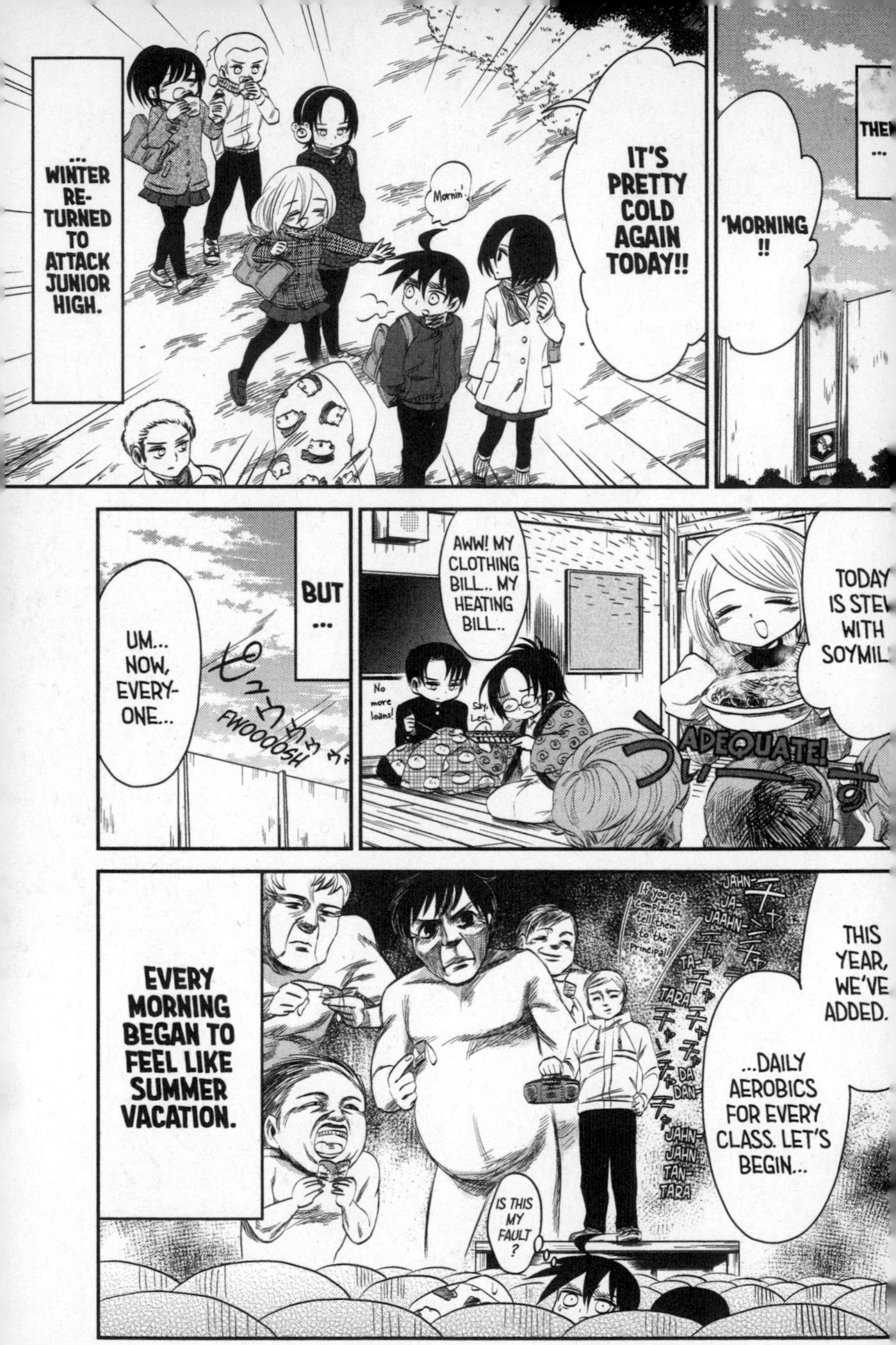
THE ...
'MORNING !!
IT'S PRETTY COLD AGAIN TODAY!!
Mornin'.
... WINTER RE-TURNED TO ATTACK JUNIOR HIGH.
TODAY IS STEW WITH SOYMIL
ADEQUATE!
AWW! MY CLOTHING BILL.. MY HEATING BILL..
Say, Levi...
No more loans!
BUT ...
UM... NOW, EVERY-ONE...
FWOOOOSH
THIS YEAR, WE'VE ADDED.
...DAILY AEROBICS FOR EVERY CLASS. LET'S BEGIN...
JAHN-JA-JAAHN-TA-TARA
DA DAN-
JAHN-JAHN TAN-TARA
If you got complaints, tell them to the principal!
IS THIS MY FAULT?
EVERY MORNING BEGAN TO FEEL LIKE SUMMER VACATION.

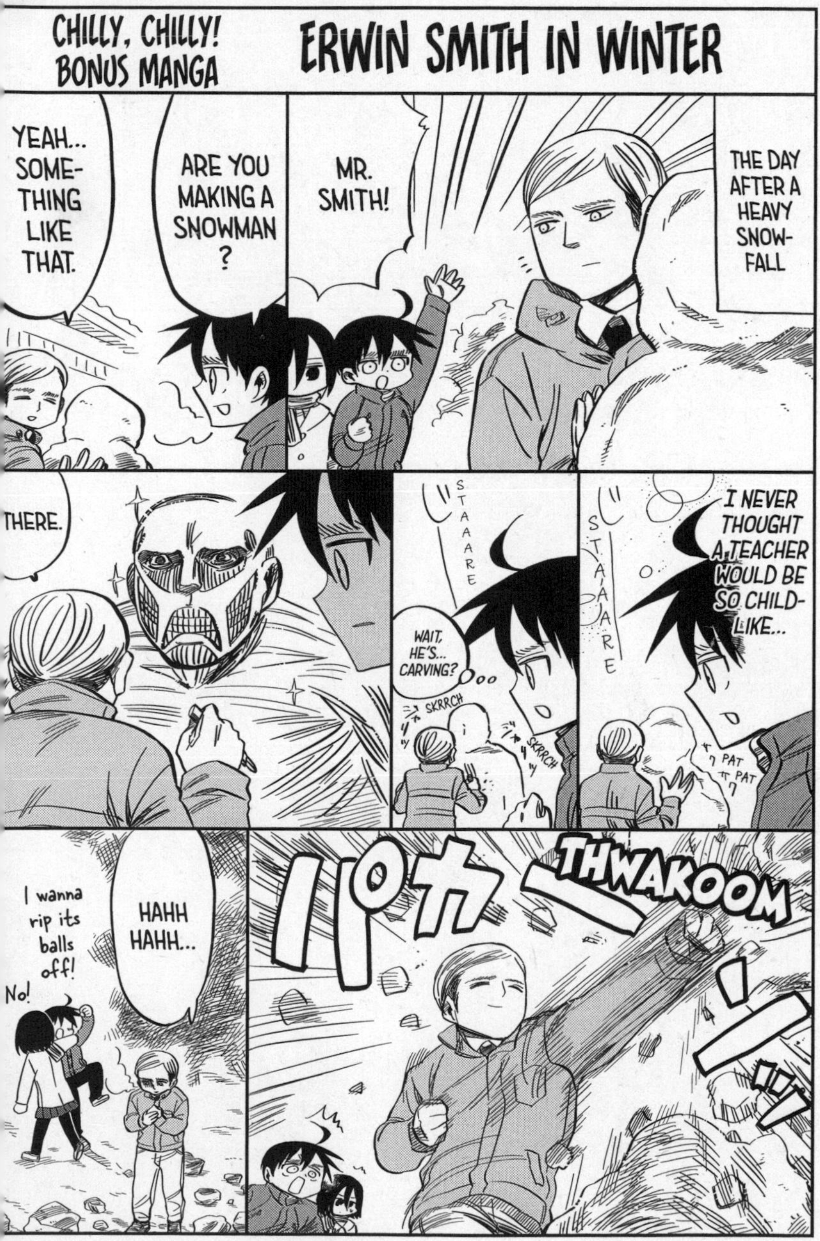
ERWIN SMITH IN WINTER
CHILLY, CHILLY! BONUS MANGA
THE DAY AFTER A HEAVY SNOW-FALL
MR. SMITH!
ARE YOU MAKING A SNOWMAN?
YEAH... SOME-THING LIKE THAT.
STAAARE
I NEVER THOUGHT A TEACHER WOULD BE SO CHILD-LIKE...
PAT PAT
STAAARE
WAIT, HE'S... CARVING?
SKRRCH
SKRRCH
THERE.
THWAKOOM
HAHH HAHH...
I wanna rip its balls off!
No!

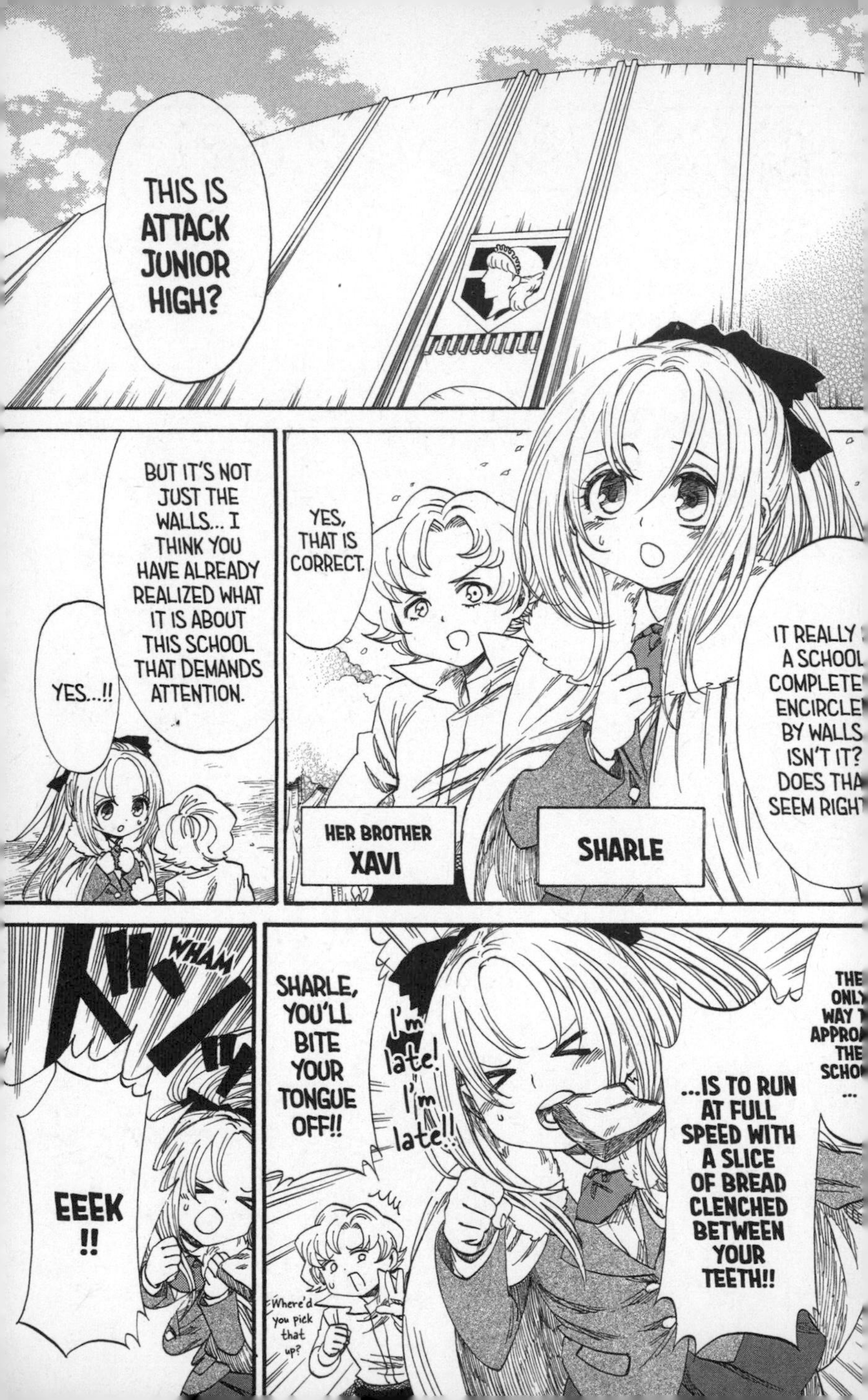
THIS IS ATTACK JUNIOR HIGH?
IT REALLY A SCHOOL COMPLETE ENCIRCLE BY WALLS ISN'T IT? DOES THA SEEM RIGHT
SHARLE
HER BROTHER XAVI
YES, THAT IS CORRECT.
BUT IT'S NOT JUST THE WALLS... I THINK YOU HAVE ALREADY REALIZED WHAT IT IS ABOUT THIS SCHOOL THAT DEMANDS ATTENTION.
YES...!!
THE ONLY WAY APPRO THE SCHO ...
...IS TO RUN AT FULL SPEED WITH A SLICE OF BREAD CLENCHED BETWEEN YOUR TEETH!!
I'm late! I'm late!!
SHARLE, YOU'LL BITE YOUR TONGUE OFF!!
Where'd you pick that up?
WHAM
EEEK !!

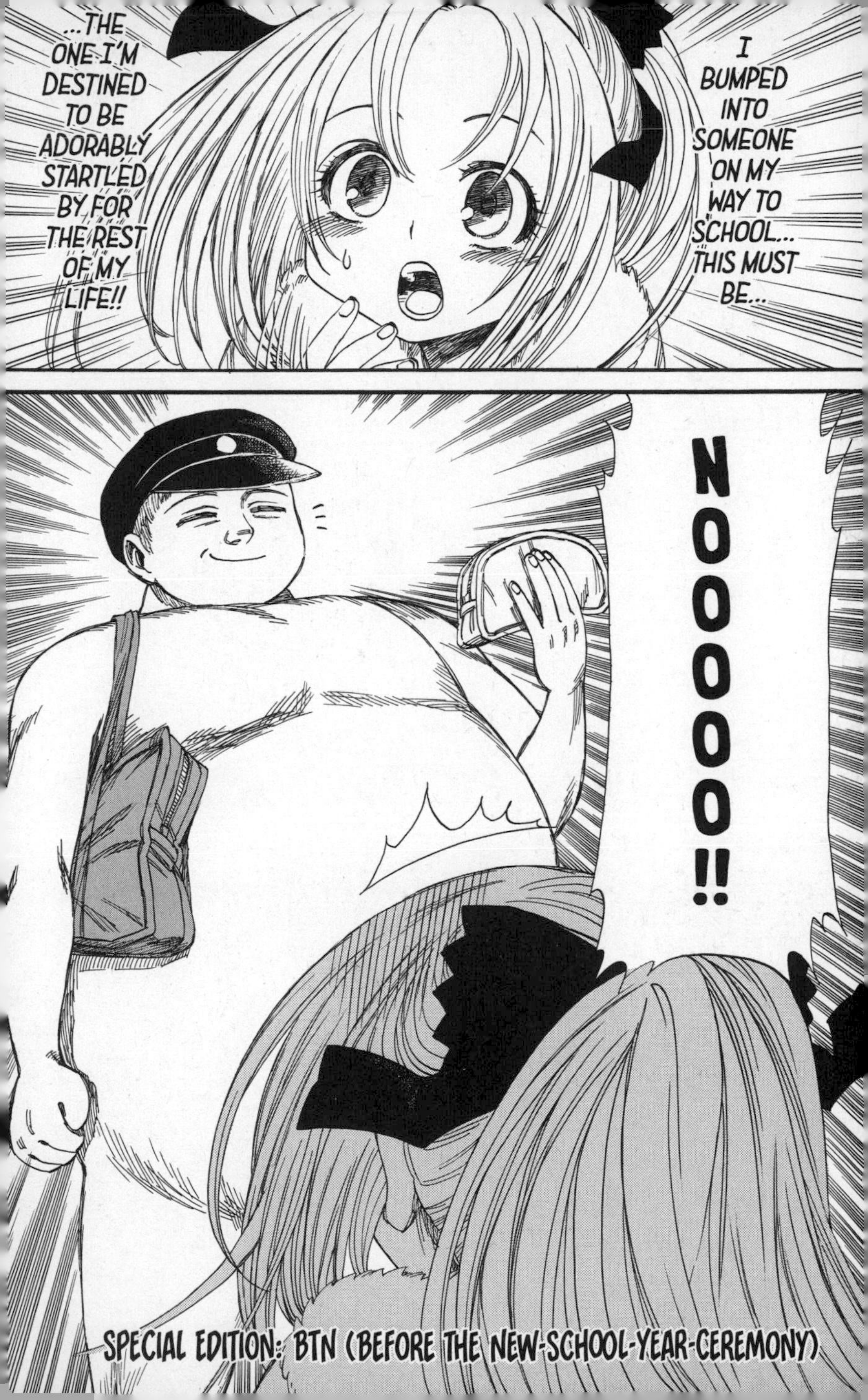
I BUMPED INTO SOMEONE ON MY WAY TO SCHOOL... THIS MUST BE...
...THE ONE I'M DESTINED TO BE ADORABLY STARTLED BY FOR THE REST OF MY LIFE!!
NOOOOO!!
SPECIAL EDITION: BTN (BEFORE THE NEW-SCHOOL-YEAR-CEREMONY)

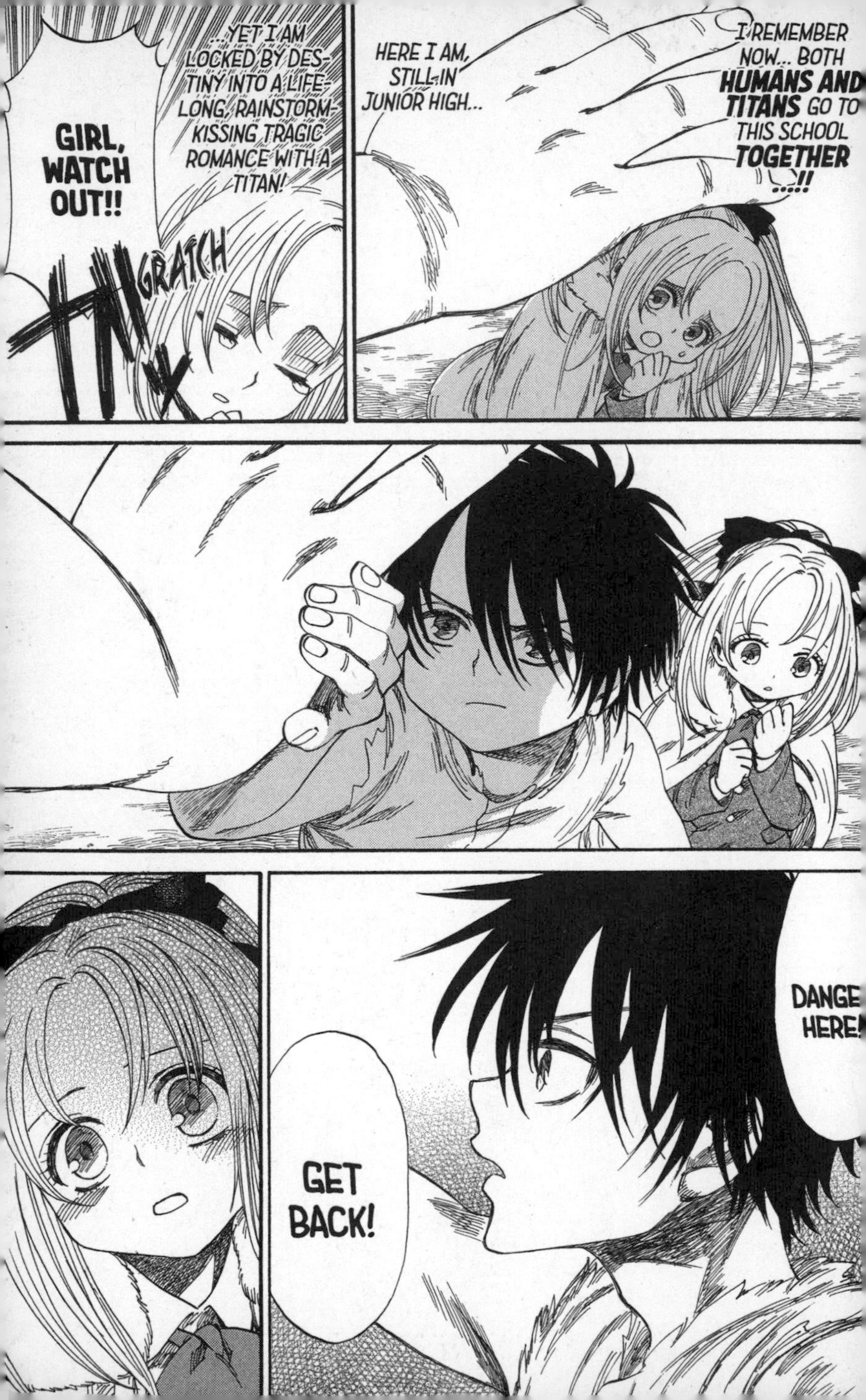
I REMEMBER NOW... BOTH HUMANS AND TITANS GO TO THIS SCHOOL TOGETHER ....!!
HERE I AM, STILL IN JUNIOR HIGH...
...YET I AM LOCKED BY DES-TINY INTO A LIFE-LONG, RAINSTORM-KISSING TRAGIC ROMANCE WITH A TITAN!
GIRL, WATCH OUT!!
GRATCH
DANGE HERE!
GET BACK!

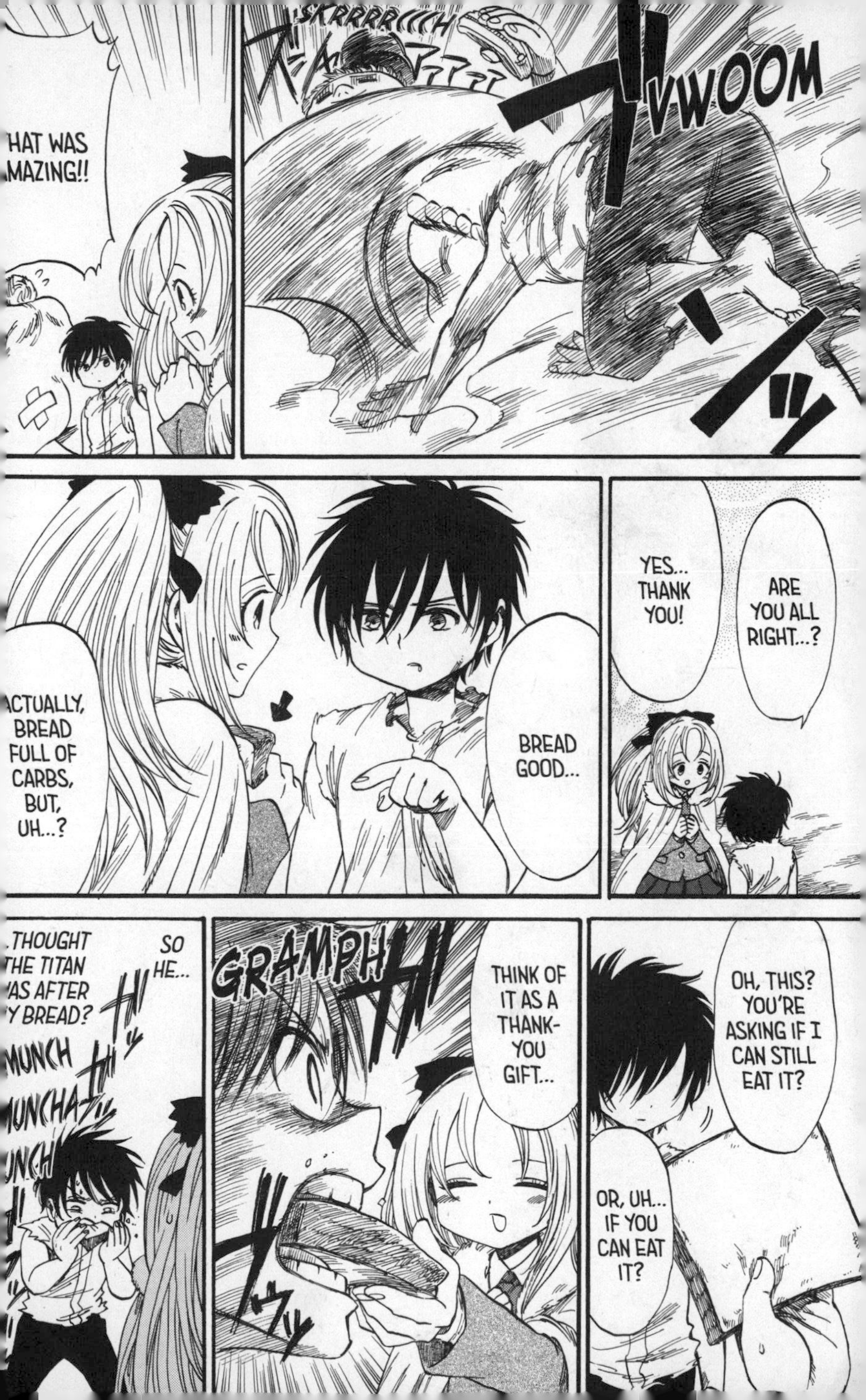
SKRRRRIIIH
VWOOM
HAT WAS AMAZING!!
ARE YOU ALL RIGHT...?
YES... THANK YOU!
BREAD GOOD...
ACTUALLY, BREAD FULL OF CARBS, BUT, UH...?
OH, THIS? YOU'RE ASKING IF I CAN STILL EAT IT?
OR, UH... IF YOU CAN EAT IT?
THINK OF IT AS A THANK-YOU GIFT...
GRAMPH
SO HE...
THOUGHT THE TITAN VAS AFTER Y BREAD?
MUNCH
MUNCHA
UNCH

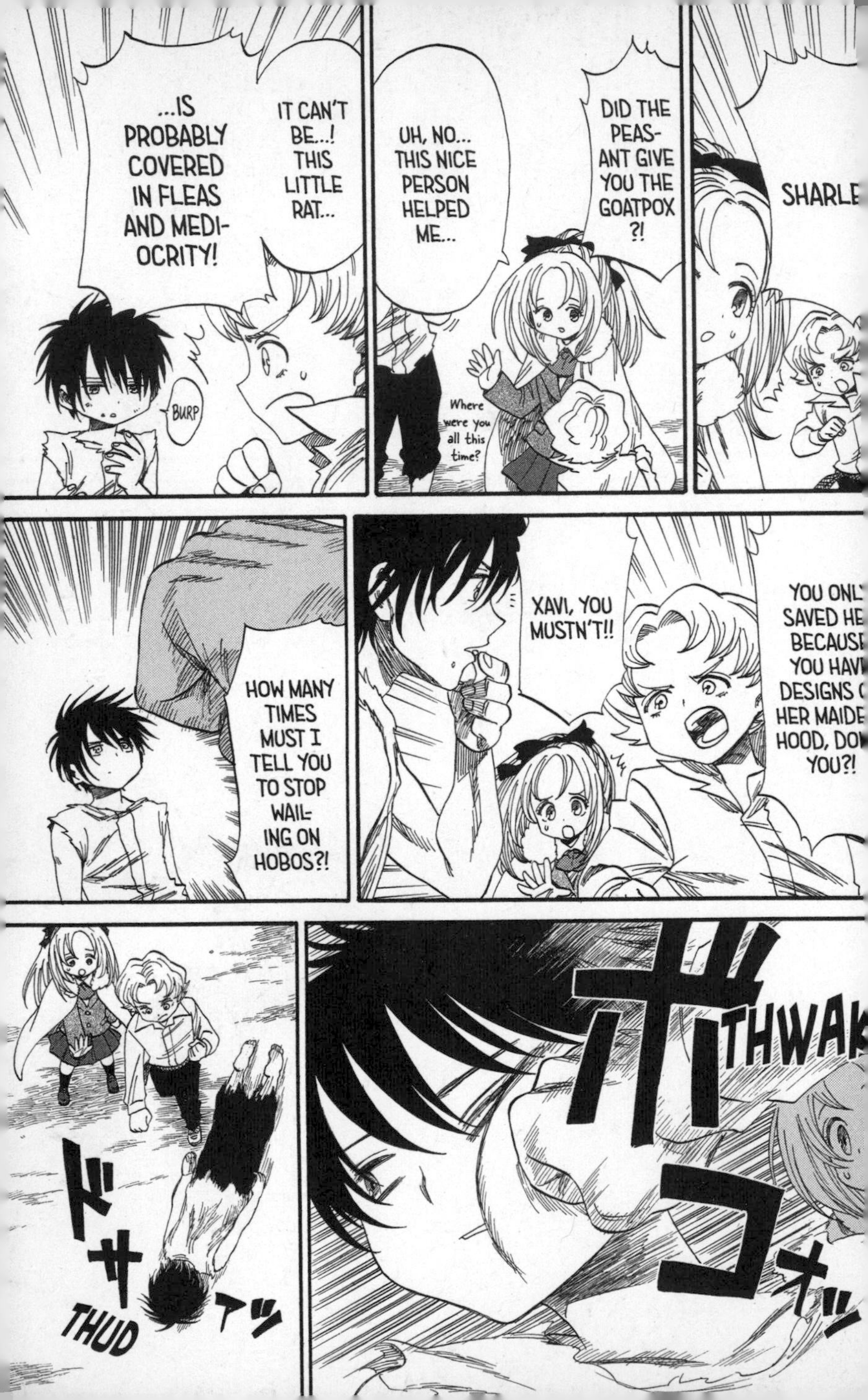
SHARLE
DID THE PEAS-ANT GIVE YOU THE GOATPOX ?!
UH, NO... THIS NICE PERSON HELPED ME...
Where were you all this time?
IT CAN'T BE...! THIS LITTLE RAT...
...IS PROBABLY COVERED IN FLEAS AND MEDI-OCRITY!
BURP
YOU ONLY SAVED HE BECAUSE YOU HAV DESIGNS O HER MAIDE HOOD, DO YOU?!
XAVI, YOU MUSTN'T!!
HOW MANY TIMES MUST I TELL YOU TO STOP WAIL-ING ON HOBOS?!
THWAK
THUD

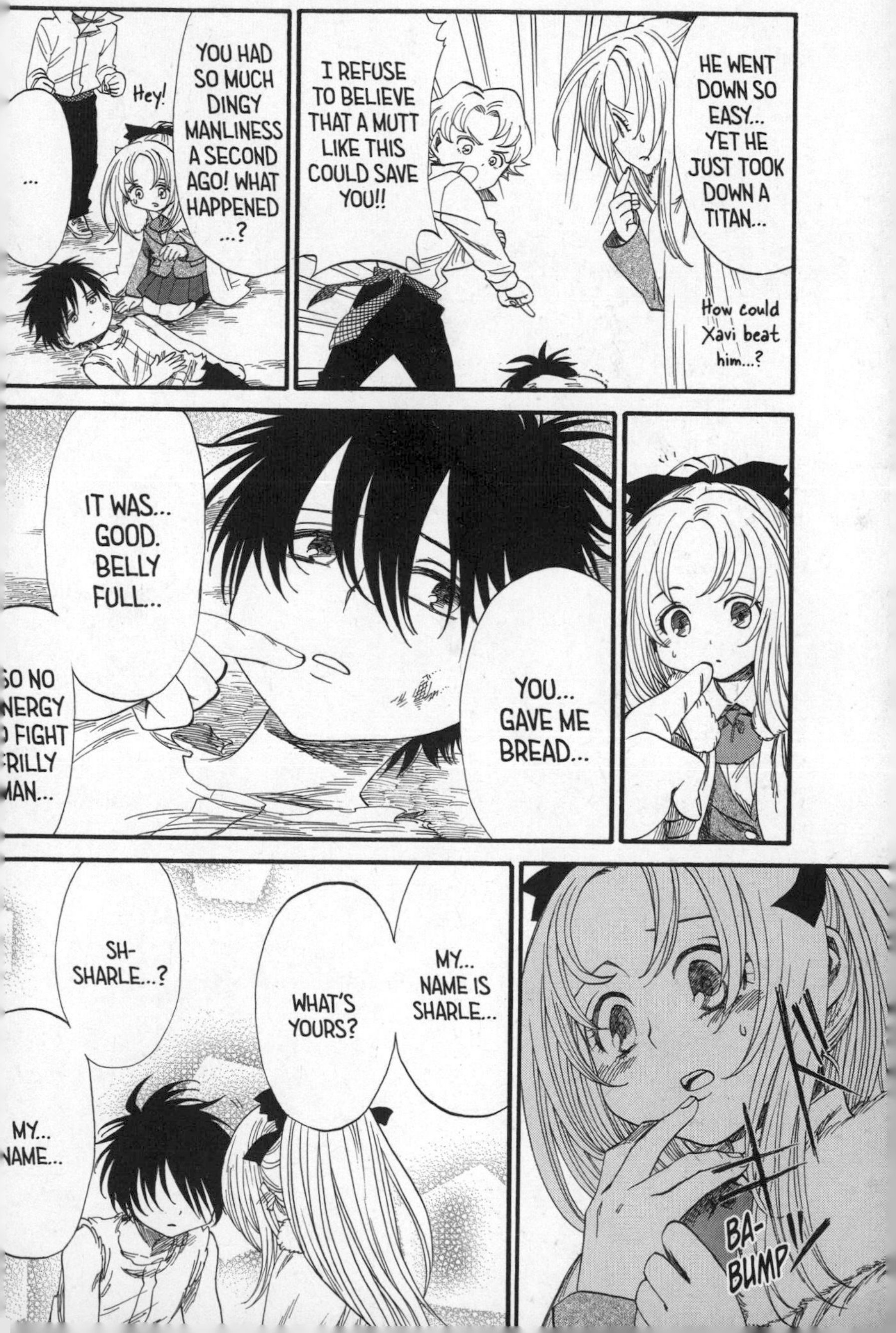
HE WENT DOWN SO EASY... YET HE JUST TOOK DOWN A TITAN...
How could Xavi beat him...?
I REFUSE TO BELIEVE THAT A MUTT LIKE THIS COULD SAVE YOU!!
YOU HAD SO MUCH DINGY MANLINESS A SECOND AGO! WHAT HAPPENED ...?
Hey!
...
YOU... GAVE ME BREAD...
IT WAS... GOOD. BELLY FULL...
SO NO NERGY FIGHT FRILLY MAN...
BA-BUMP
MY... NAME IS SHARLE...
WHAT'S YOURS?
SH-SHARLE...?
MY... NAME...

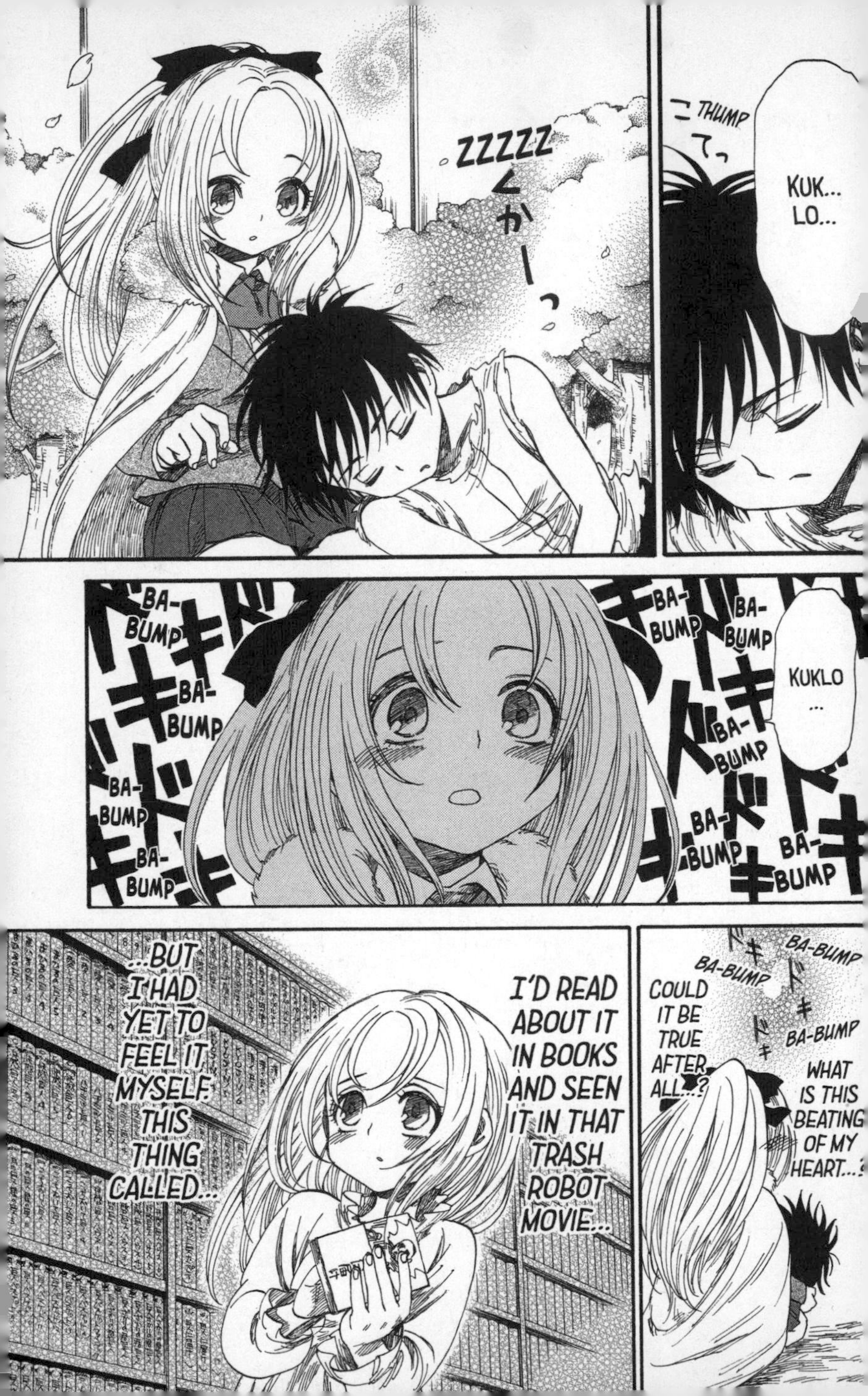
THUMP
KUK... LO...
ZZZZZ
BA-BUMP
KUKLO ...
BA-BUMP
BA-BUMP
BA-BUMP
BA-BUMP
BA-BUMP
BA-BUMP
BA-BUMP
BA-BUMP
BA-BUMP
BA-BUMP
BA-BUMP
WHAT IS THIS BEATING OF MY HEART...?
COULD IT BE TRUE AFTER ALL...?
I'D READ ABOUT IT IN BOOKS AND SEEN IT IN THAT TRASH ROBOT MOVIE...
...BUT I HAD YET TO FEEL IT MYSELF. THIS THING CALLED...

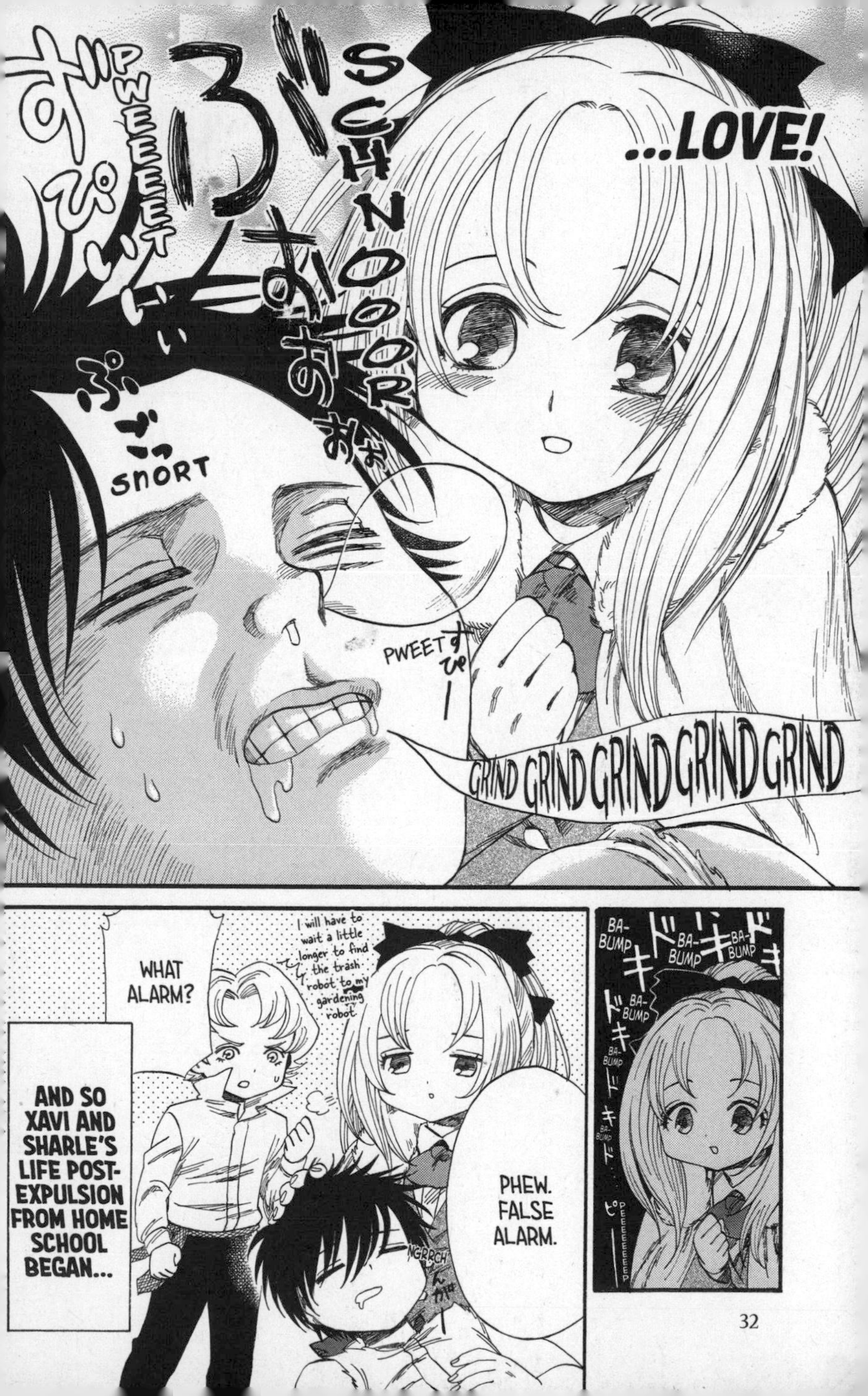
...LOVE!
SCHNOOOR
PWEEEEET
SNORT
PWEET
GRIND GRIND GRIND GRIND GRIND
BA-BUMP
BA-BUMP
BA-BUMP
BA-BUMP
BA-BUMP
BA-BUMP
PEEEEEEEEEEP
PHEW. FALSE ALARM.
I will have to wait a little longer to find the trash robot to my gardening robot.
WHAT ALARM?
NGRRCH
AND SO XAVI AND SHARLE'S LIFE POST-EXPULSION FROM HOME SCHOOL BEGAN...

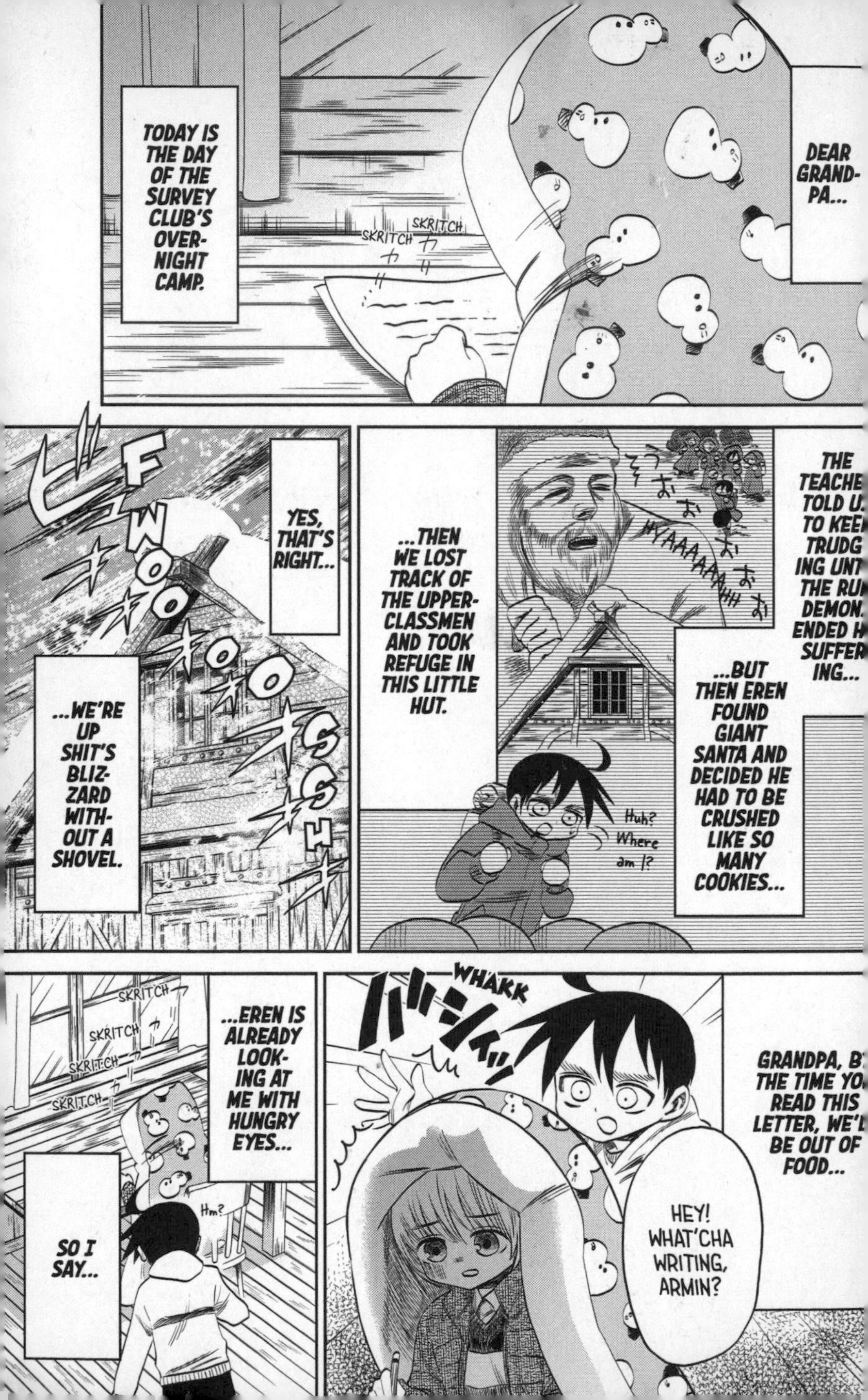
DEAR GRANDPA...
TODAY IS THE DAY OF THE SURVEY CLUB'S OVERNIGHT CAMP.
SKRITCH SKRITCH
THE TEACHE TOLD U. TO KEE TRUDG ING UNT THE RU DEMON. ENDED H SUFFER ING...
HYAAAAAAAHH
...BUT THEN EREN FOUND GIANT SANTA AND DECIDED HE HAD TO BE CRUSHED LIKE SO MANY COOKIES...
Huh? Where am I?
...THEN WE LOST TRACK OF THE UPPERCLASSMEN AND TOOK REFUGE IN THIS LITTLE HUT.
YES, THAT'S RIGHT...
FWOOOOOOSSH
...WE'RE UP SHIT'S BLIZZARD WITHOUT A SHOVEL.
GRANDPA, BY THE TIME YO READ THIS LETTER, WE'L BE OUT OF FOOD...
WHAKK
HEY! WHAT'CHA WRITING, ARMIN?
...EREN IS ALREADY LOOKING AT ME WITH HUNGRY EYES...
SKRITCH SKRITCH SKRITCH SKRITCH
Hm?
SO I SAY...

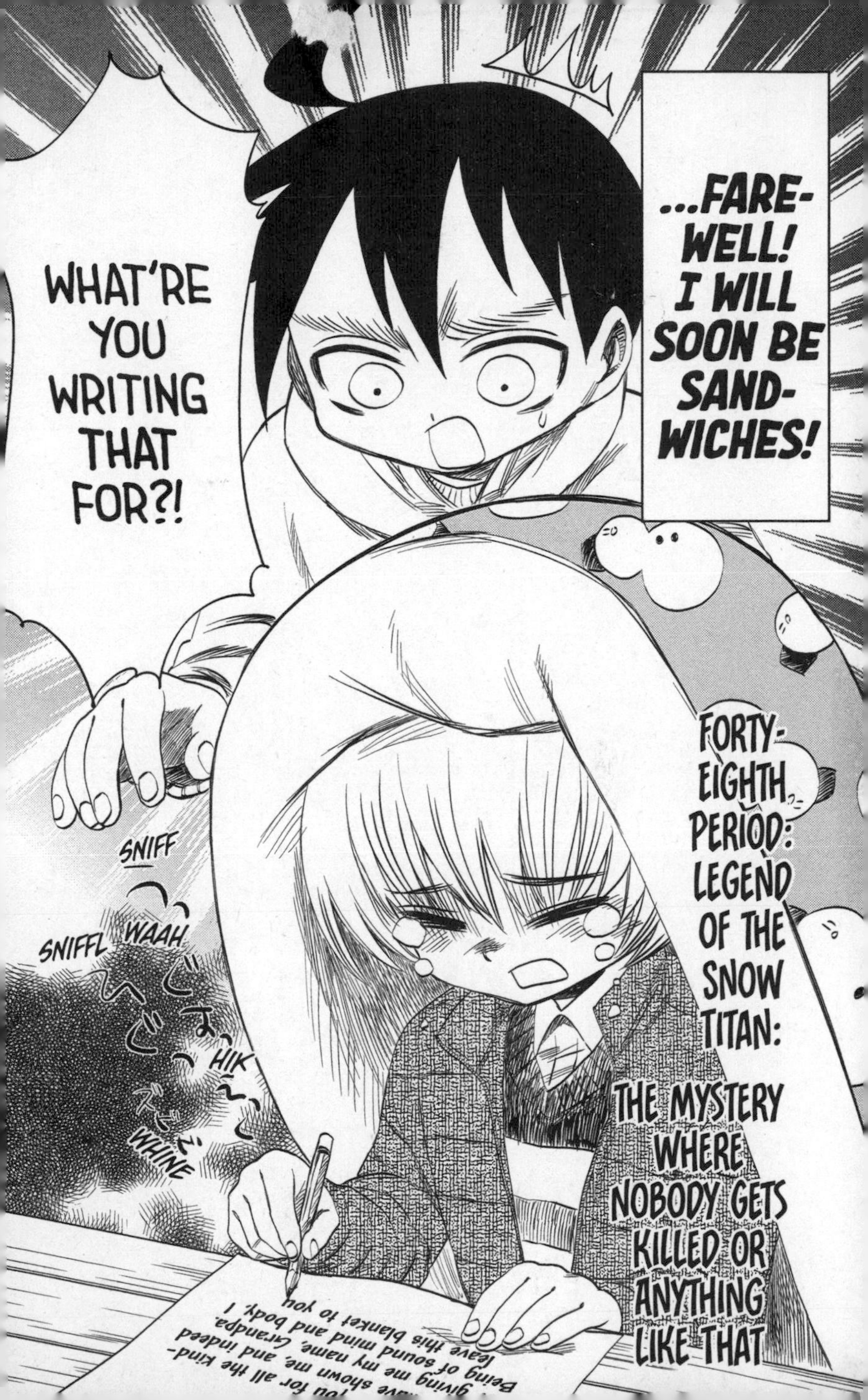
...FARE-WELL! I WILL SOON BE SAND-WICHES!
WHAT'RE YOU WRITING THAT FOR?!
FORTY-EIGHTH PERIOD: LEGEND OF THE SNOW TITAN:
THE MYSTERY WHERE NOBODY GETS KILLED OR ANYTHING LIKE THAT
SNIFF
WAAH
SNIFFL
HIK
WHINE
ou for all the kind-
ave shown me, and indeed
giving me my name, Grandpa.
Being of sound mind and body, I
leave this blanket to you

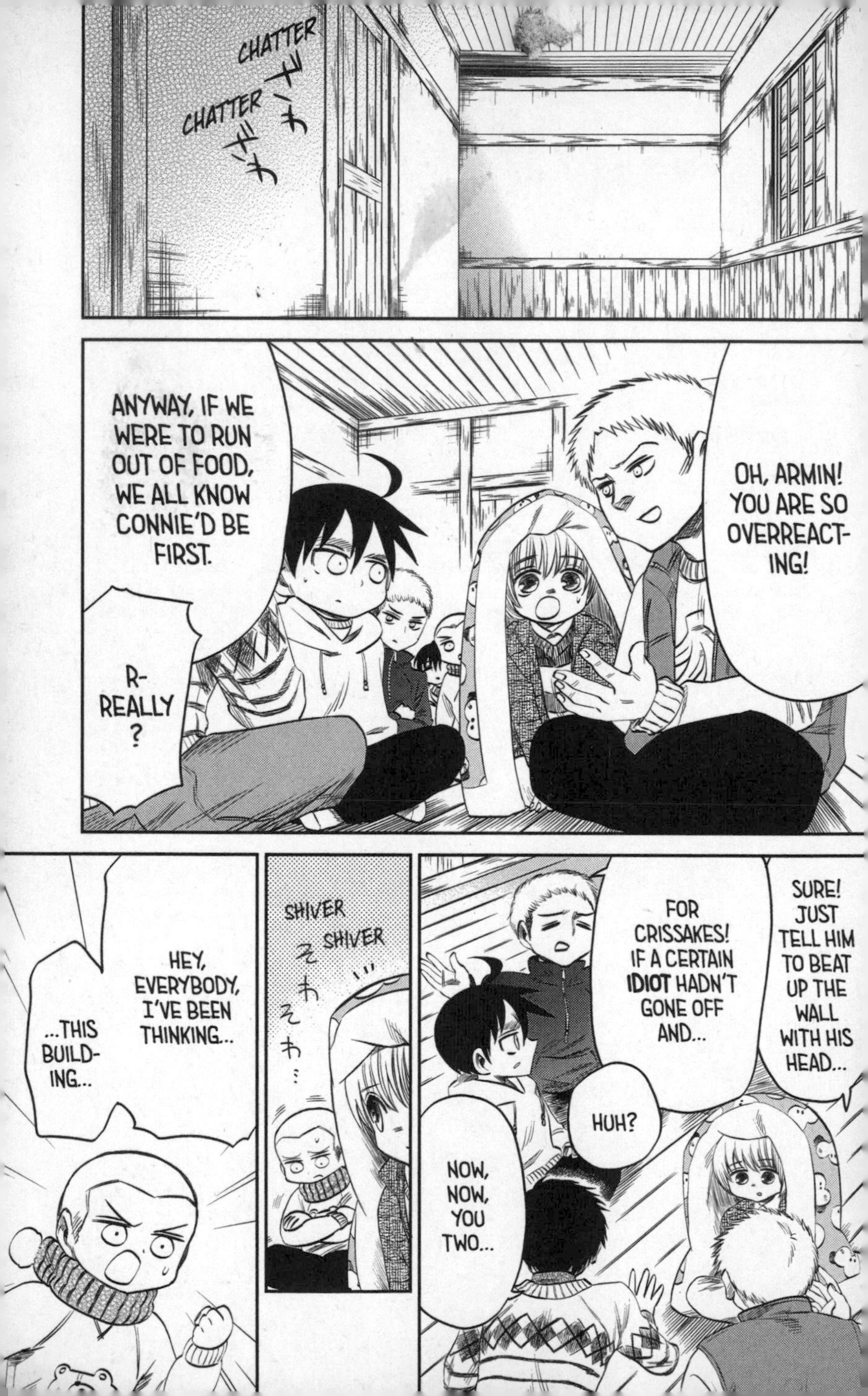
CHATTER
CHATTER
OH, ARMIN! YOU ARE SO OVERREACTING!
ANYWAY, IF WE WERE TO RUN OUT OF FOOD, WE ALL KNOW CONNIE'D BE FIRST.
R-REALLY?
SURE! JUST TELL HIM TO BEAT UP THE WALL WITH HIS HEAD...
FOR CRISSAKES! IF A CERTAIN **IDIOT** HADN'T GONE OFF AND...
HUH?
NOW, NOW, YOU TWO...
SHIVER SHIVER
そわそわ
HEY, EVERYBODY, I'VE BEEN THINKING...
...THIS BUILDING...

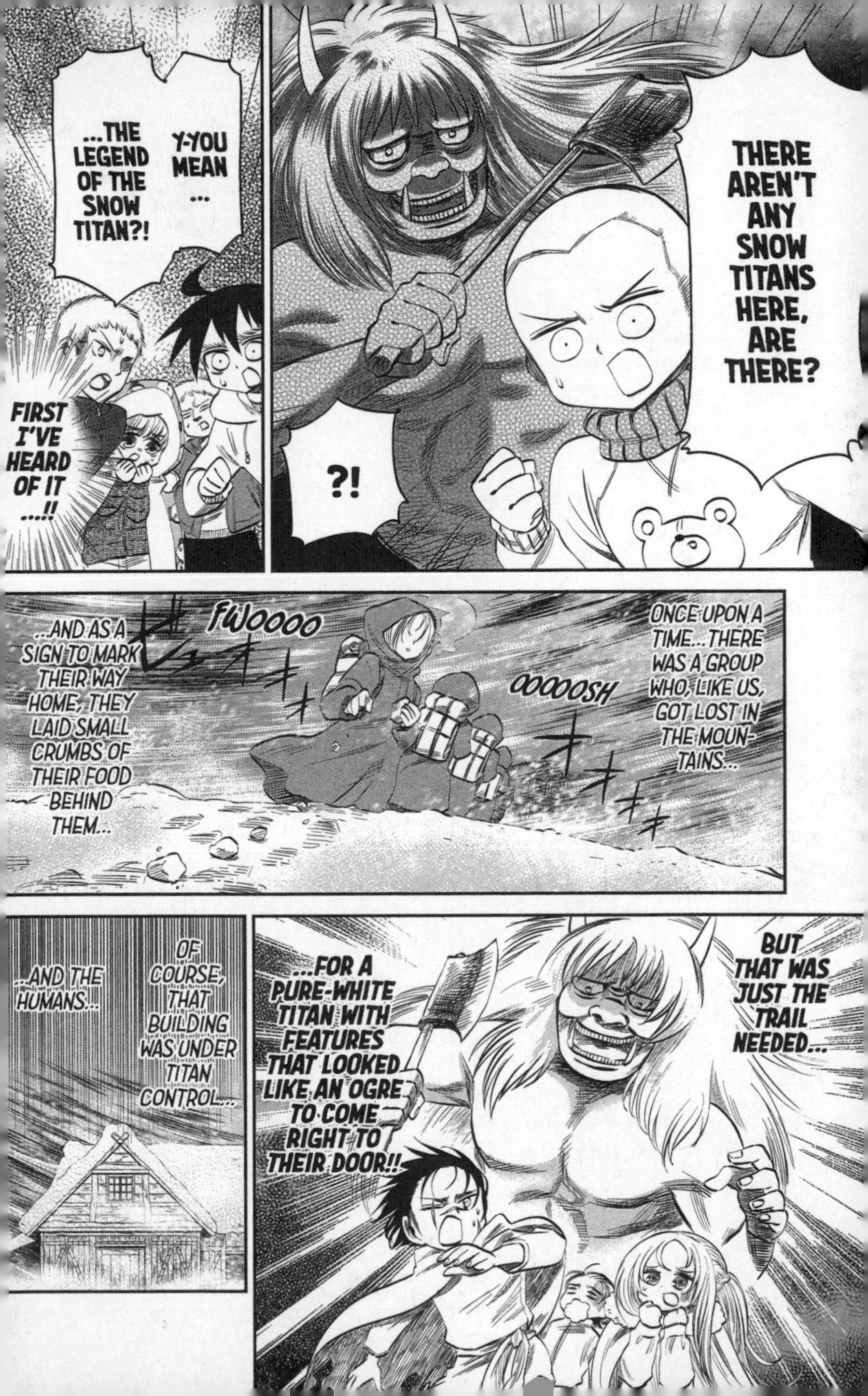
THERE AREN'T ANY SNOW TITANS HERE, ARE THERE?
?!
Y-YOU MEAN ...
...THE LEGEND OF THE SNOW TITAN?!
FIRST I'VE HEARD OF IT ...!!
ONCE UPON A TIME... THERE WAS A GROUP WHO, LIKE US, GOT LOST IN THE MOUNTAINS...
FWOOOO
OOOOOSH
...AND AS A SIGN TO MARK THEIR WAY HOME, THEY LAID SMALL CRUMBS OF THEIR FOOD BEHIND THEM...
BUT THAT WAS JUST THE TRAIL NEEDED...
...FOR A PURE-WHITE TITAN WITH FEATURES THAT LOOKED LIKE AN OGRE TO COME RIGHT TO THEIR DOOR!!
OF COURSE, THAT BUILDING WAS UNDER TITAN CONTROL...
...AND THE HUMANS...

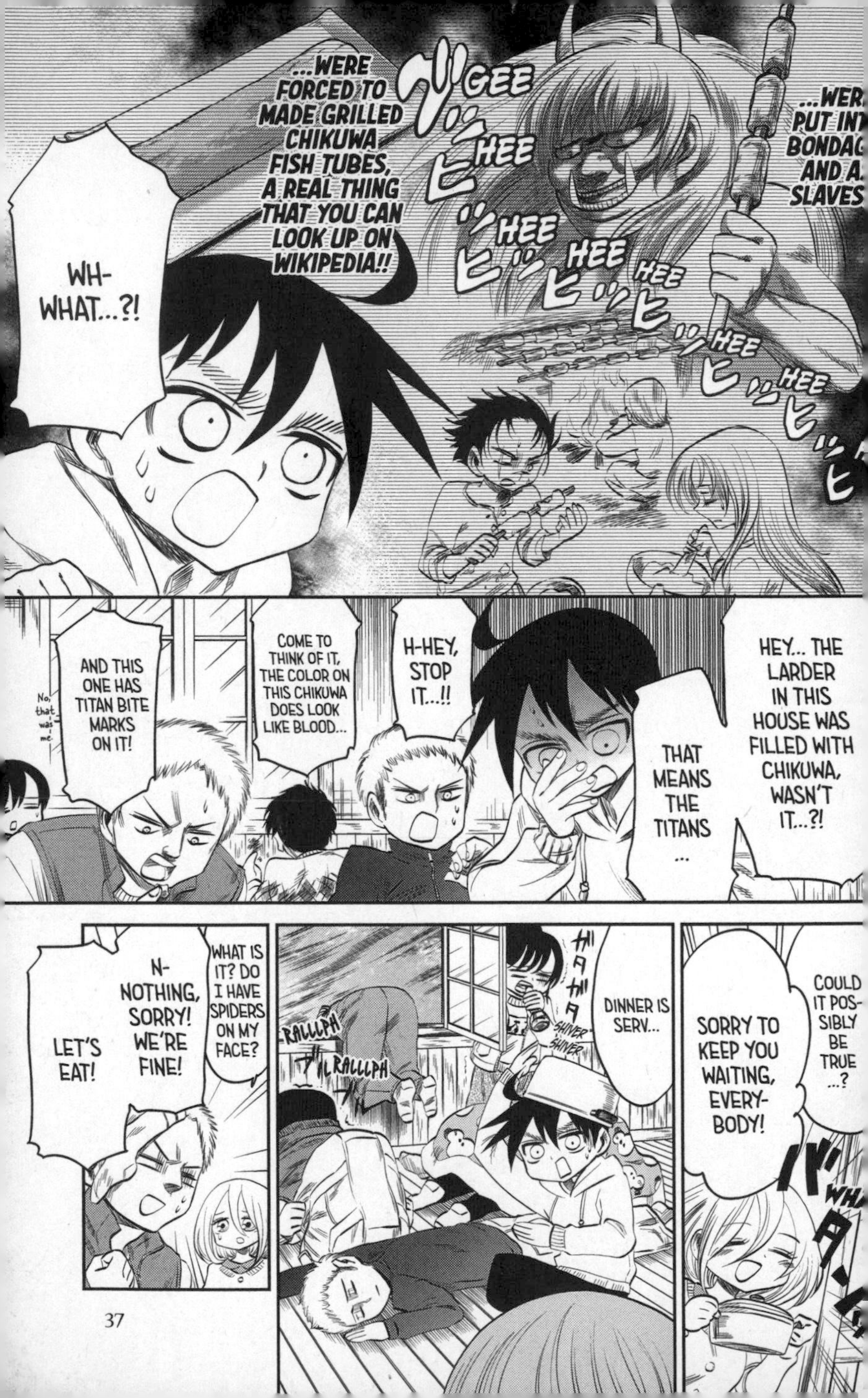
...WER PUT INT BONDAG AND A SLAVES
GEE
HEE
HEE
HEE
HEE
HEE
HEE
...WERE FORCED TO MADE GRILLED CHIKUWA FISH TUBES, A REAL THING THAT YOU CAN LOOK UP ON WIKIPEDIA!!
WH- WHAT...?!
HEY... THE LARDER IN THIS HOUSE WAS FILLED WITH CHIKUWA, WASN'T IT...?!
THAT MEANS THE TITANS ...
H-HEY, STOP IT...!!
COME TO THINK OF IT, THE COLOR ON THIS CHIKUWA DOES LOOK LIKE BLOOD...
AND THIS ONE HAS TITAN BITE MARKS ON IT!
No, that was me.
COULD IT POS- SIBLY BE TRUE ...?
SORRY TO KEEP YOU WAITING, EVERY- BODY!
WHA
DINNER IS SERV...
SHIVER SHIVER
RALLLPH
RALLLPH
WHAT IS IT? DO I HAVE SPIDERS ON MY FACE?
N- NOTHING, SORRY! WE'RE FINE!
LET'S EAT!

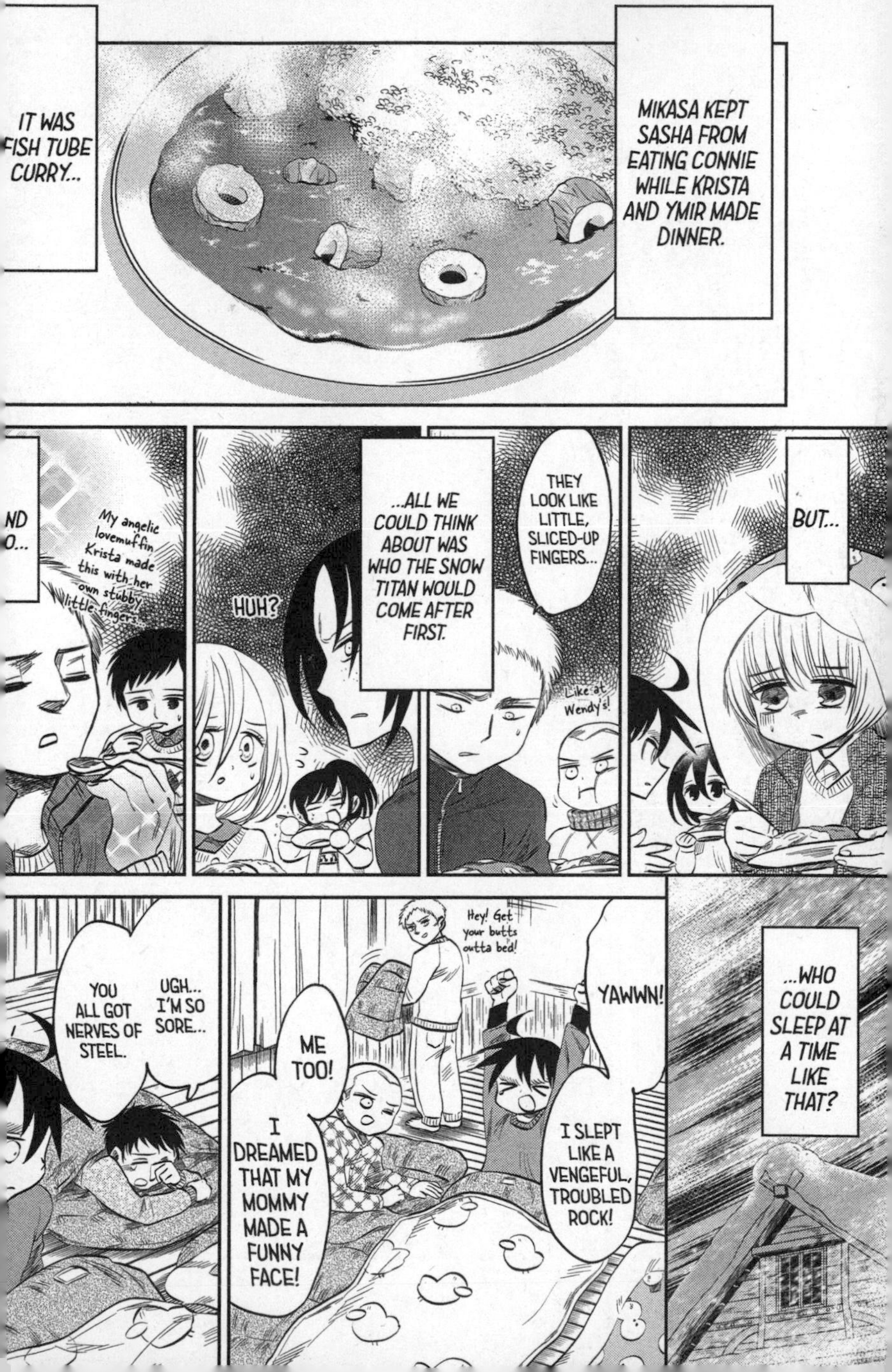
MIKASA KEPT SASHA FROM EATING CONNIE WHILE KRISTA AND YMIR MADE DINNER.
IT WAS FISH TUBE CURRY...
BUT...
THEY LOOK LIKE LITTLE, SLICED-UP FINGERS...
Like at Wendy's!
...ALL WE COULD THINK ABOUT WAS WHO THE SNOW TITAN WOULD COME AFTER FIRST.
HUH?
My angelic lovemuffin Krista made this with her own stubby little fingers...
...WHO COULD SLEEP AT A TIME LIKE THAT?
Hey! Get your butts outta bed!
YAWWN!
I SLEPT LIKE A VENGEFUL, TROUBLED ROCK!
ME TOO!
I DREAMED THAT MY MOMMY MADE A FUNNY FACE!
UGH... I'M SO SORE...
YOU ALL GOT NERVES OF STEEL.

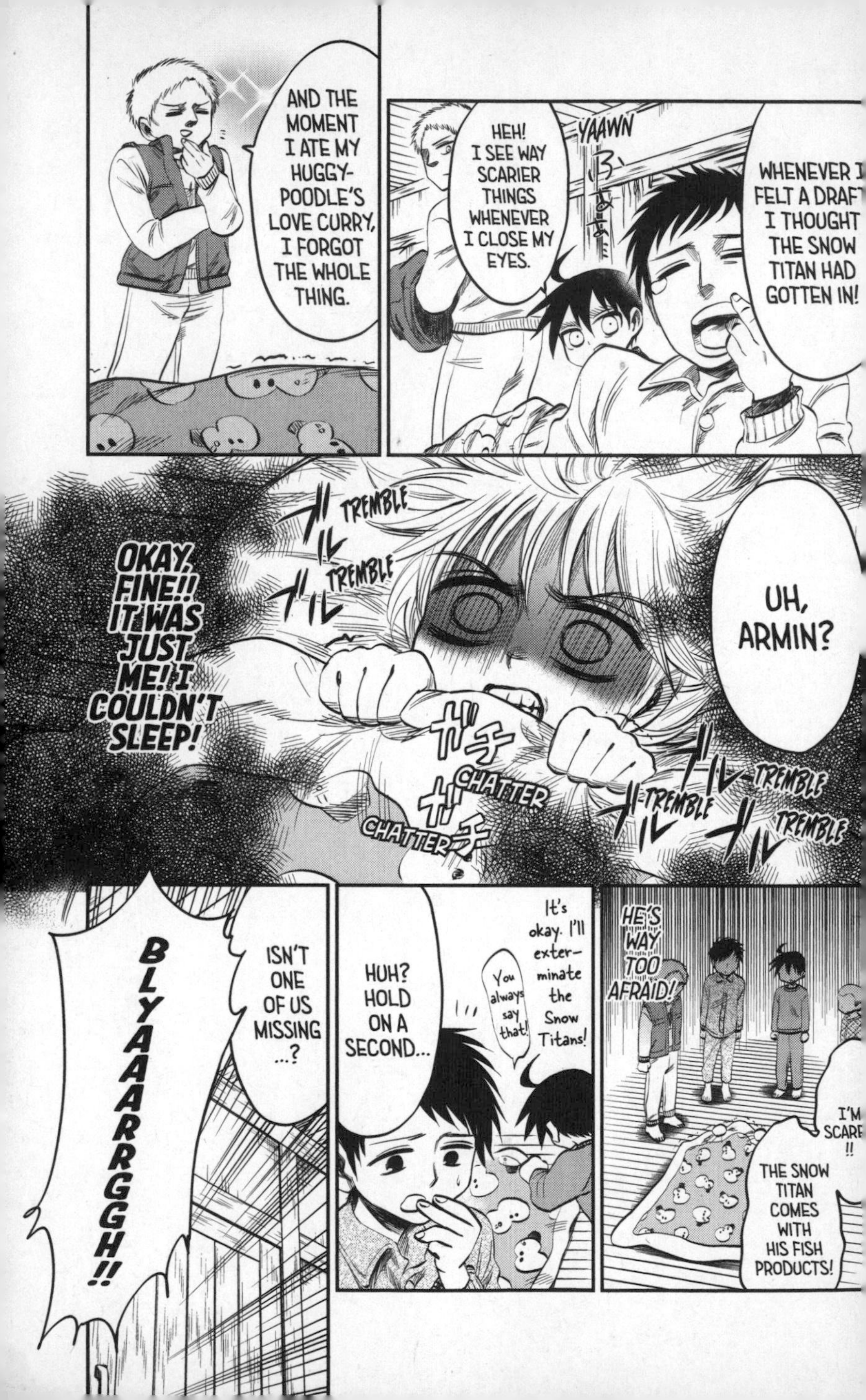
WHENEVER I FELT A DRAFT I THOUGHT THE SNOW TITAN HAD GOTTEN IN!
YAAWN
HEH! I SEE WAY SCARIER THINGS WHENEVER I CLOSE MY EYES.
AND THE MOMENT I ATE MY HUGGY-POODLE'S LOVE CURRY, I FORGOT THE WHOLE THING.
UH, ARMIN?
TREMBLE
TREMBLE
TREMBLE
TREMBLE
CHATTER
CHATTER
TREMBLE
TREMBLE
OKAY, FINE!! IT WAS JUST ME! I COULDN'T SLEEP!
HE'S WAY TOO AFRAID!
I'M SCAR !!
THE SNOW TITAN COMES WITH HIS FISH PRODUCTS!
It's okay. I'll exter-minate the Snow Titans!
You always say that!
HUH? HOLD ON A SECOND...
ISN'T ONE OF US MISSING ...?
BLYAAAARRRGGH!!

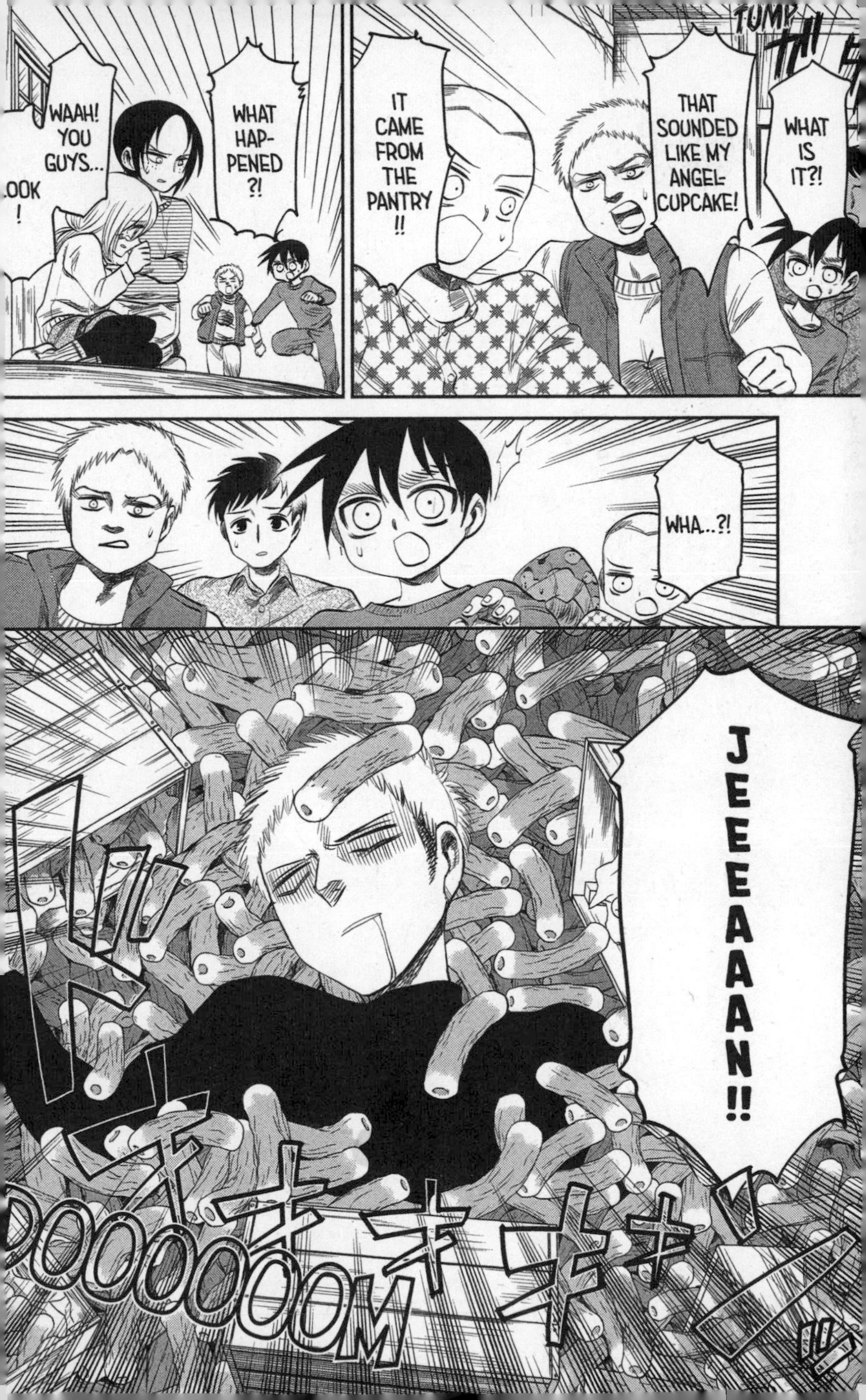
TUMP
WHAT IS IT?!
THAT SOUNDED LIKE MY ANGEL-CUPCAKE!
IT CAME FROM THE PANTRY!!
WHAT HAP-PENED?!
WAAH! YOU GUYS... .OOK!
WHA...?!
JEEEEAAAAN!!
OOOOOOOOM

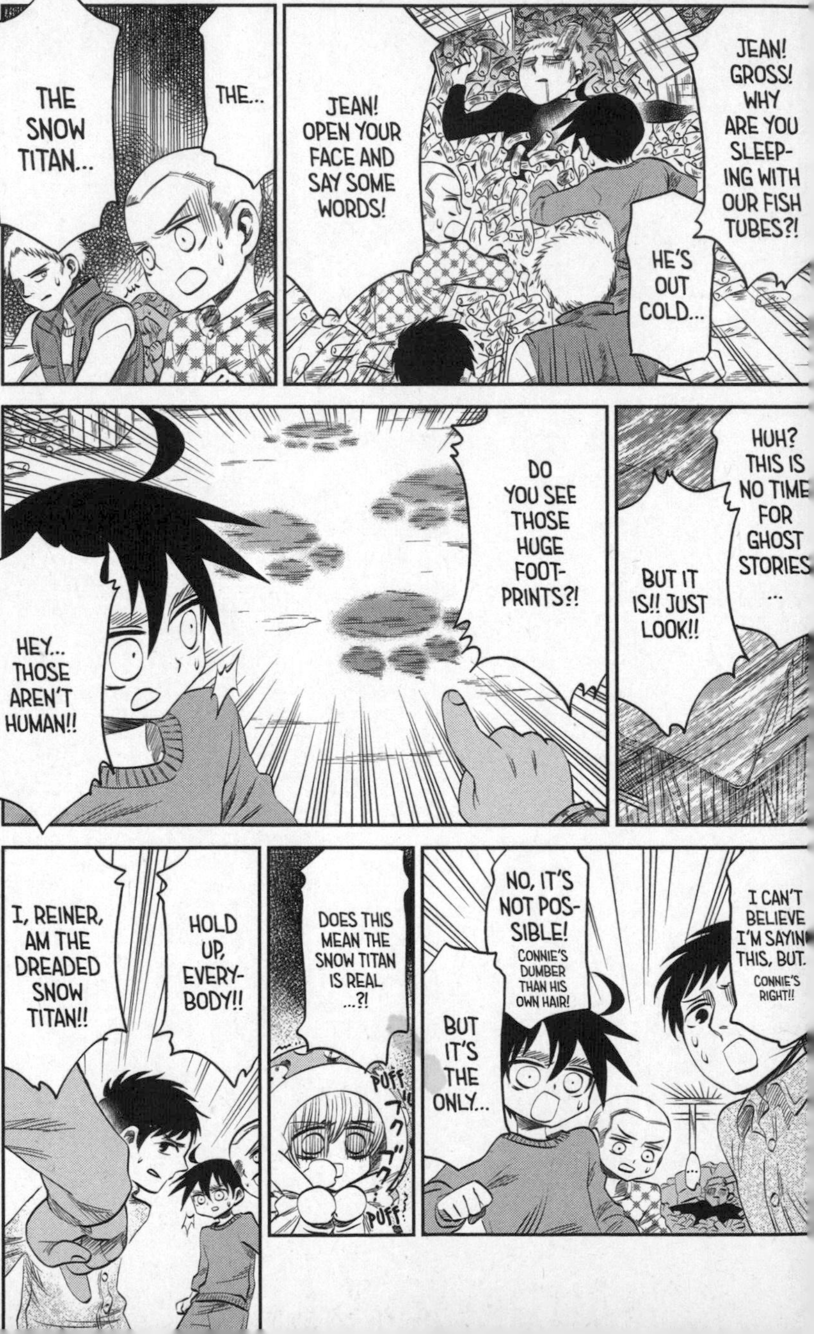

JEAN! GROSS! WHY ARE YOU SLEEP-ING WITH OUR FISH TUBES?!
HE'S OUT COLD...
JEAN! OPEN YOUR FACE AND SAY SOME WORDS!
THE...
THE SNOW TITAN...
HUH? THIS IS NO TIME FOR GHOST STORIES...
BUT IT IS!! JUST LOOK!!
DO YOU SEE THOSE HUGE FOOT-PRINTS?!
HEY... THOSE AREN'T HUMAN!!
I CAN'T BELIEVE I'M SAYIN THIS, BUT...
CONNIE'S RIGHT!!
NO, IT'S NOT POS-SIBLE!
CONNIE'S DUMBER THAN HIS OWN HAIR!
BUT IT'S THE ONLY...
...
DOES THIS MEAN THE SNOW TITAN IS REAL...?!
PUFF
PUFF
HOLD UP, EVERY-BODY!!
I, REINER, AM THE DREADED SNOW TITAN!!

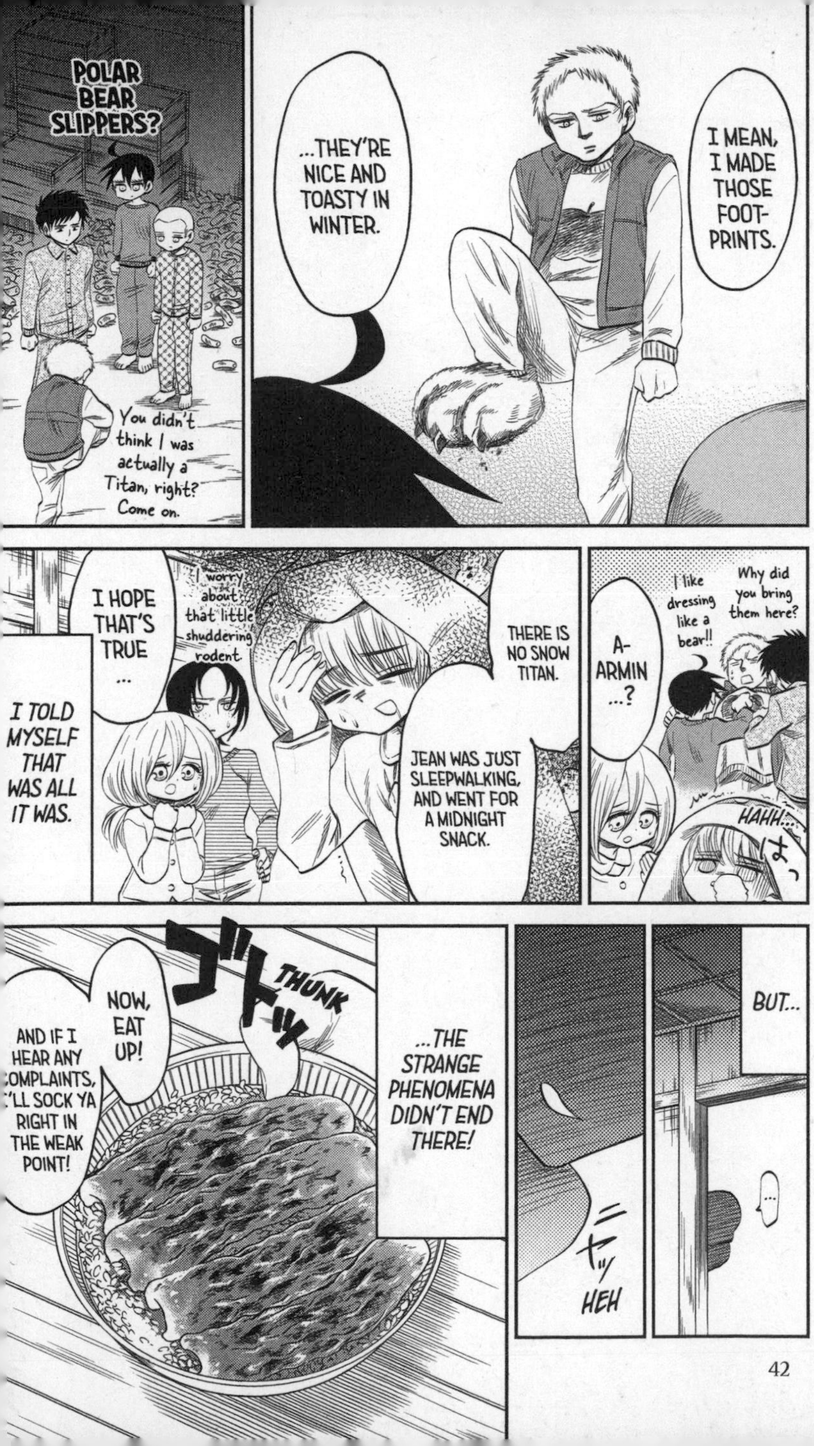

I MEAN, I MADE THOSE FOOT-PRINTS.
...THEY'RE NICE AND TOASTY IN WINTER.
POLAR BEAR SLIPPERS?
You didn't think I was actually a Titan, right? Come on.
Why did you bring them here?
I like dressing like a bear!!
A-ARMIN...?
HAHH...
THERE IS NO SNOW TITAN.
JEAN WAS JUST SLEEPWALKING, AND WENT FOR A MIDNIGHT SNACK.
I worry about that little shuddering rodent.
I HOPE THAT'S TRUE...
I TOLD MYSELF THAT WAS ALL IT WAS.
BUT...
...
HEH
...THE STRANGE PHENOMENA DIDN'T END THERE!
THUNK
NOW, EAT UP!
AND IF I HEAR ANY COMPLAINTS, 'LL SOCK YA RIGHT IN THE WEAK POINT!

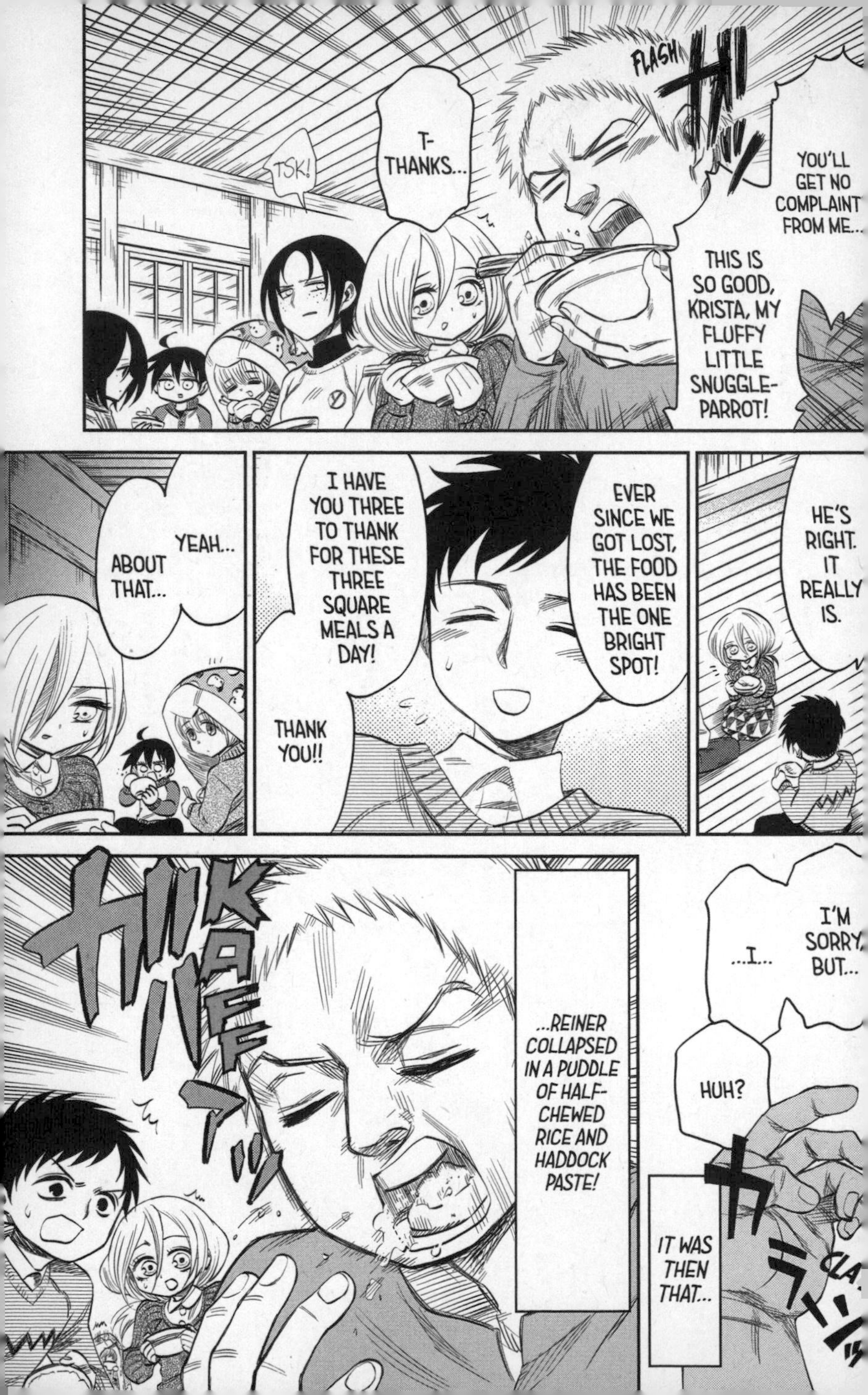
YOU'LL GET NO COMPLAINT FROM ME...
THIS IS SO GOOD, KRISTA, MY FLUFFY LITTLE SNUGGLE-PARROT!
FLASH
T-THANKS...
TSK!
HE'S RIGHT. IT REALLY IS.
EVER SINCE WE GOT LOST, THE FOOD HAS BEEN THE ONE BRIGHT SPOT!
I HAVE YOU THREE TO THANK FOR THESE THREE SQUARE MEALS A DAY!
THANK YOU!!
YEAH...
ABOUT THAT...
I'M SORRY, BUT...
...I...
HUH?
IT WAS THEN THAT...
...REINER COLLAPSED IN A PUDDLE OF HALF-CHEWED RICE AND HADDOCK PASTE!
KAFF

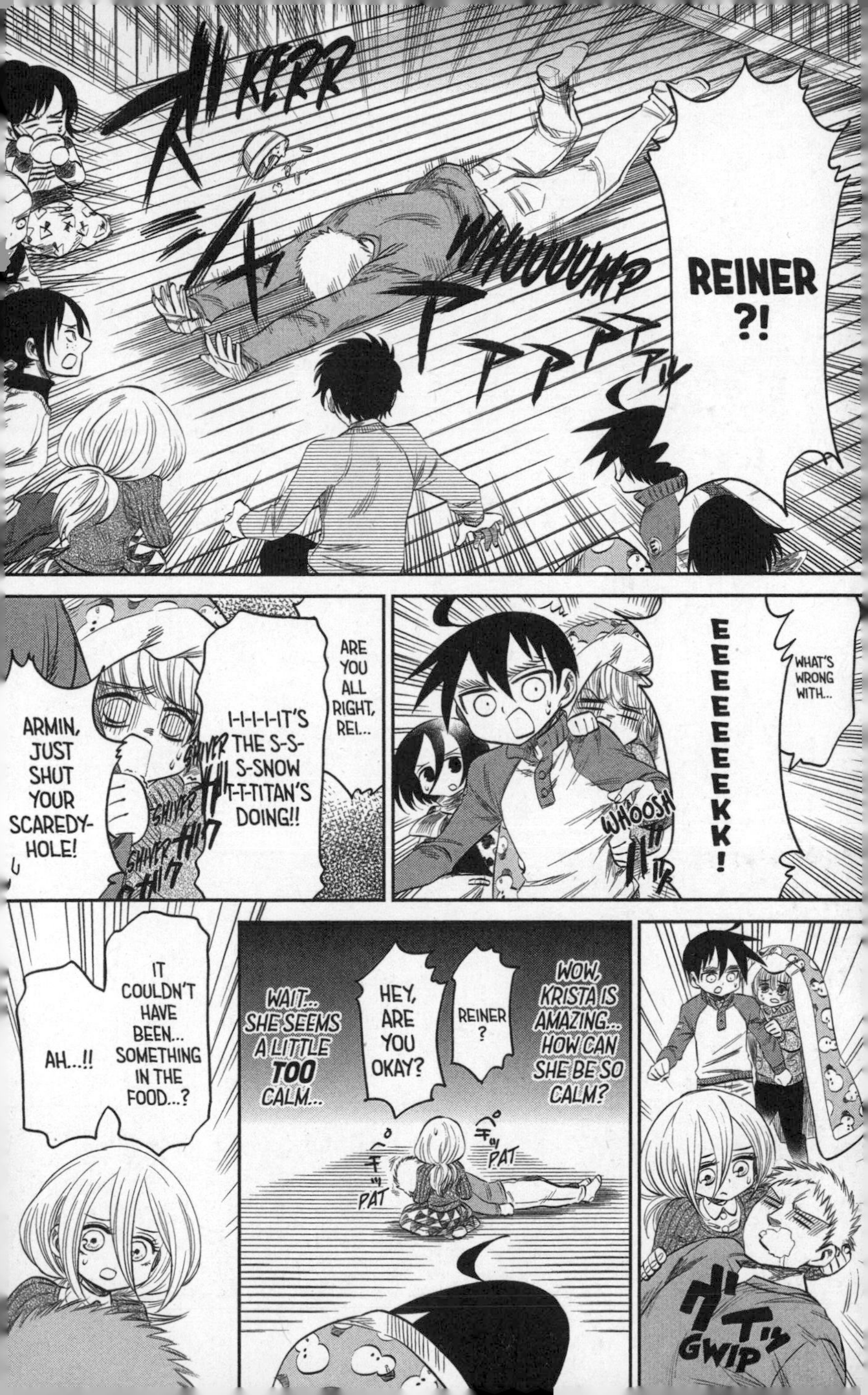
REINER ?!
WHUUUUUMP
SKERR
WHAT'S WRONG WITH...
EEEEEEEEEK!
WHOOSH
ARE YOU ALL RIGHT, REI...
I-I-I-I-IT'S THE S-S-S-SNOW T-T-TITAN'S DOING!!
SHIVER
SHIVER
SHIVER
ARMIN, JUST SHUT YOUR SCAREDY-HOLE!
GWIP
WOW, KRISTA IS AMAZING... HOW CAN SHE BE SO CALM?
REINER?
HEY, ARE YOU OKAY?
WAIT... SHE SEEMS A LITTLE TOO CALM...
PAT
PAT
IT COULDN'T HAVE BEEN... SOMETHING IN THE FOOD...?
AH...!!

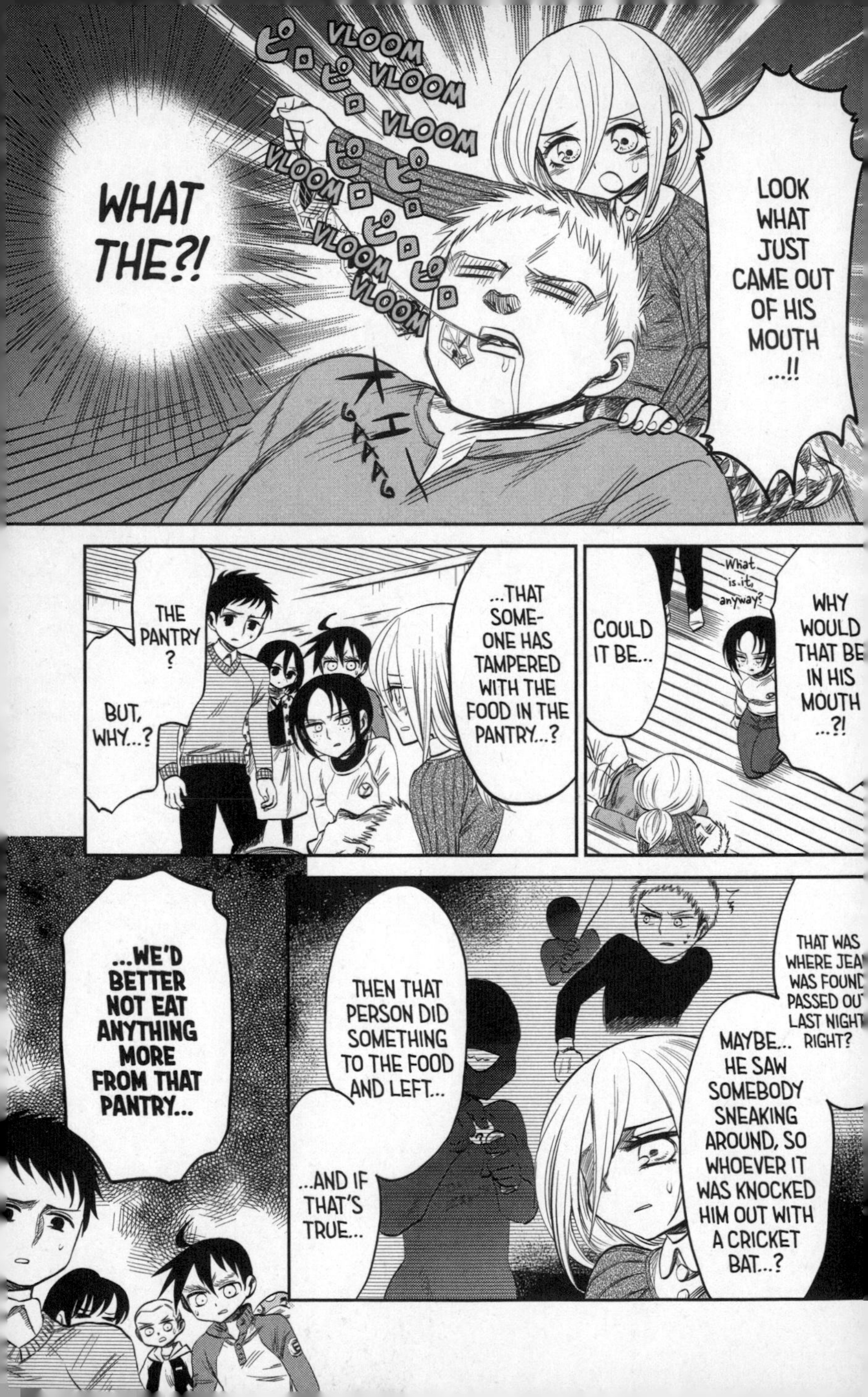
LOOK WHAT JUST CAME OUT OF HIS MOUTH ...!!
WHAT THE?!
VLOOM VLOOM VLOOM VLOOM VLOOM VLOOM
WHY WOULD THAT BE IN HIS MOUTH ...?!
What is it, anyway?
COULD IT BE...
...THAT SOME-ONE HAS TAMPERED WITH THE FOOD IN THE PANTRY...?
THE PANTRY ?
BUT, WHY...?
THAT WAS WHERE JEA WAS FOUND PASSED OU LAST NIGHT RIGHT?
MAYBE... HE SAW SOMEBODY SNEAKING AROUND, SO WHOEVER IT WAS KNOCKED HIM OUT WITH A CRICKET BAT...?
THEN THAT PERSON DID SOMETHING TO THE FOOD AND LEFT...
...AND IF THAT'S TRUE...
...WE'D BETTER NOT EAT ANYTHING MORE FROM THAT PANTRY...

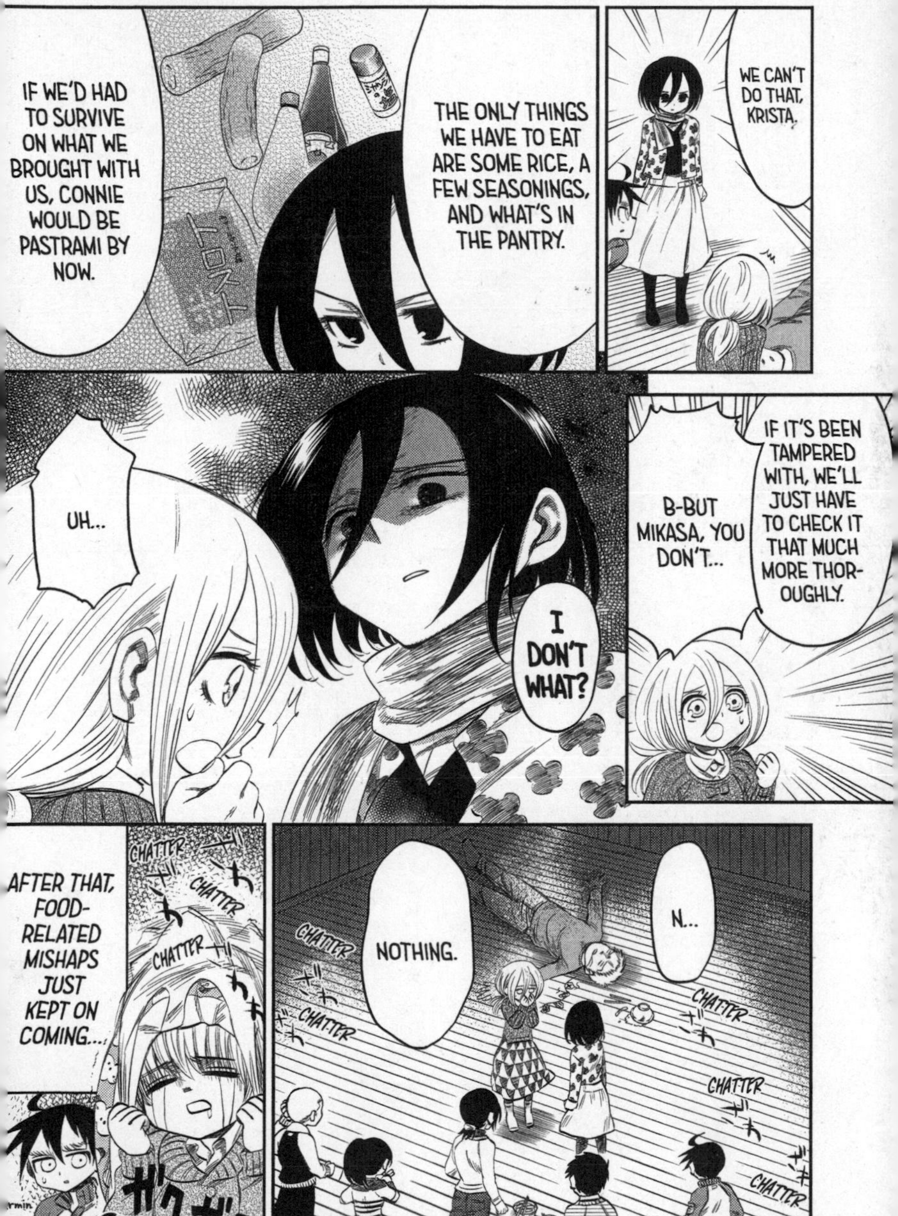
WE CAN'T DO THAT, KRISTA.
THE ONLY THINGS WE HAVE TO EAT ARE SOME RICE, A FEW SEASONINGS, AND WHAT'S IN THE PANTRY.
IF WE'D HAD TO SURVIVE ON WHAT WE BROUGHT WITH US, CONNIE WOULD BE PASTRAMI BY NOW.
IF IT'S BEEN TAMPERED WITH, WE'LL JUST HAVE TO CHECK IT THAT MUCH MORE THOROUGHLY.
B-BUT MIKASA, YOU DON'T...
I DON'T WHAT?
UH...
N...
NOTHING.
CHATTER
CHATTER
CHATTER
CHATTER
CHATTER
AFTER THAT, FOOD-RELATED MISHAPS JUST KEPT ON COMING...
CHATTER
CHATTER
CHATTER
SHIVER
SHIVER

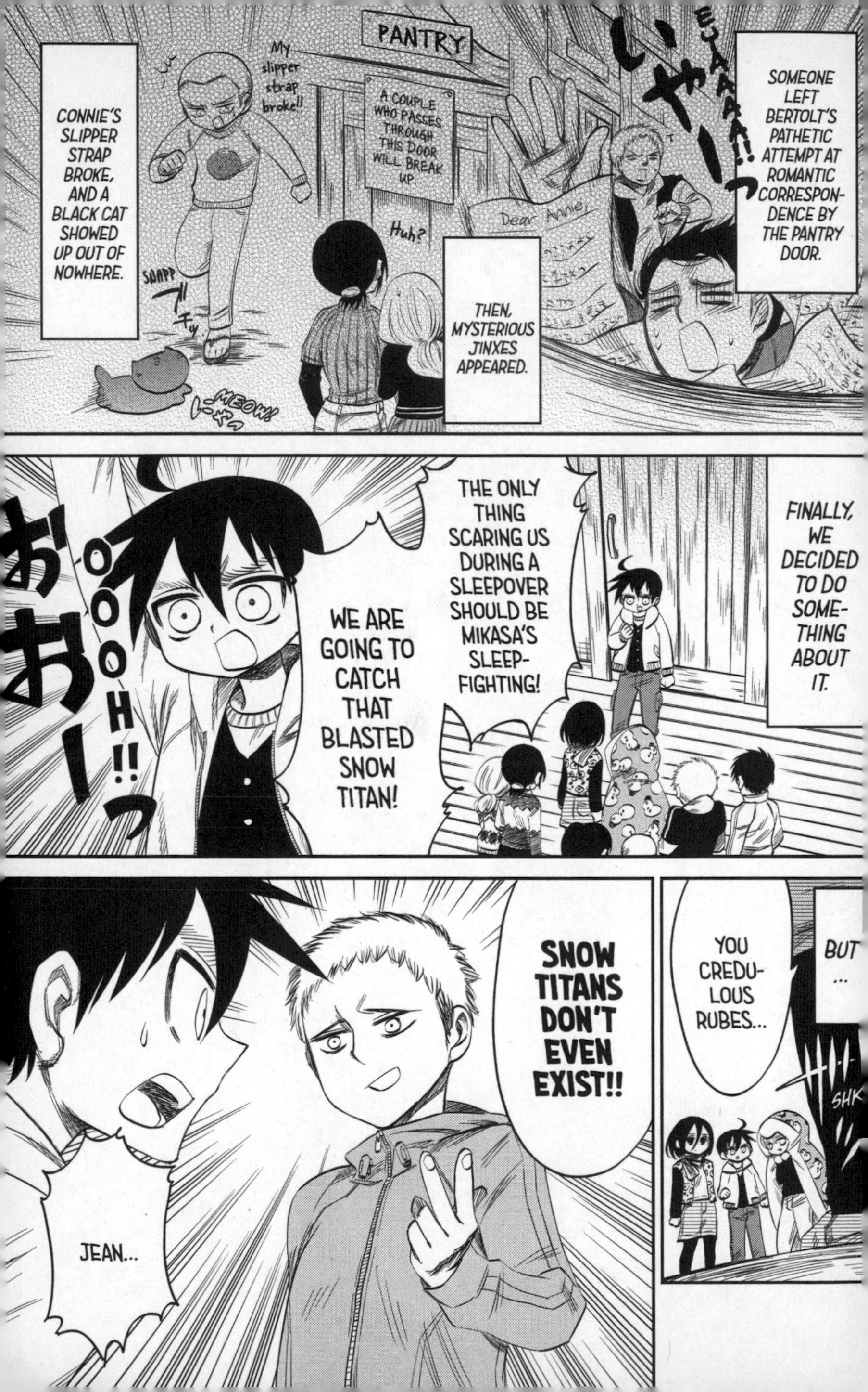

SOMEONE LEFT BERTOLT'S PATHETIC ATTEMPT AT ROMANTIC CORRESPONDENCE BY THE PANTRY DOOR.
EIJAAAAA!!
いやーっ
Dear Annie
PANTRY
A COUPLE WHO PASSES THROUGH THIS DOOR WILL BREAK UP
Huh?
THEN, MYSTERIOUS JINXES APPEARED.
My slipper strap broke!!
CONNIE'S SLIPPER STRAP BROKE, AND A BLACK CAT SHOWED UP OUT OF NOWHERE.
SNAPP
MEOW!
FINALLY, WE DECIDED TO DO SOMETHING ABOUT IT.
THE ONLY THING SCARING US DURING A SLEEPOVER SHOULD BE MIKASA'S SLEEP-FIGHTING!
WE ARE GOING TO CATCH THAT BLASTED SNOW TITAN!
OOOOH!!
おおーっ
BUT ...
YOU CREDULOUS RUBES...
SHK
SNOW TITANS DON'T EVEN EXIST!!
JEAN...

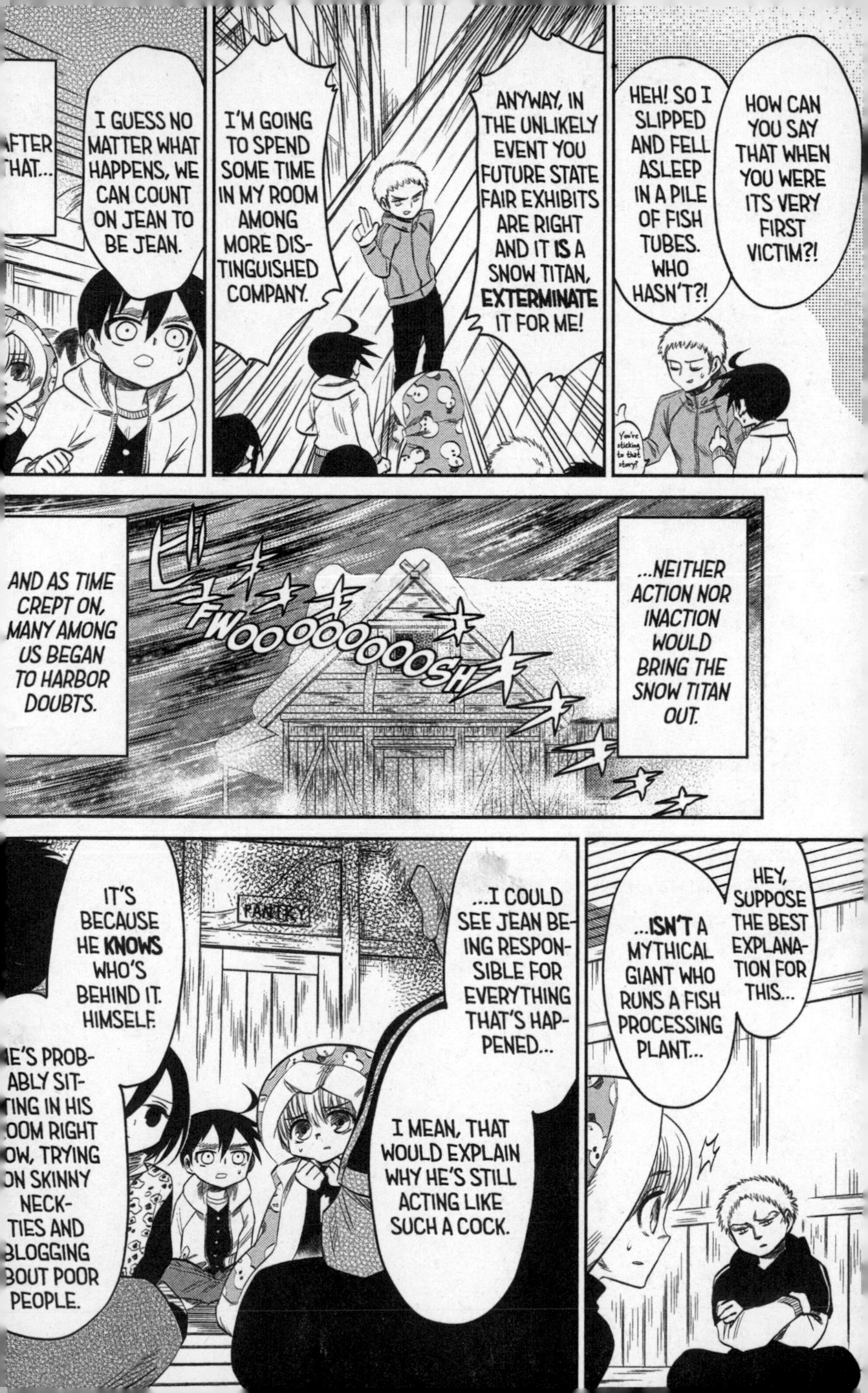
HOW CAN YOU SAY THAT WHEN YOU WERE ITS VERY FIRST VICTIM?!
HEH! SO I SLIPPED AND FELL ASLEEP IN A PILE OF FISH TUBES. WHO HASN'T?!
You're sticking to that story?
ANYWAY, IN THE UNLIKELY EVENT YOU FUTURE STATE FAIR EXHIBITS ARE RIGHT AND IT **IS** A SNOW TITAN, **EXTERMINATE** IT FOR ME!
I'M GOING TO SPEND SOME TIME IN MY ROOM AMONG MORE DISTINGUISHED COMPANY.
I GUESS NO MATTER WHAT HAPPENS, WE CAN COUNT ON JEAN TO BE JEAN.
AFTER THAT...
...NEITHER ACTION NOR INACTION WOULD BRING THE SNOW TITAN OUT.
FWOOOOOOOOOSH
AND AS TIME CREPT ON, MANY AMONG US BEGAN TO HARBOR DOUBTS.
HEY, SUPPOSE THE BEST EXPLANATION FOR THIS...
...**ISN'T** A MYTHICAL GIANT WHO RUNS A FISH PROCESSING PLANT...
...I COULD SEE JEAN BEING RESPONSIBLE FOR EVERYTHING THAT'S HAPPENED...
PANTRY
IT'S BECAUSE HE **KNOWS** WHO'S BEHIND IT. HIMSELF.
I MEAN, THAT WOULD EXPLAIN WHY HE'S STILL ACTING LIKE SUCH A COCK.
HE'S PROBABLY SITTING IN HIS ROOM RIGHT NOW, TRYING ON SKINNY NECKTIES AND BLOGGING ABOUT POOR PEOPLE.

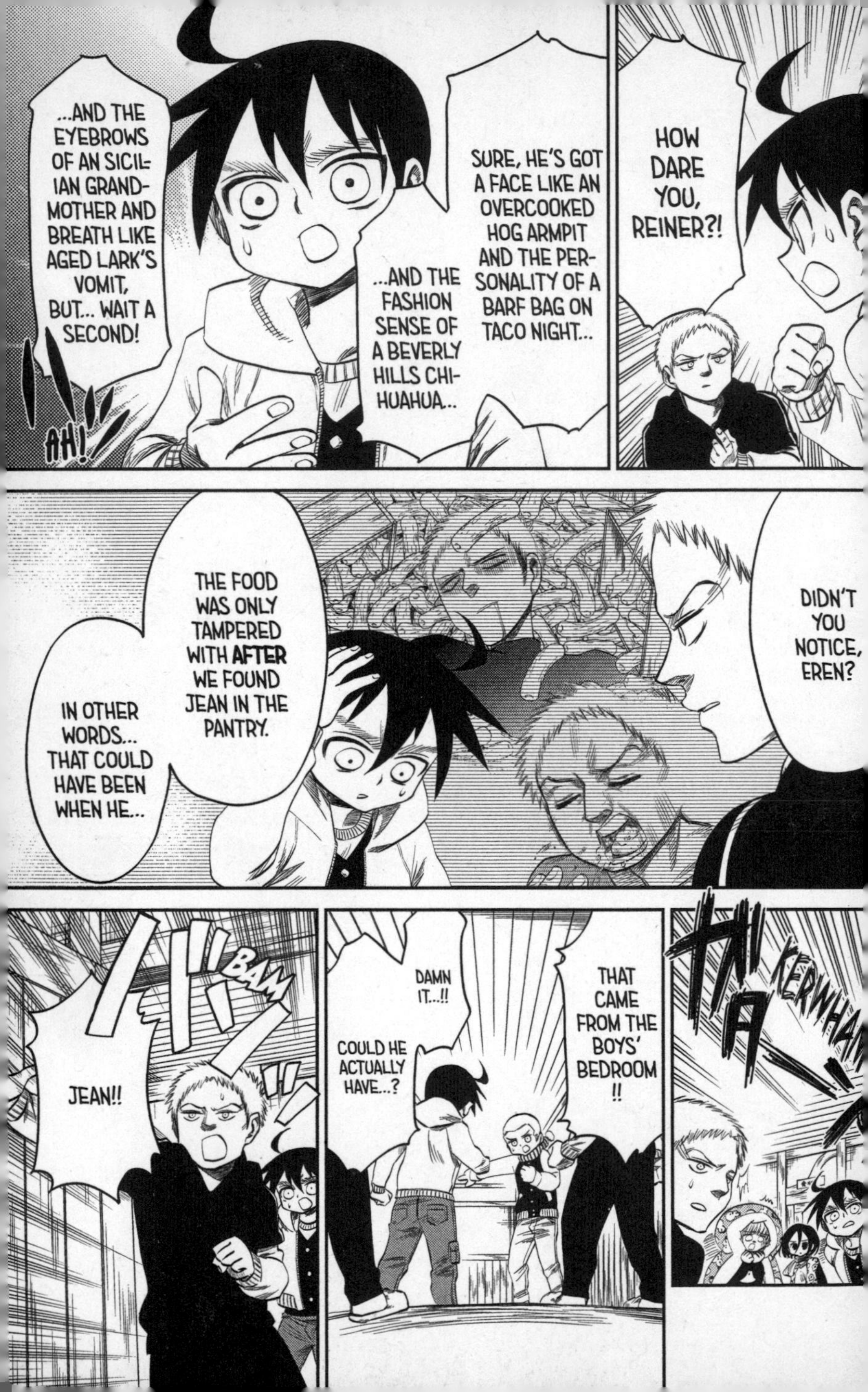
HOW DARE YOU, REINER?!
SURE, HE'S GOT A FACE LIKE AN OVERCOOKED HOG ARMPIT AND THE PERSONALITY OF A BARF BAG ON TACO NIGHT...
...AND THE FASHION SENSE OF A BEVERLY HILLS CHIHUAHUA...
...AND THE EYEBROWS OF AN SICILIAN GRANDMOTHER AND BREATH LIKE AGED LARK'S VOMIT, BUT... WAIT A SECOND!
AH!!
DIDN'T YOU NOTICE, EREN?
THE FOOD WAS ONLY TAMPERED WITH **AFTER** WE FOUND JEAN IN THE PANTRY.
IN OTHER WORDS... THAT COULD HAVE BEEN WHEN HE...
THAT CAME FROM THE BOYS' BEDROOM !!
DAMN IT...!!
COULD HE ACTUALLY HAVE...?
BAM
JEAN!!

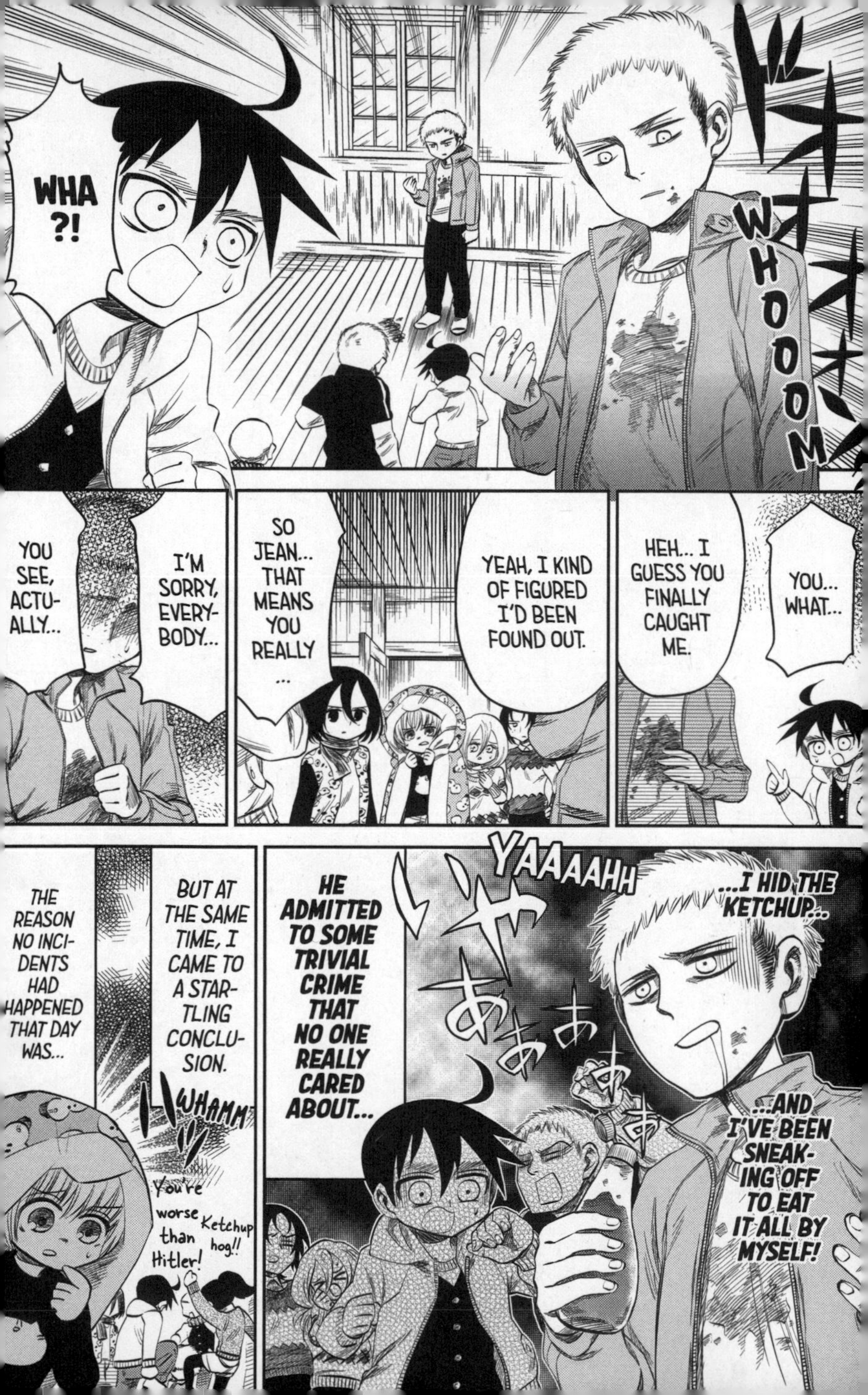
WHOOOM
WHA ?!
YOU... WHAT...
HEH... I GUESS YOU FINALLY CAUGHT ME.
YEAH, I KIND OF FIGURED I'D BEEN FOUND OUT.
SO JEAN... THAT MEANS YOU REALLY ...
I'M SORRY, EVERYBODY...
YOU SEE, ACTUALLY...
...I HID THE KETCHUP...
...AND I'VE BEEN SNEAKING OFF TO EAT IT ALL BY MYSELF!
YAAAAHH
HE ADMITTED TO SOME TRIVIAL CRIME THAT NO ONE REALLY CARED ABOUT...
BUT AT THE SAME TIME, I CAME TO A STARTLING CONCLUSION.
THE REASON NO INCIDENTS HAD HAPPENED THAT DAY WAS...
WHAMM
Ketchup hog!!
You're worse than Hitler!

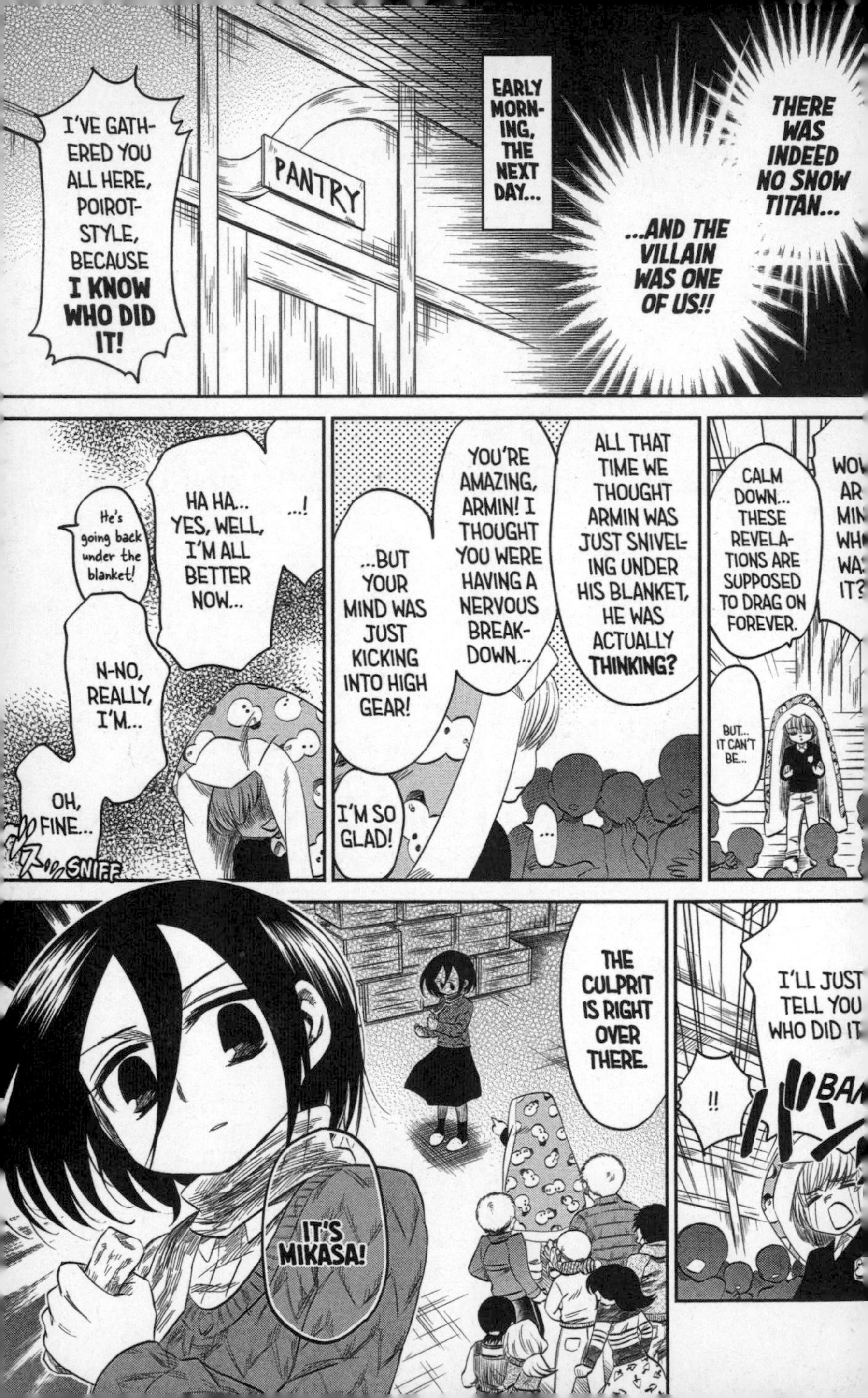
THERE WAS INDEED NO SNOW TITAN...
...AND THE VILLAIN WAS ONE OF US!!
EARLY MORNING, THE NEXT DAY...
PANTRY
I'VE GATHERED YOU ALL HERE, POIROT-STYLE, BECAUSE I KNOW WHO DID IT!
WO AR MIN WH WA IT?
CALM DOWN... THESE REVELATIONS ARE SUPPOSED TO DRAG ON FOREVER.
BUT... IT CAN'T BE...
ALL THAT TIME WE THOUGHT ARMIN WAS JUST SNIVELING UNDER HIS BLANKET, HE WAS ACTUALLY THINKING?
YOU'RE AMAZING, ARMIN! I THOUGHT YOU WERE HAVING A NERVOUS BREAKDOWN...
...BUT YOUR MIND WAS JUST KICKING INTO HIGH GEAR!
...
I'M SO GLAD!
...!
HA HA... YES, WELL, I'M ALL BETTER NOW...
He's going back under the blanket!
N-NO, REALLY, I'M...
OH, FINE...
SNIFF
I'LL JUST TELL YOU WHO DID IT
!!
THE CULPRIT IS RIGHT OVER THERE.
IT'S MIKASA!

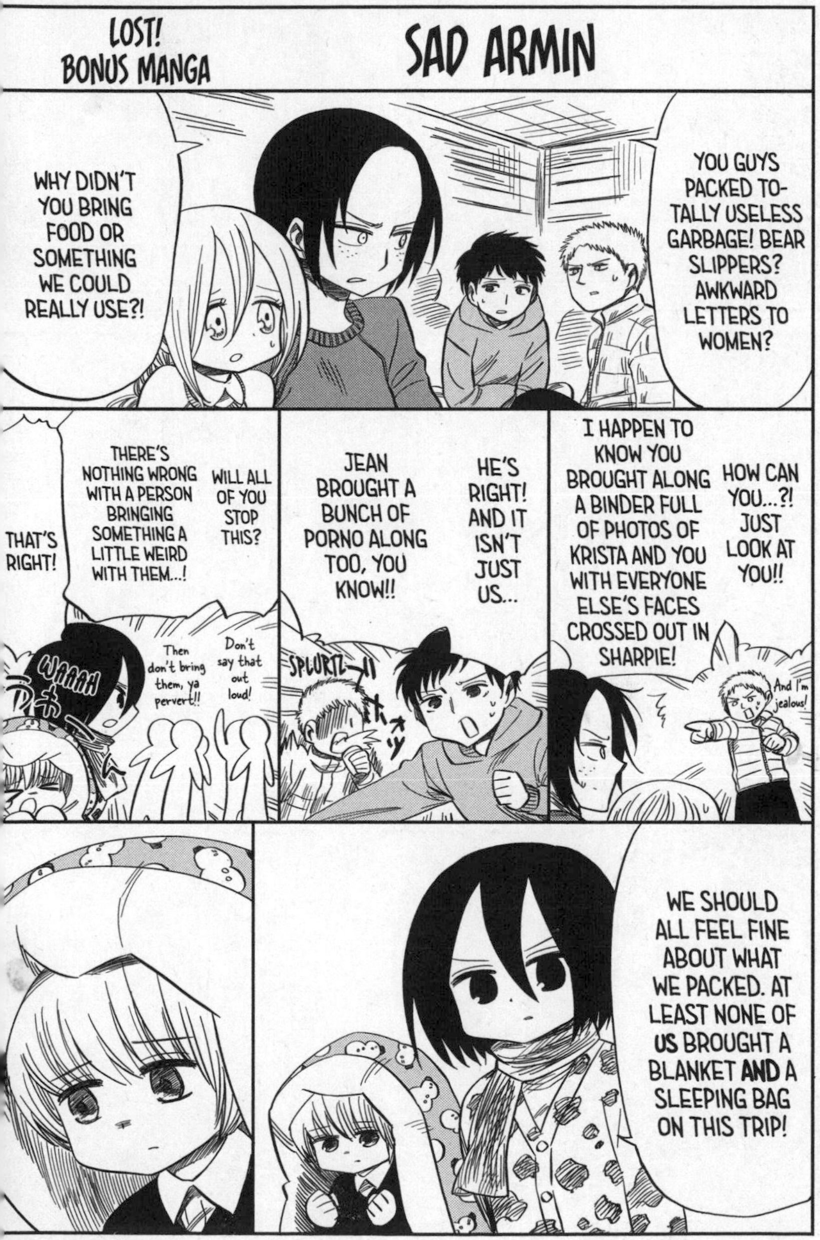
LOST! BONUS MANGA
SAD ARMIN
YOU GUYS PACKED TO-TALLY USELESS GARBAGE! BEAR SLIPPERS? AWKWARD LETTERS TO WOMEN?
WHY DIDN'T YOU BRING FOOD OR SOMETHING WE COULD REALLY USE?!
I HAPPEN TO KNOW YOU BROUGHT ALONG A BINDER FULL OF PHOTOS OF KRISTA AND YOU WITH EVERYONE ELSE'S FACES CROSSED OUT IN SHARPIE!
HOW CAN YOU...?! JUST LOOK AT YOU!!
And I'm jealous!
HE'S RIGHT! AND IT ISN'T JUST US...
JEAN BROUGHT A BUNCH OF PORNO ALONG TOO, YOU KNOW!!
SPLURTZ
WILL ALL OF YOU STOP THIS?
THERE'S NOTHING WRONG WITH A PERSON BRINGING SOMETHING A LITTLE WEIRD WITH THEM...!
THAT'S RIGHT!
Don't say that out loud!
Then don't bring them, ya pervert!!
WAAAH
WE SHOULD ALL FEEL FINE ABOUT WHAT WE PACKED. AT LEAST NONE OF US BROUGHT A BLANKET AND A SLEEPING BAG ON THIS TRIP!

FORTY-NINTH PERIOD: LEGEND OF THE SNOW TITAN (AND SO ON): ALL THE ANSWERS

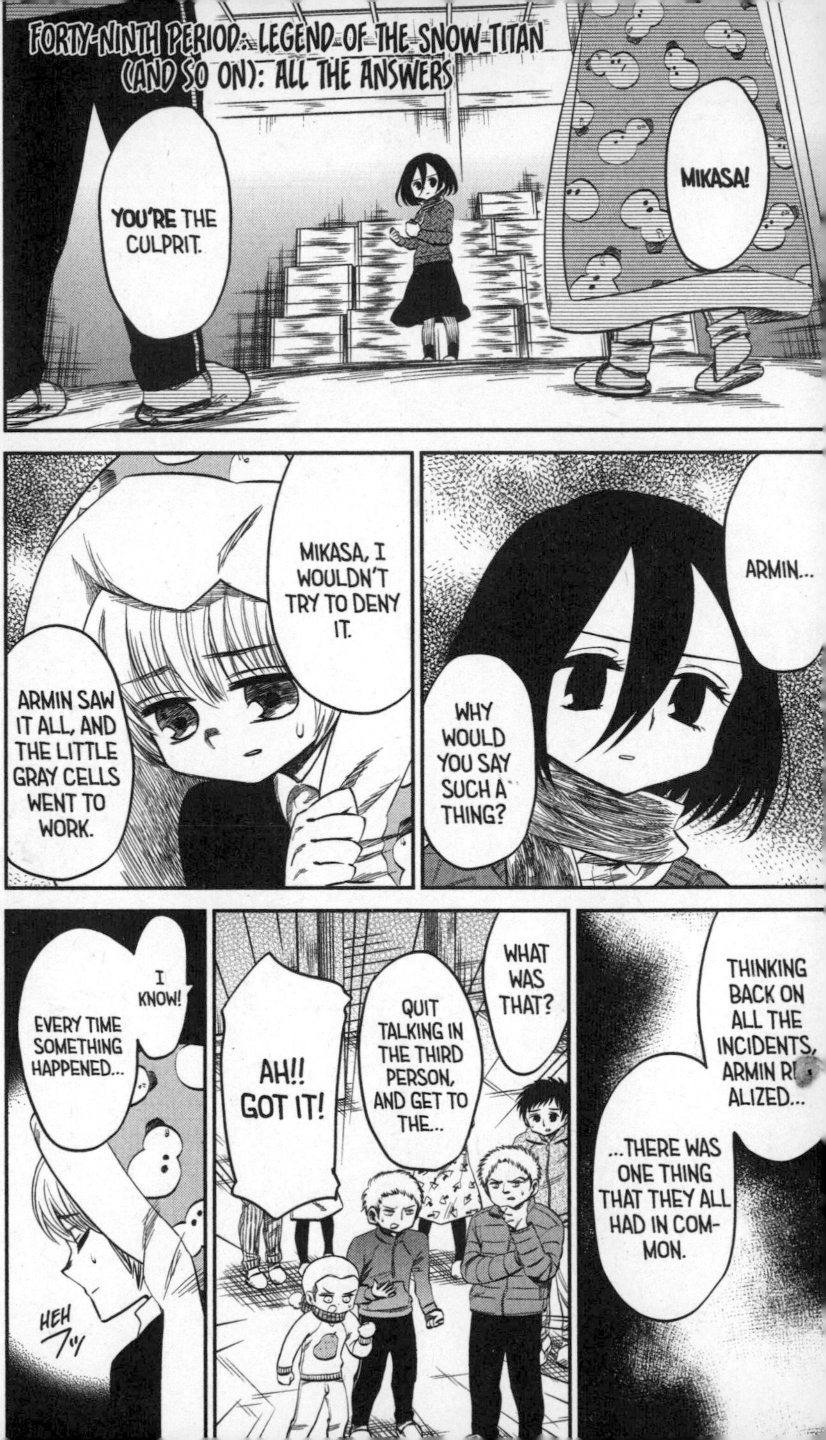
MIKASA!
YOU'RE THE CULPRIT.
ARMIN...
WHY WOULD YOU SAY SUCH A THING?
MIKASA, I WOULDN'T TRY TO DENY IT.
ARMIN SAW IT ALL, AND THE LITTLE GRAY CELLS WENT TO WORK.
THINKING BACK ON ALL THE INCIDENTS, ARMIN REALIZED...
...THERE WAS ONE THING THAT THEY ALL HAD IN COMMON.
WHAT WAS THAT?
QUIT TALKING IN THE THIRD PERSON, AND GET TO THE...
AH!! GOT IT!
I KNOW!
EVERY TIME SOMETHING HAPPENED...
HEH
フッ

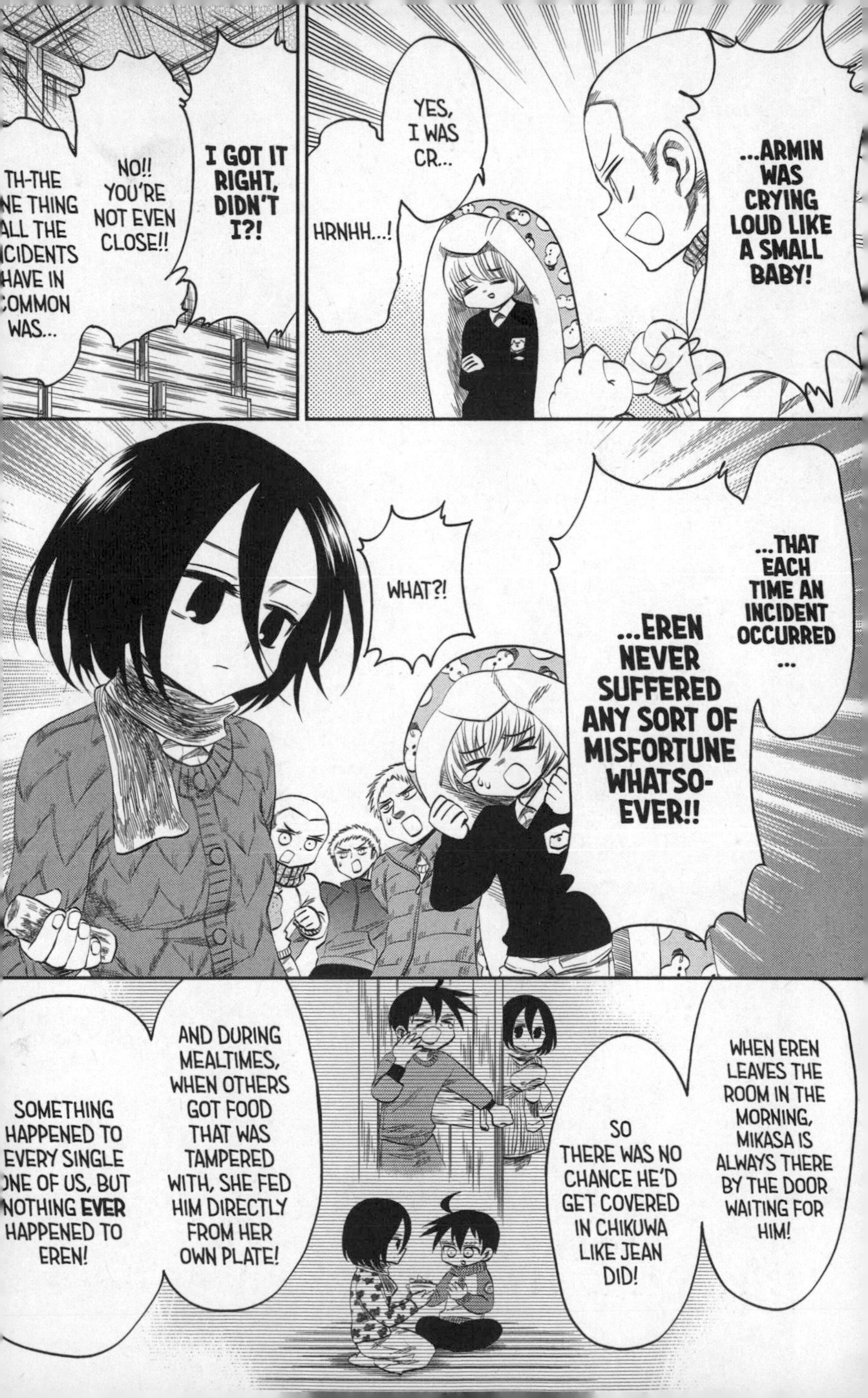
...ARMIN WAS CRYING LOUD LIKE A SMALL BABY!
YES, I WAS CR...
HRNHH...!
I GOT IT RIGHT, DIDN'T I?!
NO!! YOU'RE NOT EVEN CLOSE!!
TH-THE NE THING LL THE CIDENTS HAVE IN OMMON WAS...
...THAT EACH TIME AN INCIDENT OCCURRED...
...EREN NEVER SUFFERED ANY SORT OF MISFORTUNE WHATSO-EVER!!
WHAT?!
WHEN EREN LEAVES THE ROOM IN THE MORNING, MIKASA IS ALWAYS THERE BY THE DOOR WAITING FOR HIM!
SO THERE WAS NO CHANCE HE'D GET COVERED IN CHIKUWA LIKE JEAN DID!
AND DURING MEALTIMES, WHEN OTHERS GOT FOOD THAT WAS TAMPERED WITH, SHE FED HIM DIRECTLY FROM HER OWN PLATE!
SOMETHING HAPPENED TO VERY SINGLE NE OF US, BUT NOTHING **EVER** HAPPENED TO EREN!

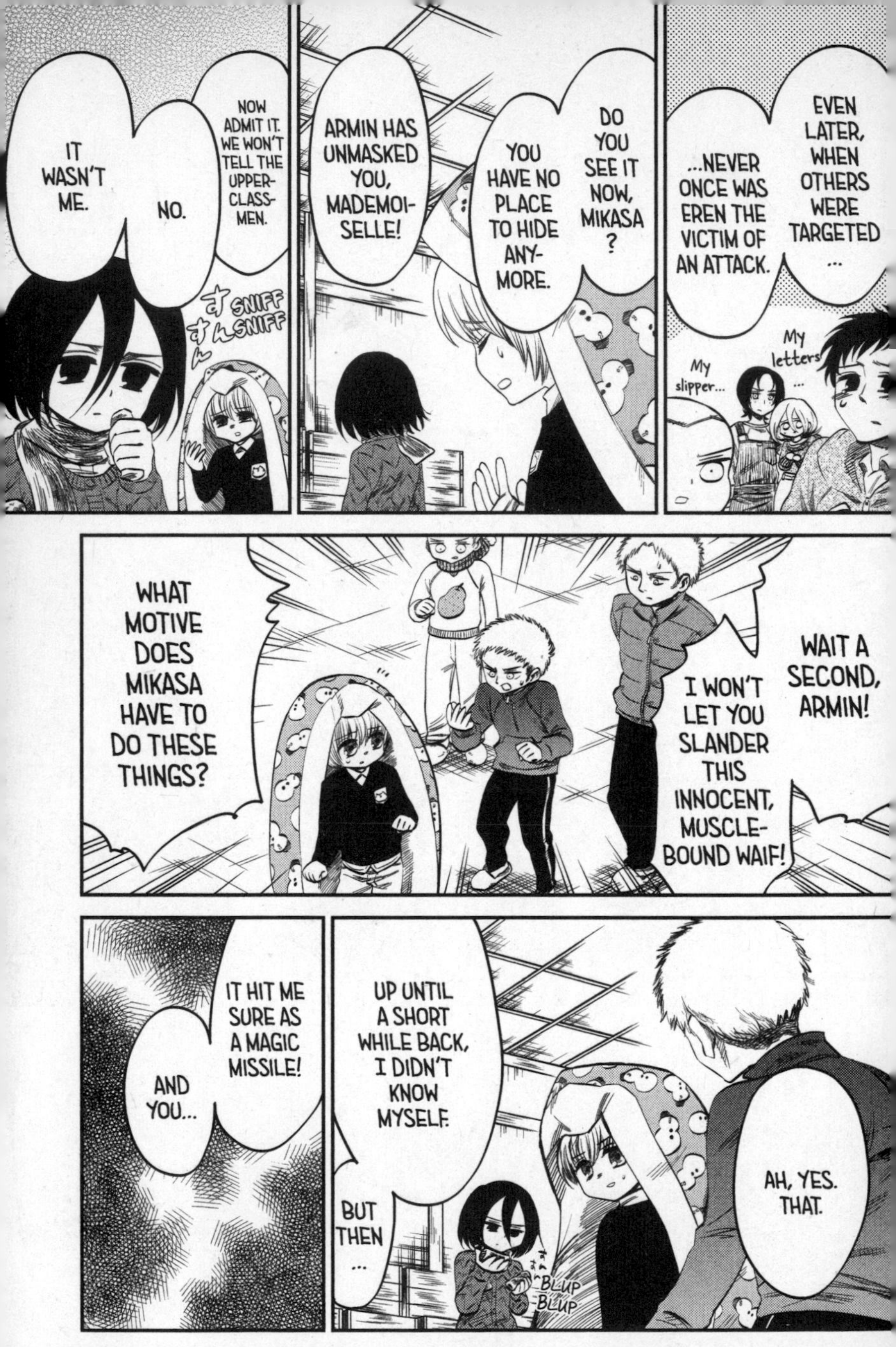
EVEN LATER, WHEN OTHERS WERE TARGETED ...
...NEVER ONCE WAS EREN THE VICTIM OF AN ATTACK.
My letters ...
My slipper...
DO YOU SEE IT NOW, MIKASA ?
YOU HAVE NO PLACE TO HIDE ANY-MORE.
ARMIN HAS UNMASKED YOU, MADEMOI-SELLE!
NOW ADMIT IT. WE WON'T TELL THE UPPER-CLASS-MEN.
SNIFF SNIFF
NO.
IT WASN'T ME.
WAIT A SECOND, ARMIN!
I WON'T LET YOU SLANDER THIS INNOCENT, MUSCLE-BOUND WAIF!
WHAT MOTIVE DOES MIKASA HAVE TO DO THESE THINGS?
AH, YES. THAT.
UP UNTIL A SHORT WHILE BACK, I DIDN'T KNOW MYSELF.
BUT THEN ...
BLUP BLUP
IT HIT ME SURE AS A MAGIC MISSILE!
AND YOU...

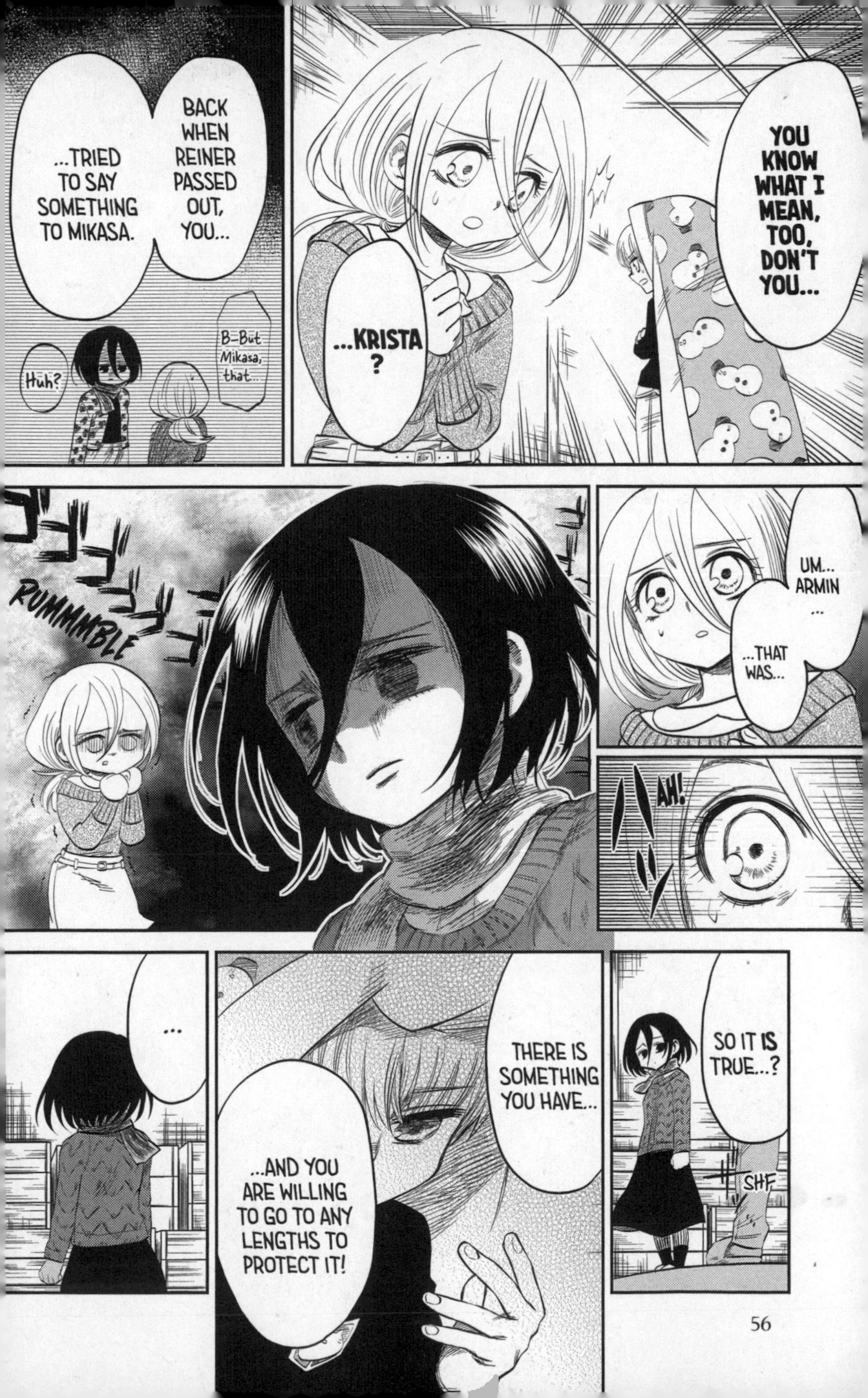
YOU KNOW WHAT I MEAN, TOO, DON'T YOU...
...KRISTA?
BACK WHEN REINER PASSED OUT, YOU...
...TRIED TO SAY SOMETHING TO MIKASA.
B-But Mikasa, that...
Huh?
UM... ARMIN ...
...THAT WAS...
AH!
RUMMMBLE
SO IT IS TRUE...?
SHF
THERE IS SOMETHING YOU HAVE...
...AND YOU ARE WILLING TO GO TO ANY LENGTHS TO PROTECT IT!
...

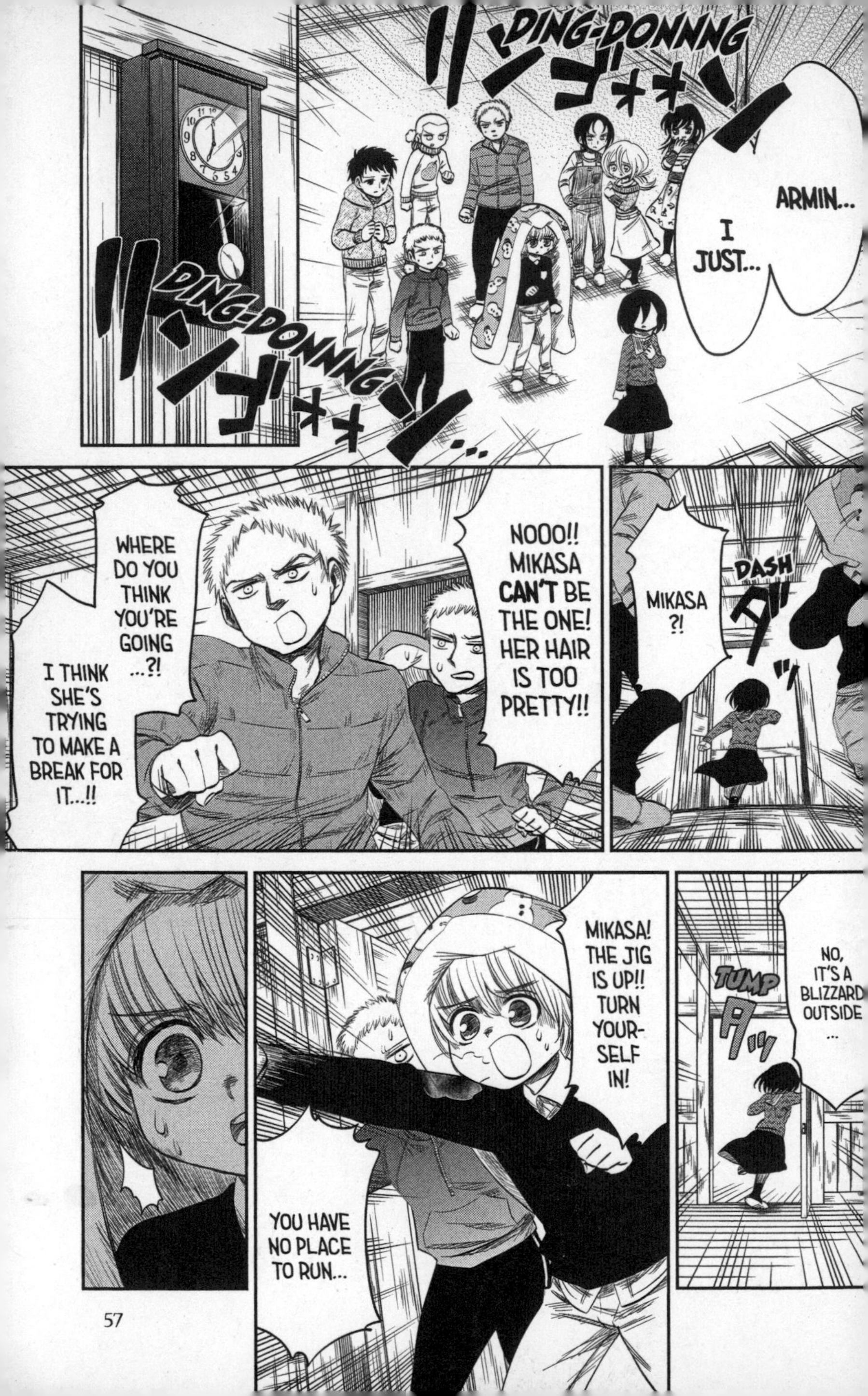
DING-DONNNG
ARMIN...
I JUST...
DING-DONNNG...
MIKASA ?!
DASH
NOOO!! MIKASA CAN'T BE THE ONE! HER HAIR IS TOO PRETTY!!
WHERE DO YOU THINK YOU'RE GOING ...?!
I THINK SHE'S TRYING TO MAKE A BREAK FOR IT...!!
NO, IT'S A BLIZZARD OUTSIDE ...
TUMP
MIKASA! THE JIG IS UP!! TURN YOUR-SELF IN!
YOU HAVE NO PLACE TO RUN...

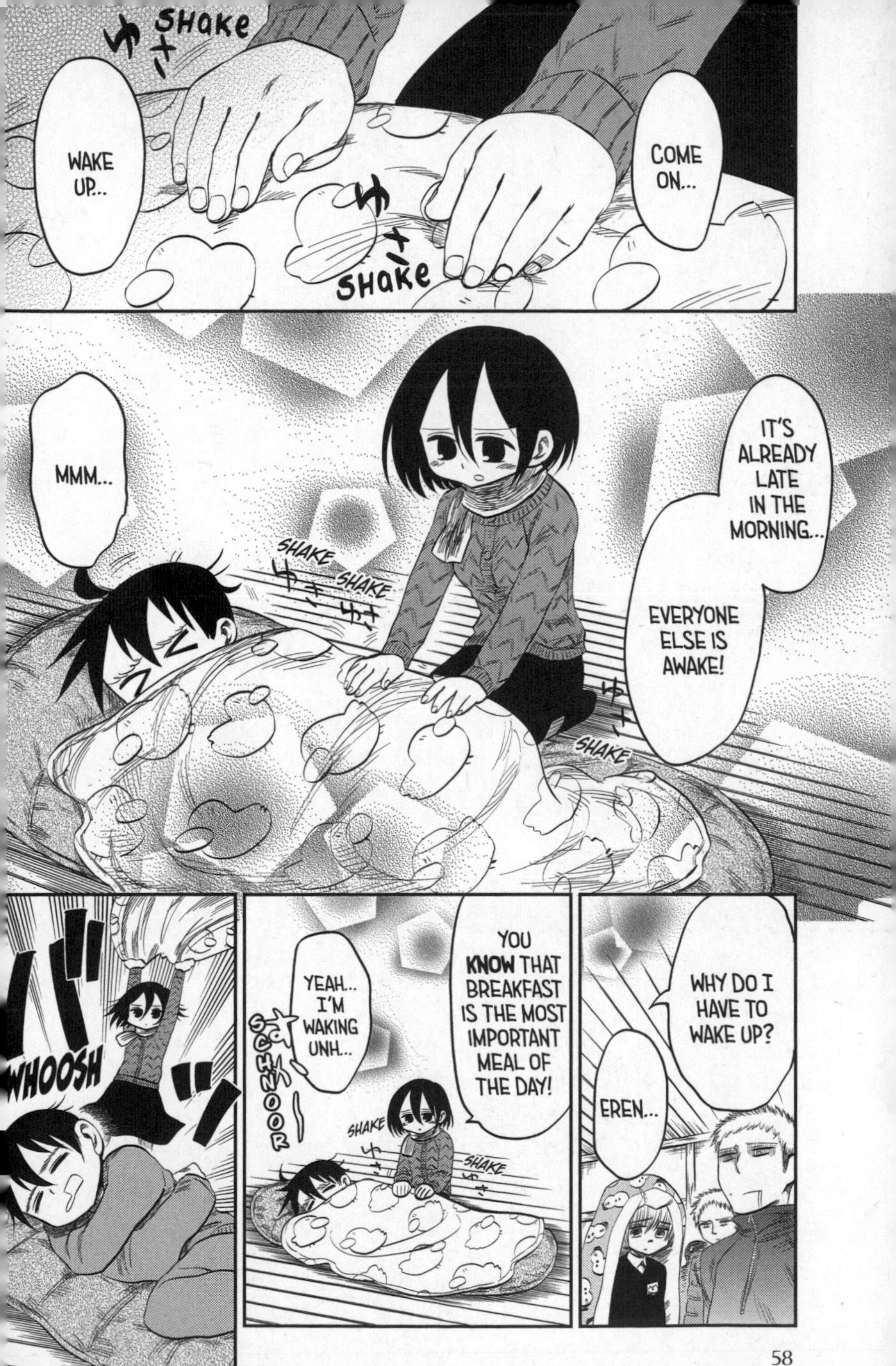
SHAKE
COME ON...
WAKE UP...
SHAKE
IT'S ALREADY LATE IN THE MORNING...
EVERYONE ELSE IS AWAKE!
SHAKE
SHAKE SHAKE
MMM...
WHY DO I HAVE TO WAKE UP?
EREN...
YOU **KNOW** THAT BREAKFAST IS THE MOST IMPORTANT MEAL OF THE DAY!
SHAKE SHAKE
YEAH... I'M WAKING UNH...
SCHNOOOR
WHOOSH

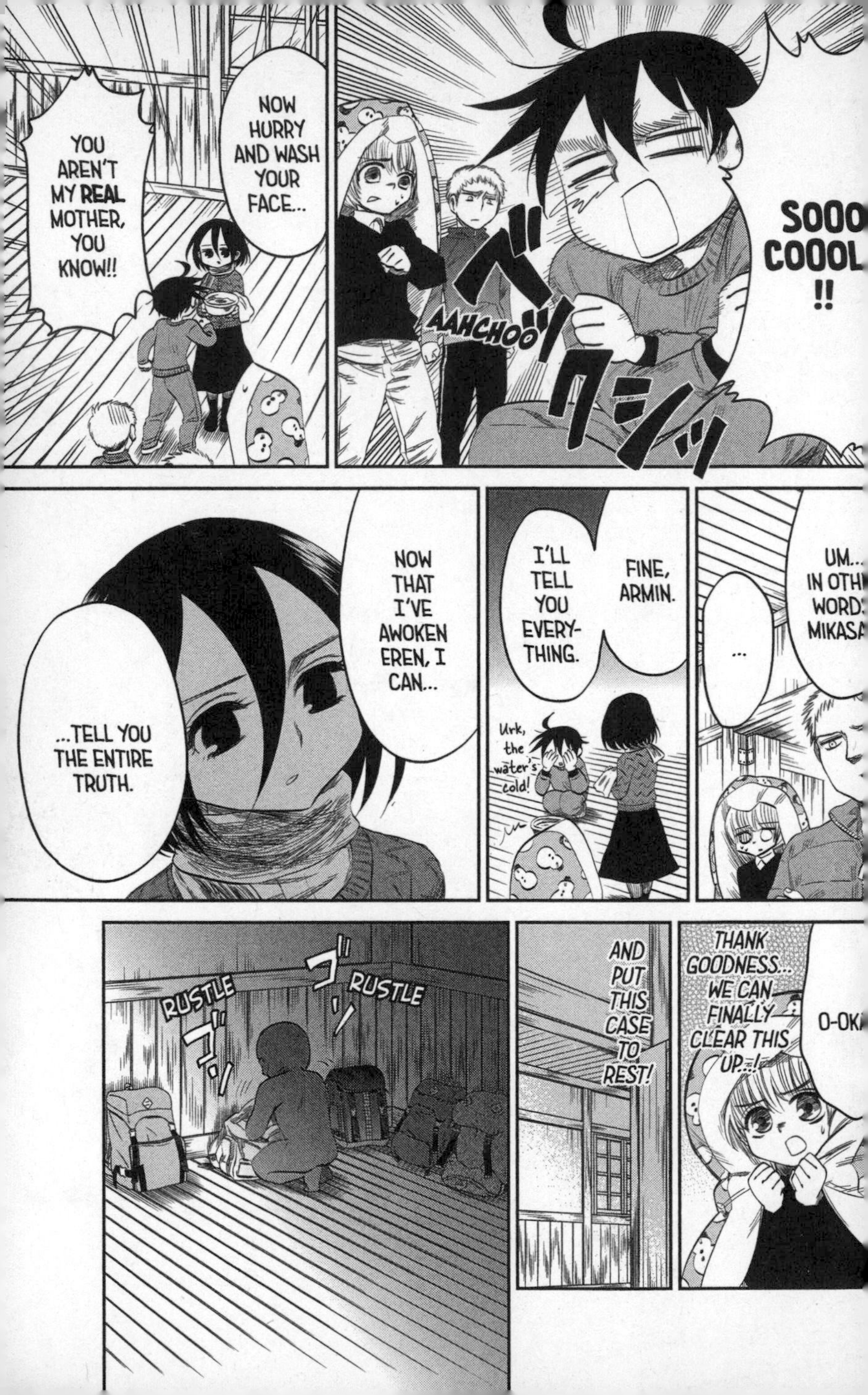
SOOO COOOL!!
AAHCHOO
NOW HURRY AND WASH YOUR FACE...
YOU AREN'T MY **REAL** MOTHER, YOU KNOW!!
UM... IN OTH WORD: MIKASA
...
FINE, ARMIN.
I'LL TELL YOU EVERY-THING.
Urk, the water's cold!
NOW THAT I'VE AWOKEN EREN, I CAN...
...TELL YOU THE ENTIRE TRUTH.
O-OKA
THANK GOODNESS... WE CAN FINALLY CLEAR THIS UP...!
AND PUT THIS CASE TO REST!
RUSTLE
RUSTLE

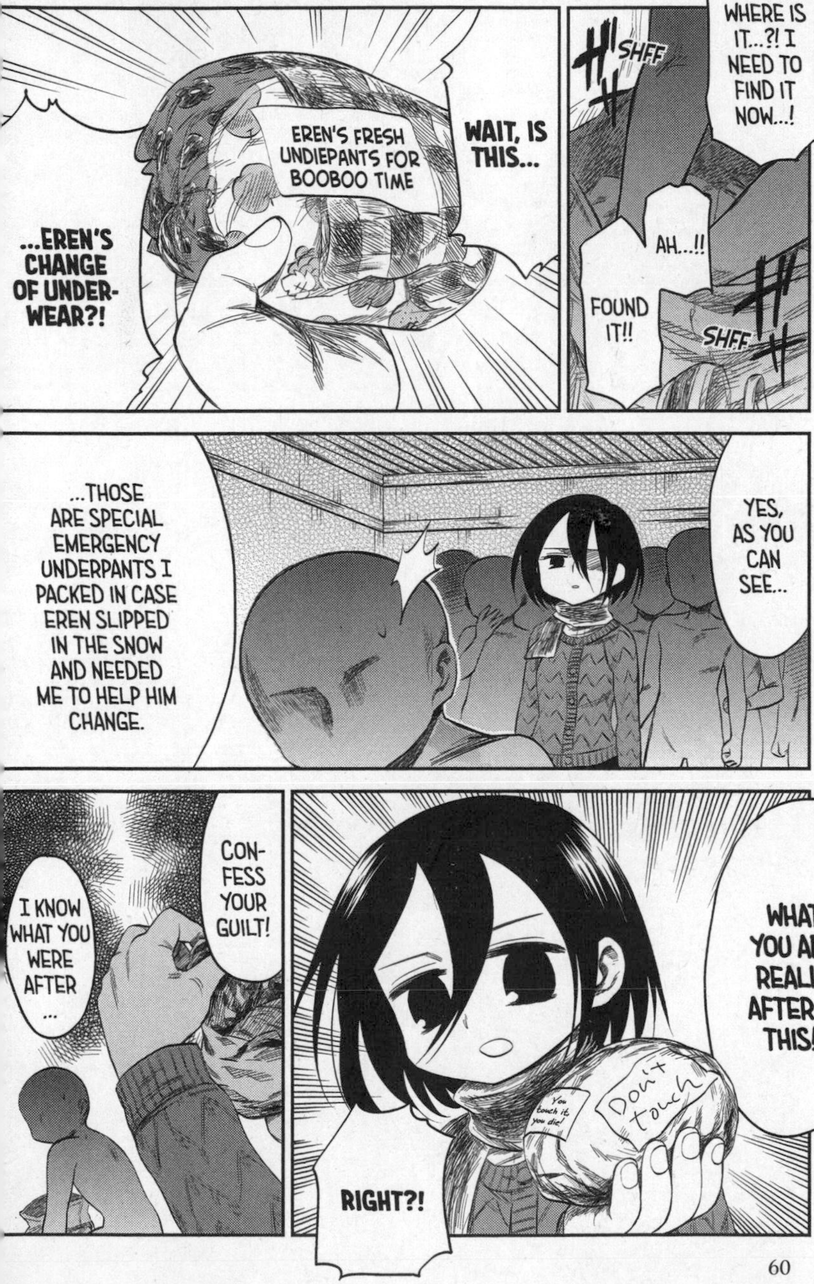
WHERE? WHERE IS IT...?! I NEED TO FIND IT NOW...!
SHFF
AH...!!
FOUND IT!!
SHFF
WAIT, IS THIS...
EREN'S FRESH UNDIEPANTS FOR BOOBOO TIME
...EREN'S CHANGE OF UNDER-WEAR?!
YES, AS YOU CAN SEE...
...THOSE ARE SPECIAL EMERGENCY UNDERPANTS I PACKED IN CASE EREN SLIPPED IN THE SNOW AND NEEDED ME TO HELP HIM CHANGE.
WHAT YOU ARE REALLY AFTER IS THIS!!
Don't touch
You touch it you die!
RIGHT?!
CON-FESS YOUR GUILT!
I KNOW WHAT YOU WERE AFTER ...

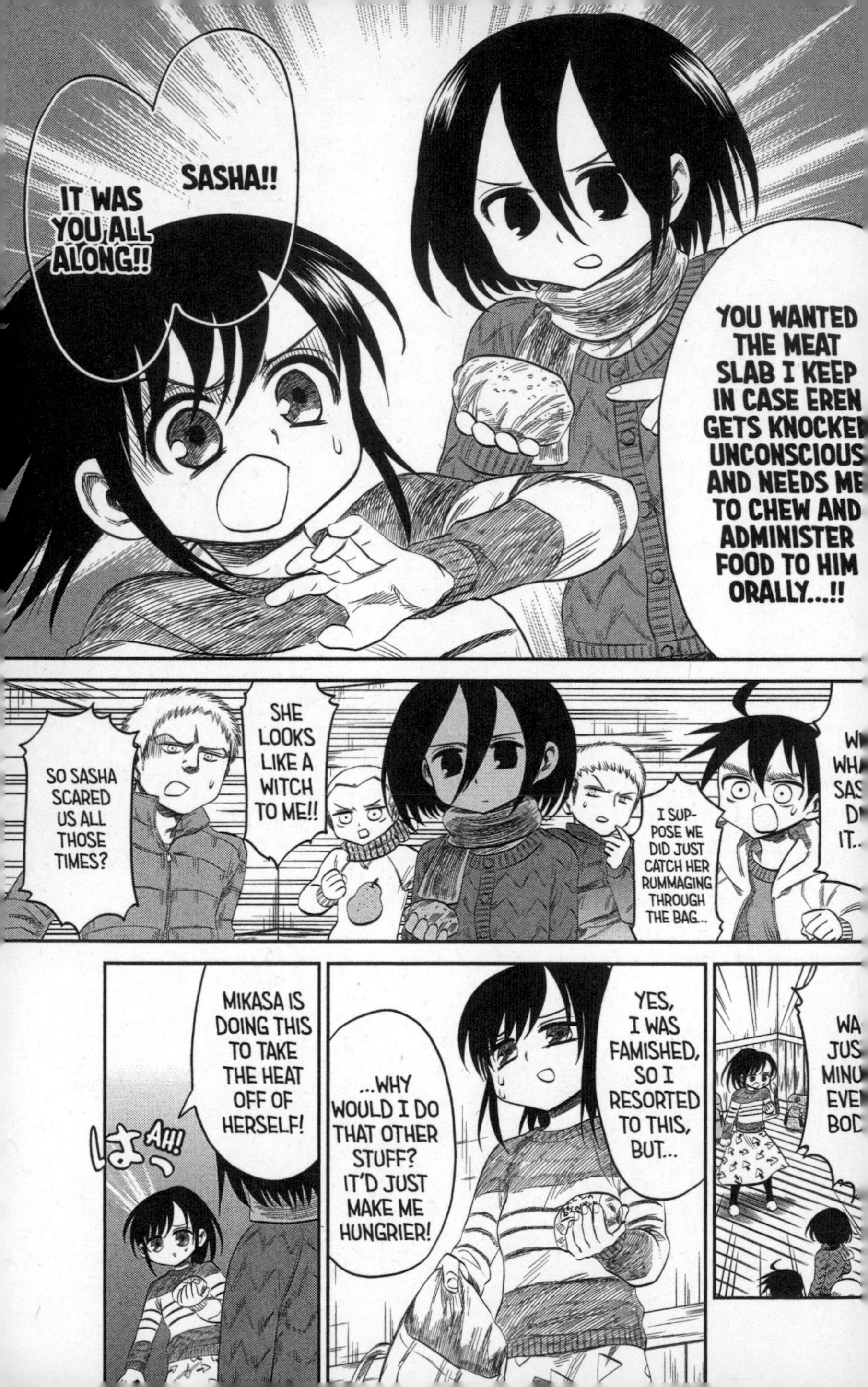
YOU WANTED THE MEAT SLAB I KEEP IN CASE EREN GETS KNOCKE UNCONSCIOUS AND NEEDS ME TO CHEW AND ADMINISTER FOOD TO HIM ORALLY...!!
SASHA!! IT WAS YOU ALL ALONG!!
I SUPPOSE WE DID JUST CATCH HER RUMMAGING THROUGH THE BAG...
SHE LOOKS LIKE A WITCH TO ME!!
SO SASHA SCARED US ALL THOSE TIMES?
YES, I WAS FAMISHED, SO I RESORTED TO THIS, BUT...
...WHY WOULD I DO THAT OTHER STUFF? IT'D JUST MAKE ME HUNGRIER!
MIKASA IS DOING THIS TO TAKE THE HEAT OFF OF HERSELF!
はっ AH!

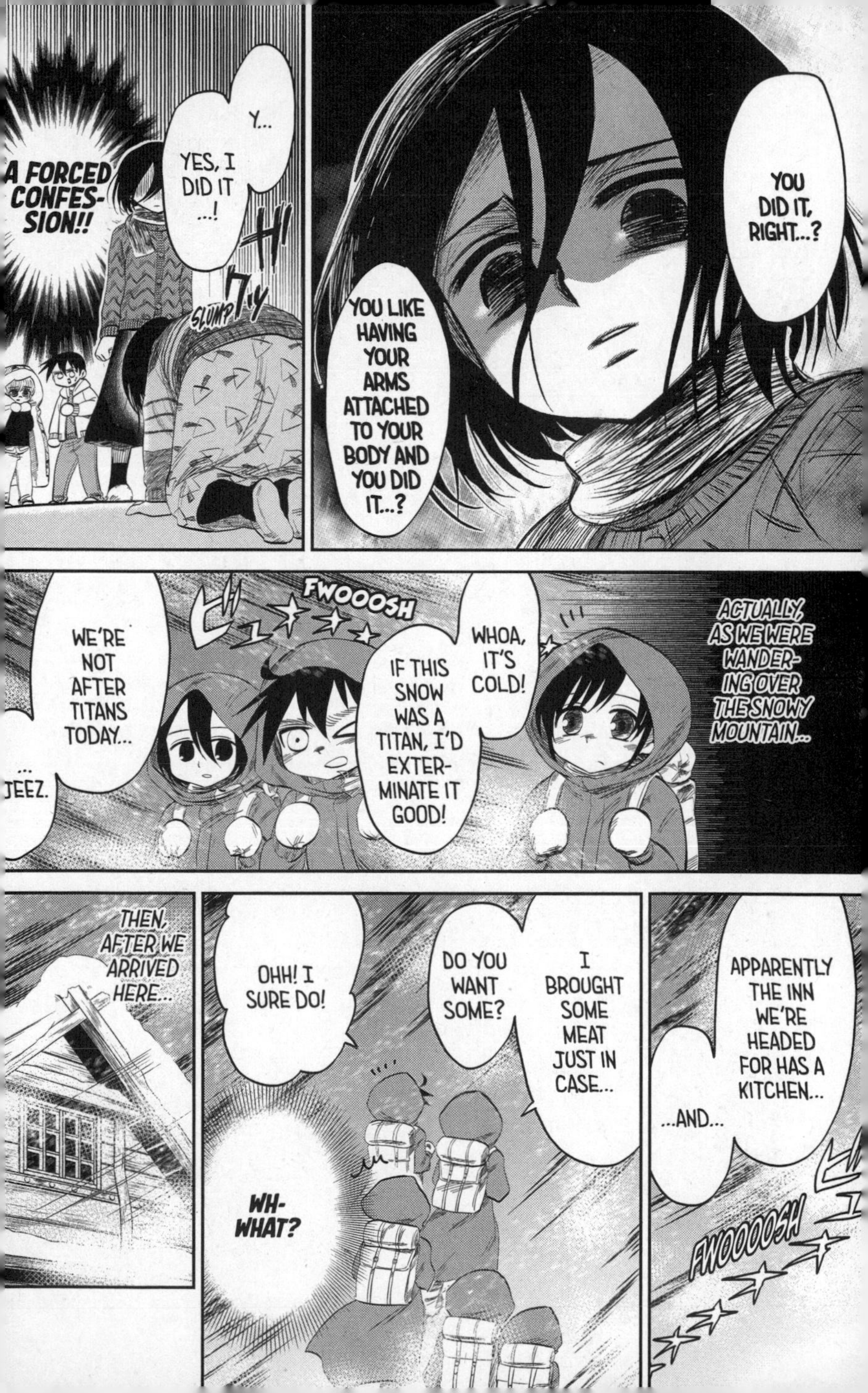
YOU DID IT, RIGHT...?
YOU LIKE HAVING YOUR ARMS ATTACHED TO YOUR BODY AND YOU DID IT...?
Y...
YES, I DID IT ...!
A FORCED CONFESSION!!
SLUMP
ACTUALLY, AS WE WERE WANDERING OVER THE SNOWY MOUNTAIN...
WHOA, IT'S COLD!
FWOOOSH
IF THIS SNOW WAS A TITAN, I'D EXTERMINATE IT GOOD!
WE'RE NOT AFTER TITANS TODAY...
... JEEZ.
APPARENTLY THE INN WE'RE HEADED FOR HAS A KITCHEN...
...AND...
FWOOOOSH
I BROUGHT SOME MEAT JUST IN CASE...
DO YOU WANT SOME?
OHH! I SURE DO!
WH-WHAT?
THEN, AFTER WE ARRIVED HERE...

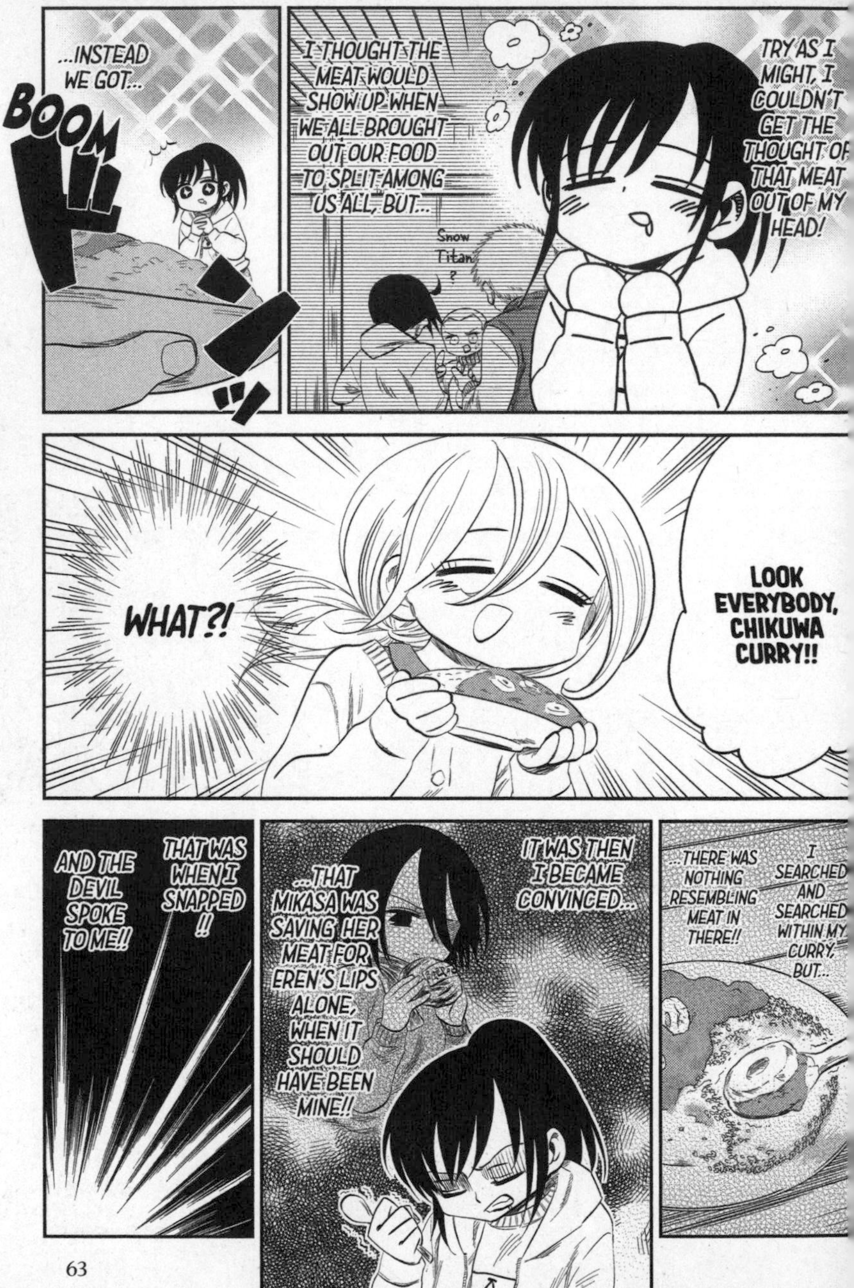
TRY AS I MIGHT, I COULDN'T GET THE THOUGHT OF THAT MEAT OUT OF MY HEAD!
I THOUGHT THE MEAT WOULD SHOW UP WHEN WE ALL BROUGHT OUT OUR FOOD TO SPLIT AMONG US ALL, BUT...
Snow Titan ?
...INSTEAD WE GOT...
BOOM
LOOK EVERYBODY, CHIKUWA CURRY!!
WHAT?!
I SEARCHED AND SEARCHED WITHIN MY CURRY, BUT...
...THERE WAS NOTHING RESEMBLING MEAT IN THERE!!
IT WAS THEN I BECAME CONVINCED...
...THAT MIKASA WAS SAVING HER MEAT FOR EREN'S LIPS ALONE, WHEN IT SHOULD HAVE BEEN MINE!!
THAT WAS WHEN I SNAPPED!!
AND THE DEVIL SPOKE TO ME!!

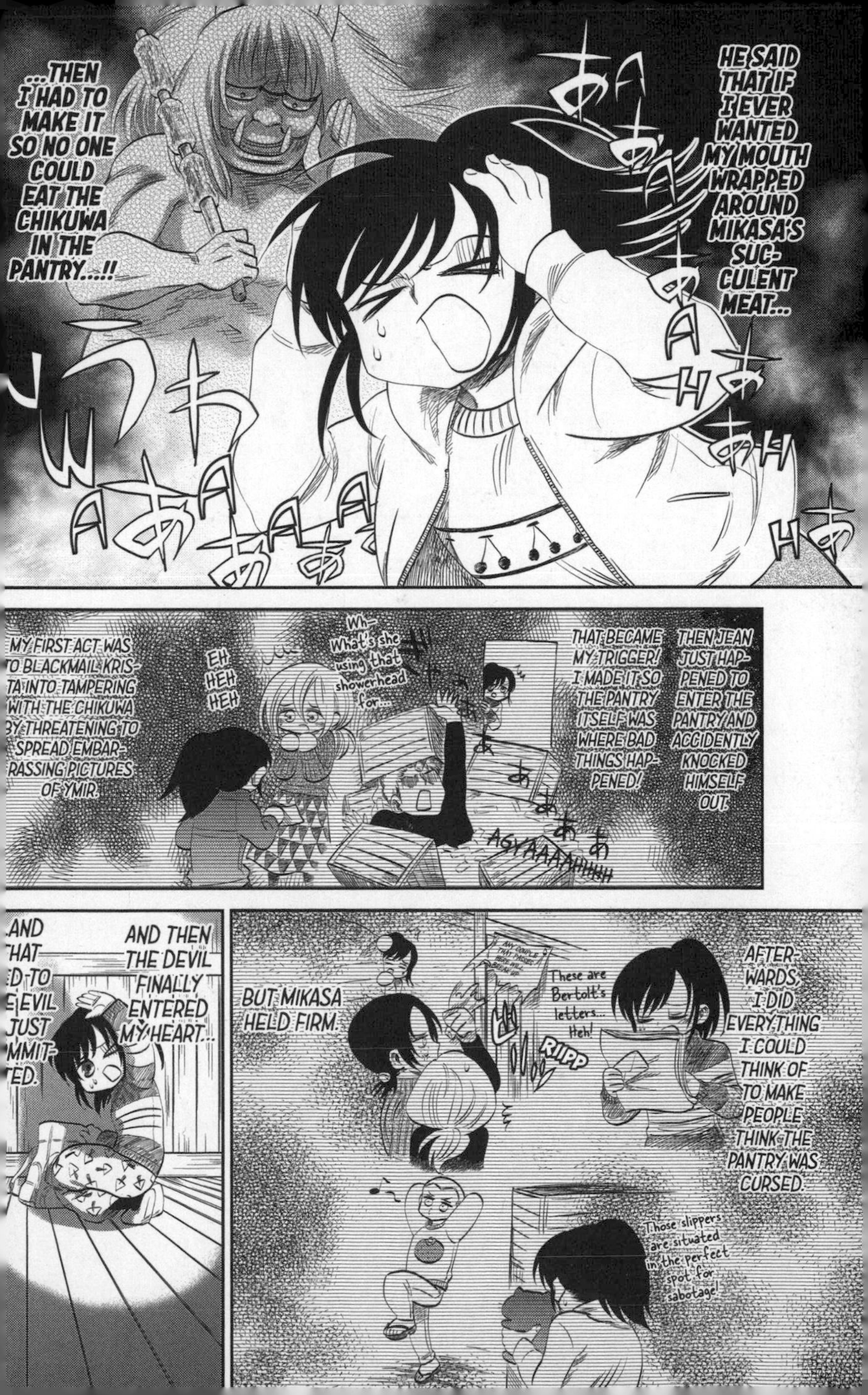
HE SAID THAT IF I EVER WANTED MY MOUTH WRAPPED AROUND MIKASA'S SUC-CULENT MEAT...
...THEN I HAD TO MAKE IT SO NO ONE COULD EAT THE CHIKUWA IN THE PANTRY...!!
THEN JEAN JUST HAP-PENED TO ENTER THE PANTRY AND ACCIDENTLY KNOCKED HIMSELF OUT.
THAT BECAME MY TRIGGER! I MADE IT SO THE PANTRY ITSELF WAS WHERE BAD THINGS HAP-PENED!
Wh- What's she using that showerhead for...
AGYAAAAAHHHH
EH HEH HEH
MY FIRST ACT WAS TO BLACKMAIL KRIS-TA INTO TAMPERING WITH THE CHIKUWA BY THREATENING TO SPREAD EMBAR-RASSING PICTURES OF YMIR.
AFTER-WARDS, I DID EVERYTHING I COULD THINK OF TO MAKE PEOPLE THINK THE PANTRY WAS CURSED.
These are Bertolt's letters... Heh!
RIIPP
BUT MIKASA HELD FIRM.
Those slippers are situated in the perfect spot for sabotage!
AND THEN THE DEVIL FINALLY ENTERED MY HEART...

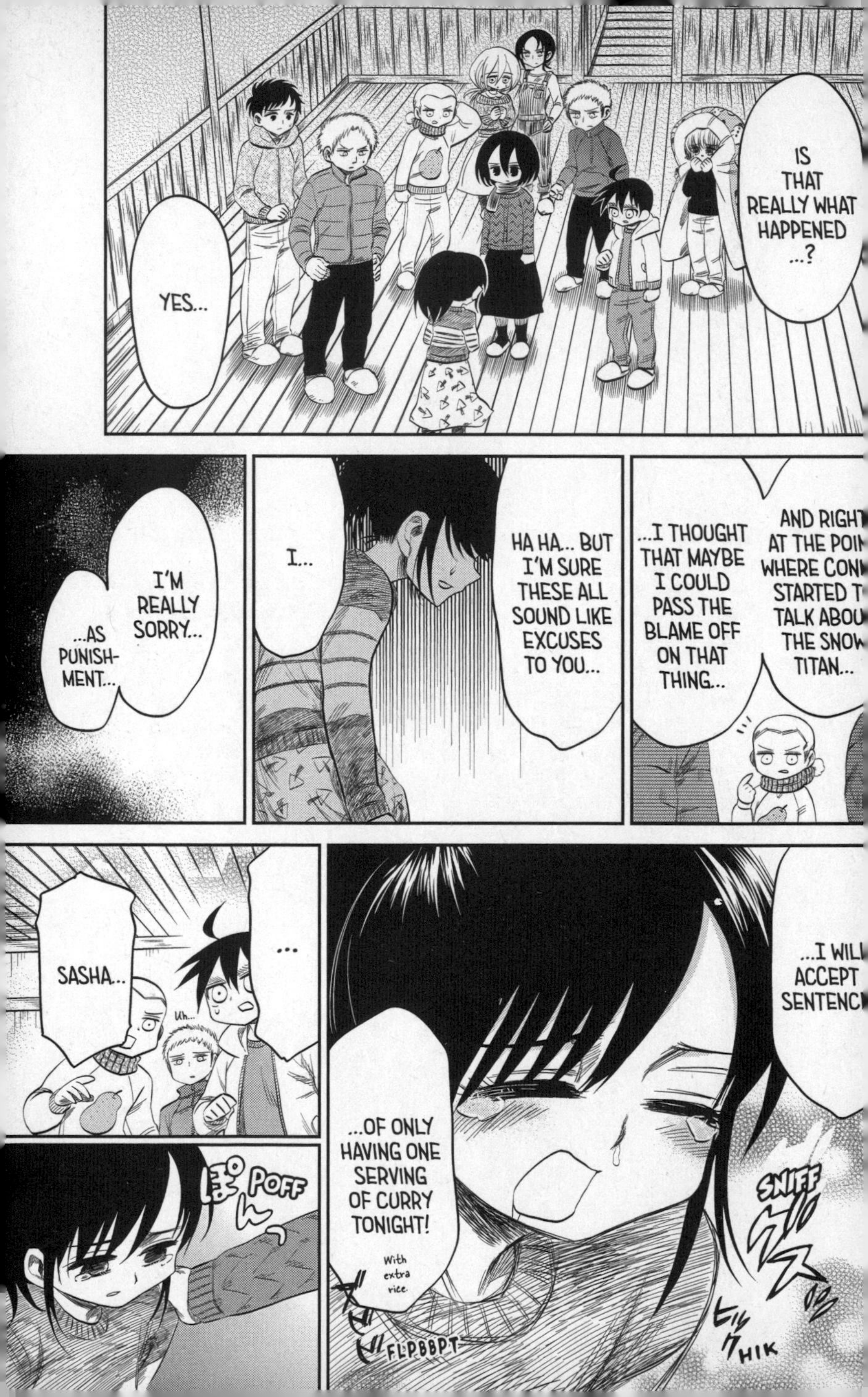
IS THAT REALLY WHAT HAPPENED ...?
YES...
AND RIGH AT THE POI WHERE CON STARTED T TALK ABOU THE SNOW TITAN...
...I THOUGHT THAT MAYBE I COULD PASS THE BLAME OFF ON THAT THING...
HA HA... BUT I'M SURE THESE ALL SOUND LIKE EXCUSES TO YOU...
I...
I'M REALLY SORRY...
...AS PUNISH-MENT...
...I WIL ACCEPT SENTENC
...OF ONLY HAVING ONE SERVING OF CURRY TONIGHT!
With extra rice.
SNIFF
HIK
FLPBBPT
...
SASHA...
Uh...
POFF

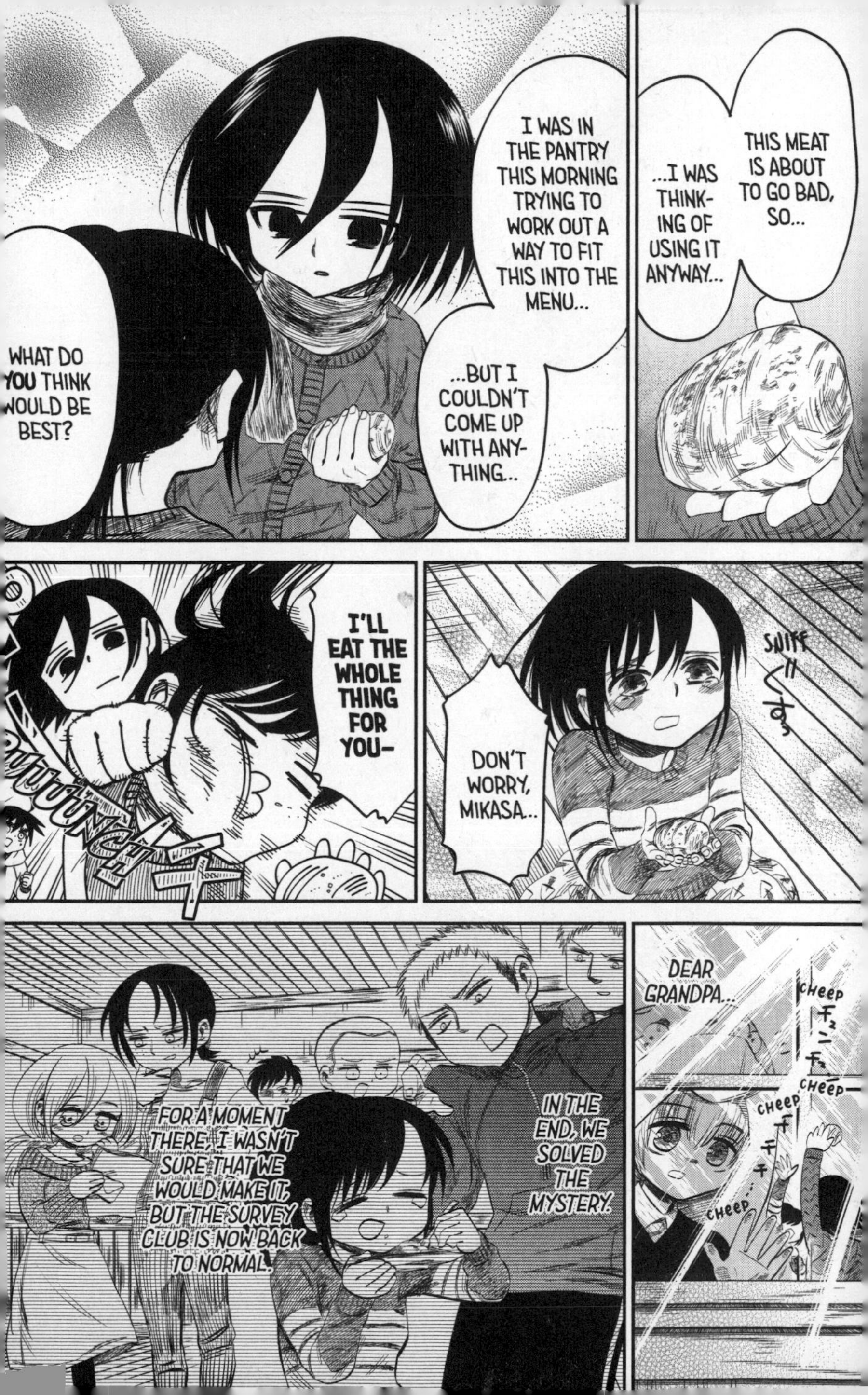
THIS MEAT IS ABOUT TO GO BAD, SO...
...I WAS THINKING OF USING IT ANYWAY...
I WAS IN THE PANTRY THIS MORNING TRYING TO WORK OUT A WAY TO FIT THIS INTO THE MENU...
...BUT I COULDN'T COME UP WITH ANYTHING...
WHAT DO YOU THINK WOULD BE BEST?
SNIFF
DON'T WORRY, MIKASA...
I'LL EAT THE WHOLE THING FOR YOU–
DEAR GRANDPA...
CHEEP
CHEEP
CHEEP
CHEEP
IN THE END, WE SOLVED THE MYSTERY.
FOR A MOMENT THERE, I WASN'T SURE THAT WE WOULD MAKE IT, BUT THE SURVEY CLUB IS NOW BACK TO NORMAL.

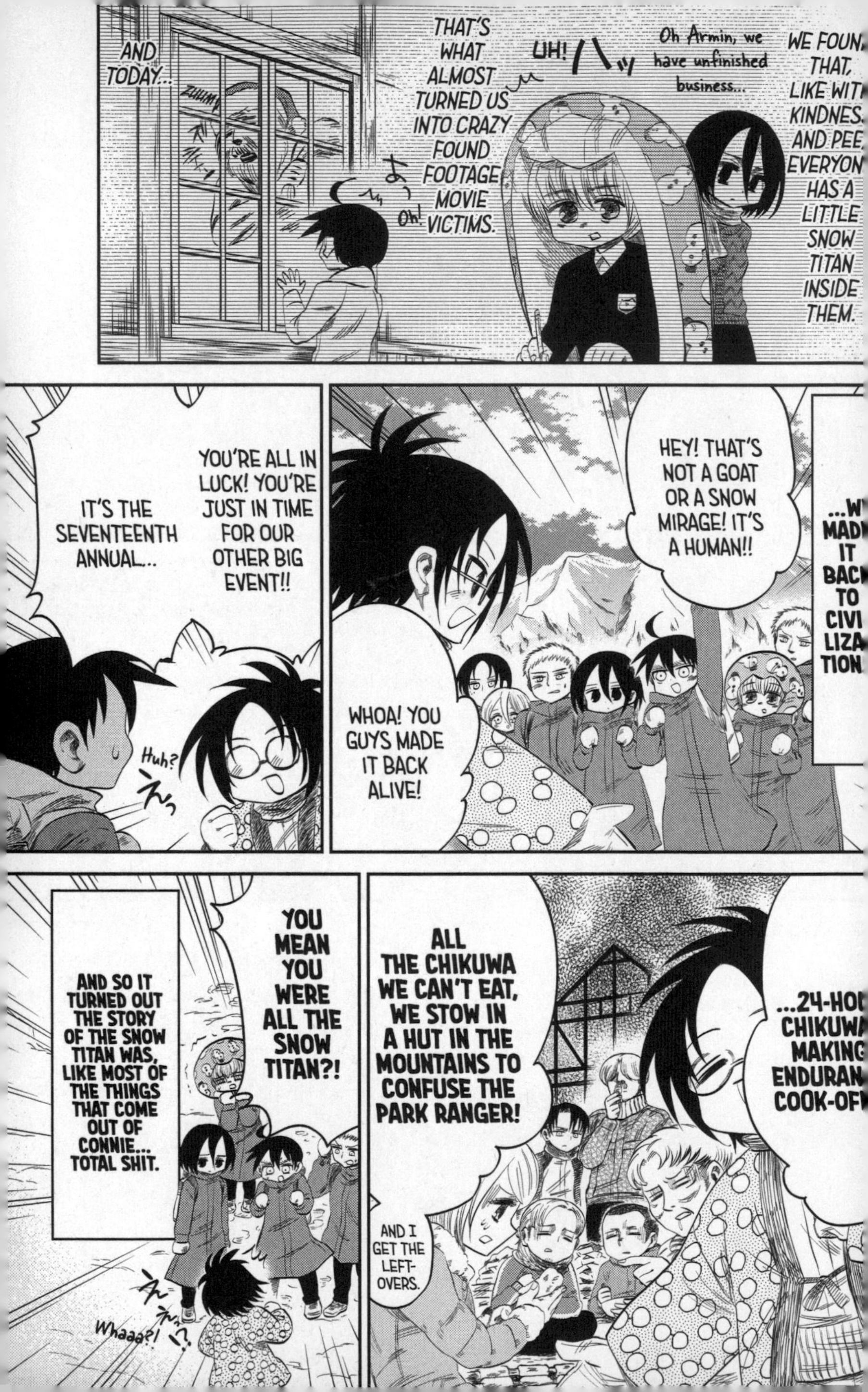
WE FOUN THAT, LIKE WIT KINDNES AND PEE EVERYON HAS A LITTLE SNOW TITAN INSIDE THEM.
Oh Armin, we have unfinished business...
UH!
THAT'S WHAT ALMOST TURNED US INTO CRAZY FOUND FOOTAGE MOVIE VICTIMS.
Oh!
AND TODAY...
...W MAD IT BAC TO CIVI LIZA TION
HEY! THAT'S NOT A GOAT OR A SNOW MIRAGE! IT'S A HUMAN!!
WHOA! YOU GUYS MADE IT BACK ALIVE!
YOU'RE ALL IN LUCK! YOU'RE JUST IN TIME FOR OUR OTHER BIG EVENT!!
IT'S THE SEVENTEENTH ANNUAL...
Huh?
...24-HO CHIKUWA MAKING ENDURAN COOK-OF
ALL THE CHIKUWA WE CAN'T EAT, WE STOW IN A HUT IN THE MOUNTAINS TO CONFUSE THE PARK RANGER!
AND I GET THE LEFT-OVERS.
YOU MEAN YOU WERE ALL THE SNOW TITAN?!
AND SO IT TURNED OUT THE STORY OF THE SNOW TITAN WAS, LIKE MOST OF THE THINGS THAT COME OUT OF CONNIE... TOTAL SHIT.
Whaaa?!

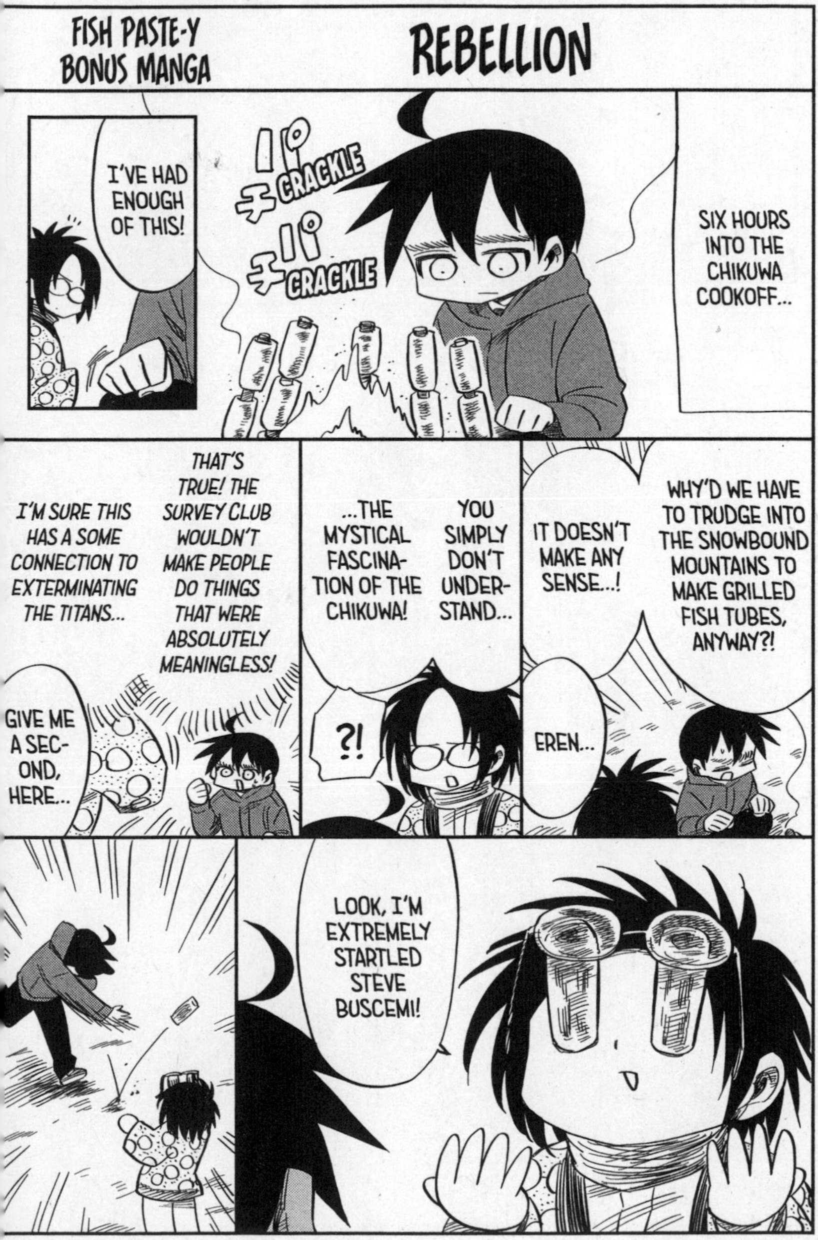
REBELLION
FISH PASTE-Y BONUS MANGA
SIX HOURS INTO THE CHIKUWA COOKOFF...
CRACKLE
CRACKLE
I'VE HAD ENOUGH OF THIS!
WHY'D WE HAVE TO TRUDGE INTO THE SNOWBOUND MOUNTAINS TO MAKE GRILLED FISH TUBES, ANYWAY?!
IT DOESN'T MAKE ANY SENSE...!
EREN...
YOU SIMPLY DON'T UNDERSTAND...
...THE MYSTICAL FASCINATION OF THE CHIKUWA!
?!
THAT'S TRUE! THE SURVEY CLUB WOULDN'T MAKE PEOPLE DO THINGS THAT WERE ABSOLUTELY MEANINGLESS!
I'M SURE THIS HAS A SOME CONNECTION TO EXTERMINATING THE TITANS...
GIVE ME A SEC-OND, HERE...
LOOK, I'M EXTREMELY STARTLED STEVE BUSCEMI!

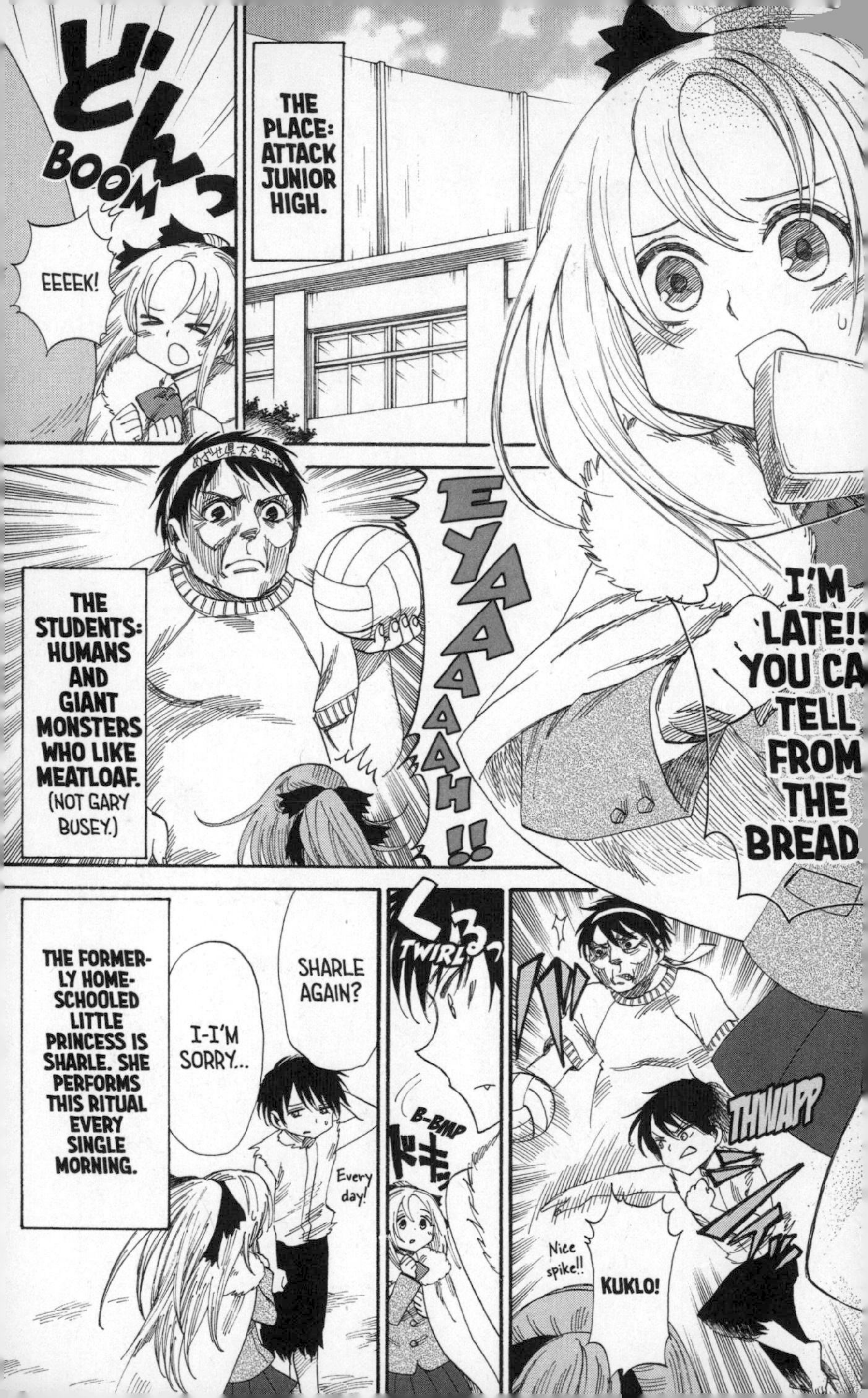
I'M LATE!! YOU CA TELL FROM THE BREAD
THE PLACE: ATTACK JUNIOR HIGH.
どんっ
BOOM
EEEEK!
EYAAAAAH!!
THE STUDENTS: HUMANS AND GIANT MONSTERS WHO LIKE MEATLOAF. (NOT GARY BUSEY.)
THWAPP
Nice spike!!
KUKLO!
くるっ
TWIRL
B-BMP
ドキッ
SHARLE AGAIN?
I-I'M SORRY...
Every day!
THE FORMERLY HOME-SCHOOLED LITTLE PRINCESS IS SHARLE. SHE PERFORMS THIS RITUAL EVERY SINGLE MORNING.

SPECIAL EDITION: GIMME BREAD, WHOA WHOA

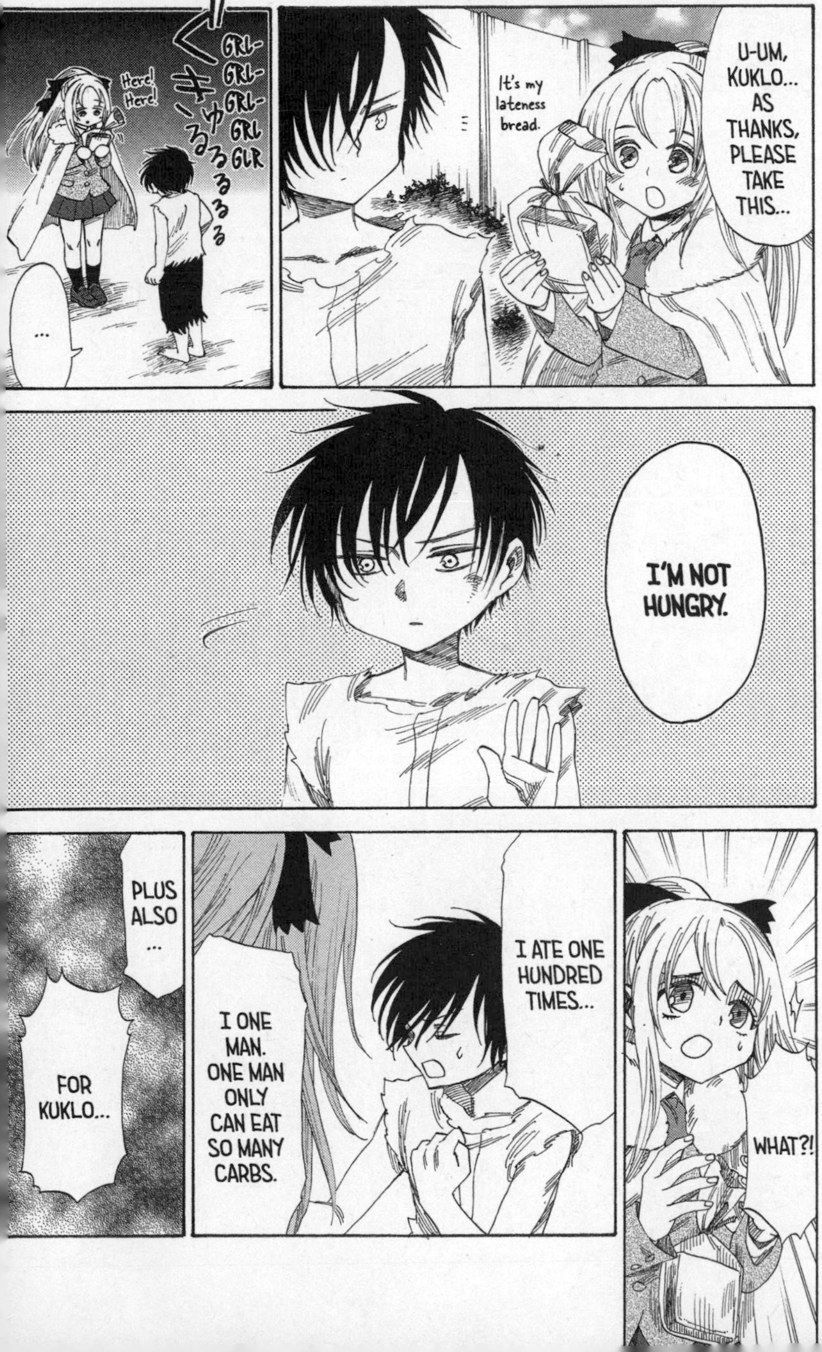
U-UM, KUKLO... AS THANKS, PLEASE TAKE THIS...
It's my lateness bread.
GRL-GRL-GRL-GRL GLR
Here! Here!
...
I'M NOT HUNGRY.
WHAT?!
I ATE ONE HUNDRED TIMES...
I ONE MAN. ONE MAN ONLY CAN EAT SO MANY CARBS.
PLUS ALSO ...
FOR KUKLO...

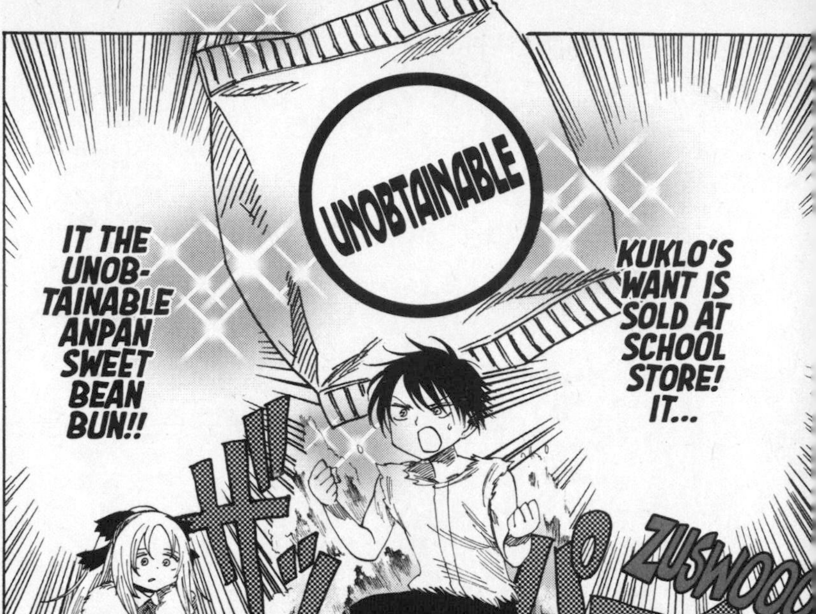
UNOBTAINABLE
KUKLO'S WANT IS SOLD AT SCHOOL STORE! IT...
IT THE UNOB-TAINABLE ANPAN SWEET BEAN BUN!!
ZUSWOOO

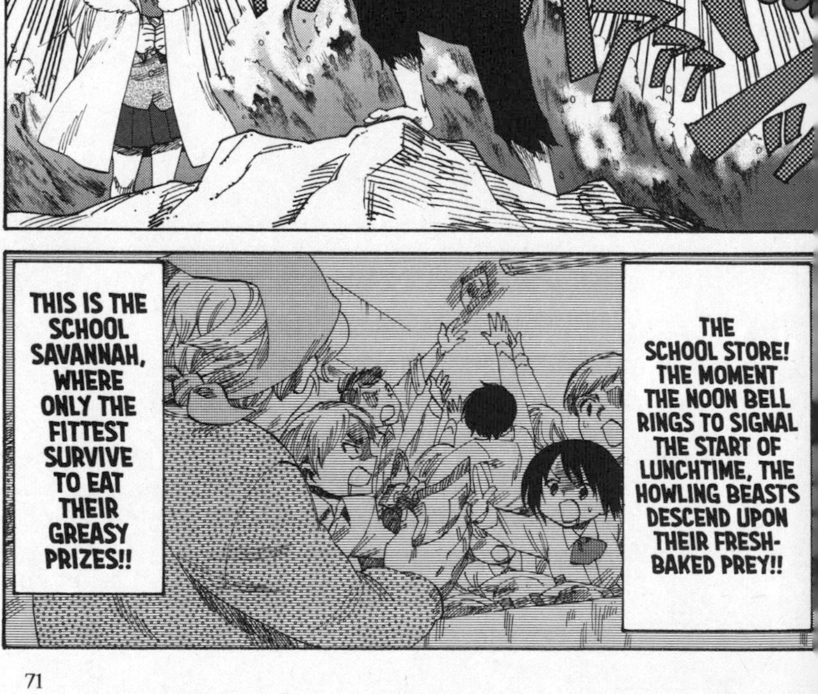
THE SCHOOL STORE! THE MOMENT THE NOON BELL RINGS TO SIGNAL THE START OF LUNCHTIME, THE HOWLING BEASTS DESCEND UPON THEIR FRESH-BAKED PREY!!
THIS IS THE SCHOOL SAVANNAH, WHERE ONLY THE FITTEST SURVIVE TO EAT THEIR GREASY PRIZES!!

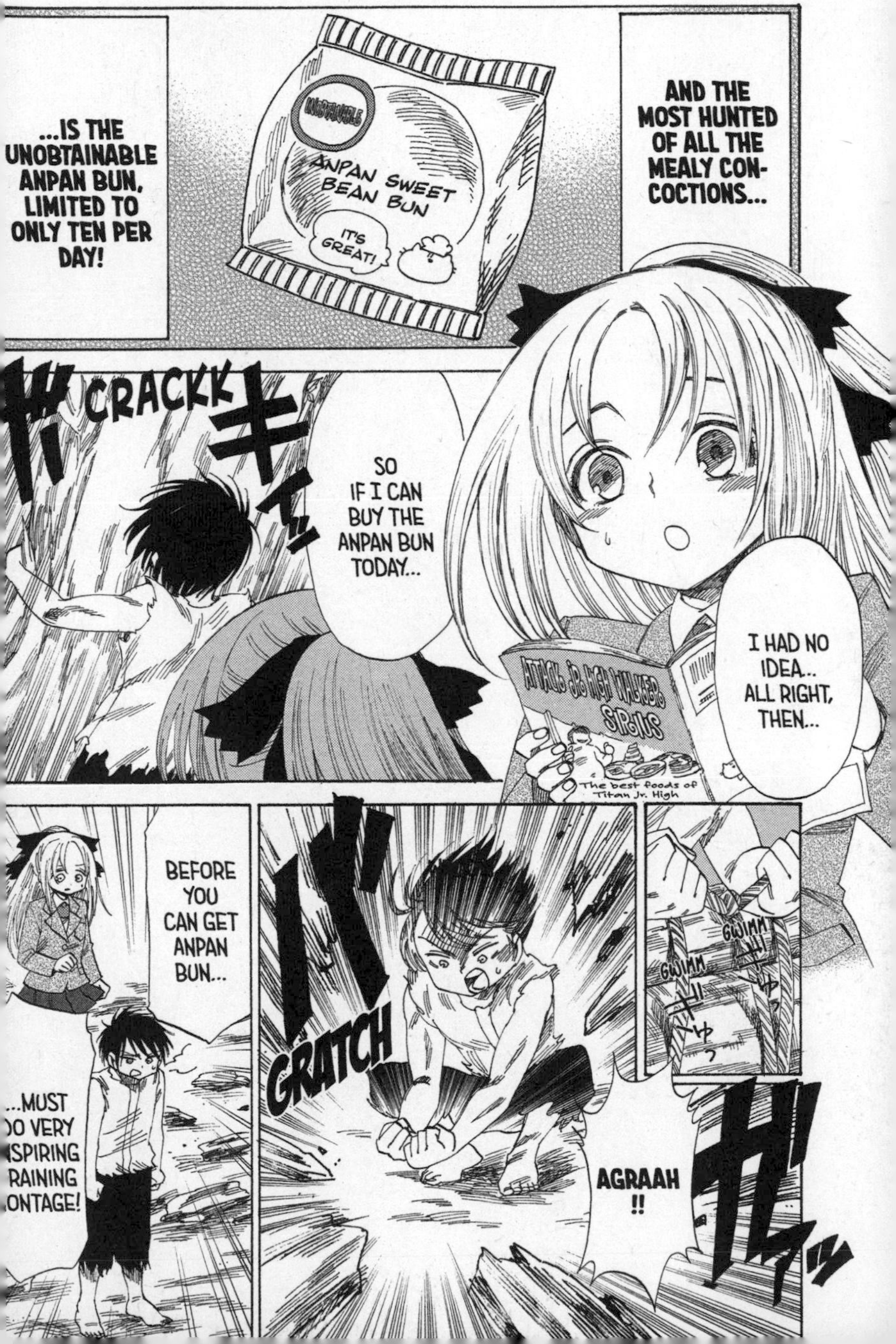
AND THE MOST HUNTED OF ALL THE MEALY CON-COCTIONS...
UNOBTAINABLE
ANPAN SWEET BEAN BUN
IT'S GREAT!
...IS THE UNOBTAINABLE ANPAN BUN, LIMITED TO ONLY TEN PER DAY!
I HAD NO IDEA.. ALL RIGHT, THEN...
The best foods of Titan Jr. High
SO IF I CAN BUY THE ANPAN BUN TODAY...
CRACKK
GWIMM
GWIMM
AGRAAH!!
GRATCH
BEFORE YOU CAN GET ANPAN BUN...
...MUST
O VERY
SPIRING
RAINING
ONTAGE!

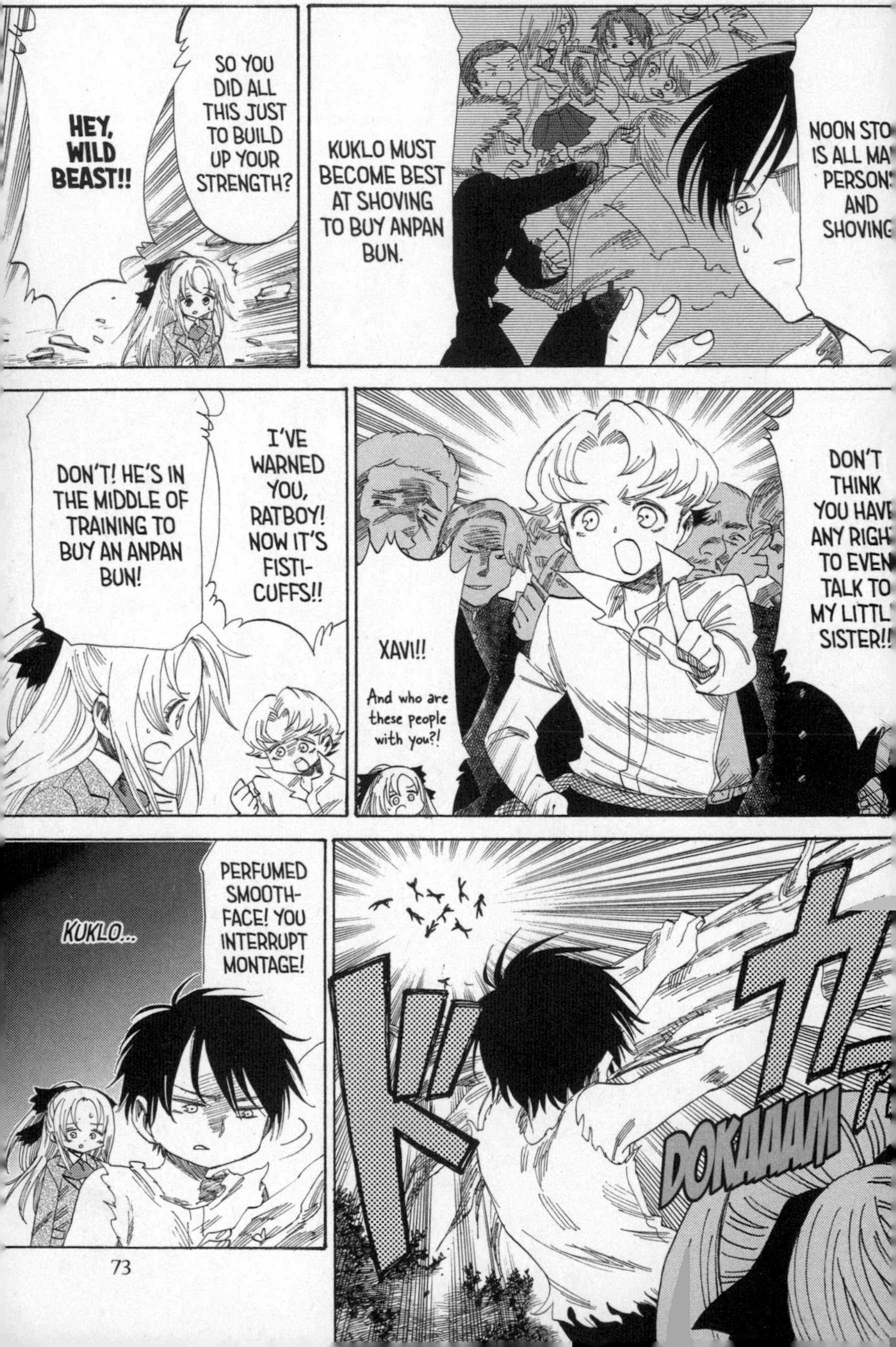
NOON STO IS ALL MA PERSON AND SHOVING
KUKLO MUST BECOME BEST AT SHOVING TO BUY ANPAN BUN.
SO YOU DID ALL THIS JUST TO BUILD UP YOUR STRENGTH?
HEY, WILD BEAST!!
DON'T THINK YOU HAV ANY RIGH TO EVEN TALK TO MY LITTL SISTER!!
XAVI!!
And who are these people with you?!
I'VE WARNED YOU, RATBOY! NOW IT'S FISTI-CUFFS!!
DON'T! HE'S IN THE MIDDLE OF TRAINING TO BUY AN ANPAN BUN!
DOKAAAM
PERFUMED SMOOTH-FACE! YOU INTERRUPT MONTAGE!
KUKLO...

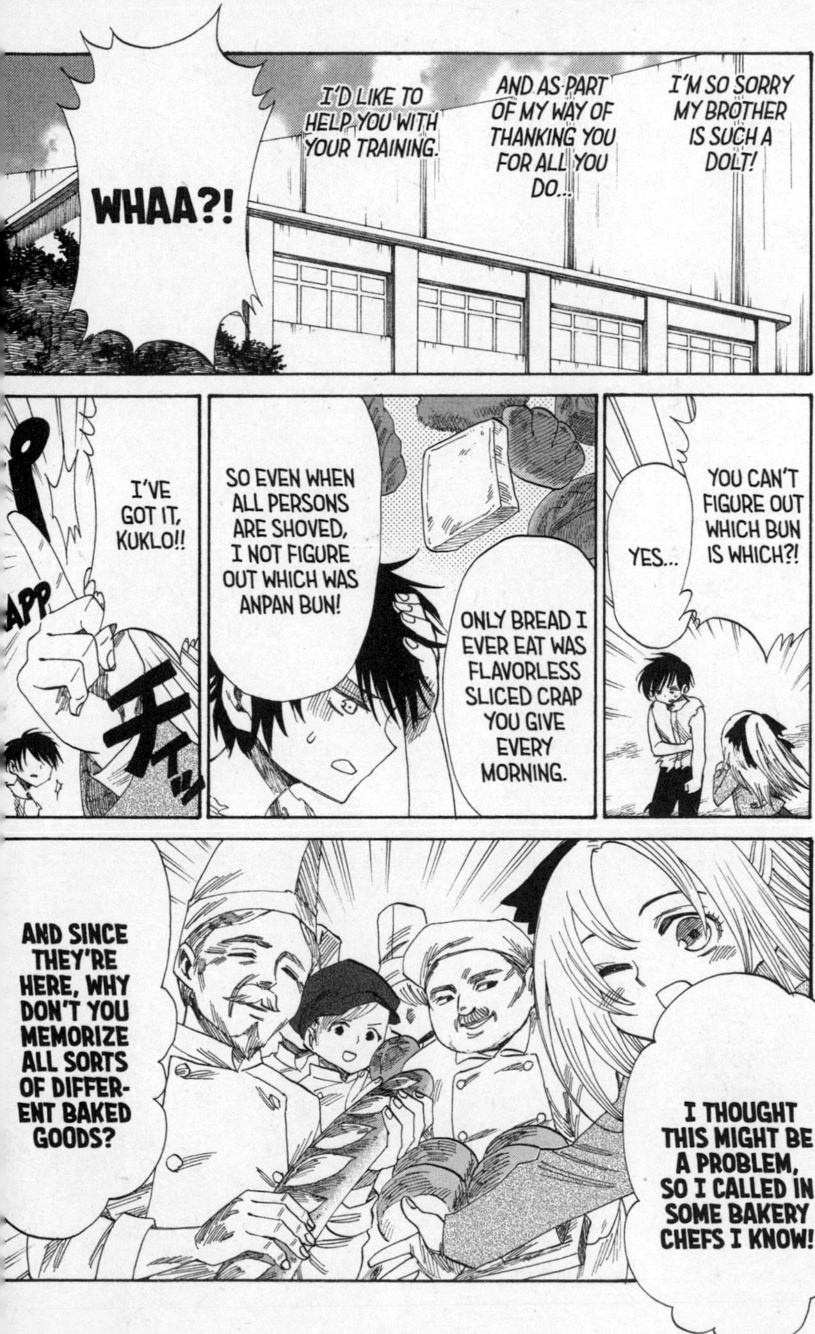
I'M SO SORRY MY BROTHER IS SUCH A DOLT!
AND AS PART OF MY WAY OF THANKING YOU FOR ALL YOU DO...
I'D LIKE TO HELP YOU WITH YOUR TRAINING.
WHAA?!
YOU CAN'T FIGURE OUT WHICH BUN IS WHICH?!
YES...
SO EVEN WHEN ALL PERSONS ARE SHOVED, I NOT FIGURE OUT WHICH WAS ANPAN BUN!
ONLY BREAD I EVER EAT WAS FLAVORLESS SLICED CRAP YOU GIVE EVERY MORNING.
I'VE GOT IT, KUKLO!!
I THOUGHT THIS MIGHT BE A PROBLEM, SO I CALLED IN SOME BAKERY CHEFS I KNOW!
AND SINCE THEY'RE HERE, WHY DON'T YOU MEMORIZE ALL SORTS OF DIFFERENT BAKED GOODS?

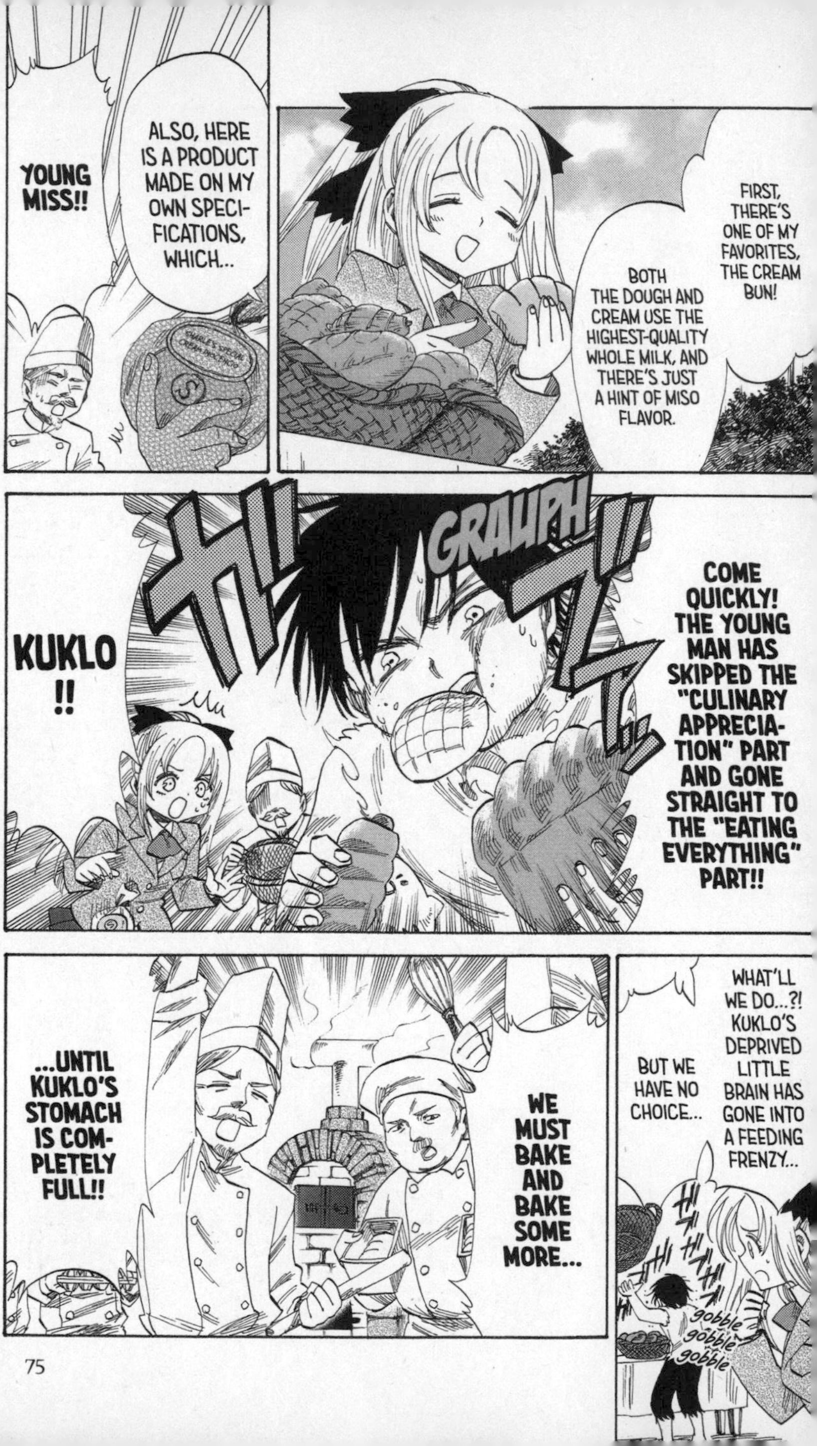
FIRST, THERE'S ONE OF MY FAVORITES, THE CREAM BUN!
BOTH THE DOUGH AND CREAM USE THE HIGHEST-QUALITY WHOLE MILK, AND THERE'S JUST A HINT OF MISO FLAVOR.
ALSO, HERE IS A PRODUCT MADE ON MY OWN SPECI-FICATIONS, WHICH...
YOUNG MISS!!
GRAUPH
COME QUICKLY! THE YOUNG MAN HAS SKIPPED THE "CULINARY APPRECIA-TION" PART AND GONE STRAIGHT TO THE "EATING EVERYTHING" PART!!
KUKLO !!
WHAT'LL WE DO...?! KUKLO'S DEPRIVED LITTLE BRAIN HAS GONE INTO A FEEDING FRENZY...
BUT WE HAVE NO CHOICE...
gobble gobble gobble
WE MUST BAKE AND BAKE SOME MORE...
...UNTIL KUKLO'S STOMACH IS COM-PLETELY FULL!!

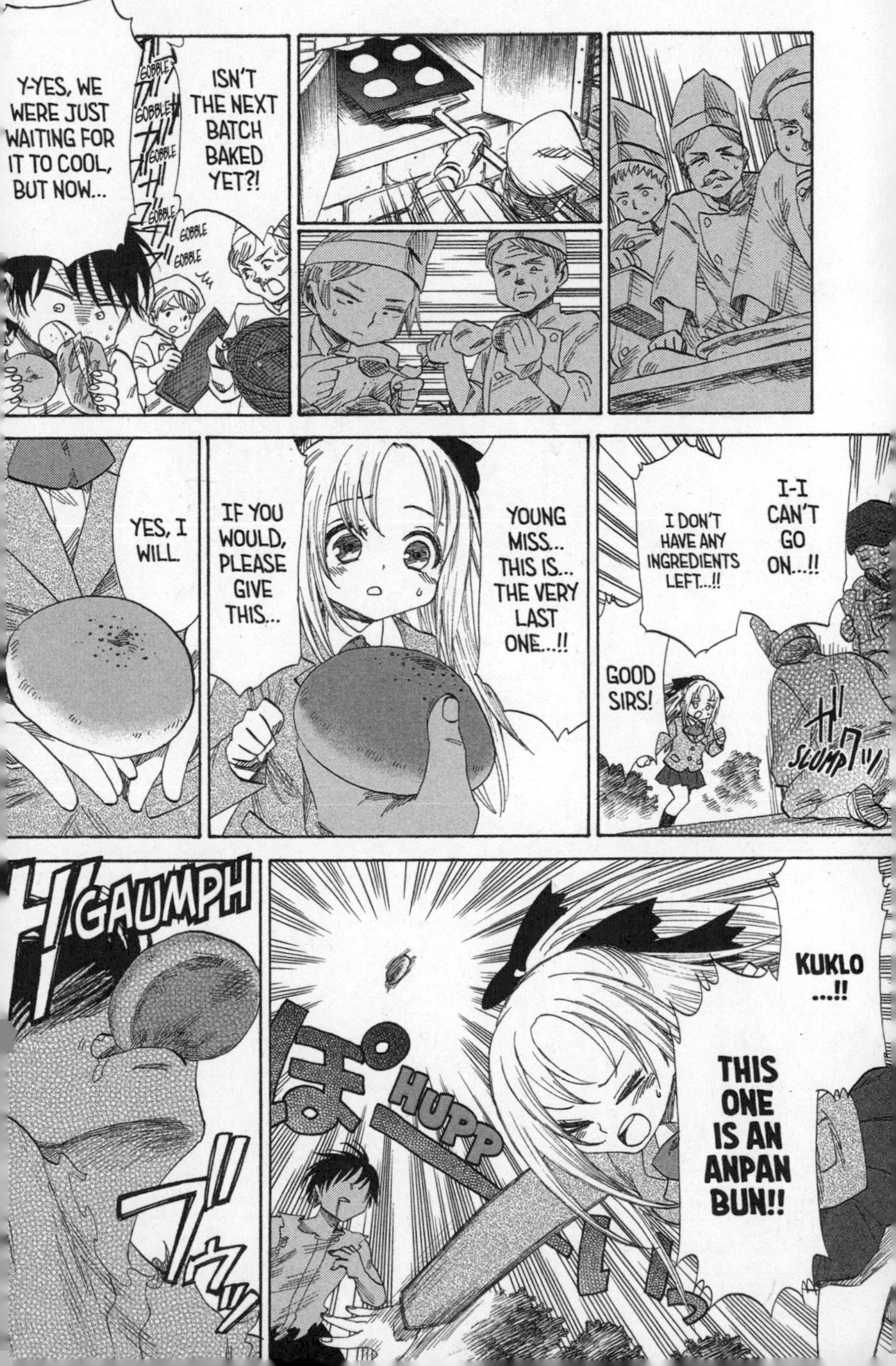
ISN'T THE NEXT BATCH BAKED YET?!
GOBBLE
GOBBLE
GOBBLE
GOBBLE
GOBBLE
GOBBLE
Y-YES, WE WERE JUST WAITING FOR IT TO COOL, BUT NOW...
I-I CAN'T GO ON...!!
I DON'T HAVE ANY INGREDIENTS LEFT...!!
SLUMP
GOOD SIRS!
YOUNG MISS... THIS IS... THE VERY LAST ONE...!!
IF YOU WOULD, PLEASE GIVE THIS...
YES, I WILL.
KUKLO ...!!
THIS ONE IS AN ANPAN BUN!!
HUPP
GAUMPH

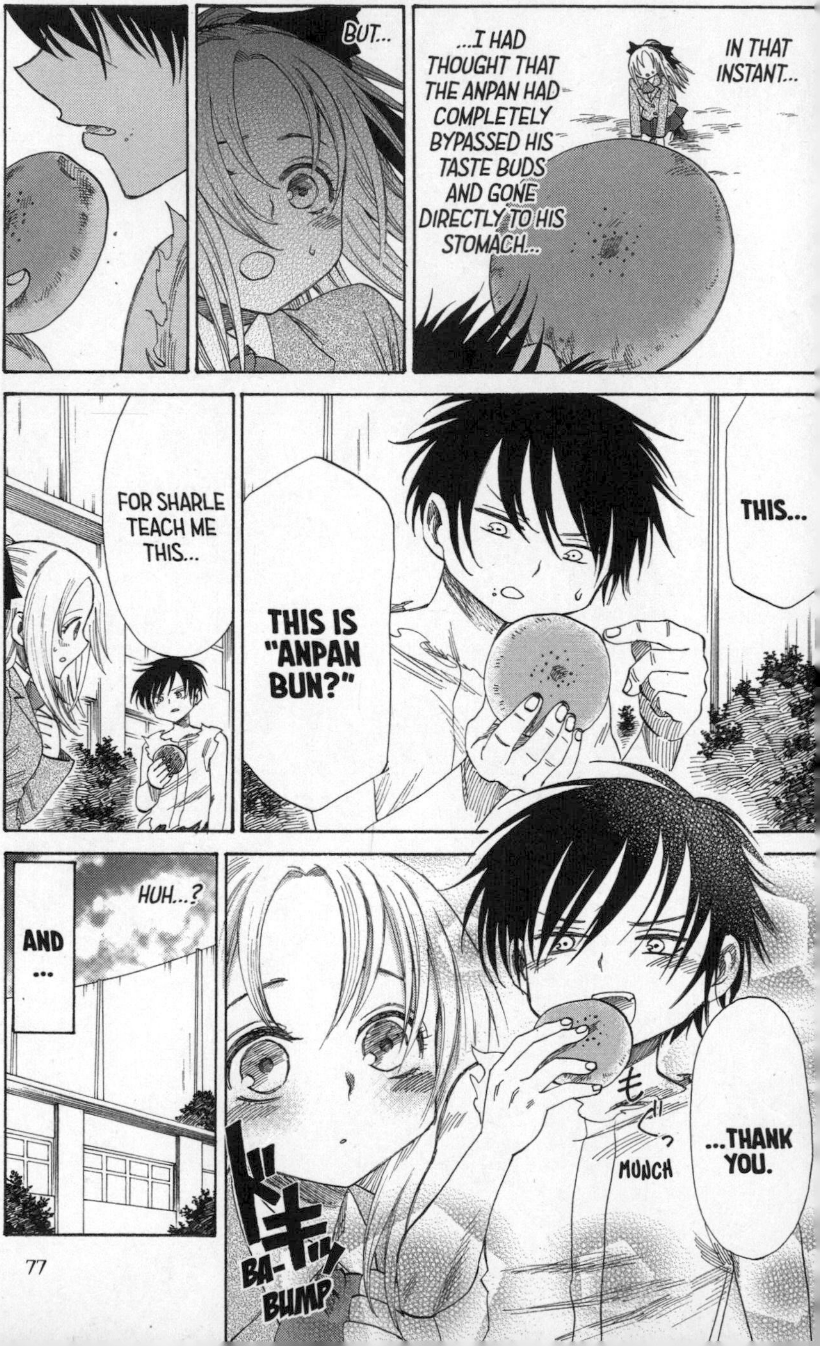
IN THAT INSTANT...
...I HAD THOUGHT THAT THE ANPAN HAD COMPLETELY BYPASSED HIS TASTE BUDS AND GONE DIRECTLY TO HIS STOMACH...
BUT...
THIS...
THIS IS "ANPAN BUN?"
FOR SHARLE TEACH ME THIS...
...THANK YOU.
もぐっ
MUNCH
ドキッ
BA-BUMP
HUH...?
AND ...

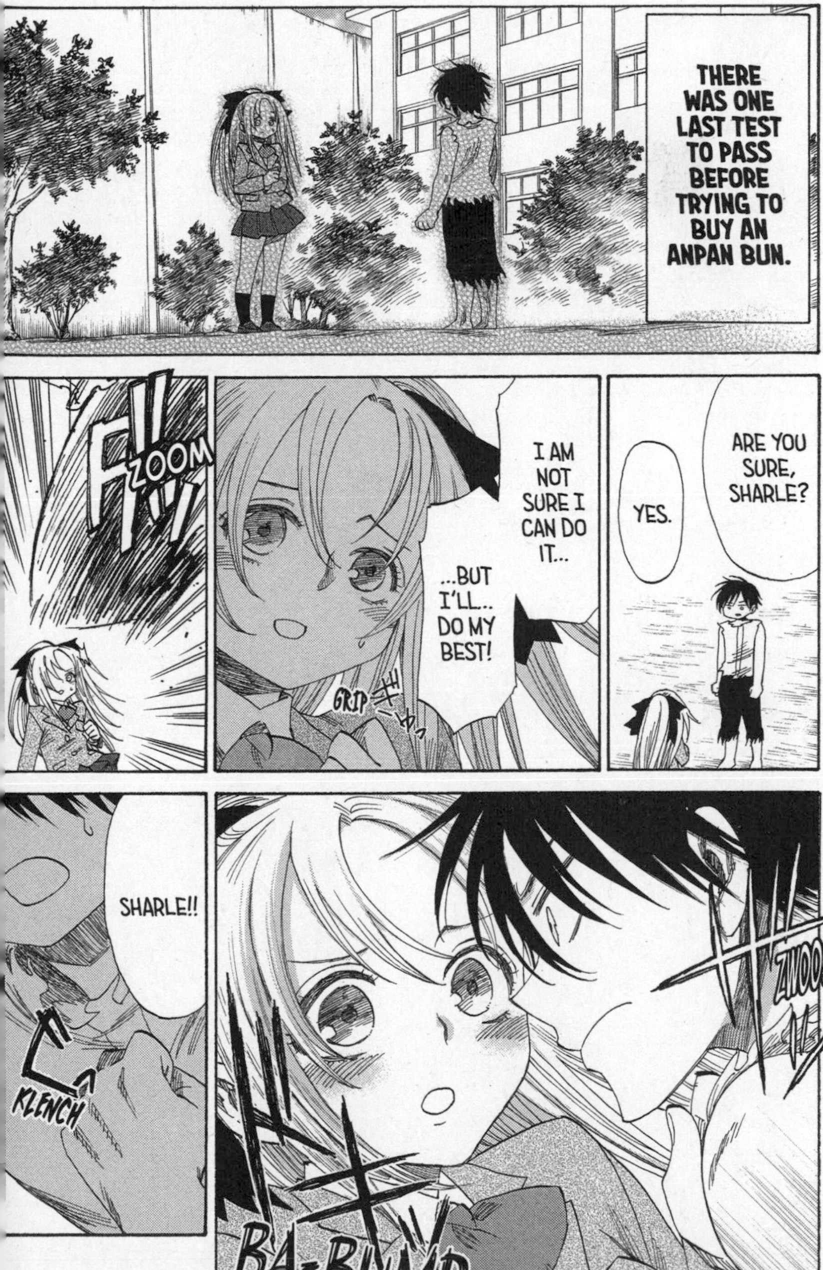
THERE WAS ONE LAST TEST TO PASS BEFORE TRYING TO BUY AN ANPAN BUN.
ARE YOU SURE, SHARLE?
YES.
I AM NOT SURE I CAN DO IT...
...BUT I'LL... DO MY BEST!
GRIP
FZOOM
ZWOOSH
BA-BUMP
SHARLE!!
KLENCH

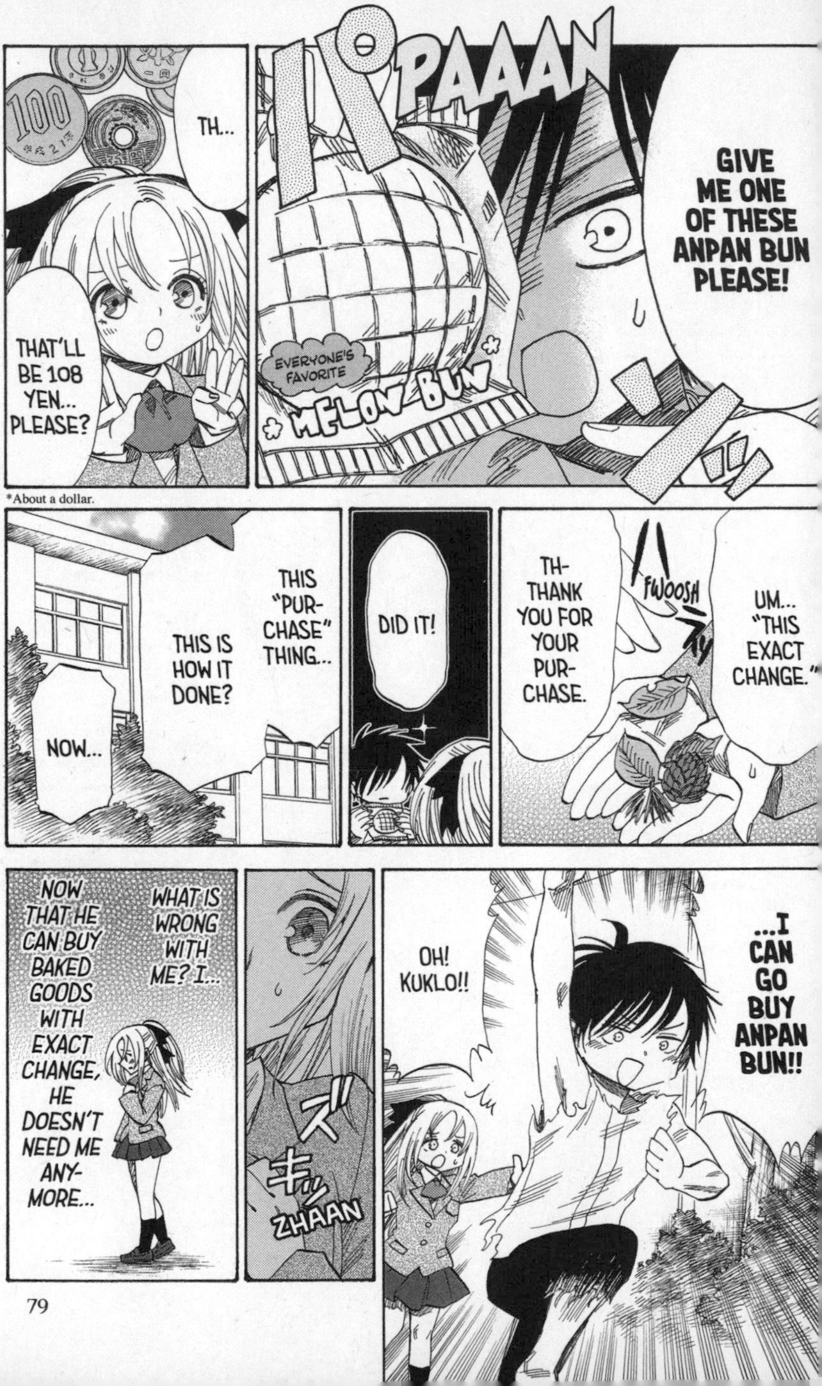
PAAAN
GIVE ME ONE OF THESE ANPAN BUN PLEASE!
EVERYONE'S FAVORITE
MELON BUN
TH...
THAT'LL BE 108 YEN... PLEASE?
UM... "THIS EXACT CHANGE."
FWOOSH
TH-THANK YOU FOR YOUR PURCHASE.
DID IT!
THIS "PURCHASE" THING...
THIS IS HOW IT DONE?
NOW...
...I CAN GO BUY ANPAN BUN!!
OH! KUKLO!!
ZHAAN
WHAT IS WRONG WITH ME? I...
NOW THAT HE CAN BUY BAKED GOODS WITH EXACT CHANGE, HE DOESN'T NEED ME ANYMORE...

*About a dollar.

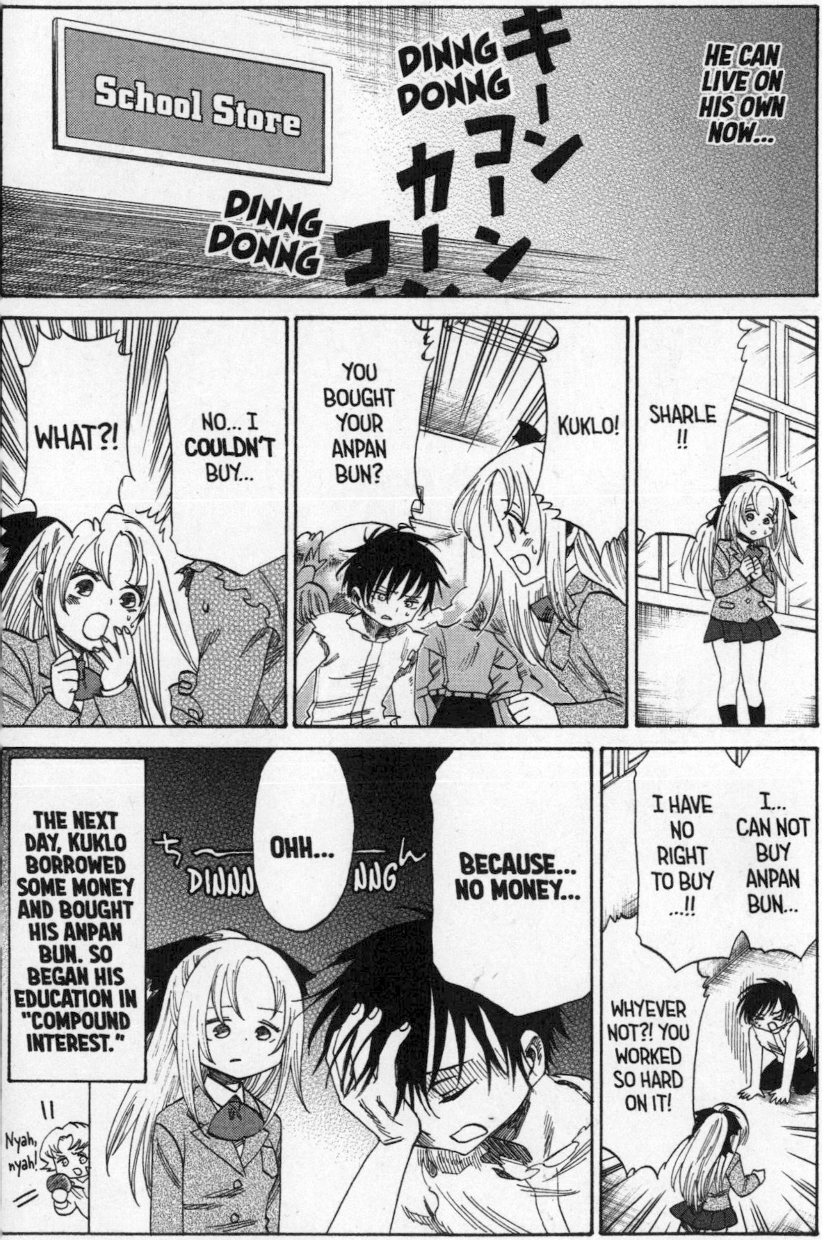
HE CAN LIVE ON HIS OWN NOW...
キーンコーン
DINNG DONNG
カーンコ
DINNG DONNG
School Store
SHARLE!!
KUKLO!
YOU BOUGHT YOUR ANPAN BUN?
NO... I COULDN'T BUY...
WHAT?!
I... CAN NOT BUY ANPAN BUN...
I HAVE NO RIGHT TO BUY ...!!
WHYEVER NOT?! YOU WORKED SO HARD ON IT!
BECAUSE... NO MONEY...
OHH...
ち〜〜ん
DINNNNG
THE NEXT DAY, KUKLO BORROWED SOME MONEY AND BOUGHT HIS ANPAN BUN. SO BEGAN HIS EDUCATION IN "COMPOUND INTEREST."
Nyah, nyah!

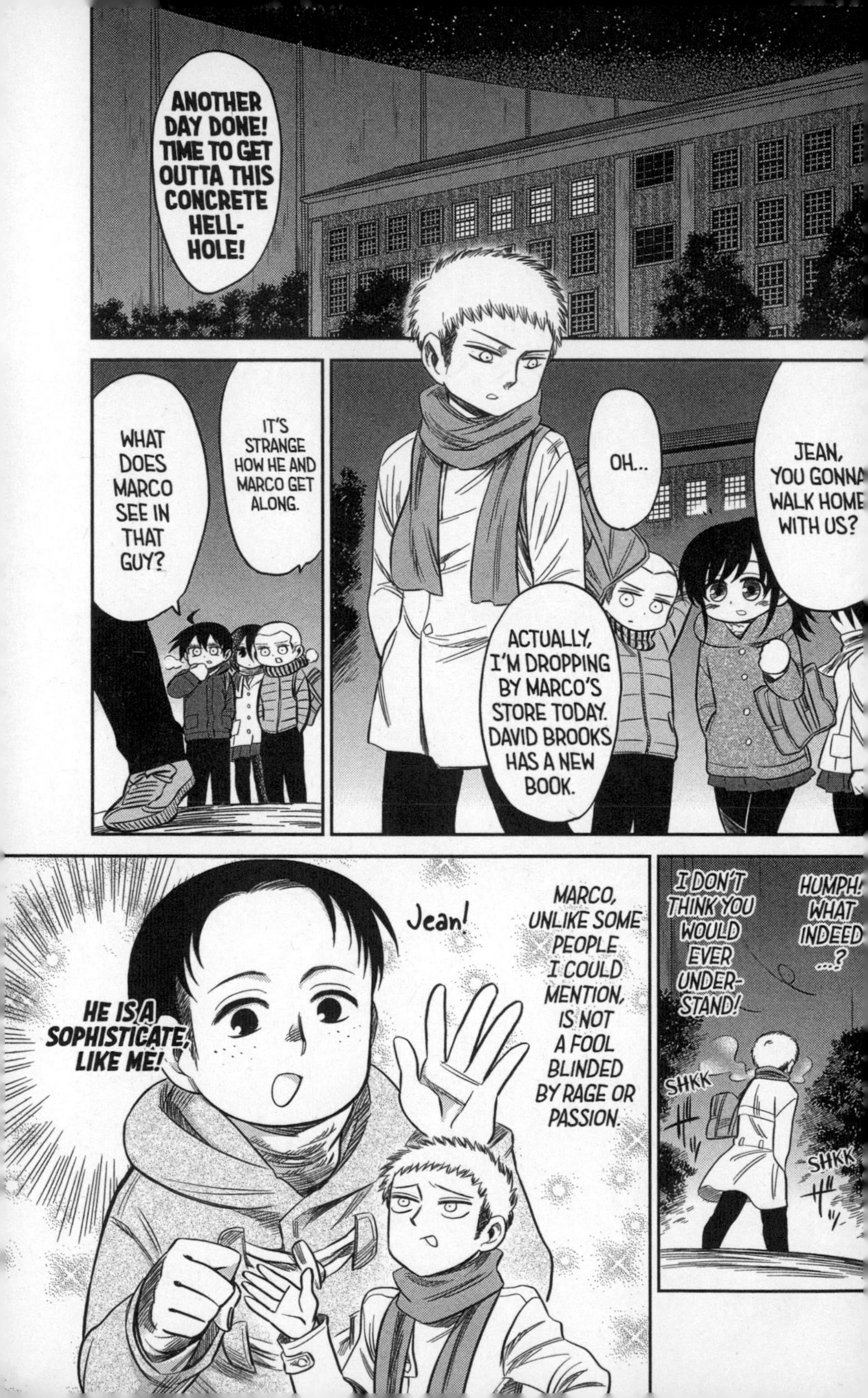
ANOTHER DAY DONE! TIME TO GET OUTTA THIS CONCRETE HELL-HOLE!
JEAN, YOU GONNA WALK HOME WITH US?
OH...
ACTUALLY, I'M DROPPING BY MARCO'S STORE TODAY. DAVID BROOKS HAS A NEW BOOK.
IT'S STRANGE HOW HE AND MARCO GET ALONG.
WHAT DOES MARCO SEE IN THAT GUY?
HUMPH! WHAT INDEED ...?
I DON'T THINK YOU WOULD EVER UNDER-STAND!
SHKK
SHKK
MARCO, UNLIKE SOME PEOPLE I COULD MENTION, IS NOT A FOOL BLINDED BY RAGE OR PASSION.
Jean!
HE IS A SOPHISTICATE, LIKE ME!

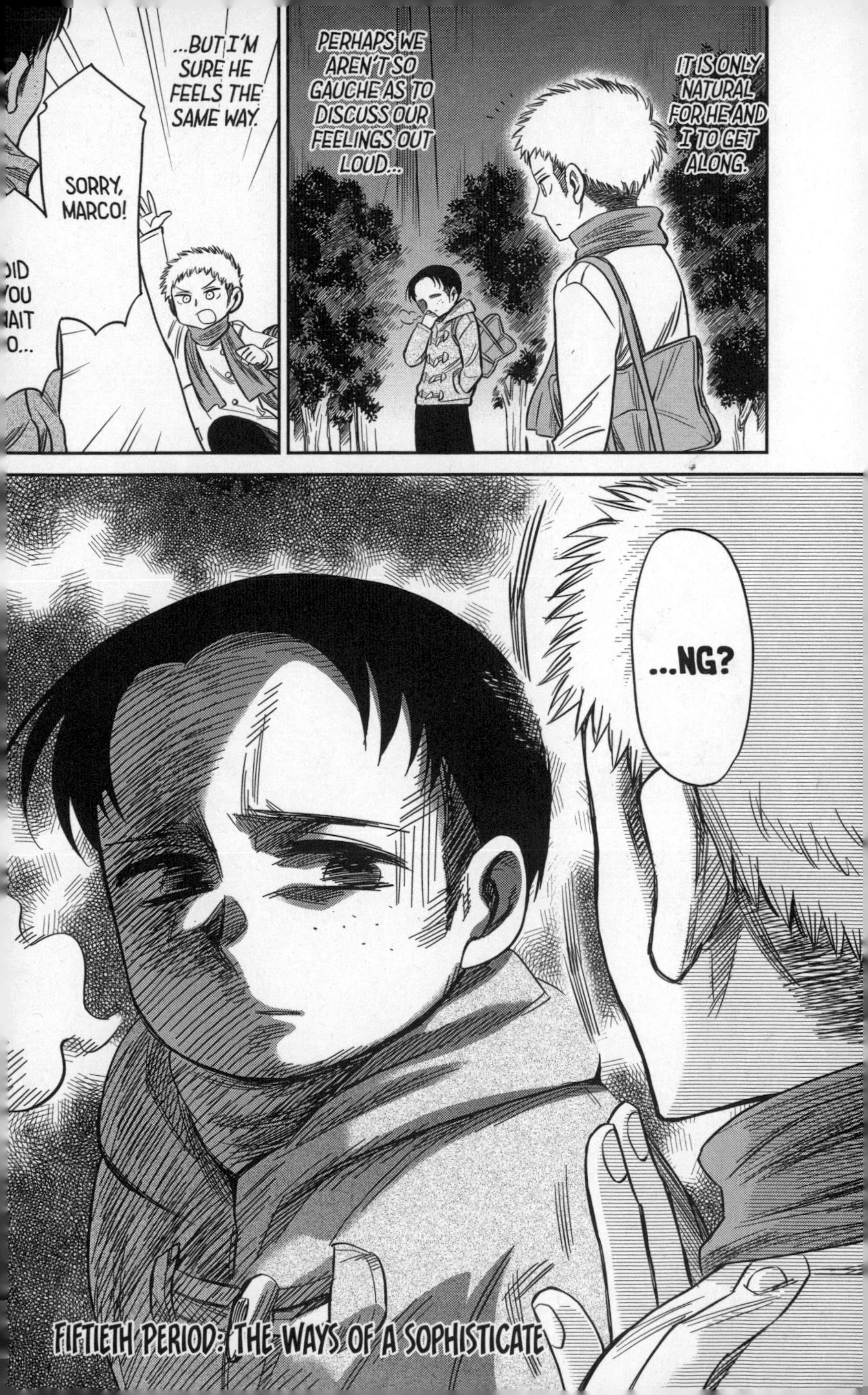
IT IS ONLY NATURAL FOR HE AND I TO GET ALONG.
PERHAPS WE AREN'T SO GAUCHE AS TO DISCUSS OUR FEELINGS OUT LOUD...
...BUT I'M SURE HE FEELS THE SAME WAY.
SORRY, MARCO!
...NG?
FIFTIETH PERIOD: THE WAYS OF A SOPHISTICATE

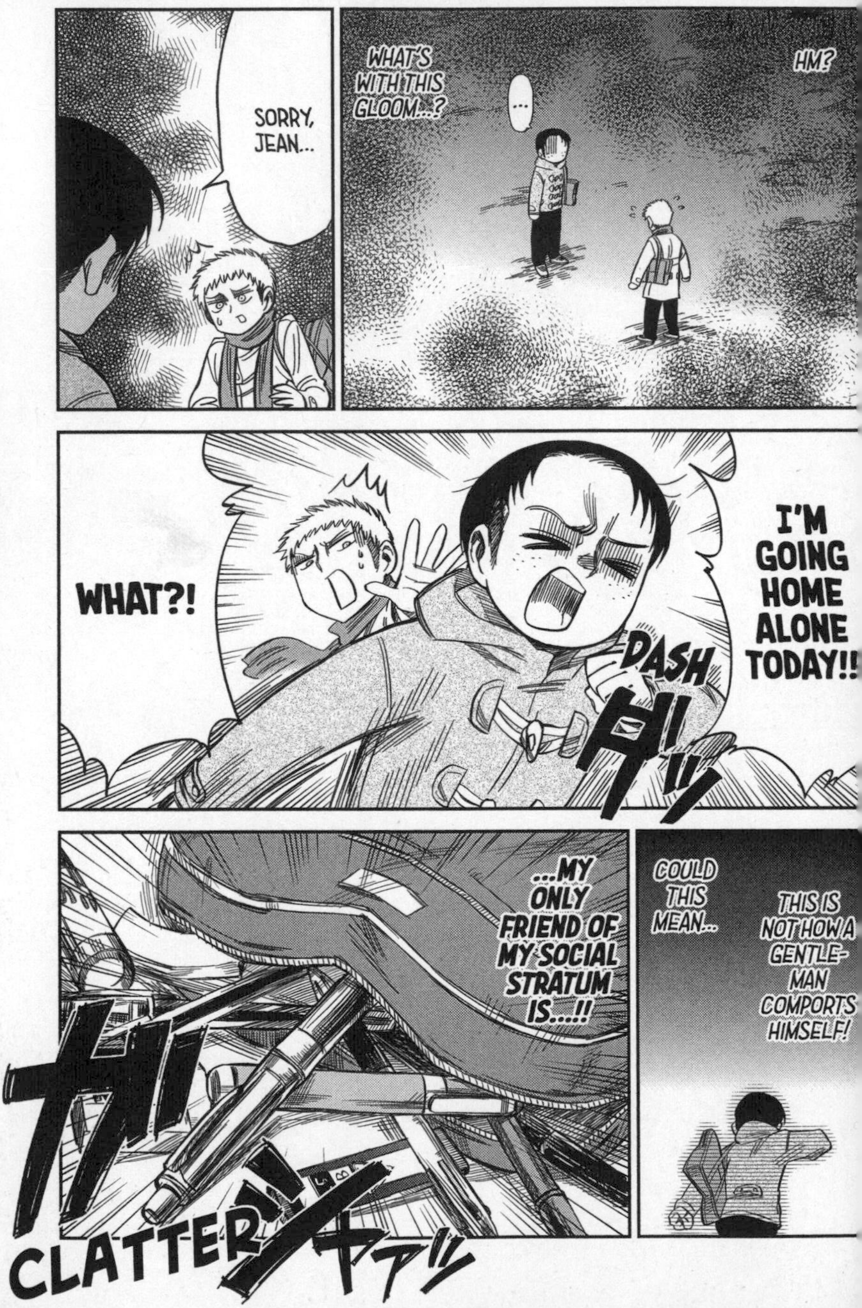
HM?
WHAT'S WITH THIS GLOOM...?
...
SORRY, JEAN...
I'M GOING HOME ALONE TODAY!!
DASH
WHAT?!
THIS IS NOT HOW A GENTLE-MAN COMPORTS HIMSELF!
COULD THIS MEAN...
...MY ONLY FRIEND OF MY SOCIAL STRATUM IS...!!
CLATTER

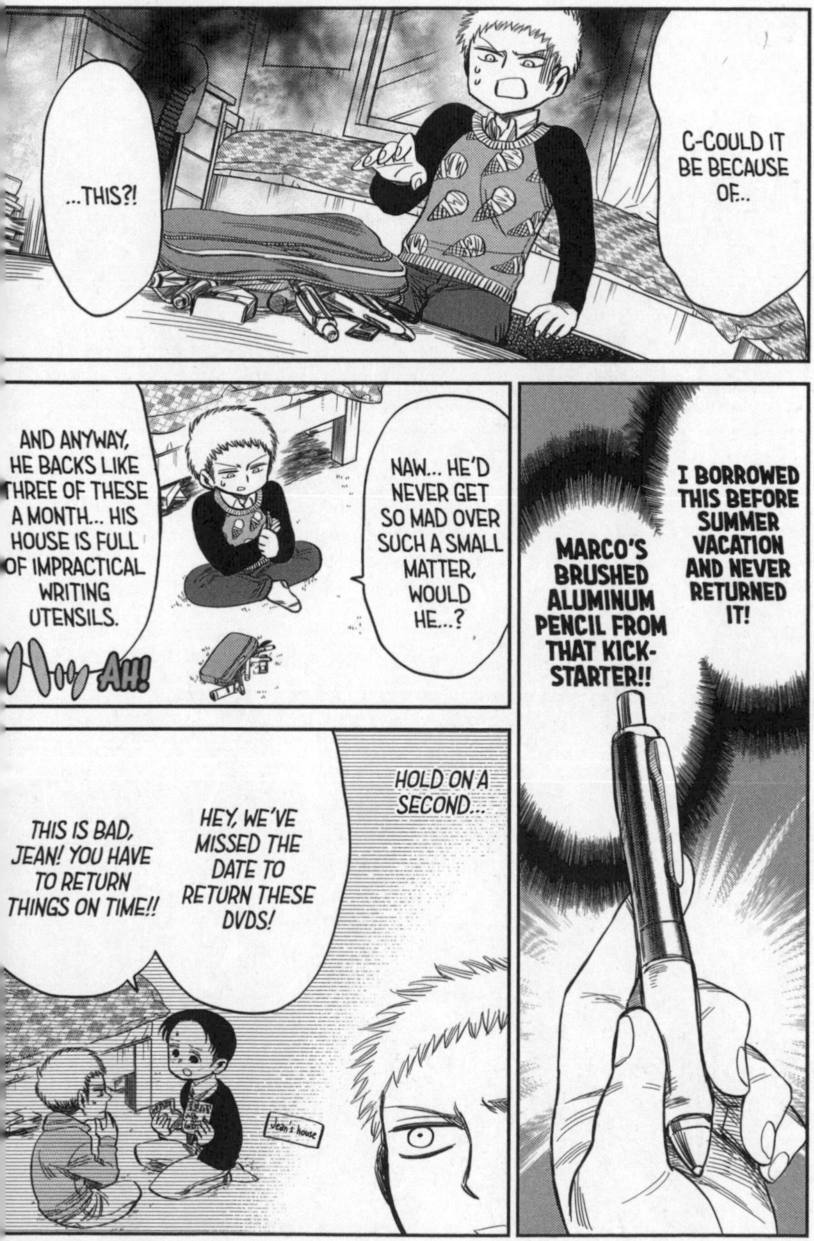
C-COULD IT BE BECAUSE OF..
...THIS?!
I BORROWED THIS BEFORE SUMMER VACATION AND NEVER RETURNED IT!
MARCO'S BRUSHED ALUMINUM PENCIL FROM THAT KICK-STARTER!!
NAW... HE'D NEVER GET SO MAD OVER SUCH A SMALL MATTER, WOULD HE...?
AND ANYWAY, HE BACKS LIKE THREE OF THESE A MONTH... HIS HOUSE IS FULL OF IMPRACTICAL WRITING UTENSILS.
AH!
HOLD ON A SECOND...
HEY, WE'VE MISSED THE DATE TO RETURN THESE DVDS!
THIS IS BAD, JEAN! YOU HAVE TO RETURN THINGS ON TIME!!
Jean's house

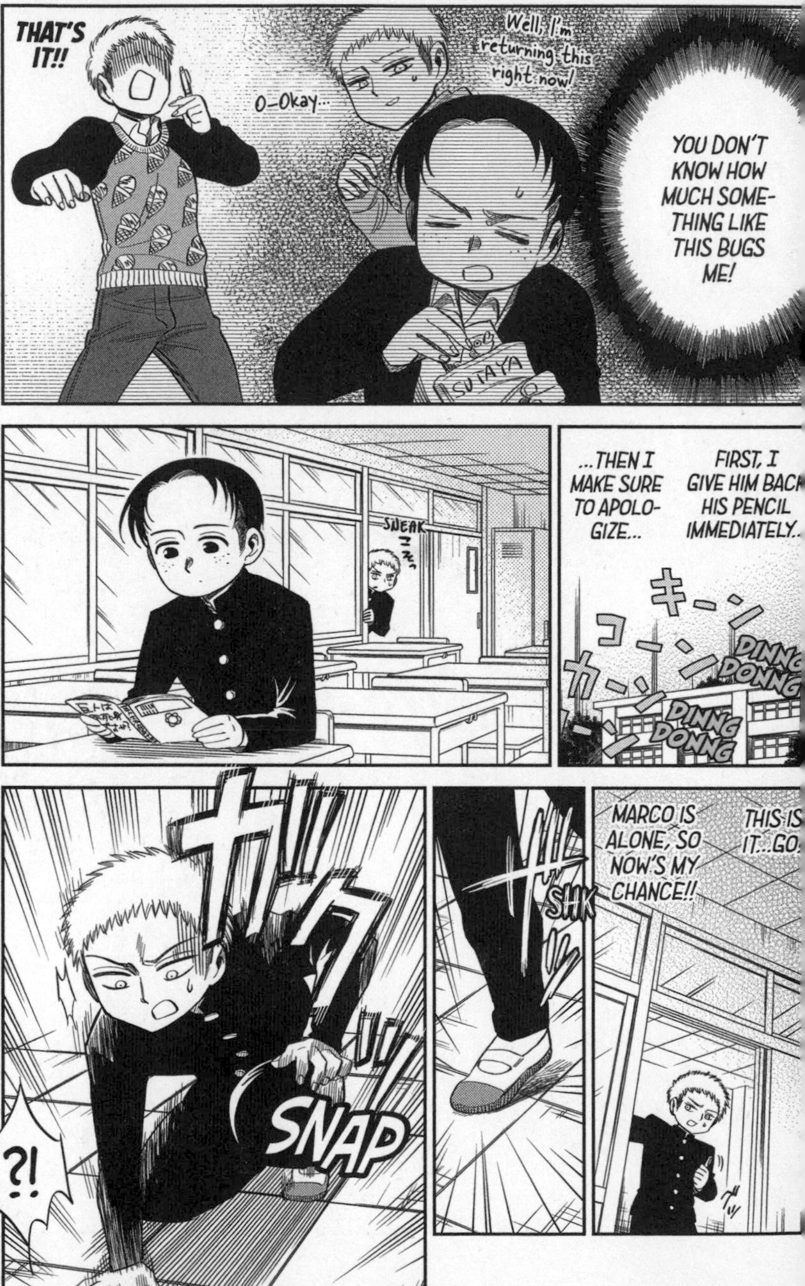
YOU DON'T KNOW HOW MUCH SOME-THING LIKE THIS BUGS ME!
Well, I'm returning this right now!
O-Okay...
THAT'S IT!!
SUTAYA
FIRST, I GIVE HIM BACK HIS PENCIL IMMEDIATELY...
...THEN I MAKE SURE TO APOLO-GIZE...
キーン
コーン
カーン
DINNG DONNG
DINNG DONNG
SNEAK
THIS IS IT...GO!
MARCO IS ALONE, SO NOW'S MY CHANCE!!
SHK
SNAP
?!

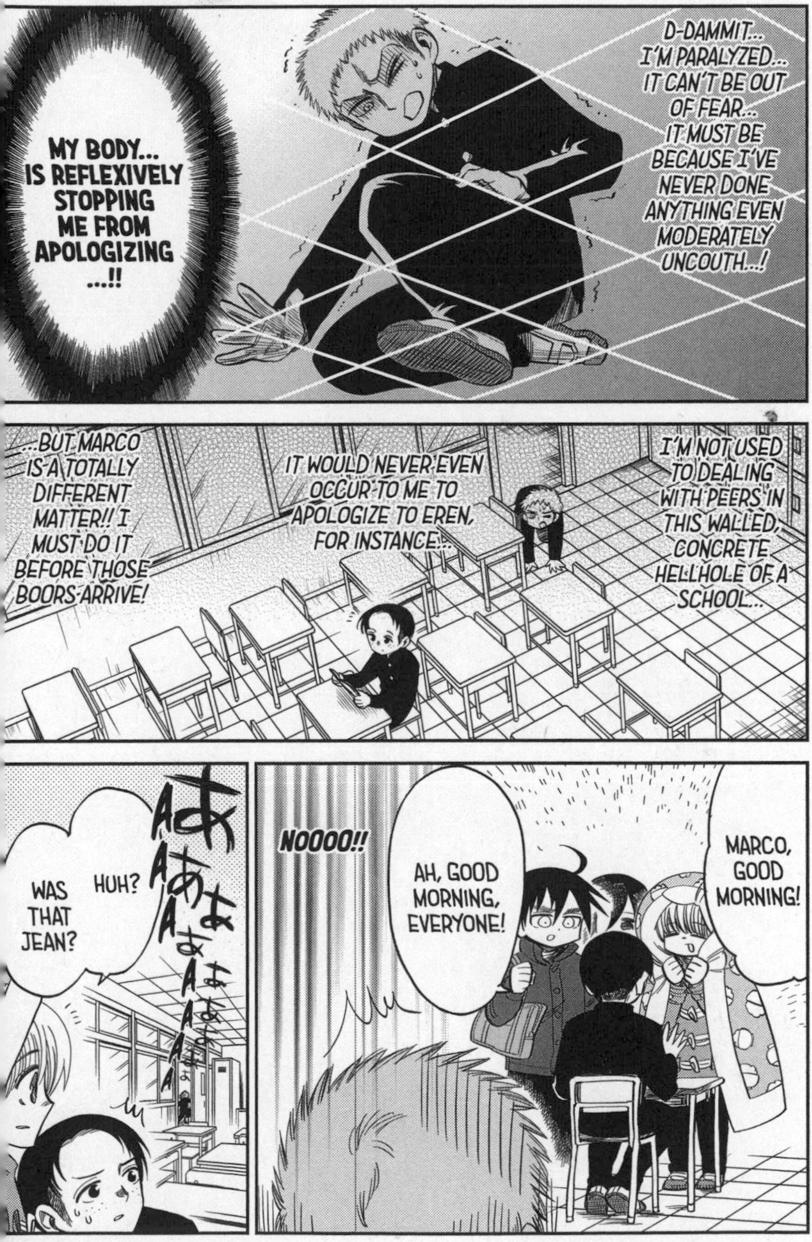
D-DAMMIT... I'M PARALYZED... IT CAN'T BE OUT OF FEAR... IT MUST BE BECAUSE I'VE NEVER DONE ANYTHING EVEN MODERATELY UNCOUTH...!
MY BODY... IS REFLEXIVELY STOPPING ME FROM APOLOGIZING ...!!
I'M NOT USED TO DEALING WITH PEERS IN THIS WALLED, CONCRETE HELLHOLE OF A SCHOOL...
IT WOULD NEVER EVEN OCCUR TO ME TO APOLOGIZE TO EREN, FOR INSTANCE...
...BUT MARCO IS A TOTALLY DIFFERENT MATTER!! I MUST DO IT BEFORE THOSE BOORS ARRIVE!
MARCO, GOOD MORNING!
AH, GOOD MORNING, EVERYONE!
NOOOO!!
AAAAA
HUH?
WAS THAT JEAN?

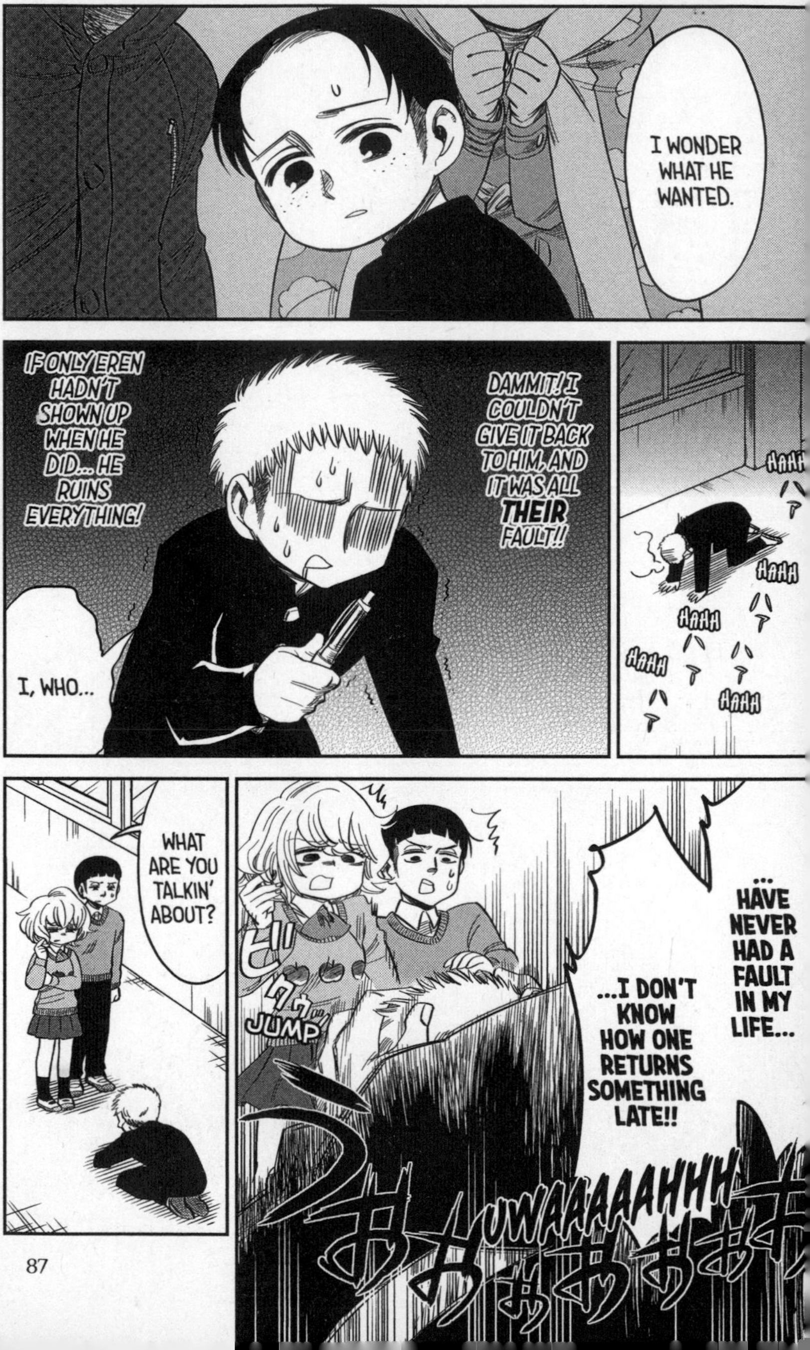
I WONDER WHAT HE WANTED.
HAHH
HAHH
HAHH
HAHH
HAHH
DAMMIT! I COULDN'T GIVE IT BACK TO HIM, AND IT WAS ALL **THEIR** FAULT!!
IF ONLY EREN HADN'T SHOWN UP WHEN HE DID... HE RUINS EVERYTHING!
I, WHO...
...HAVE NEVER HAD A FAULT IN MY LIFE...
...I DON'T KNOW HOW ONE RETURNS SOMETHING LATE!!
JUMP
UWAAAAAAHHH
WHAT ARE YOU TALKIN' ABOUT?

Marco didn't even throw his hat into the ring to be student body resident, but still, he was elected. For details see Volume 3, Period 40.

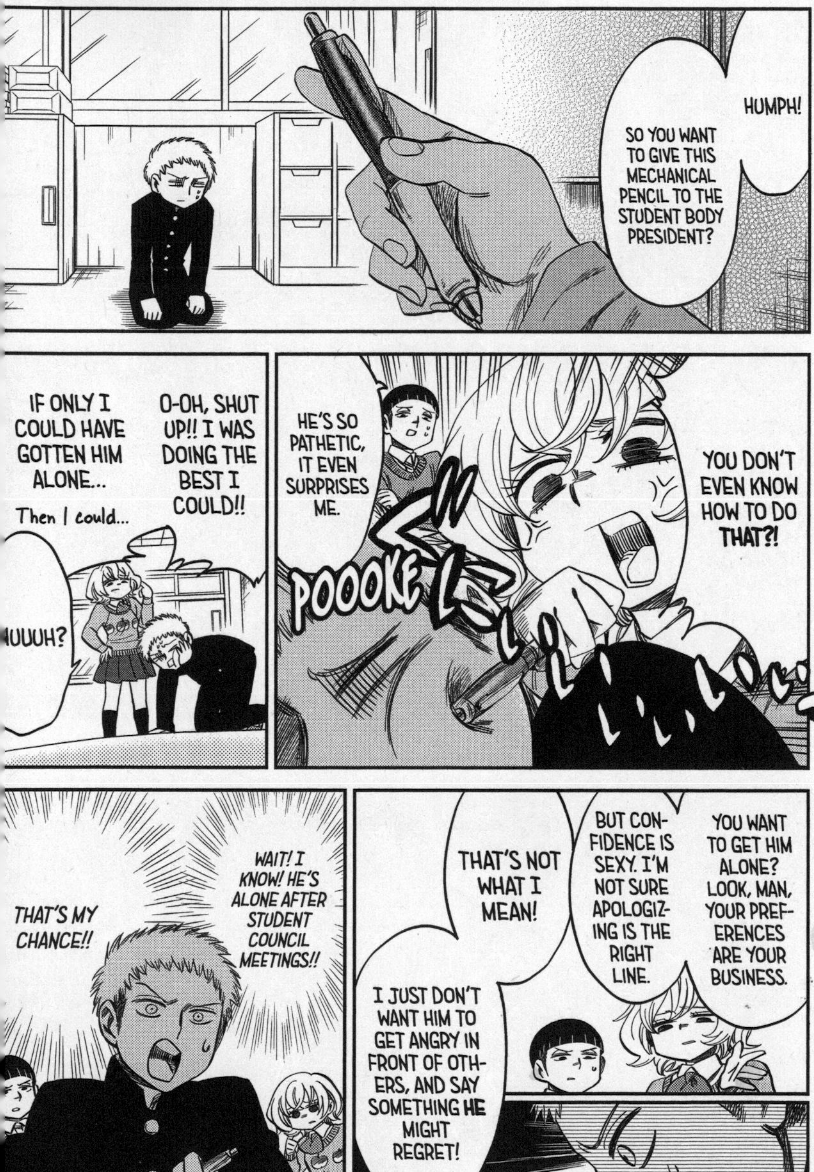
HUMPH!
SO YOU WANT TO GIVE THIS MECHANICAL PENCIL TO THE STUDENT BODY PRESIDENT?
YOU DON'T EVEN KNOW HOW TO DO THAT?!
HE'S SO PATHETIC, IT EVEN SURPRISES ME.
POOOKE
O-OH, SHUT UP!! I WAS DOING THE BEST I COULD!!
IF ONLY I COULD HAVE GOTTEN HIM ALONE...
Then I could...
HUUUH?
YOU WANT TO GET HIM ALONE? LOOK, MAN, YOUR PREFERENCES ARE YOUR BUSINESS.
BUT CONFIDENCE IS SEXY. I'M NOT SURE APOLOGIZING IS THE RIGHT LINE.
THAT'S NOT WHAT I MEAN!
I JUST DON'T WANT HIM TO GET ANGRY IN FRONT OF OTHERS, AND SAY SOMETHING HE MIGHT REGRET!
WAIT! I KNOW! HE'S ALONE AFTER STUDENT COUNCIL MEETINGS!!
THAT'S MY CHANCE!!

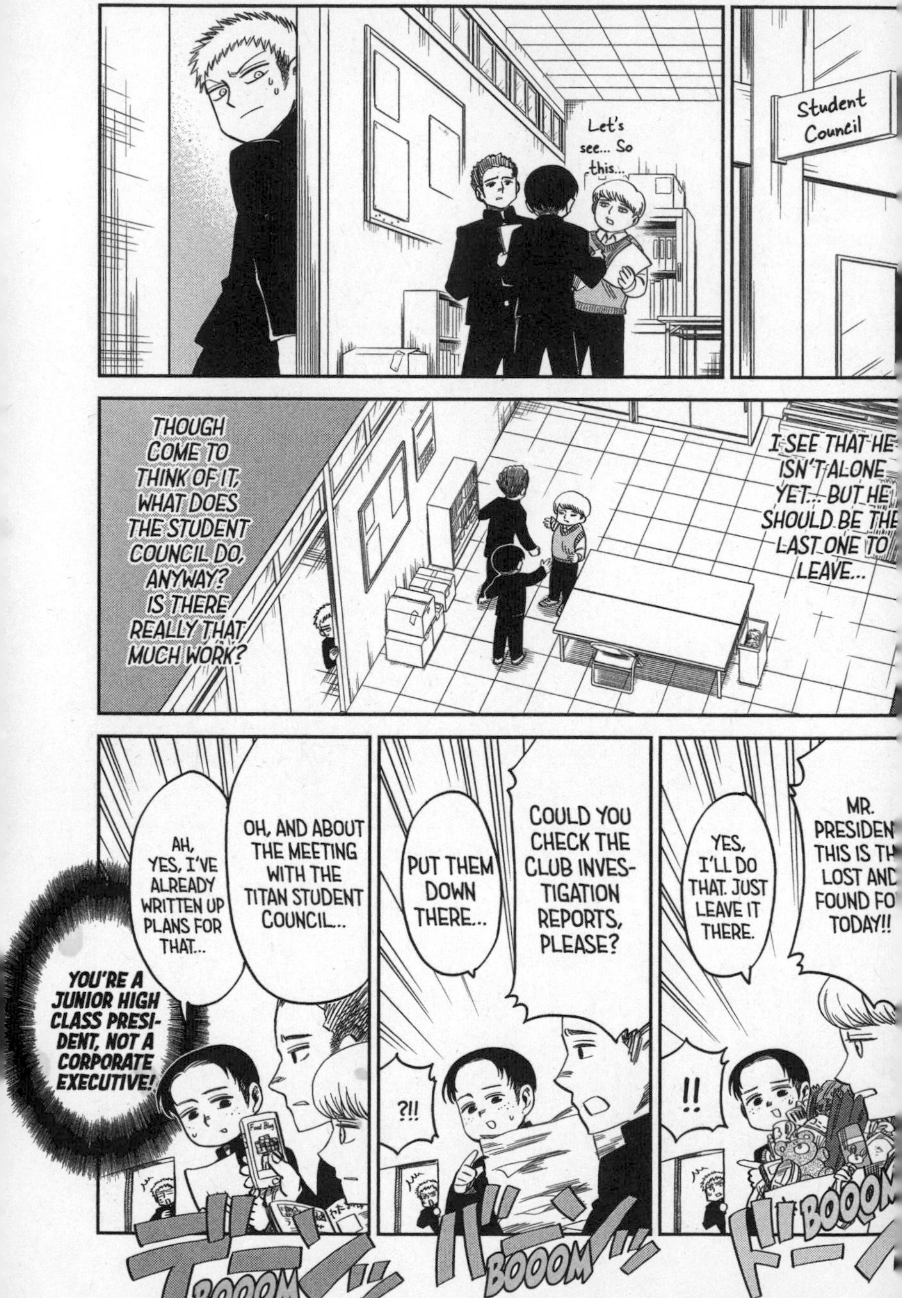
Student Council
Let's see... So this...
I SEE THAT HE ISN'T ALONE YET... BUT HE SHOULD BE THE LAST ONE TO LEAVE...
THOUGH COME TO THINK OF IT, WHAT DOES THE STUDENT COUNCIL DO, ANYWAY? IS THERE REALLY THAT MUCH WORK?
MR. PRESIDEN THIS IS TH LOST AND FOUND FO TODAY!!
YES, I'LL DO THAT. JUST LEAVE IT THERE.
!!
BOOOM
COULD YOU CHECK THE CLUB INVES-TIGATION REPORTS, PLEASE?
PUT THEM DOWN THERE...
?!!
BOOOM
OH, AND ABOUT THE MEETING WITH THE TITAN STUDENT COUNCIL...
AH, YES, I'VE ALREADY WRITTEN UP PLANS FOR THAT...
YOU'RE A JUNIOR HIGH CLASS PRESI-DENT, NOT A CORPORATE EXECUTIVE!
BOOOM

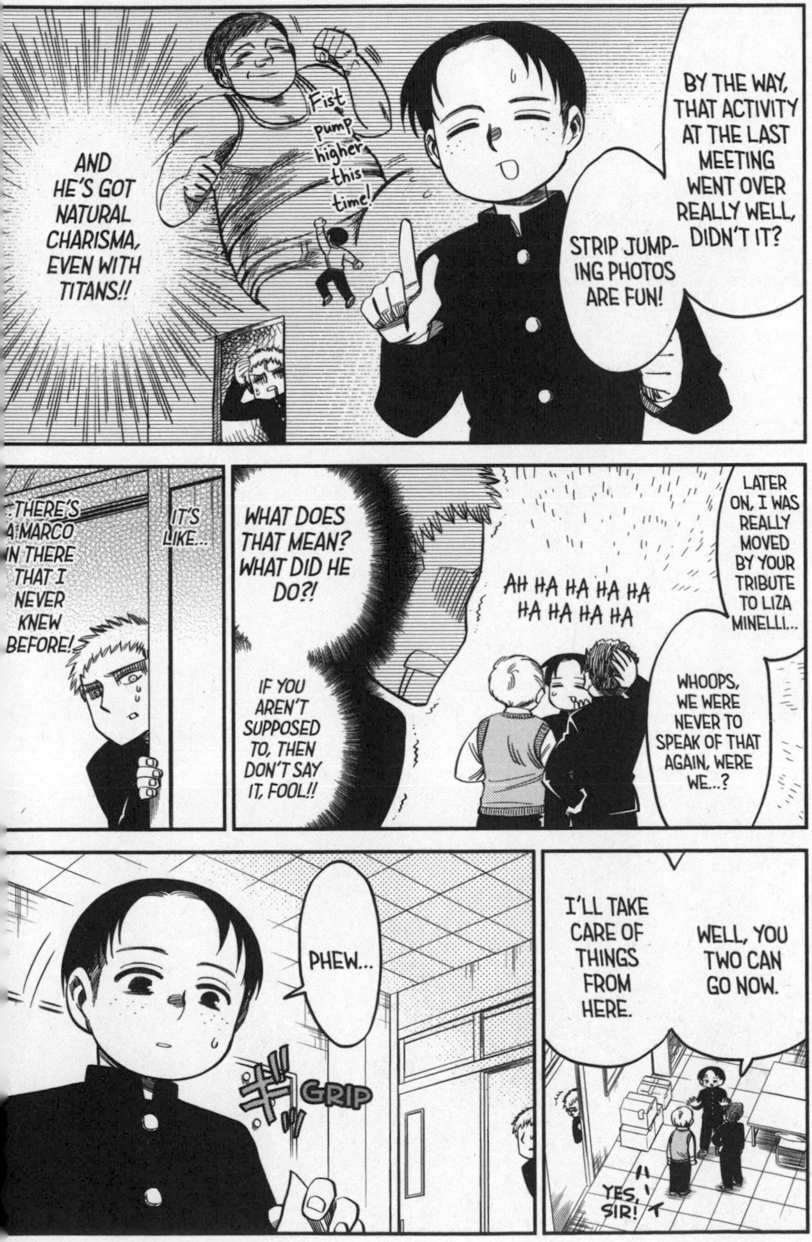
BY THE WAY, THAT ACTIVITY AT THE LAST MEETING WENT OVER REALLY WELL, DIDN'T IT?
STRIP JUMP-ING PHOTOS ARE FUN!
Fist pump higher this time!
AND HE'S GOT NATURAL CHARISMA, EVEN WITH TITANS!!
LATER ON, I WAS REALLY MOVED BY YOUR TRIBUTE TO LIZA MINELLI...
AH HA HA HA HA HA HA HA HA
WHOOPS, WE WERE NEVER TO SPEAK OF THAT AGAIN, WERE WE...?
WHAT DOES THAT MEAN? WHAT DID HE DO?!
IF YOU AREN'T SUPPOSED TO, THEN DON'T SAY IT, FOOL!!
IT'S LIKE...
...THERE'S A MARCO IN THERE THAT I NEVER KNEW BEFORE!
WELL, YOU TWO CAN GO NOW.
I'LL TAKE CARE OF THINGS FROM HERE.
YES, SIR!
PHEW...
GRIP

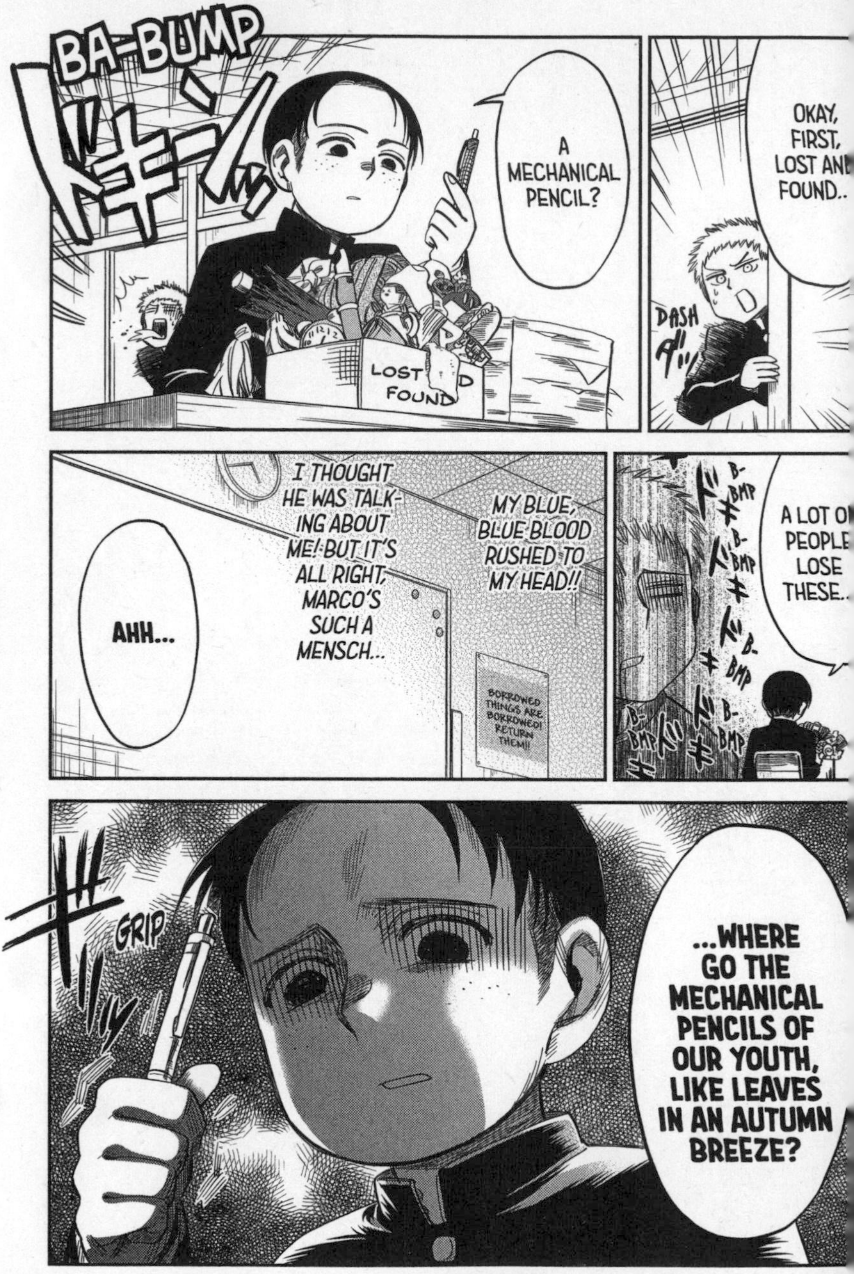
OKAY, FIRST, LOST AND FOUND..
DASH
BA-BUMP
A MECHANICAL PENCIL?
LOST FOUND
A LOT OF PEOPLE LOSE THESE...
B-BMP B-BMP B-BMP B-BMP B-BMP B-BMP
MY BLUE, BLUE BLOOD RUSHED TO MY HEAD!!
I THOUGHT HE WAS TALKING ABOUT ME! BUT IT'S ALL RIGHT, MARCO'S SUCH A MENSCH...
AHH...
BORROWED THINGS ARE BORROWED! RETURN THEM!!
...WHERE GO THE MECHANICAL PENCILS OF OUR YOUTH, LIKE LEAVES IN AN AUTUMN BREEZE?
GRIP

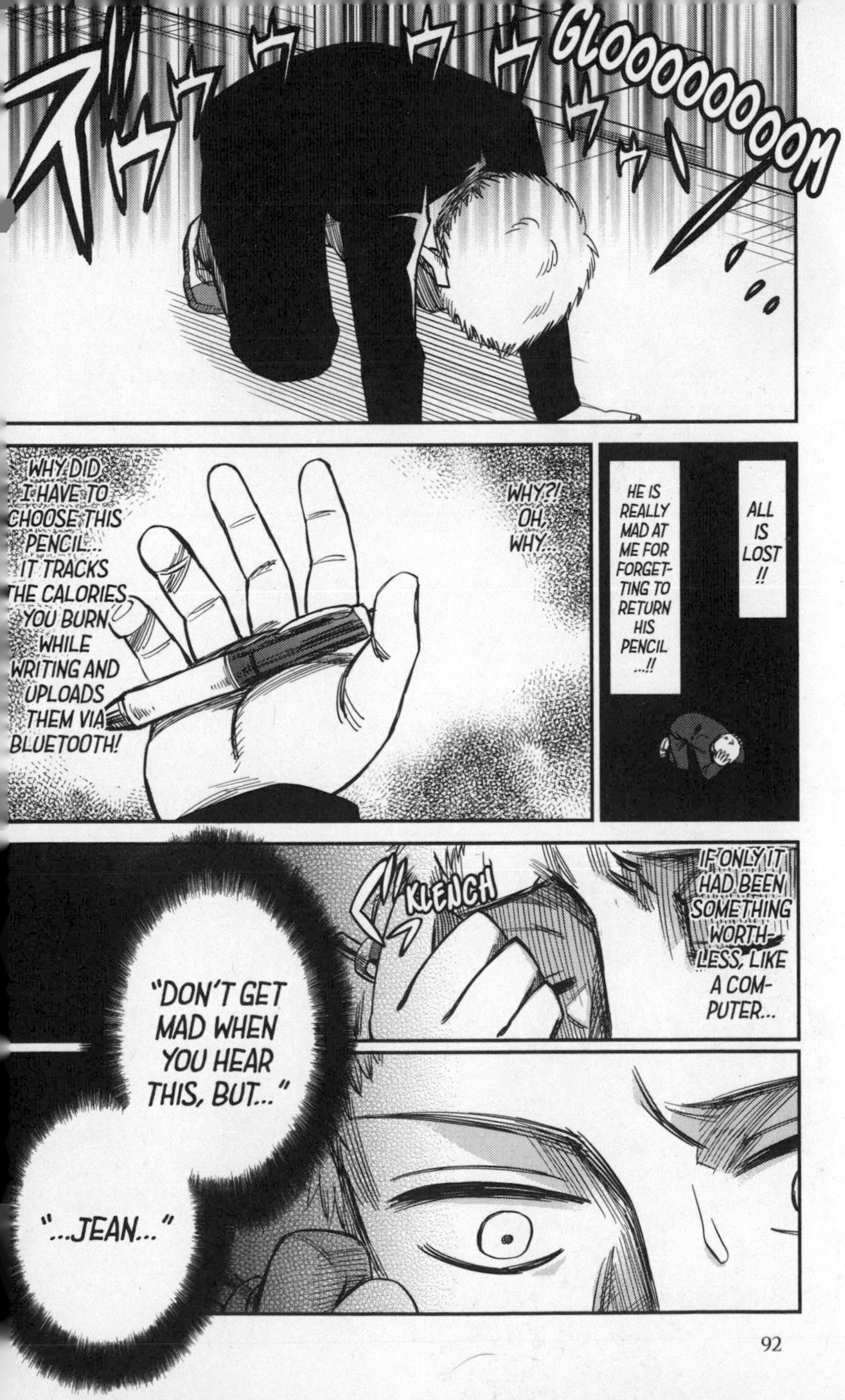
GLOOOOOOOOOM
ALL IS LOST !!
HE IS REALLY MAD AT ME FOR FORGETTING TO RETURN HIS PENCIL ...!!
WHY?! OH, WHY...
WHY DID I HAVE TO CHOOSE THIS PENCIL... IT TRACKS THE CALORIES YOU BURN WHILE WRITING AND UPLOADS THEM VIA BLUETOOTH!
IF ONLY IT HAD BEEN SOMETHING WORTHLESS, LIKE A COMPUTER...
KLENCH
"DON'T GET MAD WHEN YOU HEAR THIS, BUT..."
"...JEAN..."

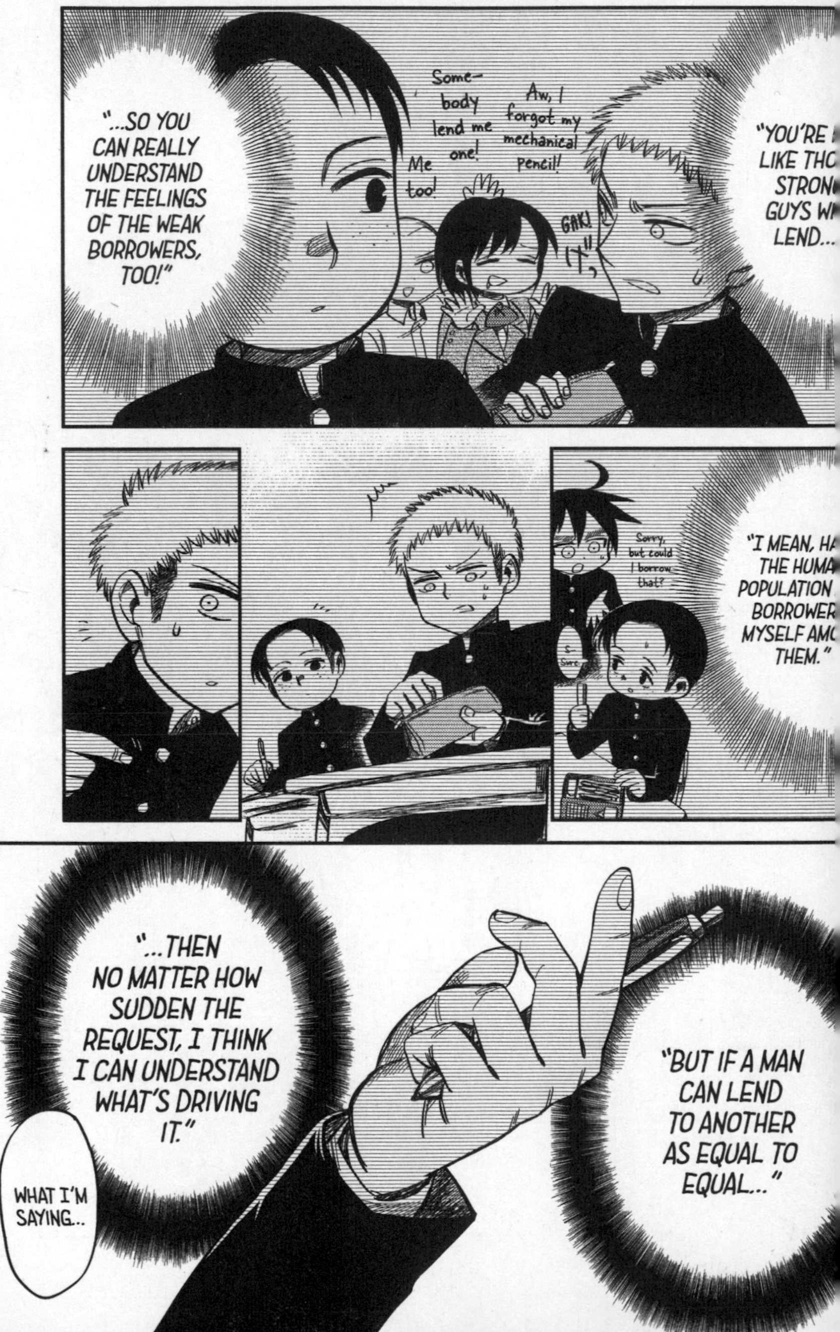
"YOU'RE
LIKE THO
STRON
GUYS WH
LEND...
Aw, I forgot my mechanical pencil!
Some-body lend me one!
Me too!
GAK!
"...SO YOU CAN REALLY UNDERSTAND THE FEELINGS OF THE WEAK BORROWERS, TOO!"
"I MEAN, HA
THE HUMA
POPULATION
BORROWER
MYSELF AM
THEM."
Sorry, but could I borrow that?
S-Sure.
"BUT IF A MAN CAN LEND TO ANOTHER AS EQUAL TO EQUAL..."
"...THEN NO MATTER HOW SUDDEN THE REQUEST, I THINK I CAN UNDERSTAND WHAT'S DRIVING IT."
WHAT I'M SAYING...

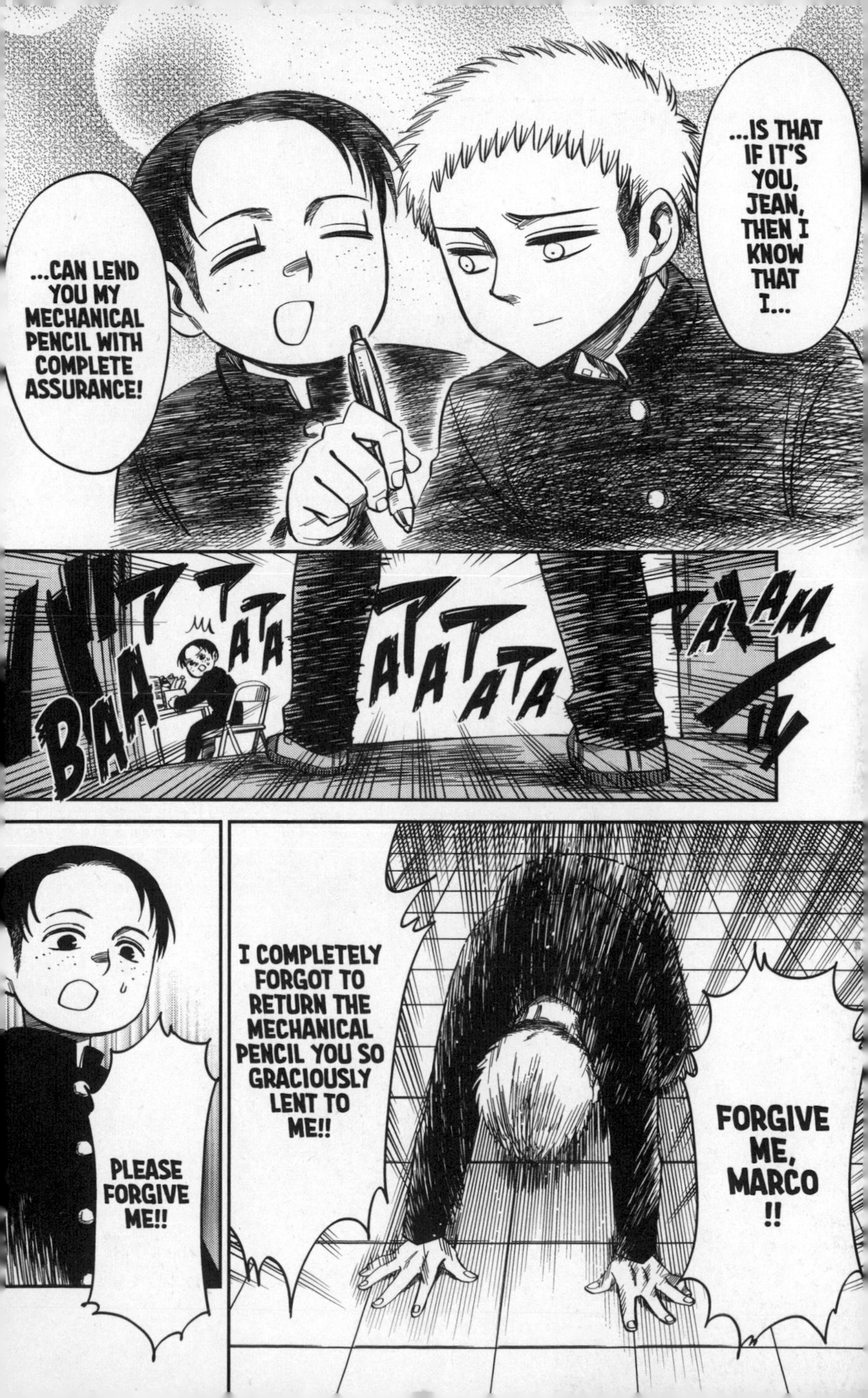
...IS THAT IF IT'S YOU, JEAN, THEN I KNOW THAT I...
...CAN LEND YOU MY MECHANICAL PENCIL WITH COMPLETE ASSURANCE!
BAATATATATATATATA
I COMPLETELY FORGOT TO RETURN THE MECHANICAL PENCIL YOU SO GRACIOUSLY LENT TO ME!!
FORGIVE ME, MARCO !!
PLEASE FORGIVE ME!!

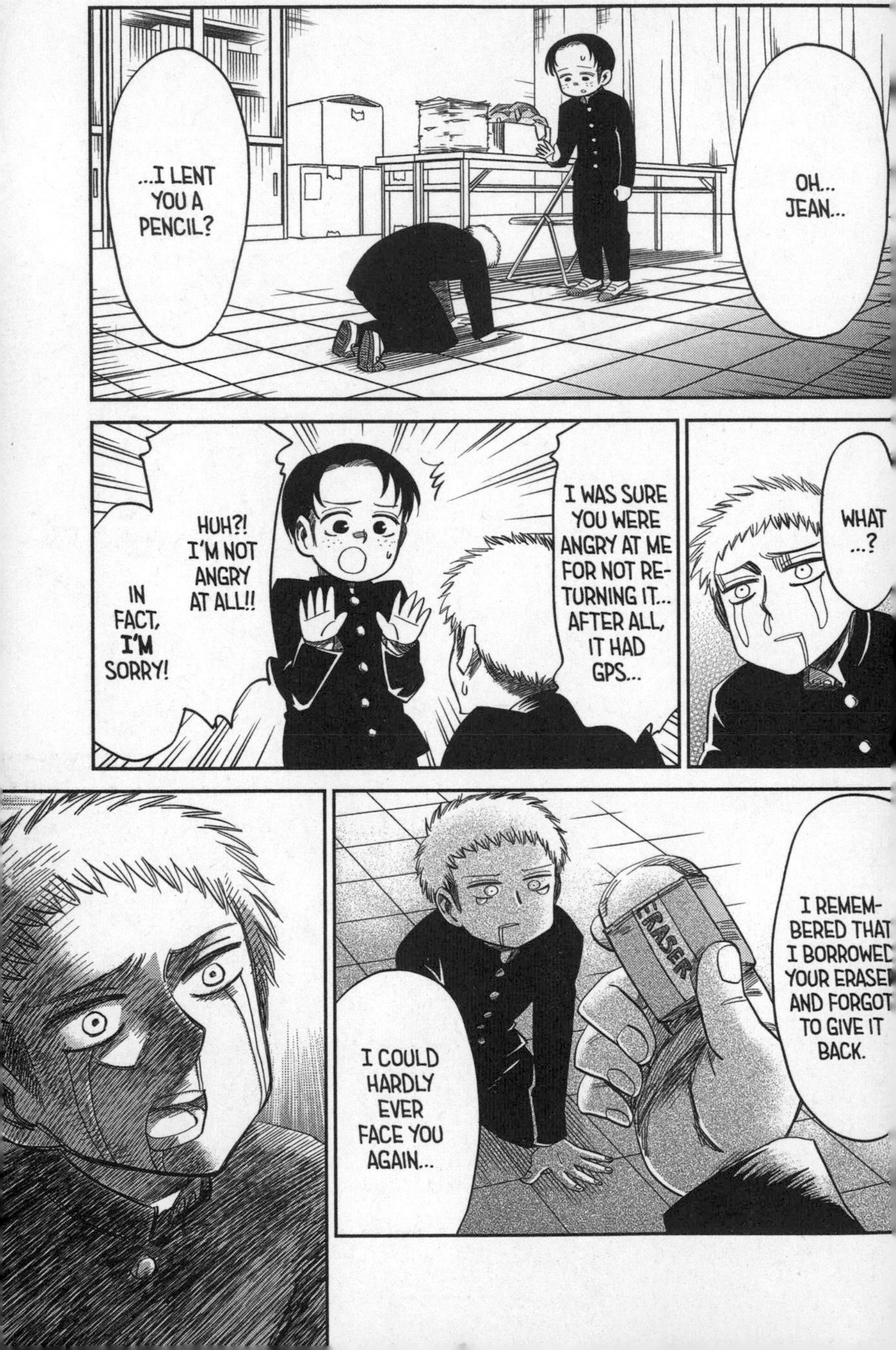
OH... JEAN...
...I LENT YOU A PENCIL?
WHAT ...?
I WAS SURE YOU WERE ANGRY AT ME FOR NOT RE-TURNING IT... AFTER ALL, IT HAD GPS...
HUH?! I'M NOT ANGRY AT ALL!!
IN FACT, **I'M** SORRY!
I REMEM-BERED THAT I BORROWED YOUR ERASER AND FORGOT TO GIVE IT BACK.
ERASER
I COULD HARDLY EVER FACE YOU AGAIN...

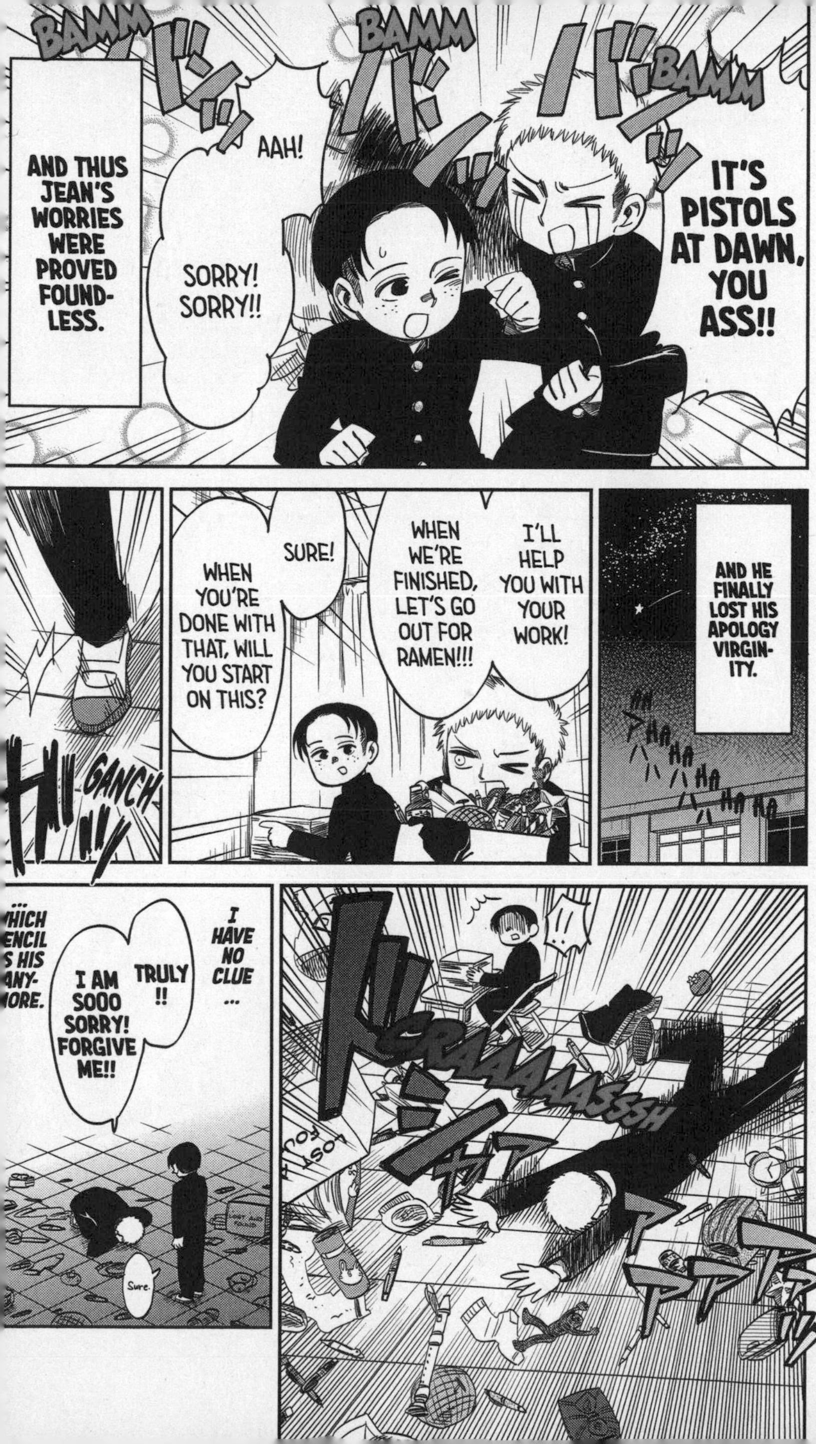
BAMM
BAMM
BAMM
IT'S PISTOLS AT DAWN, YOU ASS!!
AAH!
SORRY! SORRY!!
AND THUS JEAN'S WORRIES WERE PROVED FOUND-LESS.
AND HE FINALLY LOST HIS APOLOGY VIRGIN-ITY.
HA HA HA HA HA HA HA
I'LL HELP YOU WITH YOUR WORK!
WHEN WE'RE FINISHED, LET'S GO OUT FOR RAMEN!!!
SURE!
WHEN YOU'RE DONE WITH THAT, WILL YOU START ON THIS?
GANCH
CRAAAAAASSSH
I HAVE NO CLUE ...
TRULY!!
I AM SOOO SORRY! FORGIVE ME!!
...
HICH
ENCIL
S HIS
ANY-
ORE.
Sure.

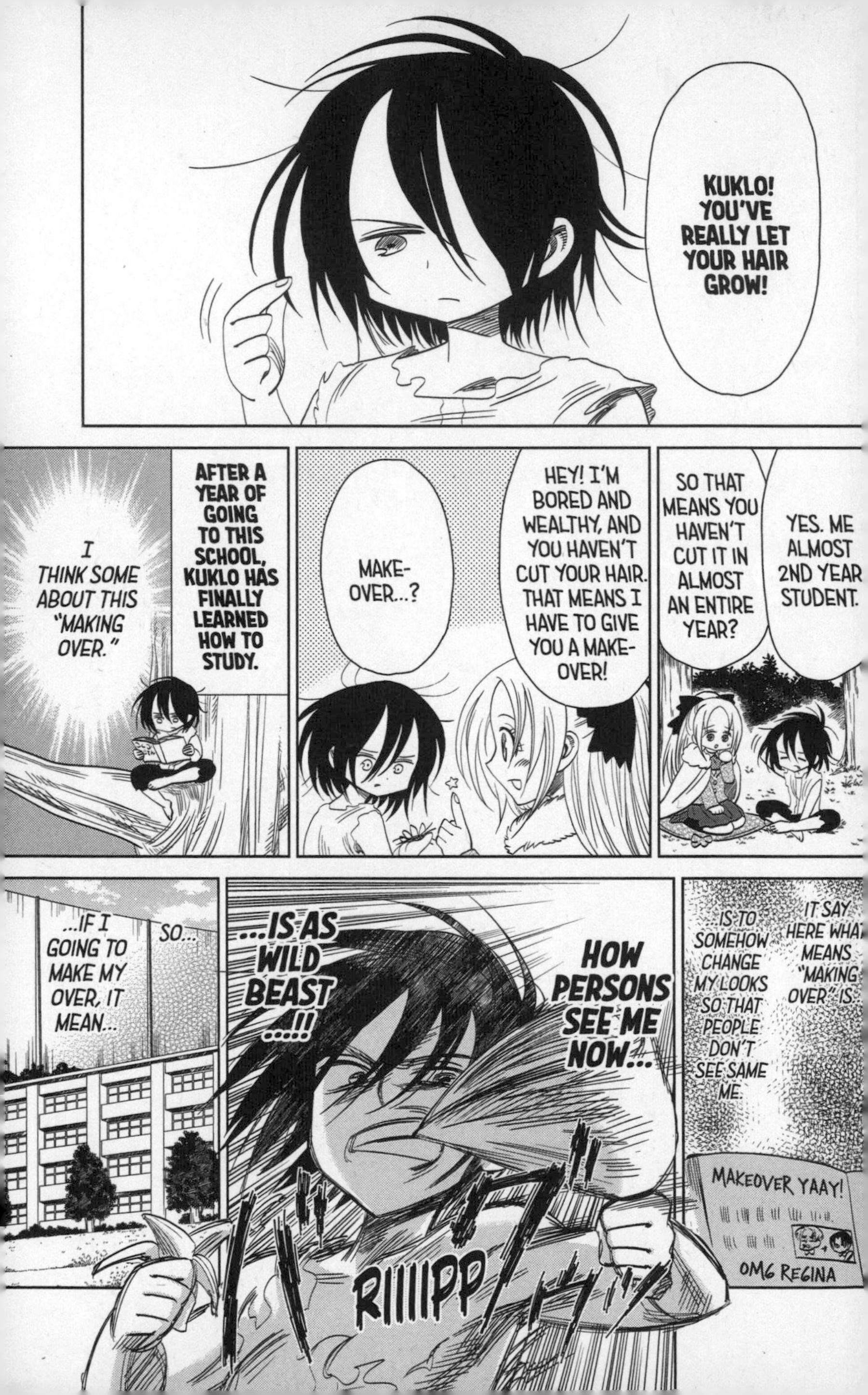
KUKLO! YOU'VE REALLY LET YOUR HAIR GROW!
YES. ME ALMOST 2ND YEAR STUDENT.
SO THAT MEANS YOU HAVEN'T CUT IT IN ALMOST AN ENTIRE YEAR?
HEY! I'M BORED AND WEALTHY, AND YOU HAVEN'T CUT YOUR HAIR. THAT MEANS I HAVE TO GIVE YOU A MAKE-OVER!
MAKE-OVER...?
AFTER A YEAR OF GOING TO THIS SCHOOL, KUKLO HAS FINALLY LEARNED HOW TO STUDY.
I THINK SOME ABOUT THIS "MAKING OVER."
IT SAY HERE WHA MEANS "MAKING OVER" IS...
...IS TO SOMEHOW CHANGE MY LOOKS SO THAT PEOPLE DON'T SEE SAME ME.
MAKEOVER YAAY!
OMG REGINA
HOW PERSONS SEE ME NOW...
...IS AS WILD BEAST...!!
RIIIPP
SO...
...IF I GOING TO MAKE MY OVER, IT MEAN...

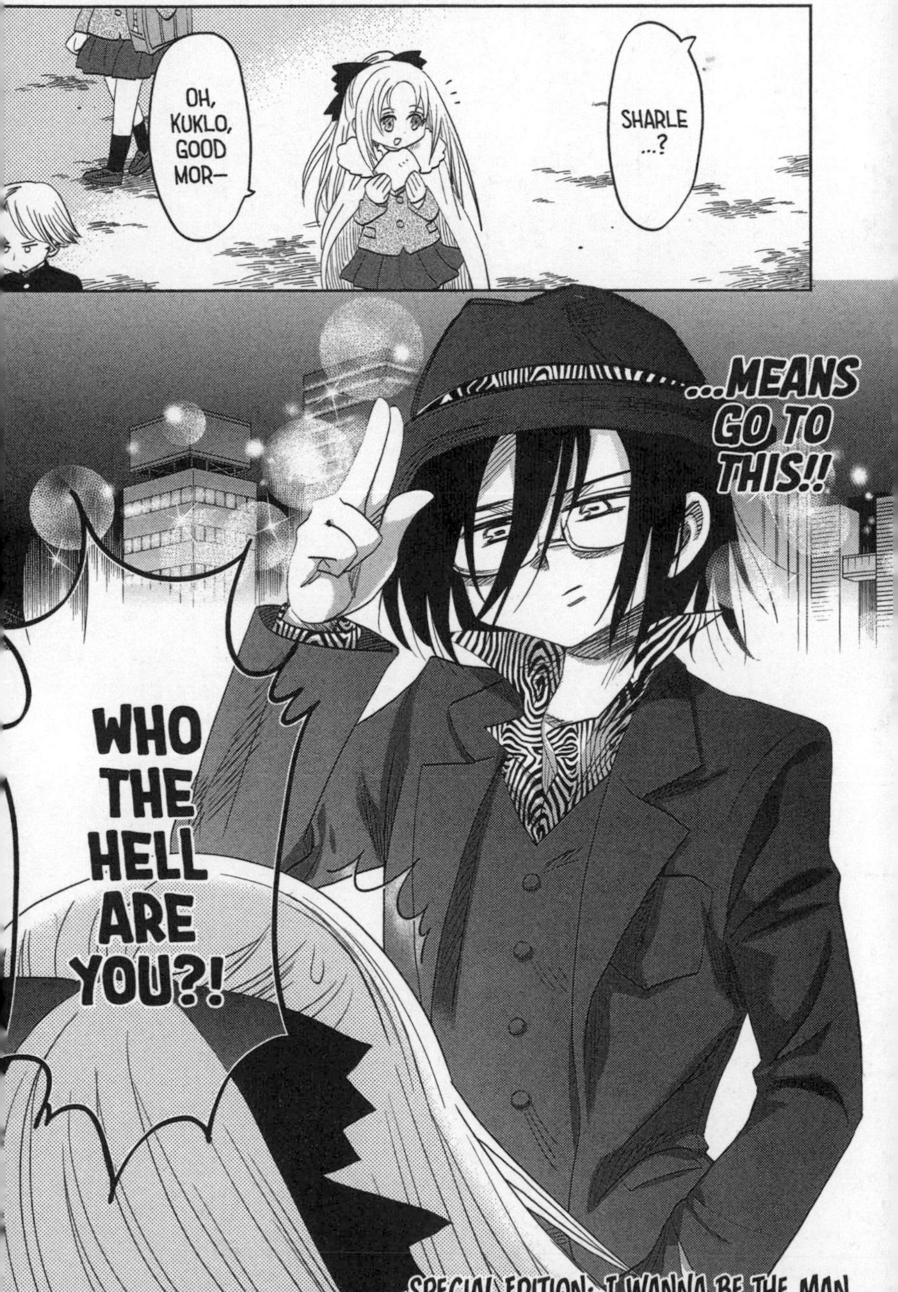
SHARLE ...?
OH, KUKLO, GOOD MOR—
...MEANS GO TO THIS!!
WHO THE HELL ARE YOU?!
SPECIAL EDITION: I WANNA BE THE MAN

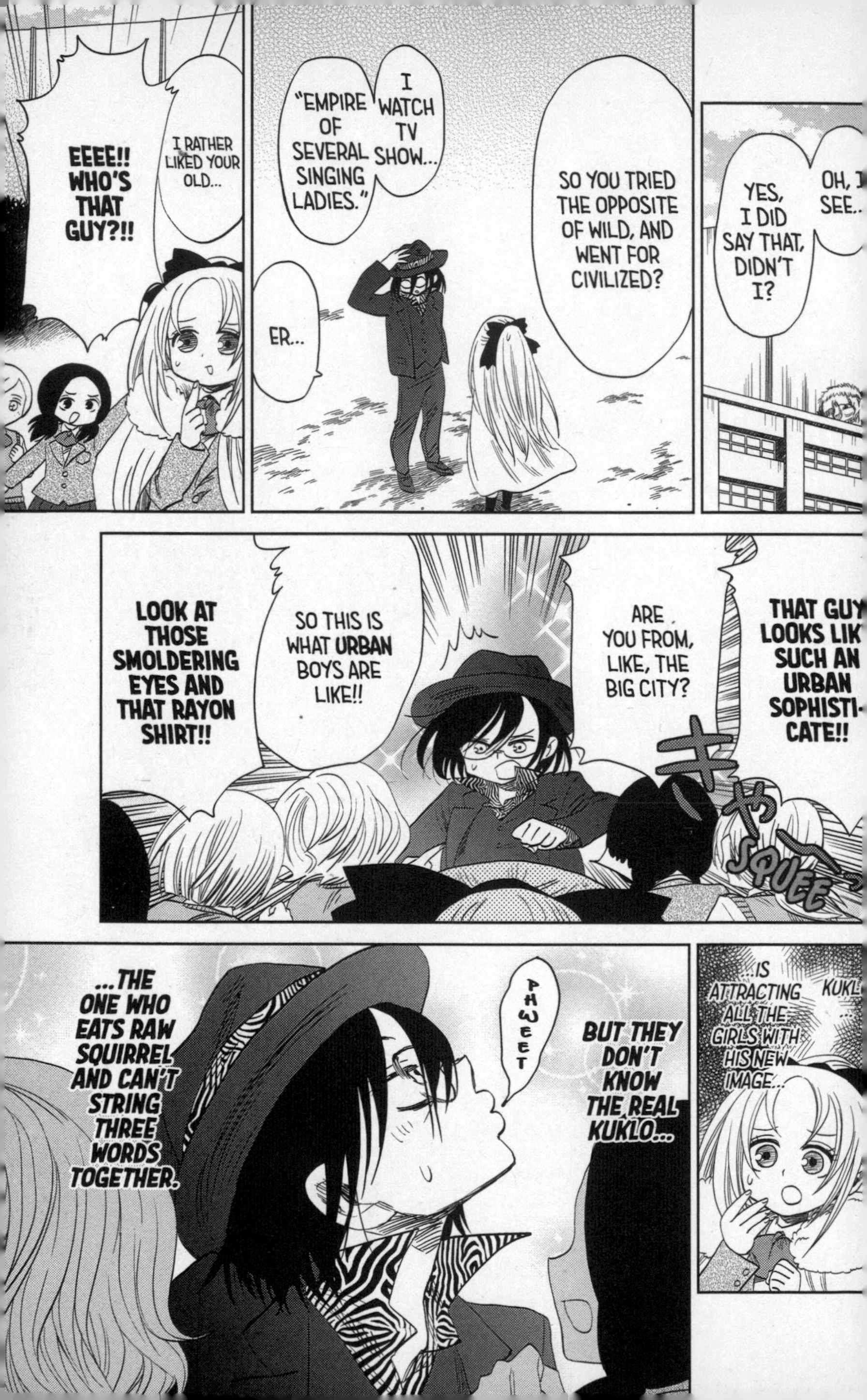
OH, I SEE...
YES, I DID SAY THAT, DIDN'T I?
SO YOU TRIED THE OPPOSITE OF WILD, AND WENT FOR CIVILIZED?
I WATCH TV SHOW...
"EMPIRE OF SEVERAL SINGING LADIES."
ER...
I RATHER LIKED YOUR OLD...
EEEE!! WHO'S THAT GUY?!!
THAT GUY LOOKS LIK SUCH AN URBAN SOPHISTI-CATE!!
キャ～
SQUEE
ARE YOU FROM, LIKE, THE BIG CITY?
SO THIS IS WHAT URBAN BOYS ARE LIKE!!
LOOK AT THOSE SMOLDERING EYES AND THAT RAYON SHIRT!!
KUKL...
...IS ATTRACTING ALL THE GIRLS WITH HIS NEW IMAGE...
BUT THEY DON'T KNOW THE REAL KUKLO...
PHWEET
...THE ONE WHO EATS RAW SQUIRREL AND CAN'T STRING THREE WORDS TOGETHER.

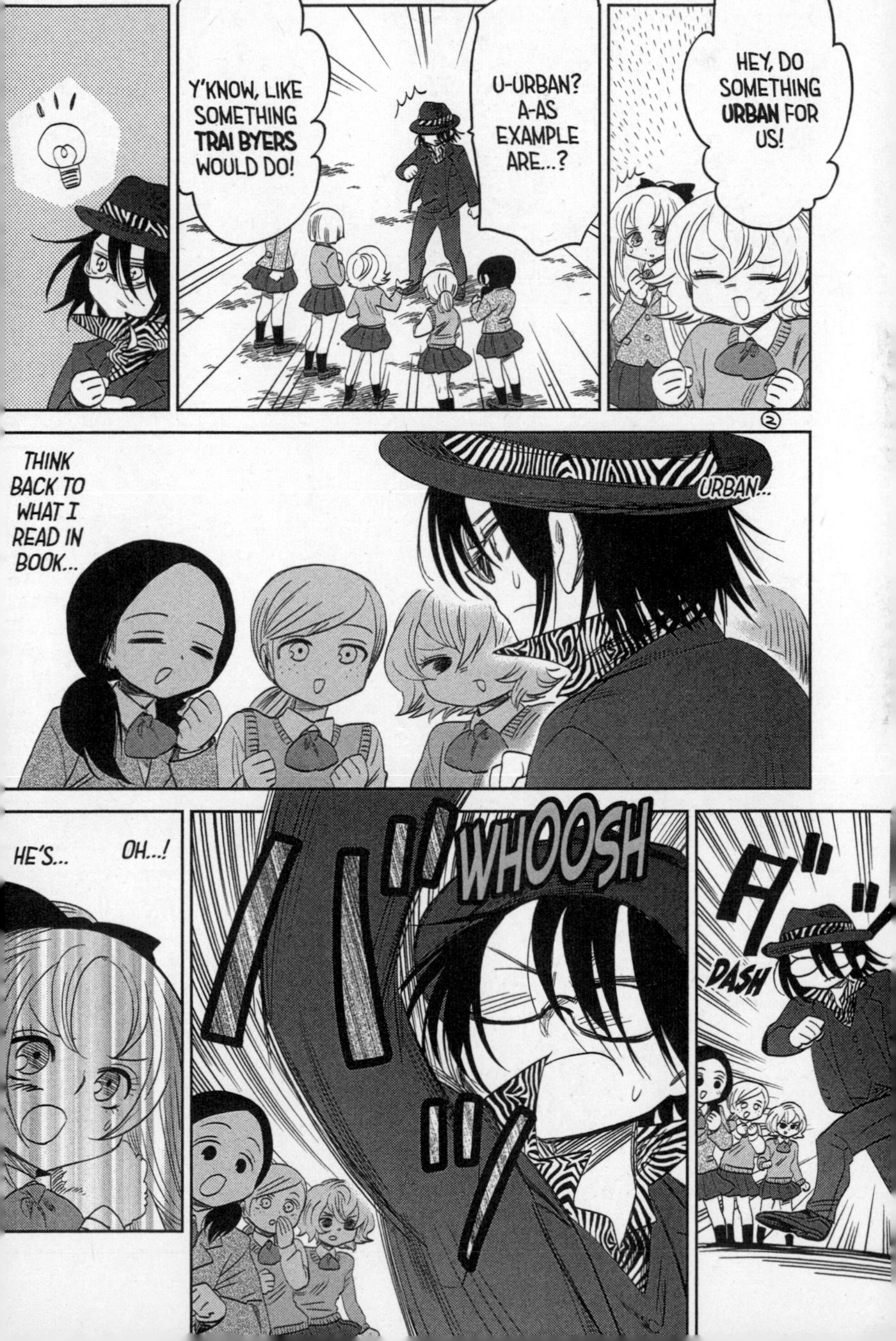
HEY, DO SOMETHING URBAN FOR US!
U-URBAN? A-AS EXAMPLE ARE...?
Y'KNOW, LIKE SOMETHING TRAI BYERS WOULD DO!
URBAN...
THINK BACK TO WHAT I READ IN BOOK...
DASH
WHOOSH
OH...!
HE'S...

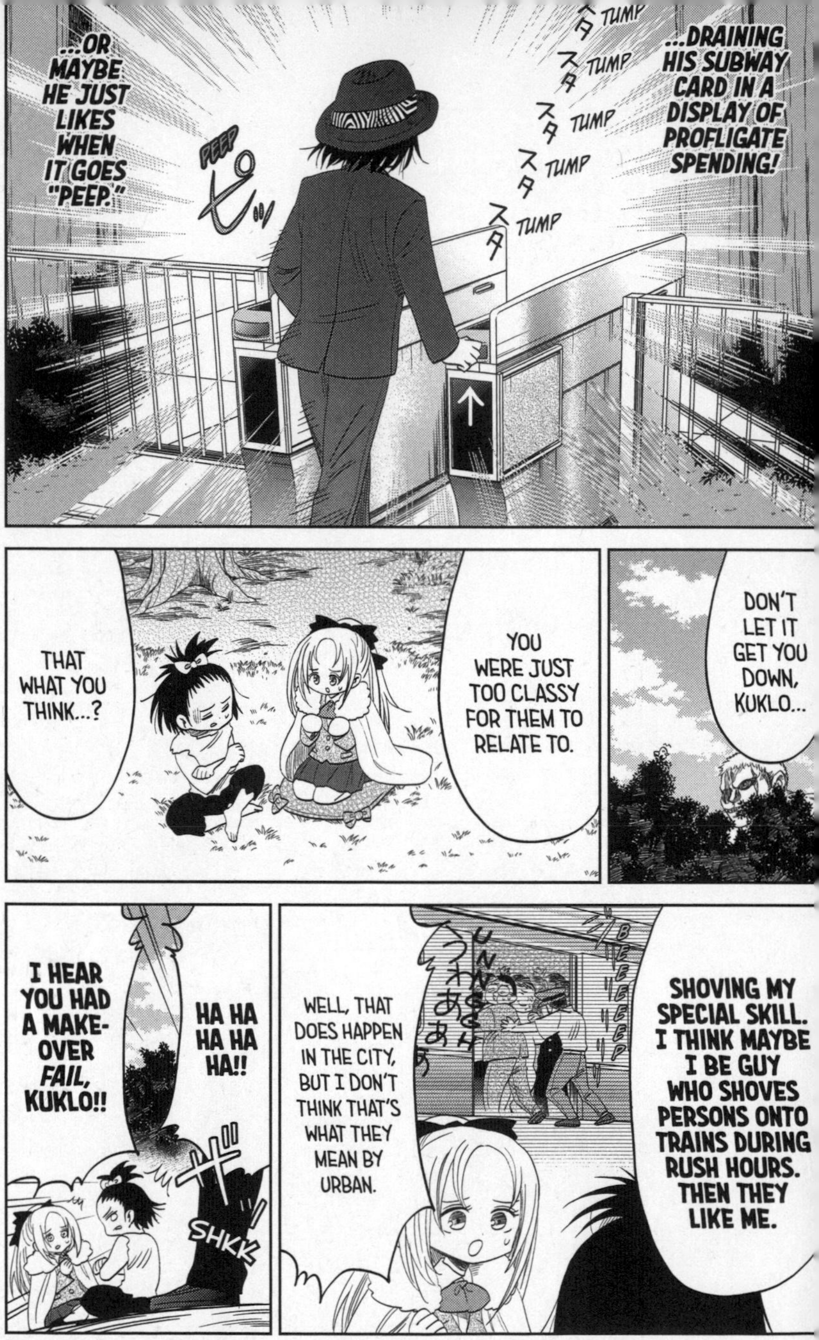

...DRAINING HIS SUBWAY CARD IN A DISPLAY OF PROFLIGATE SPENDING!
スタ TUMP スタ TUMP スタ TUMP スタ TUMP スタ TUMP
PEEP ピッ
...OR MAYBE HE JUST LIKES WHEN IT GOES "PEEP."
DON'T LET IT GET YOU DOWN, KUKLO...
YOU WERE JUST TOO CLASSY FOR THEM TO RELATE TO.
THAT WHAT YOU THINK...?
SHOVING MY SPECIAL SKILL. I THINK MAYBE I BE GUY WHO SHOVES PERSONS ONTO TRAINS DURING RUSH HOURS. THEN THEY LIKE ME.
BEEEEEEP
UNNGGH うわああ
WELL, THAT DOES HAPPEN IN THE CITY, BUT I DON'T THINK THAT'S WHAT THEY MEAN BY URBAN.
HA HA HA HA HA!!
I HEAR YOU HAD A MAKE-OVER *FAIL*, KUKLO!!
SHKK

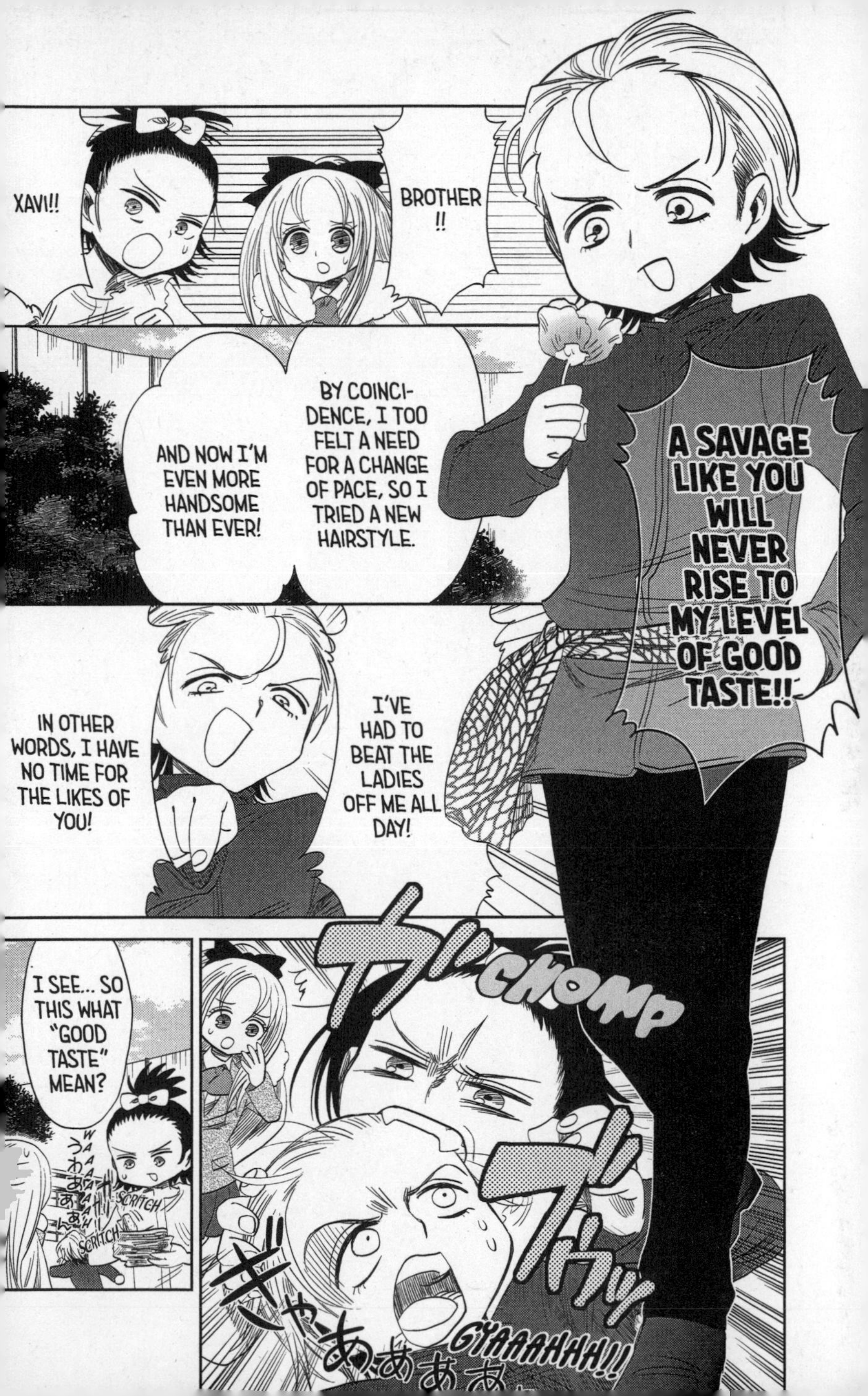
A SAVAGE LIKE YOU WILL NEVER RISE TO MY LEVEL OF GOOD TASTE!!
BROTHER !!
XAVI!!
BY COINCI-DENCE, I TOO FELT A NEED FOR A CHANGE OF PACE, SO I TRIED A NEW HAIRSTYLE.
AND NOW I'M EVEN MORE HANDSOME THAN EVER!
I'VE HAD TO BEAT THE LADIES OFF ME ALL DAY!
IN OTHER WORDS, I HAVE NO TIME FOR THE LIKES OF YOU!
CHOMP
GYAAAAHHH!!
I SEE... SO THIS WHAT "GOOD TASTE" MEAN?
WAAAAAAH!!
SCRITCH
SCRITCH

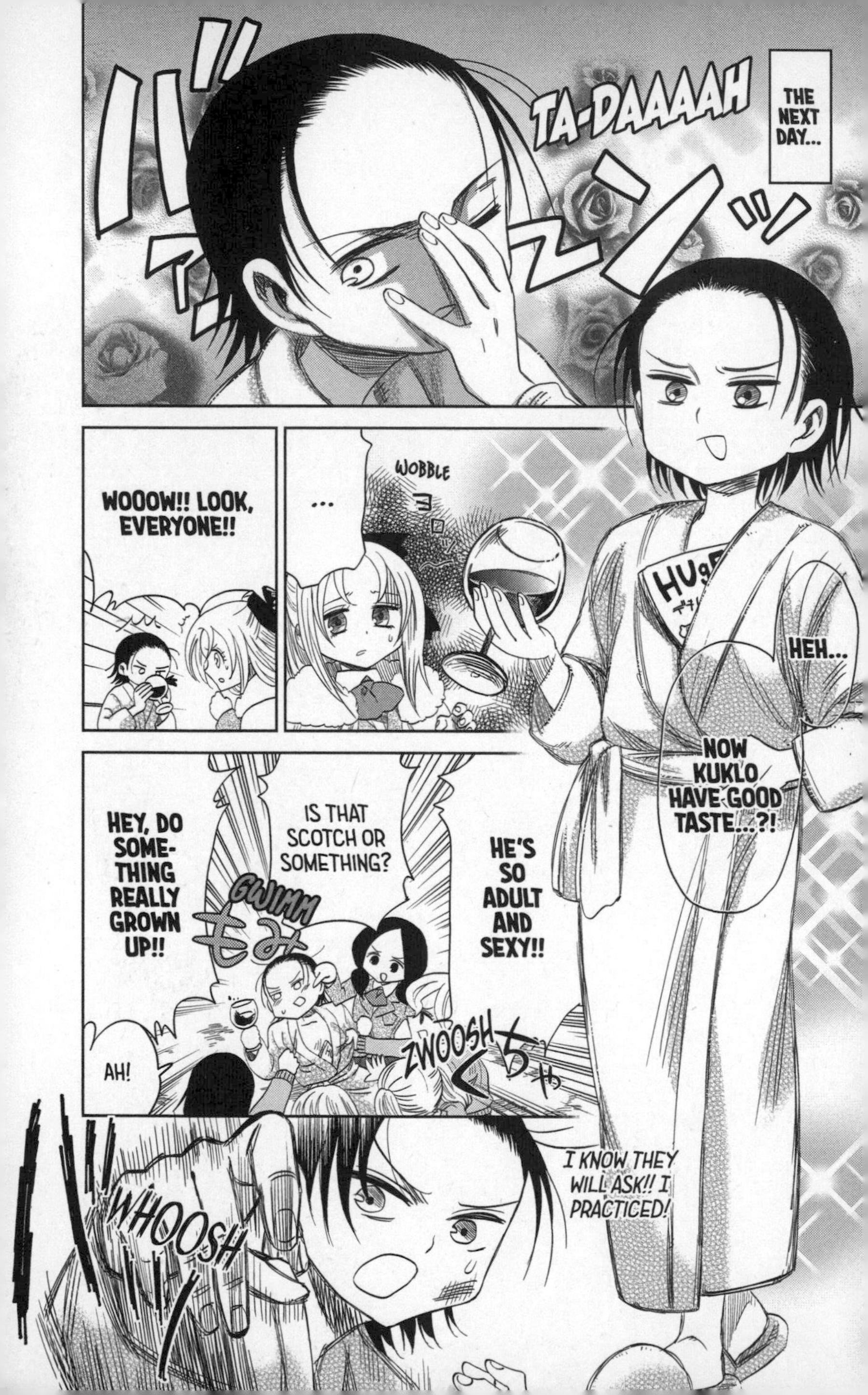
THE NEXT DAY...
TA-DAAAAH
HEH...
NOW KUKLO HAVE GOOD TASTE...?!
I KNOW THEY WILL ASK!! I PRACTICED!
WOBBLE
...
WOOOW!! LOOK, EVERYONE!!
HE'S SO ADULT AND SEXY!!
IS THAT SCOTCH OR SOMETHING?
HEY, DO SOME-THING REALLY GROWN UP!!
GWIMM
ZWOOSH
AH!
WHOOSH

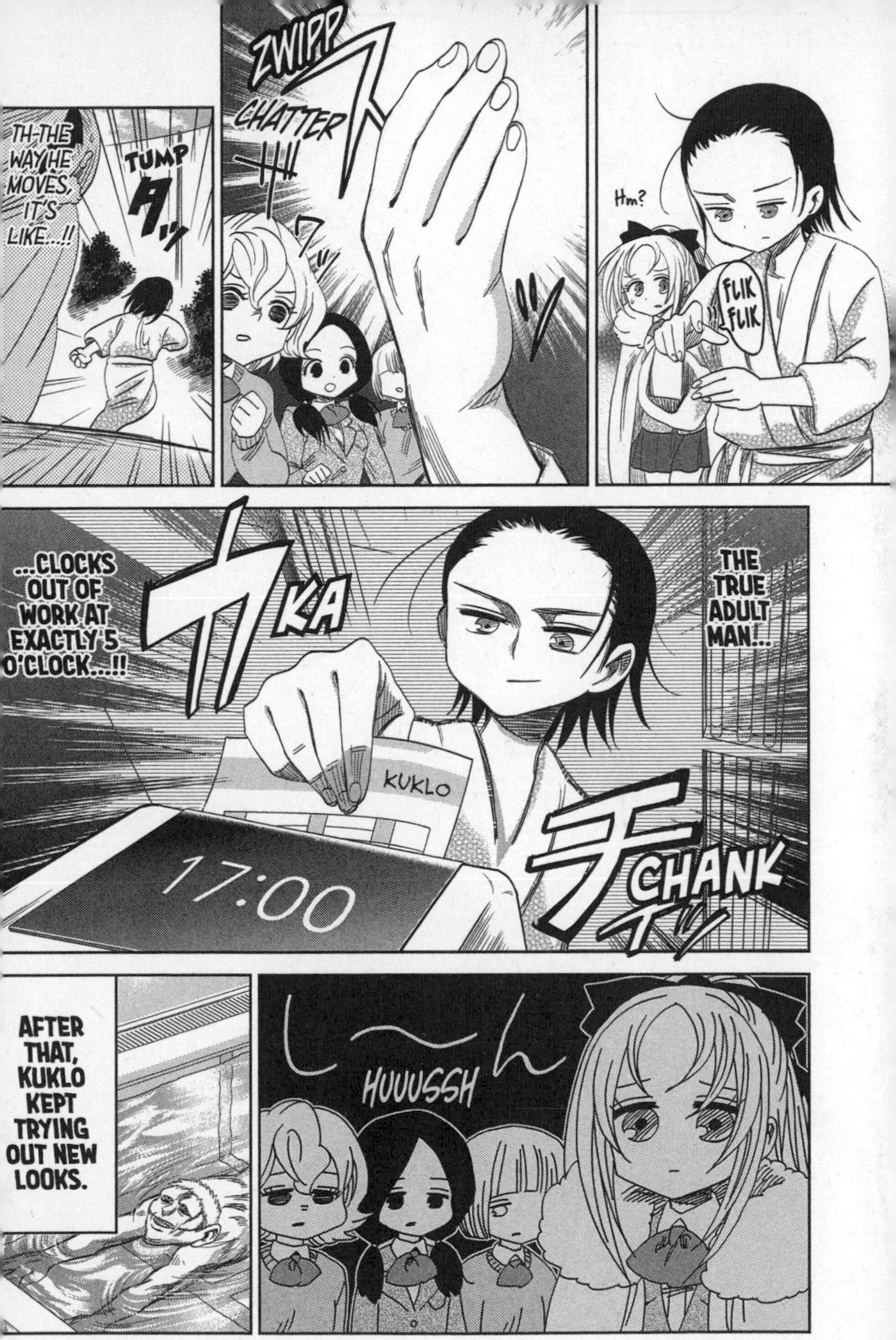
Hm?
FLIK FLIK
ZWIPP
CHATTER
TUMP
TH-THE WAY HE MOVES, IT'S LIKE...!!
THE TRUE ADULT MAN...
KA
...CLOCKS OUT OF WORK AT EXACTLY 5 O'CLOCK...!!
KUKLO
17:00
CHANK
HUUUSSH
AFTER THAT, KUKLO KEPT TRYING OUT NEW LOOKS.

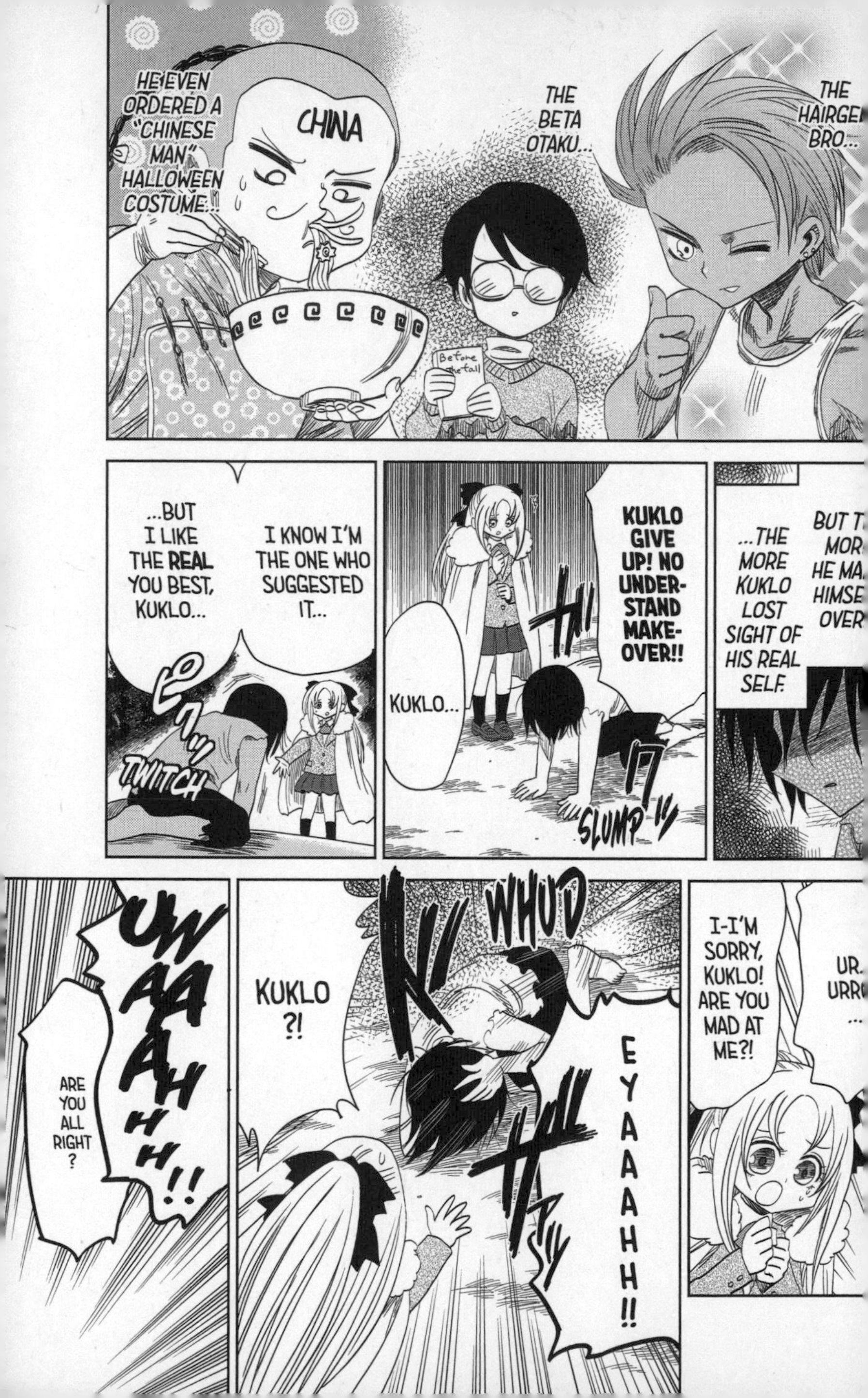
THE HAIRGE BRO...
THE BETA OTAKU...
HE EVEN ORDERED A "CHINESE MAN" HALLOWEEN COSTUME!!
CHINA
Before the fall
BUT T MOR HE MA HIMSE OVER
...THE MORE KUKLO LOST SIGHT OF HIS REAL SELF.
KUKLO GIVE UP! NO UNDERSTAND MAKE-OVER!!
KUKLO...
SLUMP
I KNOW I'M THE ONE WHO SUGGESTED IT...
...BUT I LIKE THE REAL YOU BEST, KUKLO...
TWITCH
UR... URR ...
I-I'M SORRY, KUKLO! ARE YOU MAD AT ME?!
WHUD
EYAAAAHH!!
KUKLO ?!
UWAAAAHHH!!
ARE YOU ALL RIGHT ?

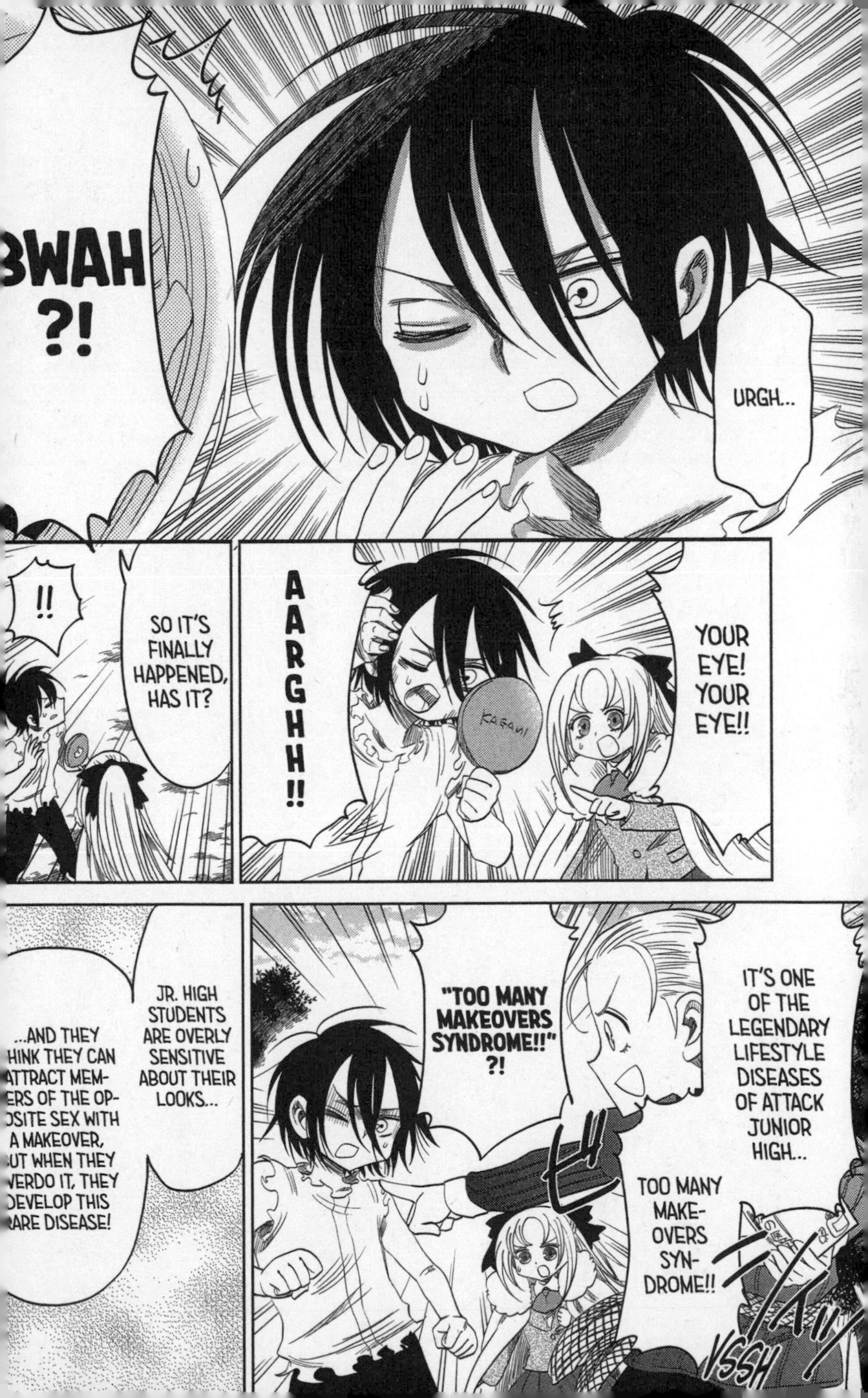
URGH...
BWAH ?!
YOUR EYE! YOUR EYE!!
AARGHH!!
KAGAMI
SO IT'S FINALLY HAPPENED, HAS IT?
!!
IT'S ONE OF THE LEGENDARY LIFESTYLE DISEASES OF ATTACK JUNIOR HIGH...
"TOO MANY MAKEOVERS SYNDROME!!" ?!
TOO MANY MAKE-OVERS SYN-DROME!!
VSSH
JR. HIGH STUDENTS ARE OVERLY SENSITIVE ABOUT THEIR LOOKS...
...AND THEY HINK THEY CAN ATTRACT MEM-ERS OF THE OP-OSITE SEX WITH A MAKEOVER, UT WHEN THEY VERDO IT, THEY DEVELOP THIS ARE DISEASE!

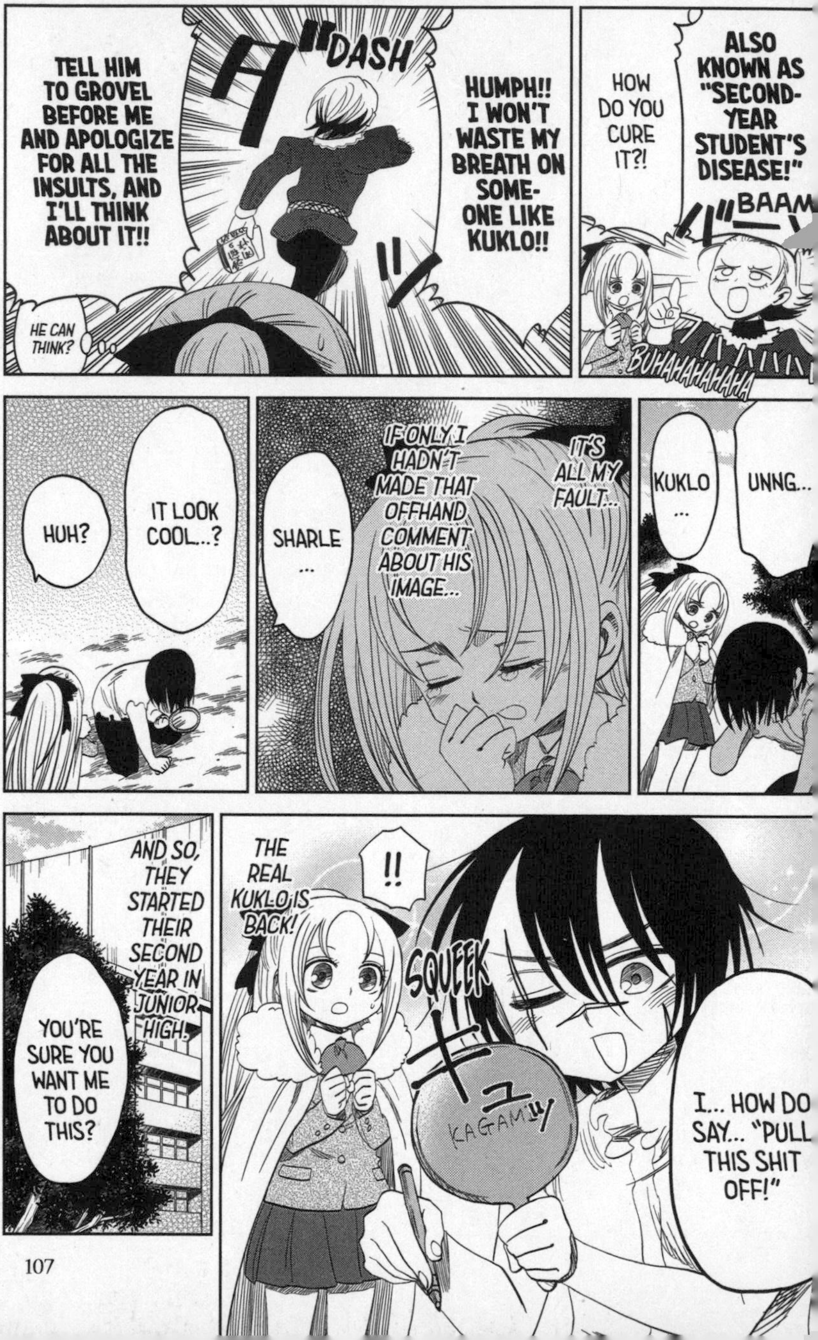
ALSO KNOWN AS "SECOND-YEAR STUDENT'S DISEASE!"
HOW DO YOU CURE IT?!
BAAM
BUHAHAHAHAHA
HUMPH!! I WON'T WASTE MY BREATH ON SOME-ONE LIKE KUKLO!!
DASH
TELL HIM TO GROVEL BEFORE ME AND APOLOGIZE FOR ALL THE INSULTS, AND I'LL THINK ABOUT IT!!
HE CAN THINK?
UNNG...
KUKLO...
IT'S ALL MY FAULT...
IF ONLY I HADN'T MADE THAT OFFHAND COMMENT ABOUT HIS IMAGE...
SHARLE...
IT LOOK COOL...?
HUH?
!!
THE REAL KUKLO IS BACK!
SQUEEK
KAGAMI
I... HOW DO SAY... "PULL THIS SHIT OFF!"
AND SO, THEY STARTED THEIR SECOND YEAR IN JUNIOR HIGH.
YOU'RE SURE YOU WANT ME TO DO THIS?

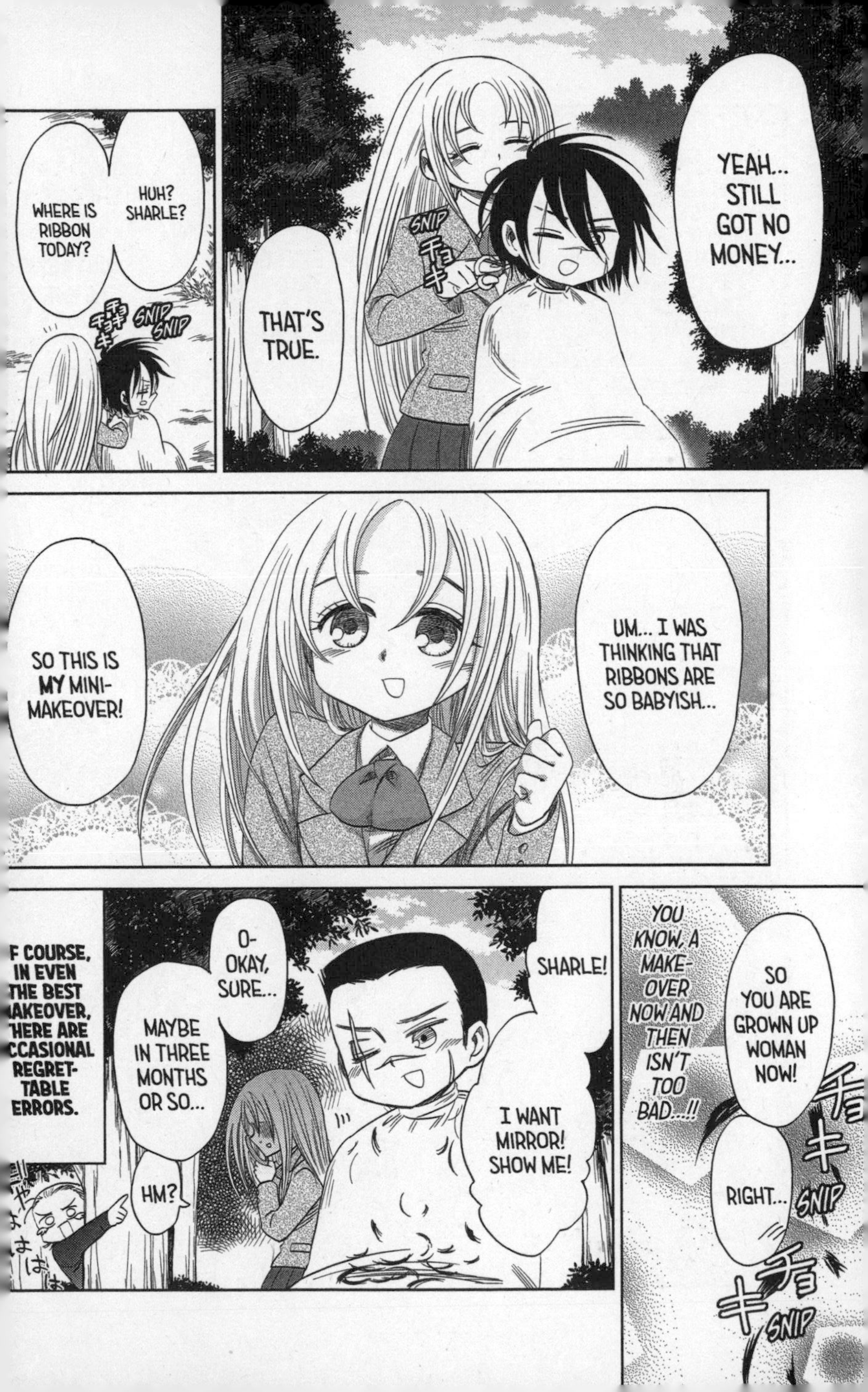
YEAH... STILL GOT NO MONEY...
SNIP
チョキ
THAT'S TRUE.
HUH? SHARLE?
WHERE IS RIBBON TODAY?
チョキチョキ
SNIP SNIP
UM... I WAS THINKING THAT RIBBONS ARE SO BABYISH...
SO THIS IS MY MINI-MAKEOVER!
YOU KNOW, A MAKE-OVER NOW AND THEN ISN'T TOO BAD...!!
SO YOU ARE GROWN UP WOMAN NOW!
チョキ
RIGHT...
SNIP
チョキ
SNIP
SHARLE!
O-OKAY, SURE...
MAYBE IN THREE MONTHS OR SO...
I WANT MIRROR! SHOW ME!
HM?
F COURSE, IN EVEN THE BEST AKEOVER, HERE ARE CCASIONAL REGRET-TABLE ERRORS.

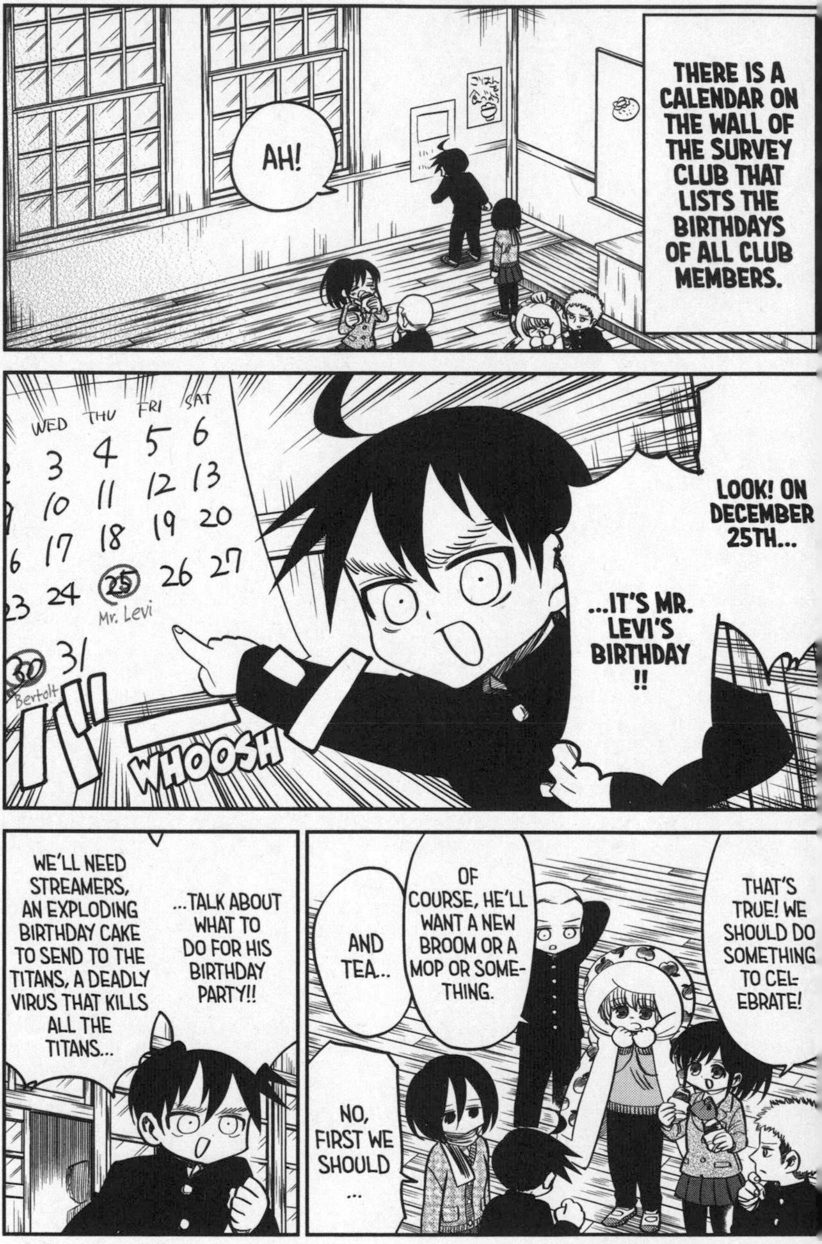
THERE IS A CALENDAR ON THE WALL OF THE SURVEY CLUB THAT LISTS THE BIRTHDAYS OF ALL CLUB MEMBERS.
AH!
LOOK! ON DECEMBER 25TH...
...IT'S MR. LEVI'S BIRTHDAY !!
WED THU FRI SAT
3 4 5 6
10 11 12 13
17 18 19 20
24 25 26 27
Mr. Levi
30 31
Bertolt
WHOOSH
THAT'S TRUE! WE SHOULD DO SOMETHING TO CEL-EBRATE!
OF COURSE, HE'LL WANT A NEW BROOM OR A MOP OR SOME-THING.
AND TEA...
NO, FIRST WE SHOULD ...
...TALK ABOUT WHAT TO DO FOR HIS BIRTHDAY PARTY!!
WE'LL NEED STREAMERS, AN EXPLODING BIRTHDAY CAKE TO SEND TO THE TITANS, A DEADLY VIRUS THAT KILLS ALL THE TITANS...

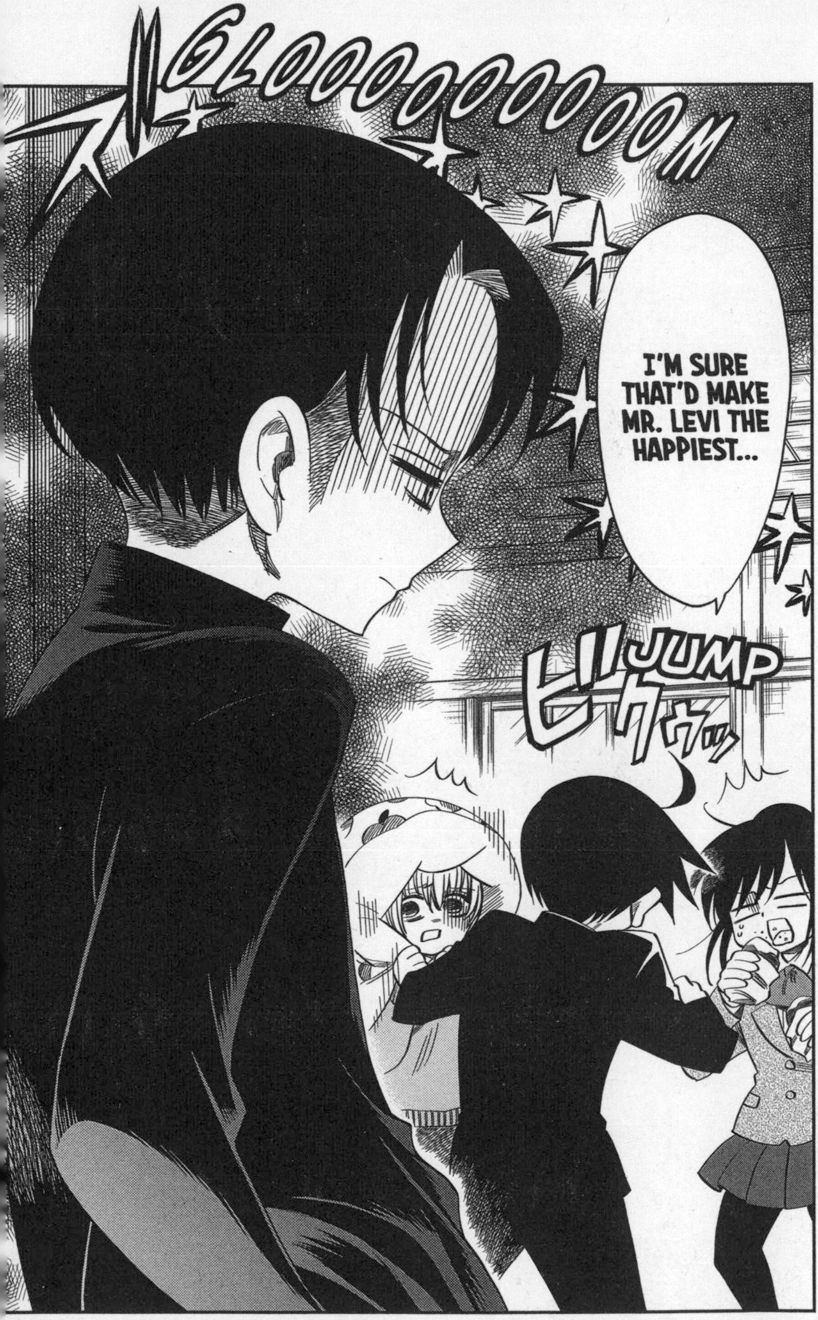
GLOOOOOOOOOM
I'M SURE THAT'D MAKE MR. LEVI THE HAPPIEST...
JUMP

FIFTY-FIRST PERIOD: ONLY COMES ONCE A YEAR

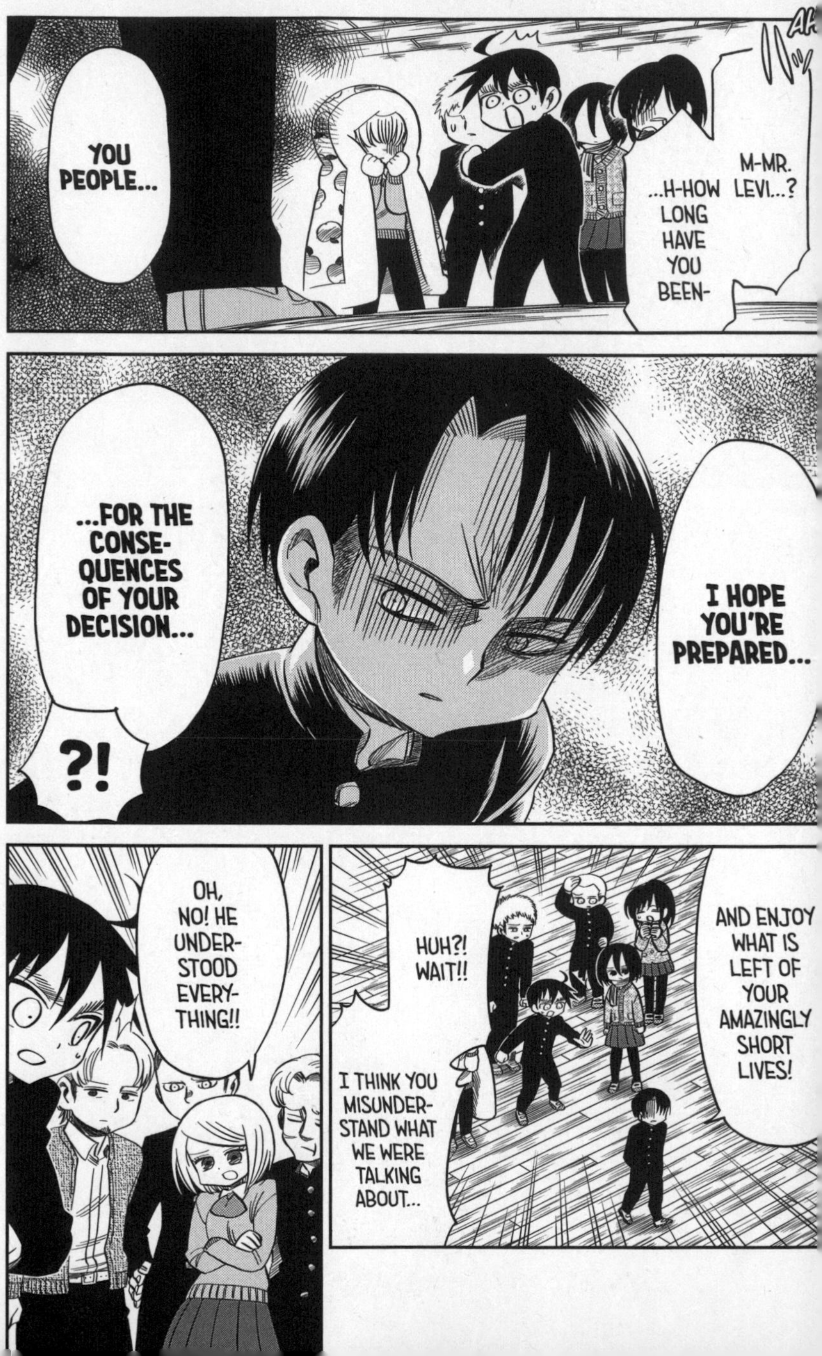
M-MR. LEVI...?
...H-HOW LONG HAVE YOU BEEN-
YOU PEOPLE...
I HOPE YOU'RE PREPARED...
...FOR THE CONSE-QUENCES OF YOUR DECISION...
?!
AND ENJOY WHAT IS LEFT OF YOUR AMAZINGLY SHORT LIVES!
HUH?! WAIT!!
I THINK YOU MISUNDER-STAND WHAT WE WERE TALKING ABOUT...
OH, NO! HE UNDER-STOOD EVERY-THING!!

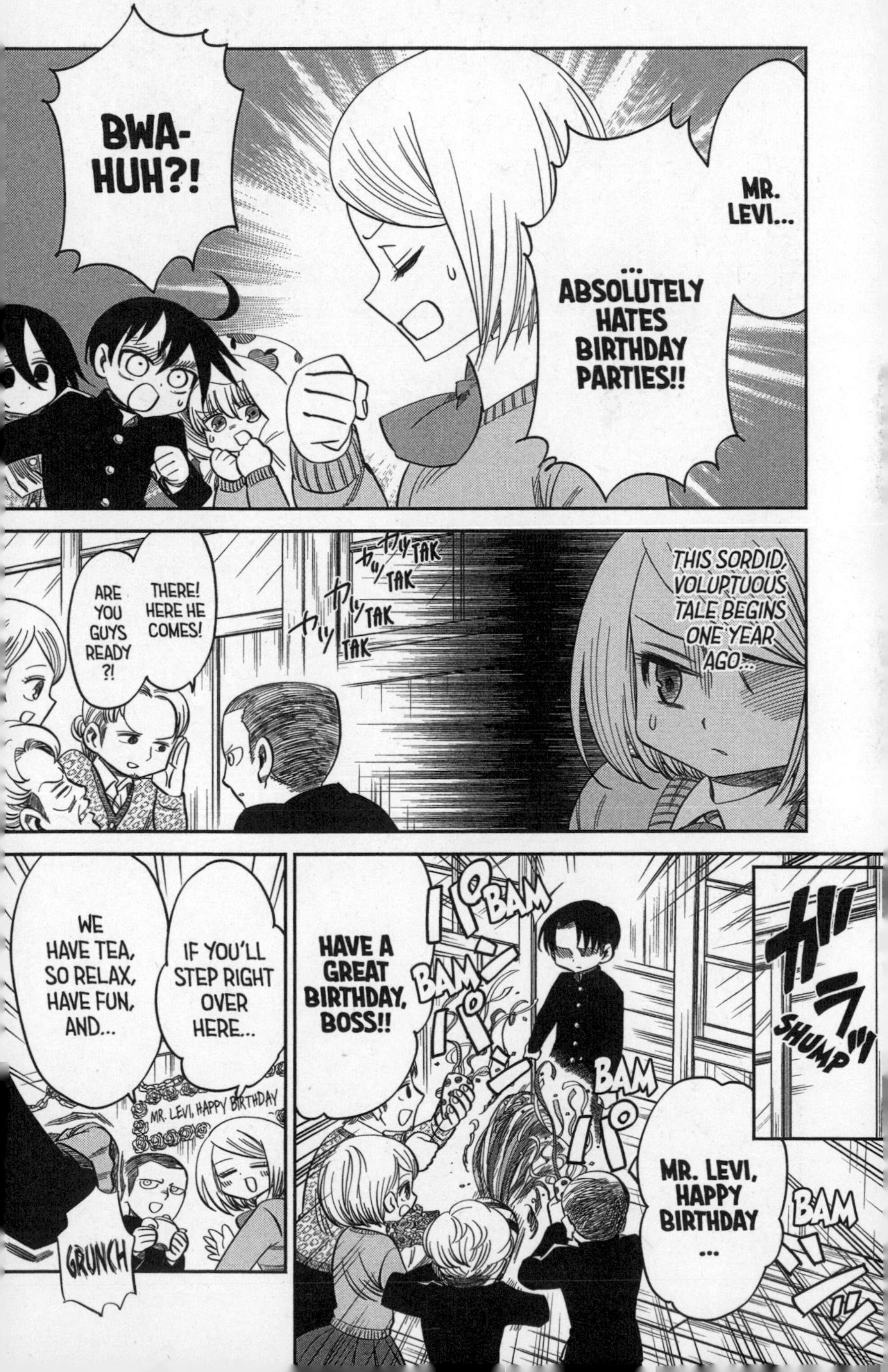
MR. LEVI...
...ABSOLUTELY HATES BIRTHDAY PARTIES!!
BWA-HUH?!
THIS SORDID, VOLUPTUOUS TALE BEGINS ONE YEAR AGO...
カッ TAK
カッ TAK
カッ TAK
カッ TAK
THERE! HERE HE COMES!
ARE YOU GUYS READY?!
ガラッ SHUMP
BAM
MR. LEVI, HAPPY BIRTHDAY...
BAM
BAM
BAM
HAVE A GREAT BIRTHDAY, BOSS!!
IF YOU'LL STEP RIGHT OVER HERE...
WE HAVE TEA, SO RELAX, HAVE FUN, AND...
MR. LEVI, HAPPY BIRTHDAY
GRUNCH

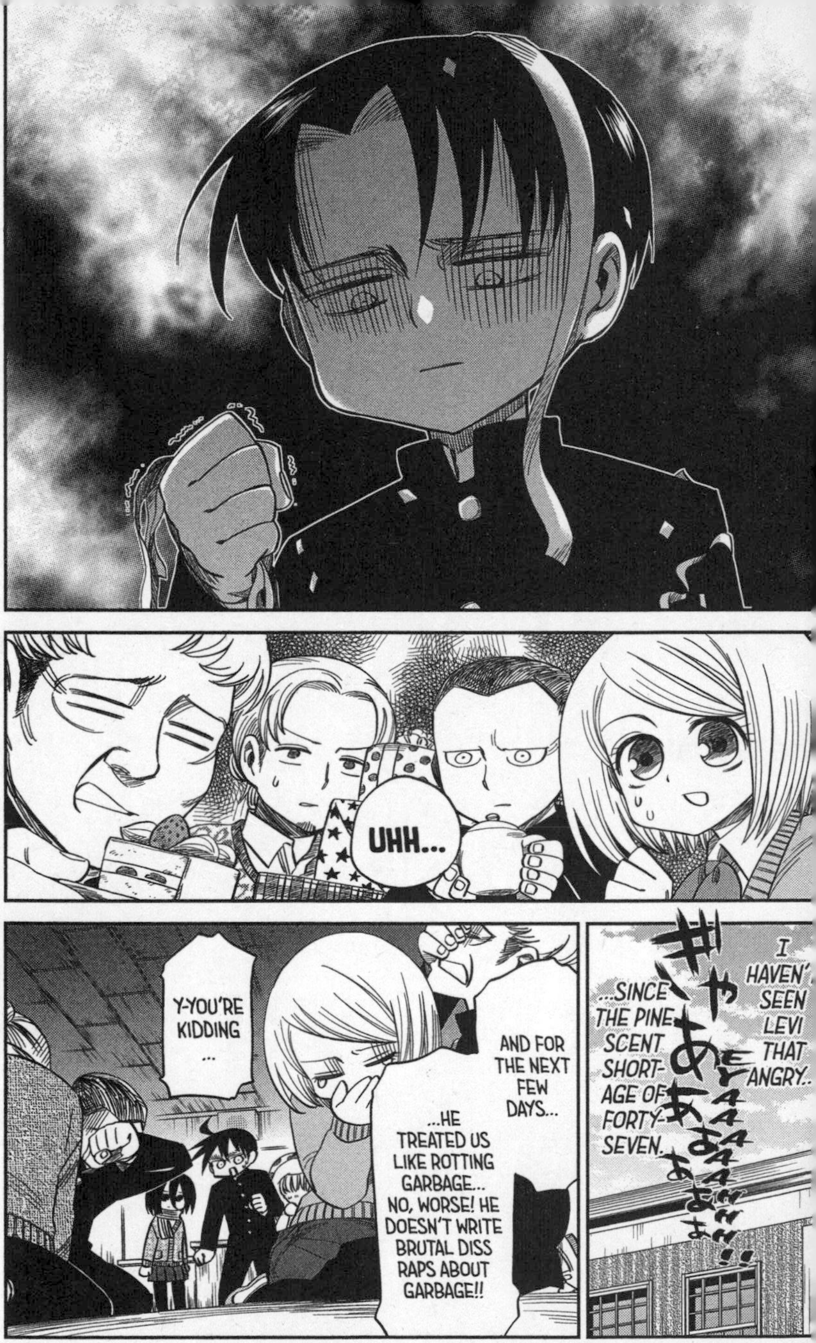
UHH...
I HAVEN'T SEEN LEVI THAT ANGRY...
...SINCE THE PINE SCENT SHORTAGE OF FORTY-SEVEN.
EYAAAAAAAHHH!!
AND FOR THE NEXT FEW DAYS...
...HE TREATED US LIKE ROTTING GARBAGE... NO, WORSE! HE DOESN'T WRITE BRUTAL DISS RAPS ABOUT GARBAGE!!
Y-YOU'RE KIDDING...

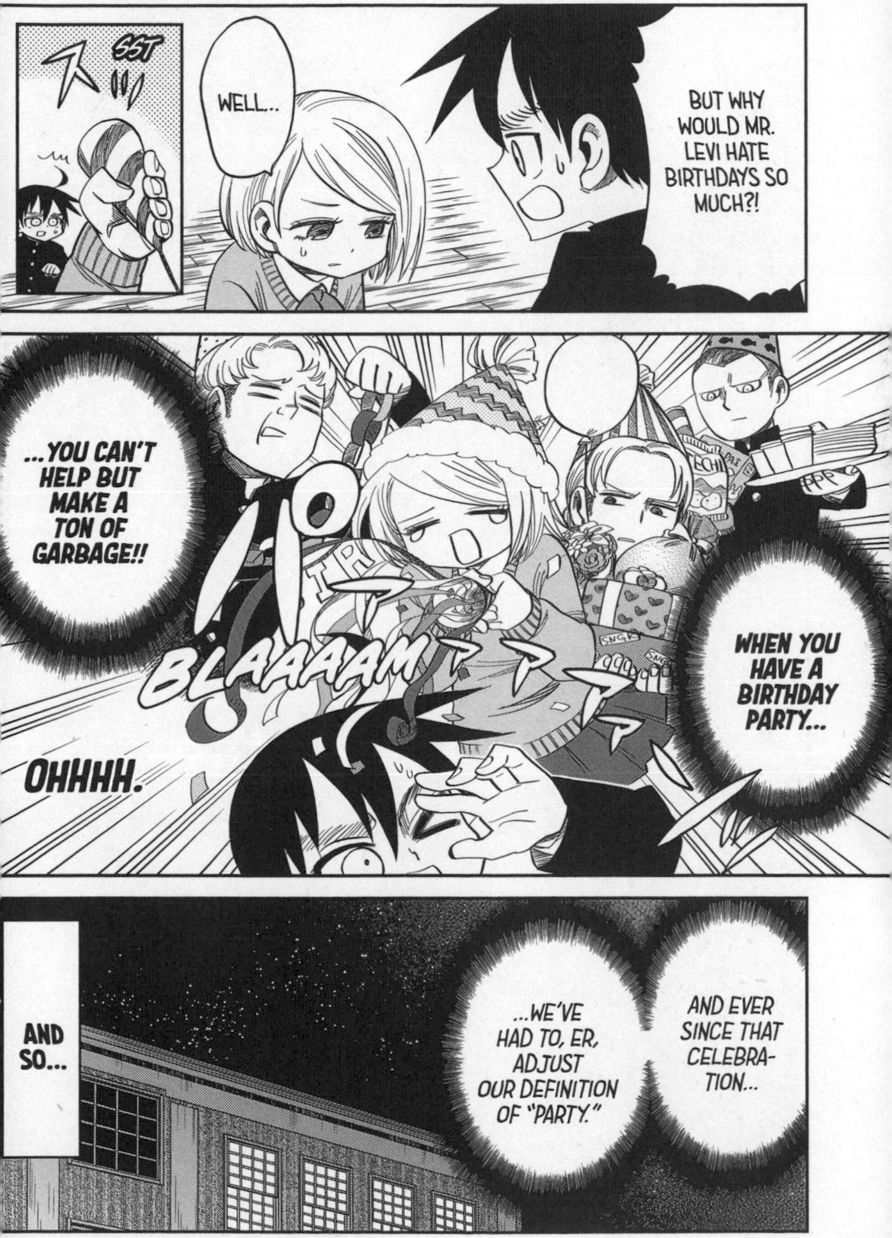

BUT WHY WOULD MR. LEVI HATE BIRTHDAYS SO MUCH?!
WELL...
SST
WHEN YOU HAVE A BIRTHDAY PARTY...
...YOU CAN'T HELP BUT MAKE A TON OF GARBAGE!!
BLAAAAM
OHHHH.
AND EVER SINCE THAT CELEBRATION...
...WE'VE HAD TO, ER, ADJUST OUR DEFINITION OF "PARTY."
AND SO...

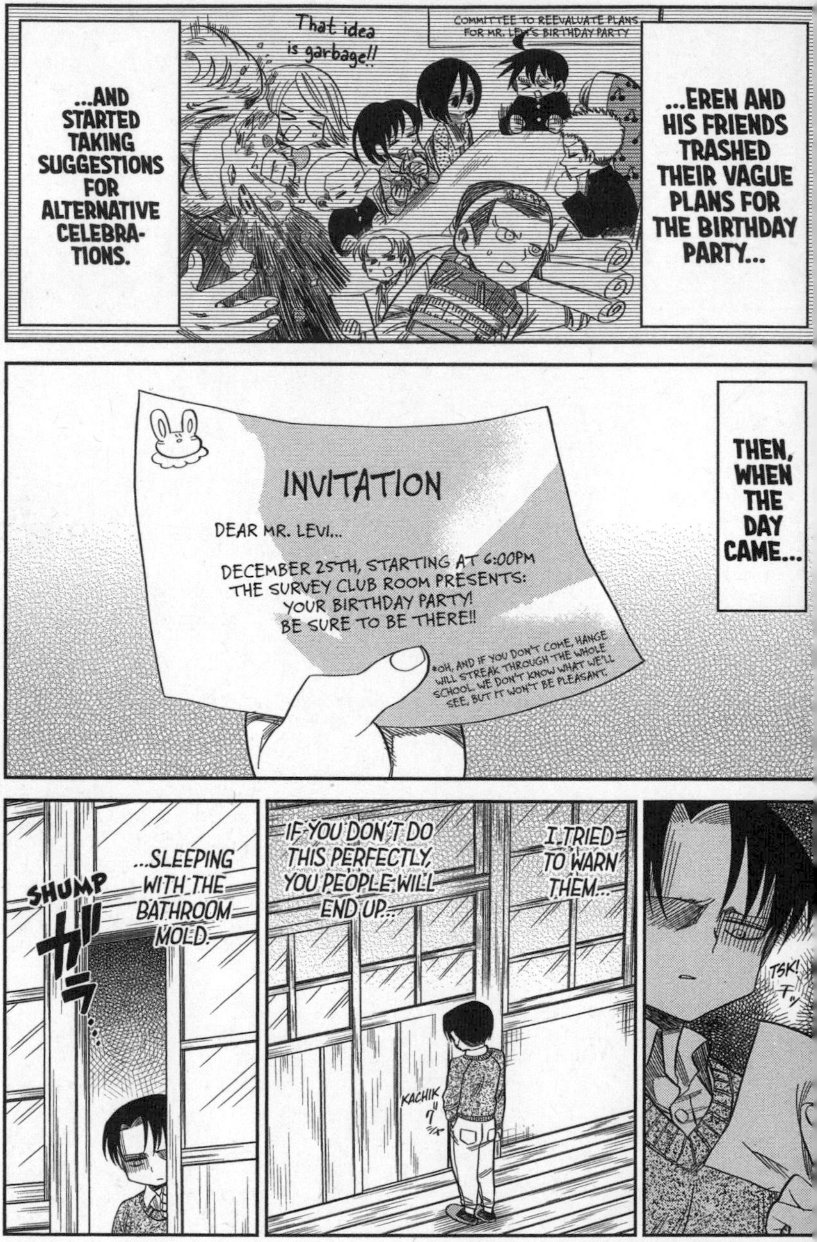
...EREN AND HIS FRIENDS TRASHED THEIR VAGUE PLANS FOR THE BIRTHDAY PARTY...
COMMITTEE TO REEVALUATE PLANS FOR MR. LEVI'S BIRTHDAY PARTY
That idea is garbage!!
...AND STARTED TAKING SUGGESTIONS FOR ALTERNATIVE CELEBRA-TIONS.
THEN, WHEN THE DAY CAME...
INVITATION
DEAR MR. LEVI...
DECEMBER 25TH, STARTING AT 6:00PM
THE SURVEY CLUB ROOM PRESENTS:
YOUR BIRTHDAY PARTY!
BE SURE TO BE THERE!!
*OH, AND IF YOU DON'T COME, HANGE WILL STREAK THROUGH THE WHOLE SCHOOL. WE DON'T KNOW WHAT WE'LL SEE, BUT IT WON'T BE PLEASANT.
TSK!
I TRIED TO WARN THEM...
IF YOU DON'T DO THIS PERFECTLY, YOU PEOPLE WILL END UP...
KACHIK
...SLEEPING WITH THE BATHROOM MOLD.
SHUMP

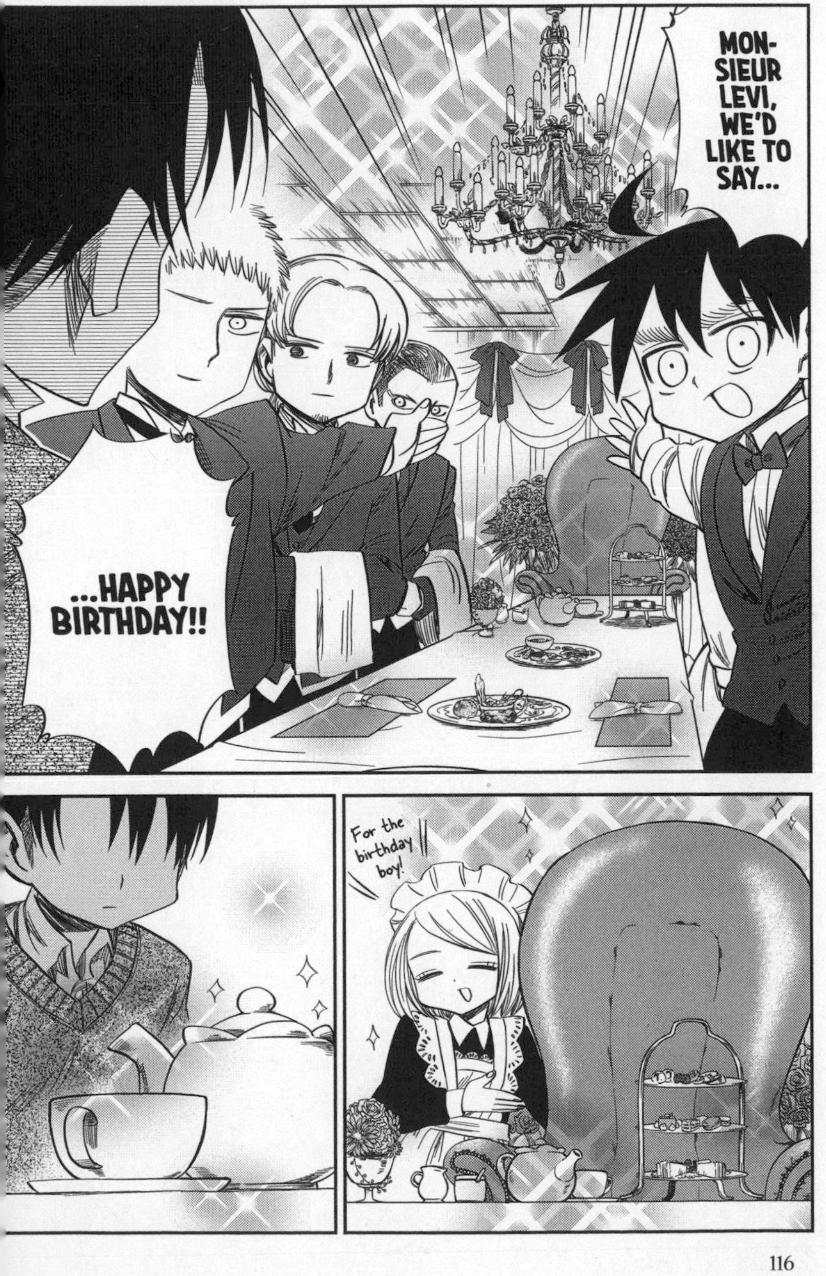
MON-SIEUR LEVI, WE'D LIKE TO SAY...
...HAPPY BIRTHDAY!!
For the birthday boy!

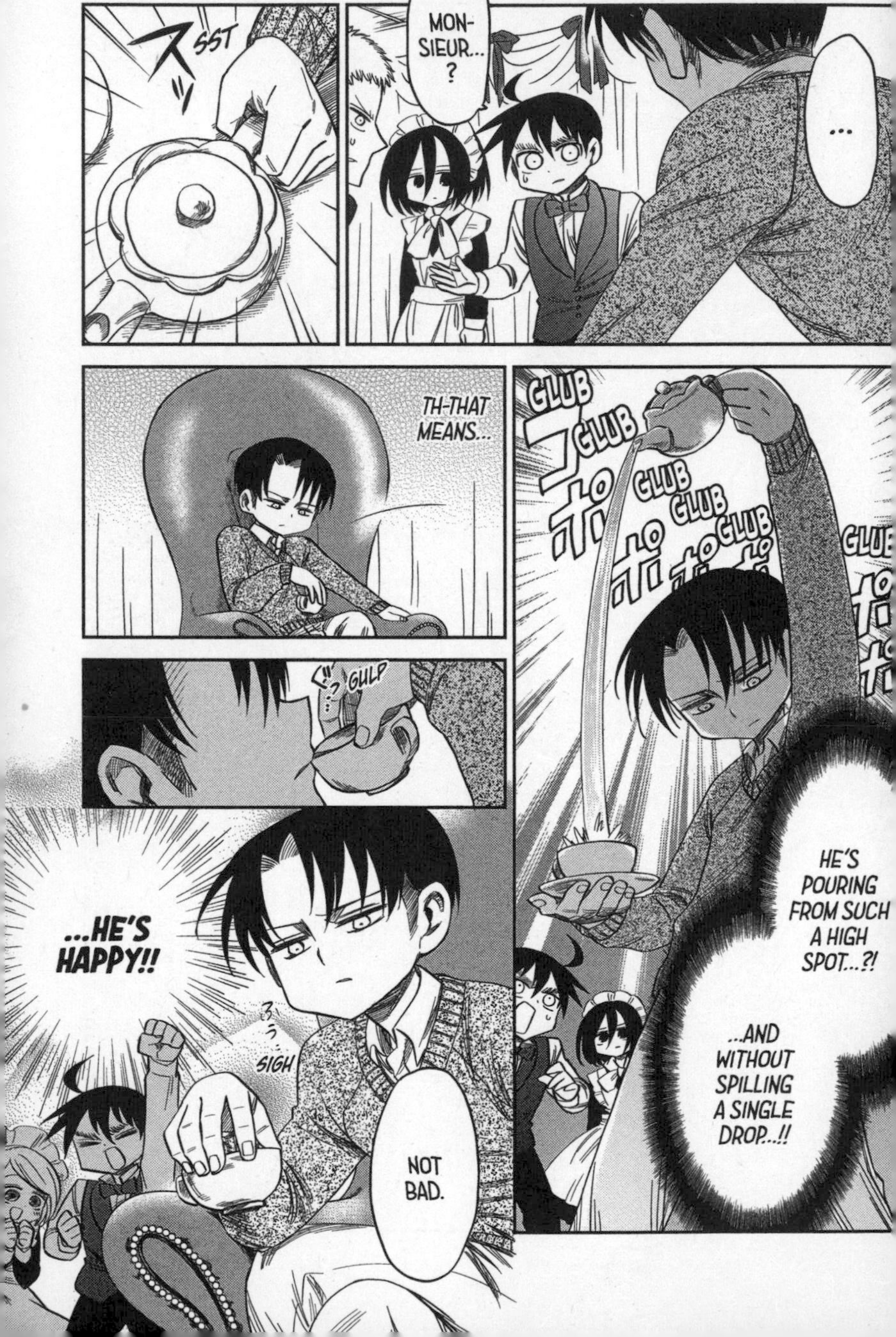
...
MON-
SIEUR...
?
SST
GLUB
GLUB
GLUB
GLUB
GLUB
GLUB
HE'S
POURING
FROM SUCH
A HIGH
SPOT...?!
...AND
WITHOUT
SPILLING
A SINGLE
DROP...!!
TH-THAT
MEANS...
GULP
SIGH
NOT
BAD.
...HE'S
HAPPY!!

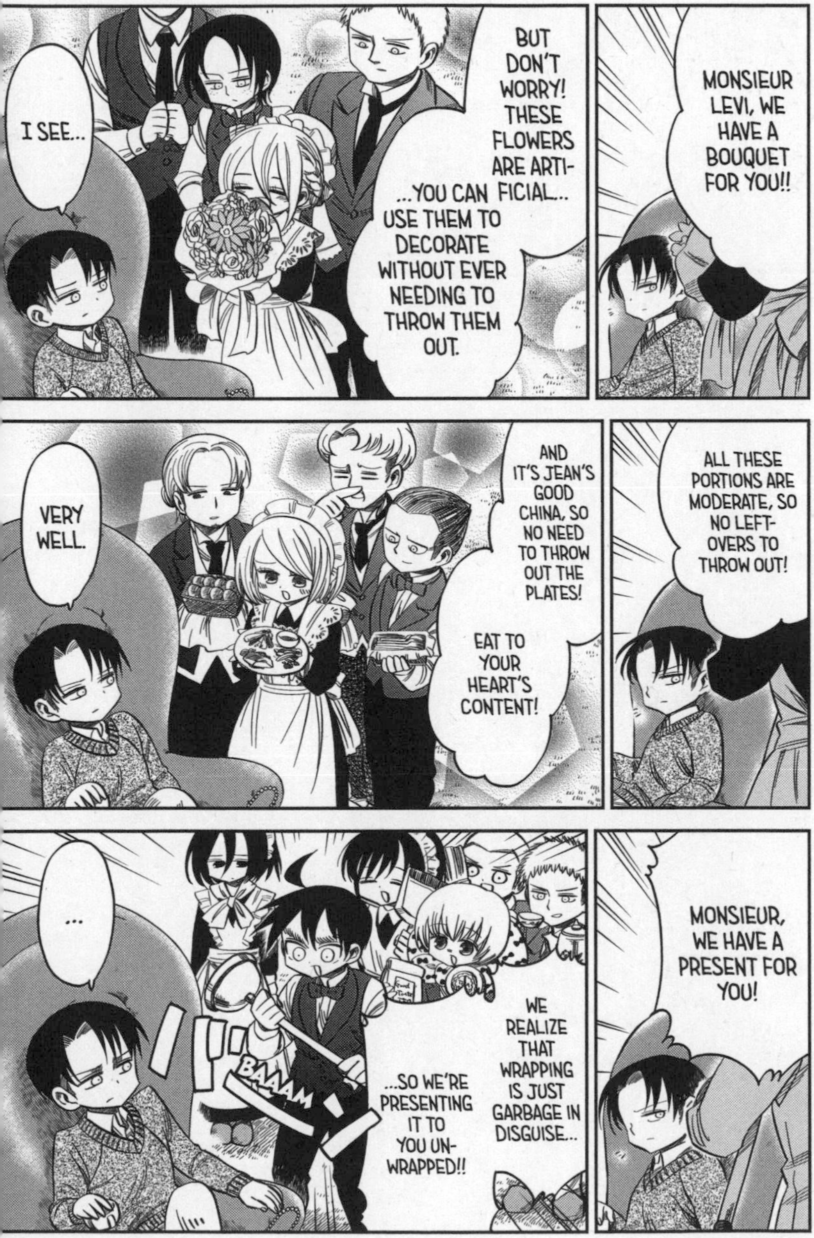
MONSIEUR LEVI, WE HAVE A BOUQUET FOR YOU!!
BUT DON'T WORRY! THESE FLOWERS ARE ARTIFICIAL...
...YOU CAN USE THEM TO DECORATE WITHOUT EVER NEEDING TO THROW THEM OUT.
I SEE...
ALL THESE PORTIONS ARE MODERATE, SO NO LEFTOVERS TO THROW OUT!
AND IT'S JEAN'S GOOD CHINA, SO NO NEED TO THROW OUT THE PLATES!
EAT TO YOUR HEART'S CONTENT!
VERY WELL.
MONSIEUR, WE HAVE A PRESENT FOR YOU!
WE REALIZE THAT WRAPPING IS JUST GARBAGE IN DISGUISE...
...SO WE'RE PRESENTING IT TO YOU UNWRAPPED!!
BAAAAM
...

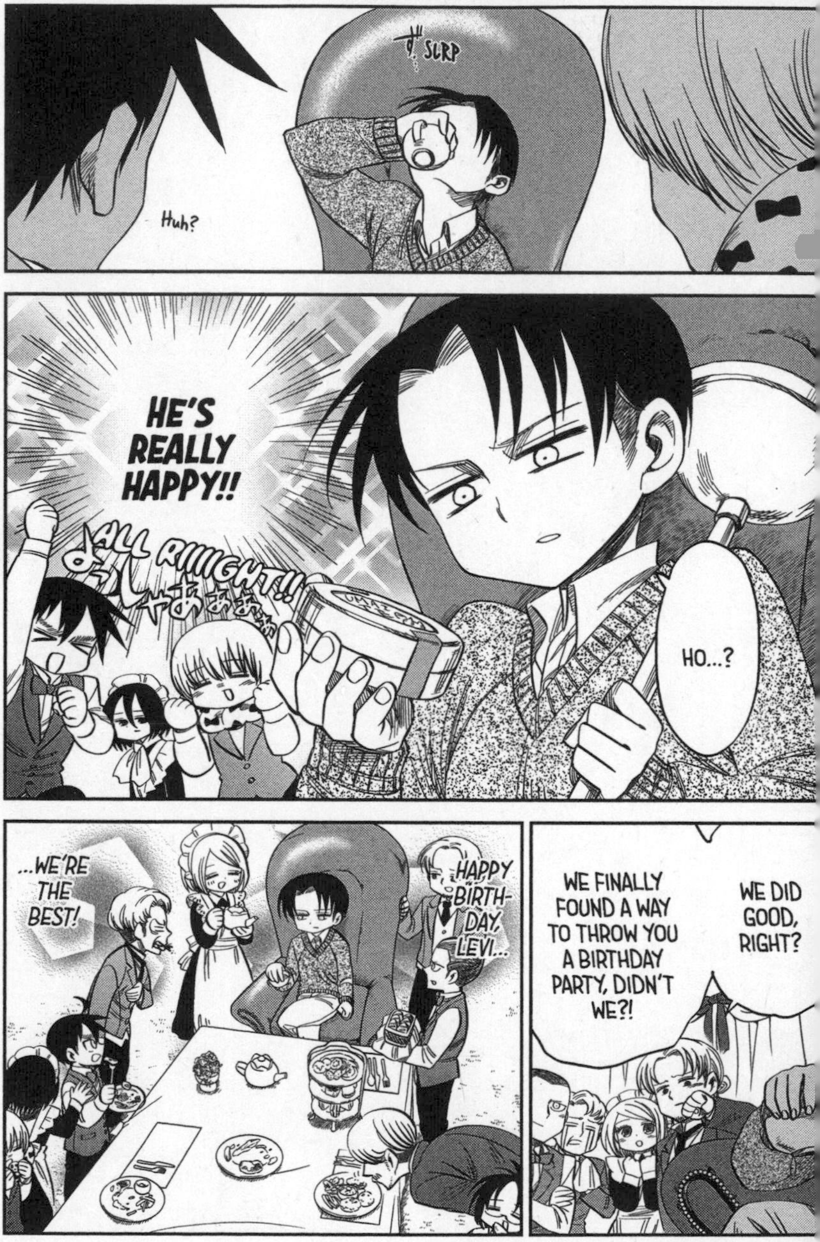
ず SCRP
Huh?
HO...?
HE'S REALLY HAPPY!!
ALL RIIIGHT!!
よっしゃあああ
WE DID GOOD, RIGHT?
WE FINALLY FOUND A WAY TO THROW YOU A BIRTHDAY PARTY, DIDN'T WE?!
HAPPY BIRTHDAY, LEVI...
...WE'RE THE BEST!

LET US EAT CAKE!!
OOH! THE MAIN DISH HAS MADE ITS ENTRANCE!
GEH HEH HEH
JUST WHAT WE'VE BEEN WAITING FOR!!
AND THE PER-FECT THING...
...TO FIN-ISH OFF A BIRTHDAY CAKE IS...
AH!
NO, EREN!
YOU CAN'T DO THAT—
DONE!!
NOW, MONSIEUR, IF YOU'LL JUST...
...BLOW OUT THE CANDLES!!

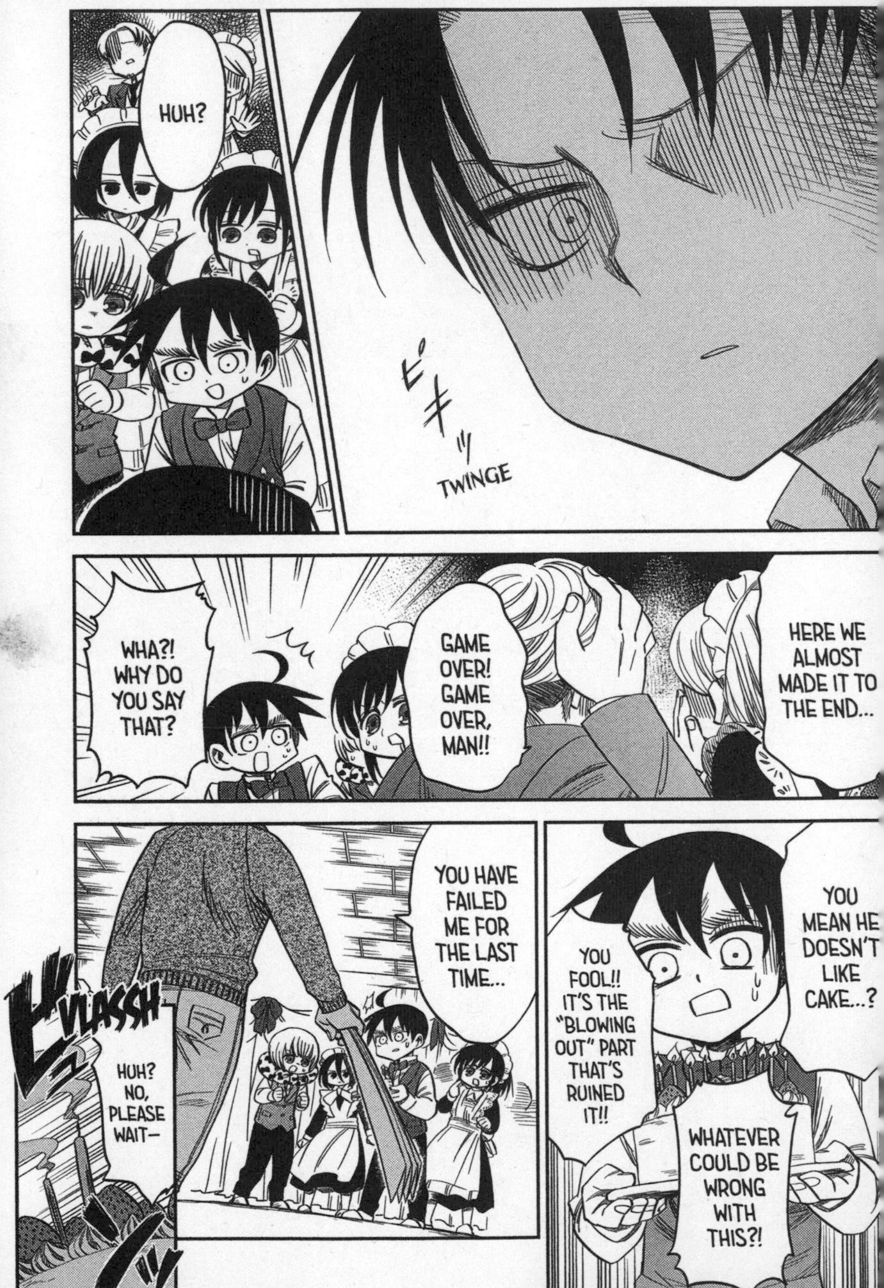
ピキッ
TWINGE
HUH?
HERE WE ALMOST MADE IT TO THE END...
GAME OVER! GAME OVER, MAN!!
WHA?! WHY DO YOU SAY THAT?
YOU MEAN HE DOESN'T LIKE CAKE...?
YOU FOOL!! IT'S THE "BLOWING OUT" PART THAT'S RUINED IT!!
WHATEVER COULD BE WRONG WITH THIS?!
YOU HAVE FAILED ME FOR THE LAST TIME...
VLASSH
HUH? NO, PLEASE WAIT—

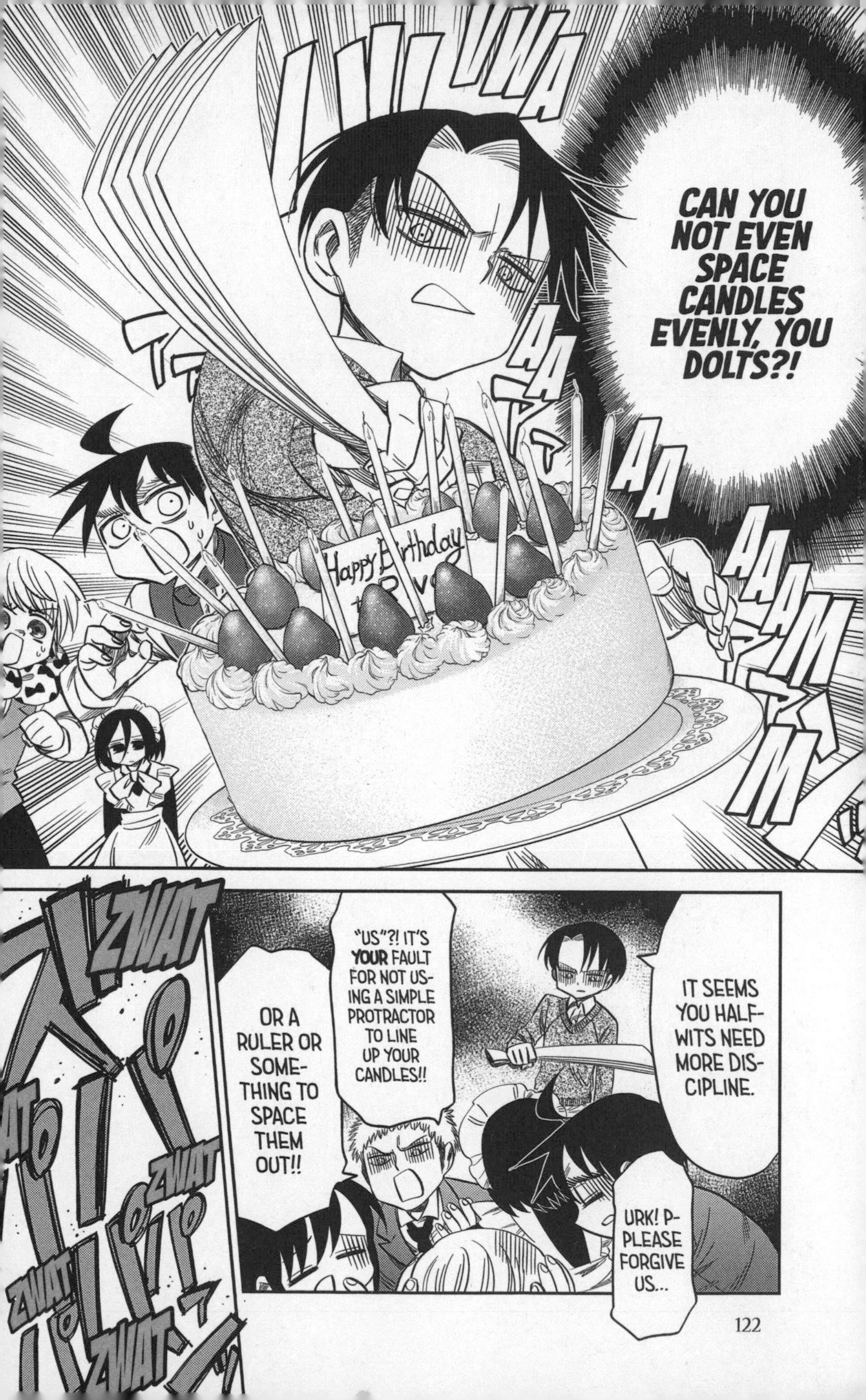
CAN YOU NOT EVEN SPACE CANDLES EVENLY, YOU DOLTS?!
Happy Birthday
IT SEEMS YOU HALF-WITS NEED MORE DISCIPLINE.
URK! P-PLEASE FORGIVE US...
"US"?! IT'S **YOUR** FAULT FOR NOT USING A SIMPLE PROTRACTOR TO LINE UP YOUR CANDLES!!
OR A RULER OR SOMETHING TO SPACE THEM OUT!!
ZWAT
ZWAT
ZWAT
ZWAT

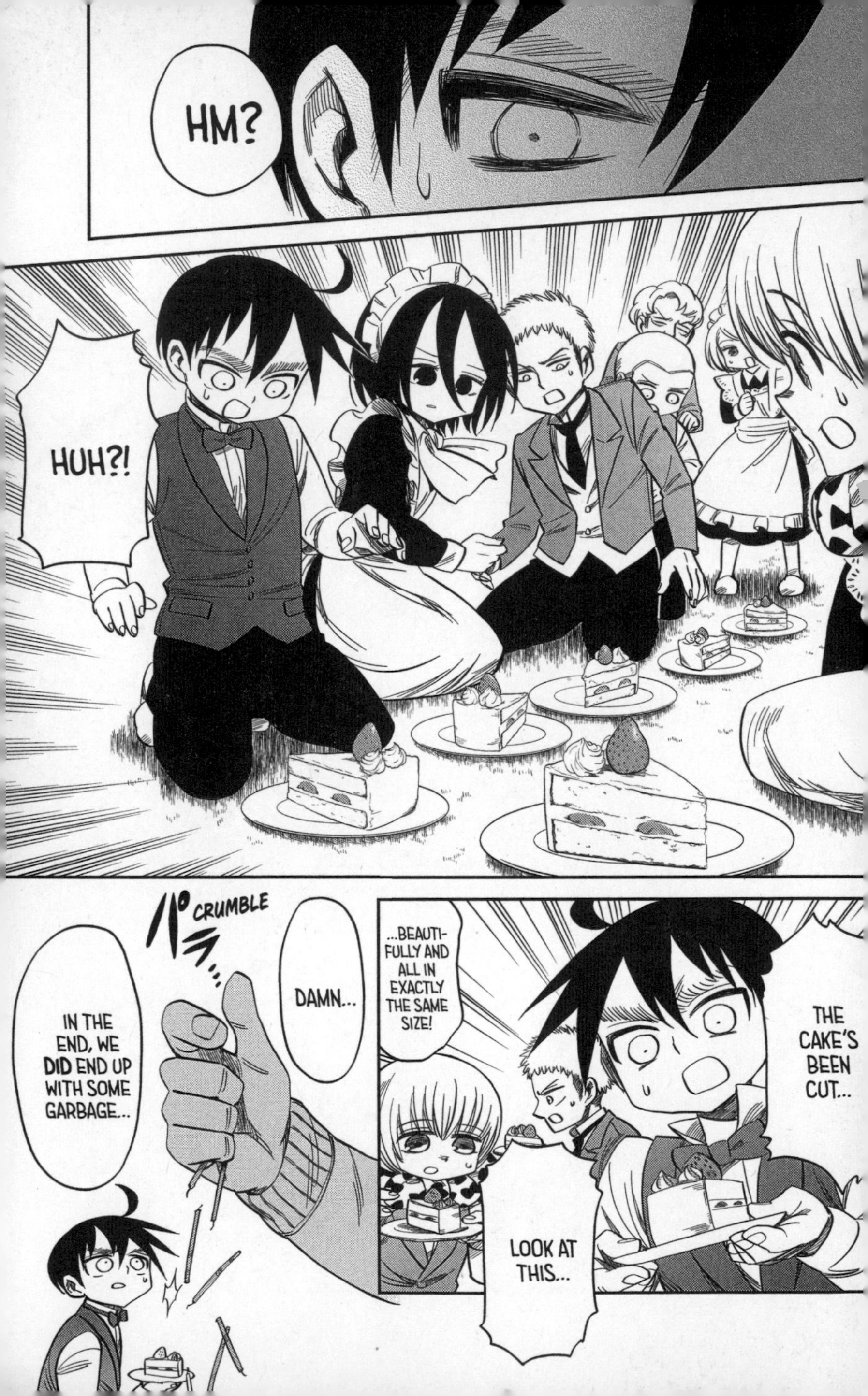
HM?
HUH?!
THE CAKE'S BEEN CUT...
...BEAUTIFULLY AND ALL IN EXACTLY THE SAME SIZE!
LOOK AT THIS...
DAMN...
CRUMBLE
IN THE END, WE **DID** END UP WITH SOME GARBAGE...

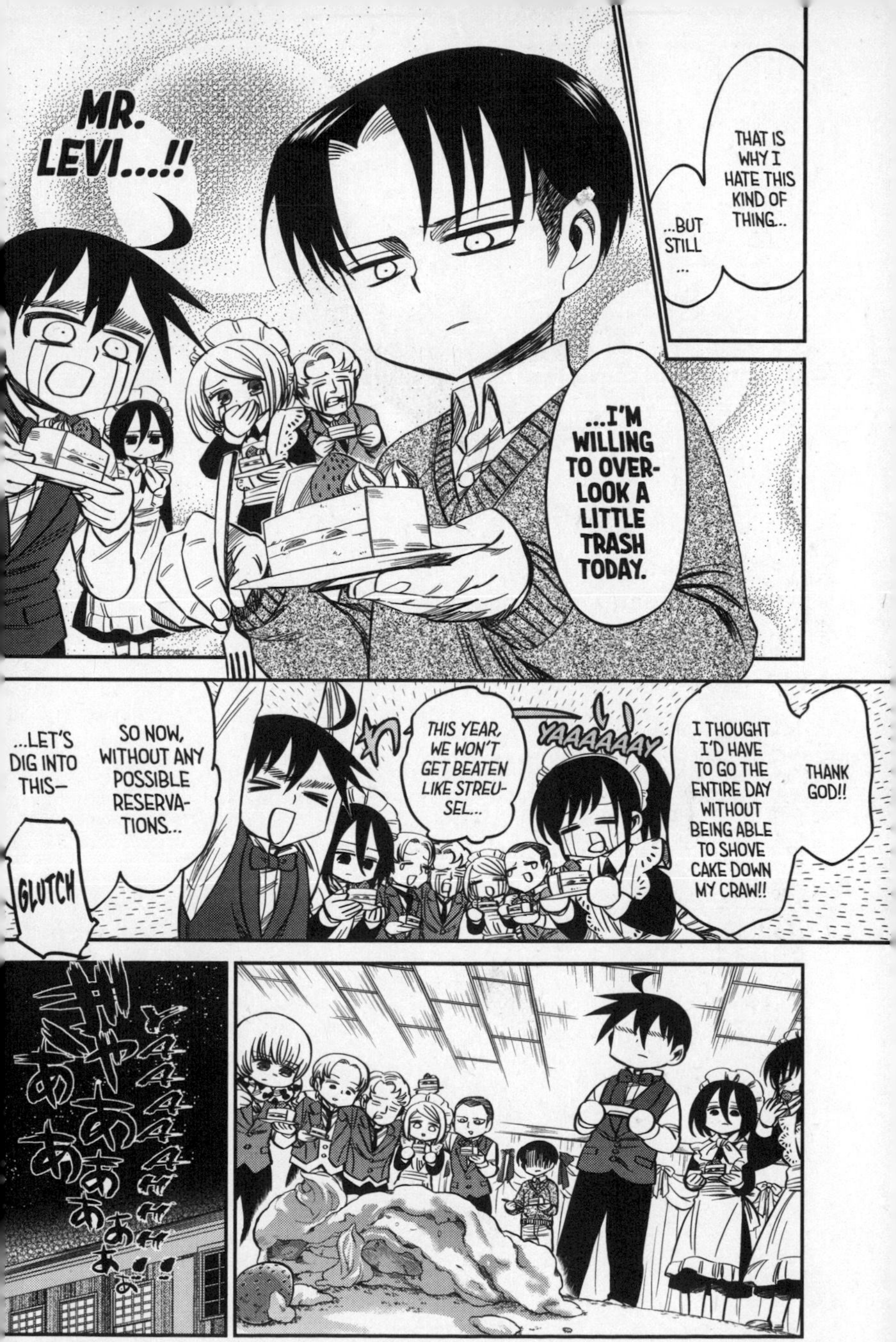
THAT IS WHY I HATE THIS KIND OF THING...
...BUT STILL ...
...I'M WILLING TO OVER-LOOK A LITTLE TRASH TODAY.
MR. LEVI...!!
THANK GOD!!
I THOUGHT I'D HAVE TO GO THE ENTIRE DAY WITHOUT BEING ABLE TO SHOVE CAKE DOWN MY CRAW!!
YAAAAAAY
THIS YEAR, WE WON'T GET BEATEN LIKE STREU-SEL...
SO NOW, WITHOUT ANY POSSIBLE RESERVA-TIONS...
...LET'S DIG INTO THIS—
GLUTCH
YAAAAAHHH!!

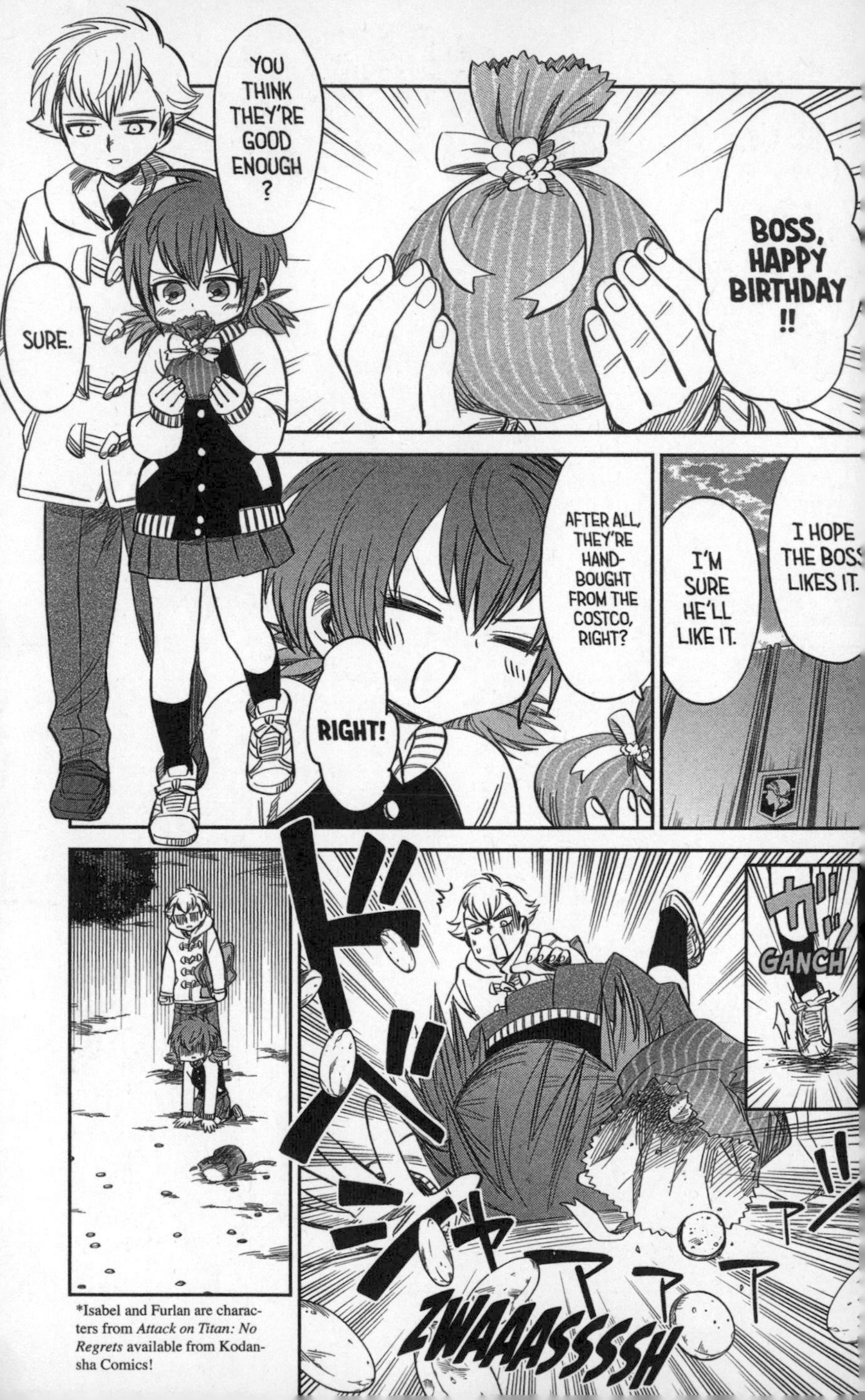
BOSS, HAPPY BIRTHDAY !!
I HOPE THE BOSS LIKES IT.
I'M SURE HE'LL LIKE IT.
AFTER ALL, THEY'RE HAND-BOUGHT FROM THE COSTCO, RIGHT?
RIGHT!
YOU THINK THEY'RE GOOD ENOUGH ?
SURE.
GANCH
ZWAAASSSSH

*Isabel and Furlan are characters from *Attack on Titan: No Regrets* available from Kodansha Comics!

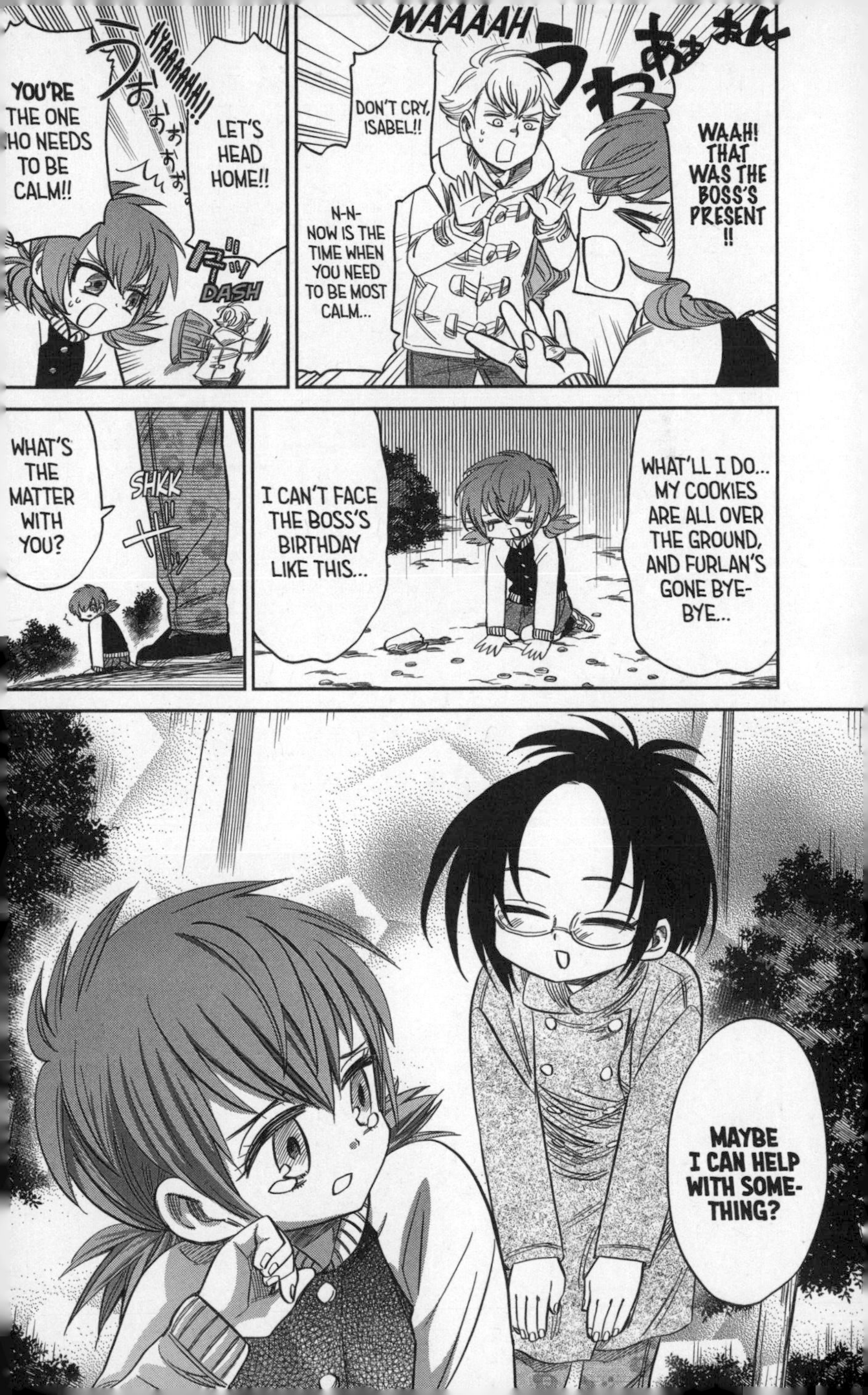
WAAAAH
WAAH! THAT WAS THE BOSS'S PRESENT!!
DON'T CRY, ISABEL!!
N-N-NOW IS THE TIME WHEN YOU NEED TO BE MOST CALM...
LET'S HEAD HOME!!
HYAAAAAAAH!!
DASH
YOU'RE THE ONE HO NEEDS TO BE CALM!!
WHAT'LL I DO... MY COOKIES ARE ALL OVER THE GROUND, AND FURLAN'S GONE BYE-BYE...
I CAN'T FACE THE BOSS'S BIRTHDAY LIKE THIS...
WHAT'S THE MATTER WITH YOU?
SHKK
MAYBE I CAN HELP WITH SOME-THING?

SPECIAL EDITION: UNDERCLASSMAN-FLAVORED COOKIES

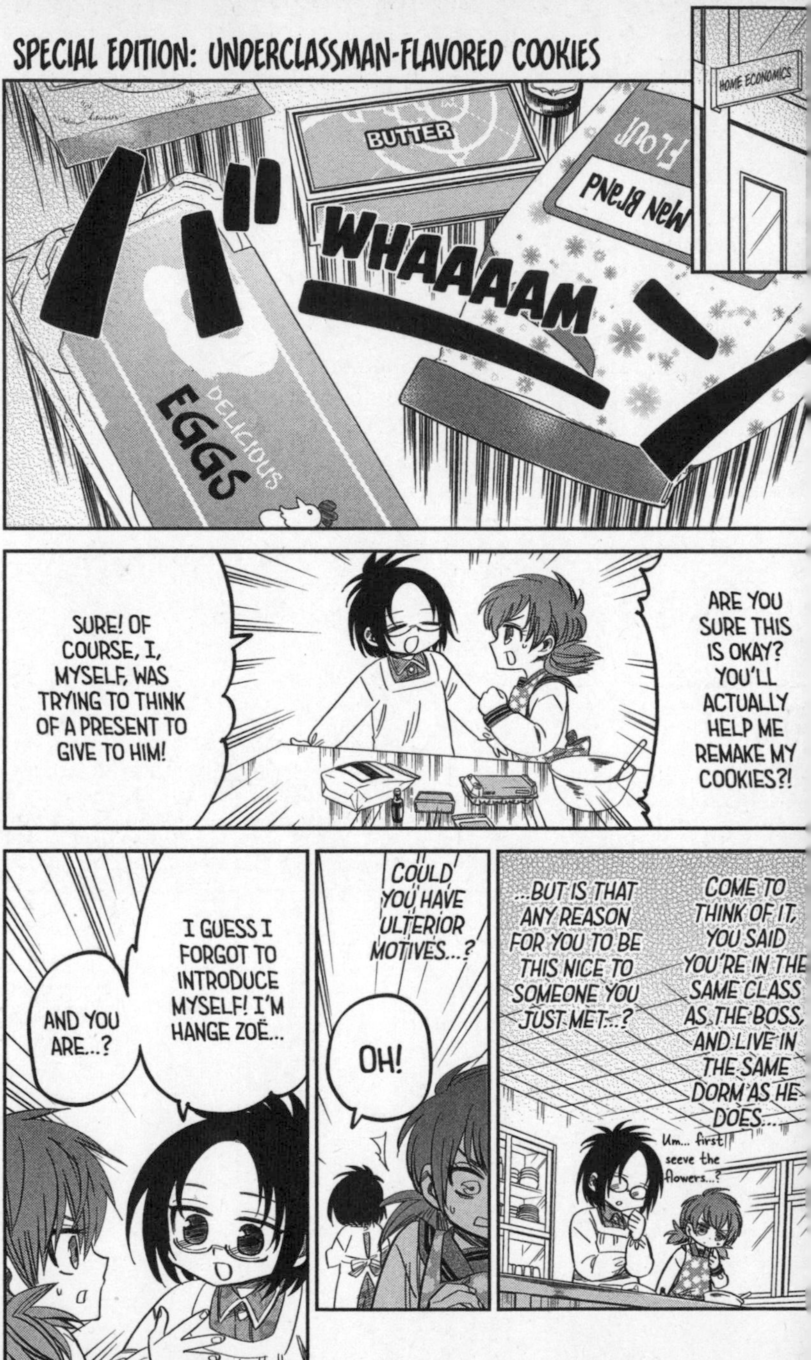
HOME ECONOMICS
BUTTER
FLOUR
New Brand
WHAAAAM
DELICIOUS
EGGS
ARE YOU SURE THIS IS OKAY? YOU'LL ACTUALLY HELP ME REMAKE MY COOKIES?!
SURE! OF COURSE, I, MYSELF, WAS TRYING TO THINK OF A PRESENT TO GIVE TO HIM!
COME TO THINK OF IT, YOU SAID YOU'RE IN THE SAME CLASS AS THE BOSS, AND LIVE IN THE SAME DORM AS HE DOES...
...BUT IS THAT ANY REASON FOR YOU TO BE THIS NICE TO SOMEONE YOU JUST MET...?
Um... first seeve the flowers...?
COULD YOU HAVE ULTERIOR MOTIVES...?
OH!
I GUESS I FORGOT TO INTRODUCE MYSELF! I'M HANGE ZOË...
AND YOU ARE...?

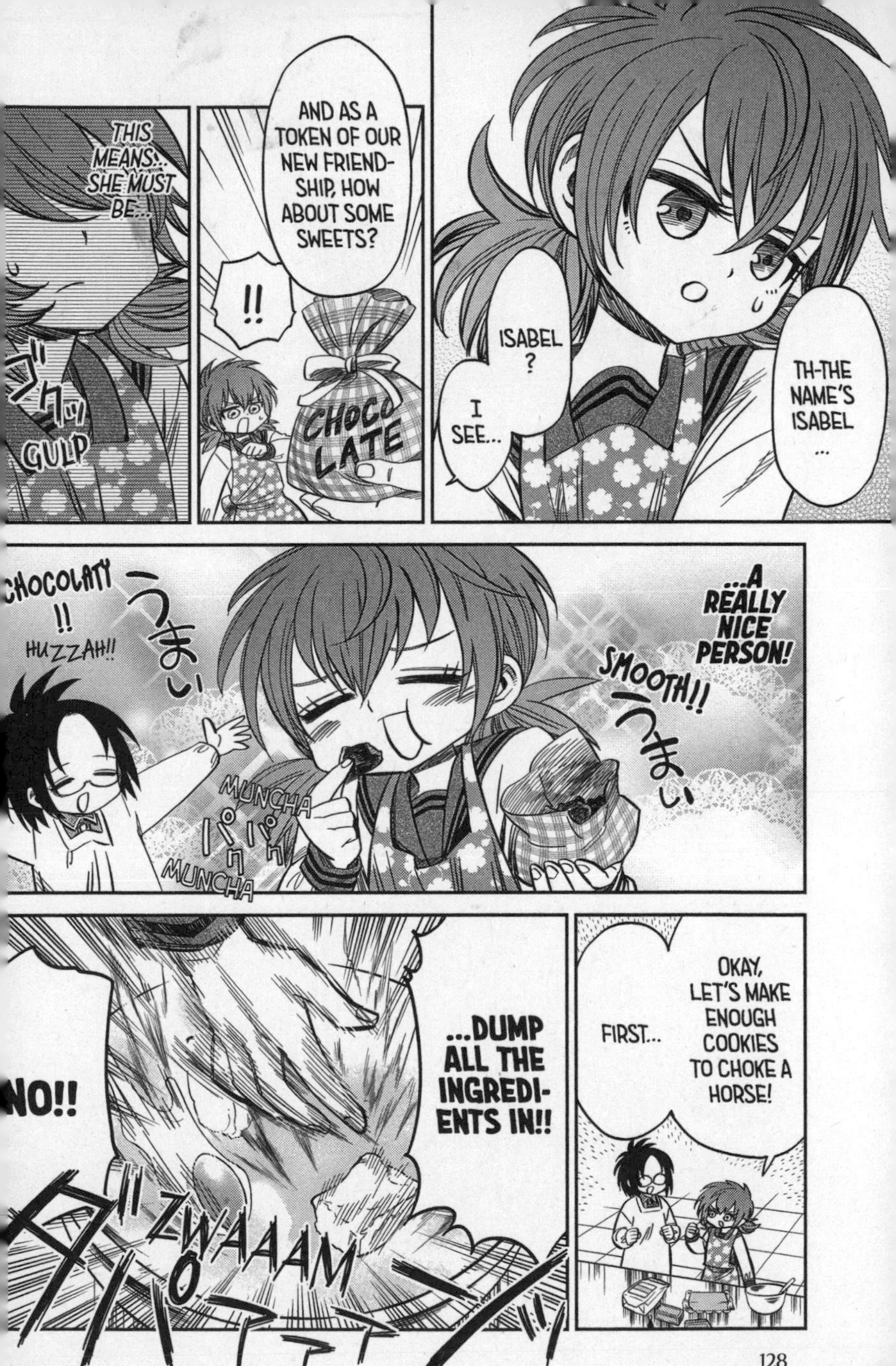
TH-THE NAME'S ISABEL ...
ISABEL ? I SEE...
AND AS A TOKEN OF OUR NEW FRIENDSHIP, HOW ABOUT SOME SWEETS?
!!
CHOCOLATE
THIS MEANS... SHE MUST BE...
ゴクッ
GULP
...A REALLY NICE PERSON!
SMOOTH!!
うまい
MUNCHA
MUNCHA
うまい
CHOCOLATY !!
HUZZAH!!
OKAY, LET'S MAKE ENOUGH COOKIES TO CHOKE A HORSE!
FIRST...
...DUMP ALL THE INGREDIENTS IN!!
NO!!
ZWAAAAM

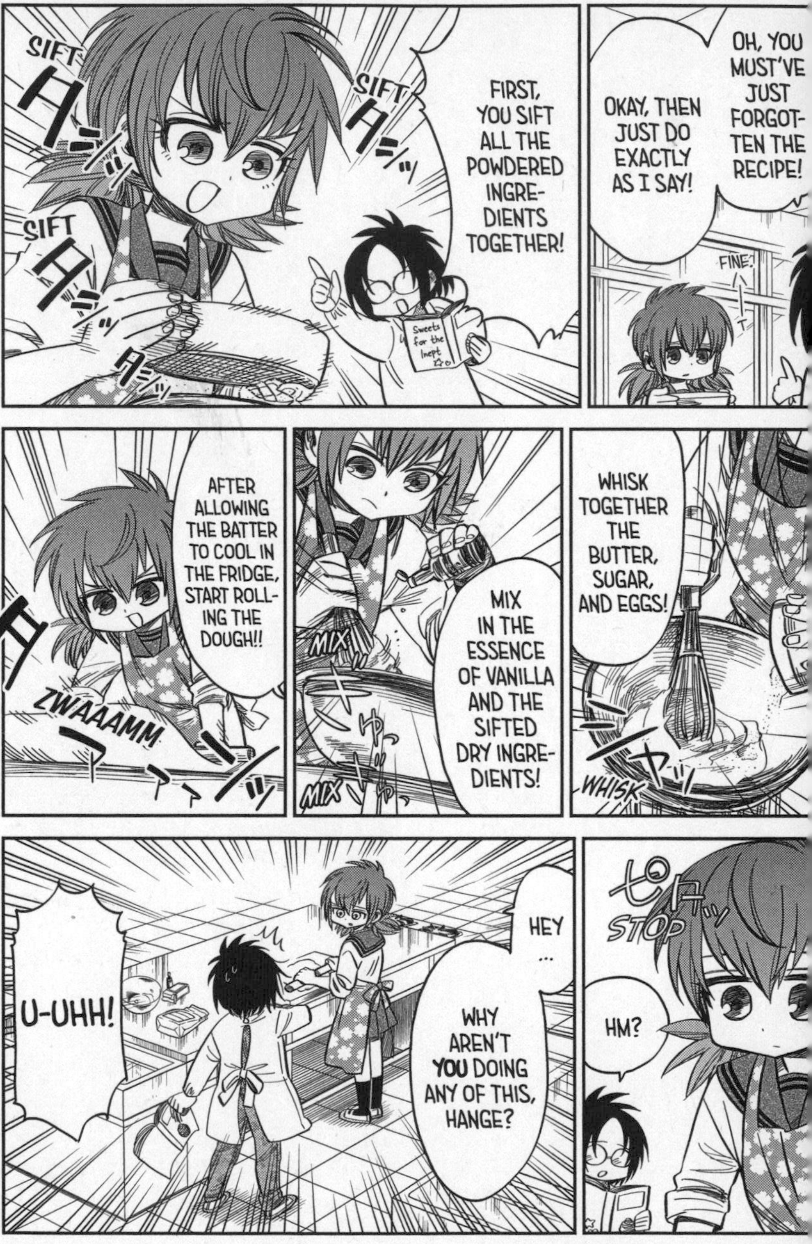
OH, YOU MUST'VE JUST FORGOT-TEN THE RECIPE!
OKAY, THEN JUST DO EXACTLY AS I SAY!
FINE!
SIFT
SIFT
FIRST, YOU SIFT ALL THE POWDERED INGRE-DIENTS TOGETHER!
SIFT
Sweets for the Inept
WHISK TOGETHER THE BUTTER, SUGAR, AND EGGS!
WHISK
MIX IN THE ESSENCE OF VANILLA AND THE SIFTED DRY INGRE-DIENTS!
MIX
MIX
AFTER ALLOWING THE BATTER TO COOL IN THE FRIDGE, START ROLL-ING THE DOUGH!!
ZWAAAMM
STOP
HM?
HEY...
WHY AREN'T YOU DOING ANY OF THIS, HANGE?
U-UHH!

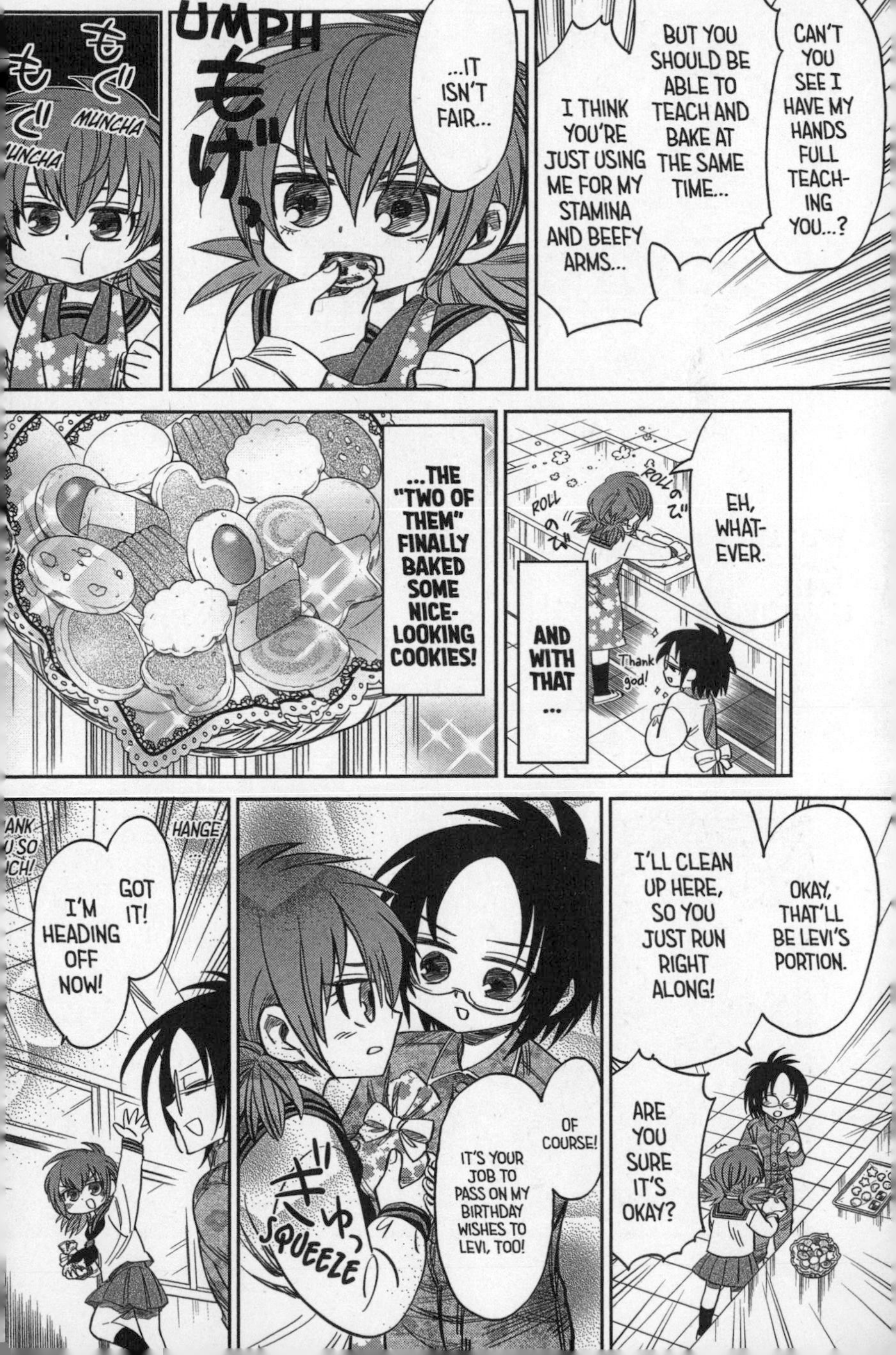
CAN'T YOU SEE I HAVE MY HANDS FULL TEACHING YOU...?
BUT YOU SHOULD BE ABLE TO TEACH AND BAKE AT THE SAME TIME...
I THINK YOU'RE JUST USING ME FOR MY STAMINA AND BEEFY ARMS...
...IT ISN'T FAIR...
UMPH
もげっ
もぐ もぐ
MUNCHA
EH, WHATEVER.
ROLL のび
ROLL のび
Thank god!
AND WITH THAT...
...THE "TWO OF THEM" FINALLY BAKED SOME NICE-LOOKING COOKIES!
OKAY, THAT'LL BE LEVI'S PORTION.
I'LL CLEAN UP HERE, SO YOU JUST RUN RIGHT ALONG!
ARE YOU SURE IT'S OKAY?
OF COURSE!
IT'S YOUR JOB TO PASS ON MY BIRTHDAY WISHES TO LEVI, TOO!
ぎゅっ
SQUEEZE
HANGE...
GOT IT! I'M HEADING OFF NOW!

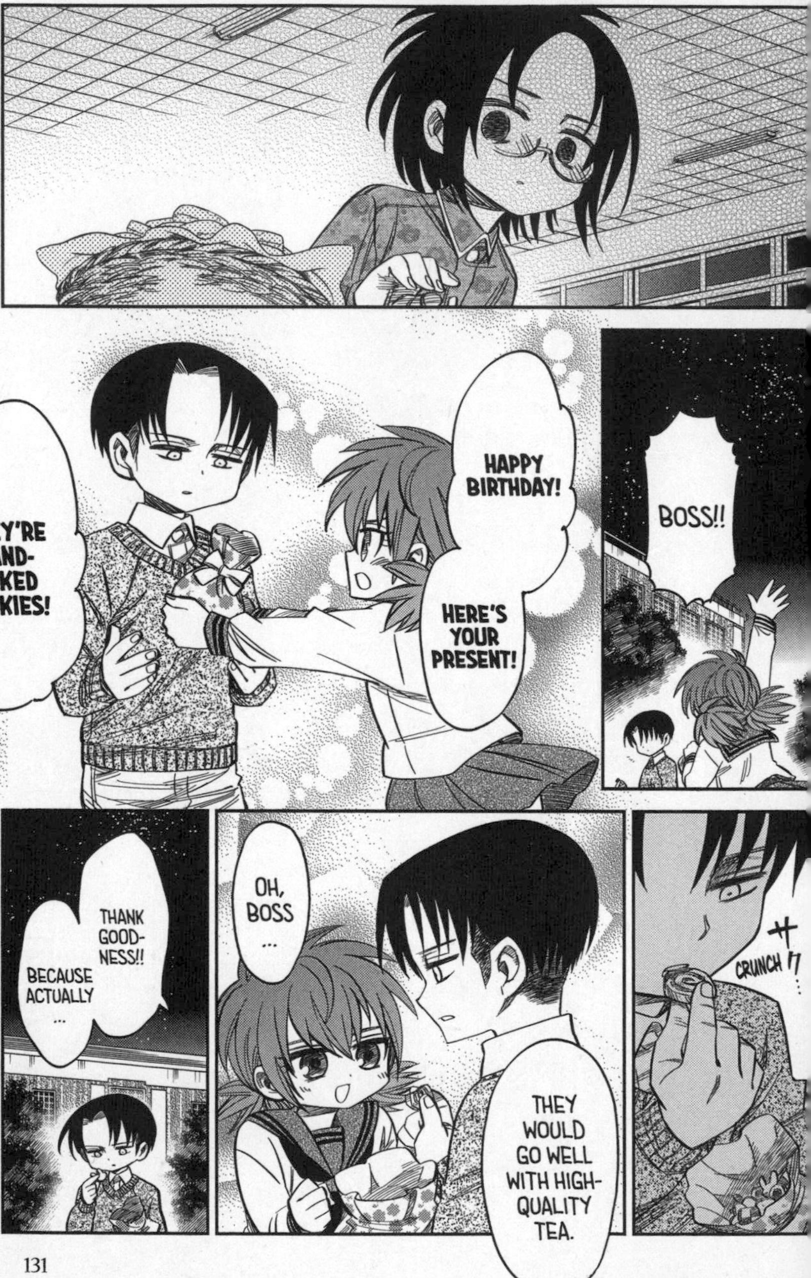
BOSS!!
HAPPY BIRTHDAY!
HERE'S YOUR PRESENT!
THEY'RE HAND-BAKED COOKIES!
CRUNCH !!
OH, BOSS ...
THEY WOULD GO WELL WITH HIGH-QUALITY TEA.
THANK GOODNESS!!
BECAUSE ACTUALLY ...

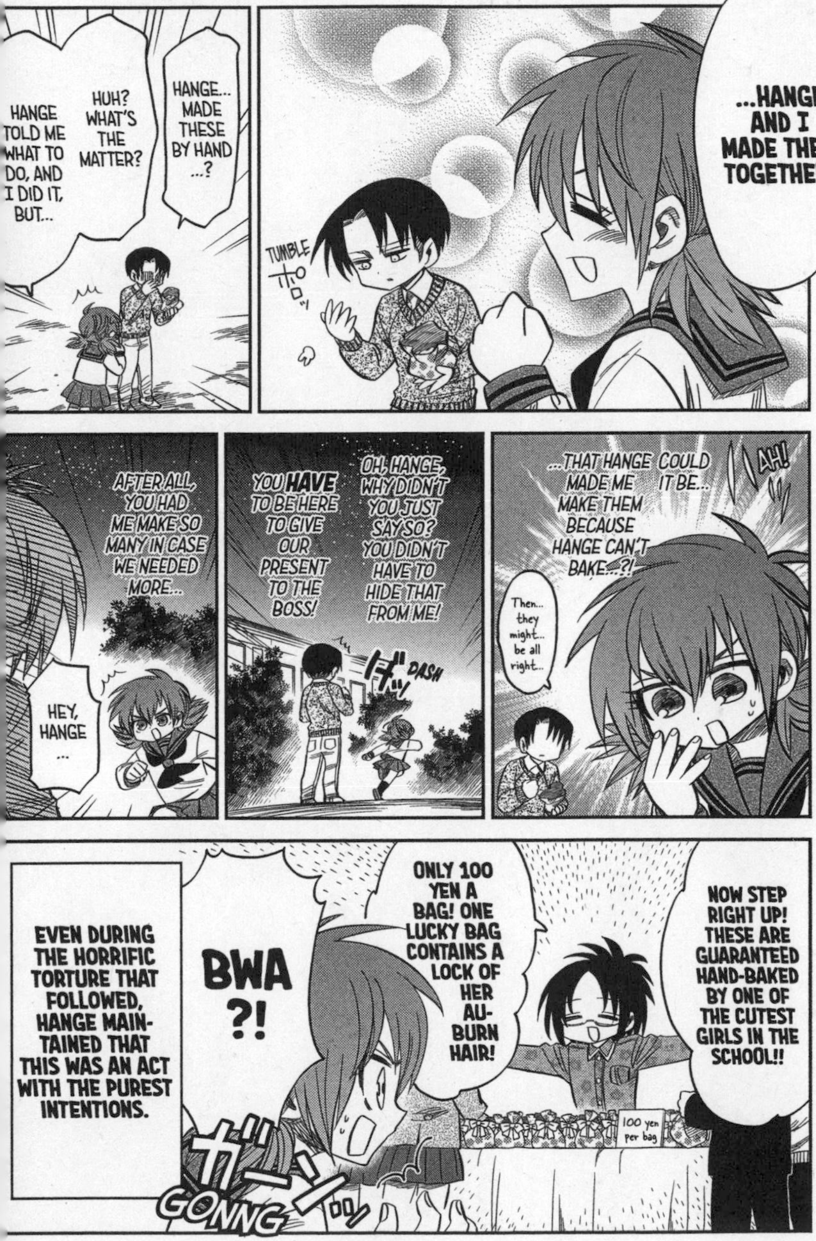
...HANGE AND I MADE THEM TOGETHER!
TUMBLE
HANGE... MADE THESE BY HAND ...?
HUH? WHAT'S THE MATTER?
HANGE TOLD ME WHAT TO DO, AND I DID IT, BUT...
AH!
COULD IT BE...
...THAT HANGE MADE ME MAKE THEM BECAUSE HANGE CAN'T BAKE...?!
Then... they might... be all right...
OH, HANGE, WHY DIDN'T YOU JUST SAY SO? YOU DIDN'T HAVE TO HIDE THAT FROM ME!
YOU HAVE TO BE HERE TO GIVE OUR PRESENT TO THE BOSS!
DASH
AFTER ALL, YOU HAD ME MAKE SO MANY IN CASE WE NEEDED MORE...
HEY, HANGE ...
NOW STEP RIGHT UP! THESE ARE GUARANTEED HAND-BAKED BY ONE OF THE CUTEST GIRLS IN THE SCHOOL!!
ONLY 100 YEN A BAG! ONE LUCKY BAG CONTAINS A LOCK OF HER AU-BURN HAIR!
100 yen per bag
BWA ?!
GONNG
EVEN DURING THE HORRIFIC TORTURE THAT FOLLOWED, HANGE MAIN-TAINED THAT THIS WAS AN ACT WITH THE PUREST INTENTIONS.

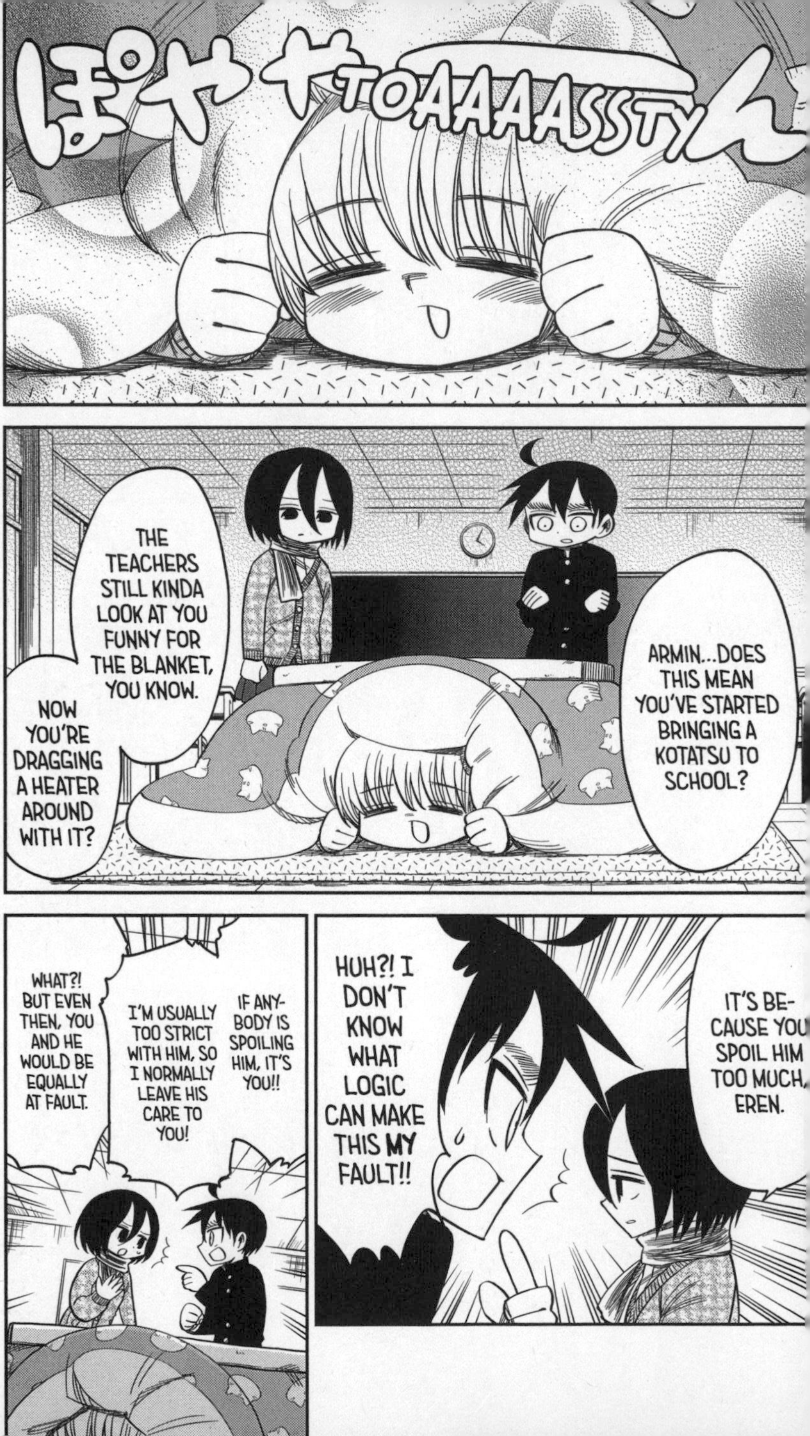
ぽややTOAAAAASSTYん
ARMIN...DOES THIS MEAN YOU'VE STARTED BRINGING A KOTATSU TO SCHOOL?
THE TEACHERS STILL KINDA LOOK AT YOU FUNNY FOR THE BLANKET, YOU KNOW.
NOW YOU'RE DRAGGING A HEATER AROUND WITH IT?
IT'S BE-CAUSE YOU SPOIL HIM TOO MUCH, EREN.
HUH?! I DON'T KNOW WHAT LOGIC CAN MAKE THIS MY FAULT!!
IF ANY-BODY IS SPOILING HIM, IT'S YOU!!
I'M USUALLY TOO STRICT WITH HIM, SO I NORMALLY LEAVE HIS CARE TO YOU!
WHAT?! BUT EVEN THEN, YOU AND HE WOULD BE EQUALLY AT FAULT.

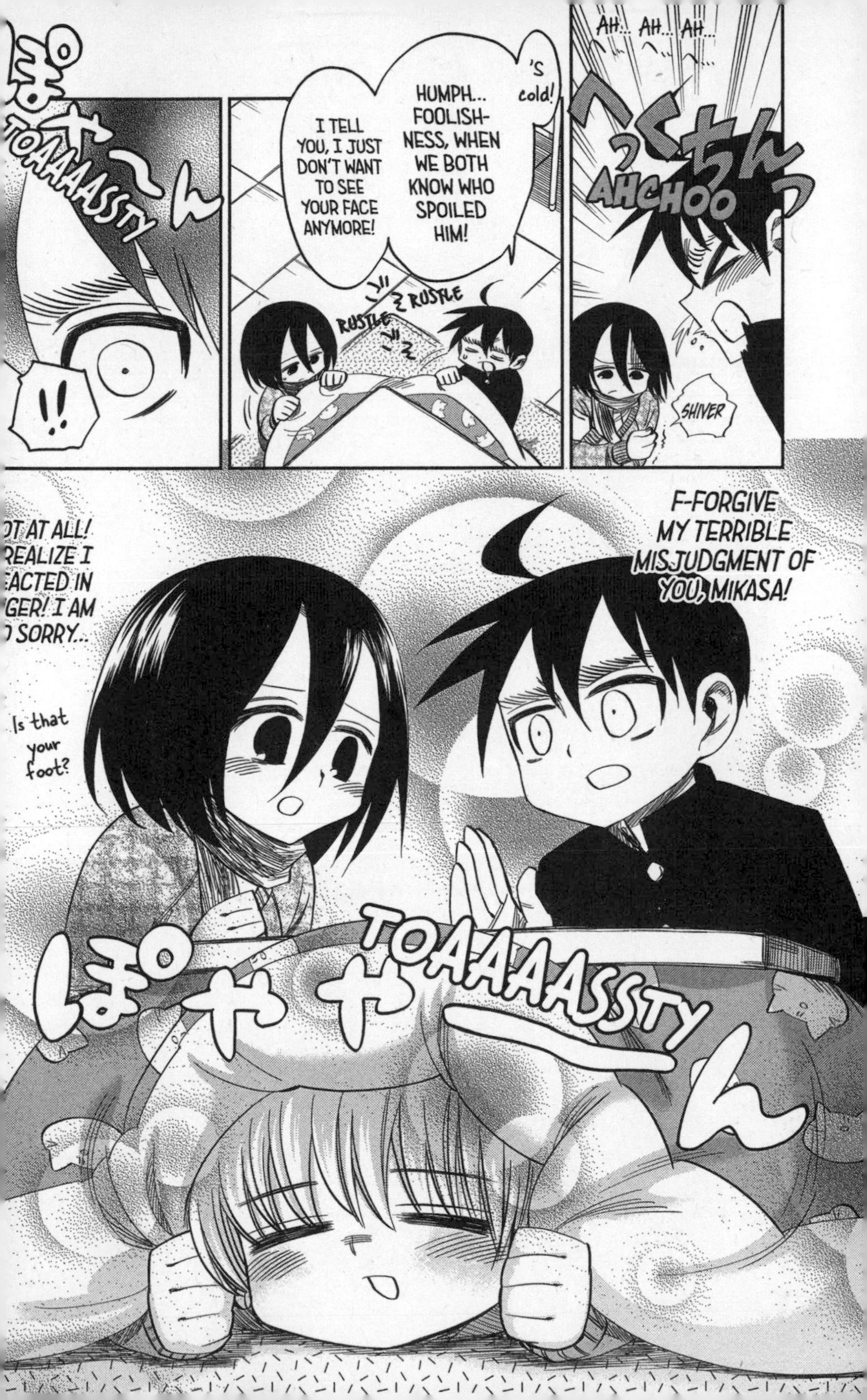
AH... AH... AH...
へっくちん
AHCHOO
SHIVER
HUMPH... FOOLISHNESS, WHEN WE BOTH KNOW WHO SPOILED HIM!
I TELL YOU, I JUST DON'T WANT TO SEE YOUR FACE ANYMORE!
'S cold!
RUSTLE
RUSTLE
ぽやーん
TOAAAASSTY
!!
F-FORGIVE MY TERRIBLE MISJUDGMENT OF YOU, MIKASA!
OT AT ALL! REALIZE I EACTED IN GER! I AM O SORRY...
Is that your foot?
ぽやーん
TOAAAAASSTY

FIFTY-SECOND PERIOD: KOTATSU IS PEACE

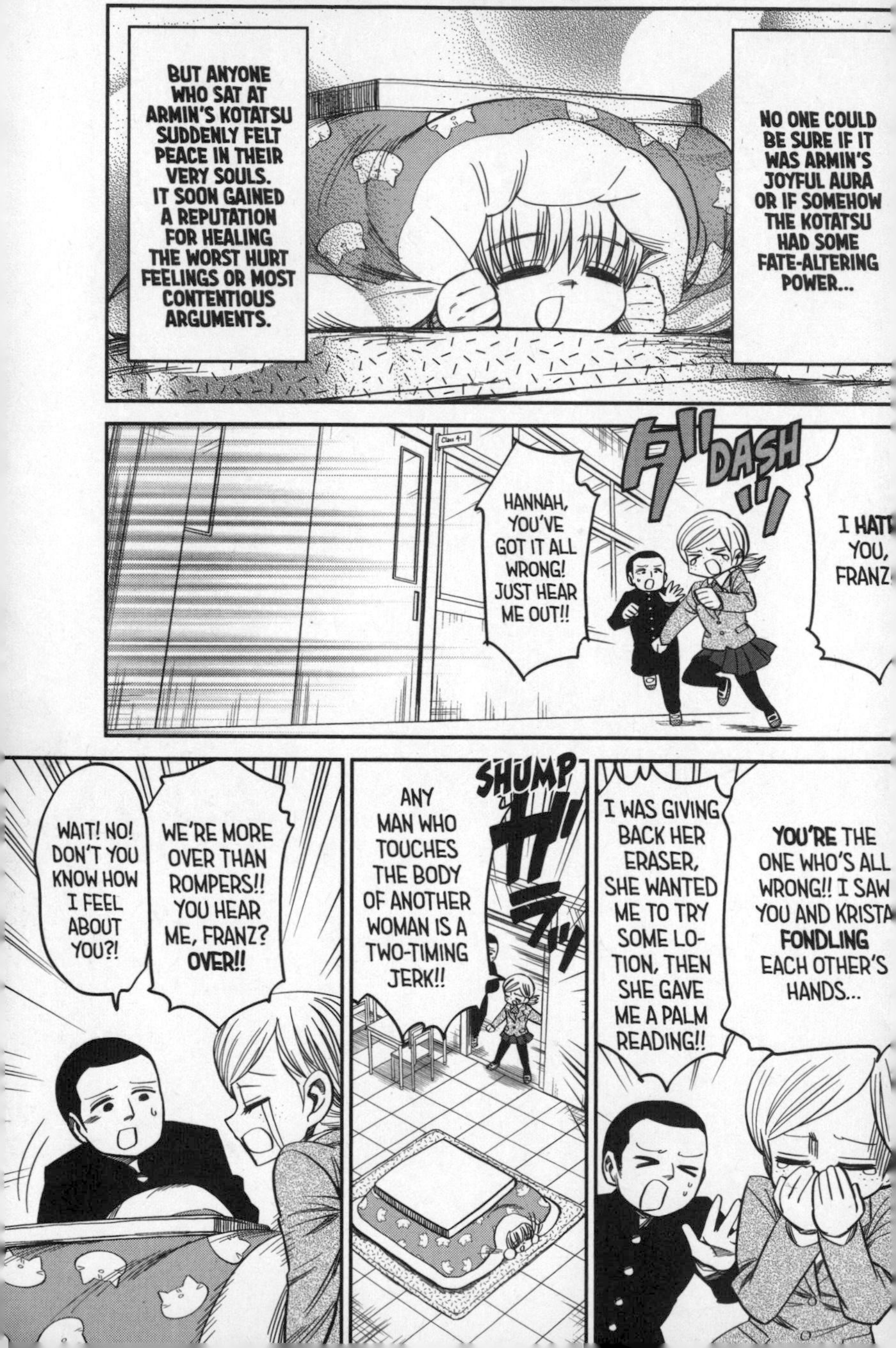
NO ONE COULD BE SURE IF IT WAS ARMIN'S JOYFUL AURA OR IF SOMEHOW THE KOTATSU HAD SOME FATE-ALTERING POWER...
BUT ANYONE WHO SAT AT ARMIN'S KOTATSU SUDDENLY FELT PEACE IN THEIR VERY SOULS. IT SOON GAINED A REPUTATION FOR HEALING THE WORST HURT FEELINGS OR MOST CONTENTIOUS ARGUMENTS.
I HAT
YOU,
FRANZ
DASH
HANNAH, YOU'VE GOT IT ALL WRONG! JUST HEAR ME OUT!!
YOU'RE THE ONE WHO'S ALL WRONG!! I SAW YOU AND KRISTA **FONDLING** EACH OTHER'S HANDS...
I WAS GIVING BACK HER ERASER, SHE WANTED ME TO TRY SOME LO-TION, THEN SHE GAVE ME A PALM READING!!
SHUMP
ANY MAN WHO TOUCHES THE BODY OF ANOTHER WOMAN IS A TWO-TIMING JERK!!
WE'RE MORE OVER THAN ROMPERS!! YOU HEAR ME, FRANZ? **OVER!!**
WAIT! NO! DON'T YOU KNOW HOW I FEEL ABOUT YOU?!

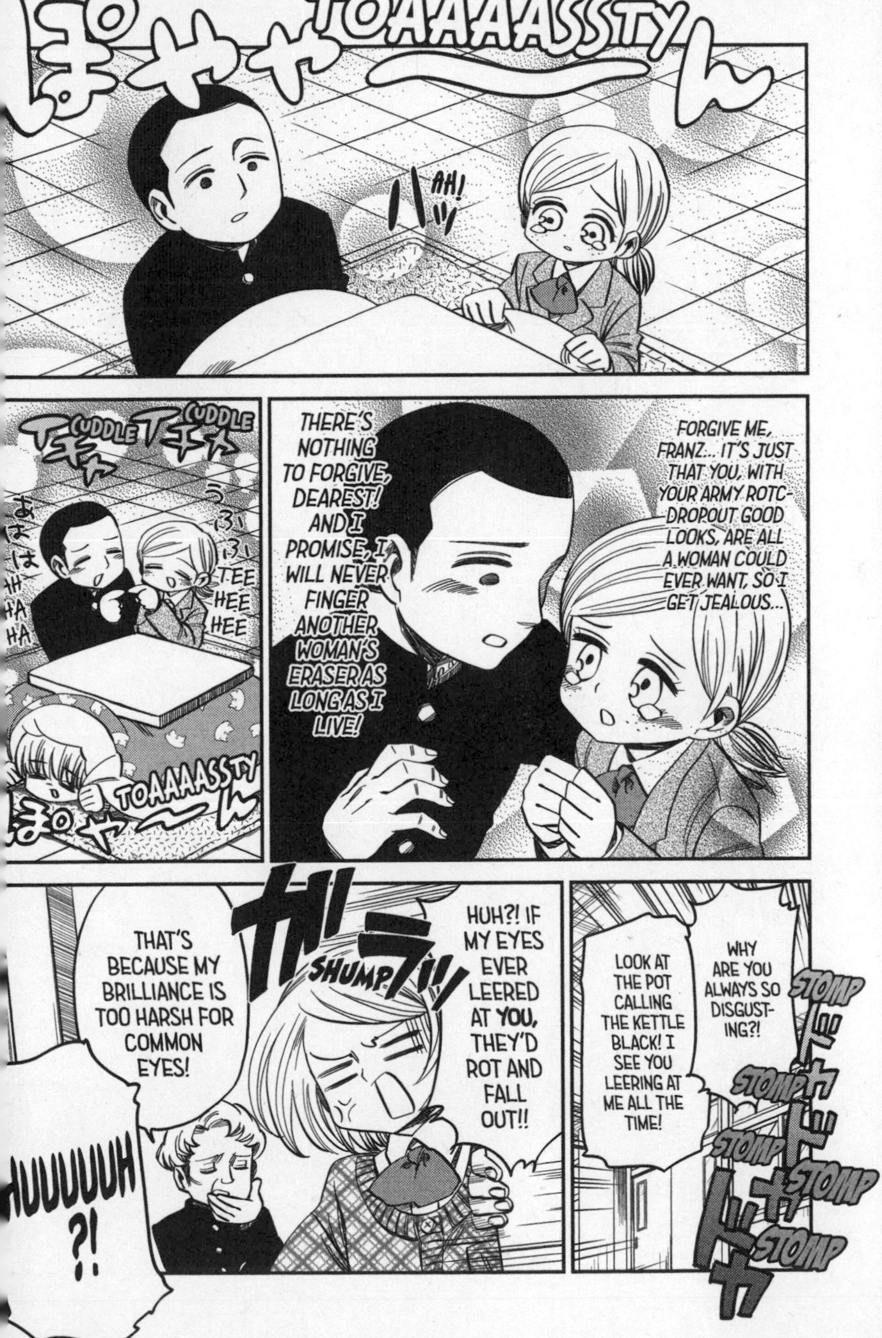
TOAAAAASSTY
AH!
FORGIVE ME, FRANZ... IT'S JUST THAT YOU, WITH YOUR ARMY ROTC-DROPOUT GOOD LOOKS, ARE ALL A WOMAN COULD EVER WANT, SO I GET JEALOUS...
THERE'S NOTHING TO FORGIVE, DEAREST! AND I PROMISE, I WILL NEVER FINGER ANOTHER WOMAN'S ERASER AS LONG AS I LIVE!
CUDDLE CUDDLE
TEE HEE HEE
HA HA HA
TOAAAASSTY
WHY ARE YOU ALWAYS SO DISGUSTING?!
LOOK AT THE POT CALLING THE KETTLE BLACK! I SEE YOU LEERING AT ME ALL THE TIME!
STOMP STOMP STOMP STOMP STOMP
HUH?! IF MY EYES EVER LEERED AT YOU, THEY'D ROT AND FALL OUT!!
SHUMP
THAT'S BECAUSE MY BRILLIANCE IS TOO HARSH FOR COMMON EYES!
HUUUUUH ?!

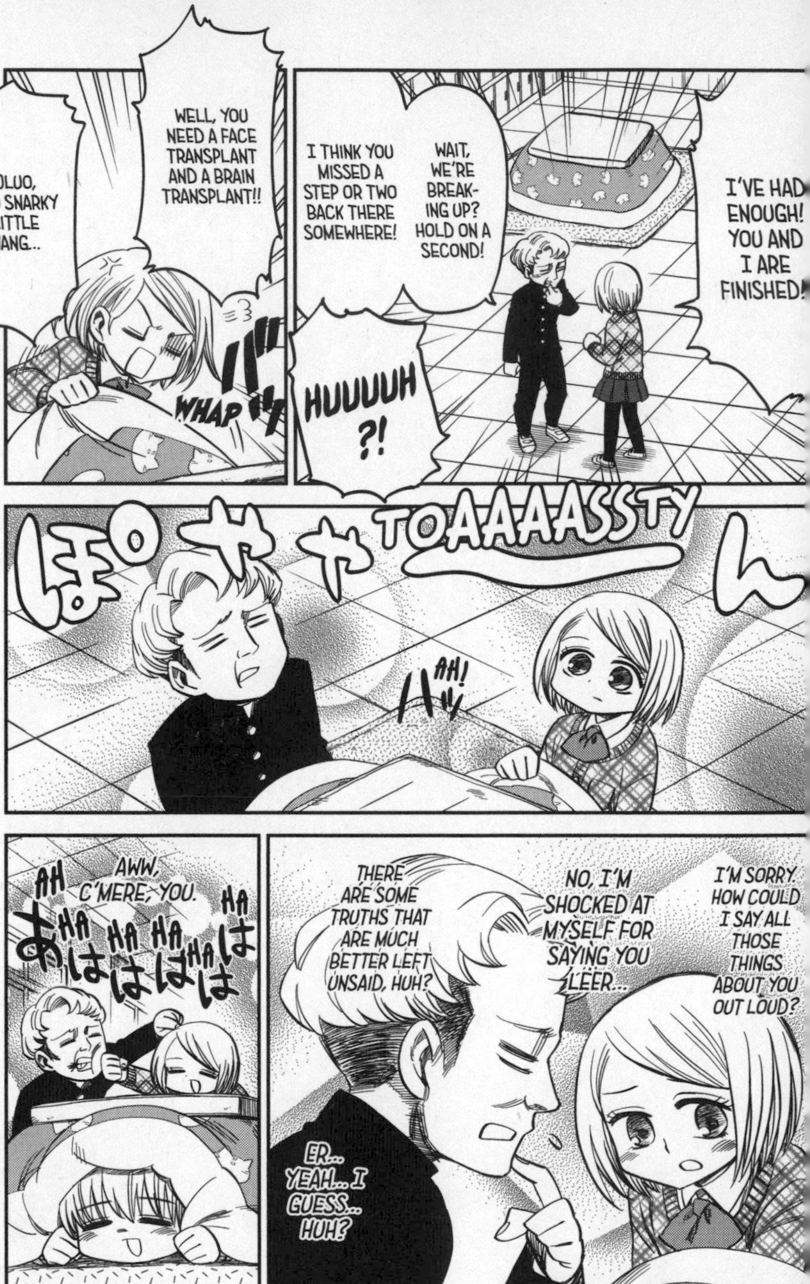
I'VE HAD ENOUGH! YOU AND I ARE FINISHED!
WAIT, WE'RE BREAK-ING UP? HOLD ON A SECOND!
I THINK YOU MISSED A STEP OR TWO BACK THERE SOMEWHERE!
HUUUUH ?!
WELL, YOU NEED A FACE TRANSPLANT AND A BRAIN TRANSPLANT!!
OLUO, YOU SNARKY LITTLE WANG..
WHAP
ぽやや
TOAAAASSTY
ん
AH!
I'M SORRY. HOW COULD I SAY ALL THOSE THINGS ABOUT YOU OUT LOUD?
NO, I'M SHOCKED AT MYSELF FOR SAYING YOU LEER...
THERE ARE SOME TRUTHS THAT ARE MUCH BETTER LEFT UNSAID, HUH?
ER... YEAH... I GUESS... HUH?
AWW, C'MERE, YOU.
AH HA HA HA HA HA
あははははは

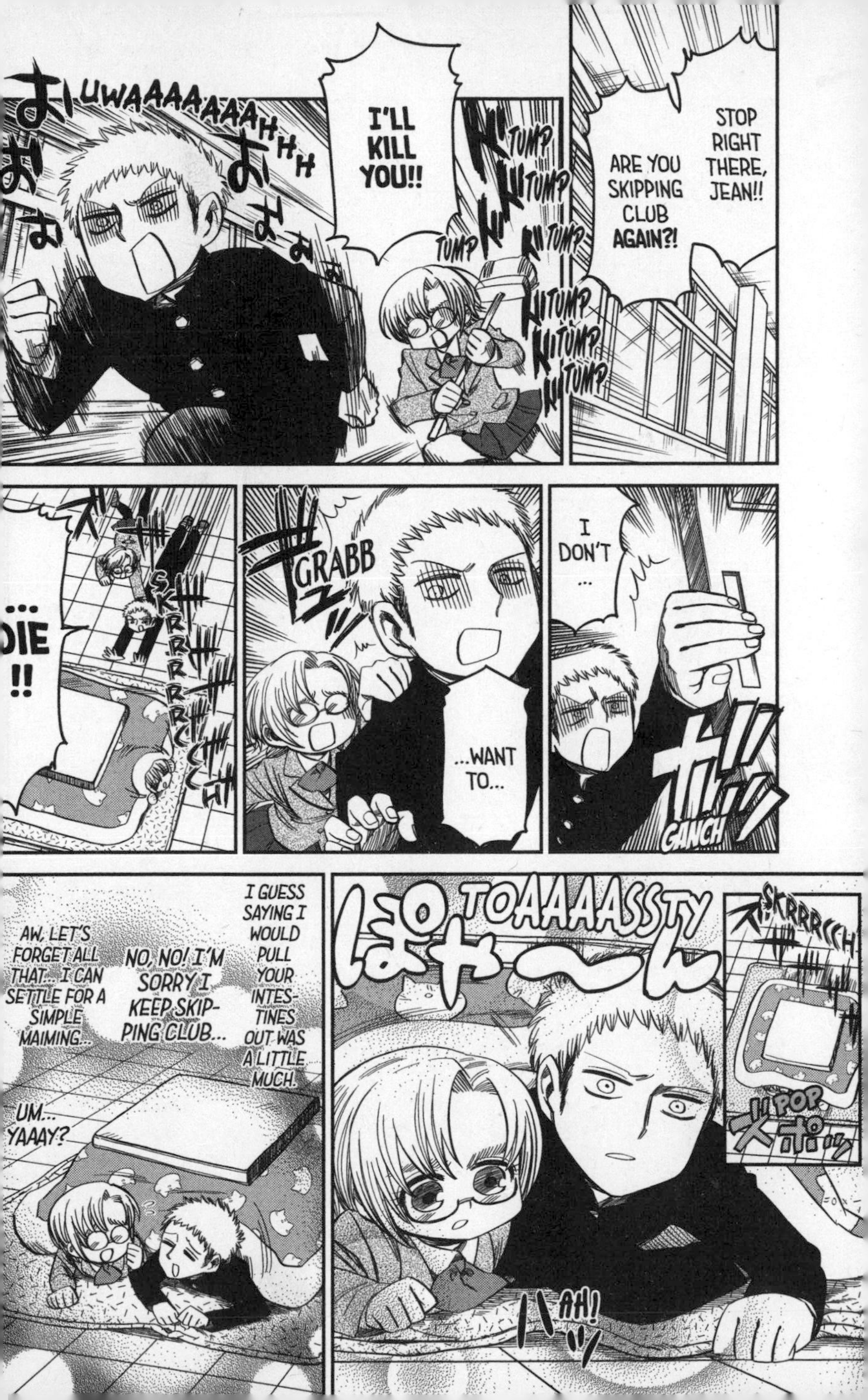
STOP RIGHT THERE, JEAN!!
ARE YOU SKIPPING CLUB AGAIN?!
TUMP TUMP TUMP TUMP TUMP TUMP TUMP
I'LL KILL YOU!!
UWAAAAAAAAAHHHH
I DON'T ...
GANCH
GRABB
...WANT TO...
...DIE!!
SKRRRRRCCH
TOAAAASSTY
SKRRRRCCH
POP
AH!
I GUESS SAYING I WOULD PULL YOUR INTES-TINES OUT WAS A LITTLE MUCH.
NO, NO! I'M SORRY I KEEP SKIP-PING CLUB...
AW, LET'S FORGET ALL THAT... I CAN SETTLE FOR A SIMPLE MAIMING...
UM... YAAAY?

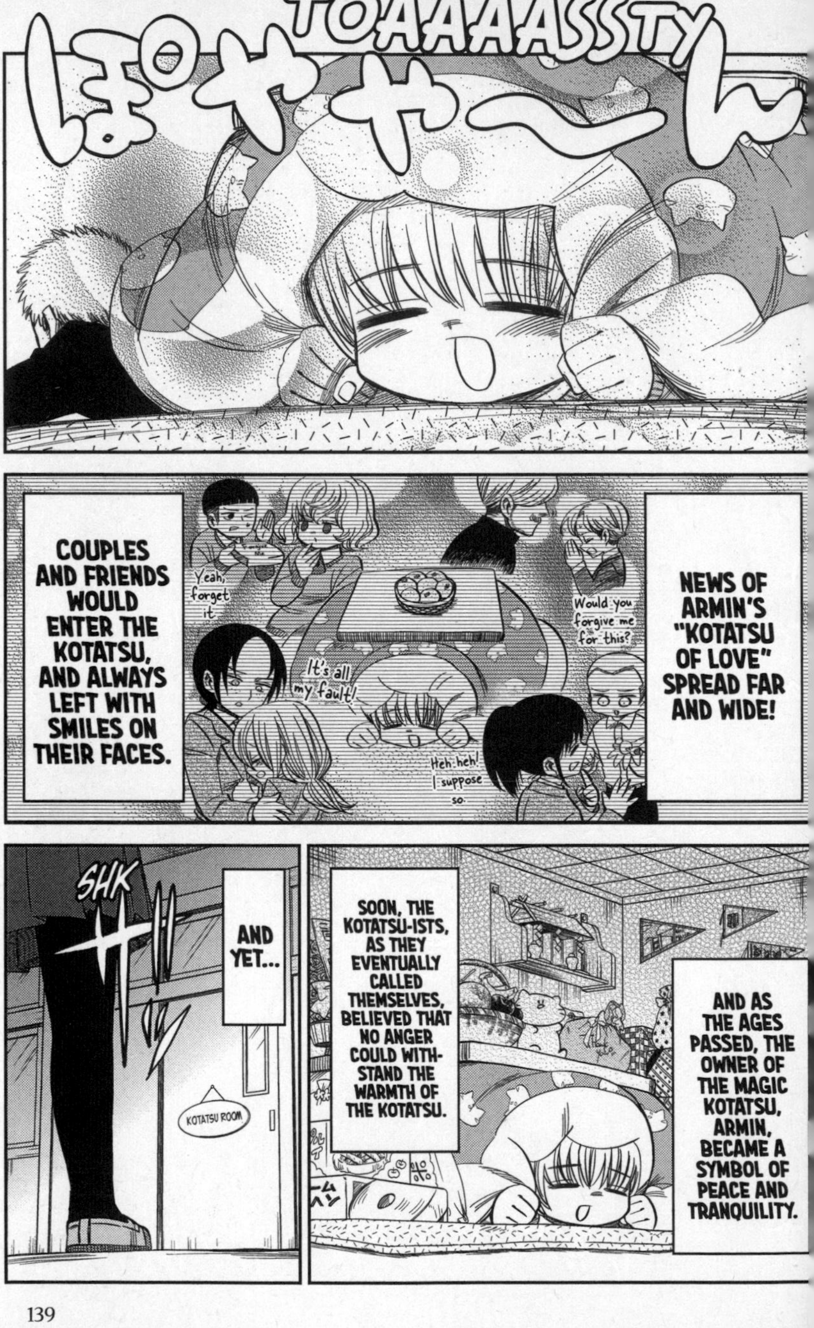
TOAAAASSTY
ほやや〜ん
NEWS OF ARMIN'S "KOTATSU OF LOVE" SPREAD FAR AND WIDE!
Would you forgive me for this?
Yeah, forget it.
It's all my fault!
Heh-heh! I suppose so.
COUPLES AND FRIENDS WOULD ENTER THE KOTATSU, AND ALWAYS LEFT WITH SMILES ON THEIR FACES.
SOON, THE KOTATSU-ISTS, AS THEY EVENTUALLY CALLED THEMSELVES, BELIEVED THAT NO ANGER COULD WITH-STAND THE WARMTH OF THE KOTATSU.
AND AS THE AGES PASSED, THE OWNER OF THE MAGIC KOTATSU, ARMIN, BECAME A SYMBOL OF PEACE AND TRANQUILITY.
AND YET...
SHK
KOTATSU ROOM

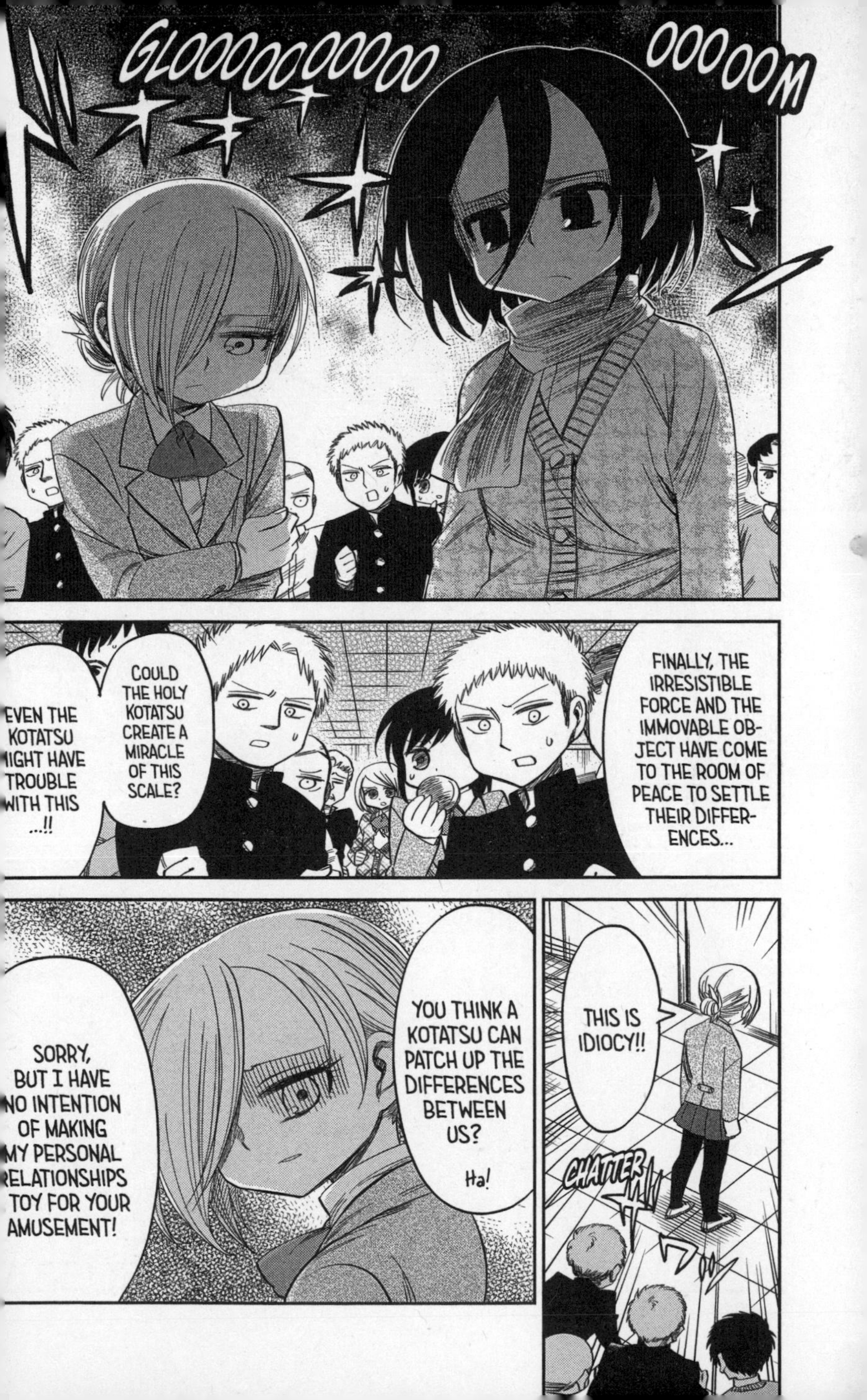
GLOOOOOOOOOO
OOOOOM
FINALLY, THE IRRESISTIBLE FORCE AND THE IMMOVABLE OBJECT HAVE COME TO THE ROOM OF PEACE TO SETTLE THEIR DIFFERENCES...
COULD THE HOLY KOTATSU CREATE A MIRACLE OF THIS SCALE?
EVEN THE KOTATSU IGHT HAVE TROUBLE WITH THIS ...!!
THIS IS IDIOCY!!
CHATTER
YOU THINK A KOTATSU CAN PATCH UP THE DIFFERENCES BETWEEN US?
Ha!
SORRY, BUT I HAVE O INTENTION OF MAKING Y PERSONAL ELATIONSHIPS TOY FOR YOUR AMUSEMENT!

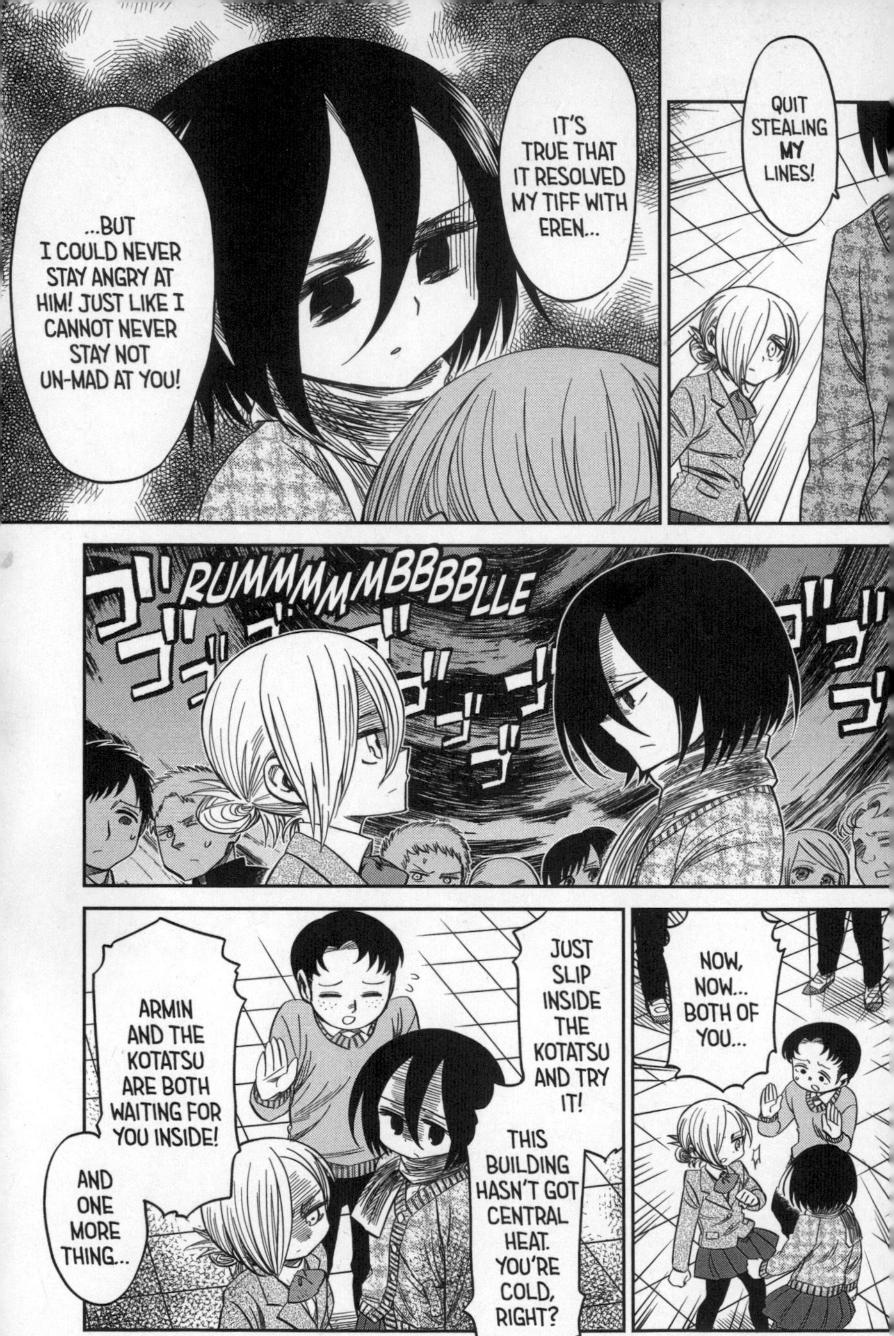
QUIT STEALING MY LINES!
IT'S TRUE THAT IT RESOLVED MY TIFF WITH EREN...
...BUT I COULD NEVER STAY ANGRY AT HIM! JUST LIKE I CANNOT NEVER STAY NOT UN-MAD AT YOU!
RUMMMMMBBBBLLE
NOW, NOW... BOTH OF YOU...
JUST SLIP INSIDE THE KOTATSU AND TRY IT!
ARMIN AND THE KOTATSU ARE BOTH WAITING FOR YOU INSIDE!
THIS BUILDING HASN'T GOT CENTRAL HEAT. YOU'RE COLD, RIGHT?
AND ONE MORE THING...

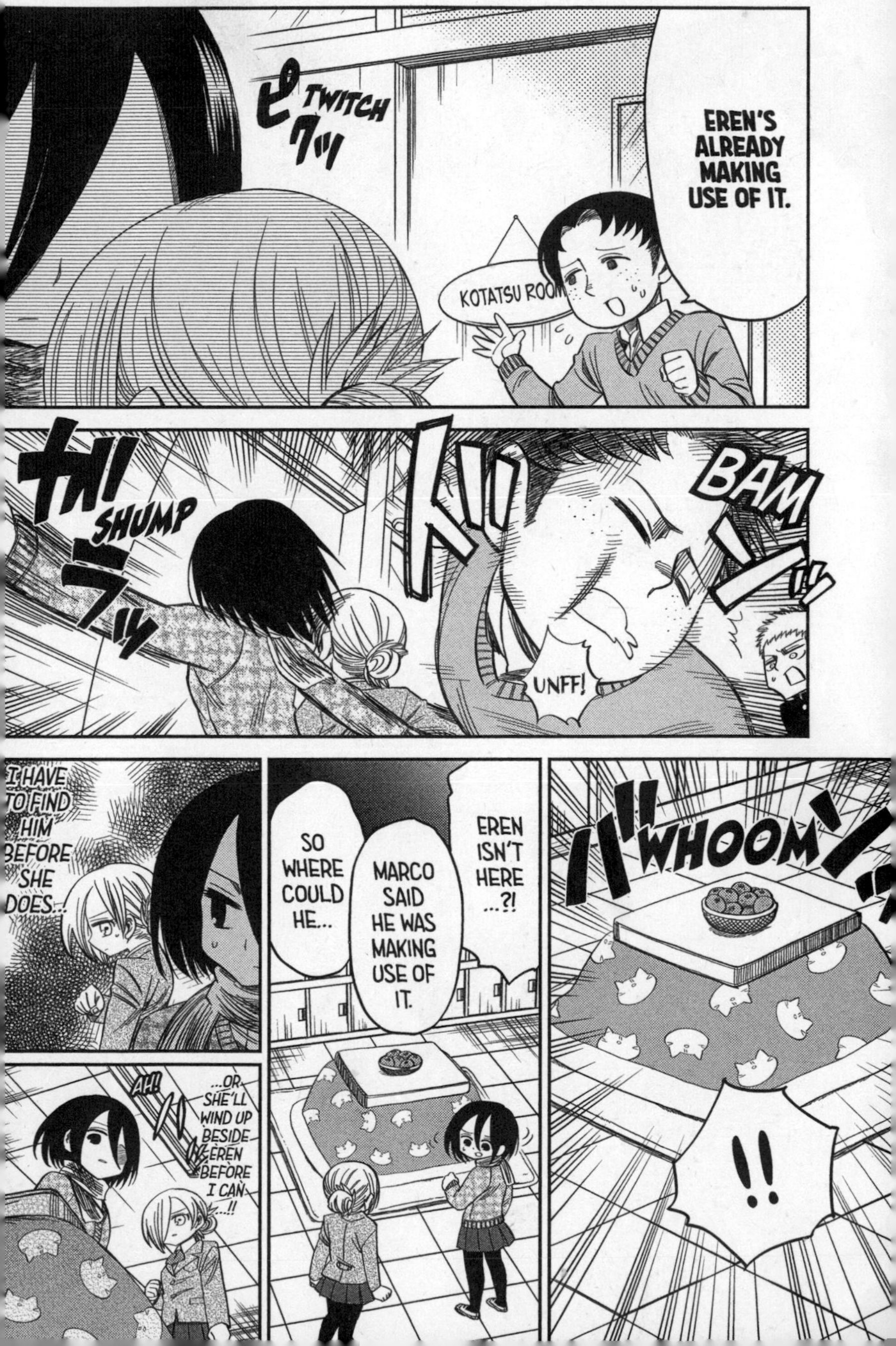
EREN'S ALREADY MAKING USE OF IT.
KOTATSU ROO
TWITCH
BAM
UNFF!
SHUMP
WHOOM
!!
EREN ISN'T HERE ...?!
MARCO SAID HE WAS MAKING USE OF IT.
SO WHERE COULD HE...
I HAVE TO FIND HIM BEFORE SHE DOES...
AH!
...OR SHE'LL WIND UP BESIDE EREN BEFORE I CAN...!!

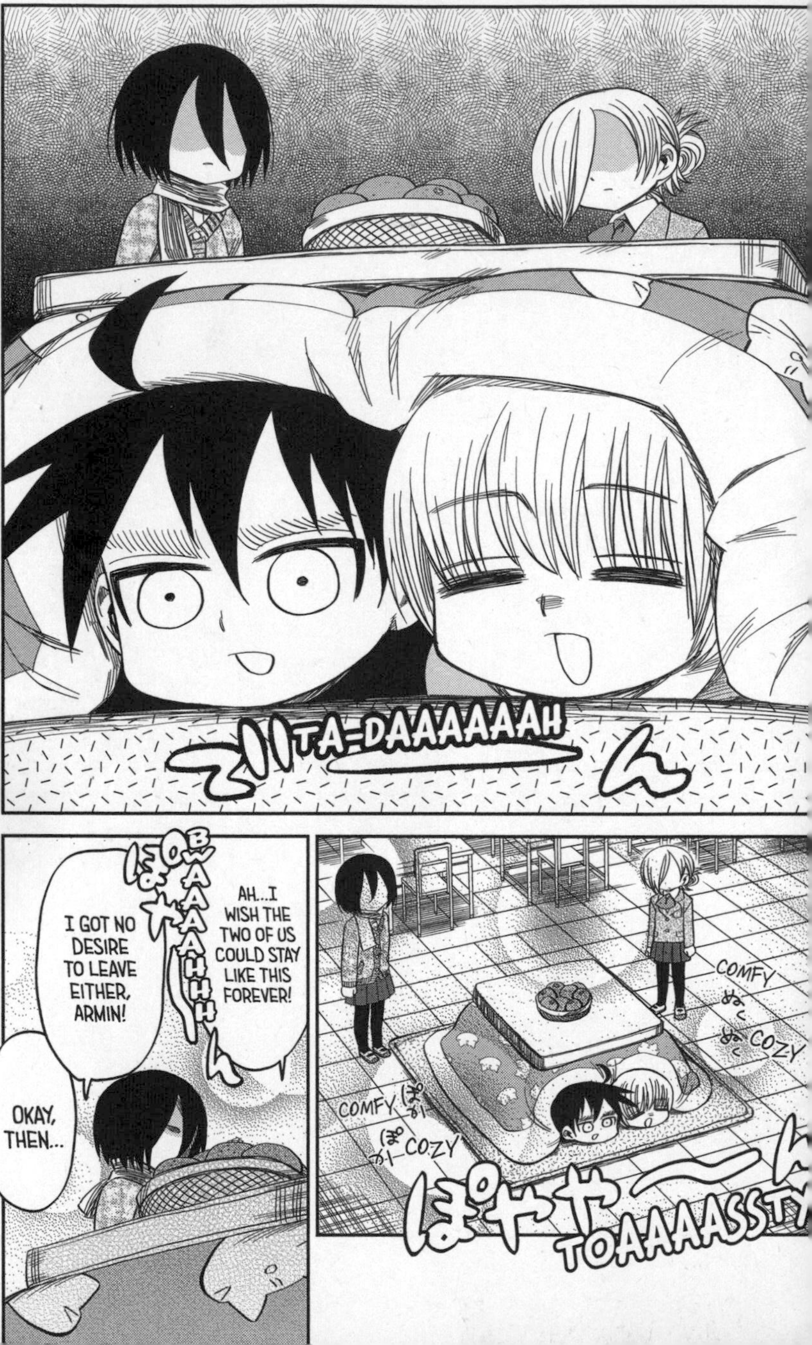
TA-DAAAAAAH
COMFY ぬく ぬく COZY
COMFY ぽか ぽか COZY
TOAAAASSTY
AH...I WISH THE TWO OF US COULD STAY LIKE THIS FOREVER!
BWAAAAAHHHH
I GOT NO DESIRE TO LEAVE EITHER, ARMIN!
OKAY, THEN...

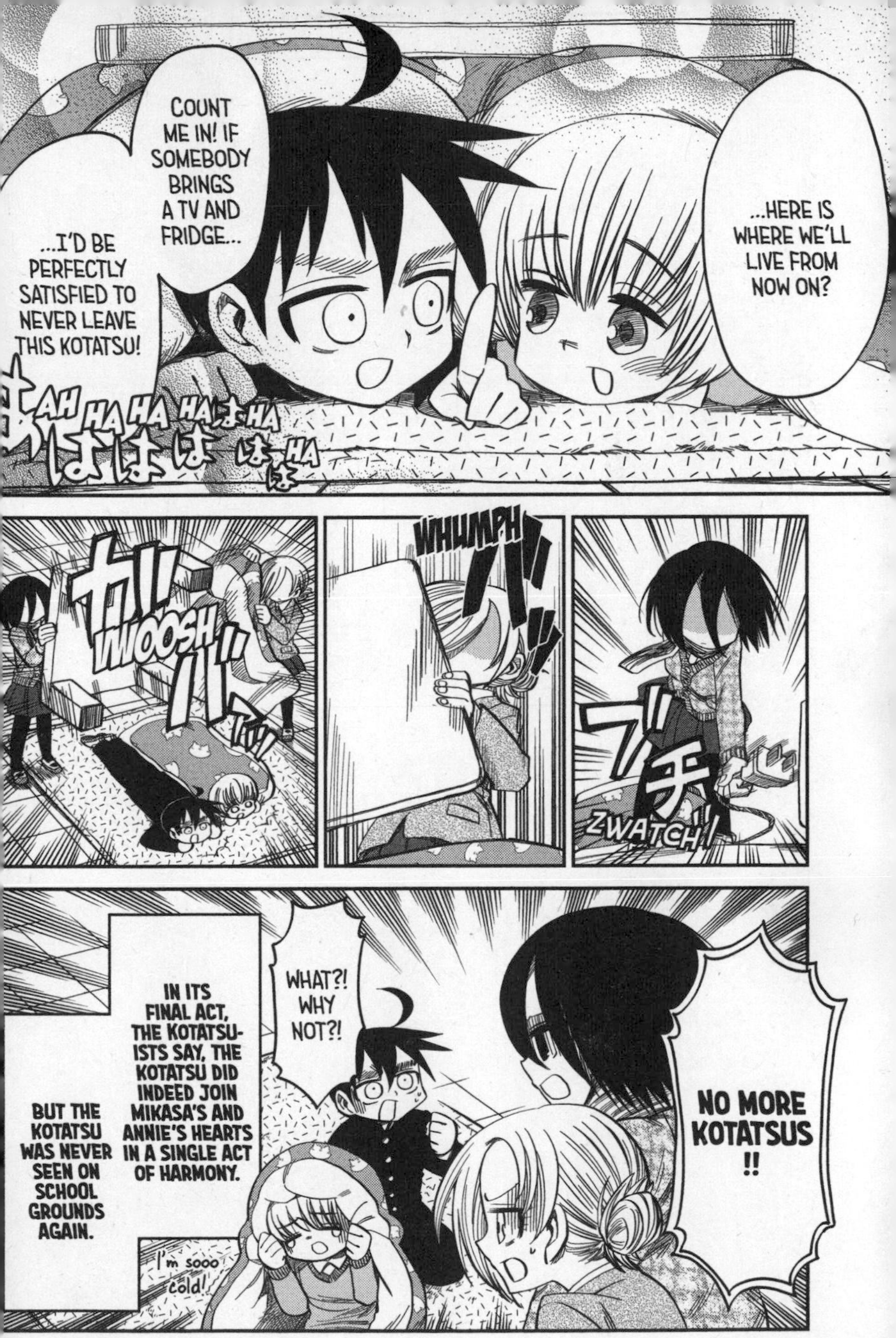
...HERE IS WHERE WE'LL LIVE FROM NOW ON?
COUNT ME IN! IF SOMEBODY BRINGS A TV AND FRIDGE...
...I'D BE PERFECTLY SATISFIED TO NEVER LEAVE THIS KOTATSU!
AH HA HA HA HA HA HA
ブチ
ZWATCH!!
WHUMPH
バッ
バッ
WOOSH!!
NO MORE KOTATSUS!!
WHAT?! WHY NOT?!
I'm sooo cold!
IN ITS FINAL ACT, THE KOTATSU-ISTS SAY, THE KOTATSU DID INDEED JOIN MIKASA'S AND ANNIE'S HEARTS IN A SINGLE ACT OF HARMONY.
BUT THE KOTATSU WAS NEVER SEEN ON SCHOOL GROUNDS AGAIN.

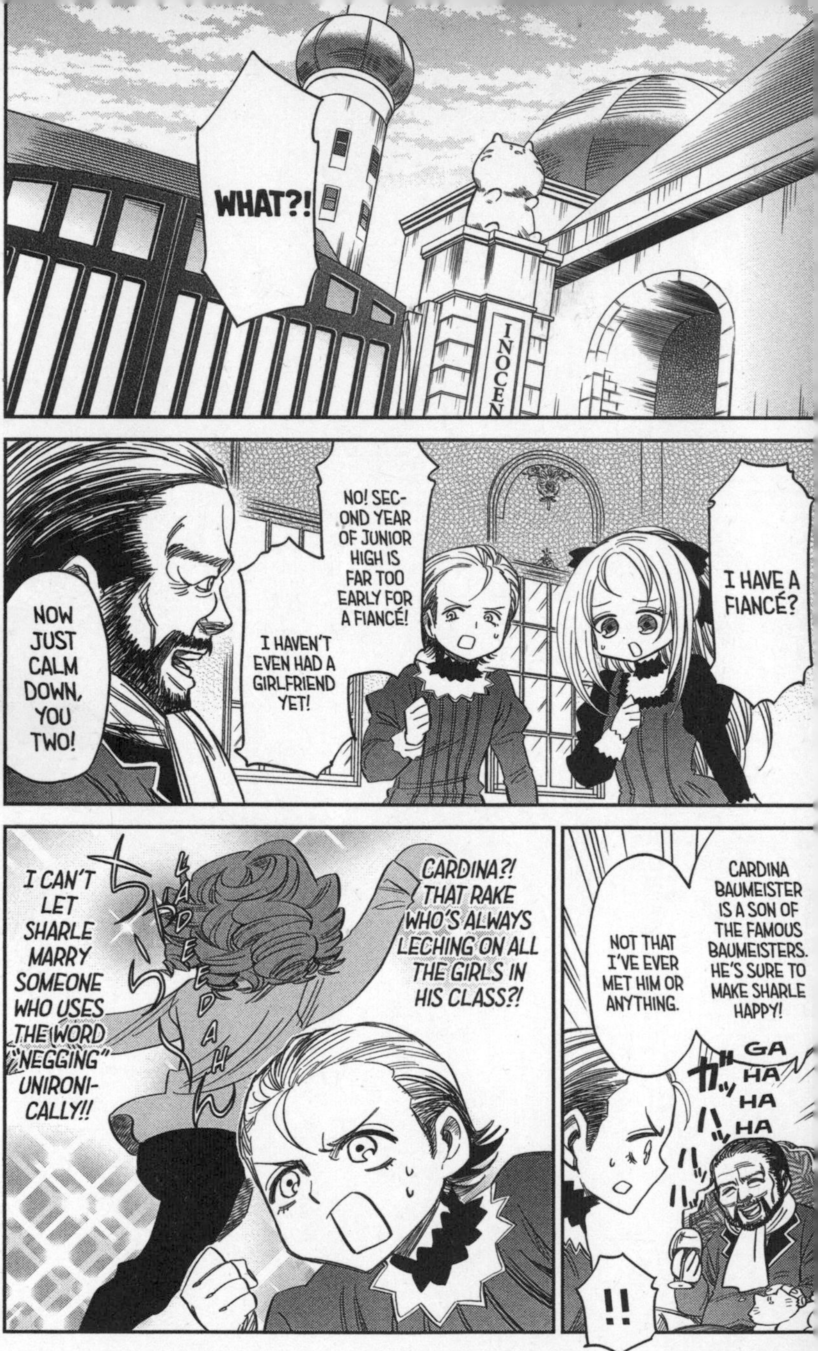
WHAT?!
INOCEN
I HAVE A FIANCÉ?
NO! SEC-OND YEAR OF JUNIOR HIGH IS FAR TOO EARLY FOR A FIANCÉ!
I HAVEN'T EVEN HAD A GIRLFRIEND YET!
NOW JUST CALM DOWN, YOU TWO!
CARDINA BAUMEISTER IS A SON OF THE FAMOUS BAUMEISTERS. HE'S SURE TO MAKE SHARLE HAPPY!
NOT THAT I'VE EVER MET HIM OR ANYTHING.
GA HA HA HA
!!
CARDINA?! THAT RAKE WHO'S ALWAYS LECHING ON ALL THE GIRLS IN HIS CLASS?!
I CAN'T LET SHARLE MARRY SOMEONE WHO USES THE WORD "NEGGING" UNIRONI-CALLY!!

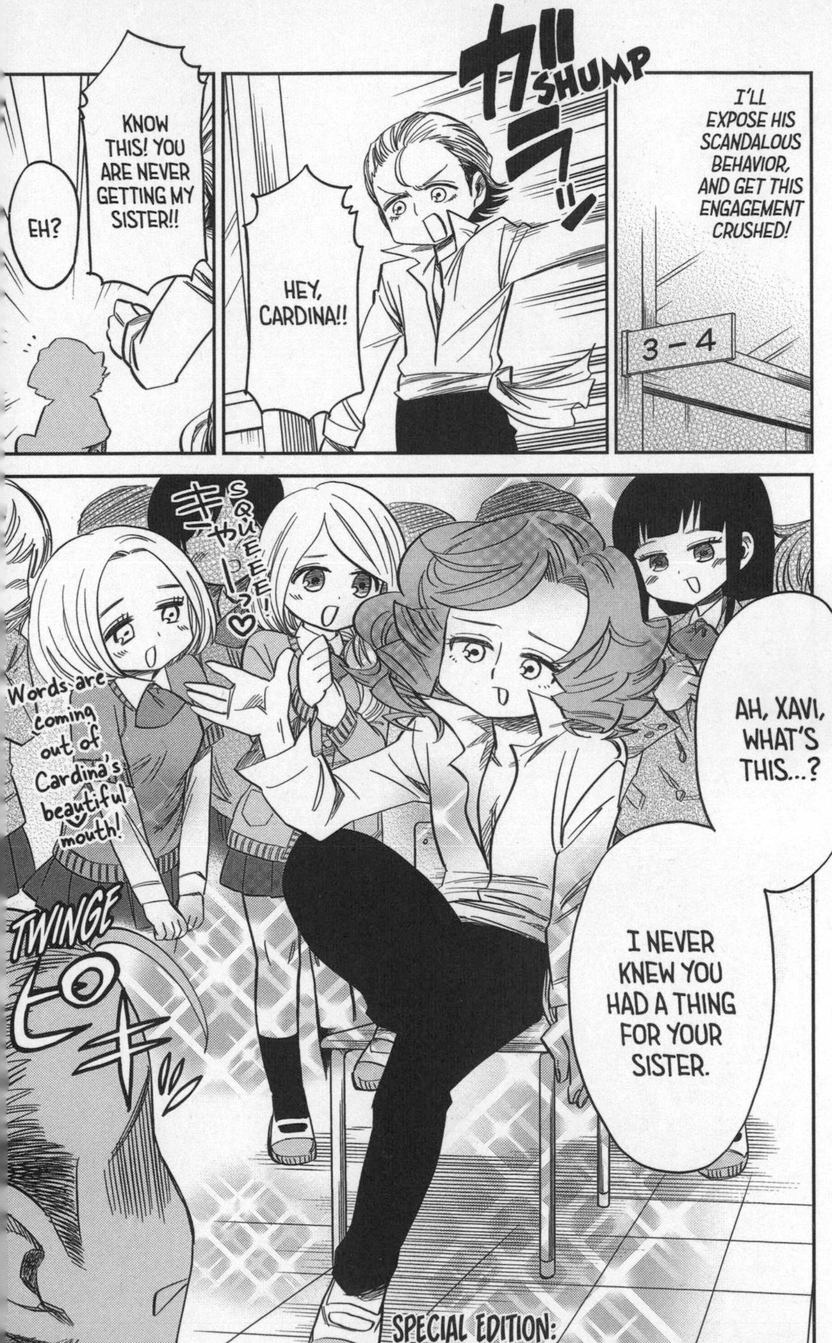
I'LL EXPOSE HIS SCANDALOUS BEHAVIOR, AND GET THIS ENGAGEMENT CRUSHED!
3 – 4
SHUMP
HEY, CARDINA!!
KNOW THIS! YOU ARE NEVER GETTING MY SISTER!!
EH?
SQUEEE!
AH, XAVI, WHAT'S THIS...?
I NEVER KNEW YOU HAD A THING FOR YOUR SISTER.
Words are coming out of Cardina's beautiful mouth!
TWINGE
SPECIAL EDITION:
THE TOWN KNOWS HIM AS A LADIES-MAN

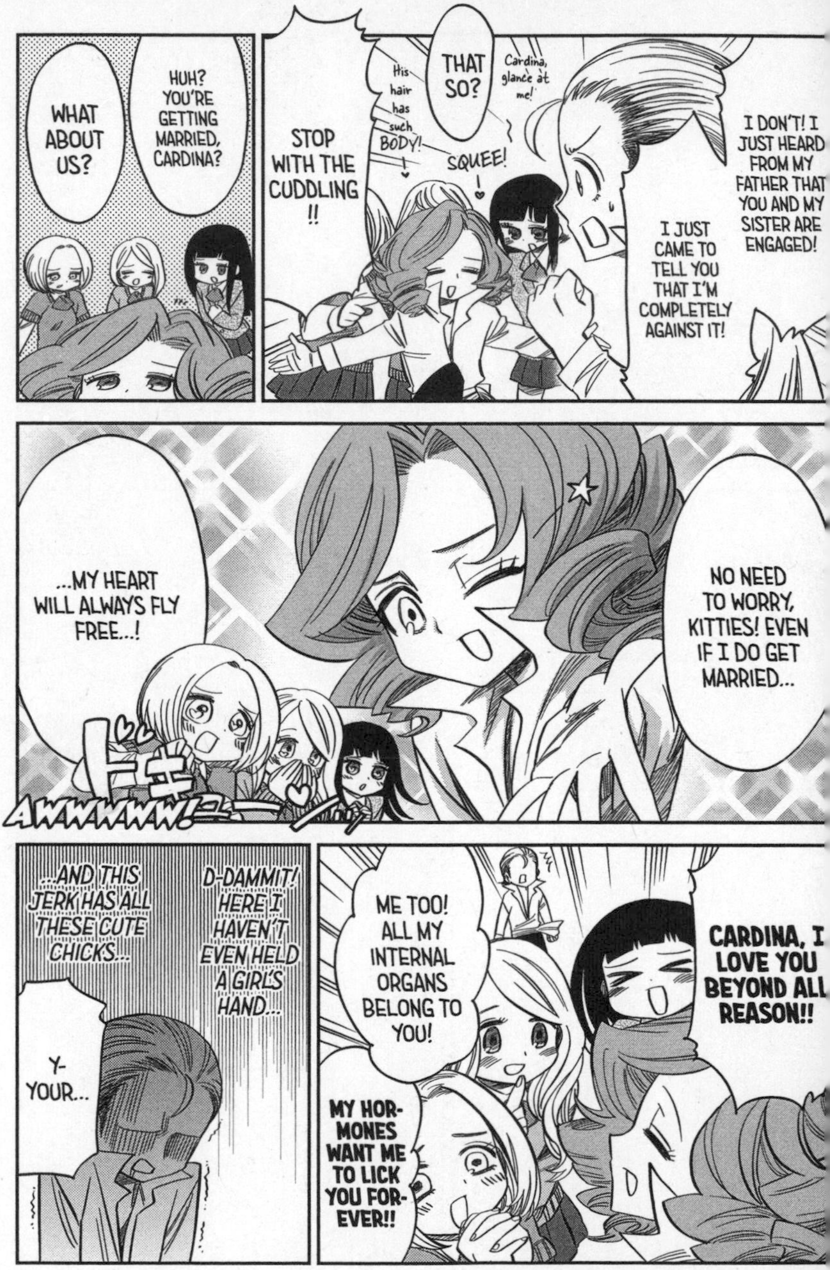
I DON'T! I JUST HEARD FROM MY FATHER THAT YOU AND MY SISTER ARE ENGAGED!
I JUST CAME TO TELL YOU THAT I'M COMPLETELY AGAINST IT!
Cardina, glance at me!
THAT SO?
SQUEE!
His hair has such BODY!
STOP WITH THE CUDDLING!!
HUH? YOU'RE GETTING MARRIED, CARDINA?
WHAT ABOUT US?
NO NEED TO WORRY, KITTIES! EVEN IF I DO GET MARRIED...
...MY HEART WILL ALWAYS FLY FREE...!
AWWWWWW!
CARDINA, I LOVE YOU BEYOND ALL REASON!!
ME TOO! ALL MY INTERNAL ORGANS BELONG TO YOU!
MY HOR-MONES WANT ME TO LICK YOU FOR-EVER!!
D-DAMMIT! HERE I HAVEN'T EVEN HELD A GIRL'S HAND...
...AND THIS JERK HAS ALL THESE CUTE CHICKS...
Y-YOUR...

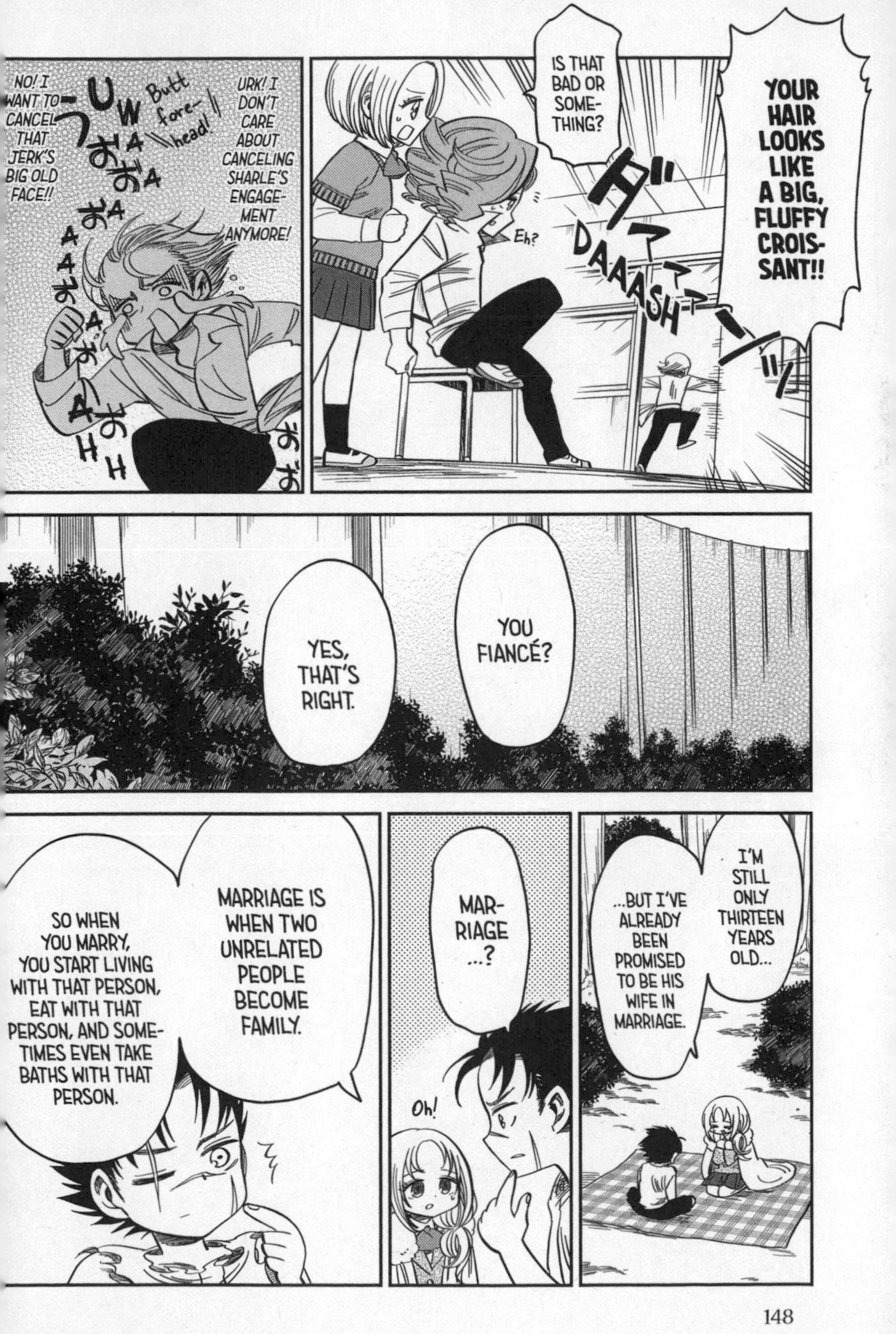
YOUR HAIR LOOKS LIKE A BIG, FLUFFY CROIS-SANT!!
IS THAT BAD OR SOME-THING?
DAAASH
Eh?
URK! I DON'T CARE ABOUT CANCELING SHARLE'S ENGAGE-MENT ANYMORE!
Butt fore-head!
NO! I WANT TO CANCEL THAT JERK'S BIG OLD FACE!!
YOU FIANCÉ?
YES, THAT'S RIGHT.
I'M STILL ONLY THIRTEEN YEARS OLD...
...BUT I'VE ALREADY BEEN PROMISED TO BE HIS WIFE IN MARRIAGE.
MAR-RIAGE ...?
Oh!
MARRIAGE IS WHEN TWO UNRELATED PEOPLE BECOME FAMILY.
SO WHEN YOU MARRY, YOU START LIVING WITH THAT PERSON, EAT WITH THAT PERSON, AND SOME-TIMES EVEN TAKE BATHS WITH THAT PERSON.

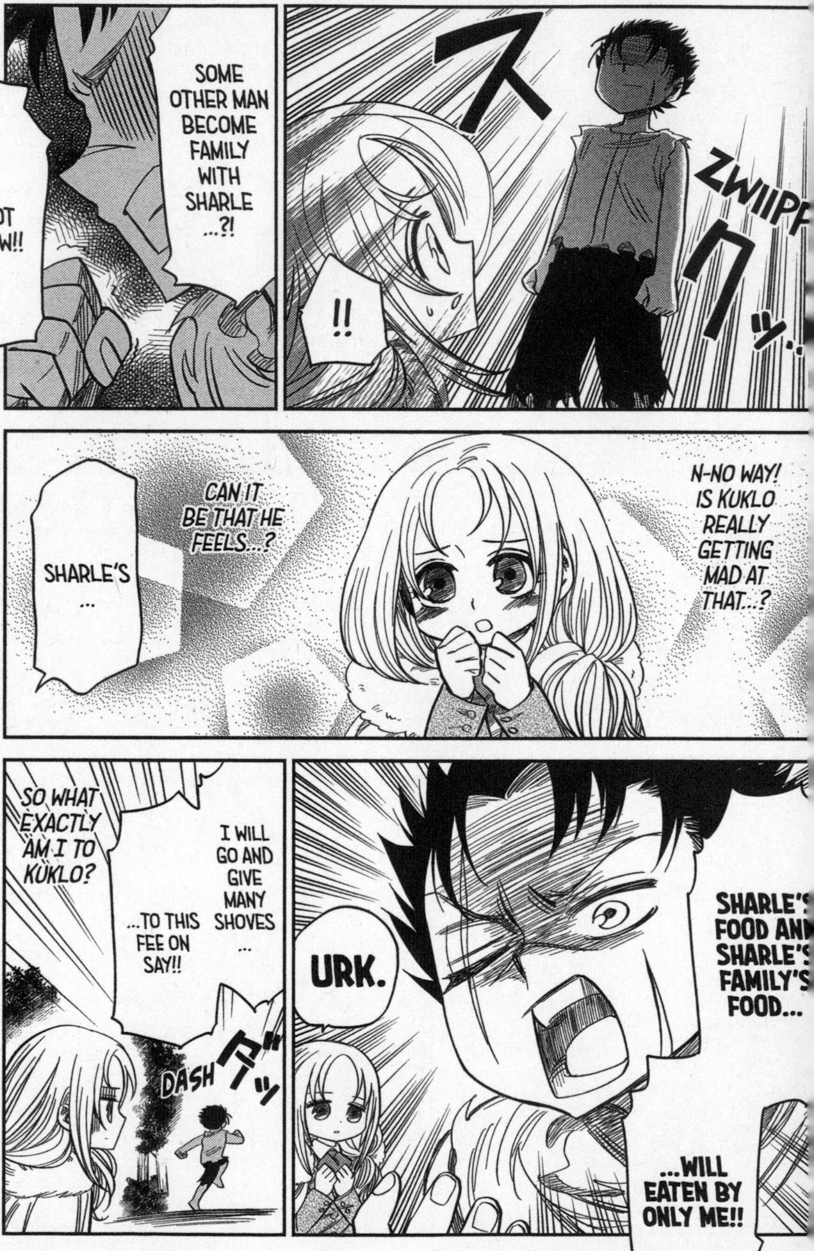
ZWIIPF
!!
SOME OTHER MAN BECOME FAMILY WITH SHARLE ...?!
I NOT ALLOW!!
N-NO WAY! IS KUKLO REALLY GETTING MAD AT THAT...?
CAN IT BE THAT HE FEELS...?
SHARLE'S ...
SHARLE'S FOOD AN SHARLE'S FAMILY'S FOOD...
URK.
...WILL EATEN BY ONLY ME!!
I WILL GO AND GIVE MANY SHOVES ...
...TO THIS FEE ON SAY!!
DASH
SO WHAT EXACTLY AM I TO KUKLO?

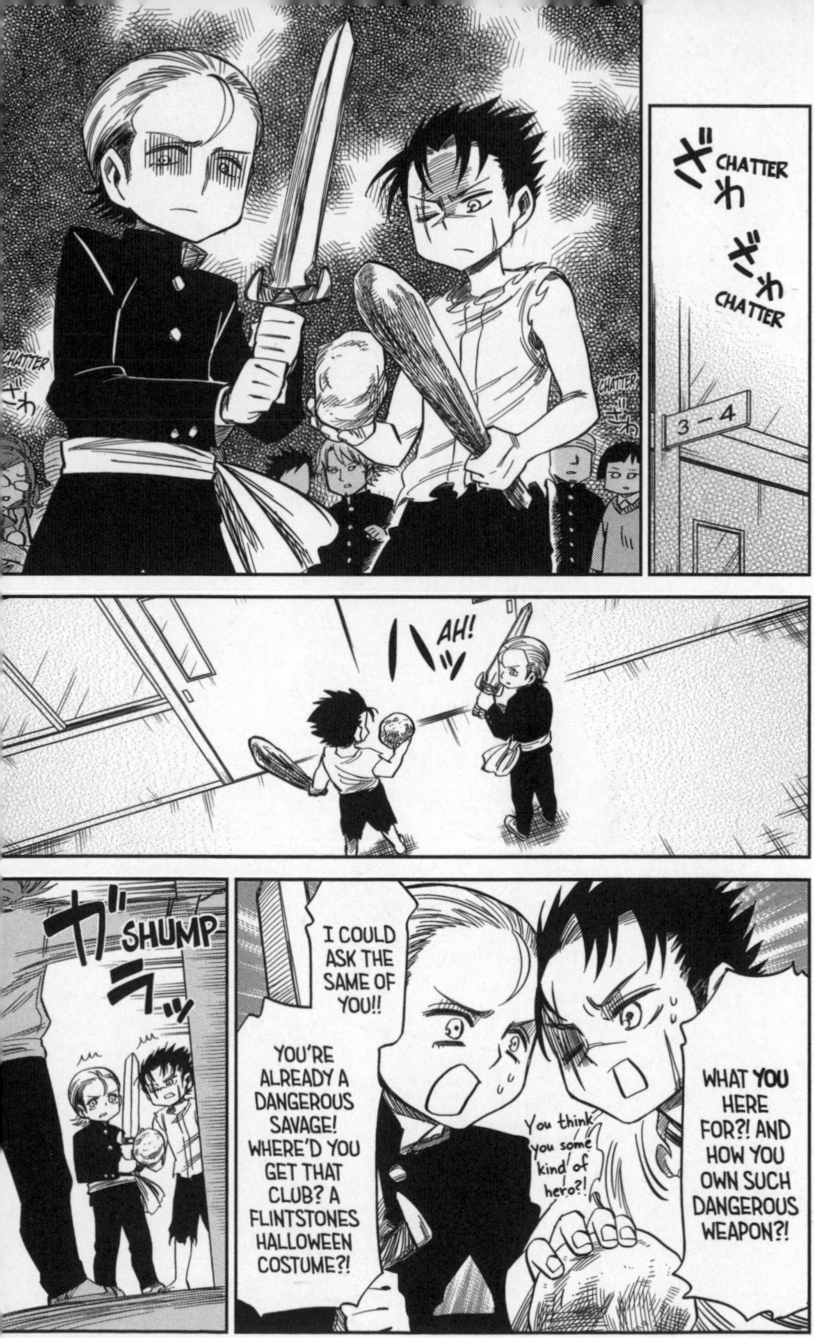
ざわ CHATTER
ざわ CHATTER
3-4
CHATTER ざわ
CHATTER ざわ
ハッ AH!
WHAT YOU HERE FOR?! AND HOW YOU OWN SUCH DANGEROUS WEAPON?!
You think you some kind of hero?!
I COULD ASK THE SAME OF YOU!!
YOU'RE ALREADY A DANGEROUS SAVAGE! WHERE'D YOU GET THAT CLUB? A FLINTSTONES HALLOWEEN COSTUME?!
ガラッ SHUMP

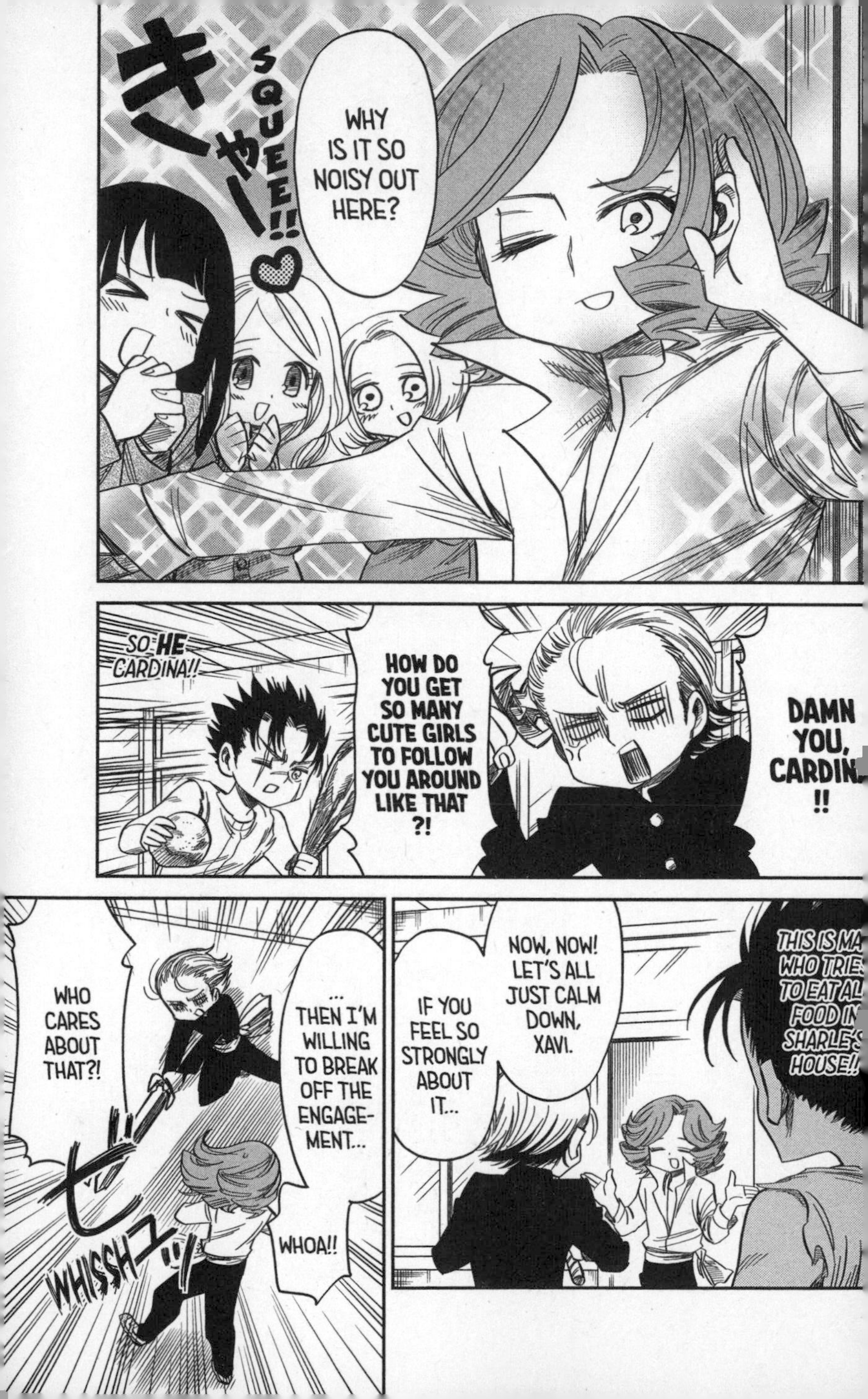
WHY IS IT SO NOISY OUT HERE?
キャー
SQUEE!!
DAMN YOU, CARDIN
!!
HOW DO YOU GET SO MANY CUTE GIRLS TO FOLLOW YOU AROUND LIKE THAT ?!
SO HE CARDINA!!
THIS IS MA WHO TRIE TO EAT AL FOOD IN SHARLE'S HOUSE!!
NOW, NOW! LET'S ALL JUST CALM DOWN, XAVI.
IF YOU FEEL SO STRONGLY ABOUT IT...
...THEN I'M WILLING TO BREAK OFF THE ENGAGE-MENT...
WHO CARES ABOUT THAT?!
WHOA!!
ヒュ
WHISSH

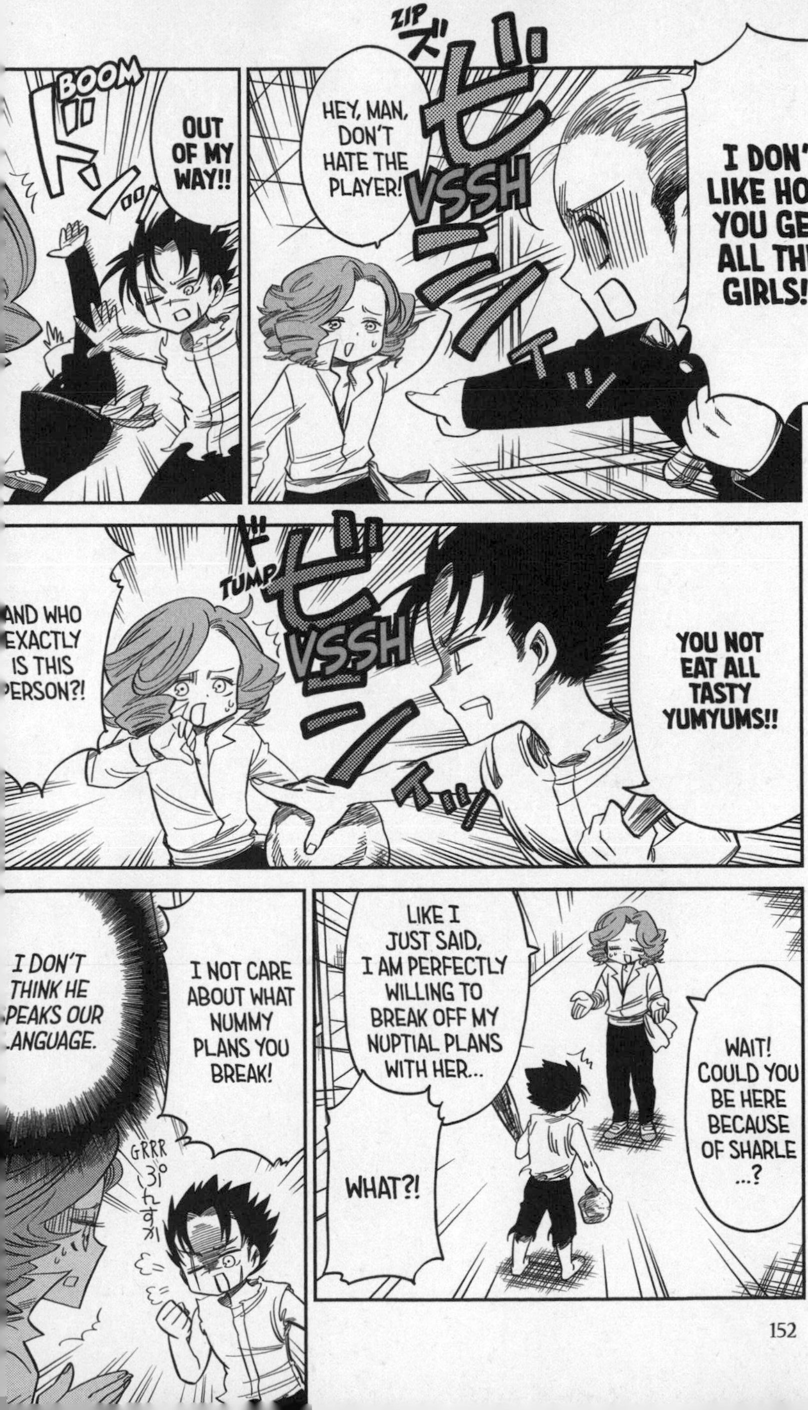

I DON'T LIKE HOW YOU GET ALL THE GIRLS!!
ZIP
VSSH
HEY, MAN, DON'T HATE THE PLAYER!
BOOM
OUT OF MY WAY!!
YOU NOT EAT ALL TASTY YUMYUMS!!
VSSH
TUMP
AND WHO EXACTLY IS THIS ERSON?!
WAIT! COULD YOU BE HERE BECAUSE OF SHARLE ...?
LIKE I JUST SAID, I AM PERFECTLY WILLING TO BREAK OFF MY NUPTIAL PLANS WITH HER...
WHAT?!
I NOT CARE ABOUT WHAT NUMMY PLANS YOU BREAK!
I DON'T THINK HE PEAKS OUR ANGUAGE.
GRRR

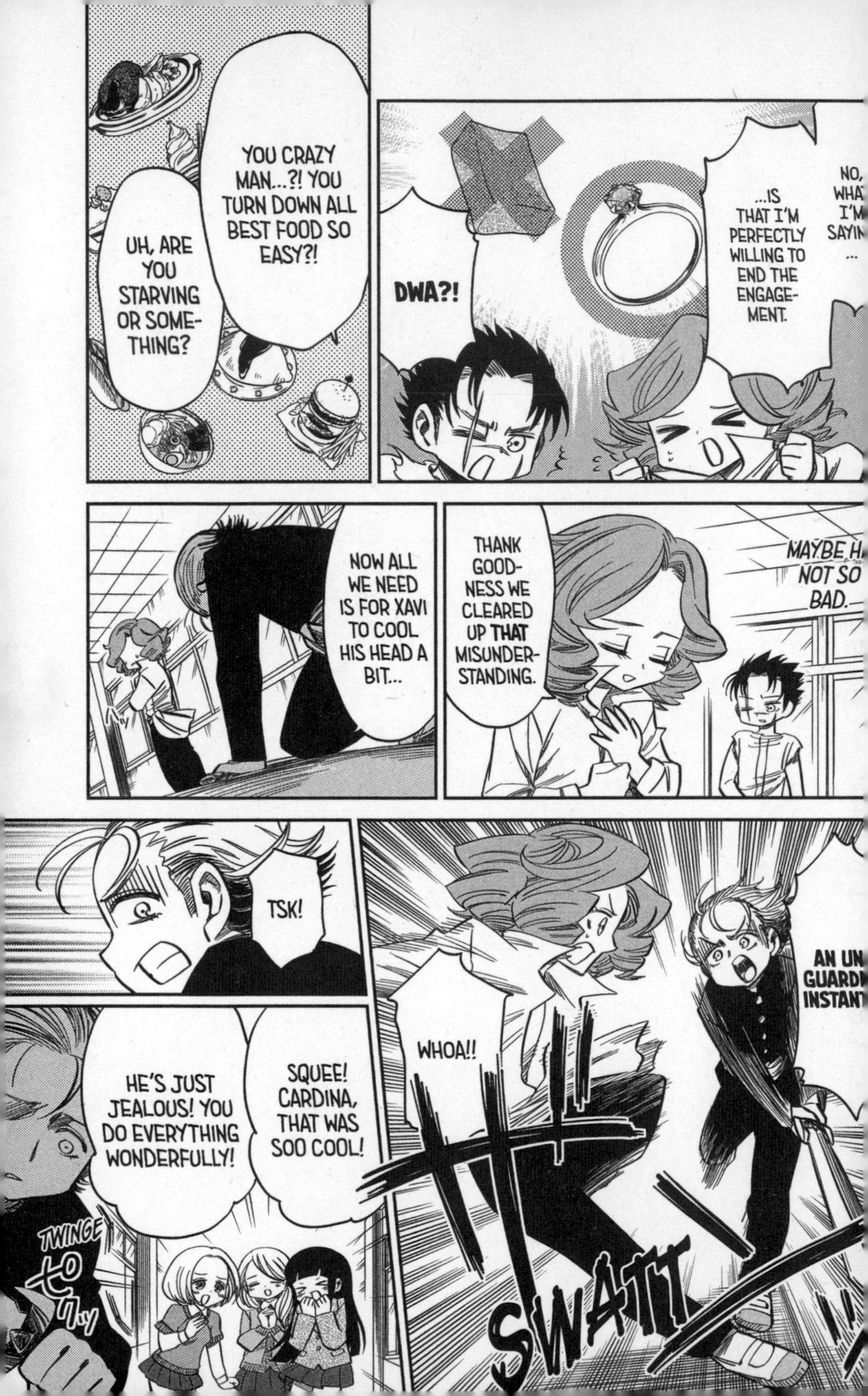
NO, WHAT I'M SAYIN...
...IS THAT I'M PERFECTLY WILLING TO END THE ENGAGEMENT.
DWA?!
YOU CRAZY MAN...?! YOU TURN DOWN ALL BEST FOOD SO EASY?!
UH, ARE YOU STARVING OR SOMETHING?
MAYBE H NOT SO BAD.
THANK GOODNESS WE CLEARED UP THAT MISUNDERSTANDING.
NOW ALL WE NEED IS FOR XAVI TO COOL HIS HEAD A BIT...
AN UN GUARD INSTANT
WHOA!!
SWATT
TSK!
SQUEE! CARDINA, THAT WAS SOO COOL!
HE'S JUST JEALOUS! YOU DO EVERYTHING WONDERFULLY!
TWINGE

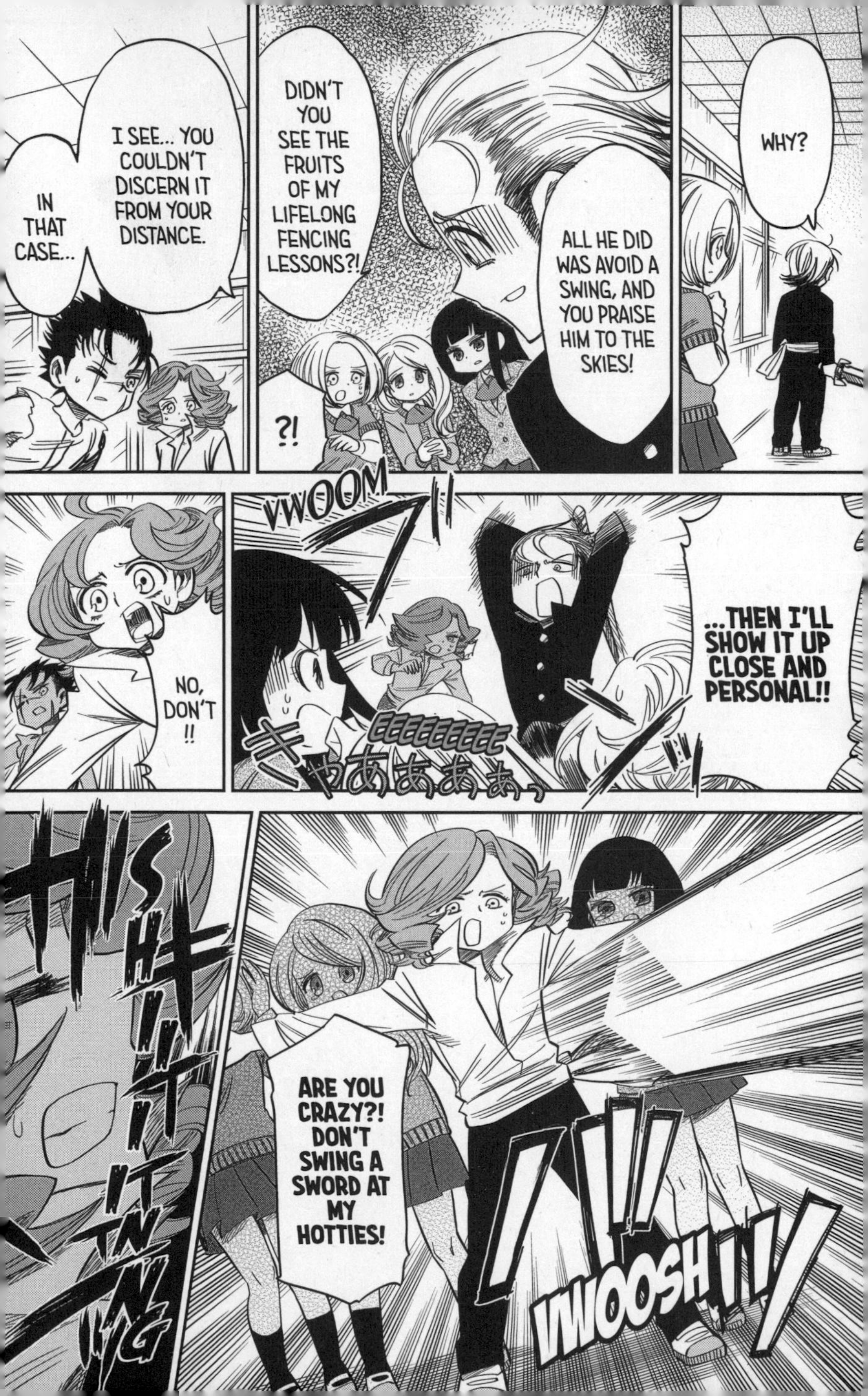
WHY?
ALL HE DID WAS AVOID A SWING, AND YOU PRAISE HIM TO THE SKIES!
DIDN'T YOU SEE THE FRUITS OF MY LIFELONG FENCING LESSONS?!
?!
I SEE... YOU COULDN'T DISCERN IT FROM YOUR DISTANCE.
IN THAT CASE...
...THEN I'LL SHOW IT UP CLOSE AND PERSONAL!!
VWOOM
EEEEEEEEE
きゃあああああっ
NO, DON'T!!
ARE YOU CRAZY?! DON'T SWING A SWORD AT MY HOTTIES!
VWOOSH

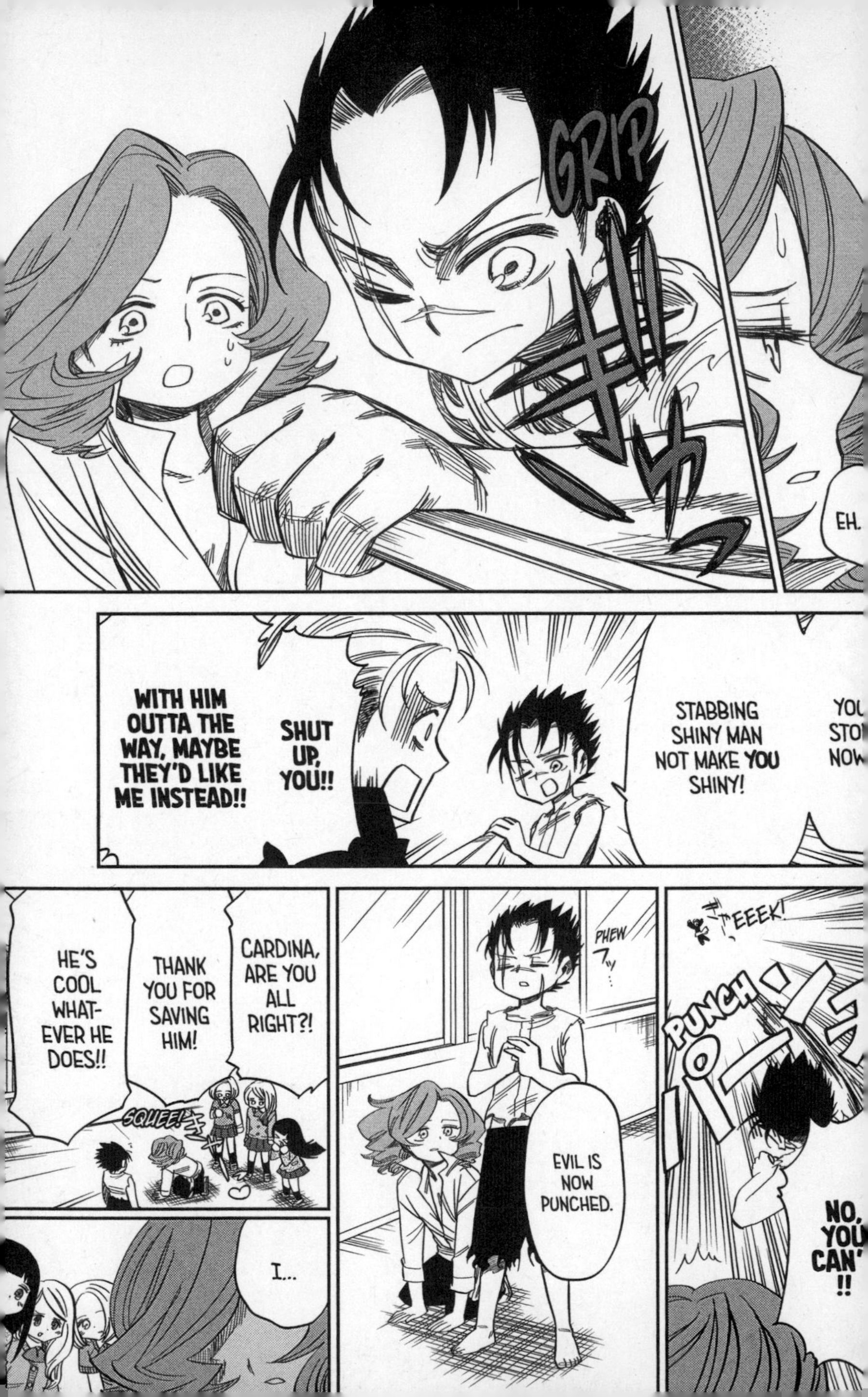
EH.
GRIP
STABBING SHINY MAN NOT MAKE YOU SHINY!
SHUT UP, YOU!!
WITH HIM OUTTA THE WAY, MAYBE THEY'D LIKE ME INSTEAD!!
EEEK!
PUNCH
NO, YOU CAN'
!!
PHEW
EVIL IS NOW PUNCHED.
CARDINA, ARE YOU ALL RIGHT?!
THANK YOU FOR SAVING HIM!
HE'S COOL WHAT-EVER HE DOES!!
SQUEE!
I...

Read about the real Sharle, Kuklo, and all the characters in *Attack on Titan: Before the Fall*, available from Kodansha Comics!

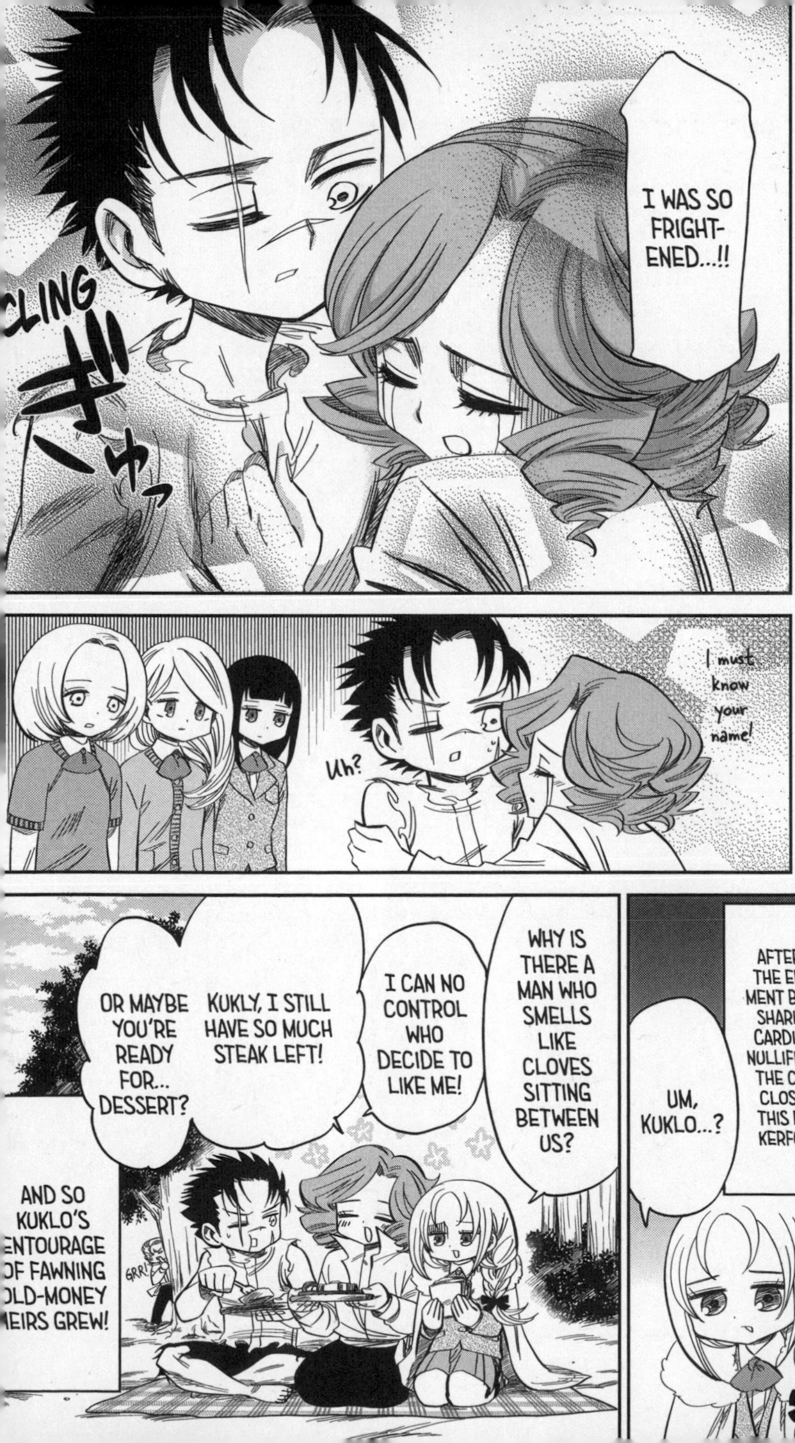
I WAS SO FRIGHT-ENED...!!
CLING
ぎゅっ
I must know your name!
Uh?
AFTER THAT, THE ENGAGE-MENT BETWEEN SHARLE AND CARDINA WAS NULLIFIED, AND THE CURTAIN CLOSED ON THIS ENTIRE KERFUFFLE.
UM, KUKLO...?
WHY IS THERE A MAN WHO SMELLS LIKE CLOVES SITTING BETWEEN US?
I CAN NO CONTROL WHO DECIDE TO LIKE ME!
KUKLY, I STILL HAVE SO MUCH STEAK LEFT!
OR MAYBE YOU'RE READY FOR... DESSERT?
GRR!
AND SO KUKLO'S ENTOURAGE OF FAWNING OLD-MONEY HEIRS GREW!

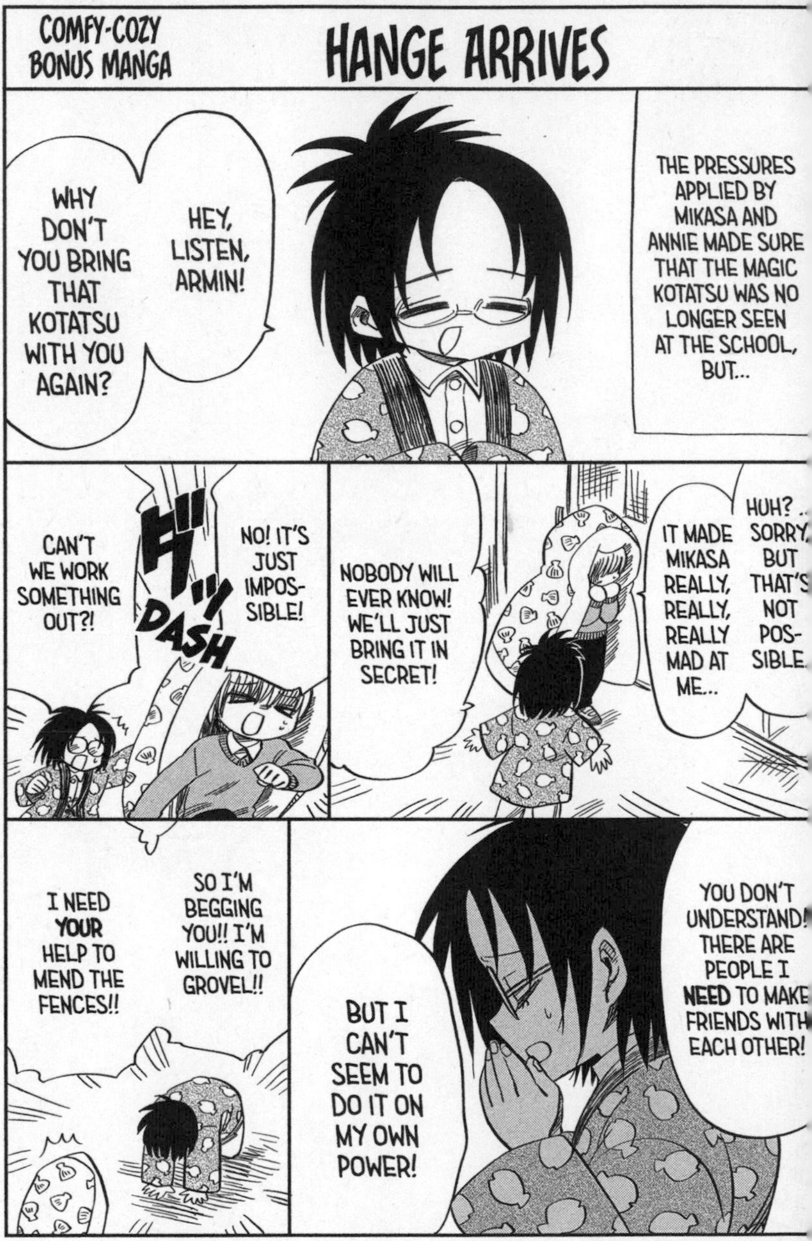
COMFY-COZY BONUS MANGA
HANGE ARRIVES
THE PRESSURES APPLIED BY MIKASA AND ANNIE MADE SURE THAT THE MAGIC KOTATSU WAS NO LONGER SEEN AT THE SCHOOL, BUT...
HEY, LISTEN, ARMIN!
WHY DON'T YOU BRING THAT KOTATSU WITH YOU AGAIN?
HUH? .. SORRY, BUT THAT'S NOT POS-SIBLE.
IT MADE MIKASA REALLY, REALLY, REALLY MAD AT ME...
NOBODY WILL EVER KNOW! WE'LL JUST BRING IT IN SECRET!
NO! IT'S JUST IMPOS-SIBLE!
DASH
CAN'T WE WORK SOMETHING OUT?!
YOU DON'T UNDERSTAND! THERE ARE PEOPLE I NEED TO MAKE FRIENDS WITH EACH OTHER!
BUT I CAN'T SEEM TO DO IT ON MY OWN POWER!
SO I'M BEGGING YOU!! I'M WILLING TO GROVEL!!
I NEED YOUR HELP TO MEND THE FENCES!!

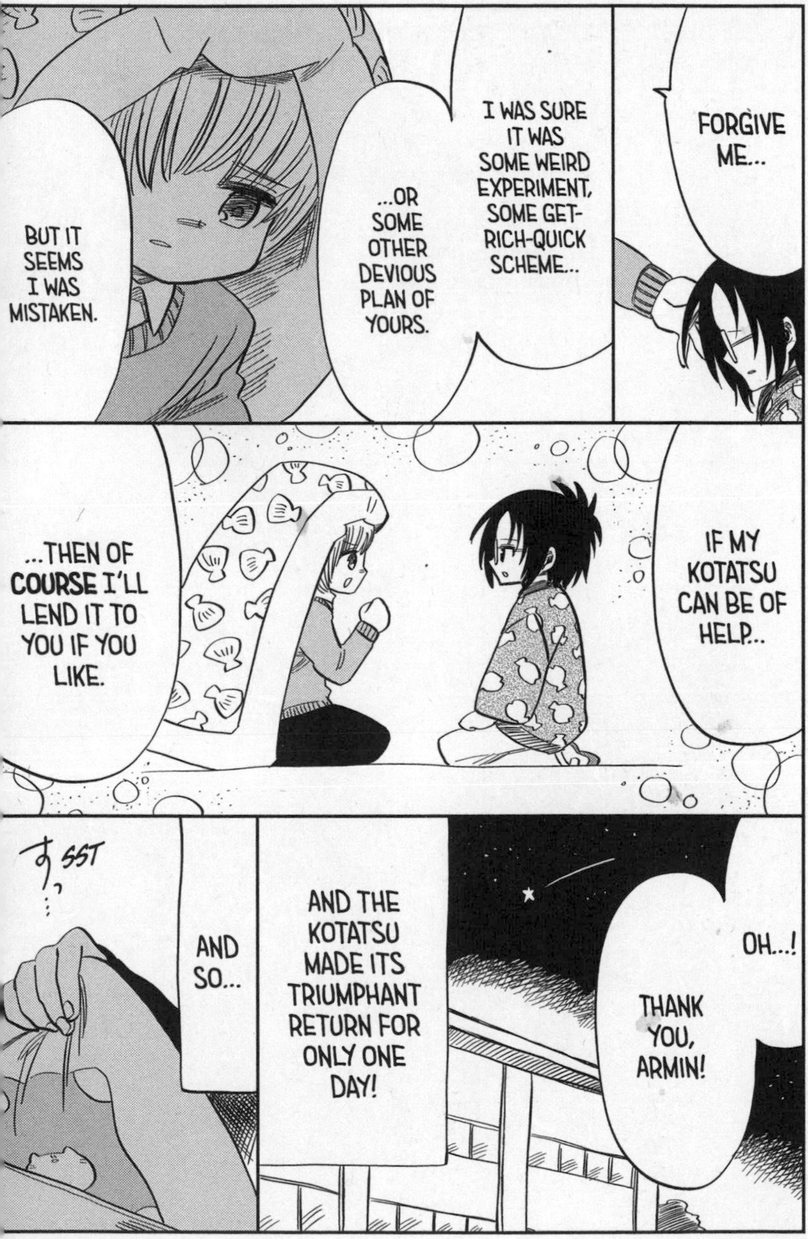
FORGIVE ME...
I WAS SURE IT WAS SOME WEIRD EXPERIMENT, SOME GET-RICH-QUICK SCHEME...
...OR SOME OTHER DEVIOUS PLAN OF YOURS.
BUT IT SEEMS I WAS MISTAKEN.
IF MY KOTATSU CAN BE OF HELP...
...THEN OF COURSE I'LL LEND IT TO YOU IF YOU LIKE.
OH...!
THANK YOU, ARMIN!
AND SO...
AND THE KOTATSU MADE ITS TRIUMPHANT RETURN FOR ONLY ONE DAY!
す SST

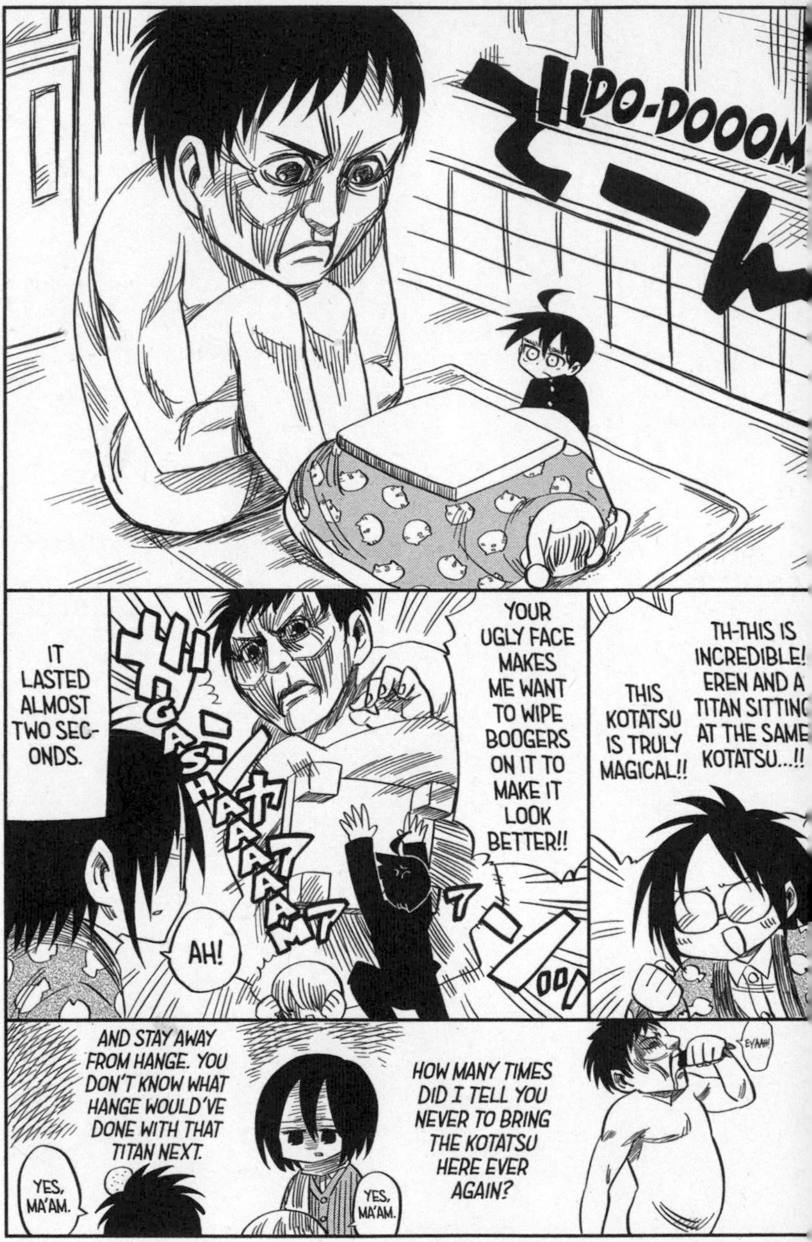
DO-DOOOM
TH-THIS IS INCREDIBLE! EREN AND A TITAN SITTIN AT THE SAME KOTATSU...!!
THIS KOTATSU IS TRULY MAGICAL!!
YOUR UGLY FACE MAKES ME WANT TO WIPE BOOGERS ON IT TO MAKE IT LOOK BETTER!!
GASHAAAAAAM
AH!
IT LASTED ALMOST TWO SECONDS.
EYAAH!
HOW MANY TIMES DID I TELL YOU NEVER TO BRING THE KOTATSU HERE EVER AGAIN?
YES, MA'AM.
AND STAY AWAY FROM HANGE. YOU DON'T KNOW WHAT HANGE WOULD'VE DONE WITH THAT TITAN NEXT.
YES, MA'AM.

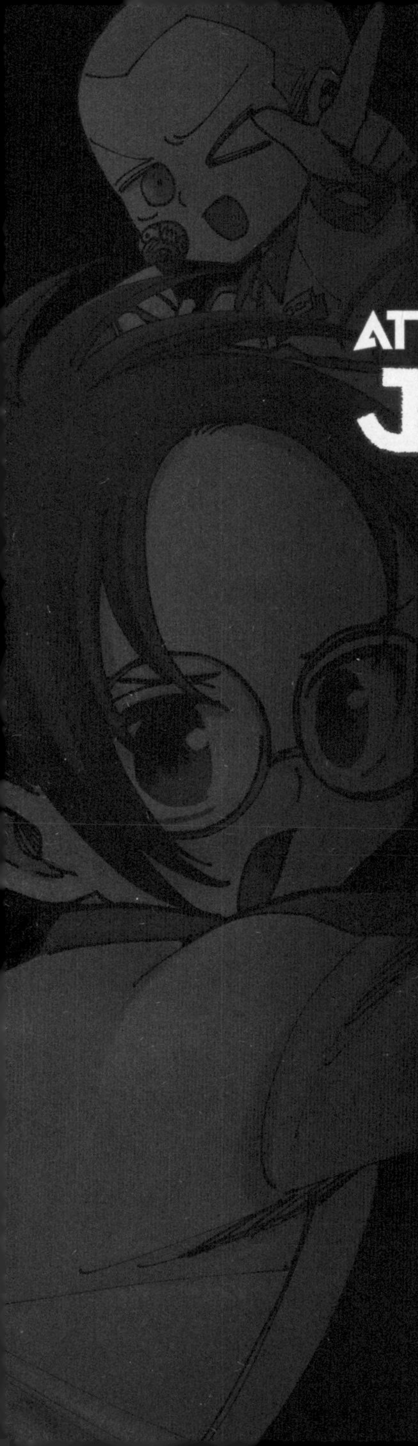

ATTACK on TITAN JUNIOR HIGH

SAKI NAKAGAWA

Based on "Attack on Titan" by
HAJIME ISAYAMA

50 YEN OFF AT THE REGISTER
30 YEN OFF AT THE REGISTER
10 YEN OFF AT THE REGISTER
HALF OFF AT THE REGISTER

Contents

SATURDAY, FEB 14

DAY DUTY: HANGE

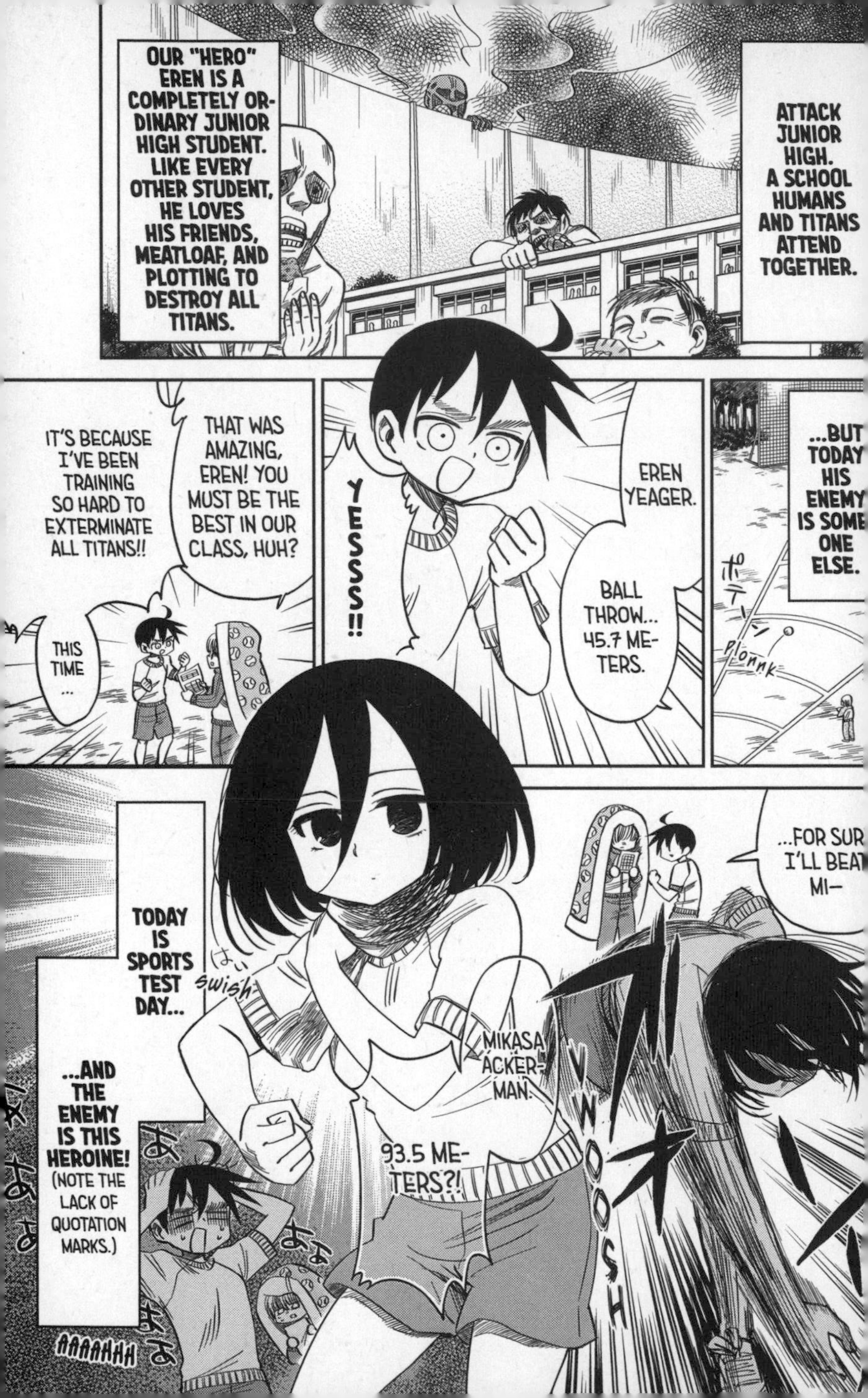
ATTACK JUNIOR HIGH. A SCHOOL HUMANS AND TITANS ATTEND TOGETHER.
OUR "HERO" EREN IS A COMPLETELY ORDINARY JUNIOR HIGH STUDENT. LIKE EVERY OTHER STUDENT, HE LOVES HIS FRIENDS, MEATLOAF, AND PLOTTING TO DESTROY ALL TITANS.
...BUT TODAY HIS ENEMY IS SOMEONE ELSE.
Plonnk
EREN YEAGER.
BALL THROW... 45.7 METERS.
YESSS!!
THAT WAS AMAZING, EREN! YOU MUST BE THE BEST IN OUR CLASS, HUH?
IT'S BECAUSE I'VE BEEN TRAINING SO HARD TO EXTERMINATE ALL TITANS!!
THIS TIME ...
...FOR SUR I'LL BEAT MI–
VWOOOSH
MIKASA ACKERMAN.
swish
TODAY IS SPORTS TEST DAY...
93.5 METERS?!
...AND THE ENEMY IS THIS HEROINE! (NOTE THE LACK OF QUOTATION MARKS.)
AAAAHHH

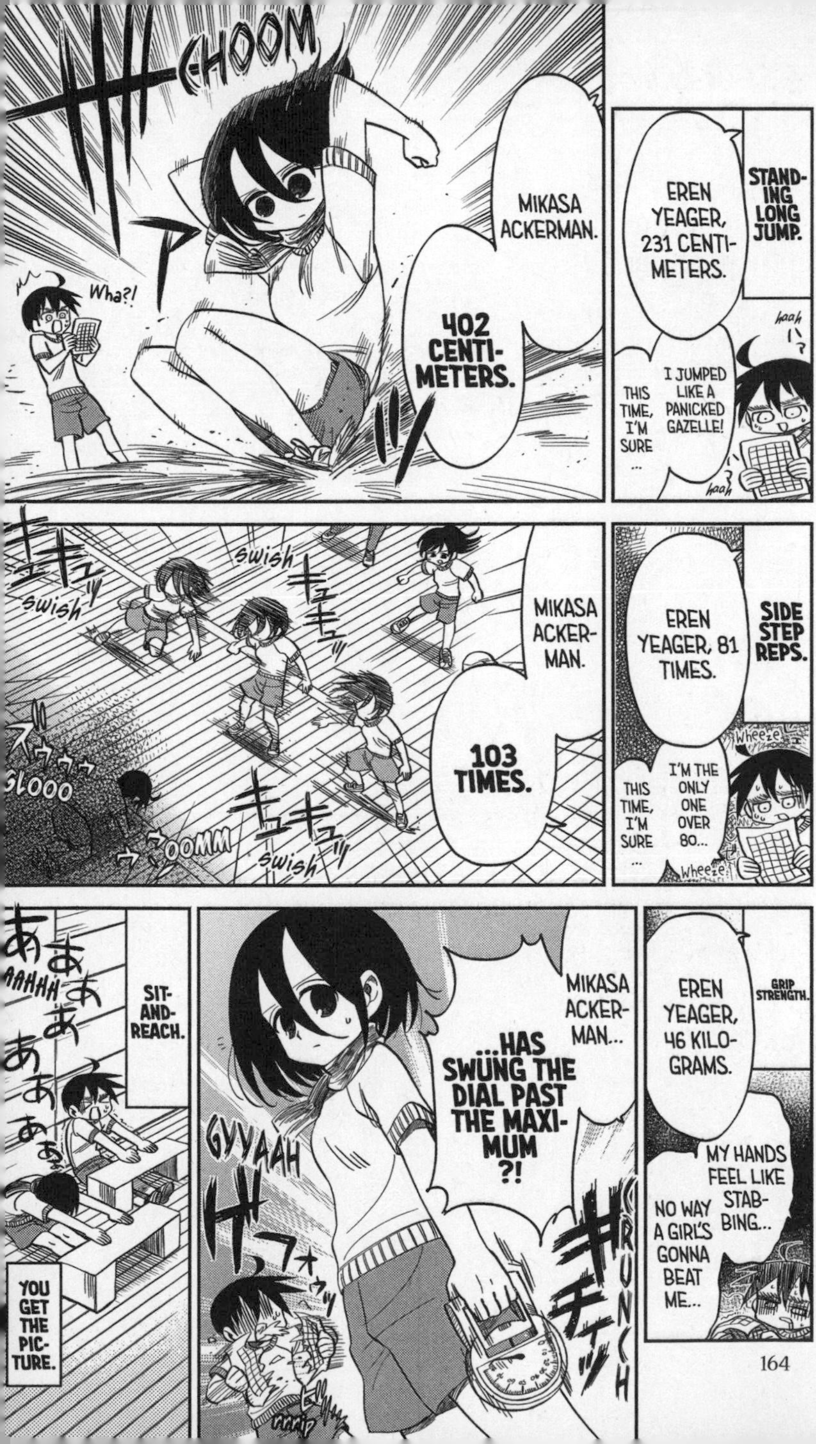
STANDING LONG JUMP.
EREN YEAGER, 231 CENTIMETERS.
I JUMPED LIKE A PANICKED GAZELLE!
THIS TIME, I'M SURE ...
haah
haah
MIKASA ACKERMAN.
402 CENTIMETERS.
CHOOM
Wha?!
SIDE STEP REPS.
EREN YEAGER, 81 TIMES.
I'M THE ONLY ONE OVER 80...
THIS TIME, I'M SURE ...
Wheeze
Wheeze
MIKASA ACKERMAN.
103 TIMES.
swish
swish
swish
GLOOO
OOMM
GRIP STRENGTH.
EREN YEAGER, 46 KILOGRAMS.
MY HANDS FEEL LIKE STABBING...
NO WAY A GIRL'S GONNA BEAT ME...
MIKASA ACKERMAN...
...HAS SWUNG THE DIAL PAST THE MAXIMUM ?!
CRUNCH
GYYAAH
SIT-AND-REACH.
AAHHH
YOU GET THE PICTURE.

SPECIAL EPISODE: SPORTS TEST OF FEAR

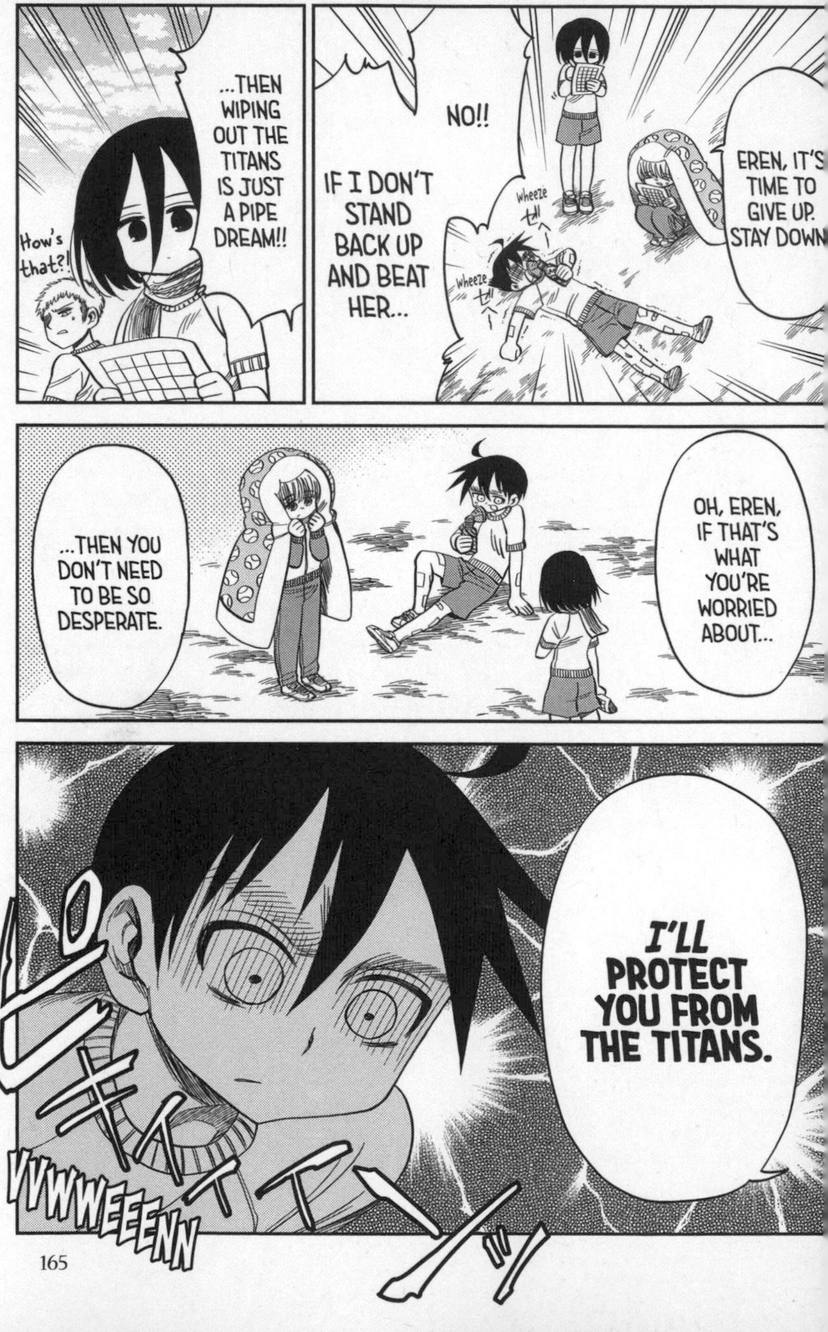
EREN, IT'S TIME TO GIVE UP. STAY DOWN
NO!!
IF I DON'T STAND BACK UP AND BEAT HER...
Wheeze
Wheeze
...THEN WIPING OUT THE TITANS IS JUST A PIPE DREAM!!
How's that?!
OH, EREN, IF THAT'S WHAT YOU'RE WORRIED ABOUT...
...THEN YOU DON'T NEED TO BE SO DESPERATE.
I'LL PROTECT YOU FROM THE TITANS.
VVWWEEENN

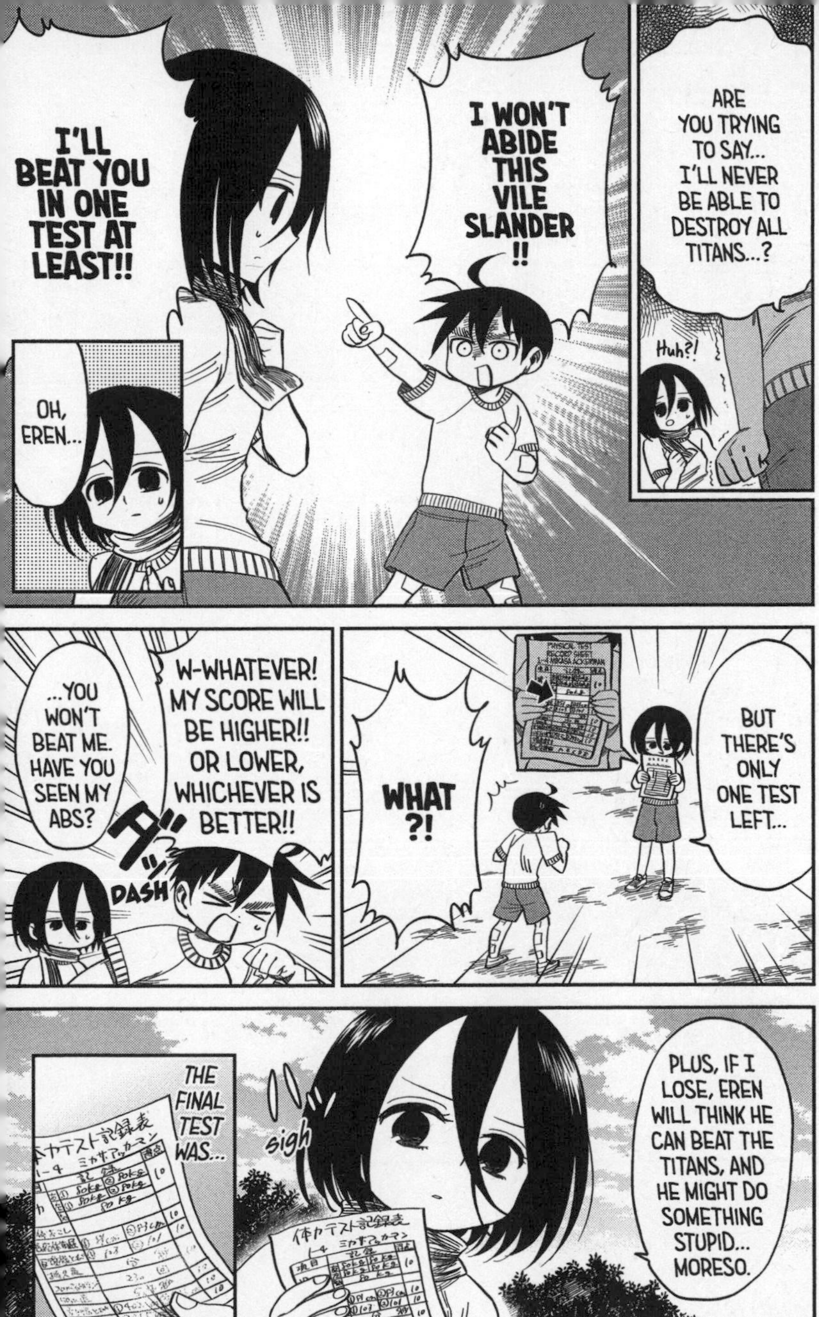
ARE YOU TRYING TO SAY... I'LL NEVER BE ABLE TO DESTROY ALL TITANS...?
Huh?!
I WON'T ABIDE THIS VILE SLANDER!!
I'LL BEAT YOU IN ONE TEST AT LEAST!!
OH, EREN...
BUT THERE'S ONLY ONE TEST LEFT...
WHAT?!
W-WHATEVER! MY SCORE WILL BE HIGHER!! OR LOWER, WHICHEVER IS BETTER!!
...YOU WON'T BEAT ME. HAVE YOU SEEN MY ABS?
DASH
PLUS, IF I LOSE, EREN WILL THINK HE CAN BEAT THE TITANS, AND HE MIGHT DO SOMETHING STUPID... MORESO.
sigh
THE FINAL TEST WAS...

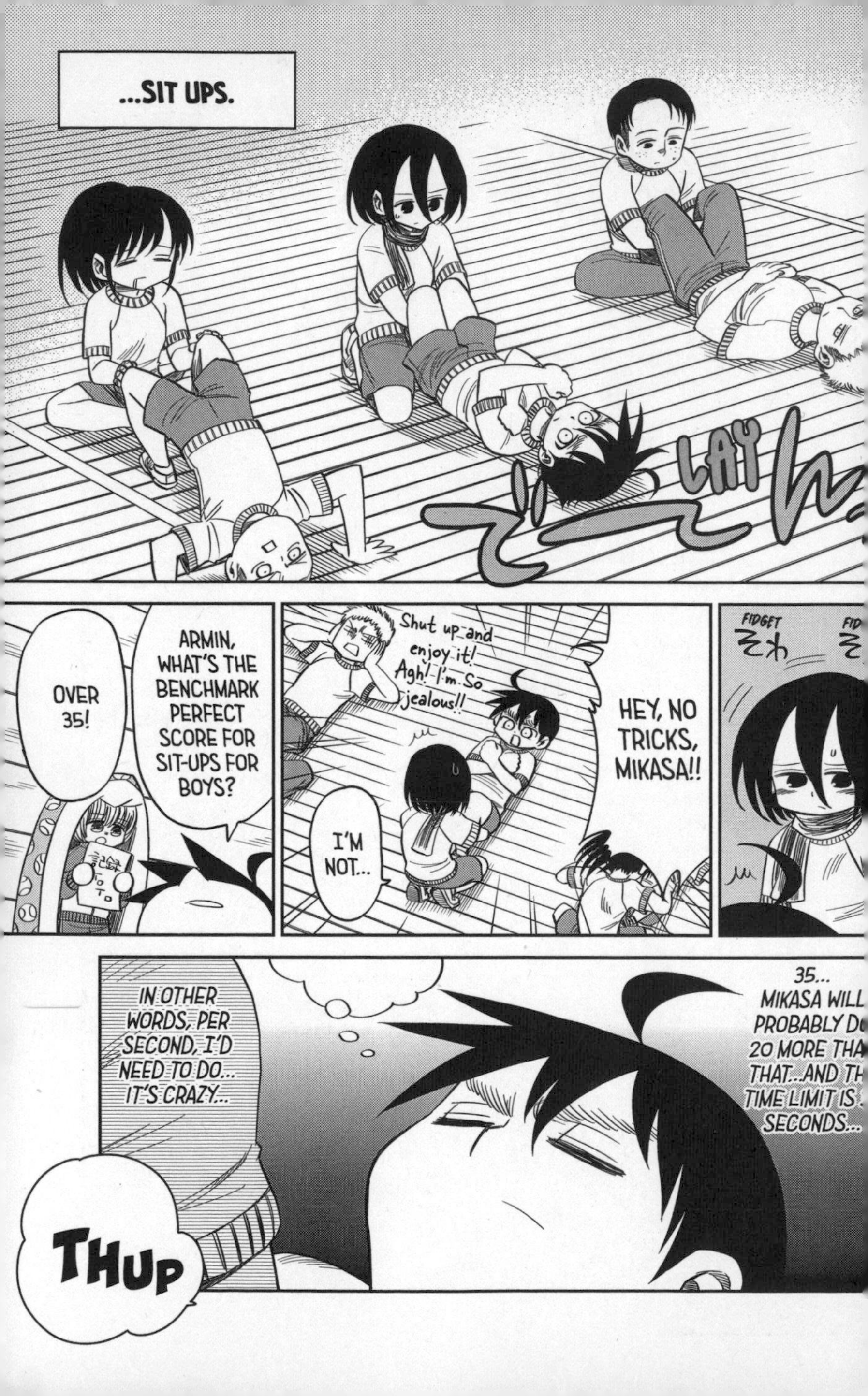

...SIT UPS.
LAY
FIDGET
そわ
FID
HEY, NO TRICKS, MIKASA!!
Shut up and enjoy it! Agh! I'm. So jealous!!
I'M NOT...
ARMIN, WHAT'S THE BENCHMARK PERFECT SCORE FOR SIT-UPS FOR BOYS?
OVER 35!
35... MIKASA WILL PROBABLY D 20 MORE THA THAT...AND TH TIME LIMIT IS SECONDS...
IN OTHER WORDS, PER SECOND, I'D NEED TO DO... IT'S CRAZY...
THUP

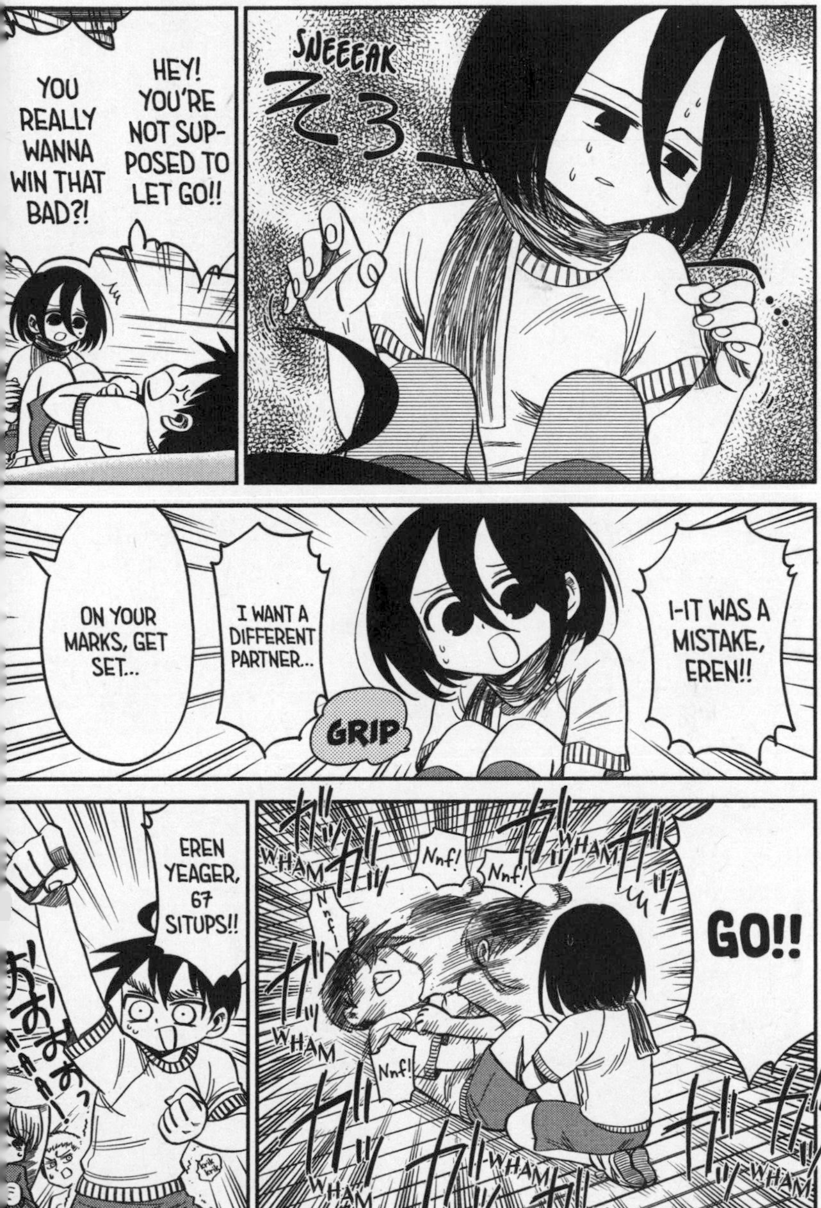
SNEEEAK
HEY! YOU'RE NOT SUP-POSED TO LET GO!!
YOU REALLY WANNA WIN THAT BAD?!
I-IT WAS A MISTAKE, EREN!!
GRIP
I WANT A DIFFERENT PARTNER...
ON YOUR MARKS, GET SET...
GO!!
WHAM
Nnf!
Nnf!
WHAM
Nnf!
WHAM
Nnf!
WHAM
WHAM
WHAM
EREN YEAGER, 67 SITUPS!!

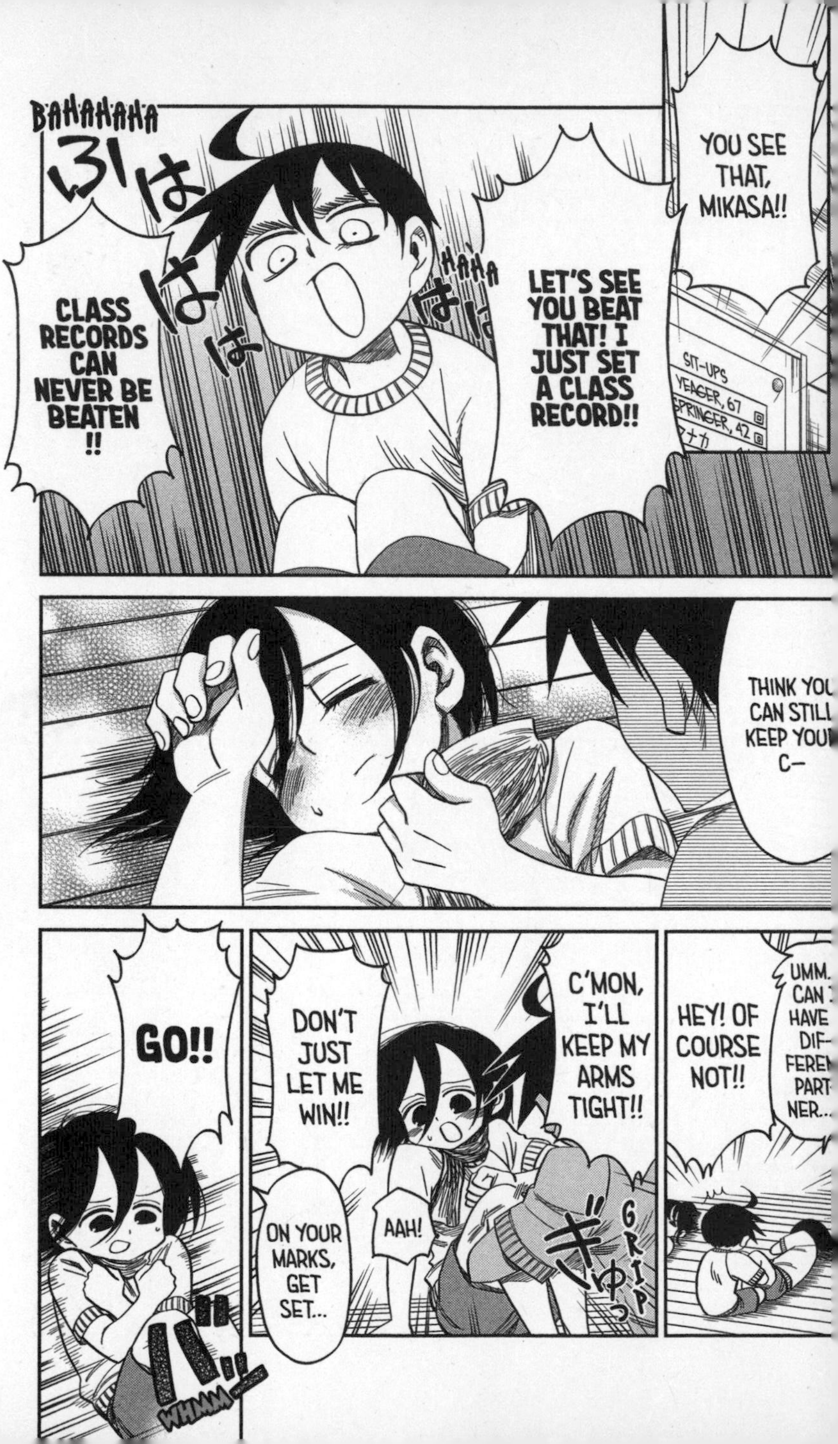
YOU SEE THAT, MIKASA!!
SIT-UPS
YEAGER, 67
SPRINGER, 42
LET'S SEE YOU BEAT THAT! I JUST SET A CLASS RECORD!!
HAHA
BAHAHAHA
CLASS RECORDS CAN NEVER BE BEATEN!!
THINK YOU CAN STILL KEEP YOUR C—
UMM... CAN I HAVE DIF-FEREN PART-NER...
HEY! OF COURSE NOT!!
C'MON, I'LL KEEP MY ARMS TIGHT!!
DON'T JUST LET ME WIN!!
AAH!
GRIP
ON YOUR MARKS, GET SET...
GO!!
WHMM

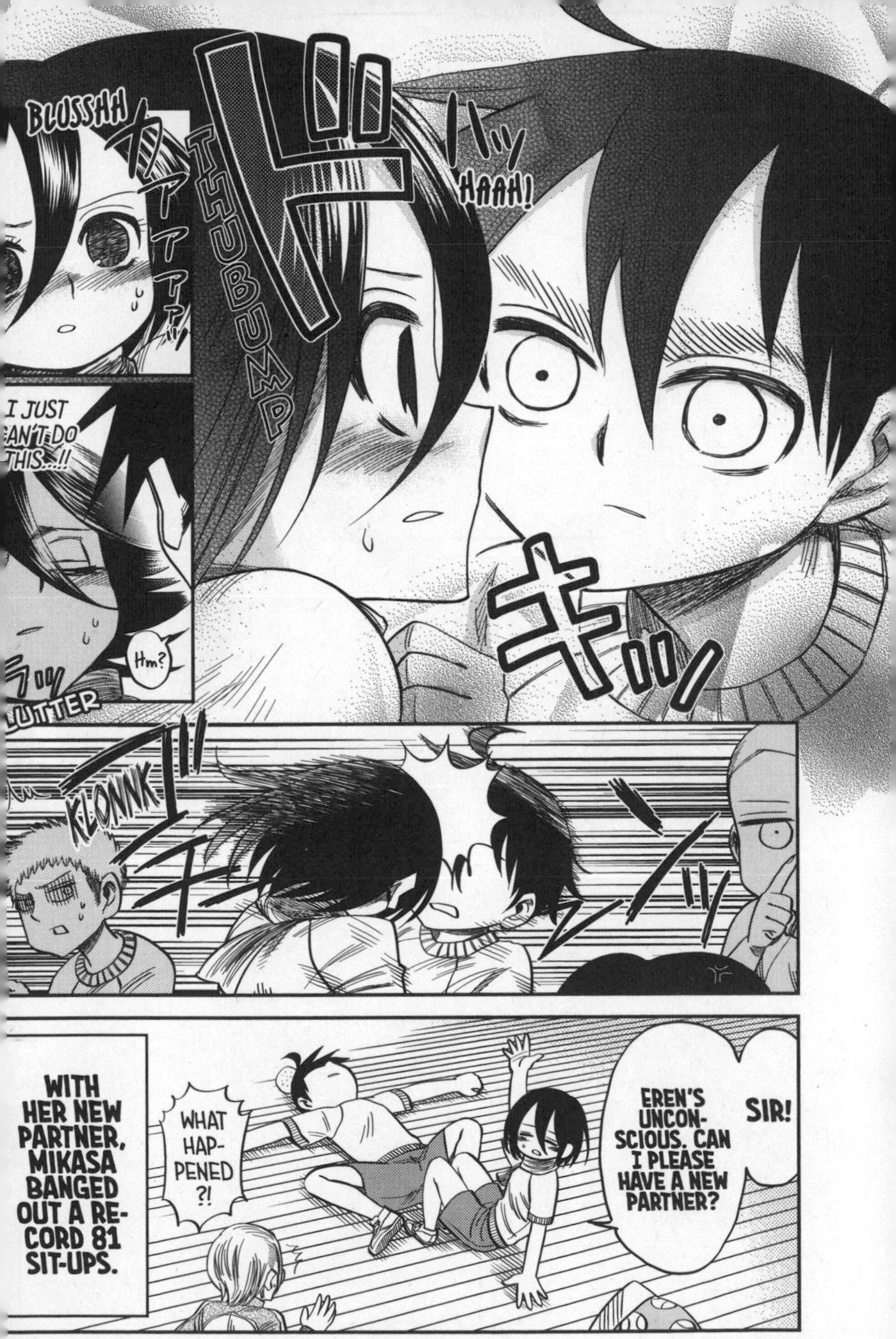
HAAH!
THUBUMP
BLOSSHH
I JUST CAN'T DO THIS...!!
Hm?
LUTTER
KLONNK
SIR!
EREN'S UNCONSCIOUS. CAN I PLEASE HAVE A NEW PARTNER?
WHAT HAPPENED?!
WITH HER NEW PARTNER, MIKASA BANGED OUT A RECORD 81 SIT-UPS.

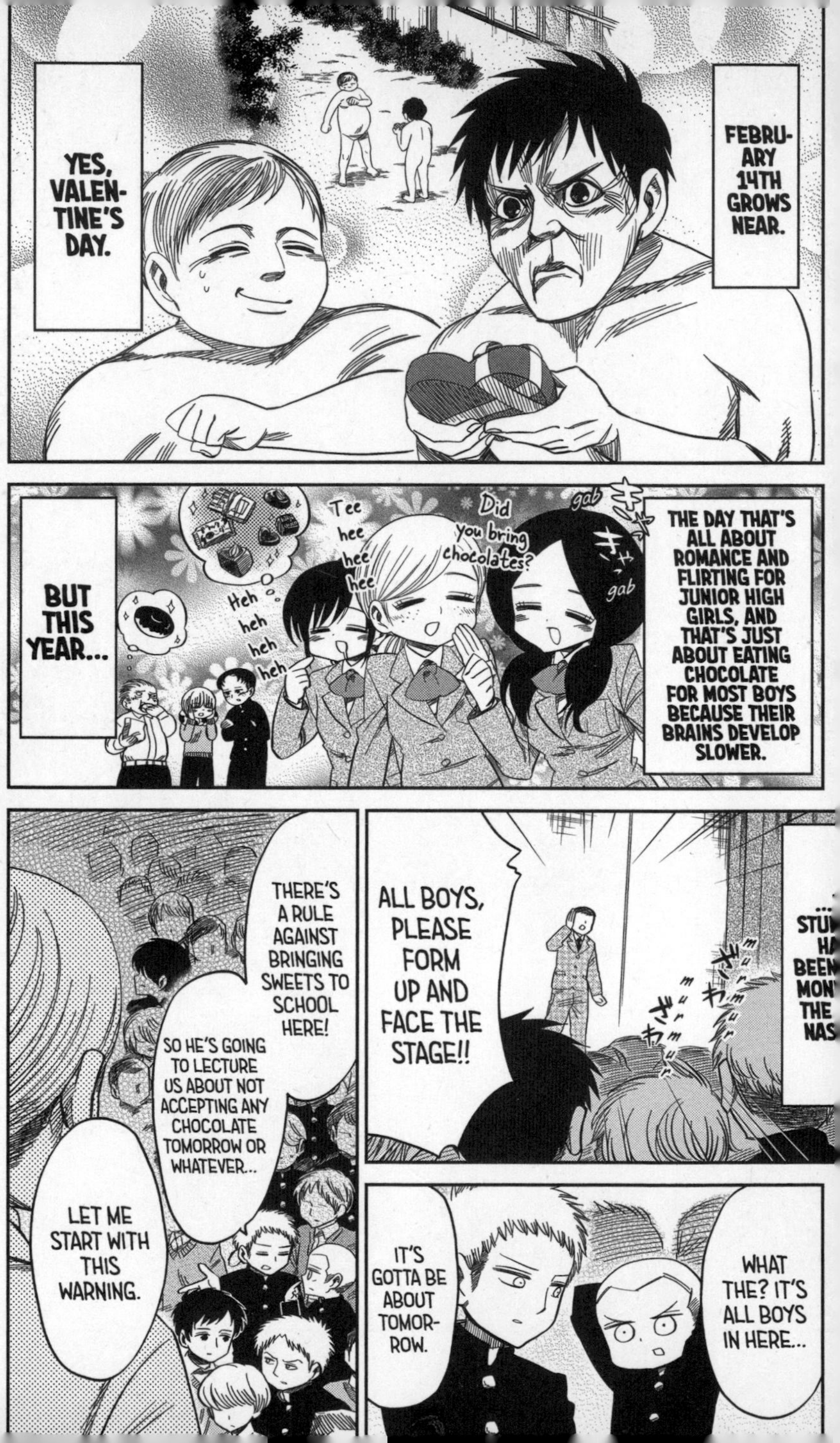
FEBRUARY 14TH GROWS NEAR.
YES, VALENTINE'S DAY.
THE DAY THAT'S ALL ABOUT ROMANCE AND FLIRTING FOR JUNIOR HIGH GIRLS, AND THAT'S JUST ABOUT EATING CHOCOLATE FOR MOST BOYS BECAUSE THEIR BRAINS DEVELOP SLOWER.
gab gab
Did you bring chocolates?
Tee hee hee hee
Heh heh heh heh
BUT THIS YEAR...
ALL BOYS, PLEASE FORM UP AND FACE THE STAGE!!
WHAT THE? IT'S ALL BOYS IN HERE...
IT'S GOTTA BE ABOUT TOMORROW.
THERE'S A RULE AGAINST BRINGING SWEETS TO SCHOOL HERE!
SO HE'S GOING TO LECTURE US ABOUT NOT ACCEPTING ANY CHOCOLATE TOMORROW OR WHATEVER...
LET ME START WITH THIS WARNING.

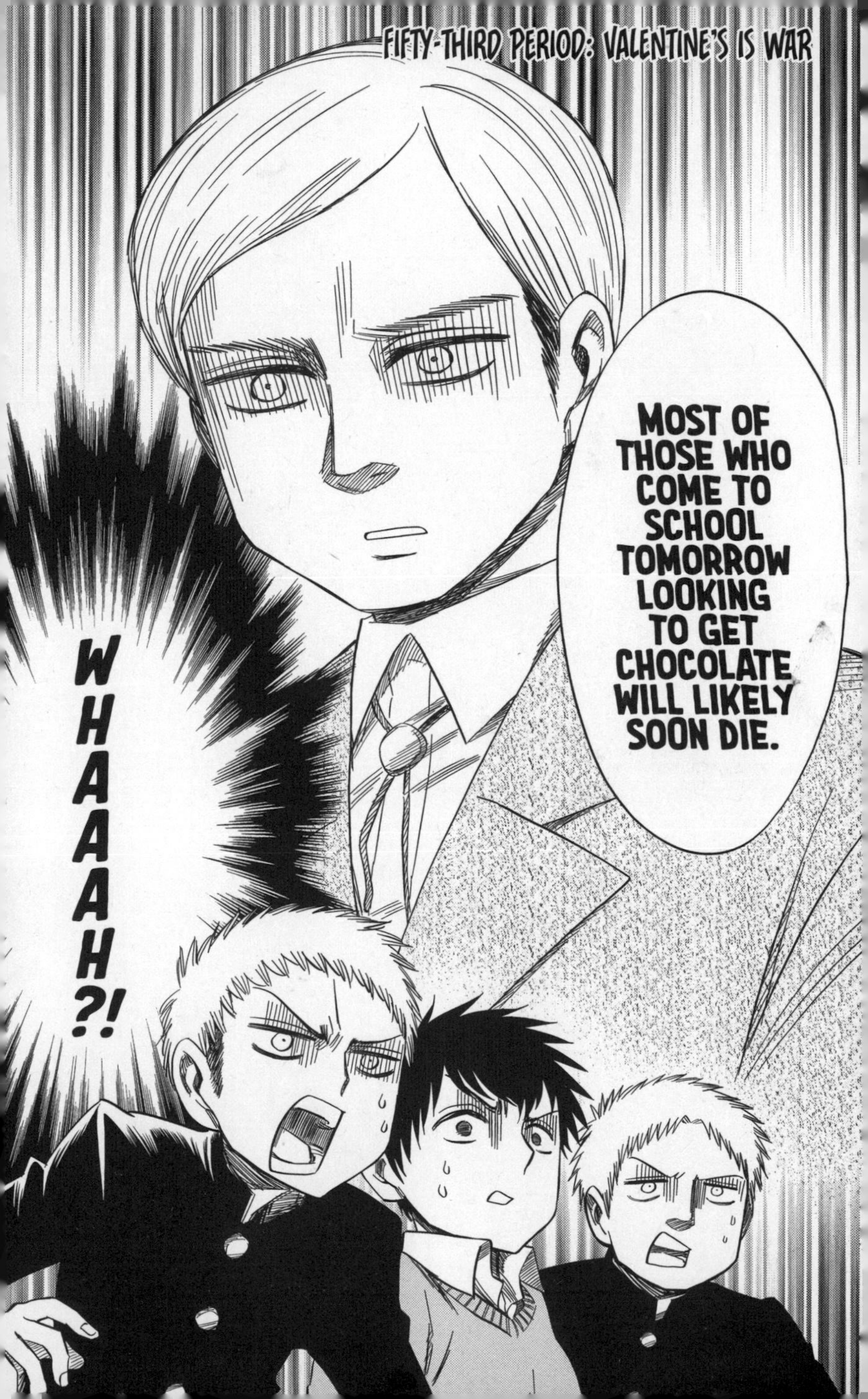
FIFTY-THIRD PERIOD: VALENTINE'S IS WAR
MOST OF THOSE WHO COME TO SCHOOL TOMORROW LOOKING TO GET CHOCOLATE WILL LIKELY SOON DIE.
WHAAAAH?!

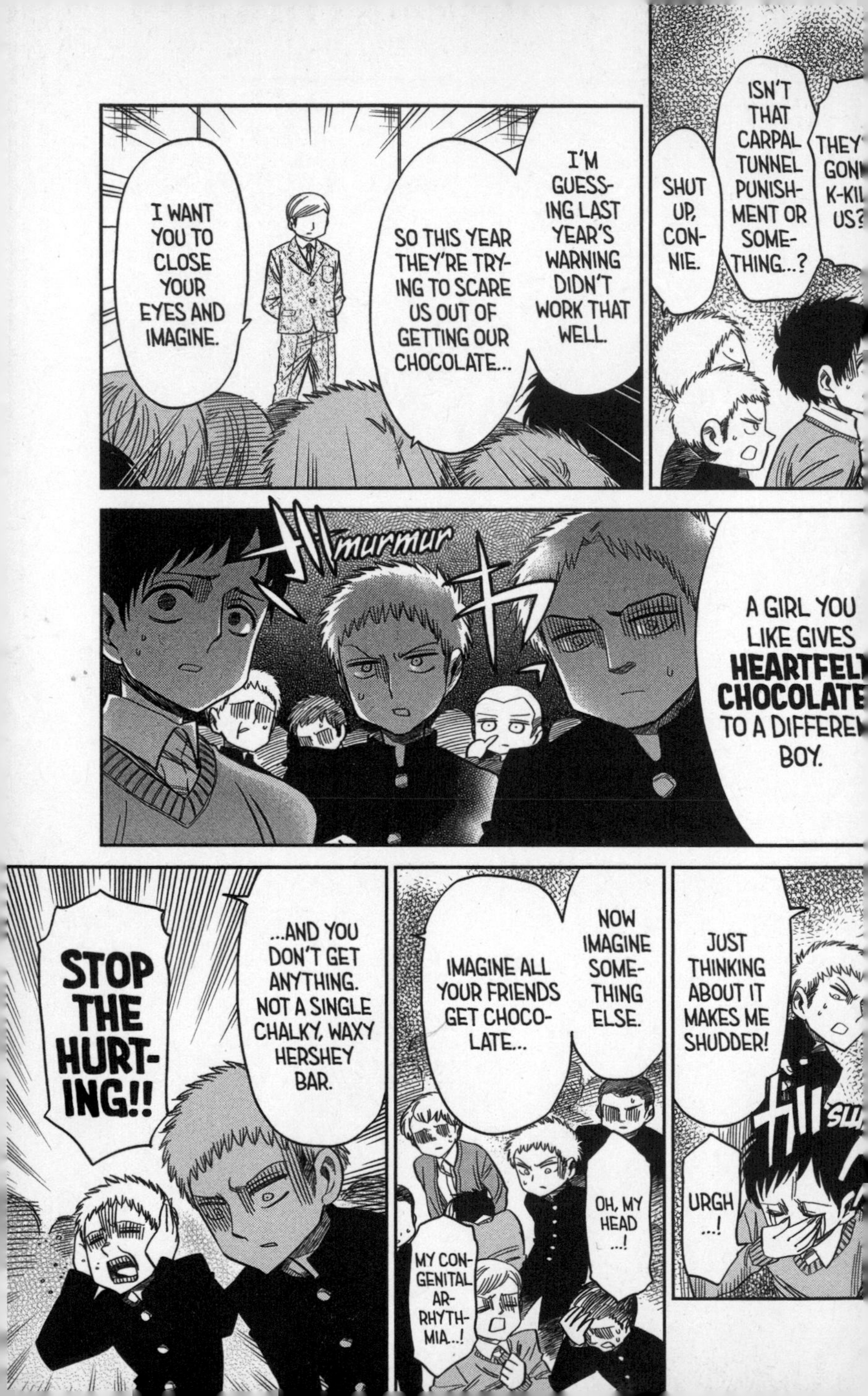
THEY' GON K-KIL US?
ISN'T THAT CARPAL TUNNEL PUNISHMENT OR SOMETHING...?
SHUT UP, CONNIE.
I'M GUESSING LAST YEAR'S WARNING DIDN'T WORK THAT WELL.
SO THIS YEAR THEY'RE TRYING TO SCARE US OUT OF GETTING OUR CHOCOLATE...
I WANT YOU TO CLOSE YOUR EYES AND IMAGINE.
A GIRL YOU LIKE GIVES **HEARTFEL CHOCOLATE** TO A DIFFERE BOY.
murmur
JUST THINKING ABOUT IT MAKES ME SHUDDER!
URGH...!
NOW IMAGINE SOMETHING ELSE.
IMAGINE ALL YOUR FRIENDS GET CHOCOLATE...
OH, MY HEAD...!
MY CONGENITAL ARRHYTHMIA...!
...AND YOU DON'T GET ANYTHING. NOT A SINGLE CHALKY, WAXY HERSHEY BAR.
STOP THE HURTING!!

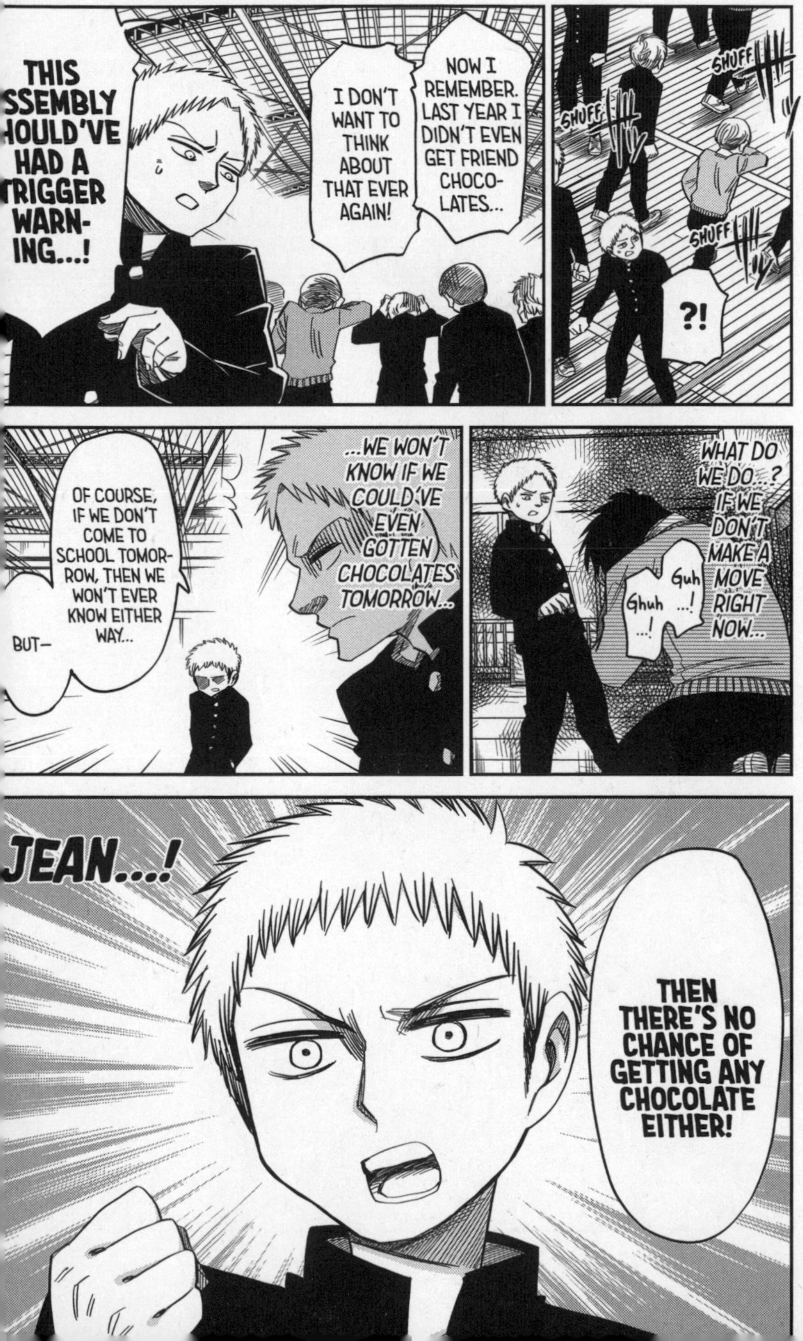
SHUFF
SHUFF
SHUFF
?!
NOW I REMEMBER. LAST YEAR I DIDN'T EVEN GET FRIEND CHOCO-LATES...
I DON'T WANT TO THINK ABOUT THAT EVER AGAIN!
THIS SSEMBLY HOULD'VE HAD A RIGGER WARN-ING...!
WHAT DO WE DO...? IF WE DON'T MAKE A MOVE RIGHT NOW...
Guh ...!
Ghuh ...!
...WE WON'T KNOW IF WE COULD'VE EVEN GOTTEN CHOCOLATES TOMORROW...
OF COURSE, IF WE DON'T COME TO SCHOOL TOMOR-ROW, THEN WE WON'T EVER KNOW EITHER WAY...
BUT—
THEN THERE'S NO CHANCE OF GETTING ANY CHOCOLATE EITHER!
JEAN...!

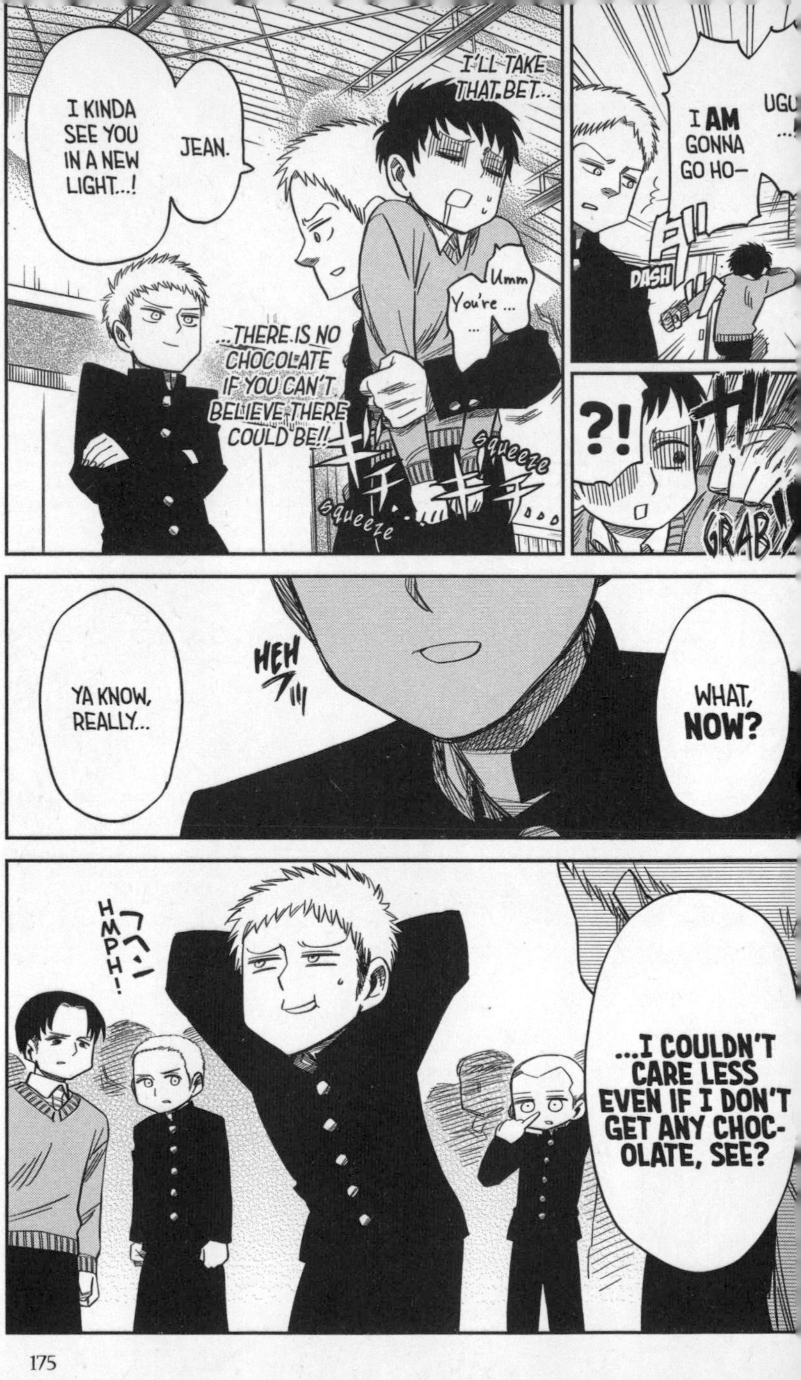
UGU...
I AM GONNA GO HO—
DASH
?!
GRAB!!
I'LL TAKE THAT BET...
Umm You're ... ...
JEAN.
I KINDA SEE YOU IN A NEW LIGHT...!
...THERE IS NO CHOCOLATE IF YOU CAN'T BELIEVE THERE COULD BE!!
squeeze
squeeze
WHAT, NOW?
HEH
YA KNOW, REALLY...
...I COULDN'T CARE LESS EVEN IF I DON'T GET ANY CHOCOLATE, SEE?
HMPH!

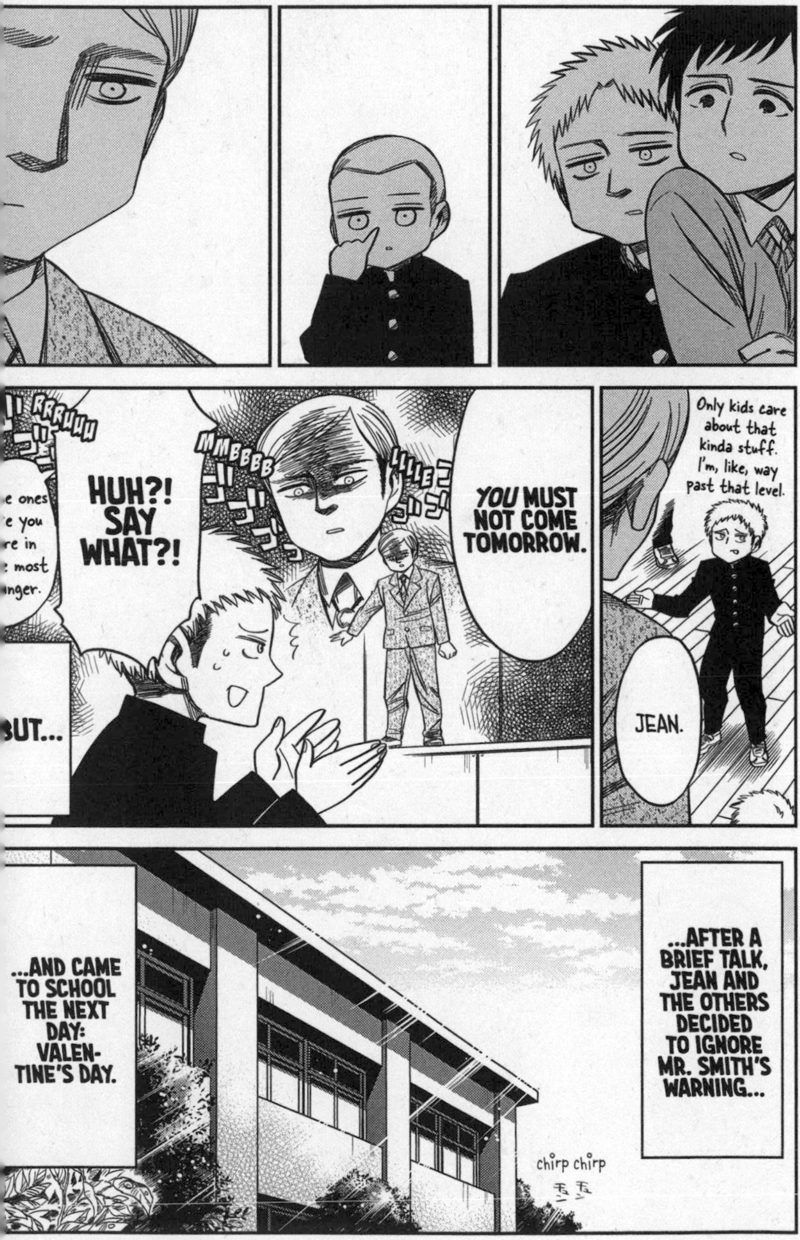
Only kids care about that kinda stuff. I'm, like, way past that level.
JEAN.
YOU MUST NOT COME TOMORROW.
LLLLE
MMBBBB
HUH?! SAY WHAT?!
...AFTER A BRIEF TALK, JEAN AND THE OTHERS DECIDED TO IGNORE MR. SMITH'S WARNING...
chirp chirp
...AND CAME TO SCHOOL THE NEXT DAY: VALEN-TINE'S DAY.

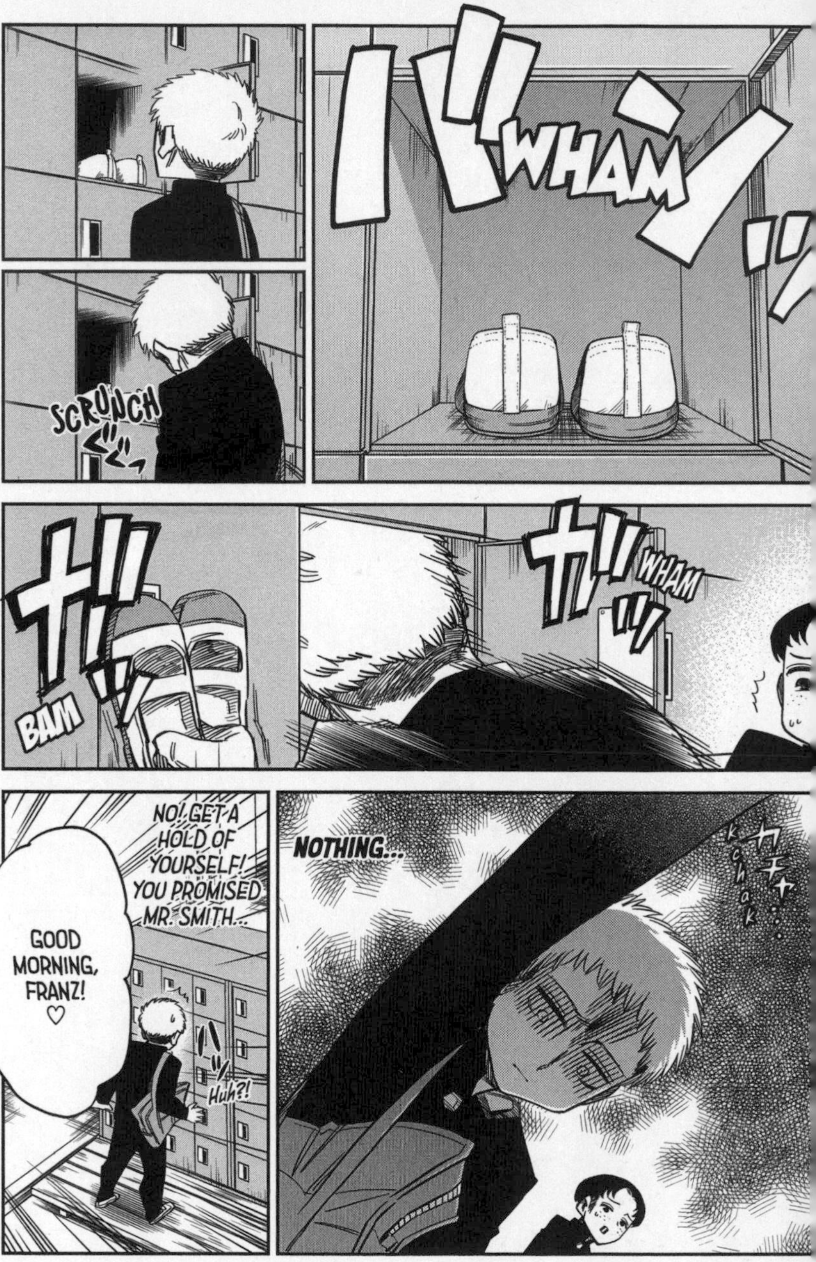
WHAM
SCRUNCH
WHAM
BAM
NOTHING...
kchak
NO! GET A HOLD OF YOURSELF! YOU PROMISED MR. SMITH...
GOOD MORNING, FRANZ! ♡
Huh?!

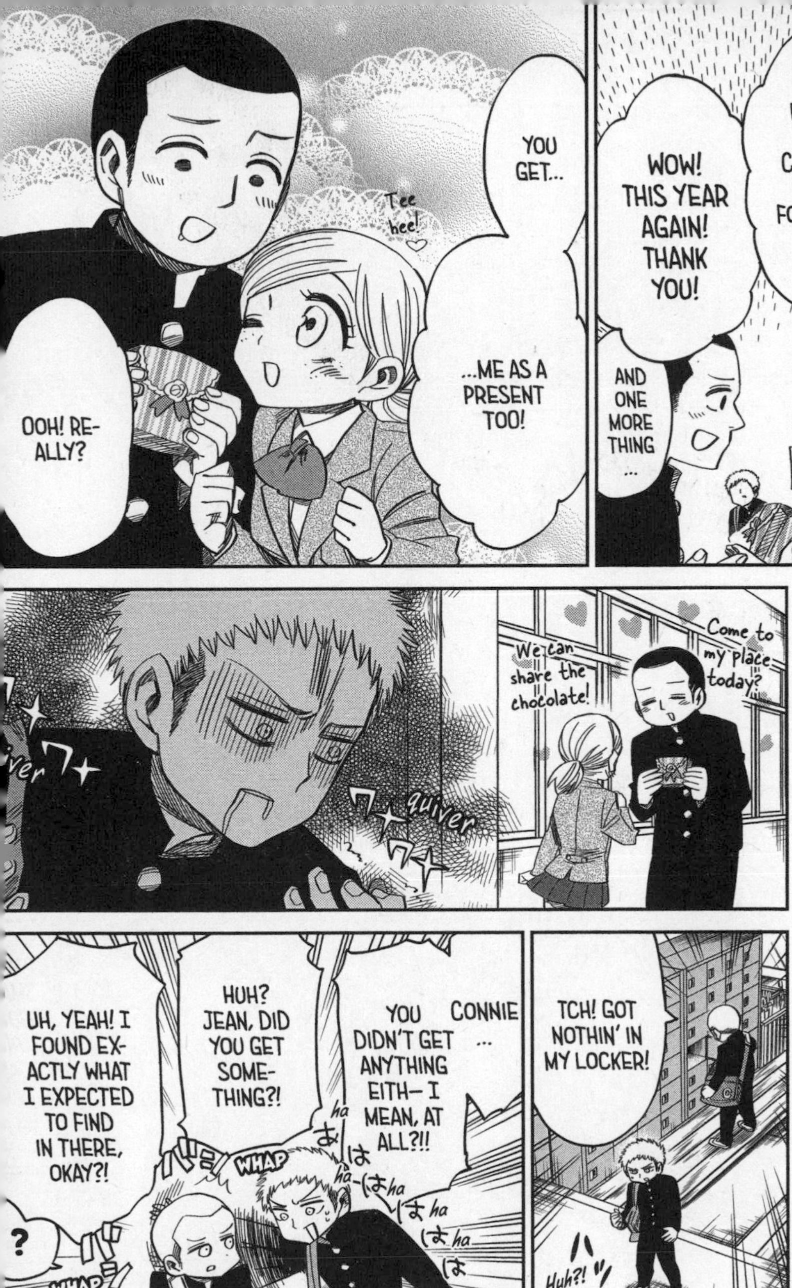
HERE! ♡ CHOCOLATE FOR YOU! ♡
WOW! THIS YEAR AGAIN! THANK YOU!
AND ONE MORE THING ...
YOU GET...
...ME AS A PRESENT TOO!
Tee hee! ♡
OOH! REALLY?
Come to my place today?
We can share the chocolate!
quiver
quiver
TCH! GOT NOTHIN' IN MY LOCKER!
Huh?!
CONNIE ...
YOU DIDN'T GET ANYTHING EITH— I MEAN, AT ALL?!!
ha ha ha ha ha
HUH? JEAN, DID YOU GET SOMETHING?!
UH, YEAH! I FOUND EXACTLY WHAT I EXPECTED TO FIND IN THERE, OKAY?!
WHAP
?
WHAP
WHAP

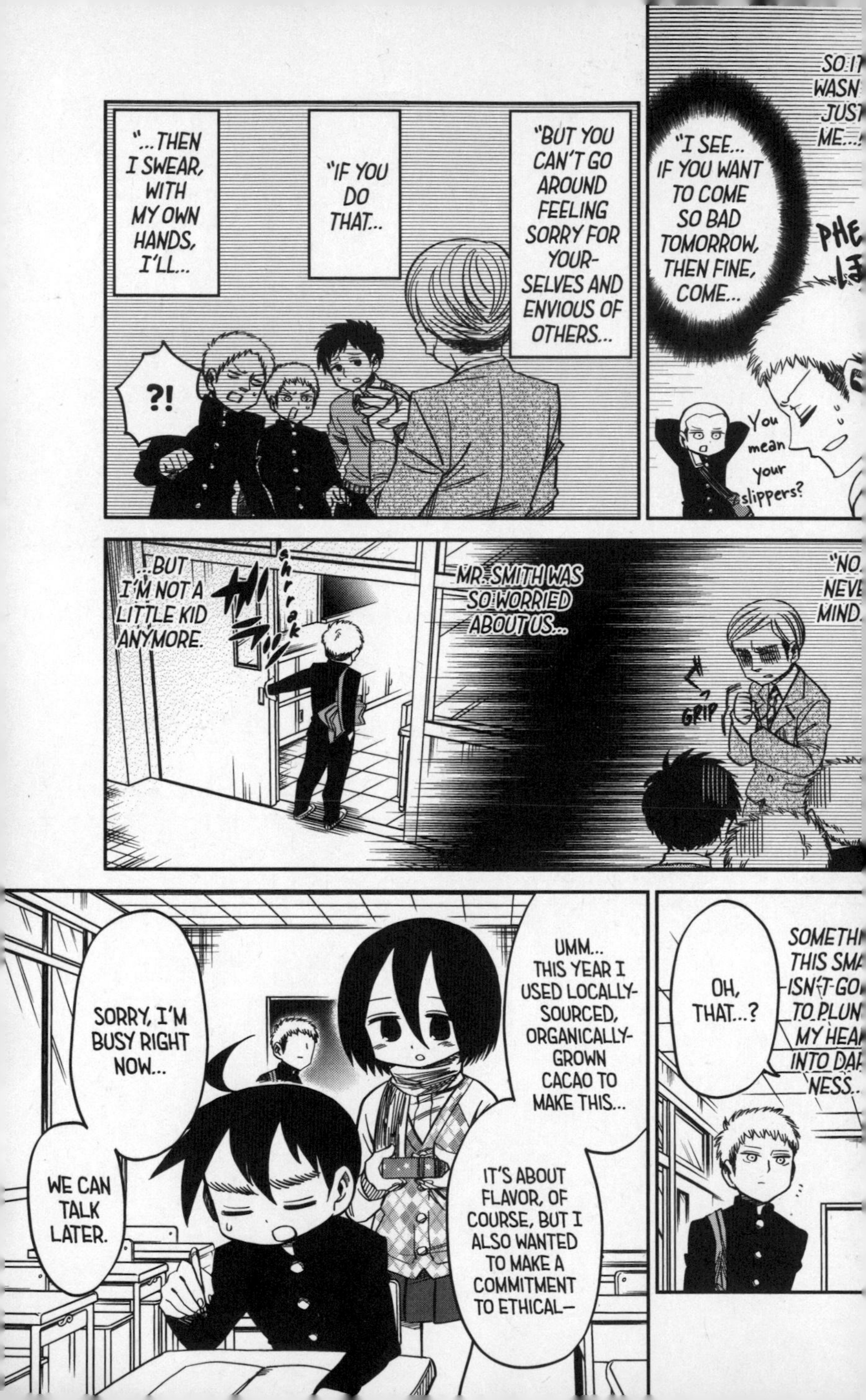
SO IT WASN JUST ME...
"I SEE... IF YOU WANT TO COME SO BAD TOMORROW, THEN FINE, COME...
PHE
You mean your slippers?
"BUT YOU CAN'T GO AROUND FEELING SORRY FOR YOURSELVES AND ENVIOUS OF OTHERS...
"IF YOU DO THAT...
"...THEN I SWEAR, WITH MY OWN HANDS, I'LL...
?!
"NO. NEVE MIND.
GRIP
MR. SMITH WAS SO WORRIED ABOUT US...
shrrak
...BUT I'M NOT A LITTLE KID ANYMORE.
SOMETH THIS SMA ISN'T GO TO PLUN MY HEA INTO DAR NESS...
OH, THAT...?
UMM... THIS YEAR I USED LOCALLY-SOURCED, ORGANICALLY-GROWN CACAO TO MAKE THIS...
IT'S ABOUT FLAVOR, OF COURSE, BUT I ALSO WANTED TO MAKE A COMMITMENT TO ETHICAL—
SORRY, I'M BUSY RIGHT NOW...
WE CAN TALK LATER.

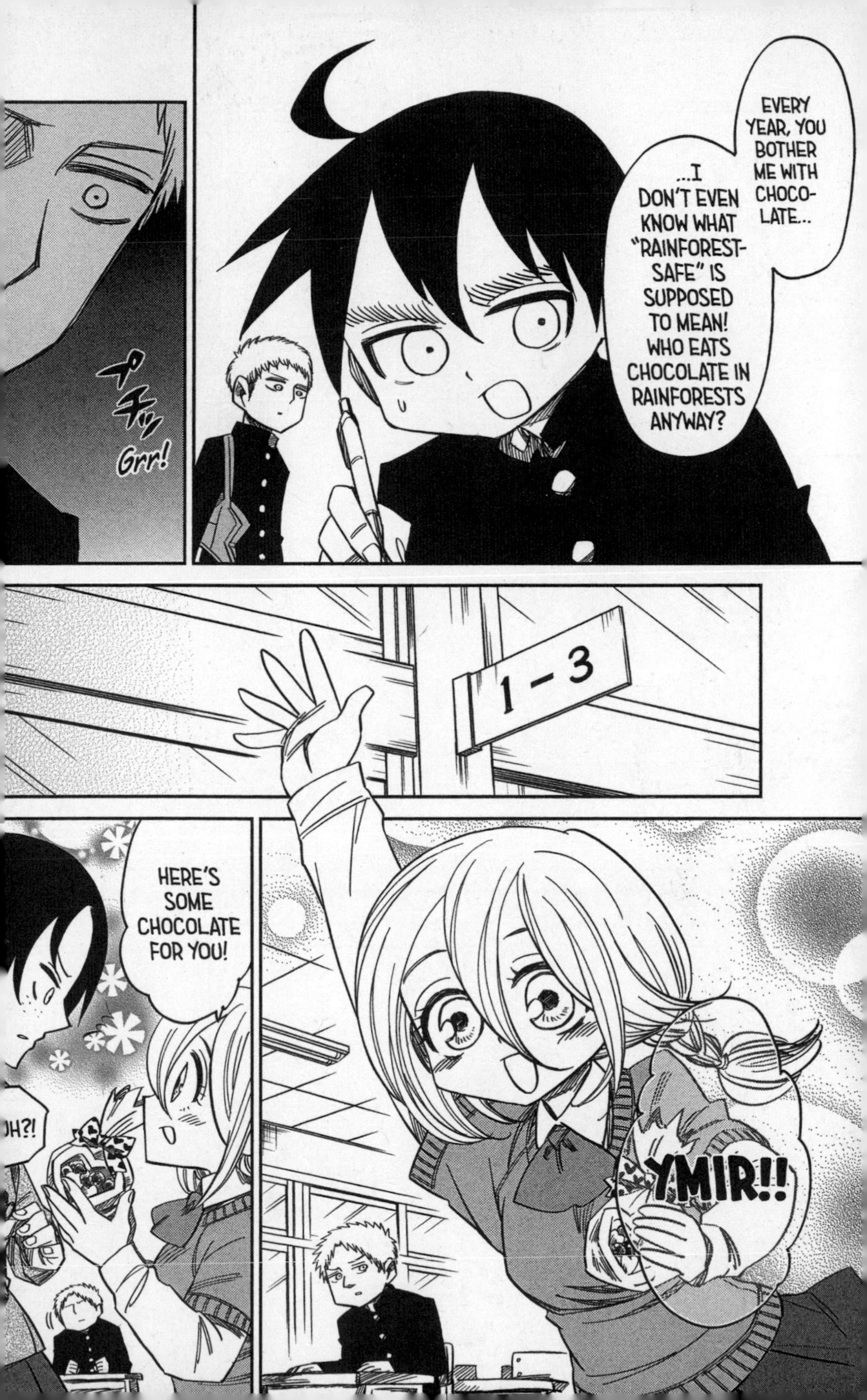

EVERY YEAR, YOU BOTHER ME WITH CHOCO-LATE...
...I DON'T EVEN KNOW WHAT "RAINFOREST-SAFE" IS SUPPOSED TO MEAN! WHO EATS CHOCOLATE IN RAINFORESTS ANYWAY?
プチッ
Grr!
1 – 3
YMIR!!
HERE'S SOME CHOCOLATE FOR YOU!

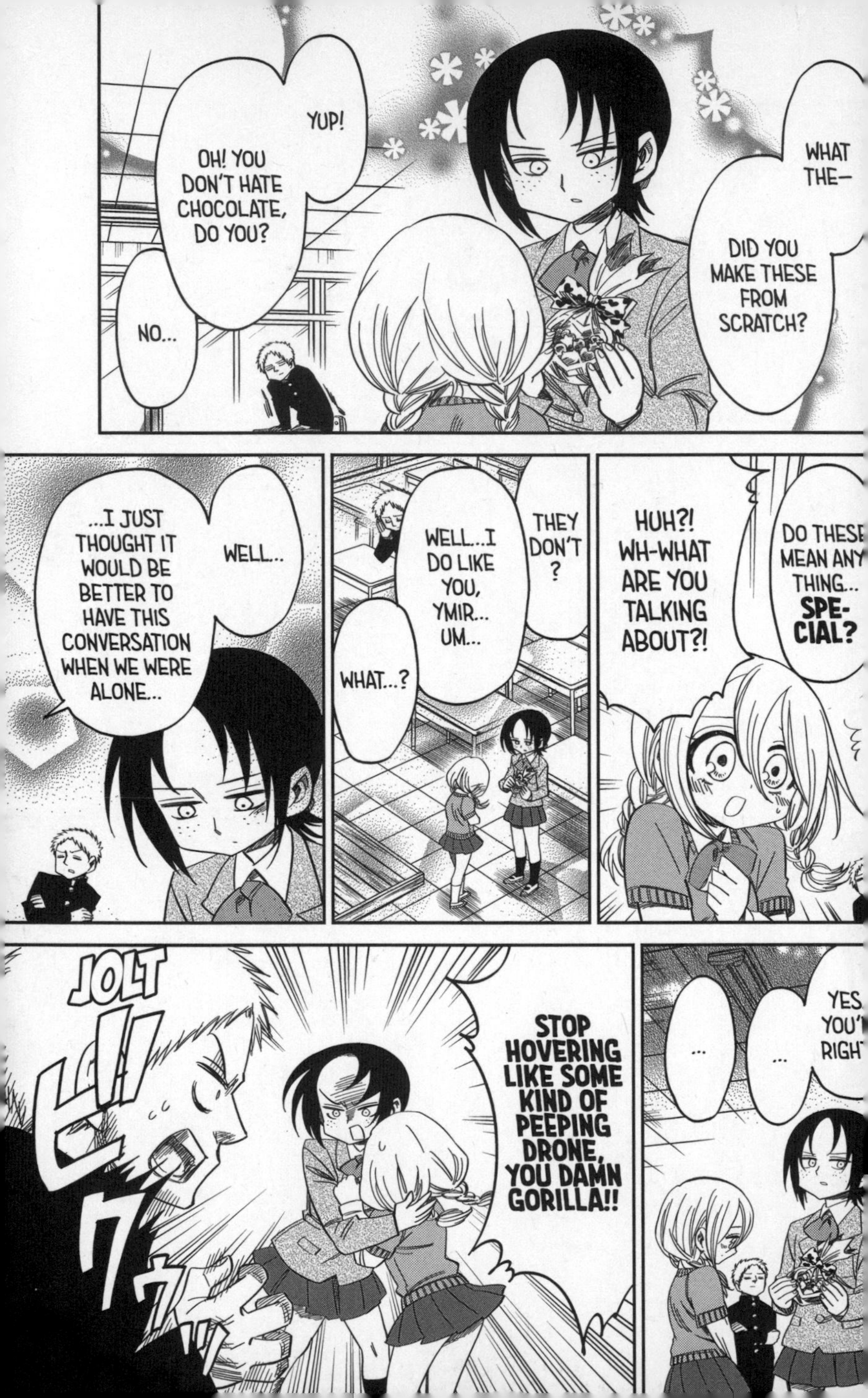
WHAT THE—
DID YOU MAKE THESE FROM SCRATCH?
YUP!
OH! YOU DON'T HATE CHOCOLATE, DO YOU?
NO...
DO THESE MEAN ANY THING... SPE- CIAL?
HUH?! WH-WHAT ARE YOU TALKING ABOUT?!
THEY DON'T ?
WELL...I DO LIKE YOU, YMIR... UM...
WHAT...?
WELL...
...I JUST THOUGHT IT WOULD BE BETTER TO HAVE THIS CONVERSATION WHEN WE WERE ALONE...
YES. YOU' RIGHT
...
...
STOP HOVERING LIKE SOME KIND OF PEEPING DRONE, YOU DAMN GORILLA!!
JOLT

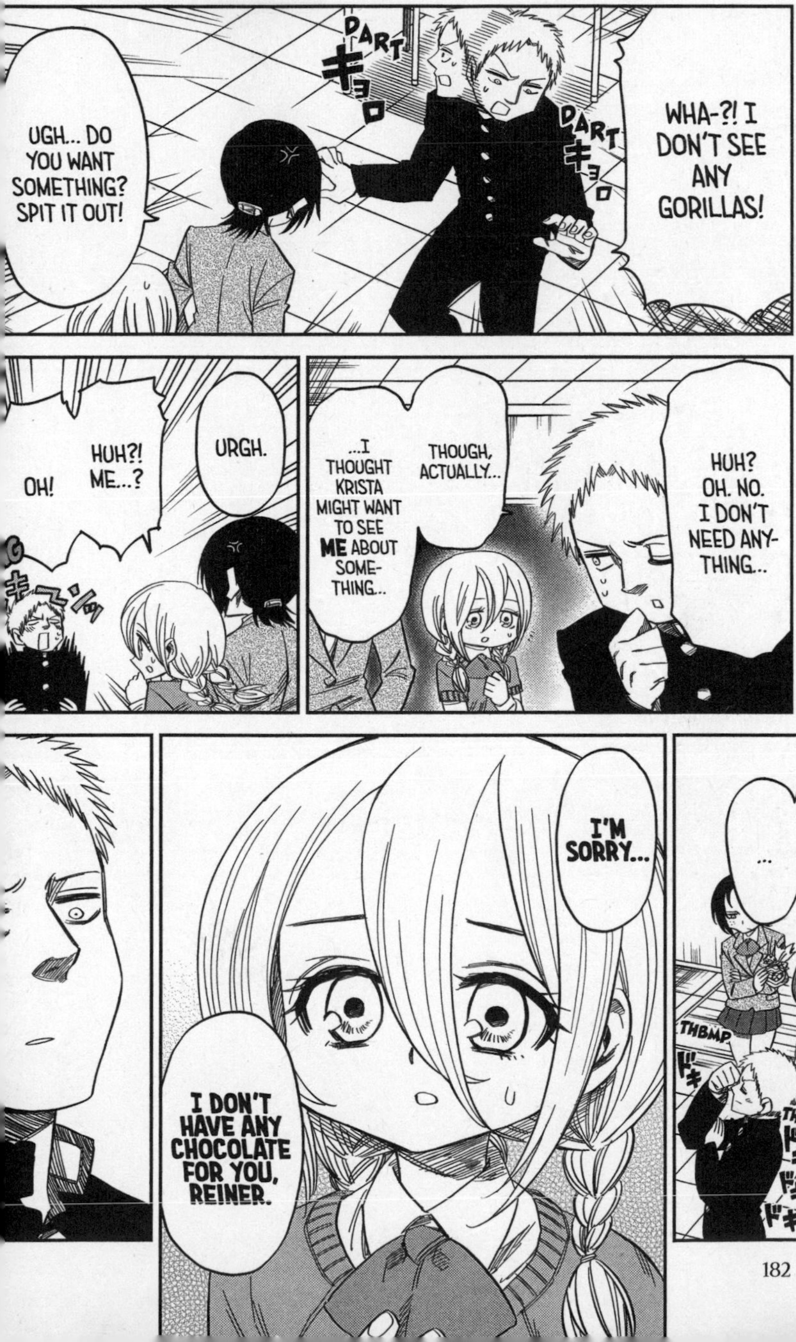
WHA-?! I DON'T SEE ANY GORILLAS!
DART
DART
UGH... DO YOU WANT SOMETHING? SPIT IT OUT!
HUH? OH. NO. I DON'T NEED ANY-THING...
THOUGH, ACTUALLY...
...I THOUGHT KRISTA MIGHT WANT TO SEE ME ABOUT SOME-THING...
URGH.
HUH?! ME...?
OH!
UMM...
...
THBMP
THBMP
THBMP
THBMP
I'M SORRY...
I DON'T HAVE ANY CHOCOLATE FOR YOU, REINER.

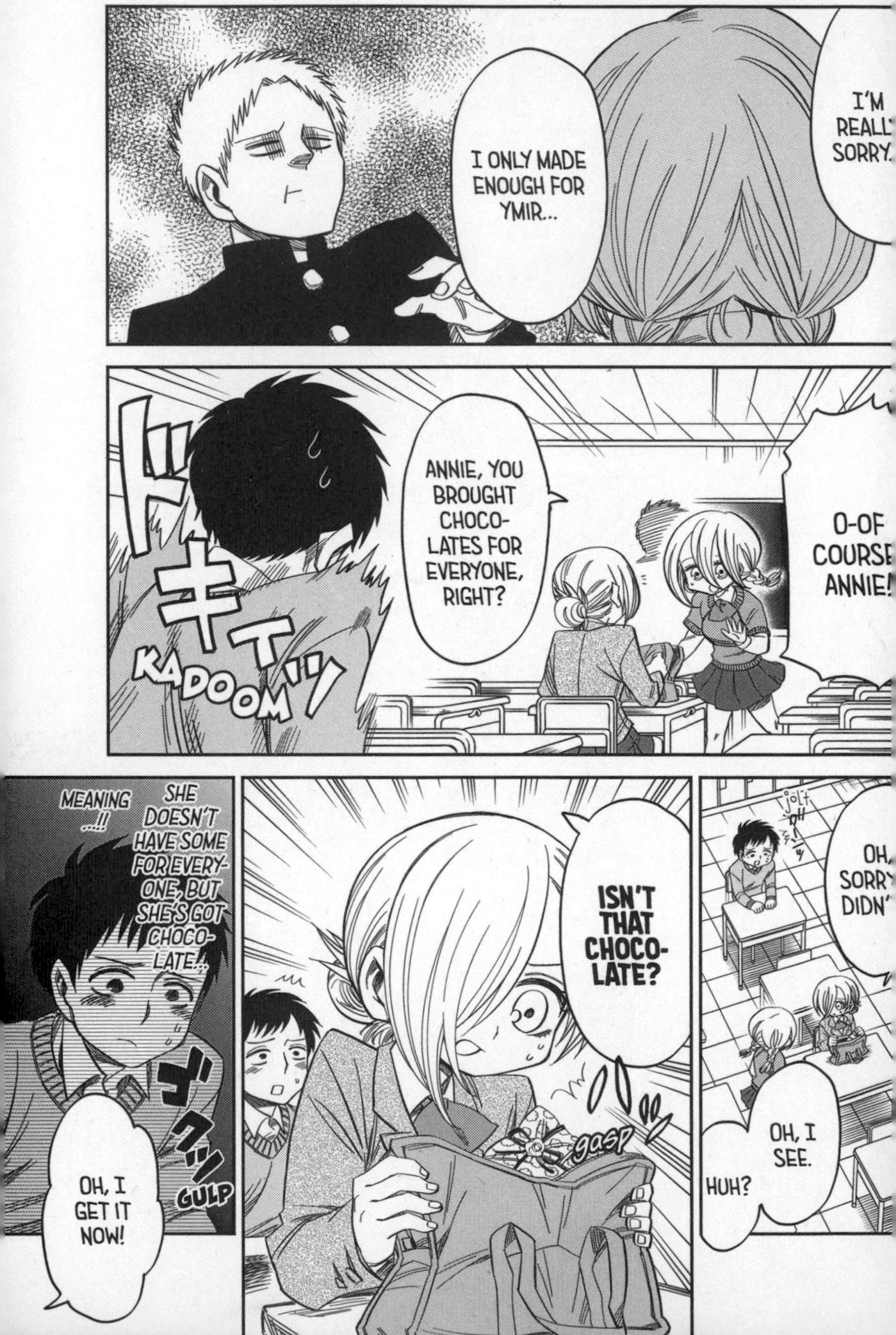
I'M REALL SORRY.
I ONLY MADE ENOUGH FOR YMIR...
O-OF COURSE ANNIE!
ANNIE, YOU BROUGHT CHOCO-LATES FOR EVERYONE, RIGHT?
ドキッ
KADOOM
jolt
OH, SORRY DIDN'
OH, I SEE.
HUH?
ISN'T THAT CHOCO-LATE?
gasp
MEANING ...!!
SHE DOESN'T HAVE SOME FOR EVERY-ONE, BUT SHE'S GOT CHOCO-LATE...
ゴクッ
GULP
OH, I GET IT NOW!

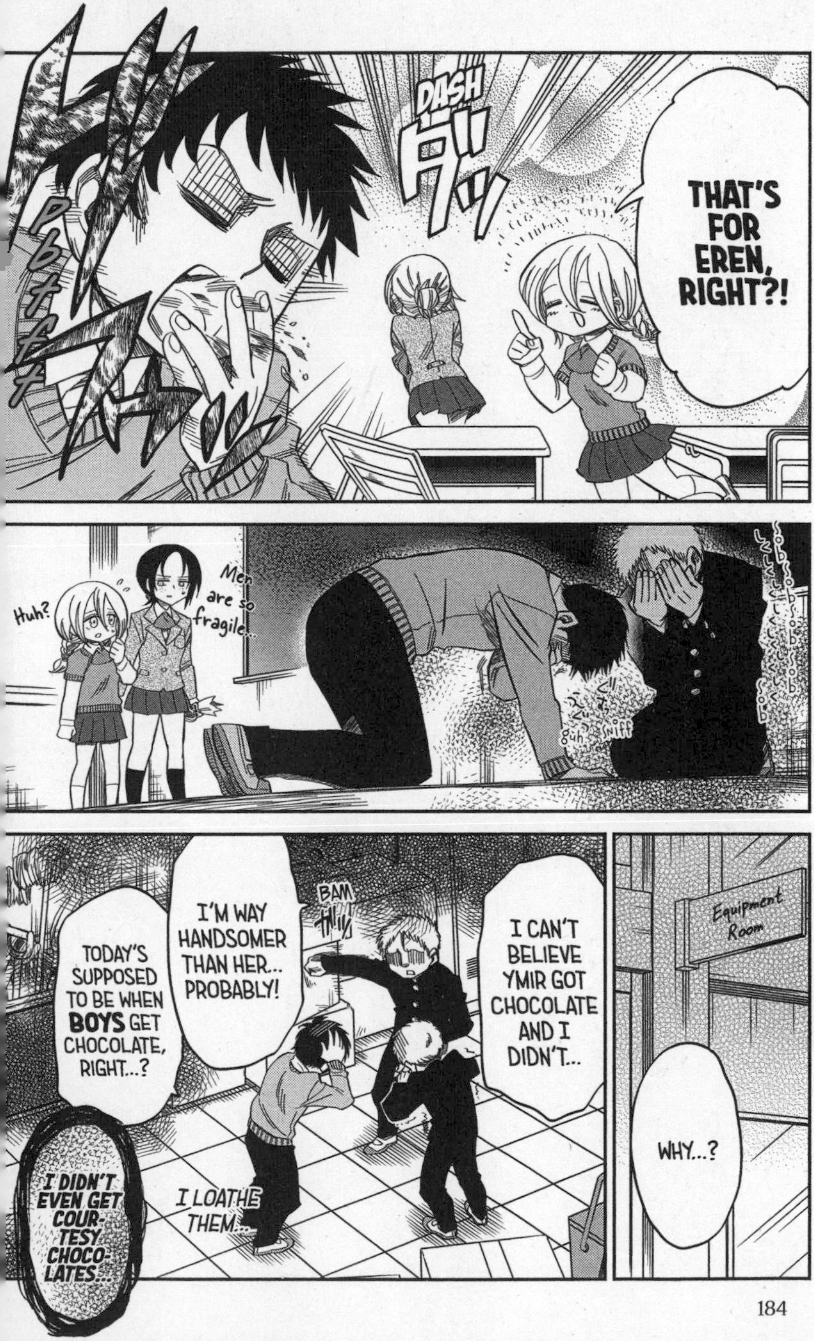
DASH
ダッ
THAT'S FOR EREN, RIGHT?!
Pbffff
sob sob sob
sniff
guh
Men are so fragile...
Huh?
Equipment Room
WHY...?
I CAN'T BELIEVE YMIR GOT CHOCOLATE AND I DIDN'T...
BAM
I'M WAY HANDSOMER THAN HER... PROBABLY!
TODAY'S SUPPOSED TO BE WHEN **BOYS** GET CHOCOLATE, RIGHT...?
I LOATHE THEM...
I DIDN'T EVEN GET COURTESY CHOCOLATES...

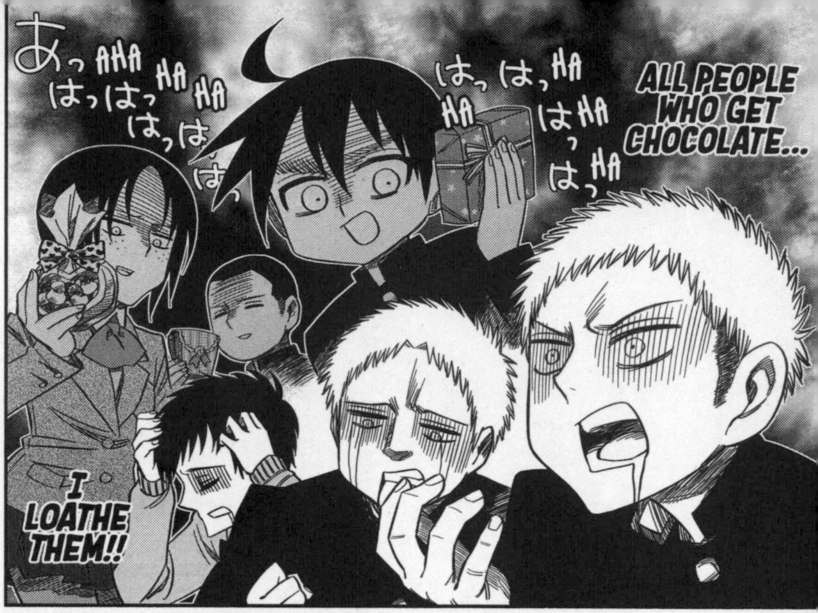
ALL PEOPLE WHO GET CHOCOLATE...
はっはっ HA HA はっ HA はっ HA はっ HA
あっ AHA はっはっ HA HA HA はっはっはっ
I LOATHE THEM!!
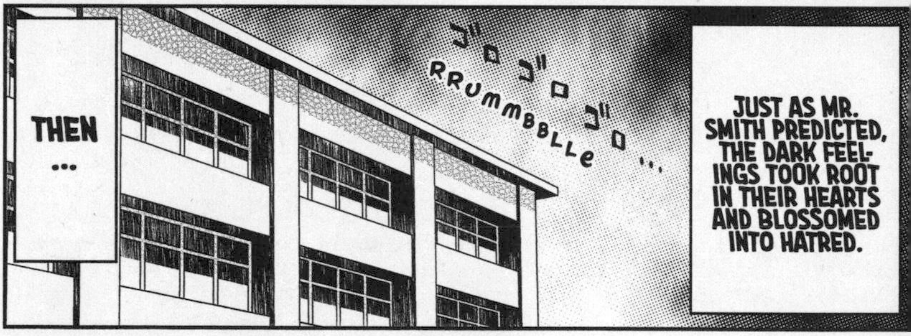
JUST AS MR. SMITH PREDICTED, THE DARK FEEL- INGS TOOK ROOT IN THEIR HEARTS AND BLOSSOMED INTO HATRED.
ゴロゴロゴロ... RRUMMBBLLE
THEN ...
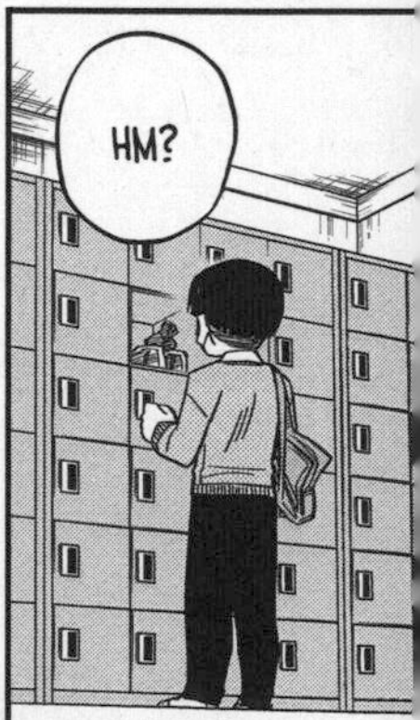
HM?
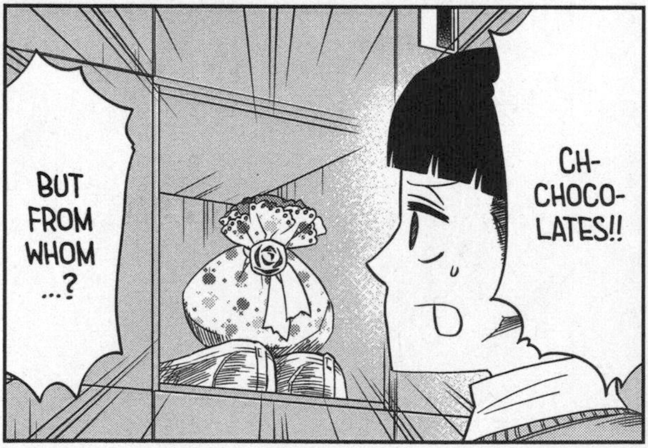
CH- CHOCO- LATES!!
BUT FROM WHOM ...?

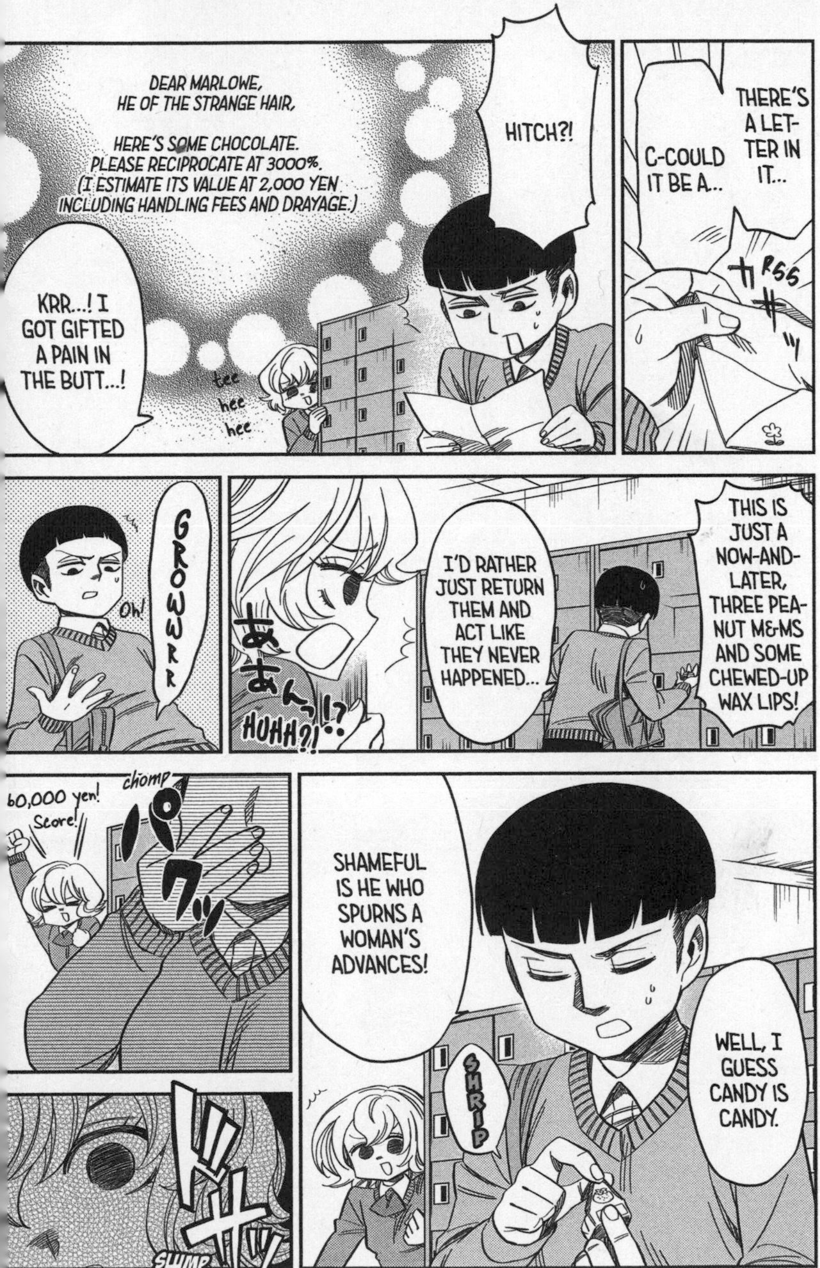

THERE'S A LET-TER IN IT...
C-COULD IT BE A...
RSS
HITCH?!
DEAR MARLOWE, HE OF THE STRANGE HAIR,
HERE'S SOME CHOCOLATE. PLEASE RECIPROCATE AT 3000%. (I ESTIMATE ITS VALUE AT 2,000 YEN INCLUDING HANDLING FEES AND DRAYAGE.)
tee hee hee
KRR...! I GOT GIFTED A PAIN IN THE BUTT...!
THIS IS JUST A NOW-AND-LATER, THREE PEA-NUT M&MS AND SOME CHEWED-UP WAX LIPS!
I'D RATHER JUST RETURN THEM AND ACT LIKE THEY NEVER HAPPENED...
あぁんっ!?
HUHH?!
GROWWRR
Oh!
SHAMEFUL IS HE WHO SPURNS A WOMAN'S ADVANCES!
WELL, I GUESS CANDY IS CANDY.
SHRIP
chomp
60,000 yen! Score!
SLUMP

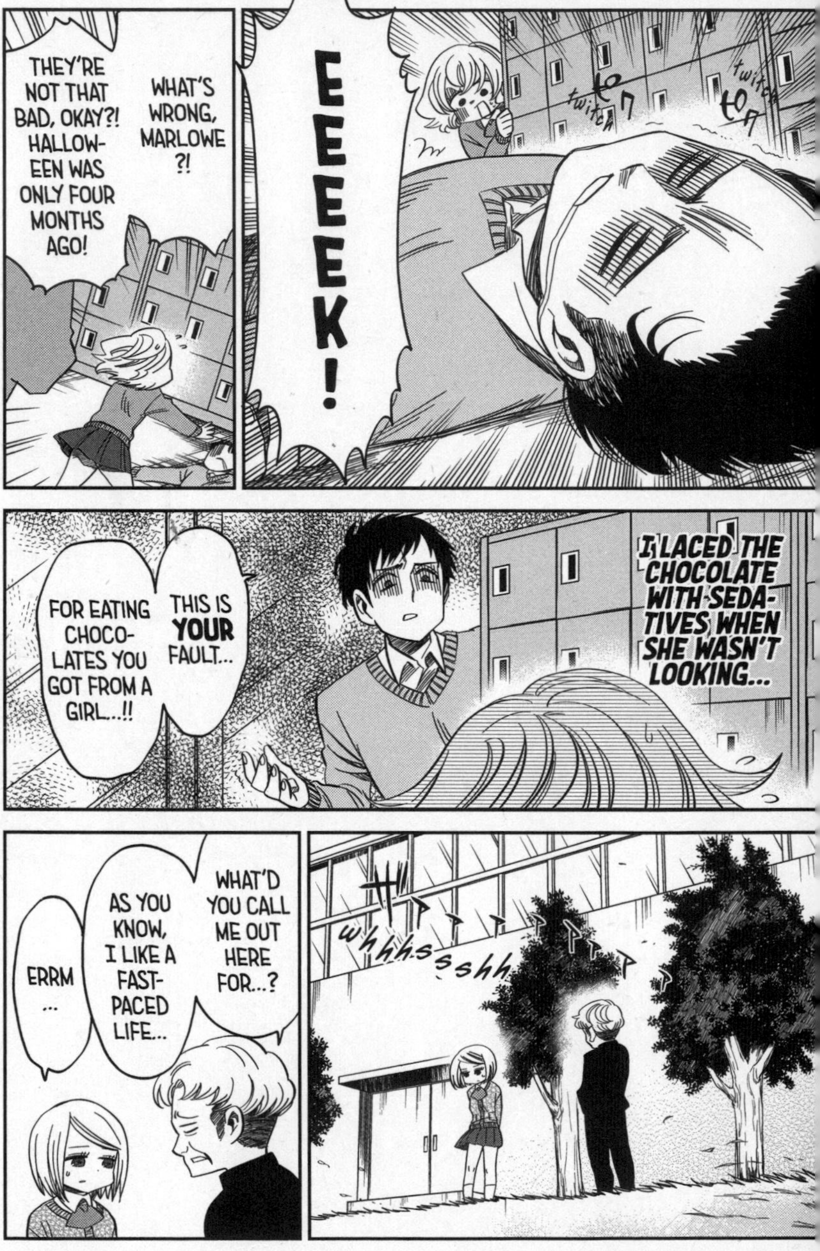
EEEEK!
twitch
twitch
WHAT'S WRONG, MARLOWE?!
THEY'RE NOT THAT BAD, OKAY?! HALLOWEEN WAS ONLY FOUR MONTHS AGO!
I LACED THE CHOCOLATE WITH SEDATIVES WHEN SHE WASN'T LOOKING...
THIS IS YOUR FAULT...
FOR EATING CHOCOLATES YOU GOT FROM A GIRL...!!
whhhsssshh
WHAT'D YOU CALL ME OUT HERE FOR...?
AS YOU KNOW, I LIKE A FAST-PACED LIFE...
ERRM...

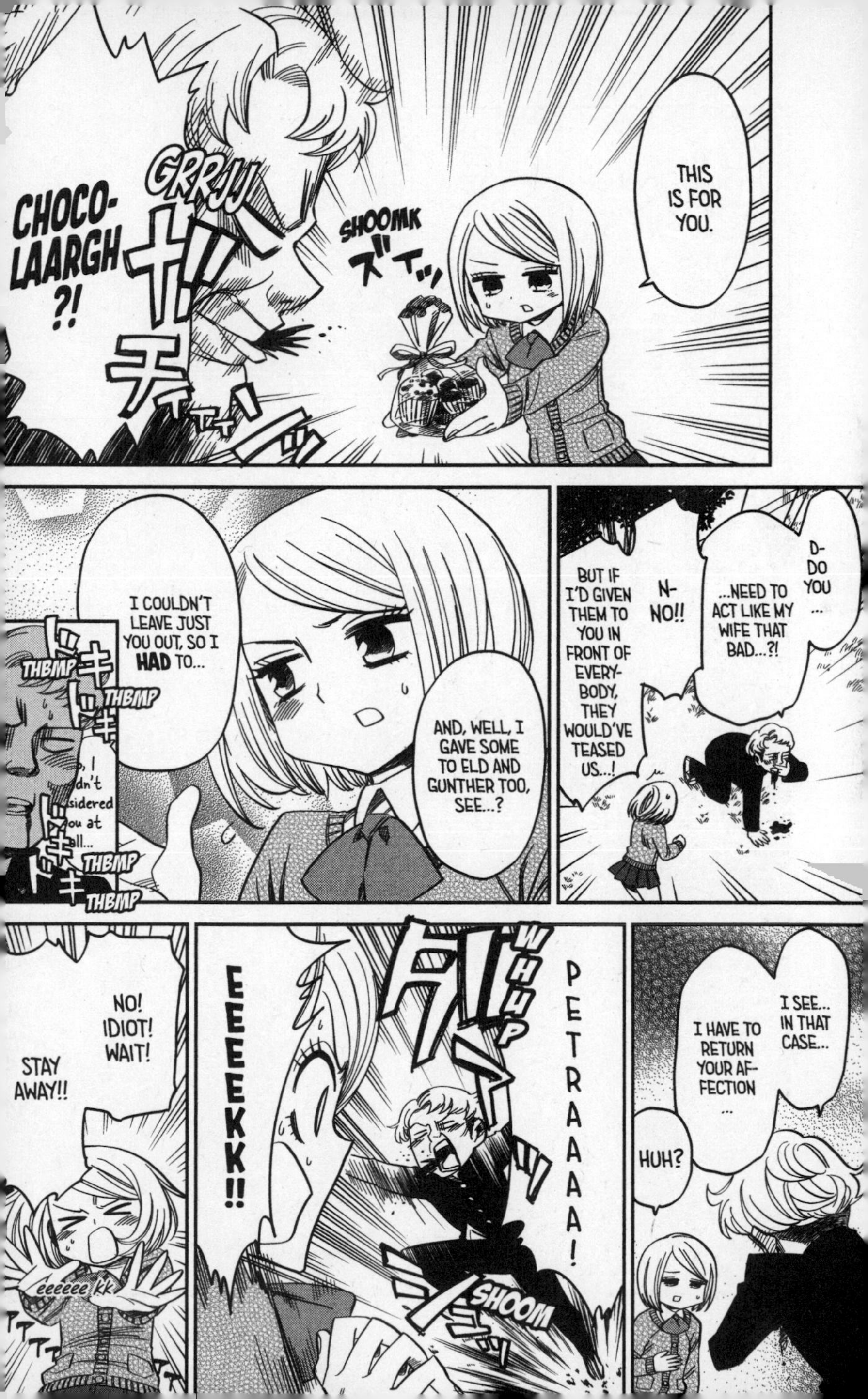
THIS IS FOR YOU.
SHOOMK
GRRJJ
CHOCO-LAARGH?!
D-DO YOU...
...NEED TO ACT LIKE MY WIFE THAT BAD...?!
N-NO!!
BUT IF I'D GIVEN THEM TO YOU IN FRONT OF EVERYBODY, THEY WOULD'VE TEASED US...!
AND, WELL, I GAVE SOME TO ELD AND GUNTHER TOO, SEE...?
I COULDN'T LEAVE JUST YOU OUT, SO I **HAD** TO...
THBMP THBMP THBMP THBMP
I SEE... IN THAT CASE...
I HAVE TO RETURN YOUR AFFECTION...
HUH?
PETRAAAA!
WHUP
EEEEEKK!!
SHOOM
NO! IDIOT! WAIT!
STAY AWAY!!
eeeeee kk

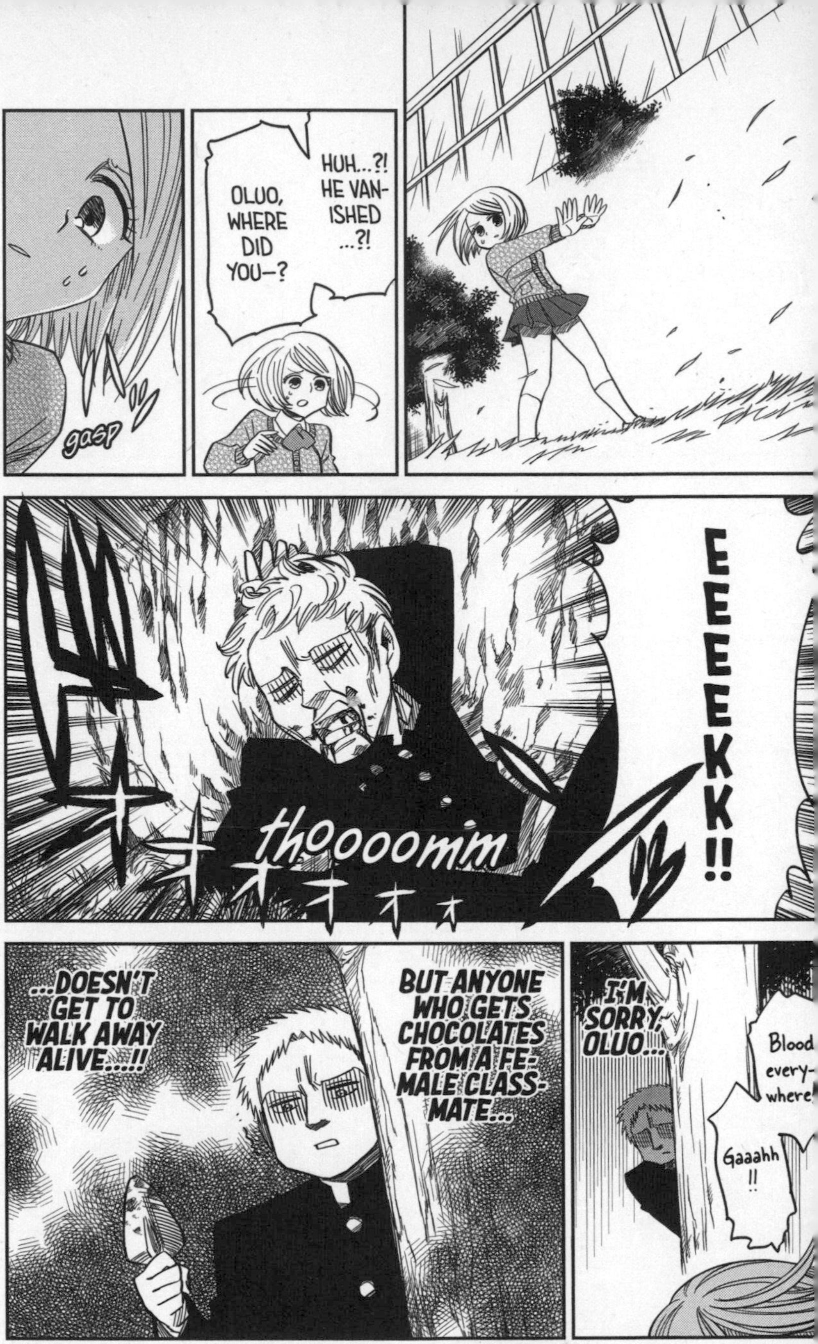
HUH...?! HE VAN-ISHED ...?!
OLUO, WHERE DID YOU--?
gasp
EEEEEKK!!
thoooomm
Blood every-where
Gaaahh !!
I'M SORRY, OLUO...
BUT ANYONE WHO GETS CHOCOLATES FROM A FE-MALE CLASS-MATE...
...DOESN'T GET TO WALK AWAY ALIVE...!!

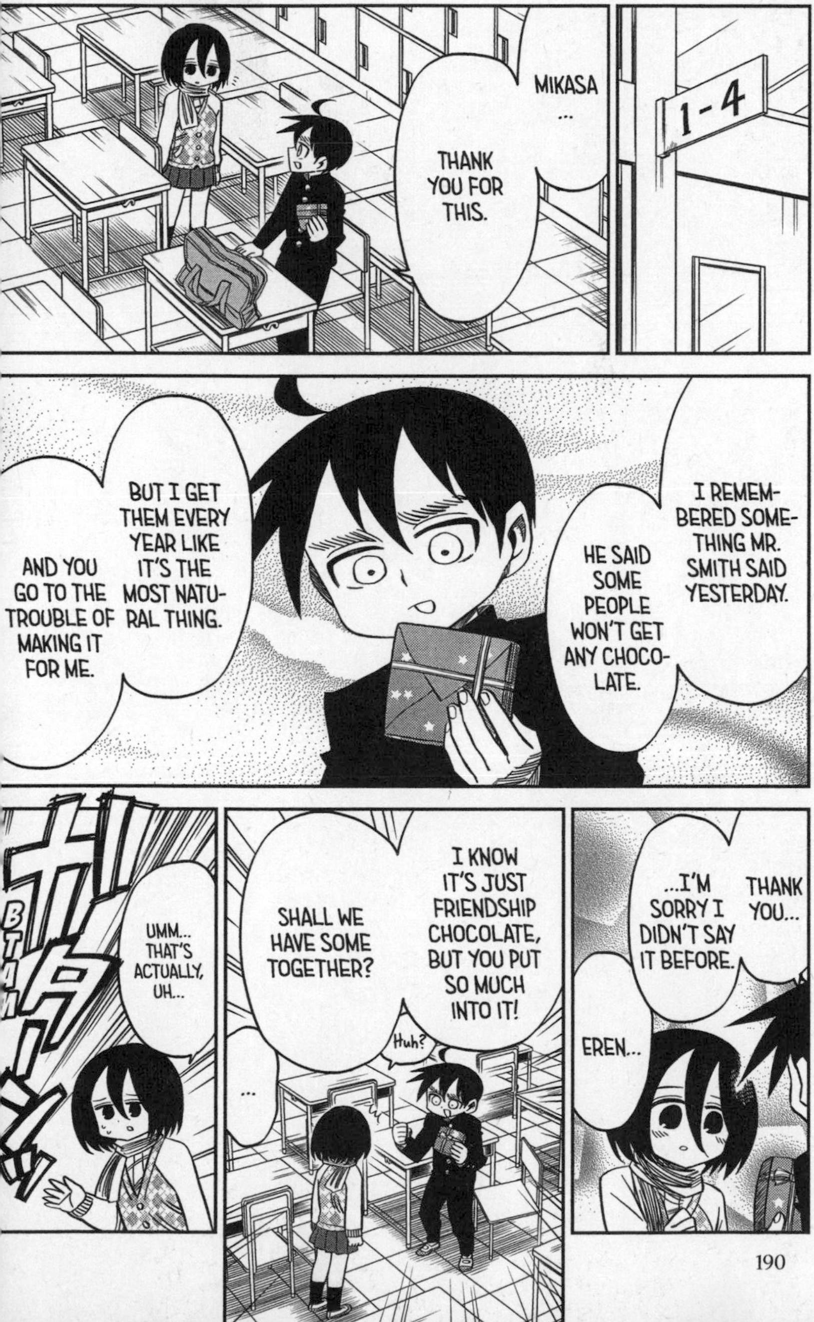
1-4
MIKASA ...
THANK YOU FOR THIS.
I REMEM-BERED SOME-THING MR. SMITH SAID YESTERDAY.
HE SAID SOME PEOPLE WON'T GET ANY CHOCO-LATE.
BUT I GET THEM EVERY YEAR LIKE IT'S THE MOST NATU-RAL THING.
AND YOU GO TO THE TROUBLE OF MAKING IT FOR ME.
THANK YOU...
...I'M SORRY I DIDN'T SAY IT BEFORE.
EREN...
I KNOW IT'S JUST FRIENDSHIP CHOCOLATE, BUT YOU PUT SO MUCH INTO IT!
SHALL WE HAVE SOME TOGETHER?
Huh?
...
UMM... THAT'S ACTUALLY, UH...
BTAN

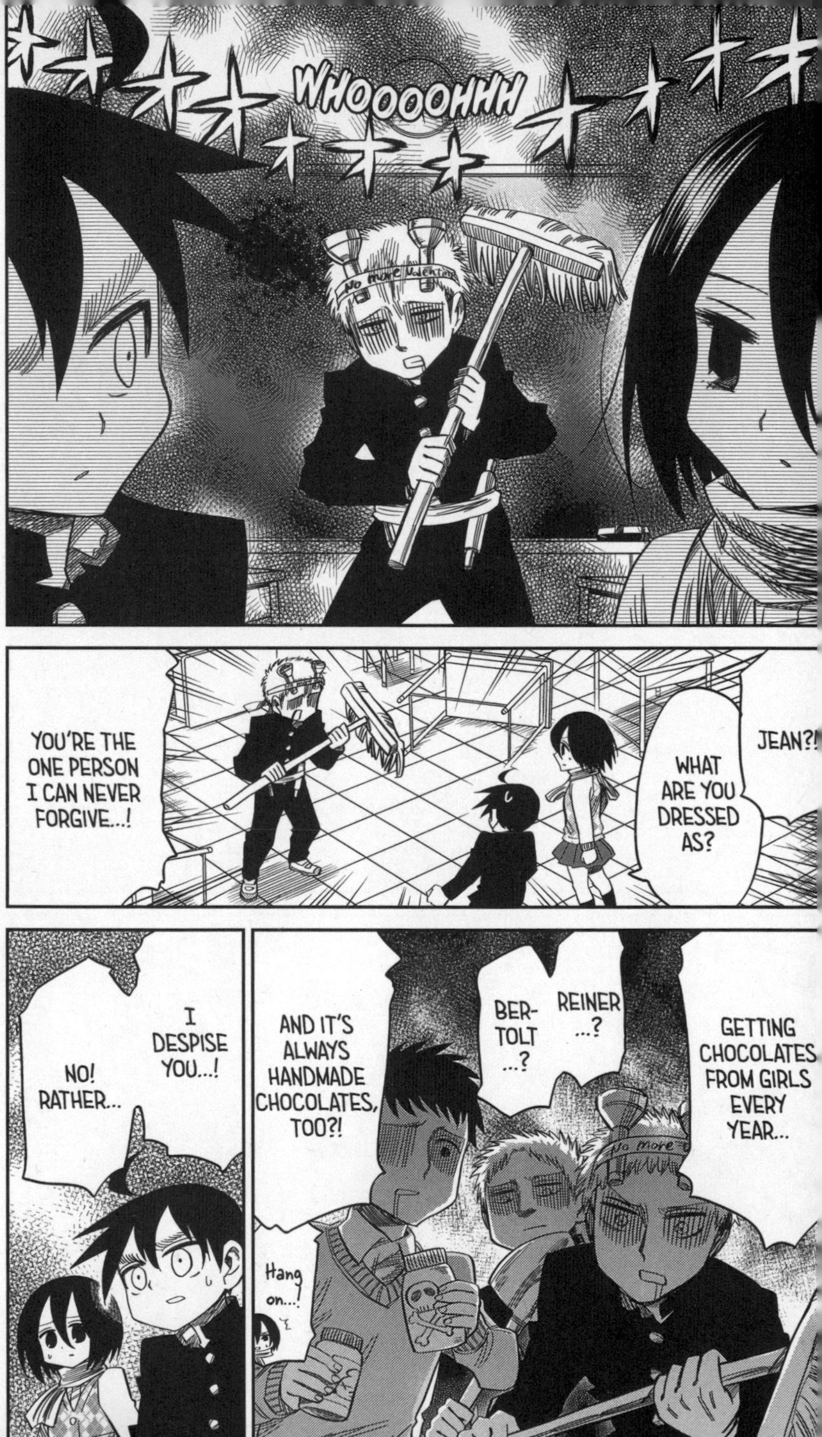
WHOOOOHHH
No more Valentine
JEAN?!
WHAT ARE YOU DRESSED AS?
YOU'RE THE ONE PERSON I CAN NEVER FORGIVE...!
GETTING CHOCOLATES FROM GIRLS EVERY YEAR...
REINER ...?
BER-TOLT ...?
AND IT'S ALWAYS HANDMADE CHOCOLATES, TOO?!
No more
Hang on...!
I DESPISE YOU...!
NO! RATHER...

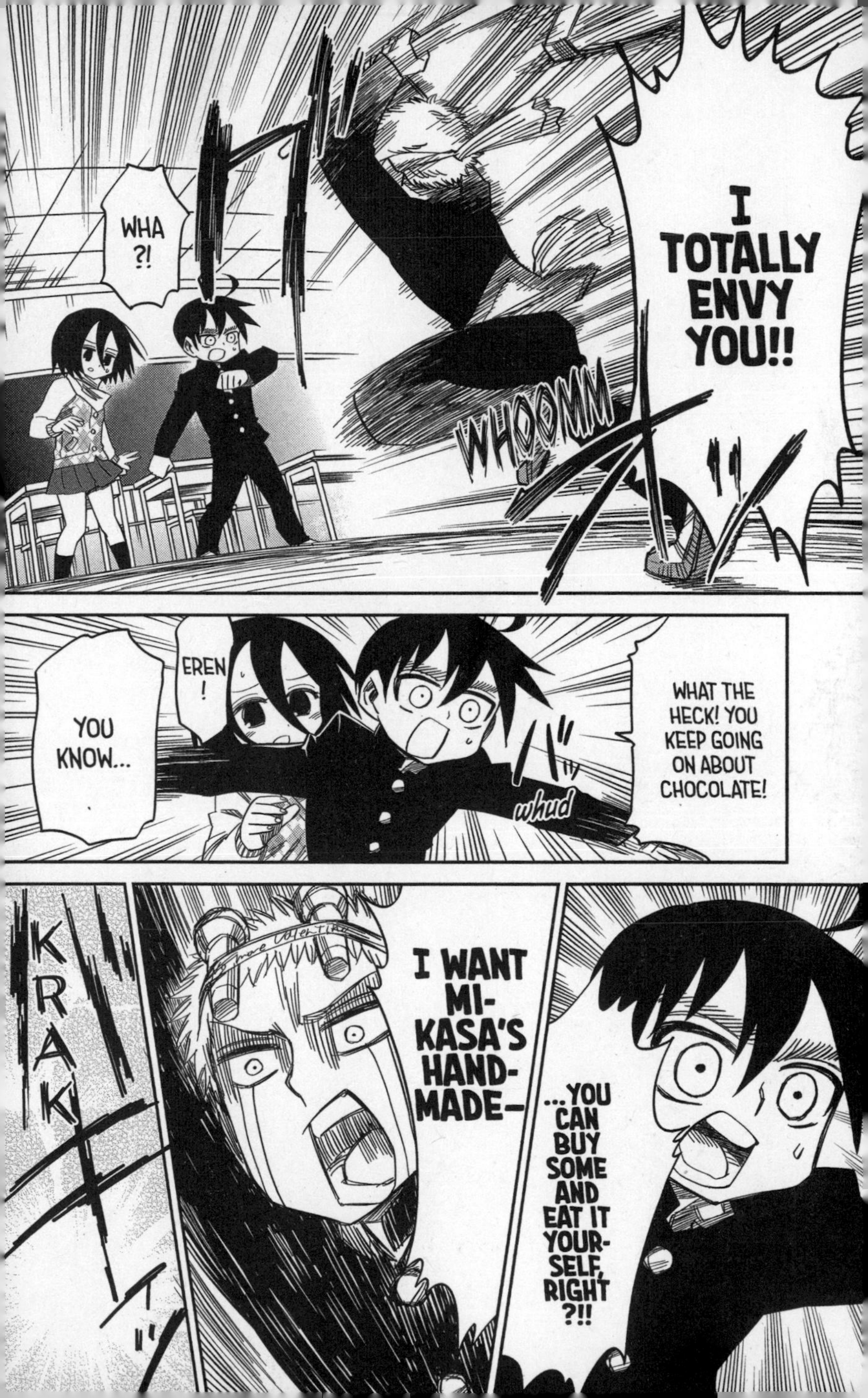
I TOTALLY ENVY YOU!!
WHOOMM
WHA ?!
WHAT THE HECK! YOU KEEP GOING ON ABOUT CHOCOLATE!
whud
EREN !
YOU KNOW...
...YOU CAN BUY SOME AND EAT IT YOUR-SELF, RIGHT?!!
I WANT MI-KASA'S HAND-MADE—
KRAK

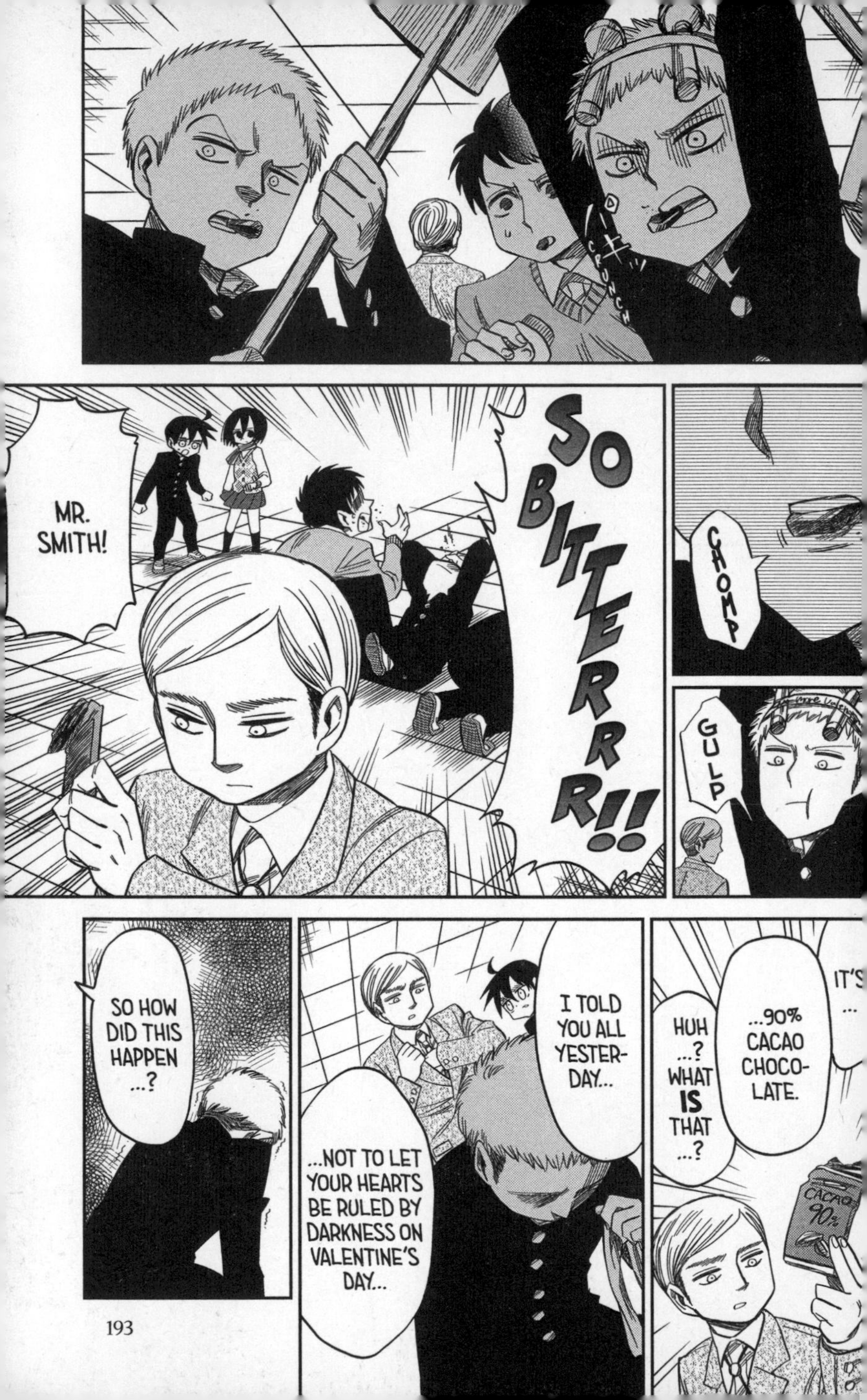
CRUNCH
CHOMP
GULP
SO BITTERRR!!
MR. SMITH!
IT'S ...
...90% CACAO CHOCOLATE.
HUH ...? WHAT IS THAT ...?
CACAO 90%
I TOLD YOU ALL YESTERDAY...
...NOT TO LET YOUR HEARTS BE RULED BY DARKNESS ON VALENTINE'S DAY...
SO HOW DID THIS HAPPEN ...?

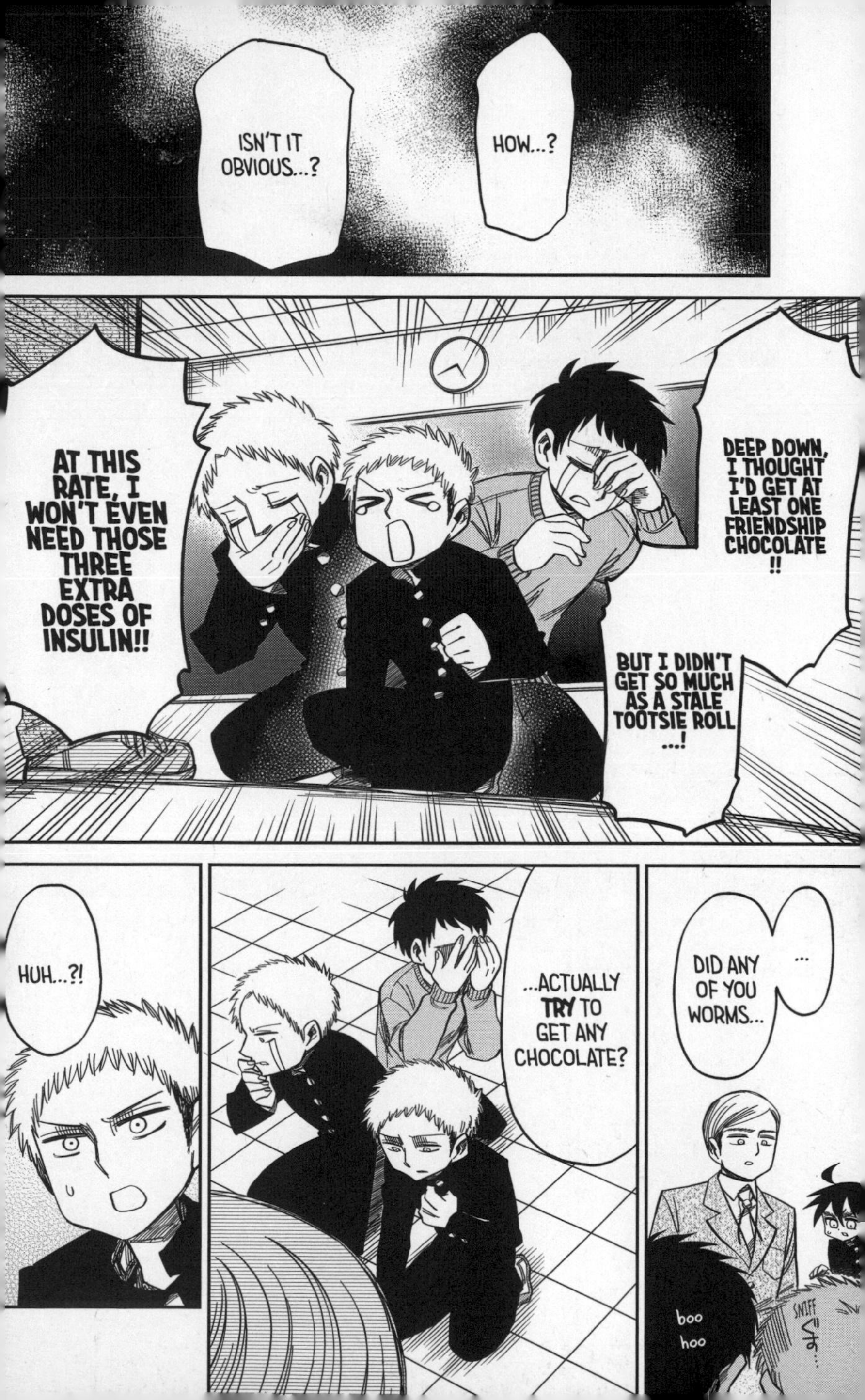
HOW...?
ISN'T IT OBVIOUS...?
DEEP DOWN, I THOUGHT I'D GET AT LEAST ONE FRIENDSHIP CHOCOLATE !!
BUT I DIDN'T GET SO MUCH AS A STALE TOOTSIE ROLL ...!
AT THIS RATE, I WON'T EVEN NEED THOSE THREE EXTRA DOSES OF INSULIN!!
...
DID ANY OF YOU WORMS...
SNIFF
boo hoo
...ACTUALLY TRY TO GET ANY CHOCOLATE?
HUH...?!

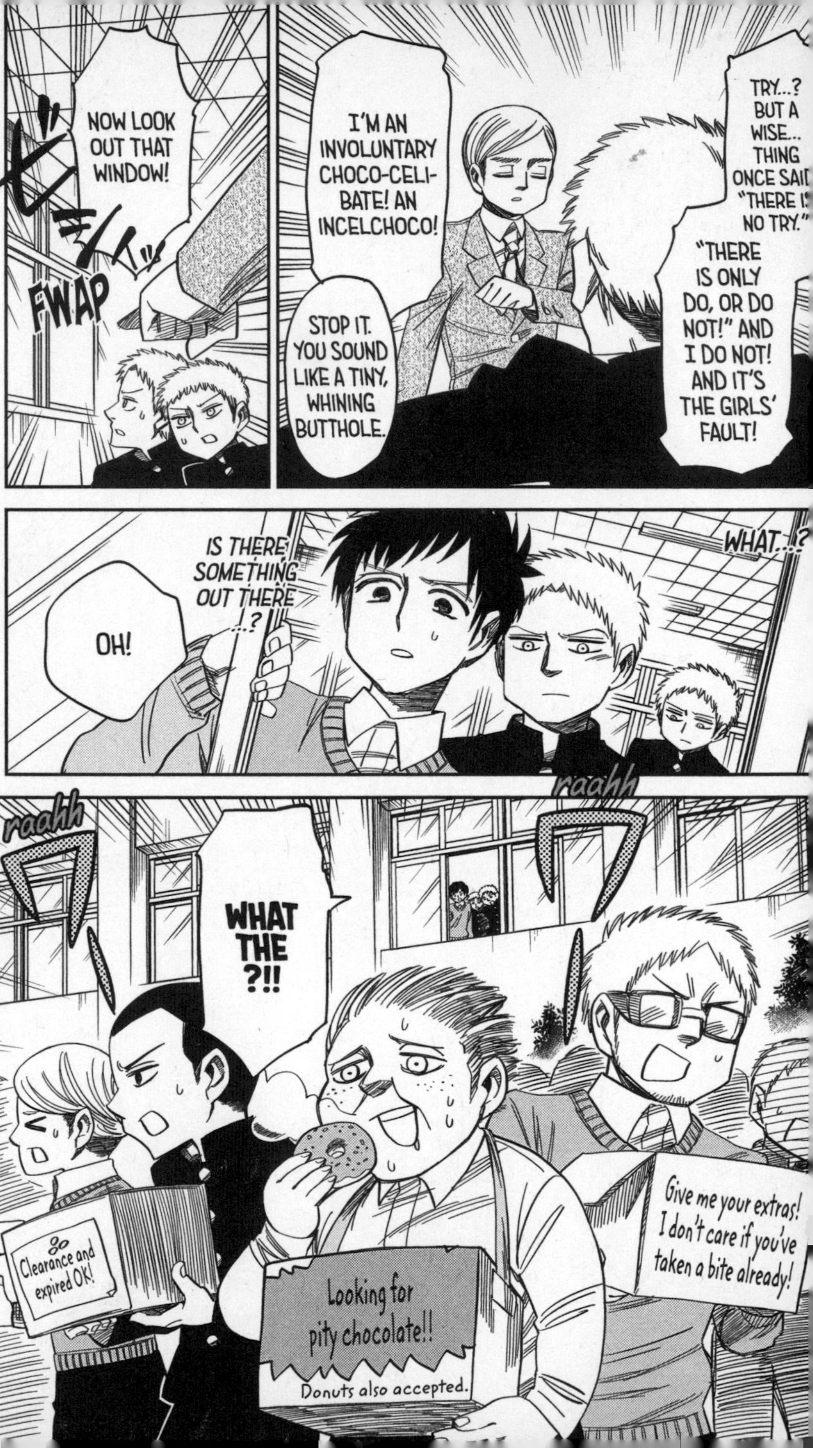
TRY...? BUT A WISE... THING ONCE SAID "THERE IS NO TRY."
"THERE IS ONLY DO, OR DO NOT!" AND I DO NOT! AND IT'S THE GIRLS' FAULT!
I'M AN INVOLUNTARY CHOCO-CELIBATE! AN INCELCHOCO!
STOP IT. YOU SOUND LIKE A TINY, WHINING BUTTHOLE.
NOW LOOK OUT THAT WINDOW!
FWAP
WHAT...?
IS THERE SOMETHING OUT THERE...?
OH!
raahh
raahh
WHAT THE?!!
Give me your extras! I don't care if you've taken a bite already!
Looking for pity chocolate!!
Donuts also accepted.
Clearance and expired OK!

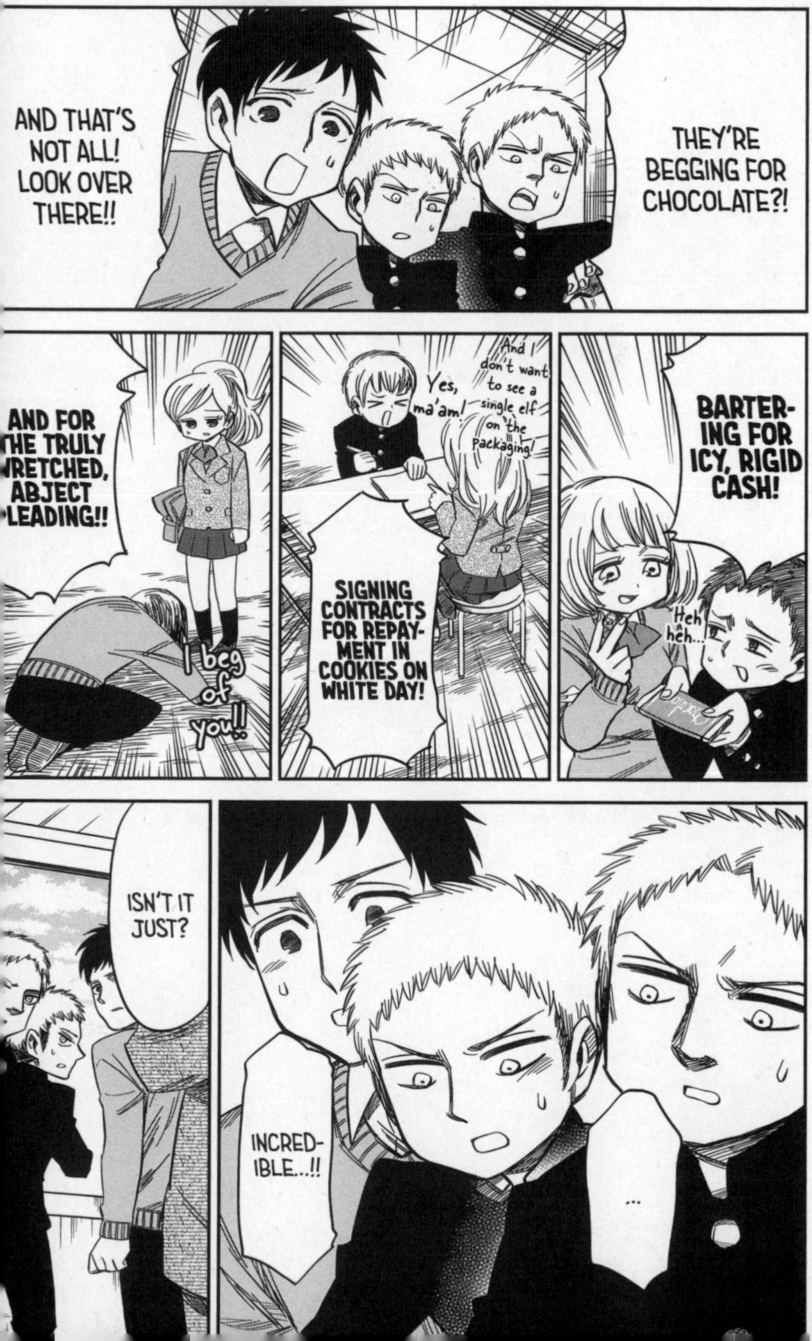
THEY'RE BEGGING FOR CHOCOLATE?!
AND THAT'S NOT ALL! LOOK OVER THERE!!
BARTER-ING FOR ICY, RIGID CASH!
Heh heh...
And I don't want to see a single elf on the packaging!
Yes, ma'am!
SIGNING CONTRACTS FOR REPAY-MENT IN COOKIES ON WHITE DAY!
AND FOR THE TRULY WRETCHED, ABJECT PLEADING!!
I beg of you!!
...
INCRED-IBLE...!!
ISN'T IT JUST?

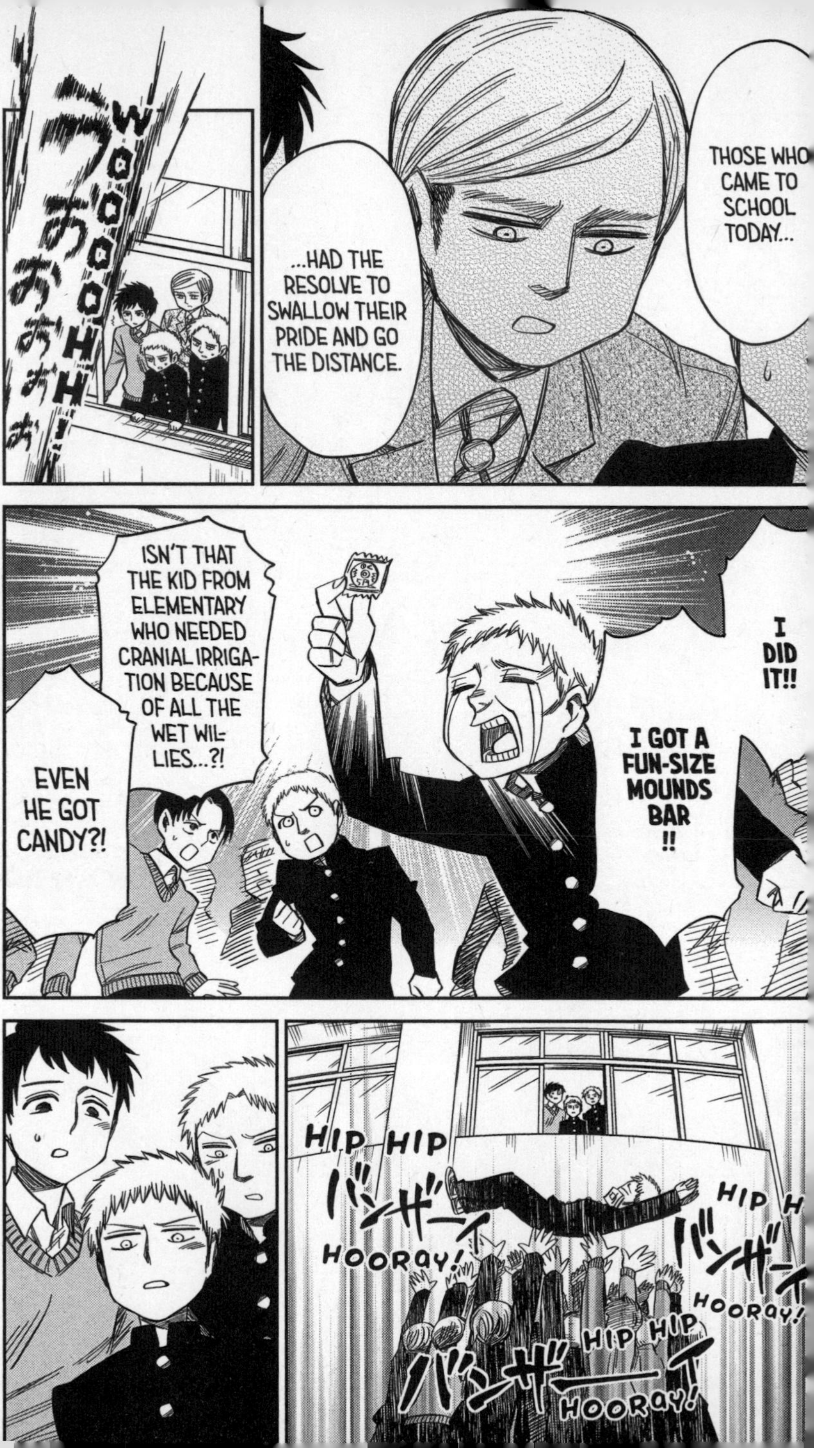
THOSE WHO CAME TO SCHOOL TODAY...
...HAD THE RESOLVE TO SWALLOW THEIR PRIDE AND GO THE DISTANCE.
WOOOOOOHH!!
I DID IT!!
I GOT A FUN-SIZE MOUNDS BAR!!
ISN'T THAT THE KID FROM ELEMENTARY WHO NEEDED CRANIAL IRRIGATION BECAUSE OF ALL THE WET WILLIES...?!
EVEN HE GOT CANDY?!
HIP HIP バンザーイ HOORAY!
HIP HIP バンザーイ HOORAY!
HIP HIP バンザーイ HOORAY!

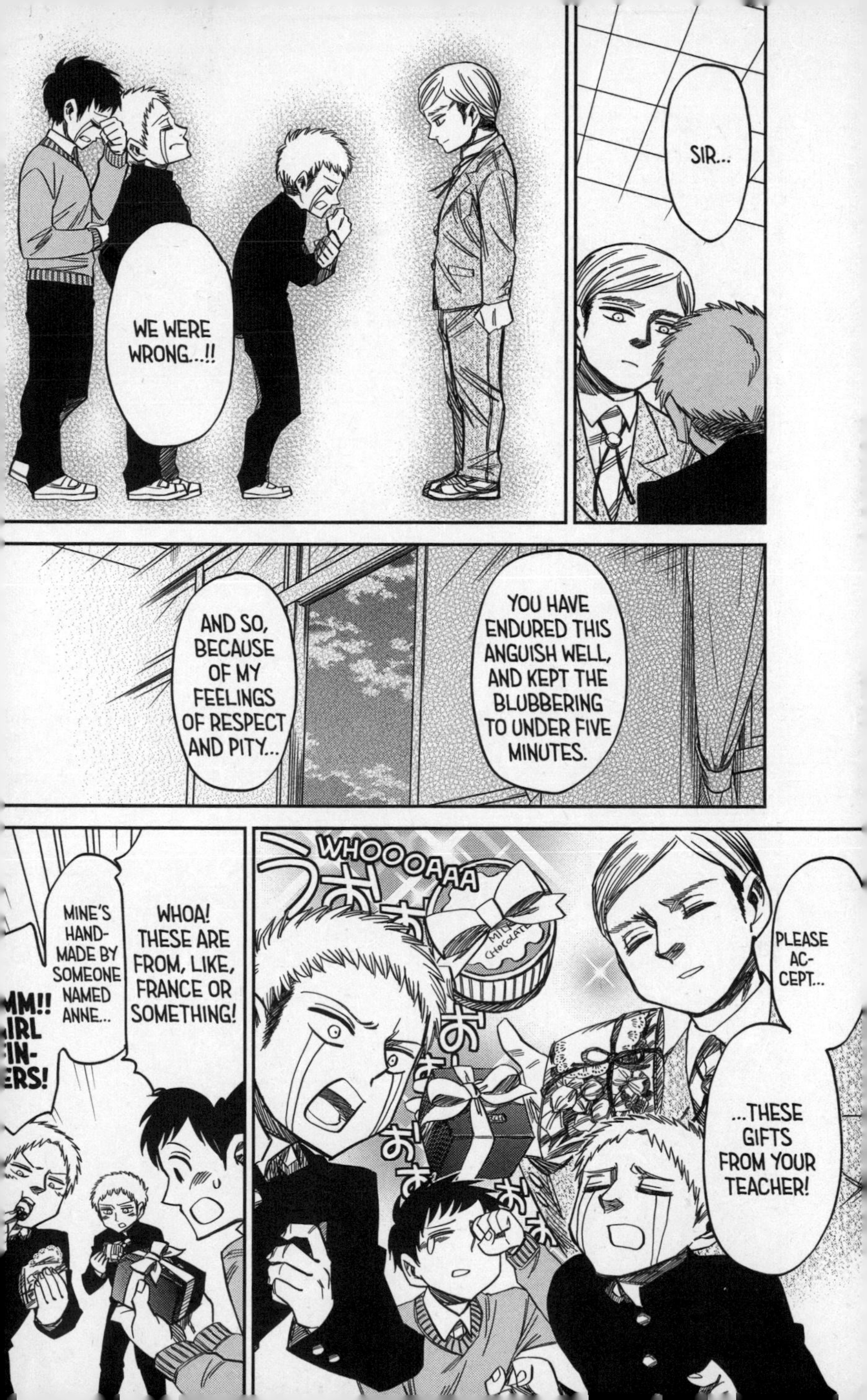
SIR...
WE WERE WRONG...!!
YOU HAVE ENDURED THIS ANGUISH WELL, AND KEPT THE BLUBBERING TO UNDER FIVE MINUTES.
AND SO, BECAUSE OF MY FEELINGS OF RESPECT AND PITY...
WHOOOAAA
PLEASE AC-CEPT...
...THESE GIFTS FROM YOUR TEACHER!
WHOA! THESE ARE FROM, LIKE, FRANCE OR SOMETHING!
MINE'S HAND-MADE BY SOMEONE NAMED ANNE...

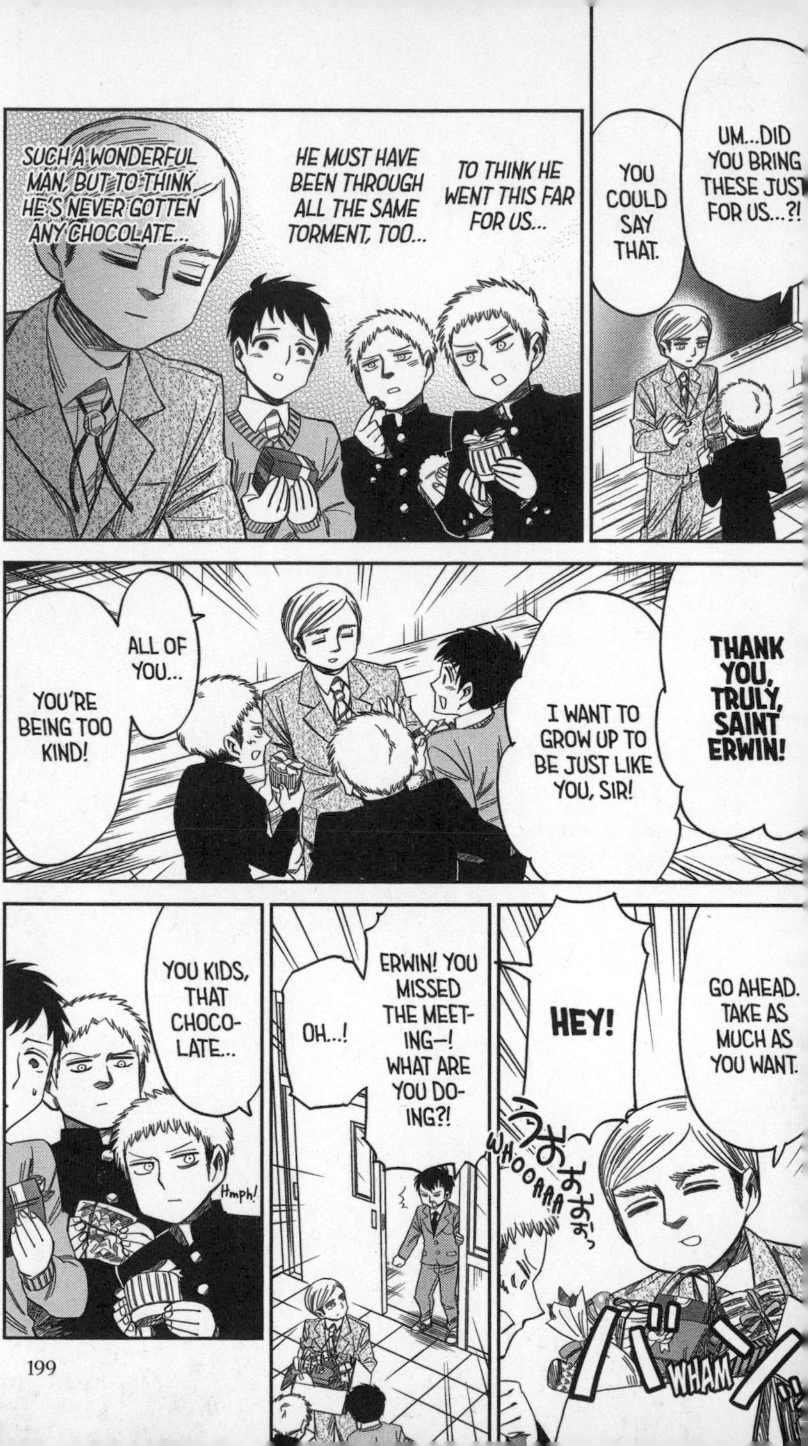
UM...DID YOU BRING THESE JUST FOR US...?!
YOU COULD SAY THAT.
TO THINK HE WENT THIS FAR FOR US...
HE MUST HAVE BEEN THROUGH ALL THE SAME TORMENT, TOO...
SUCH A WONDERFUL MAN, BUT TO THINK HE'S NEVER GOTTEN ANY CHOCOLATE...
THANK YOU, TRULY, SAINT ERWIN!
I WANT TO GROW UP TO BE JUST LIKE YOU, SIR!
ALL OF YOU...
YOU'RE BEING TOO KIND!
GO AHEAD. TAKE AS MUCH AS YOU WANT.
HEY!
WHOOAAA
WHAM
ERWIN! YOU MISSED THE MEET-ING—! WHAT ARE YOU DO-ING?!
OH...!
YOU KIDS, THAT CHOCO-LATE...
Hmph!

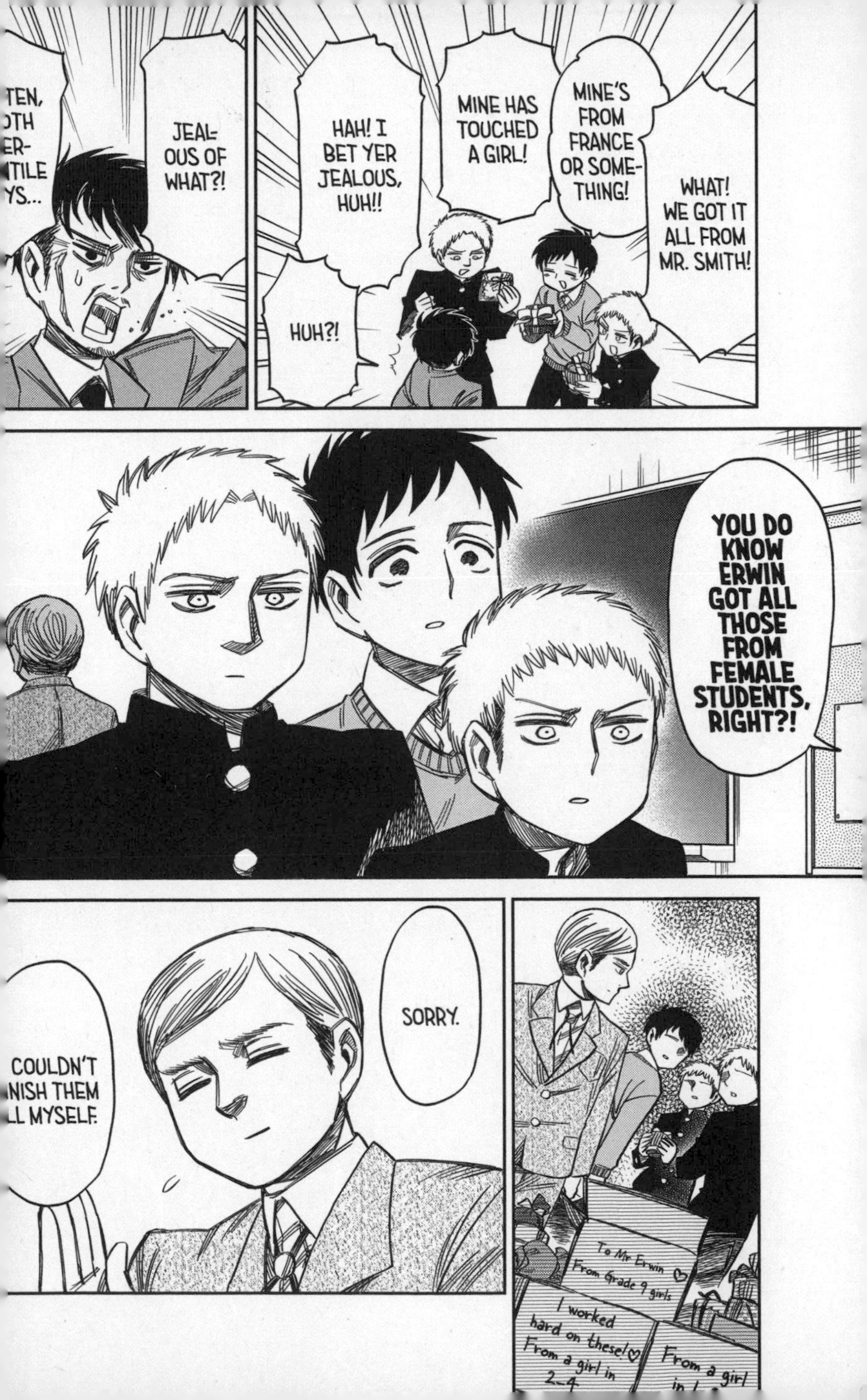
WHAT! WE GOT IT ALL FROM MR. SMITH!
MINE'S FROM FRANCE OR SOME-THING!
MINE HAS TOUCHED A GIRL!
HAH! I BET YER JEALOUS, HUH!!
HUH?!
JEAL-OUS OF WHAT?!
TEN, OTH ER- TILE YS...
YOU DO KNOW ERWIN GOT ALL THOSE FROM FEMALE STUDENTS, RIGHT?!
To Mr Erwin ♡ From Grade 9 girls
I worked hard on these!♡ From a girl in 2-4
From a girl
SORRY.
COULDN'T NISH THEM LL MYSELF.

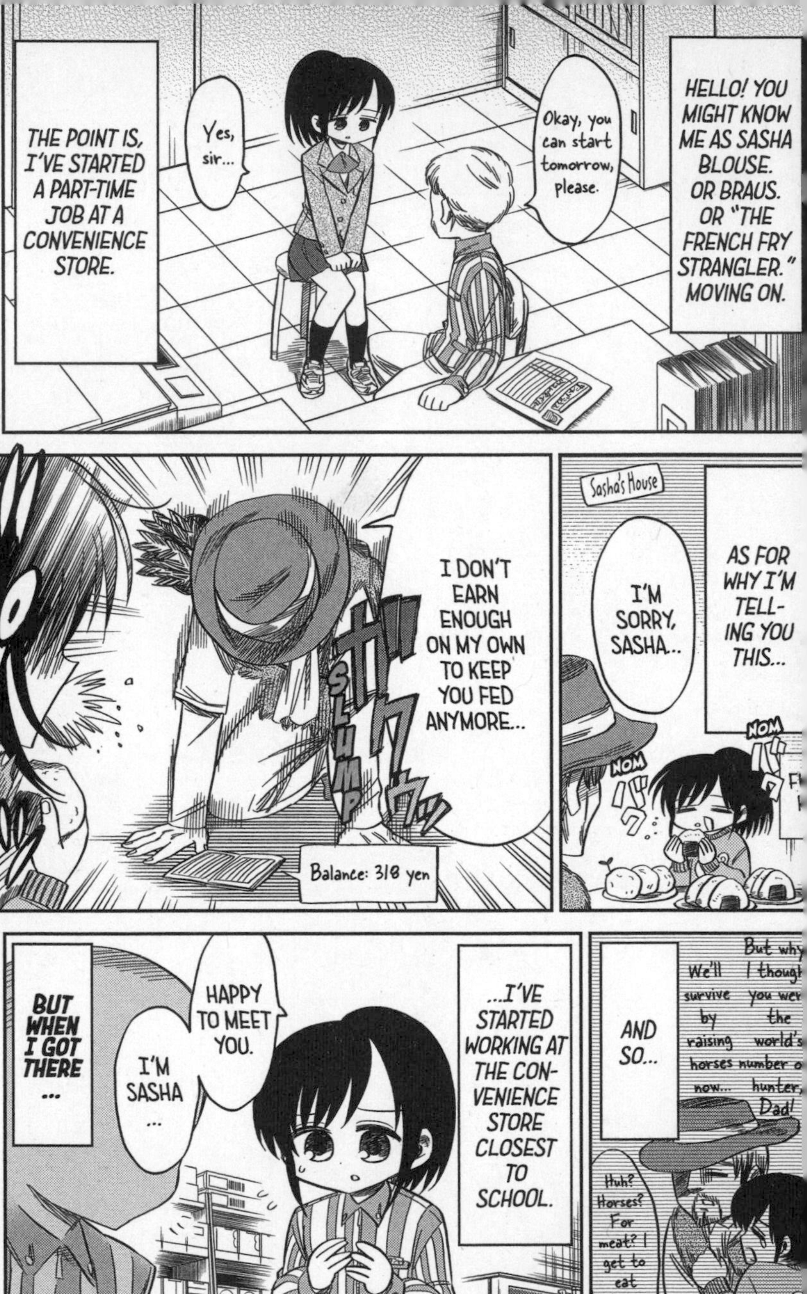
HELLO! YOU MIGHT KNOW ME AS SASHA BLOUSE. OR BRAUS. OR "THE FRENCH FRY STRANGLER." MOVING ON.
Okay, you can start tomorrow, please.
Yes, sir...
THE POINT IS, I'VE STARTED A PART-TIME JOB AT A CONVENIENCE STORE.
Sasha's House
AS FOR WHY I'M TELLING YOU THIS...
I'M SORRY, SASHA...
NOM
NOM
I DON'T EARN ENOUGH ON MY OWN TO KEEP YOU FED ANYMORE...
SLUMP
Balance: 318 yen
BFFFT
We'll survive by raising horses now...
AND SO...
Huh? Horses? For meat? I get to eat them, right?
...I'VE STARTED WORKING AT THE CONVENIENCE STORE CLOSEST TO SCHOOL.
HAPPY TO MEET YOU.
I'M SASHA...
BUT WHEN I GOT THERE...

IFTY-FOURTH PERIOD: PART-TIME JOB? NO PROB AT ATTACK JUNIOR HIGH

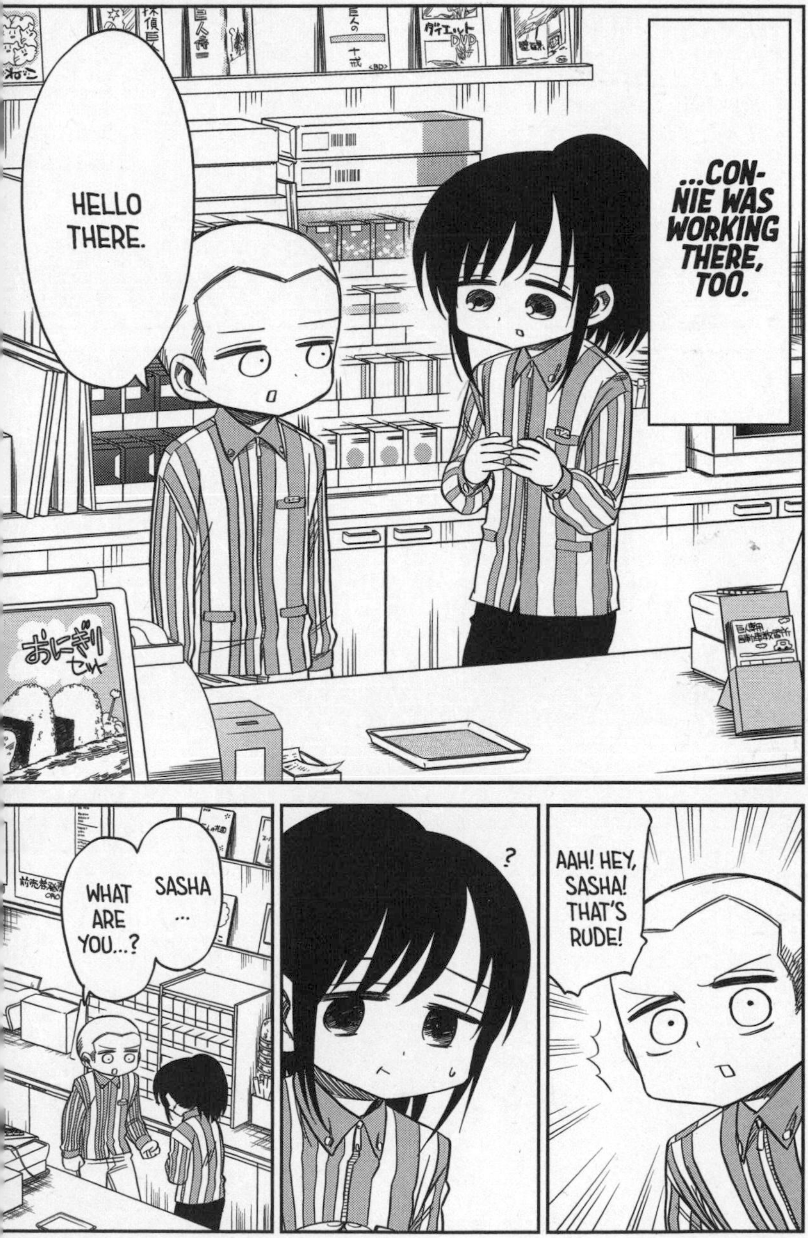
...CON-NIE WAS WORKING THERE, TOO.
HELLO THERE.
ダイエット DVD
おにぎり セット
AAH! HEY, SASHA! THAT'S RUDE!
?
SASHA ...
WHAT ARE YOU...?

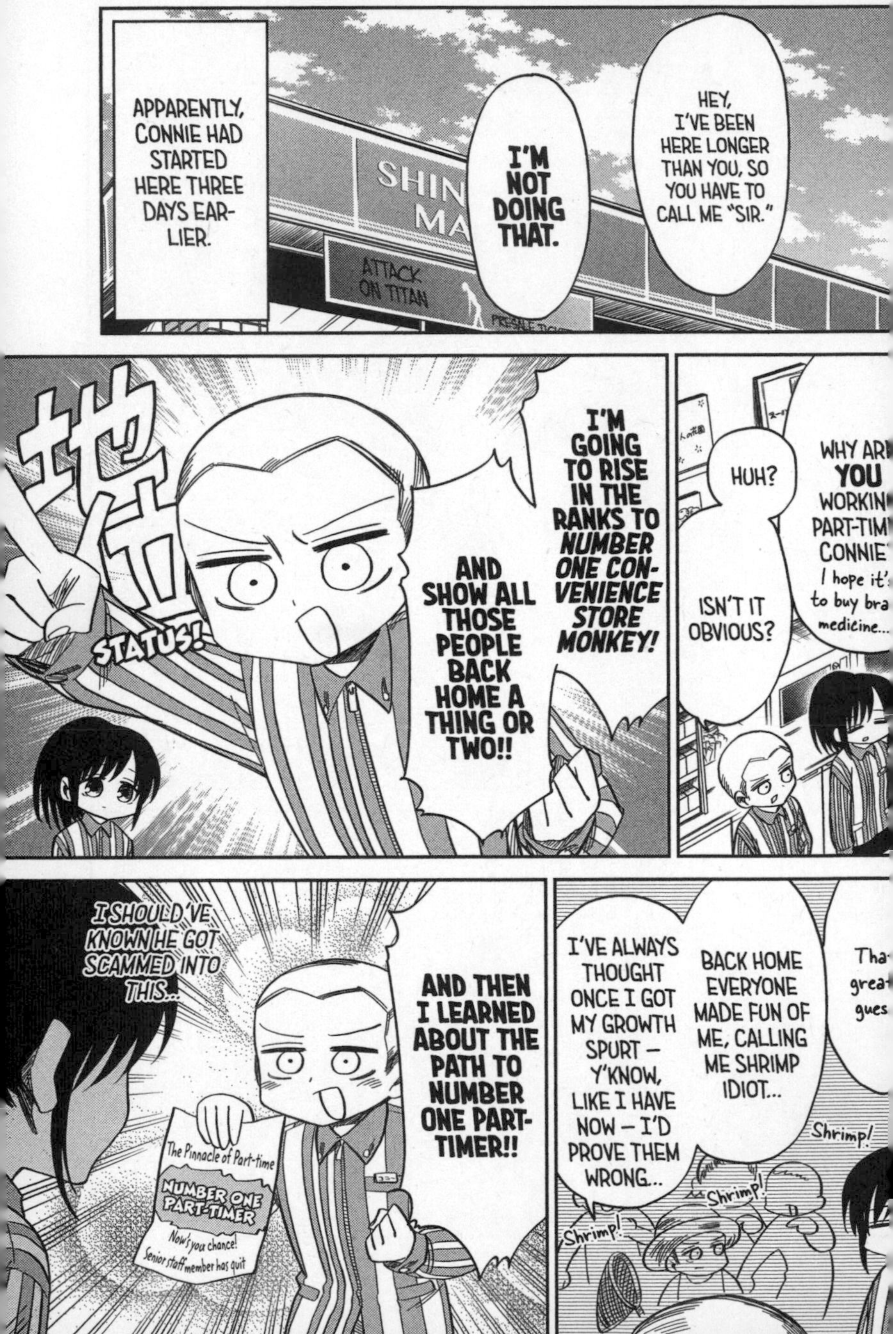
HEY, I'VE BEEN HERE LONGER THAN YOU, SO YOU HAVE TO CALL ME "SIR."
I'M NOT DOING THAT.
ATTACK ON TITAN
APPARENTLY, CONNIE HAD STARTED HERE THREE DAYS EARLIER.
WHY AR YOU WORKIN PART-TIM CONNIE
I hope it's to buy bra medicine...
HUH?
ISN'T IT OBVIOUS?
I'M GOING TO RISE IN THE RANKS TO NUMBER ONE CONVENIENCE STORE MONKEY!
AND SHOW ALL THOSE PEOPLE BACK HOME A THING OR TWO!!
STATUS!
Tha grea gues
BACK HOME EVERYONE MADE FUN OF ME, CALLING ME SHRIMP IDIOT...
I'VE ALWAYS THOUGHT ONCE I GOT MY GROWTH SPURT – Y'KNOW, LIKE I HAVE NOW – I'D PROVE THEM WRONG...
Shrimp!
Shrimp!
Shrimp!
AND THEN I LEARNED ABOUT THE PATH TO NUMBER ONE PART-TIMER!!
The Pinnacle of Part-time
NUMBER ONE PART-TIMER
Now's your chance! Senior staff member has quit
I SHOULD'VE KNOWN HE GOT SCAMMED INTO THIS...

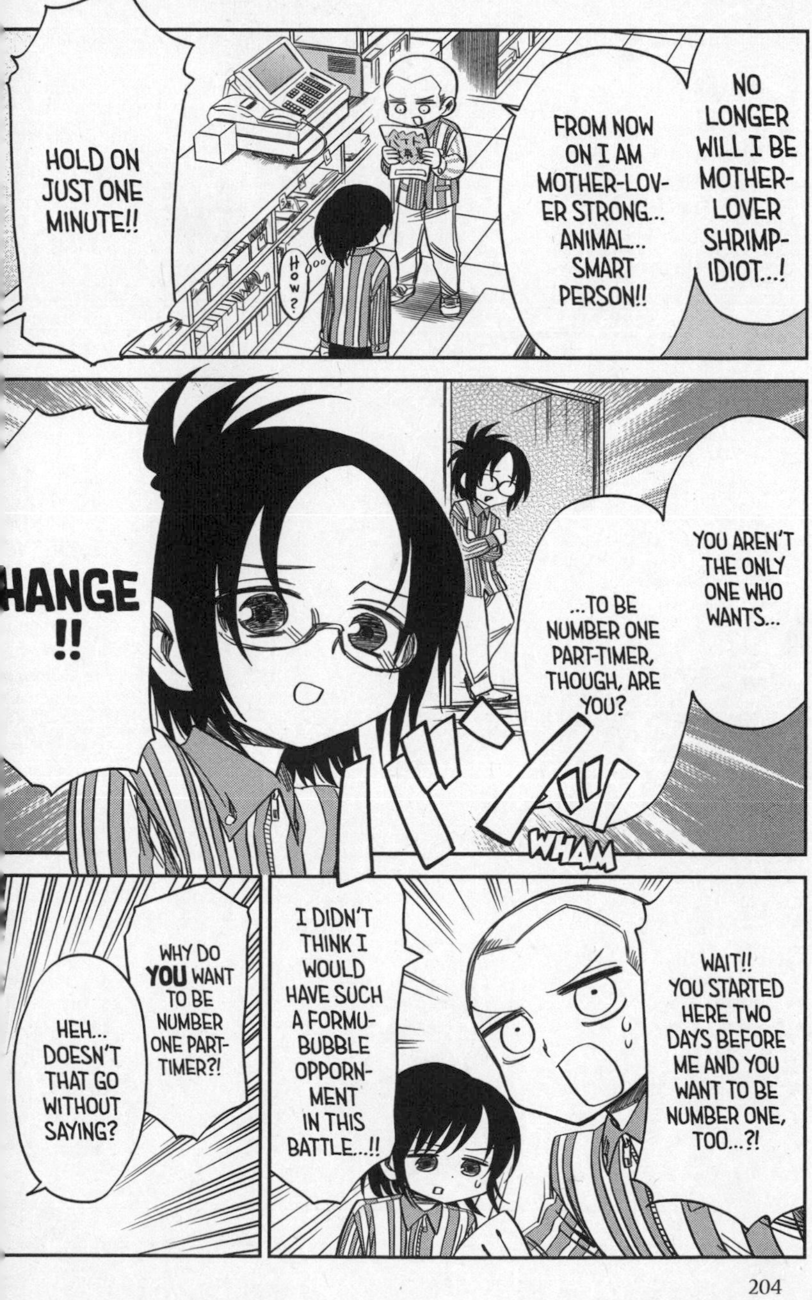
NO LONGER WILL I BE MOTHER-LOVER SHRIMP-IDIOT...!
FROM NOW ON I AM MOTHER-LOVER STRONG... ANIMAL... SMART PERSON!!
HOW?
HOLD ON JUST ONE MINUTE!!
YOU AREN'T THE ONLY ONE WHO WANTS...
...TO BE NUMBER ONE PART-TIMER, THOUGH, ARE YOU?
WHAM
HANGE !!
WAIT!! YOU STARTED HERE TWO DAYS BEFORE ME AND YOU WANT TO BE NUMBER ONE, TOO...?!
I DIDN'T THINK I WOULD HAVE SUCH A FORMU-BUBBLE OPPORN-MENT IN THIS BATTLE...!!
WHY DO YOU WANT TO BE NUMBER ONE PART-TIMER?!
HEH... DOESN'T THAT GO WITHOUT SAYING?

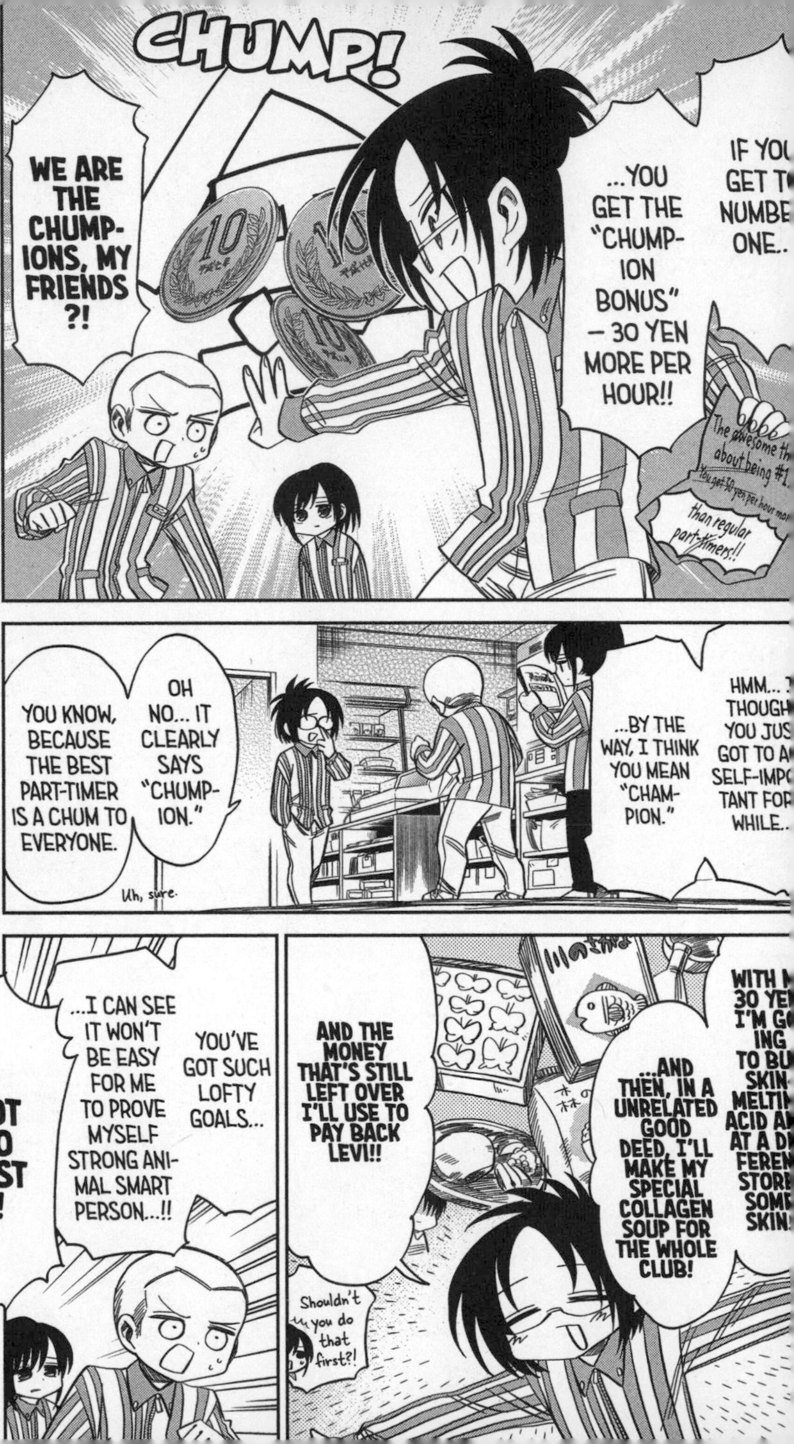
CHUMP!
IF YOU GET T NUMBE ONE..
...YOU GET THE "CHUMPION BONUS" – 30 YEN MORE PER HOUR!!
The awesome th about being #1 You get 30 yen per hour mo than regular part-timers!!
WE ARE THE CHUMPIONS, MY FRIENDS ?!
HMM... THOUGH YOU JUS GOT TO A SELF-IMPO TANT FOR WHILE..
...BY THE WAY, I THINK YOU MEAN "CHAMPION."
OH NO... IT CLEARLY SAYS "CHUMPION."
YOU KNOW, BECAUSE THE BEST PART-TIMER IS A CHUM TO EVERYONE.
Uh, sure.
WITH 30 YE I'M GO ING TO BU SKIN MELTI ACID A AT A D FEREN STORE SOME SKIN!
...AND THEN, IN A UNRELATED GOOD DEED, I'LL MAKE MY SPECIAL COLLAGEN SOUP FOR THE WHOLE CLUB!
AND THE MONEY THAT'S STILL LEFT OVER I'LL USE TO PAY BACK LEVI!!
Shouldn't you do that first?!
YOU'VE GOT SUCH LOFTY GOALS...
...I CAN SEE IT WON'T BE EASY FOR ME TO PROVE MYSELF STRONG ANIMAL SMART PERSON...!!
NOT SO FAST !!

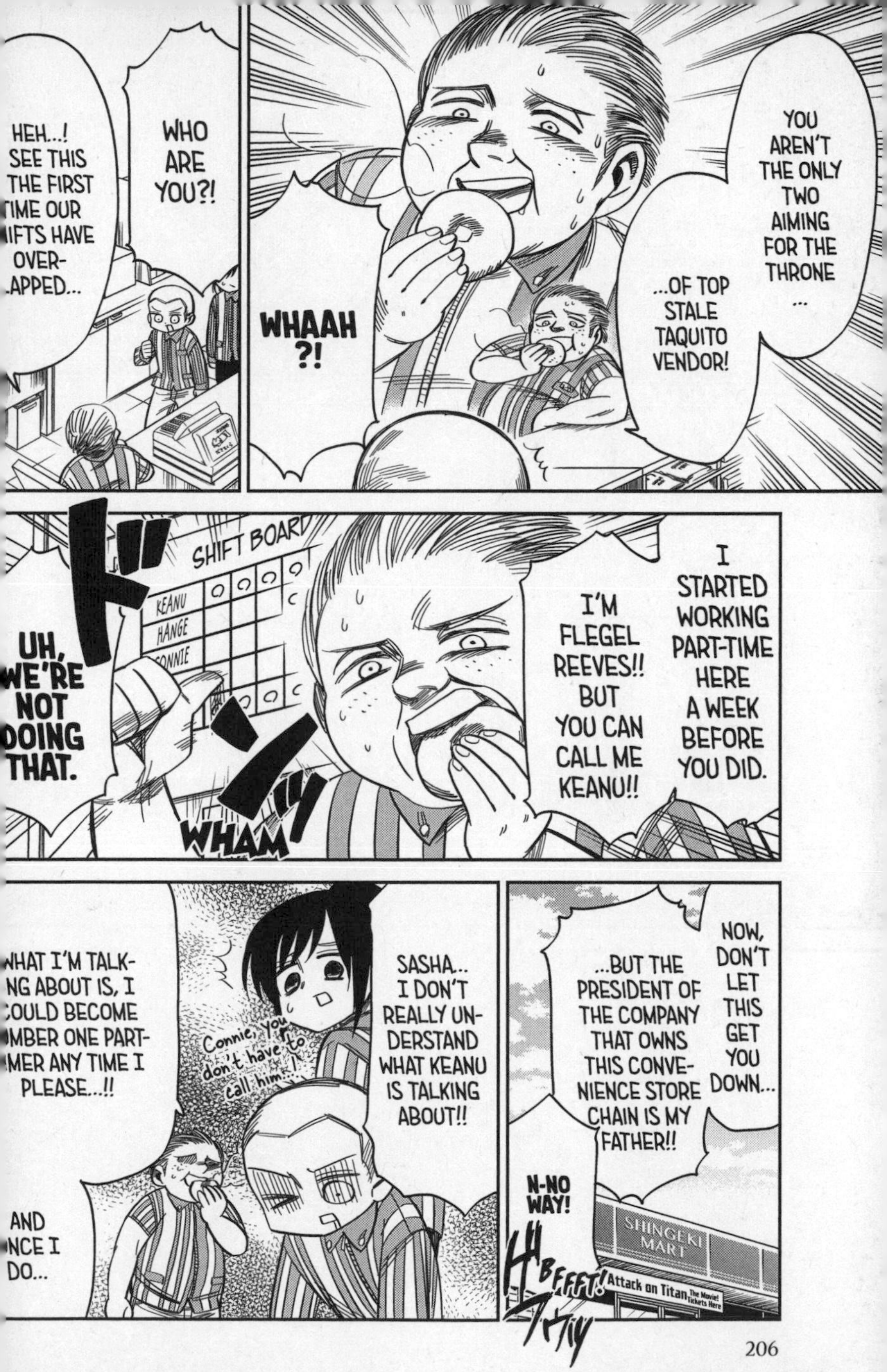
YOU AREN'T THE ONLY TWO AIMING FOR THE THRONE...
...OF TOP STALE TAQUITO VENDOR!
WHAAH?!
WHO ARE YOU?!
HEH...! SEE THIS THE FIRST TIME OUR IFTS HAVE OVER- APPED...
I STARTED WORKING PART-TIME HERE A WEEK BEFORE YOU DID.
I'M FLEGEL REEVES!! BUT YOU CAN CALL ME KEANU!!
SHIFT BOARD
KEANU
HANGE
ONNIE
WHAM
UH, WE'RE NOT DOING THAT.
NOW, DON'T LET THIS GET YOU DOWN...
...BUT THE PRESIDENT OF THE COMPANY THAT OWNS THIS CONVE- NIENCE STORE CHAIN IS MY FATHER!!
N-NO WAY!
BFFFT!
SHINGEKI MART
Attack on Titan The Movie! Tickets Here
SASHA... I DON'T REALLY UN- DERSTAND WHAT KEANU IS TALKING ABOUT!!
Connie, you don't have to call him...!
VHAT I'M TALK- NG ABOUT IS, I COULD BECOME MBER ONE PART- MER ANY TIME I PLEASE...!!
AND NCE I DO...

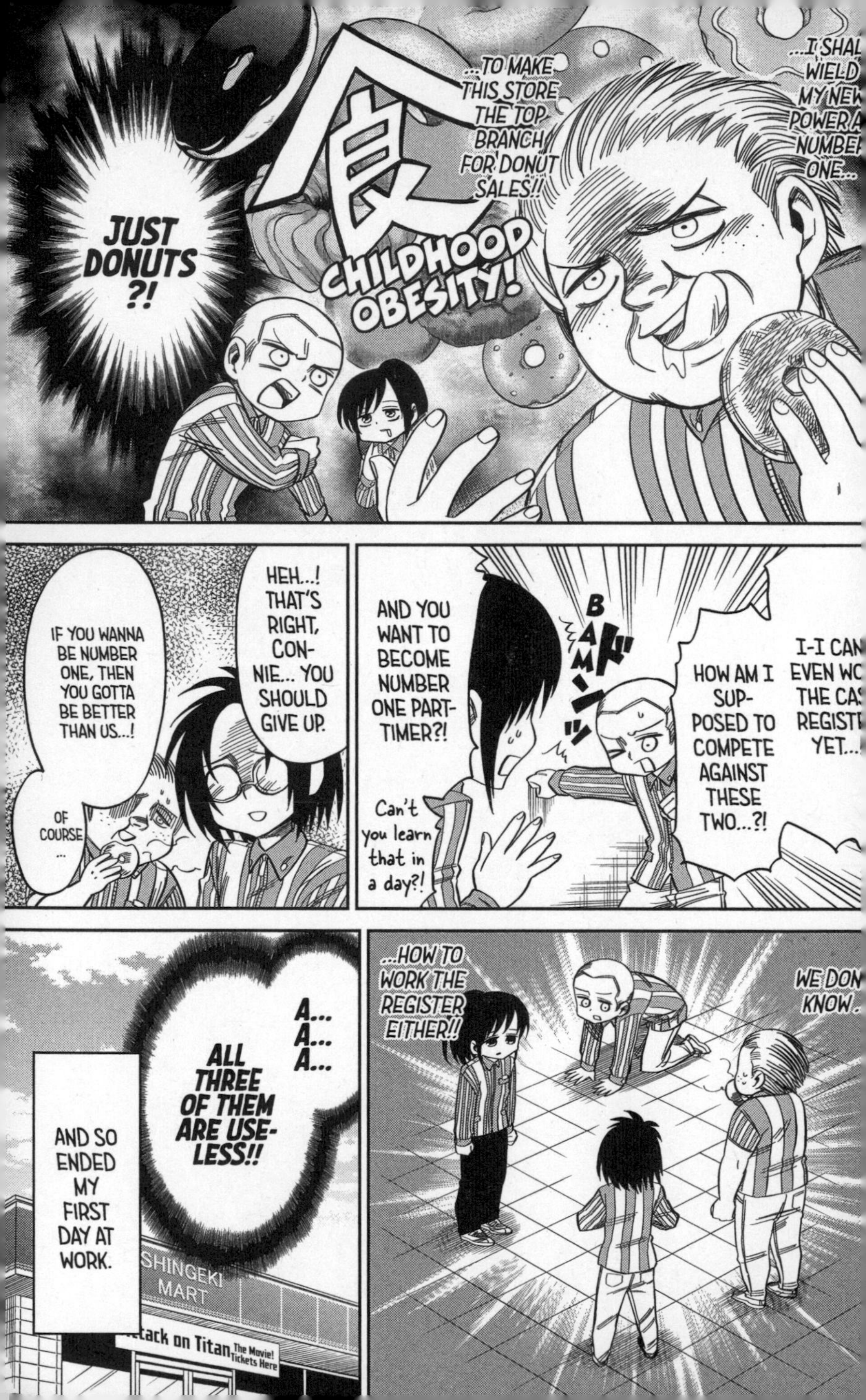

...I SHAL WIELD MY NEW POWER A NUMBE ONE...
...TO MAKE THIS STORE THE TOP BRANCH FOR DONUT SALES!!
食
CHILDHOOD OBESITY!
JUST DONUTS ?!
I-I CAN EVEN WO THE CAS REGISTE YET...
HOW AM I SUP-POSED TO COMPETE AGAINST THESE TWO...?!
BAMン
AND YOU WANT TO BECOME NUMBER ONE PART-TIMER?!
Can't you learn that in a day?!
HEH...! THAT'S RIGHT, CON-NIE... YOU SHOULD GIVE UP.
IF YOU WANNA BE NUMBER ONE, THEN YOU GOTTA BE BETTER THAN US...!
OF COURSE ...
WE DON KNOW...
...HOW TO WORK THE REGISTER EITHER!!
A... A... A...
ALL THREE OF THEM ARE USE-LESS!!
AND SO ENDED MY FIRST DAY AT WORK.
SHINGEKI MART
tack on Titan The Movie! Tickets Here

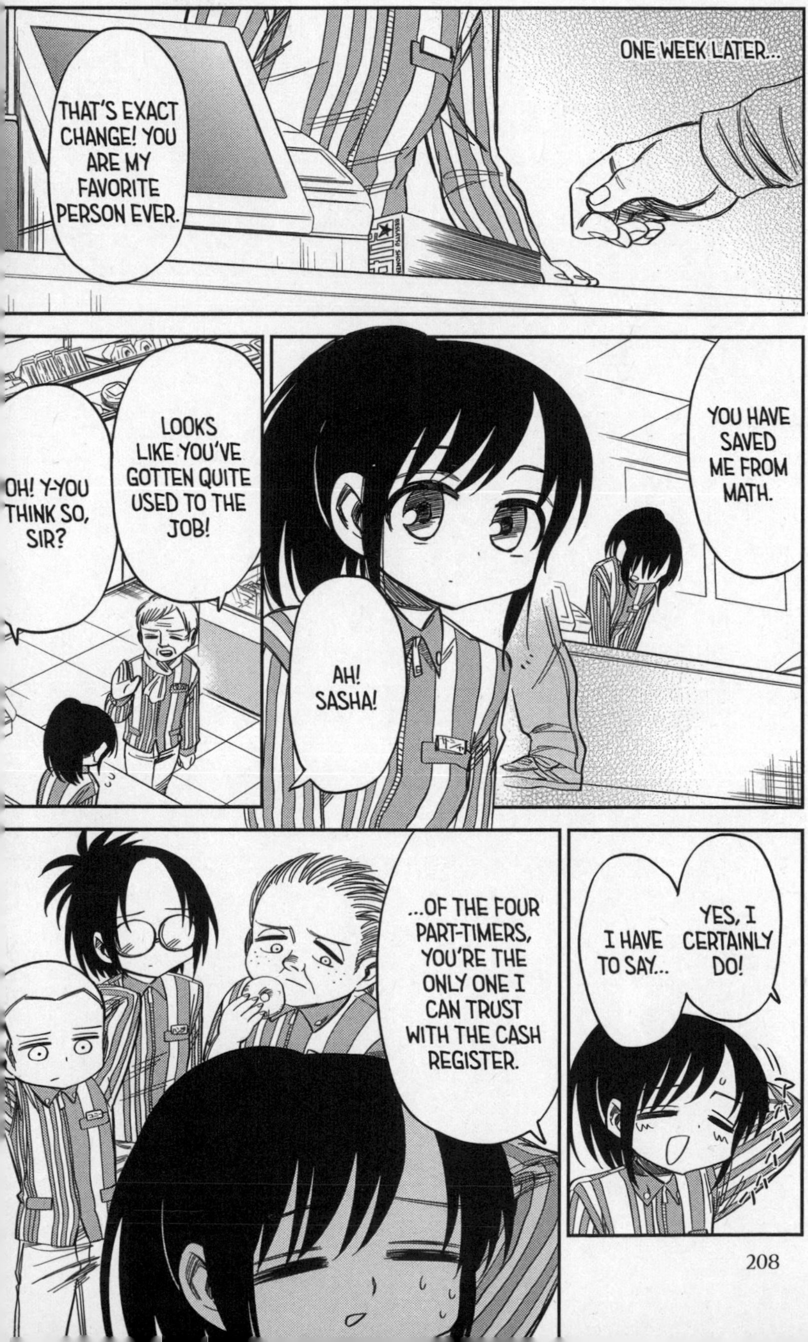
ONE WEEK LATER...
THAT'S EXACT CHANGE! YOU ARE MY FAVORITE PERSON EVER.
YOU HAVE SAVED ME FROM MATH.
AH! SASHA!
LOOKS LIKE YOU'VE GOTTEN QUITE USED TO THE JOB!
OH! Y-YOU THINK SO, SIR?
YES, I CERTAINLY DO!
I HAVE TO SAY...
...OF THE FOUR PART-TIMERS, YOU'RE THE ONLY ONE I CAN TRUST WITH THE CASH REGISTER.

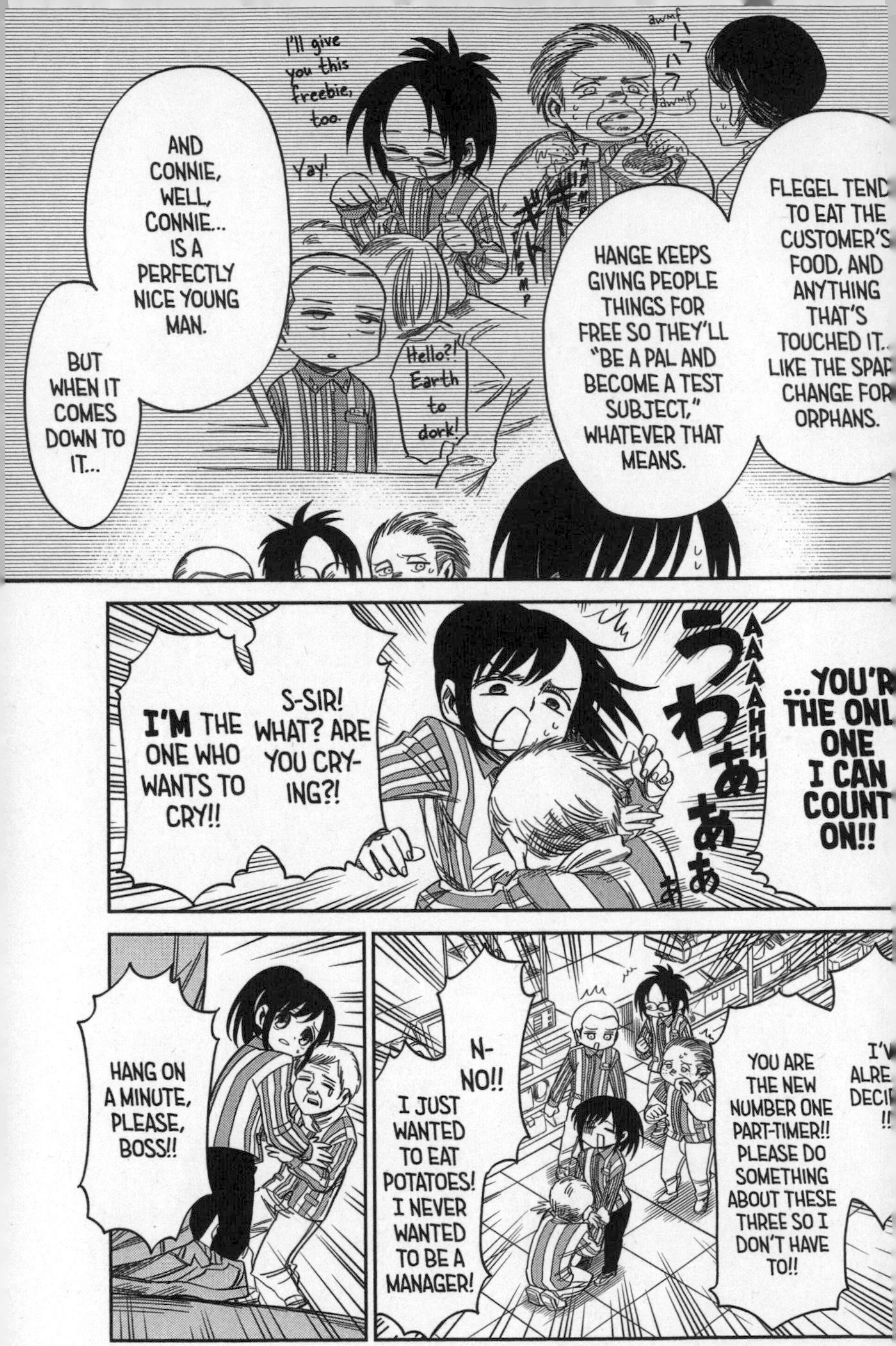
FLEGEL TEND TO EAT THE CUSTOMER'S FOOD, AND ANYTHING THAT'S TOUCHED IT.. LIKE THE SPAR CHANGE FOR ORPHANS.
awmf
awmf
HANGE KEEPS GIVING PEOPLE THINGS FOR FREE SO THEY'LL "BE A PAL AND BECOME A TEST SUBJECT," WHATEVER THAT MEANS.
THMP
I'll give you this freebie, too.
Yay!
Hello?! Earth to dork!
AND CONNIE, WELL, CONNIE... IS A PERFECTLY NICE YOUNG MAN.
BUT WHEN IT COMES DOWN TO IT...
...YOU'R THE ONL ONE I CAN COUNT ON!!
うわあああ
AAAAHH
S-SIR! WHAT? ARE YOU CRY-ING?!
I'M THE ONE WHO WANTS TO CRY!!
I'V ALRE DECI !!
YOU ARE THE NEW NUMBER ONE PART-TIMER!! PLEASE DO SOMETHING ABOUT THESE THREE SO I DON'T HAVE TO!!
N-NO!!
I JUST WANTED TO EAT POTATOES! I NEVER WANTED TO BE A MANAGER!
HANG ON A MINUTE, PLEASE, BOSS!!

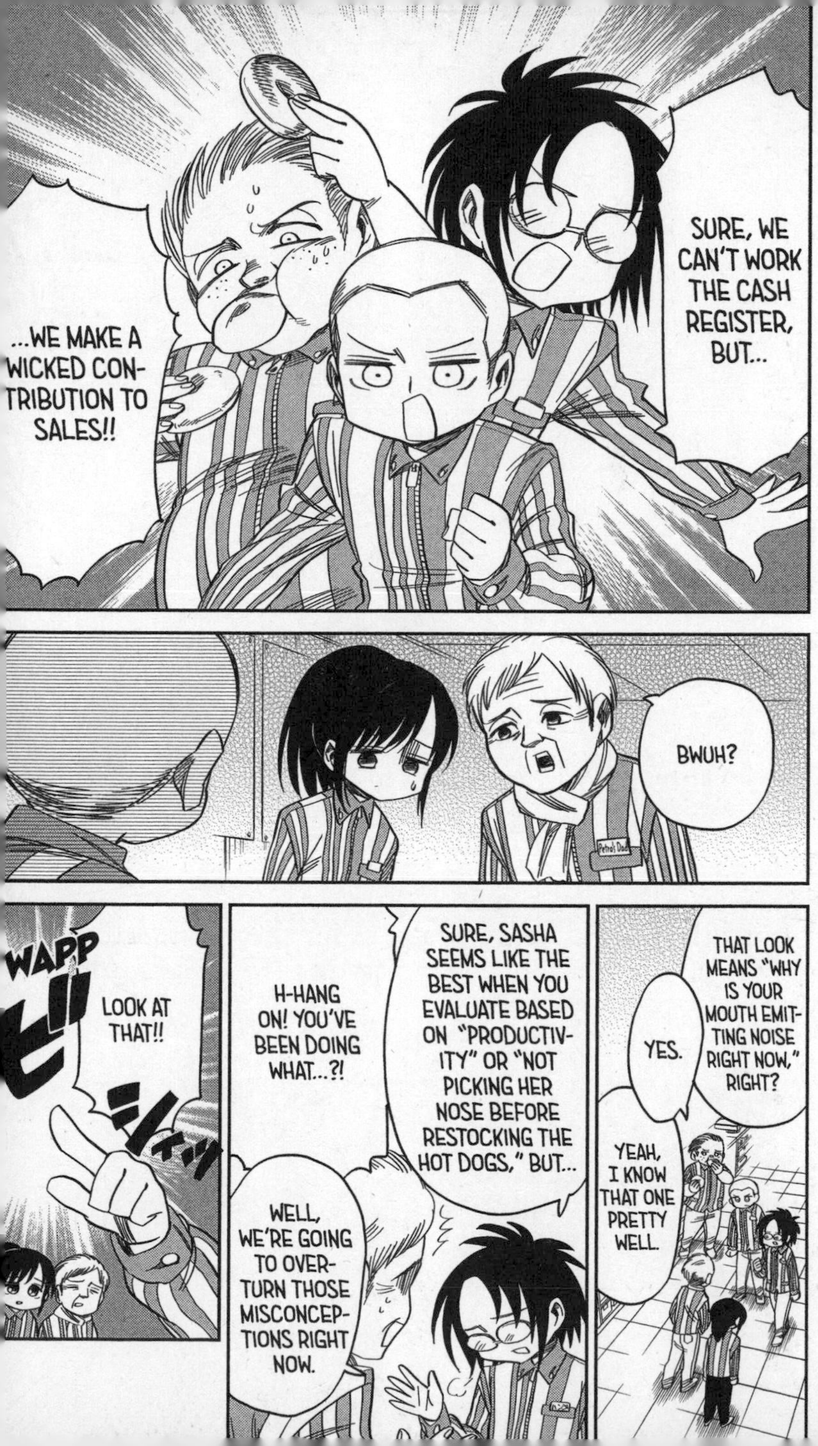
SURE, WE CAN'T WORK THE CASH REGISTER, BUT...
...WE MAKE A WICKED CONTRIBUTION TO SALES!!
BWUH?
THAT LOOK MEANS "WHY IS YOUR MOUTH EMITTING NOISE RIGHT NOW," RIGHT?
YES.
YEAH, I KNOW THAT ONE PRETTY WELL.
SURE, SASHA SEEMS LIKE THE BEST WHEN YOU EVALUATE BASED ON "PRODUCTIVITY" OR "NOT PICKING HER NOSE BEFORE RESTOCKING THE HOT DOGS," BUT...
H-HANG ON! YOU'VE BEEN DOING WHAT...?!
WELL, WE'RE GOING TO OVERTURN THOSE MISCONCEPTIONS RIGHT NOW.
WAPP
LOOK AT THAT!!

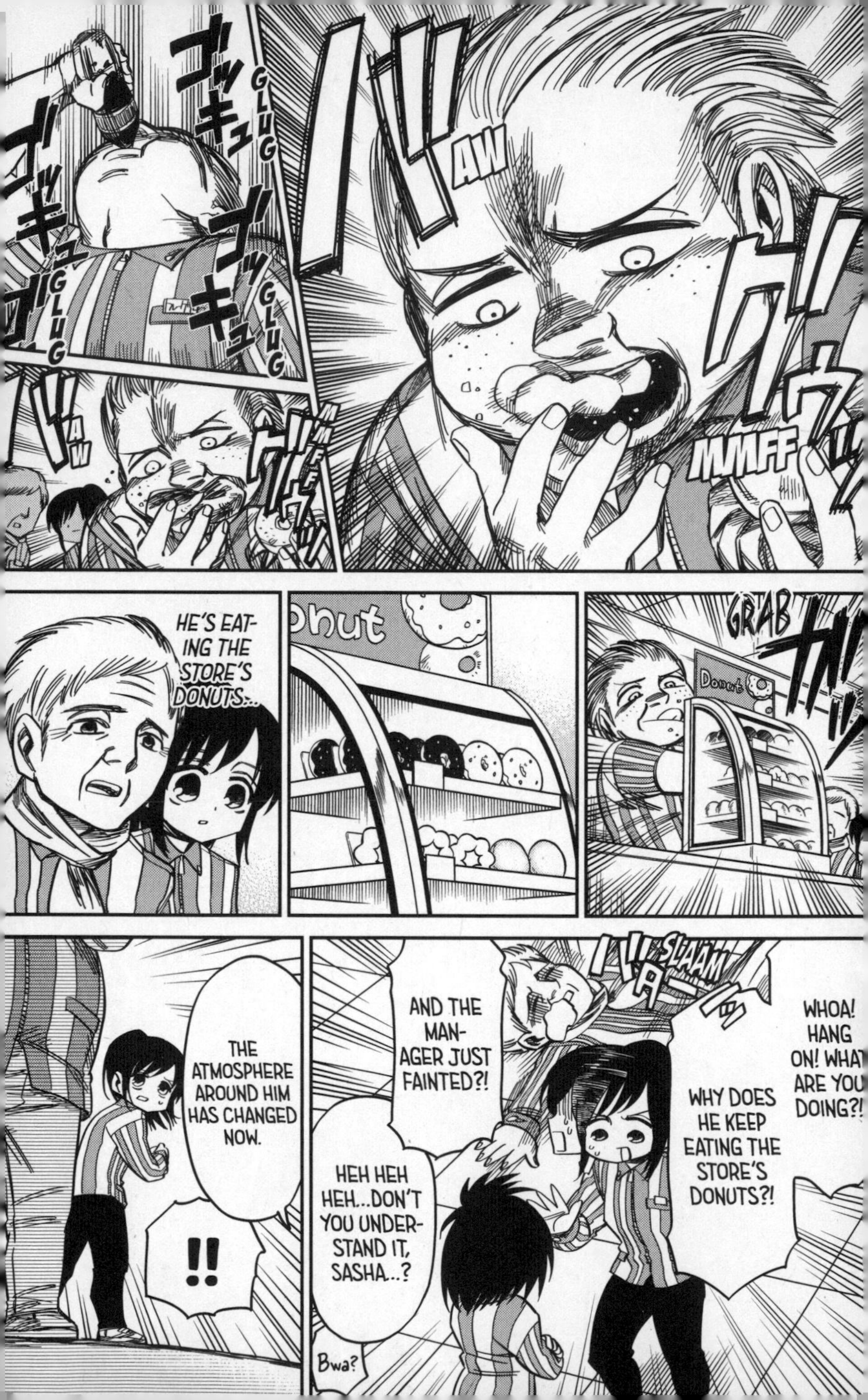

AW
MMFF
GLUG
GLUG
GLUG
GLUG
AW
MMFF
GRAB
HE'S EATING THE STORE'S DONUTS...
SLAAM
WHOA! HANG ON! WHAT ARE YOU DOING?!
WHY DOES HE KEEP EATING THE STORE'S DONUTS?!
AND THE MANAGER JUST FAINTED?!
HEH HEH HEH...DON'T YOU UNDERSTAND IT, SASHA...?
Bwa?
THE ATMOSPHERE AROUND HIM HAS CHANGED NOW.
!!

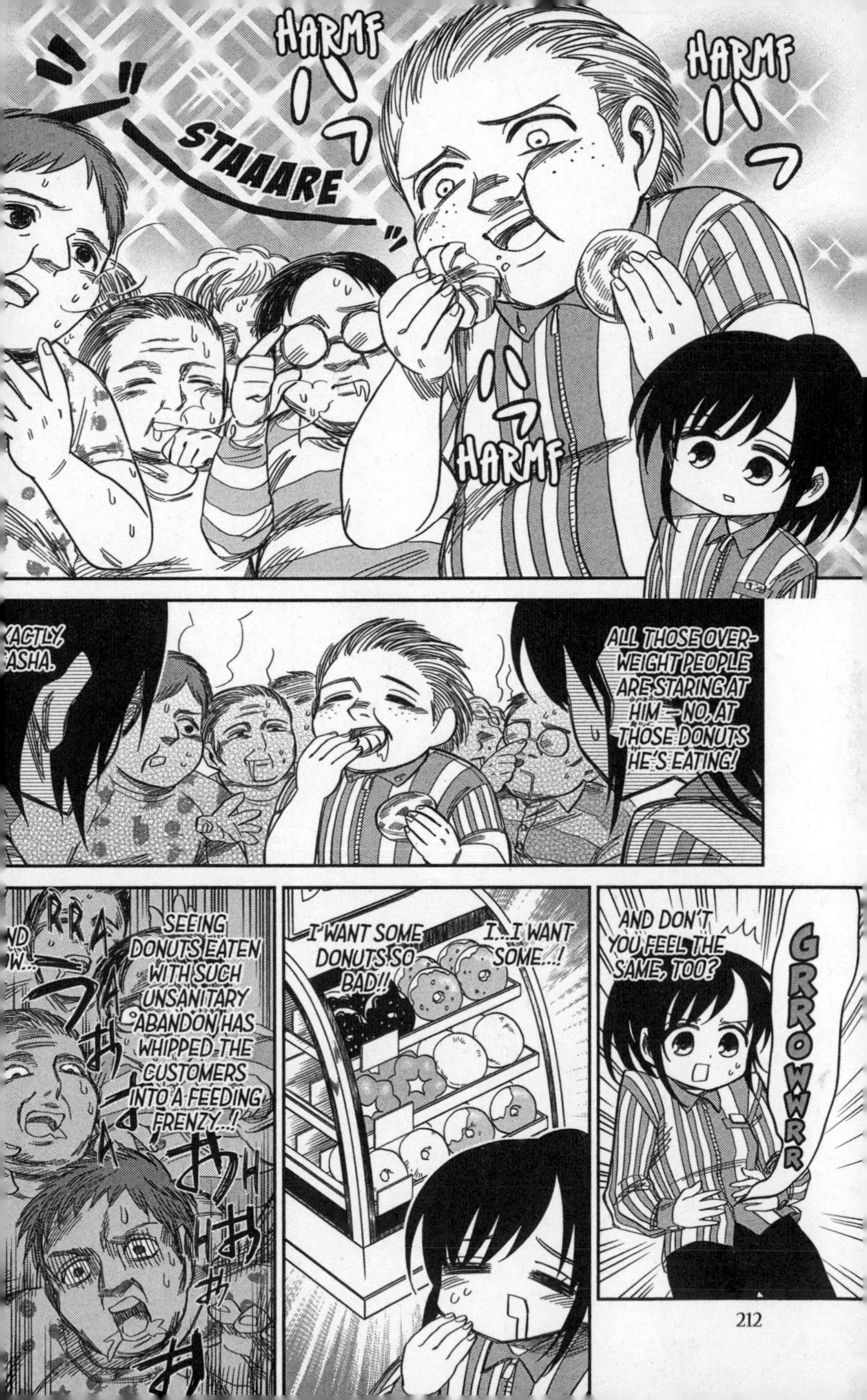
HARMF
HARMF
STAAARE
HARMF
ALL THOSE OVER-WEIGHT PEOPLE ARE STARING AT HIM — NO, AT THOSE DONUTS HE'S EATING!
XACTLY, ASHA.
AND DON'T YOU FEEL THE SAME, TOO?
GRROWWRR
I...I WANT SOME...!
I WANT SOME DONUTS SO BAD!!
SEEING DONUTS EATEN WITH SUCH UNSANITARY ABANDON HAS WHIPPED THE CUSTOMERS INTO A FEEDING FRENZY...!

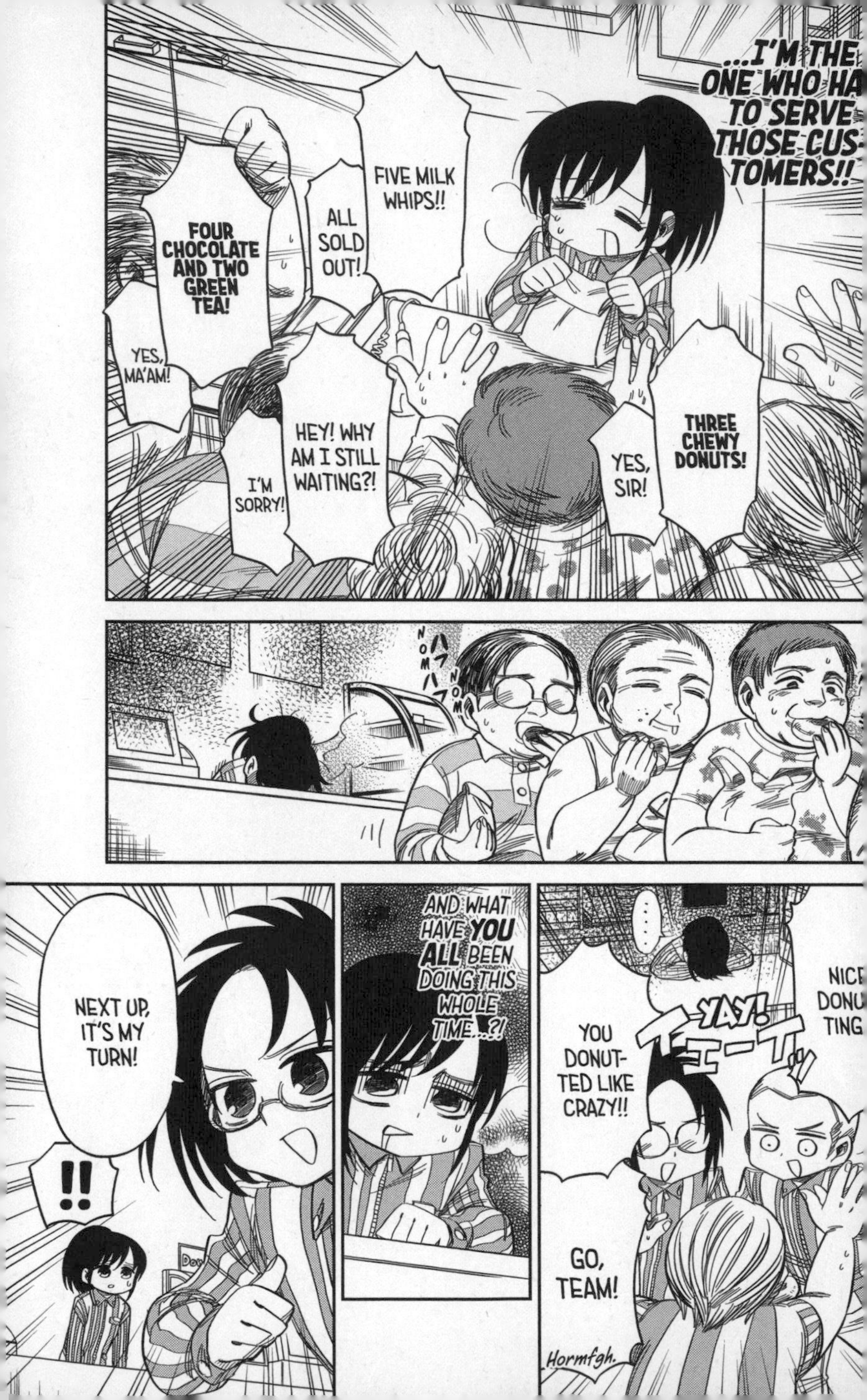
...I'M THE ONE WHO HA TO SERVE THOSE CUS-TOMERS!!
FIVE MILK WHIPS!!
ALL SOLD OUT!
FOUR CHOCOLATE AND TWO GREEN TEA!
YES, MA'AM!
THREE CHEWY DONUTS!
YES, SIR!
HEY! WHY AM I STILL WAITING?!
I'M SORRY!
NOM ハフ
NOM ハフ
NIC DONU TING
...
YAY! イエーイ!!
YOU DONUT-TED LIKE CRAZY!!
GO, TEAM!
Hormfgh.
AND WHAT HAVE YOU ALL BEEN DOING THIS WHOLE TIME...?!
NEXT UP, IT'S MY TURN!
!!

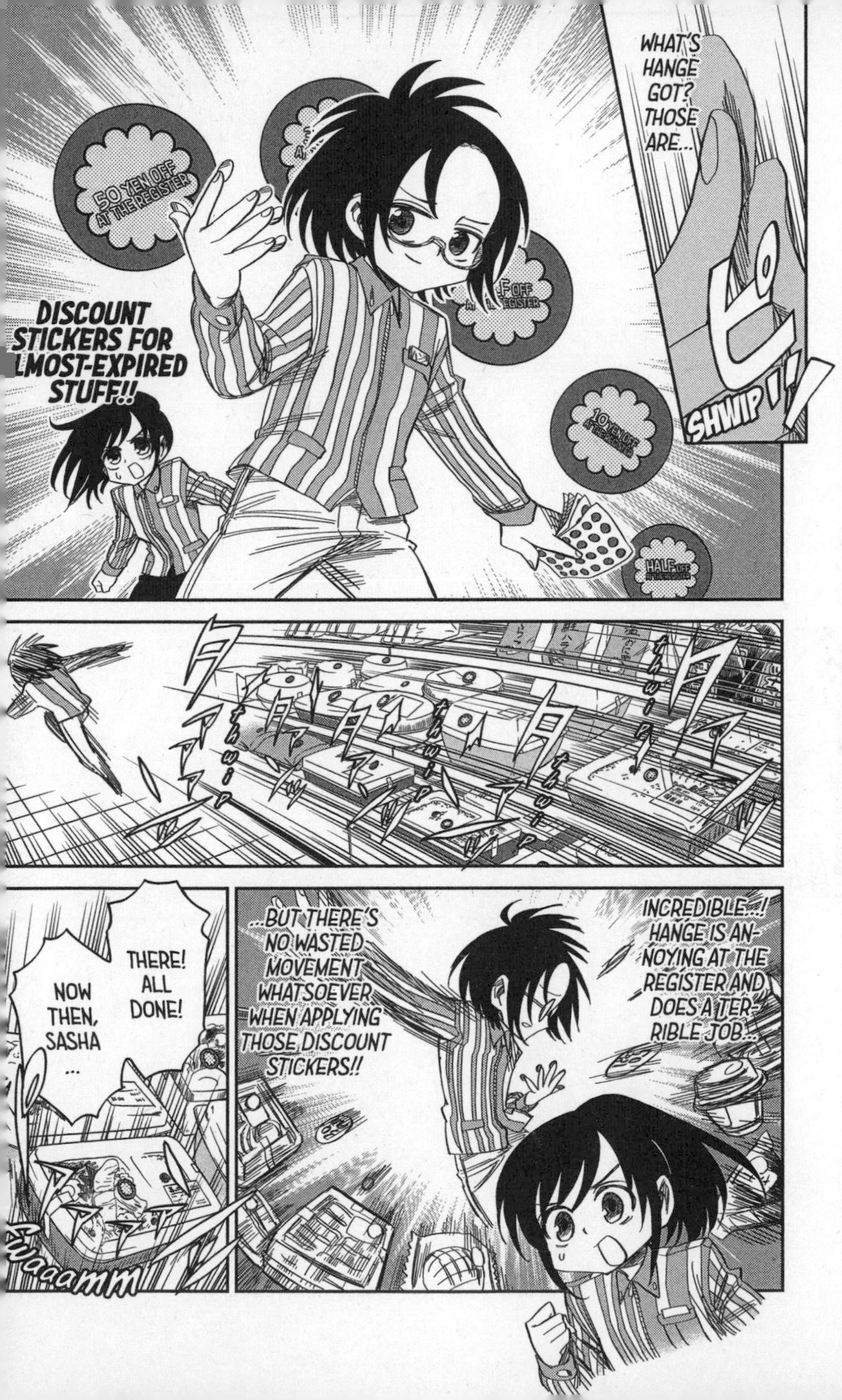
WHAT'S HANGE GOT? THOSE ARE...
SHWIP!!
50 YEN OFF AT THE REGISTER
10 YEN OFF AT THE REGISTER
DISCOUNT STICKERS FOR LMOST-EXPIRED STUFF!!
thwip
thwip
thwip
thwip
INCREDIBLE...! HANGE IS AN-NOYING AT THE REGISTER AND DOES A TER-RIBLE JOB...
...BUT THERE'S NO WASTED MOVEMENT WHATSOEVER WHEN APPLYING THOSE DISCOUNT STICKERS!!
THERE! ALL DONE!
NOW THEN, SASHA ...
Gwaaamm

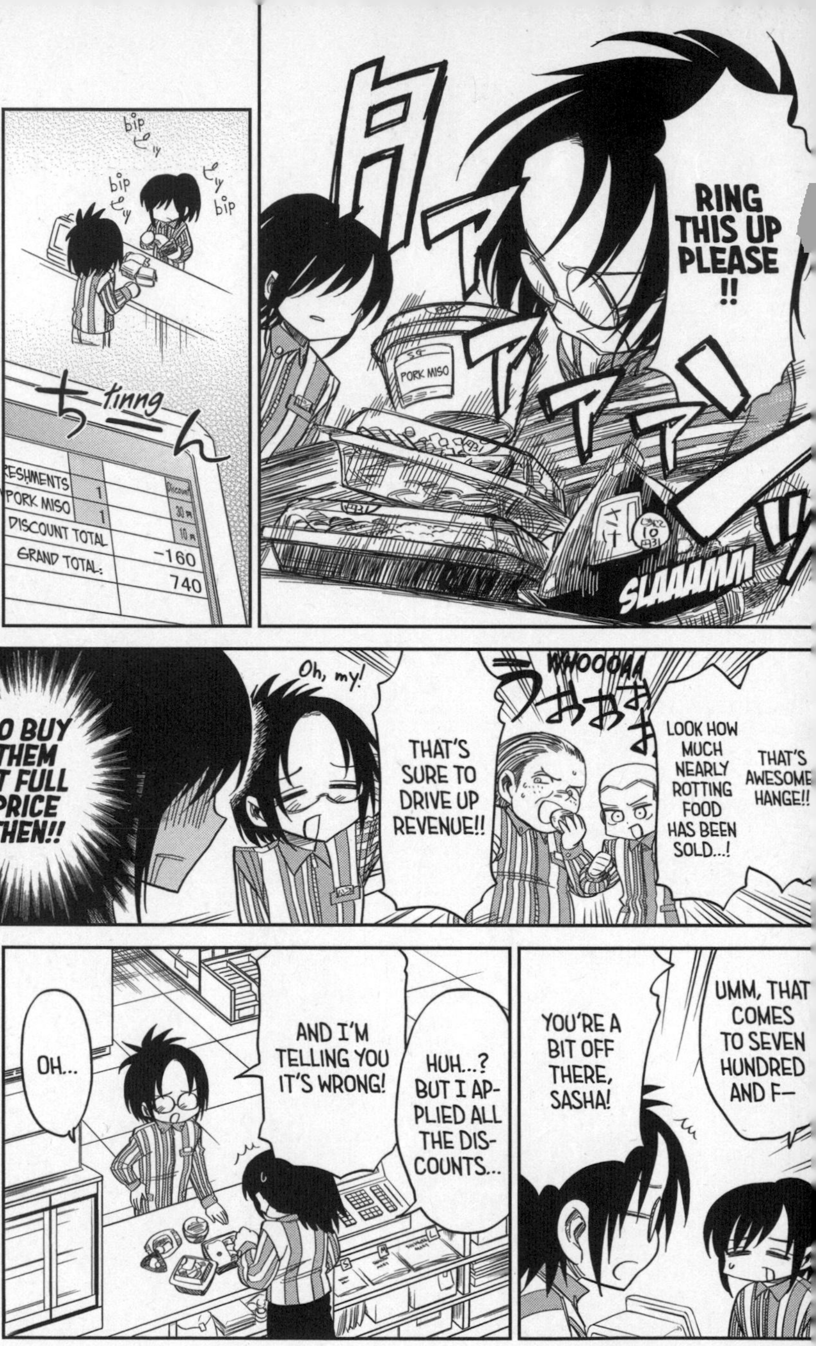
RING THIS UP PLEASE!!
SLAAAMM
PORK MISO
bip
bip
bip
tinng
RESHMENTS 1
PORK MISO 1
DISCOUNT TOTAL
GRAND TOTAL:
−160
740
THAT'S AWESOME HANGE!!
LOOK HOW MUCH NEARLY ROTTING FOOD HAS BEEN SOLD...!
WHOOOAA
THAT'S SURE TO DRIVE UP REVENUE!!
Oh, my!
SO BUY THEM AT FULL PRICE THEN!!
UMM, THAT COMES TO SEVEN HUNDRED AND F—
YOU'RE A BIT OFF THERE, SASHA!
HUH...? BUT I APPLIED ALL THE DISCOUNTS...
AND I'M TELLING YOU IT'S WRONG!
OH...

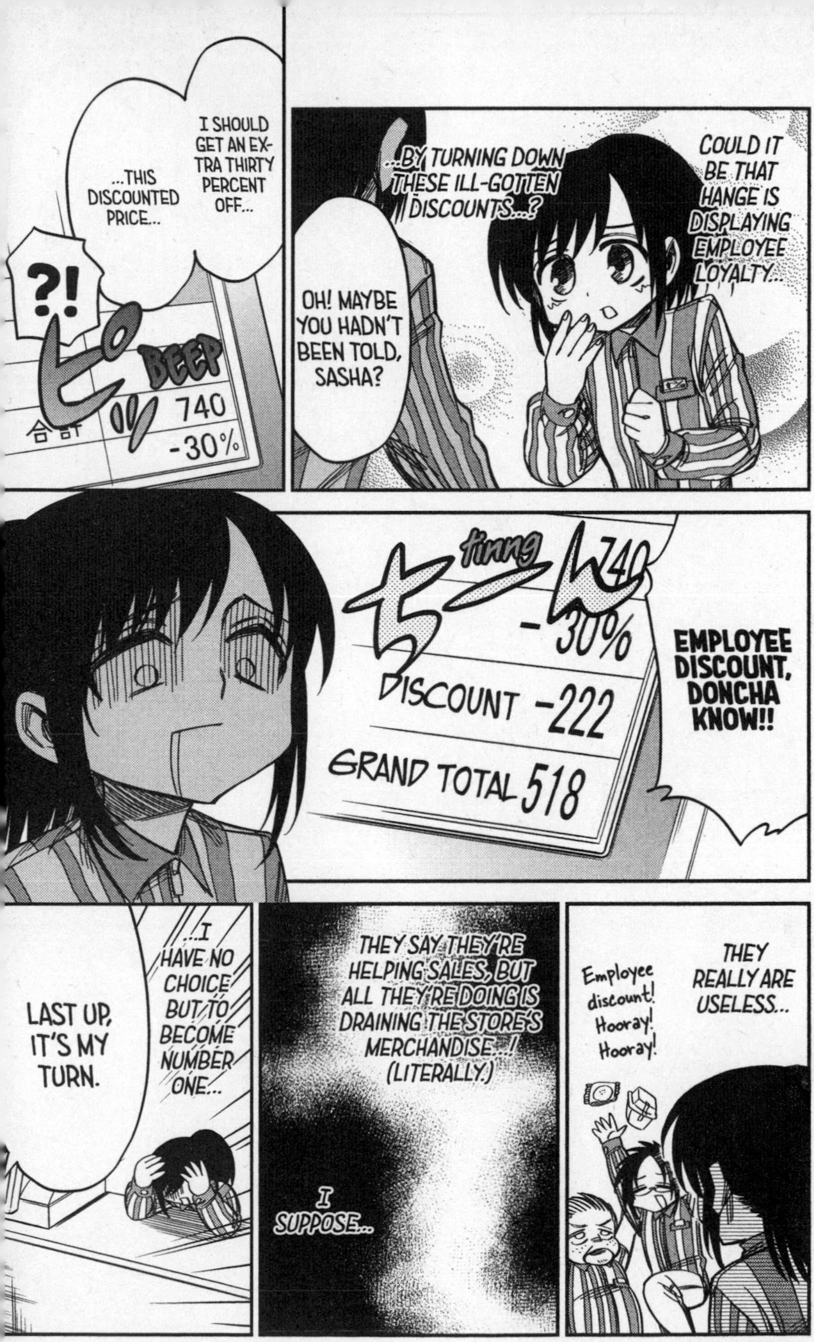
COULD IT BE THAT HANGE IS DISPLAYING EMPLOYEE LOYALTY...
...BY TURNING DOWN THESE ILL-GOTTEN DISCOUNTS...?
OH! MAYBE YOU HADN'T BEEN TOLD, SASHA?
I SHOULD GET AN EXTRA THIRTY PERCENT OFF...
...THIS DISCOUNTED PRICE...
?!
BEEP
合計 740
-30%
tinng
740
-30%
EMPLOYEE DISCOUNT, DONCHA KNOW!!
DISCOUNT -222
GRAND TOTAL 518
THEY REALLY ARE USELESS...
Employee discount! Hooray! Hooray!
THEY SAY THEY'RE HELPING SALES, BUT ALL THEY'RE DOING IS DRAINING THE STORE'S MERCHANDISE...! (LITERALLY.)
I SUPPOSE...
...I HAVE NO CHOICE BUT TO BECOME NUMBER ONE...
LAST UP, IT'S MY TURN.

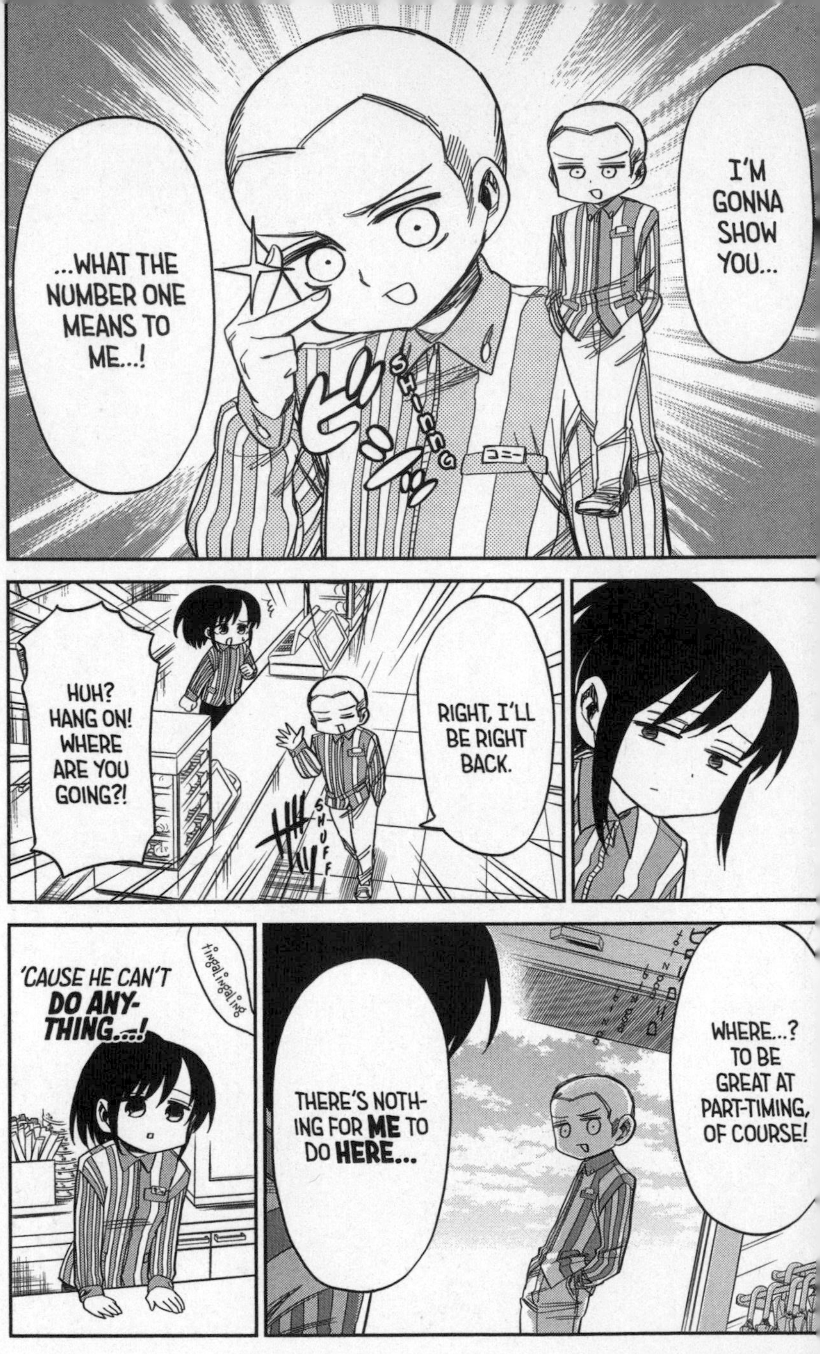
I'M GONNA SHOW YOU...
...WHAT THE NUMBER ONE MEANS TO ME...!
RIGHT, I'LL BE RIGHT BACK.
HUH? HANG ON! WHERE ARE YOU GOING?!
SHUFF
WHERE...? TO BE GREAT AT PART-TIMING, OF COURSE!
THERE'S NOTHING FOR ME TO DO HERE...
'CAUSE HE CAN'T DO ANYTHING...!

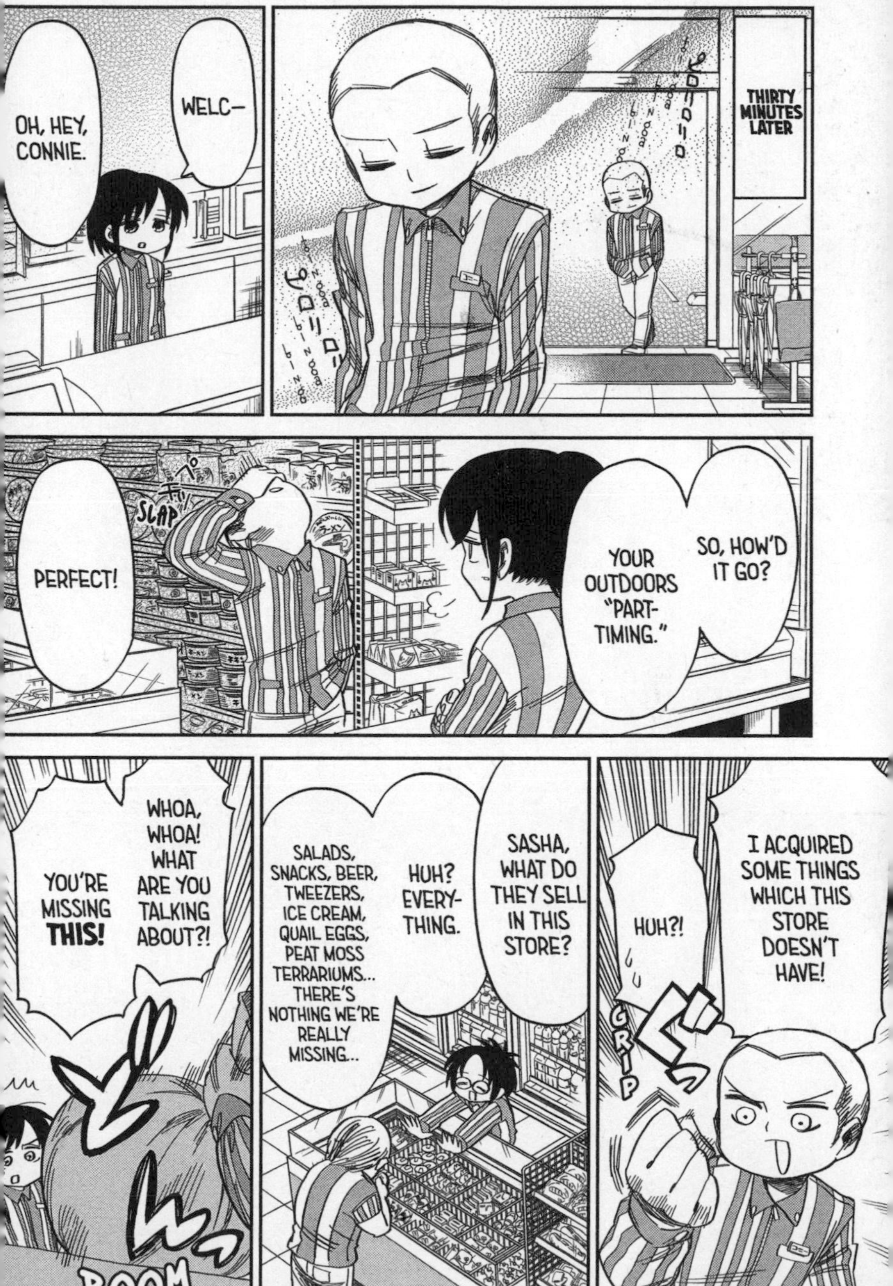
THIRTY MINUTES LATER
WELC—
OH, HEY, CONNIE.
SO, HOW'D IT GO?
YOUR OUTDOORS "PART-TIMING."
SLAP
PERFECT!
I ACQUIRED SOME THINGS WHICH THIS STORE DOESN'T HAVE!
HUH?!
GRIP
SASHA, WHAT DO THEY SELL IN THIS STORE?
HUH? EVERYTHING.
SALADS, SNACKS, BEER, TWEEZERS, ICE CREAM, QUAIL EGGS, PEAT MOSS TERRARIUMS... THERE'S NOTHING WE'RE REALLY MISSING...
WHOA, WHOA! WHAT ARE YOU TALKING ABOUT?!
YOU'RE MISSING **THIS!**
BOOM

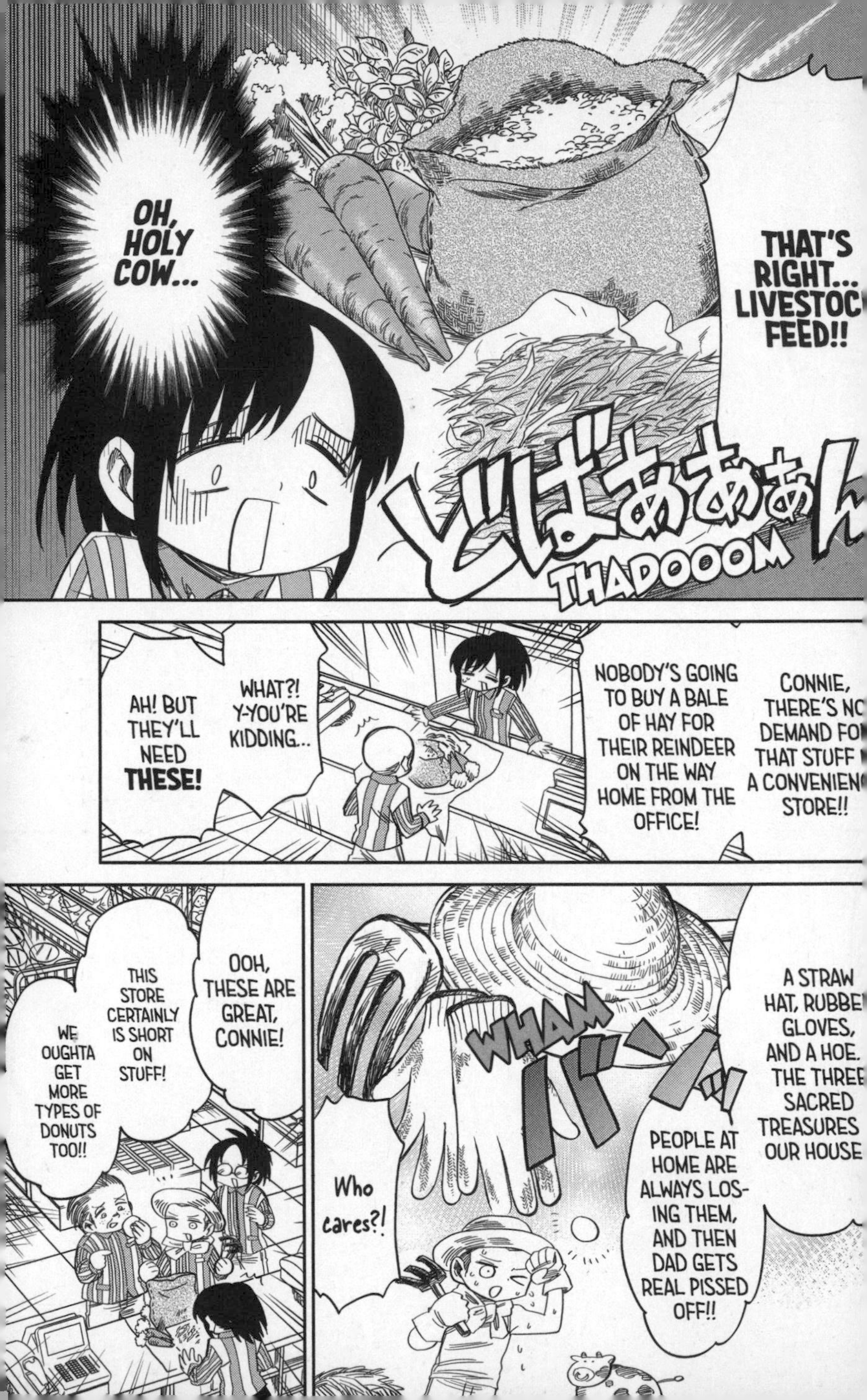
THAT'S RIGHT... LIVESTOC FEED!!
どばあああん
THADOOOM
OH, HOLY COW...
CONNIE, THERE'S NO DEMAND FO THAT STUFF A CONVENIEN STORE!!
NOBODY'S GOING TO BUY A BALE OF HAY FOR THEIR REINDEER ON THE WAY HOME FROM THE OFFICE!
WHAT?! Y-YOU'RE KIDDING...
AH! BUT THEY'LL NEED **THESE!**
A STRAW HAT, RUBBE GLOVES, AND A HOE. THE THREE SACRED TREASURES OUR HOUSE
WHAM
PEOPLE AT HOME ARE ALWAYS LOSING THEM, AND THEN DAD GETS REAL PISSED OFF!!
Who cares?!
OOH, THESE ARE GREAT, CONNIE!
THIS STORE CERTAINLY IS SHORT ON STUFF!
WE OUGHTA GET MORE TYPES OF DONUTS TOO!!

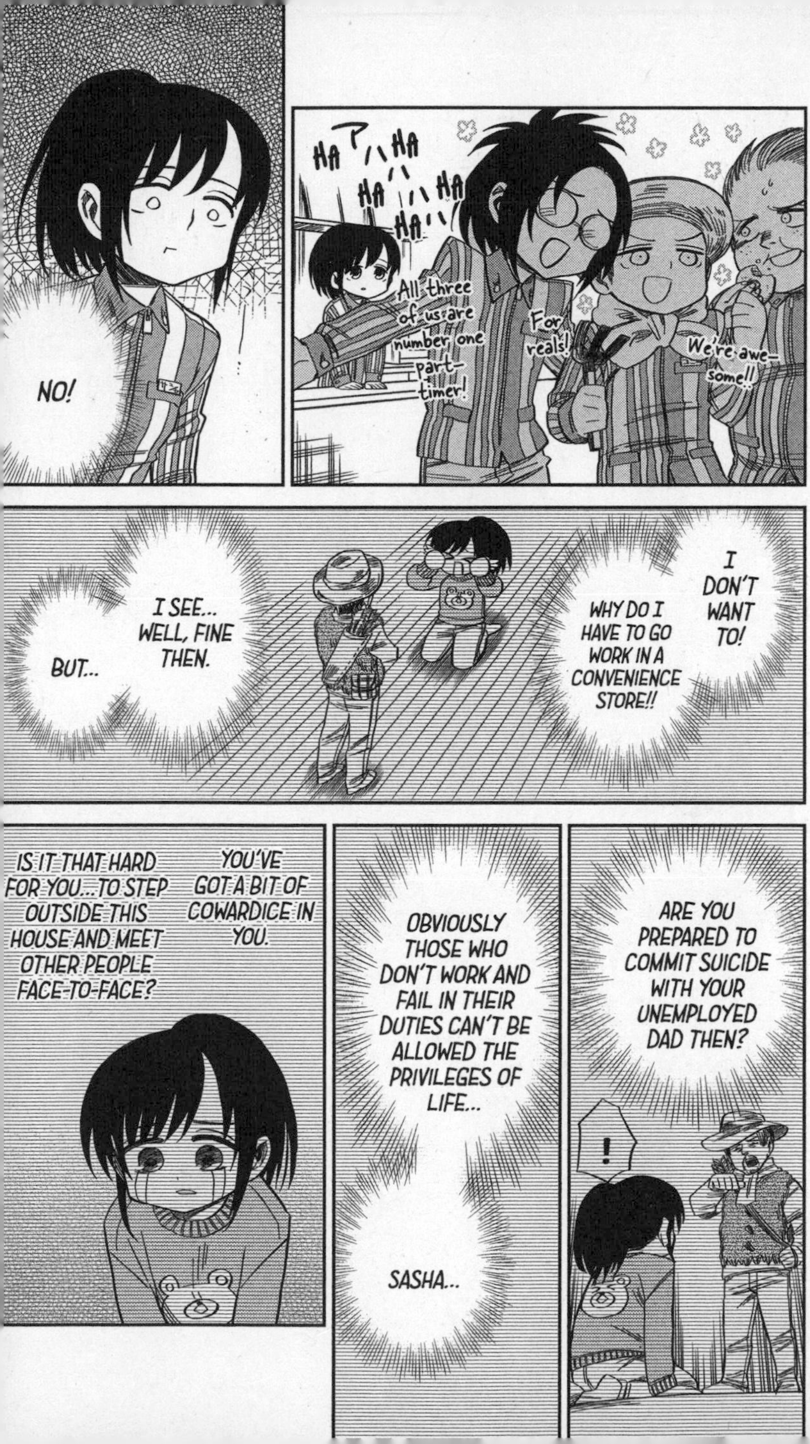

HA HA HA HA HA
All three of us are number one part-timer!
For reals!
We're awe-some!!
NO!
I DON'T WANT TO!
WHY DO I HAVE TO GO WORK IN A CONVENIENCE STORE!!
I SEE... WELL, FINE THEN.
BUT...
ARE YOU PREPARED TO COMMIT SUICIDE WITH YOUR UNEMPLOYED DAD THEN?
!
OBVIOUSLY THOSE WHO DON'T WORK AND FAIL IN THEIR DUTIES CAN'T BE ALLOWED THE PRIVILEGES OF LIFE...
SASHA...
YOU'VE GOT A BIT OF COWARDICE IN YOU.
IS IT THAT HARD FOR YOU...TO STEP OUTSIDE THIS HOUSE AND MEET OTHER PEOPLE FACE-TO-FACE?

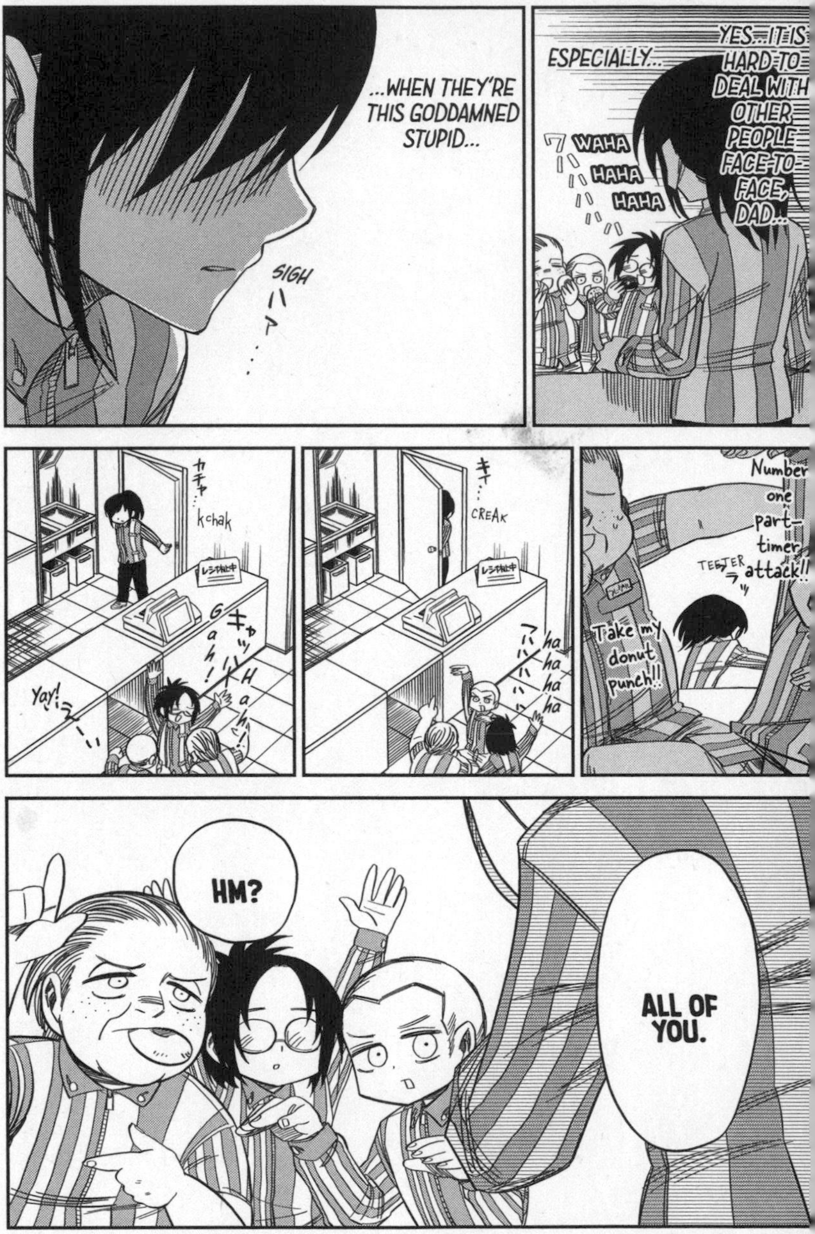
YES... IT IS HARD TO DEAL WITH OTHER PEOPLE FACE-TO-FACE, DAD...
ESPECIALLY...
WAHA HAHA HAHA
...WHEN THEY'RE THIS GODDAMNED STUPID...
SIGH
Number one part-timer attack!!
TEETER
Take my donut punch!!
CREAK
haha haha haha
kchak
Gah! Hah!
Yay!
ALL OF YOU.
HM?

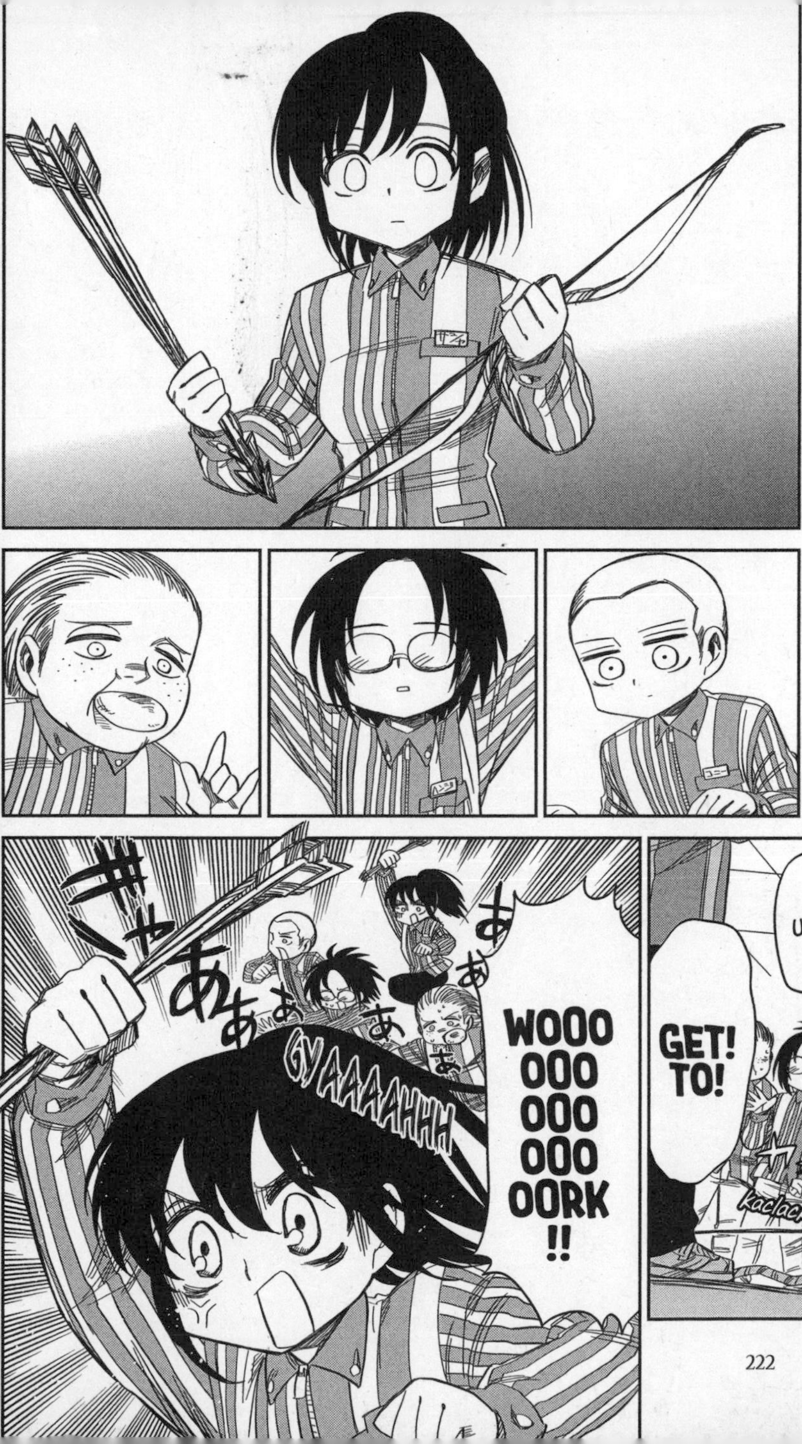
UH...
GET! TO!
kaclack
WOOO OOO OOO OOO OORK!!
GYAAAAHHH

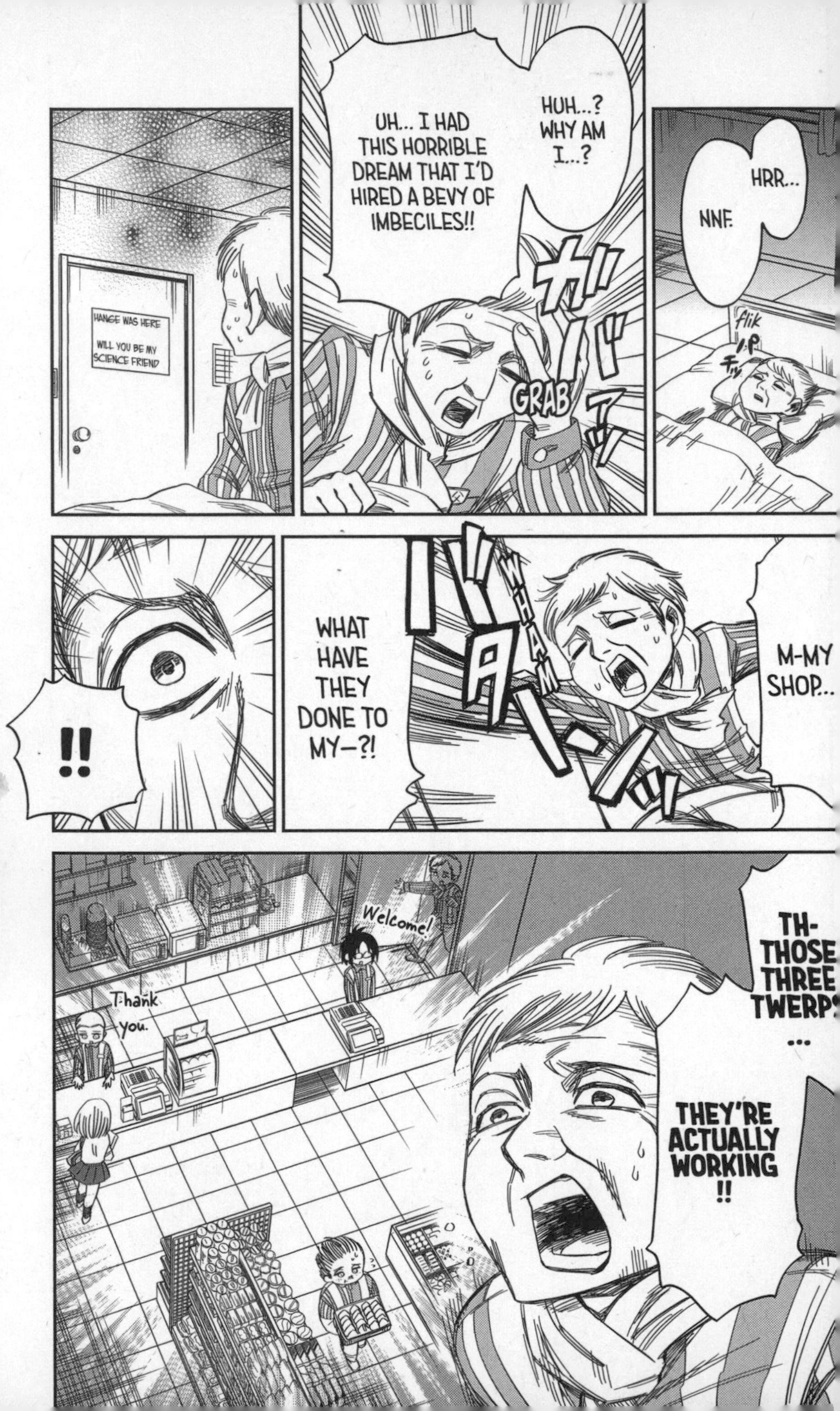
HRR...
NNF.
flik
HUH...? WHY AM I...?
UH... I HAD THIS HORRIBLE DREAM THAT I'D HIRED A BEVY OF IMBECILES!!
GRAB
HANGE WAS HERE
WILL YOU BE MY SCIENCE FRIEND
M-MY SHOP...
WHAM
WHAT HAVE THEY DONE TO MY—?!
!!
TH-THOSE THREE TWERPS...
THEY'RE ACTUALLY WORKING!!
Welcome!
Thank you.

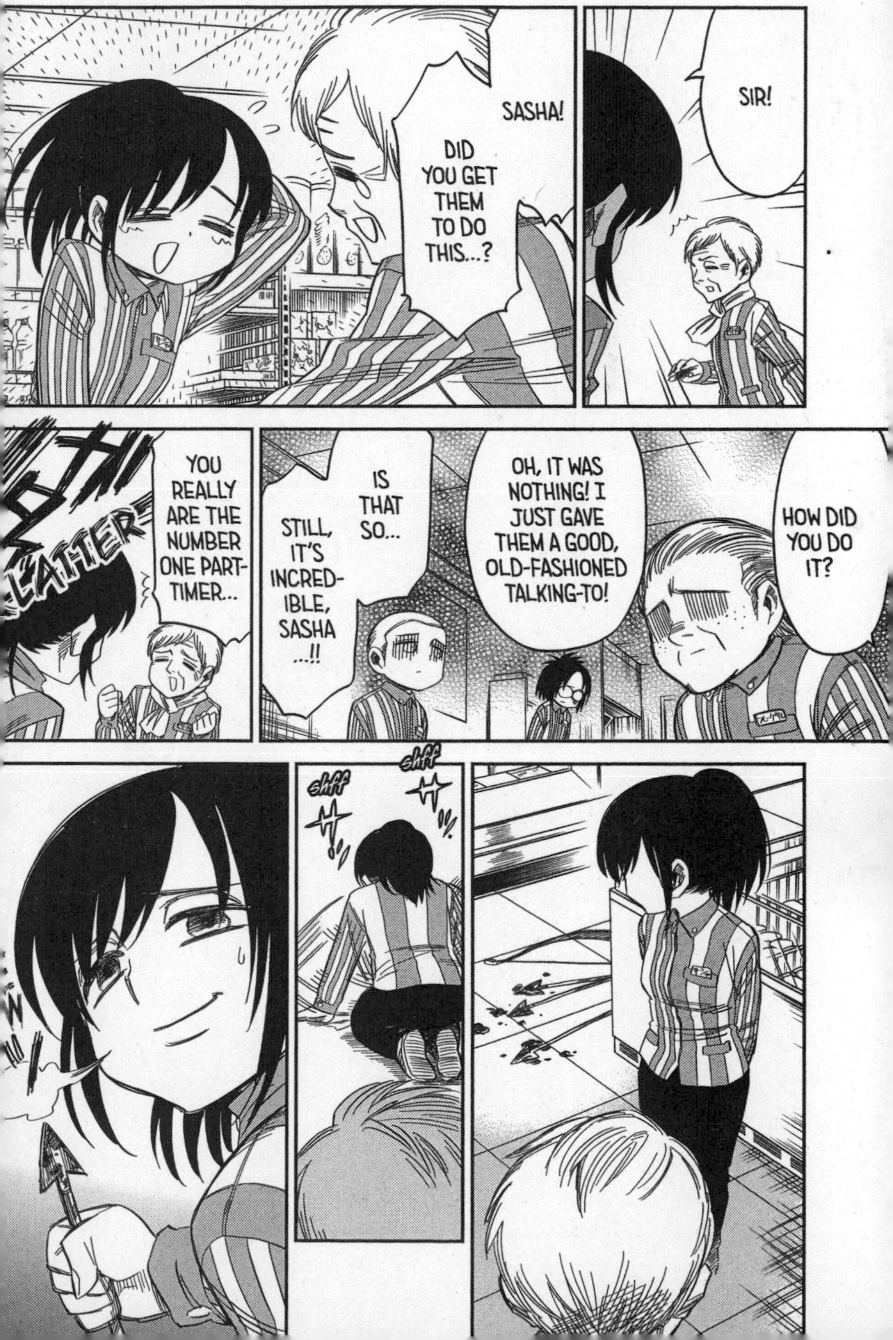
SIR!
SASHA!
DID YOU GET THEM TO DO THIS...?
HOW DID YOU DO IT?
OH, IT WAS NOTHING! I JUST GAVE THEM A GOOD, OLD-FASHIONED TALKING-TO!
IS THAT SO...
STILL, IT'S INCRED-IBLE, SASHA ...!!
YOU REALLY ARE THE NUMBER ONE PART-TIMER...
CLATTER
shff
shff

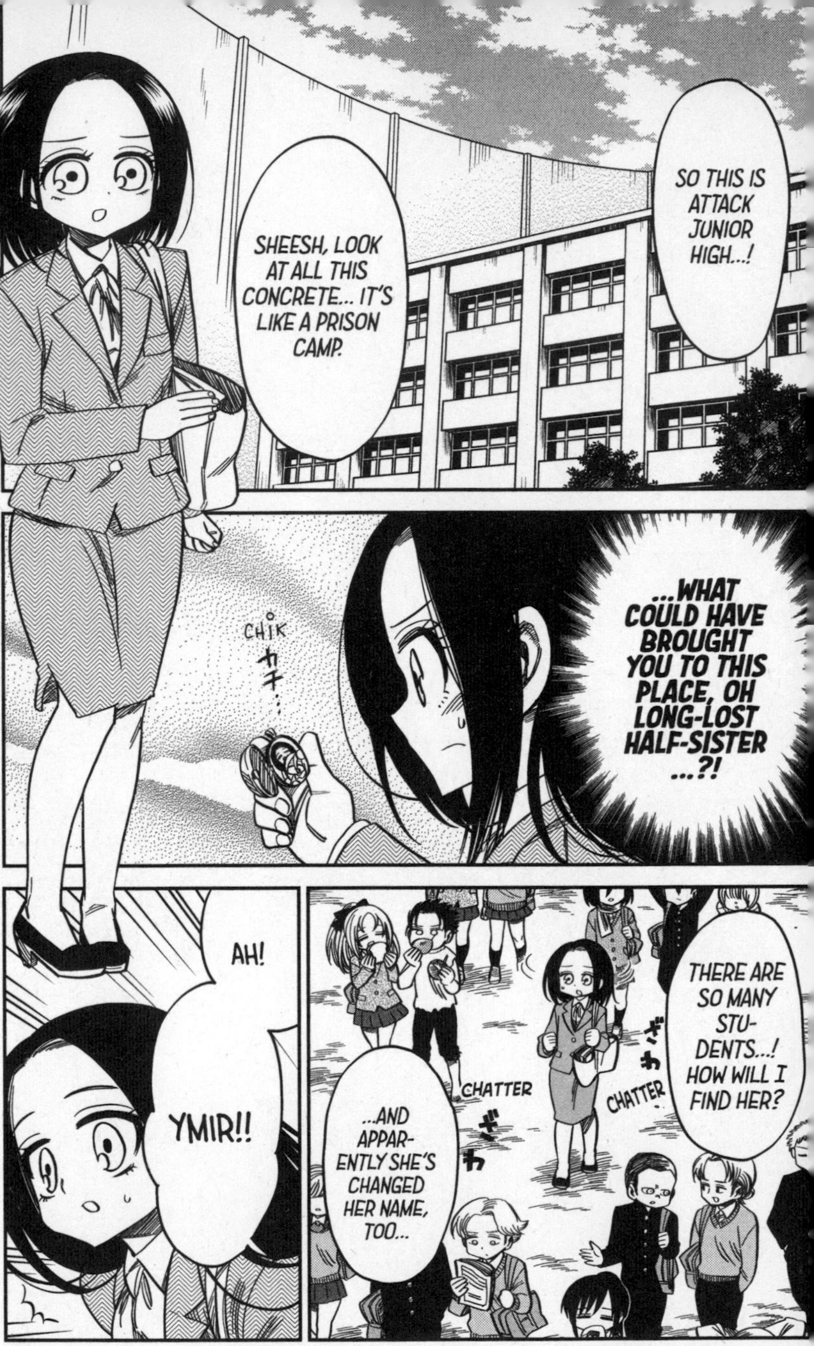
SO THIS IS ATTACK JUNIOR HIGH...!
SHEESH, LOOK AT ALL THIS CONCRETE... IT'S LIKE A PRISON CAMP.
...WHAT COULD HAVE BROUGHT YOU TO THIS PLACE, OH LONG-LOST HALF-SISTER ...?!
CHIK
THERE ARE SO MANY STU-DENTS...! HOW WILL I FIND HER?
CHATTER
CHATTER
...AND APPAR-ENTLY SHE'S CHANGED HER NAME, TOO...
AH!
YMIR!!

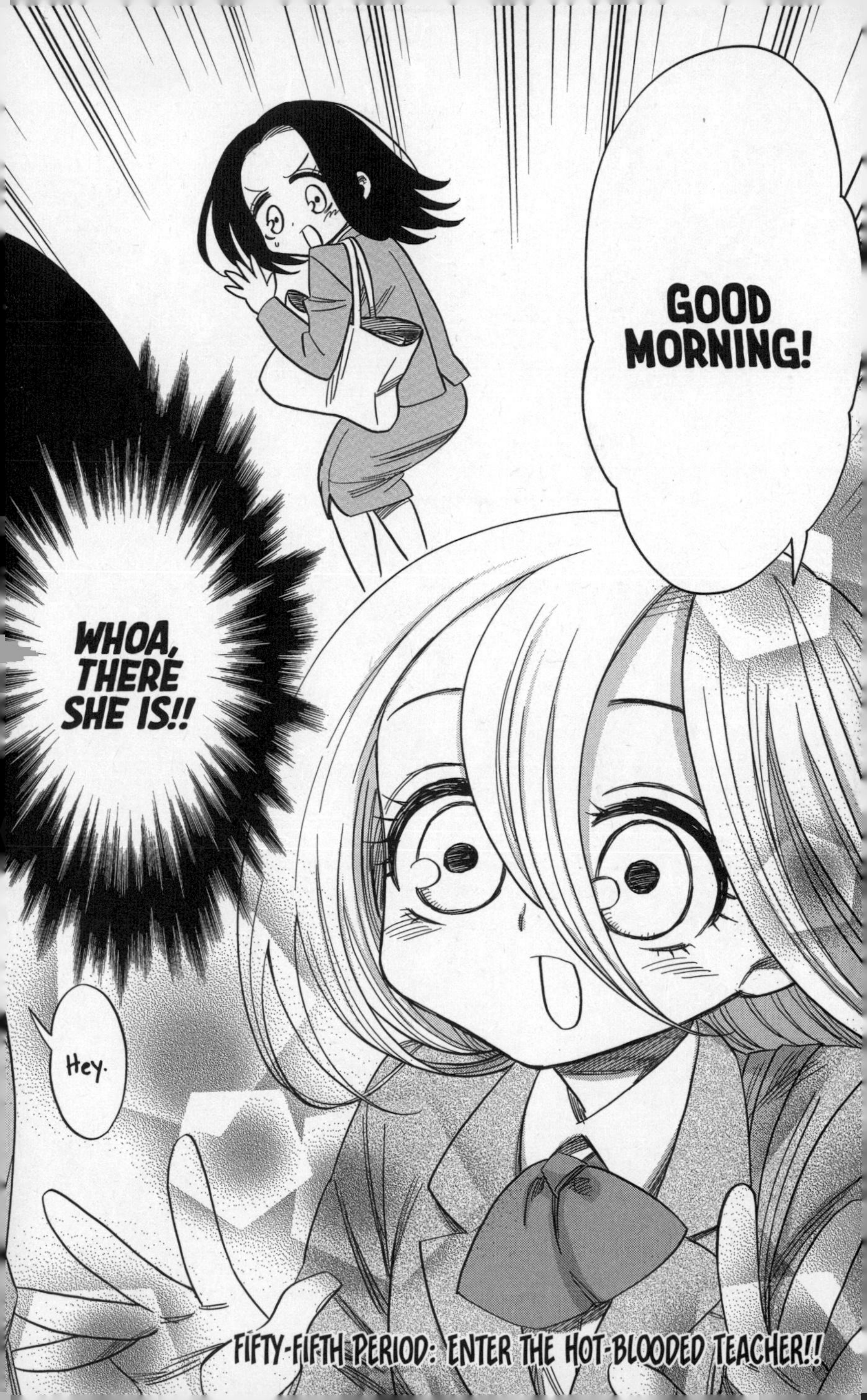
GOOD MORNING!
WHOA, THERE SHE IS!!
Hey.
FIFTY-FIFTH PERIOD: ENTER THE HOT-BLOODED TEACHER!!

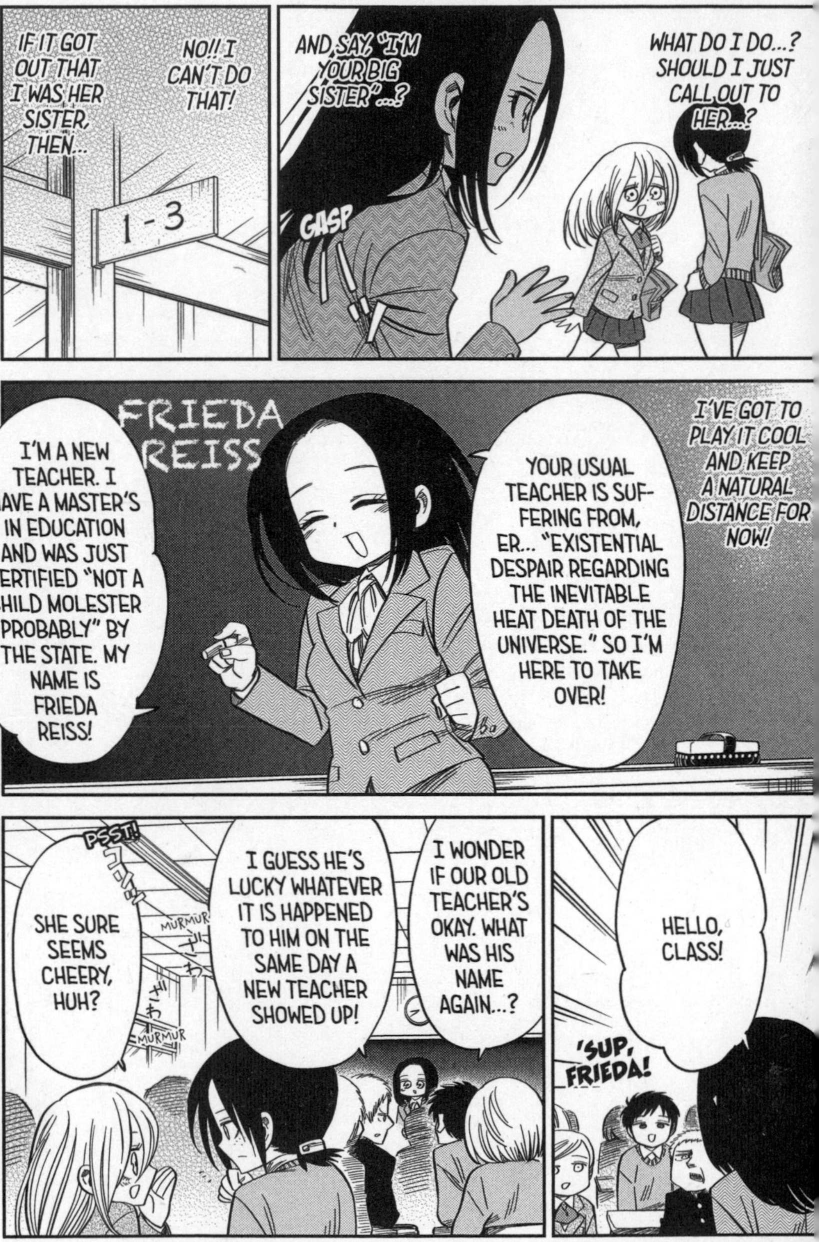
WHAT DO I DO...? SHOULD I JUST CALL OUT TO HER...?
AND SAY, "I'M YOUR BIG SISTER"...?
GASP
IF IT GOT OUT THAT I WAS HER SISTER, THEN...
NO!! I CAN'T DO THAT!
1-3
I'VE GOT TO PLAY IT COOL AND KEEP A NATURAL DISTANCE FOR NOW!
YOUR USUAL TEACHER IS SUFFERING FROM, ER... "EXISTENTIAL DESPAIR REGARDING THE INEVITABLE HEAT DEATH OF THE UNIVERSE." SO I'M HERE TO TAKE OVER!
FRIEDA REISS
I'M A NEW TEACHER. I HAVE A MASTER'S IN EDUCATION AND WAS JUST CERTIFIED "NOT A CHILD MOLESTER PROBABLY" BY THE STATE. MY NAME IS FRIEDA REISS!
HELLO, CLASS!
'SUP, FRIEDA!
I WONDER IF OUR OLD TEACHER'S OKAY. WHAT WAS HIS NAME AGAIN...?
I GUESS HE'S LUCKY WHATEVER IT IS HAPPENED TO HIM ON THE SAME DAY A NEW TEACHER SHOWED UP!
PSST!
SHE SURE SEEMS CHEERY, HUH?
MURMUR
MURMUR

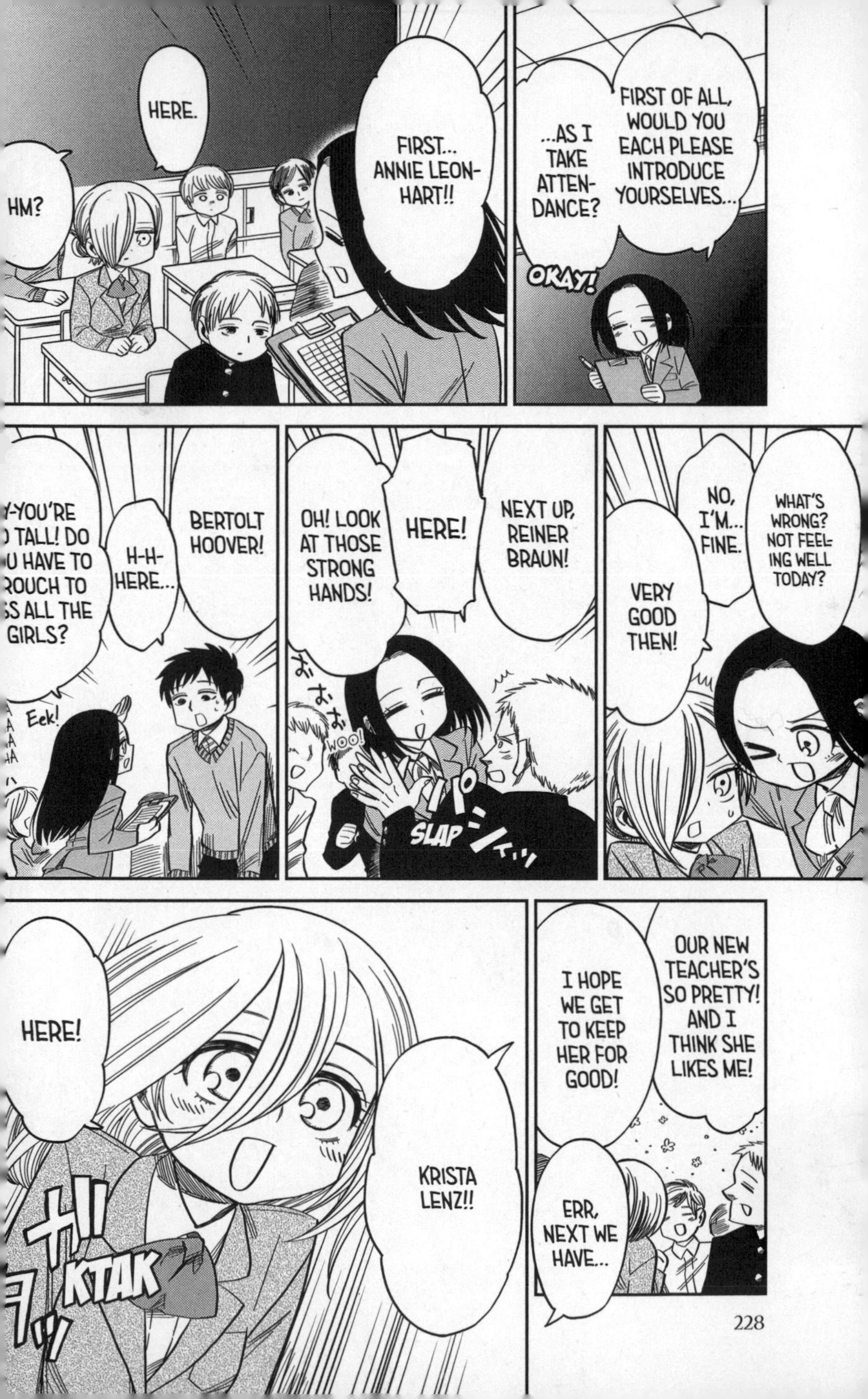
FIRST OF ALL, WOULD YOU EACH PLEASE INTRODUCE YOURSELVES...
...AS I TAKE ATTEN-DANCE?
OKAY!
FIRST... ANNIE LEON-HART!!
HERE.
HM?
WHAT'S WRONG? NOT FEEL-ING WELL TODAY?
NO, I'M... FINE.
VERY GOOD THEN!
NEXT UP, REINER BRAUN!
HERE!
OH! LOOK AT THOSE STRONG HANDS!
WOO!
SLAP
BERTOLT HOOVER!
H-H-HERE...
Y-YOU'RE O TALL! DO U HAVE TO ROUCH TO SS ALL THE GIRLS?
Eek!
OUR NEW TEACHER'S SO PRETTY! AND I THINK SHE LIKES ME!
I HOPE WE GET TO KEEP HER FOR GOOD!
ERR, NEXT WE HAVE...
KRISTA LENZ!!
HERE!
KTAK

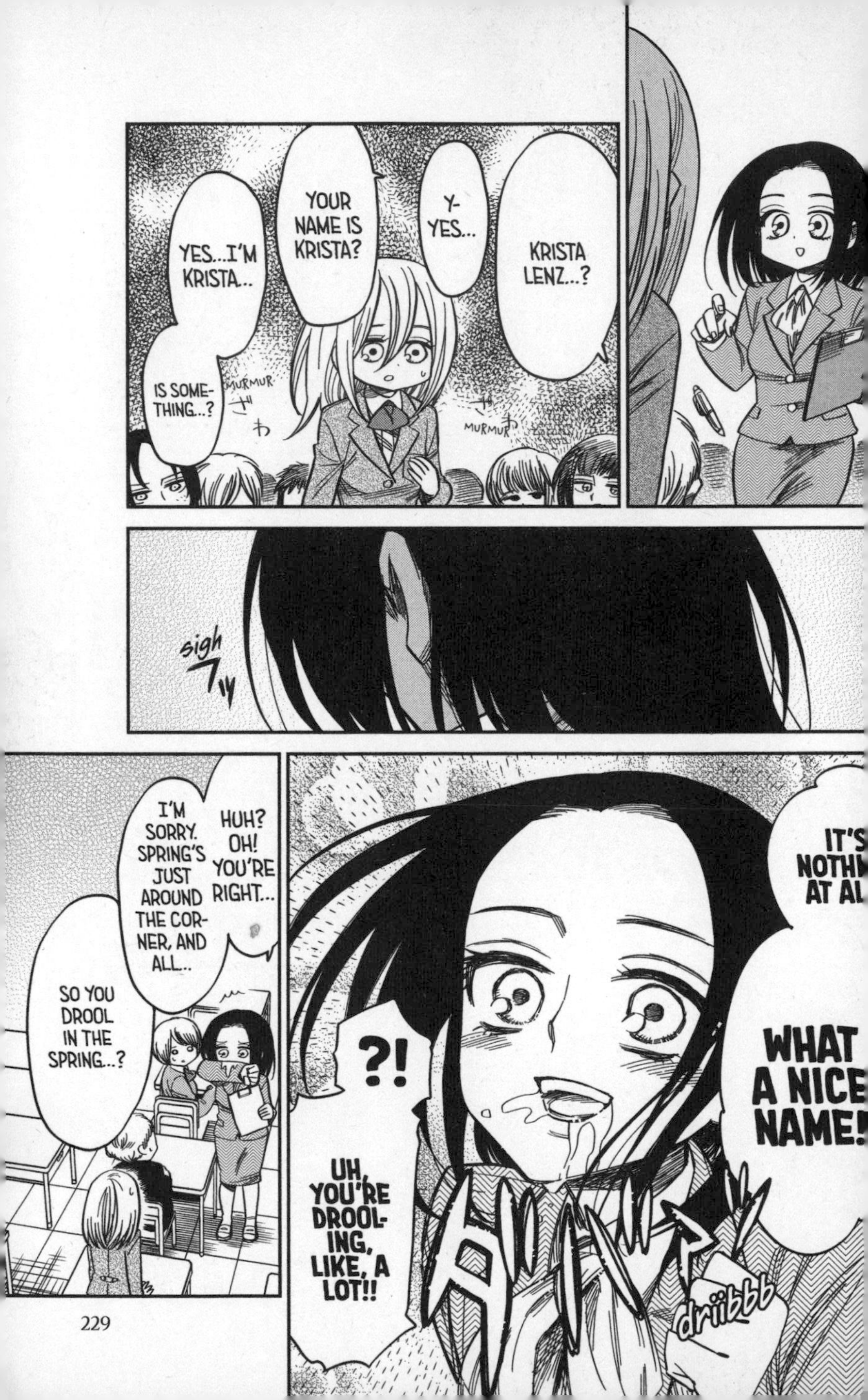
KRISTA LENZ...?
Y- YES...
YOUR NAME IS KRISTA?
YES...I'M KRISTA...
IS SOMETHING...?
MURMUR
MURMUR
sigh
IT'S NOTH AT AL
WHAT A NICE NAME!
?!
UH, YOU'RE DROOLING, LIKE, A LOT!!
driibbb
HUH? OH! YOU'RE RIGHT...
I'M SORRY. SPRING'S JUST AROUND THE CORNER, AND ALL...
SO YOU DROOL IN THE SPRING...?

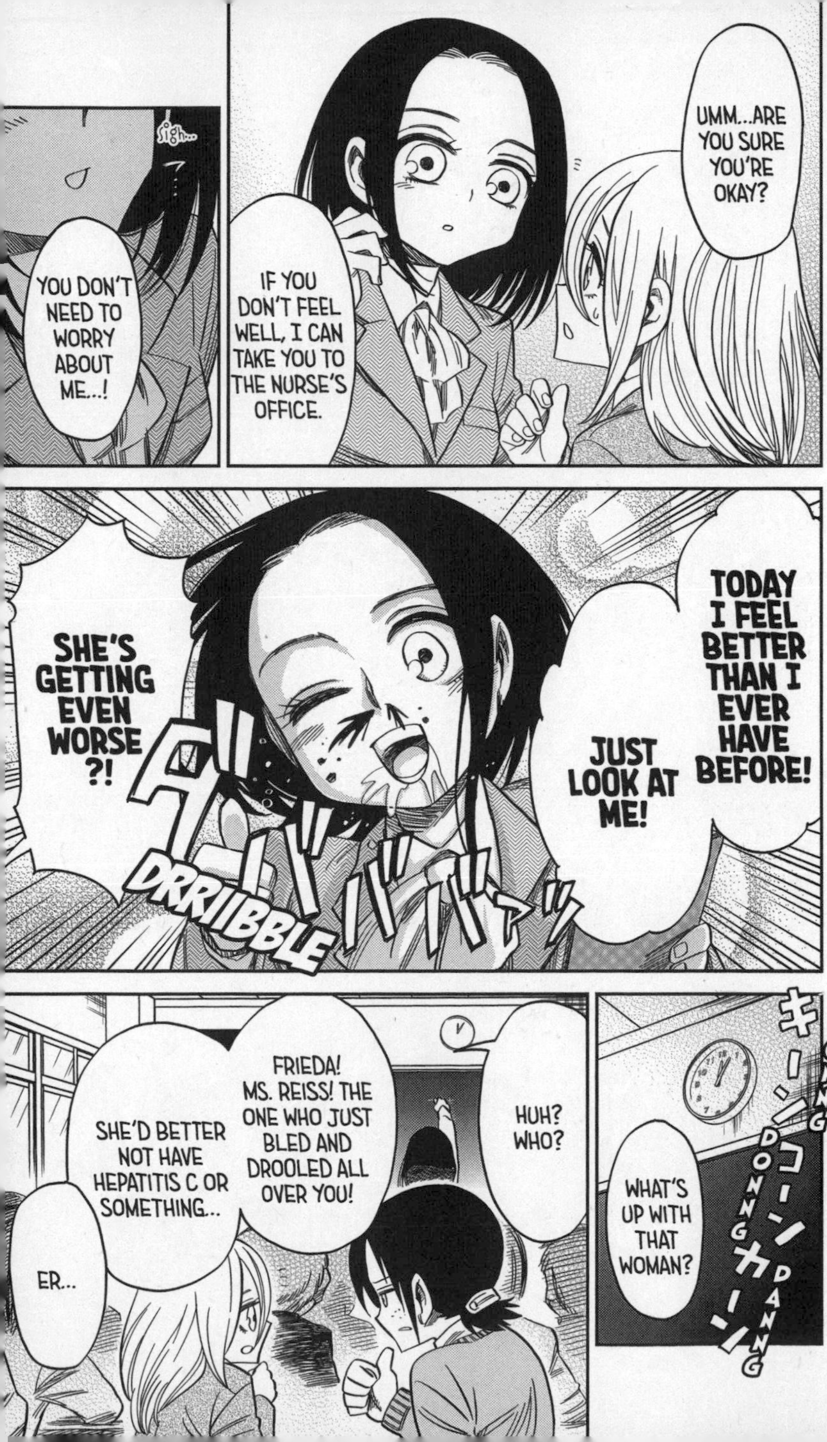
UMM...ARE YOU SURE YOU'RE OKAY?
IF YOU DON'T FEEL WELL, I CAN TAKE YOU TO THE NURSE'S OFFICE.
Sigh...
YOU DON'T NEED TO WORRY ABOUT ME...!
TODAY I FEEL BETTER THAN I EVER HAVE BEFORE!
JUST LOOK AT ME!
DRRIIBBLE
SHE'S GETTING EVEN WORSE?!
DONNG
DONNG
DANNG
WHAT'S UP WITH THAT WOMAN?
HUH? WHO?
FRIEDA! MS. REISS! THE ONE WHO JUST BLED AND DROOLED ALL OVER YOU!
SHE'D BETTER NOT HAVE HEPATITIS C OR SOMETHING...
ER...

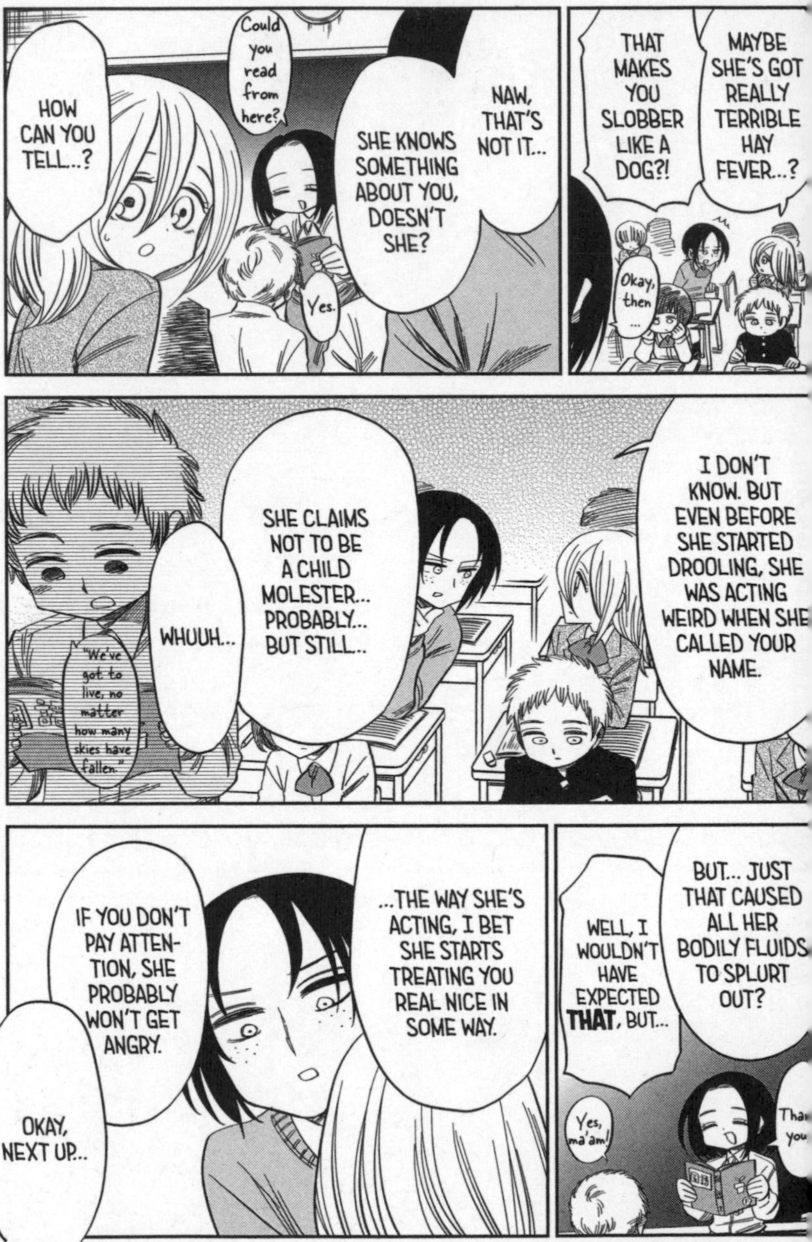
MAYBE SHE'S GOT REALLY TERRIBLE HAY FEVER...?
THAT MAKES YOU SLOBBER LIKE A DOG?!
Okay, then ...
NAW, THAT'S NOT IT...
SHE KNOWS SOMETHING ABOUT YOU, DOESN'T SHE?
Could you read from here?
Yes.
HOW CAN YOU TELL...?
I DON'T KNOW. BUT EVEN BEFORE SHE STARTED DROOLING, SHE WAS ACTING WEIRD WHEN SHE CALLED YOUR NAME.
SHE CLAIMS NOT TO BE A CHILD MOLESTER... PROBABLY... BUT STILL...
WHUUH...
"We've got to live, no matter how many skies have fallen."
BUT... JUST THAT CAUSED ALL HER BODILY FLUIDS TO SPLURT OUT?
WELL, I WOULDN'T HAVE EXPECTED **THAT**, BUT...
Yes, ma'am!
...THE WAY SHE'S ACTING, I BET SHE STARTS TREATING YOU REAL NICE IN SOME WAY.
IF YOU DON'T PAY ATTENTION, SHE PROBABLY WON'T GET ANGRY.
OKAY, NEXT UP...

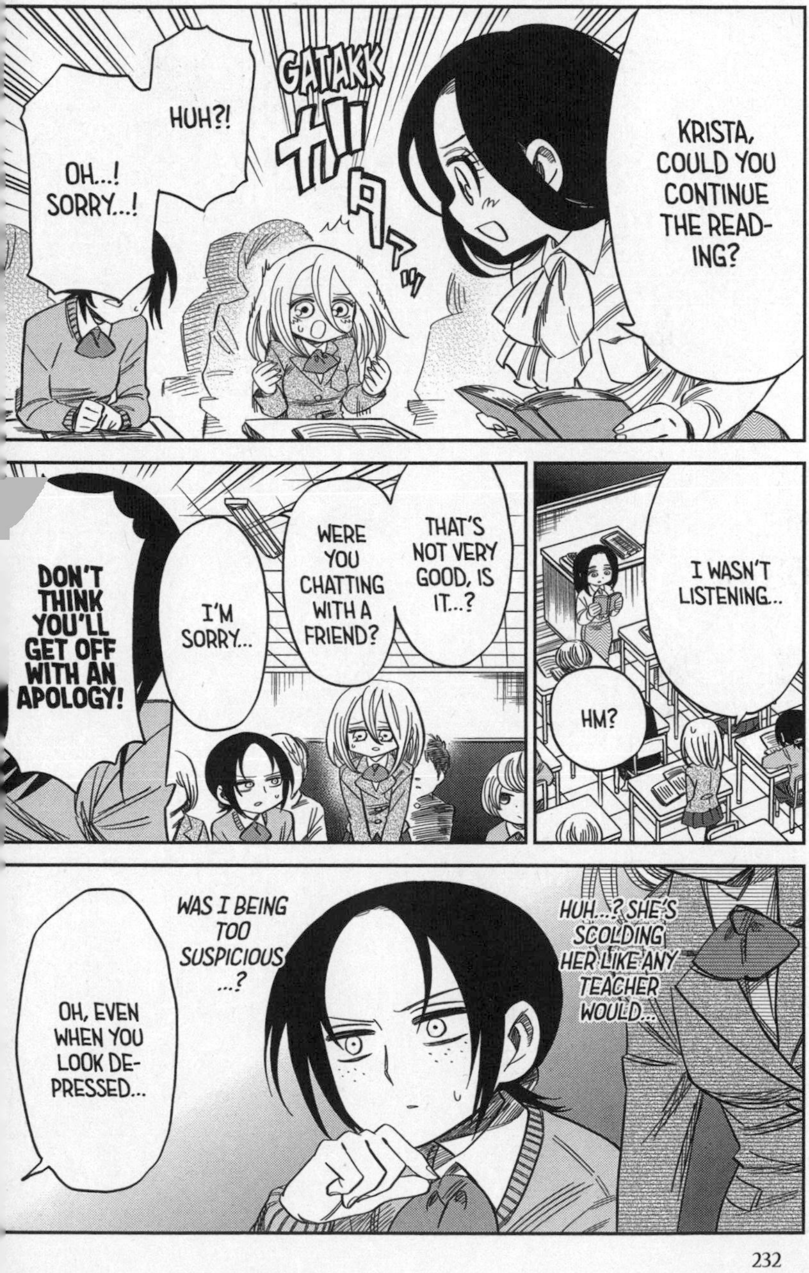
KRISTA, COULD YOU CONTINUE THE READING?
GATAKK
ガタッ
HUH?!
OH...! SORRY...!
I WASN'T LISTENING...
HM?
THAT'S NOT VERY GOOD, IS IT...?
WERE YOU CHATTING WITH A FRIEND?
I'M SORRY...
DON'T THINK YOU'LL GET OFF WITH AN APOLOGY!
HUH...? SHE'S SCOLDING HER LIKE ANY TEACHER WOULD...
WAS I BEING TOO SUSPICIOUS ...?
OH, EVEN WHEN YOU LOOK DEPRESSED...

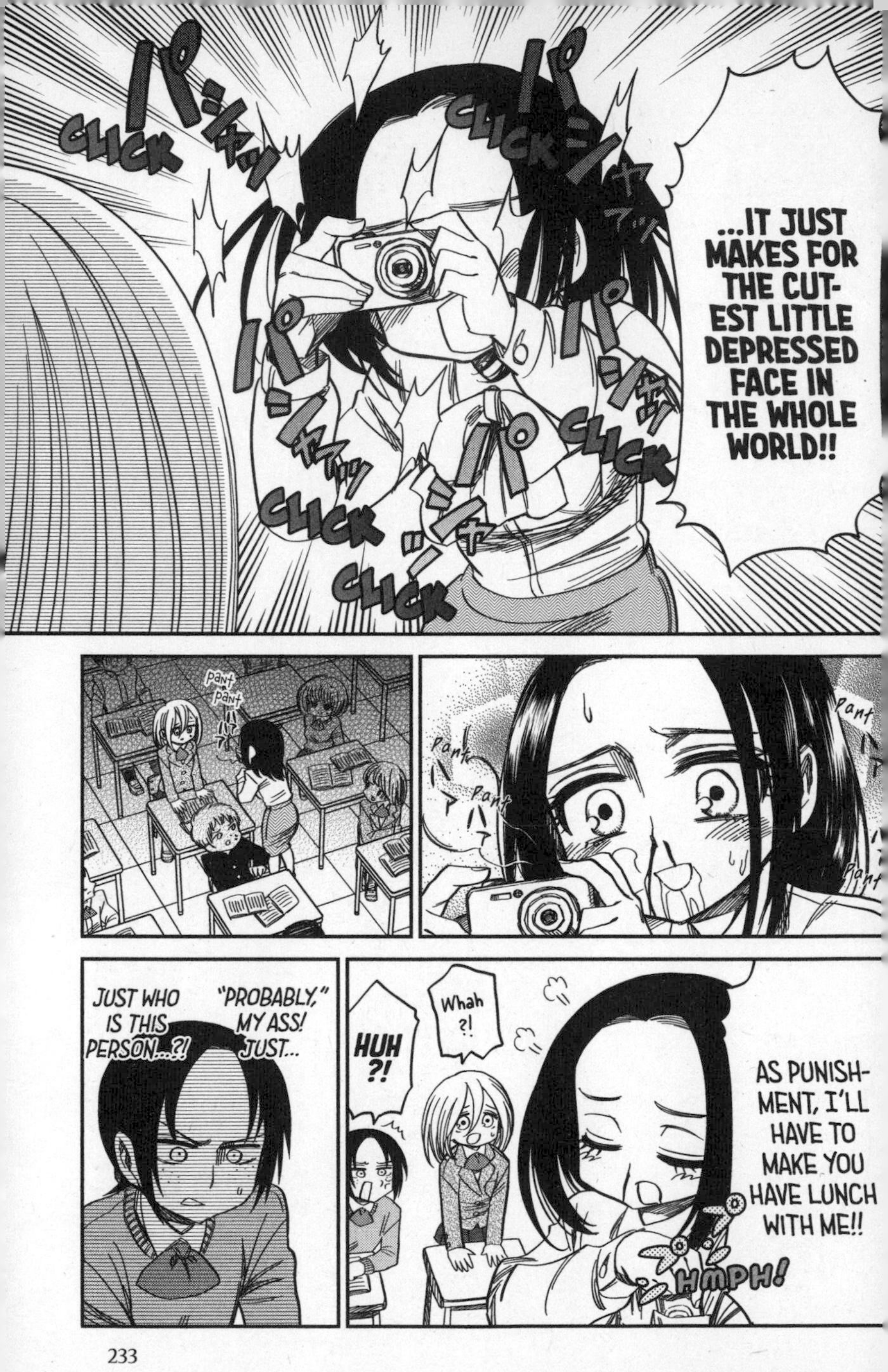
CLICK
CLICK
...IT JUST MAKES FOR THE CUT-EST LITTLE DEPRESSED FACE IN THE WHOLE WORLD!!
CLICK
CLICK
CLICK
Pant
Pant
Pant
Pant
pant
pant
AS PUNISH-MENT, I'LL HAVE TO MAKE YOU HAVE LUNCH WITH ME!!
HMPH!
Whah ?!
HUH ?!
"PROBABLY," MY ASS! JUST...
JUST WHO IS THIS PERSON...?!

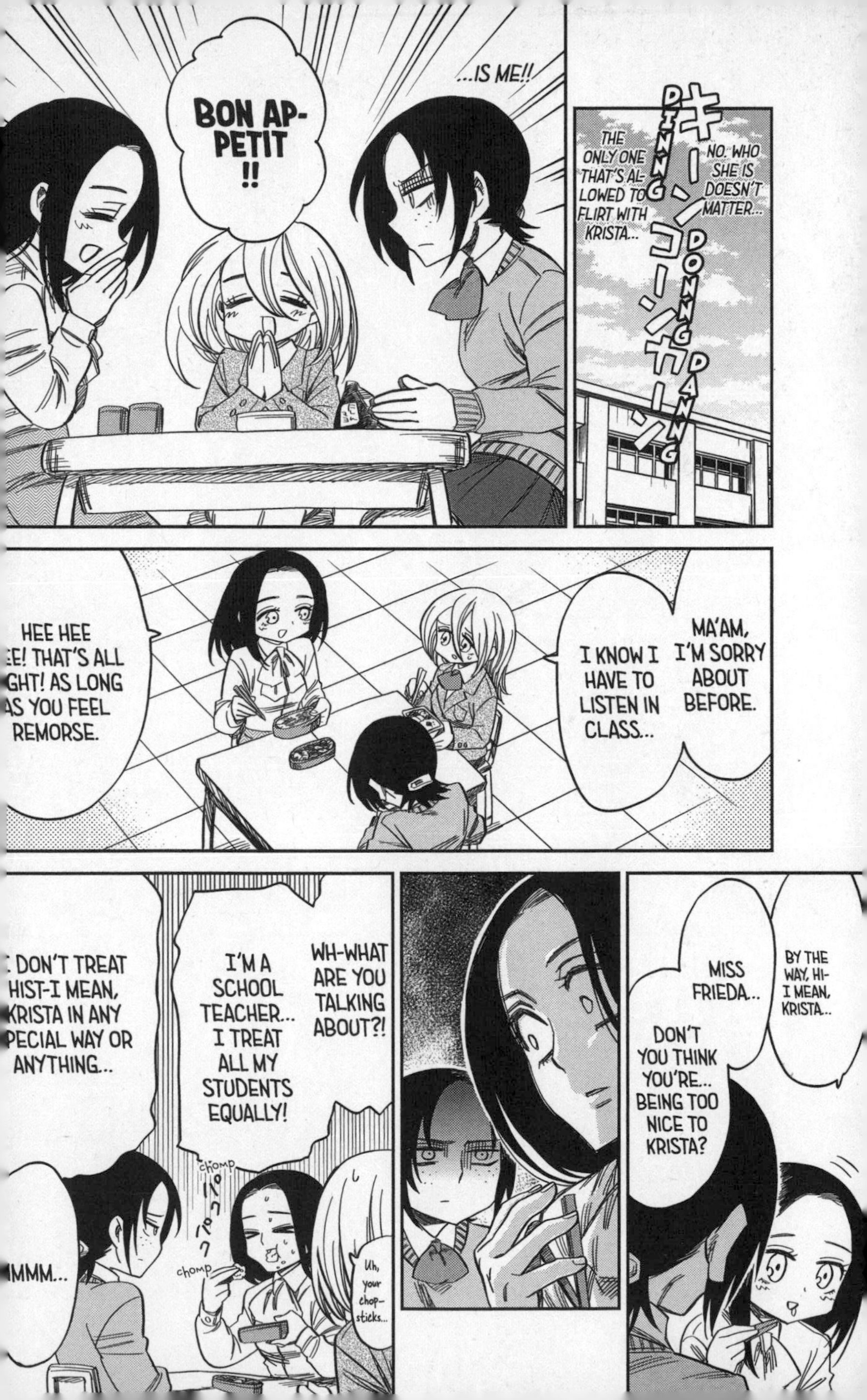
キーンコーンカーン
DINNG DONNG DANNG
NO. WHO SHE IS DOESN'T MATTER...
THE ONLY ONE THAT'S ALLOWED TO FLIRT WITH KRISTA...
...IS ME!!
BON APPETIT!!
MA'AM, I'M SORRY ABOUT BEFORE.
I KNOW I HAVE TO LISTEN IN CLASS...
HEE HEE EE! THAT'S ALL GHT! AS LONG AS YOU FEEL REMORSE.
BY THE WAY, HI- I MEAN, KRISTA...
MISS FRIEDA...
DON'T YOU THINK YOU'RE... BEING TOO NICE TO KRISTA?
WH-WHAT ARE YOU TALKING ABOUT?!
I'M A SCHOOL TEACHER... I TREAT ALL MY STUDENTS EQUALLY!
DON'T TREAT HIST-I MEAN, KRISTA IN ANY PECIAL WAY OR ANYTHING...
chomp
chomp
Uh, your chopsticks...
MMMM...

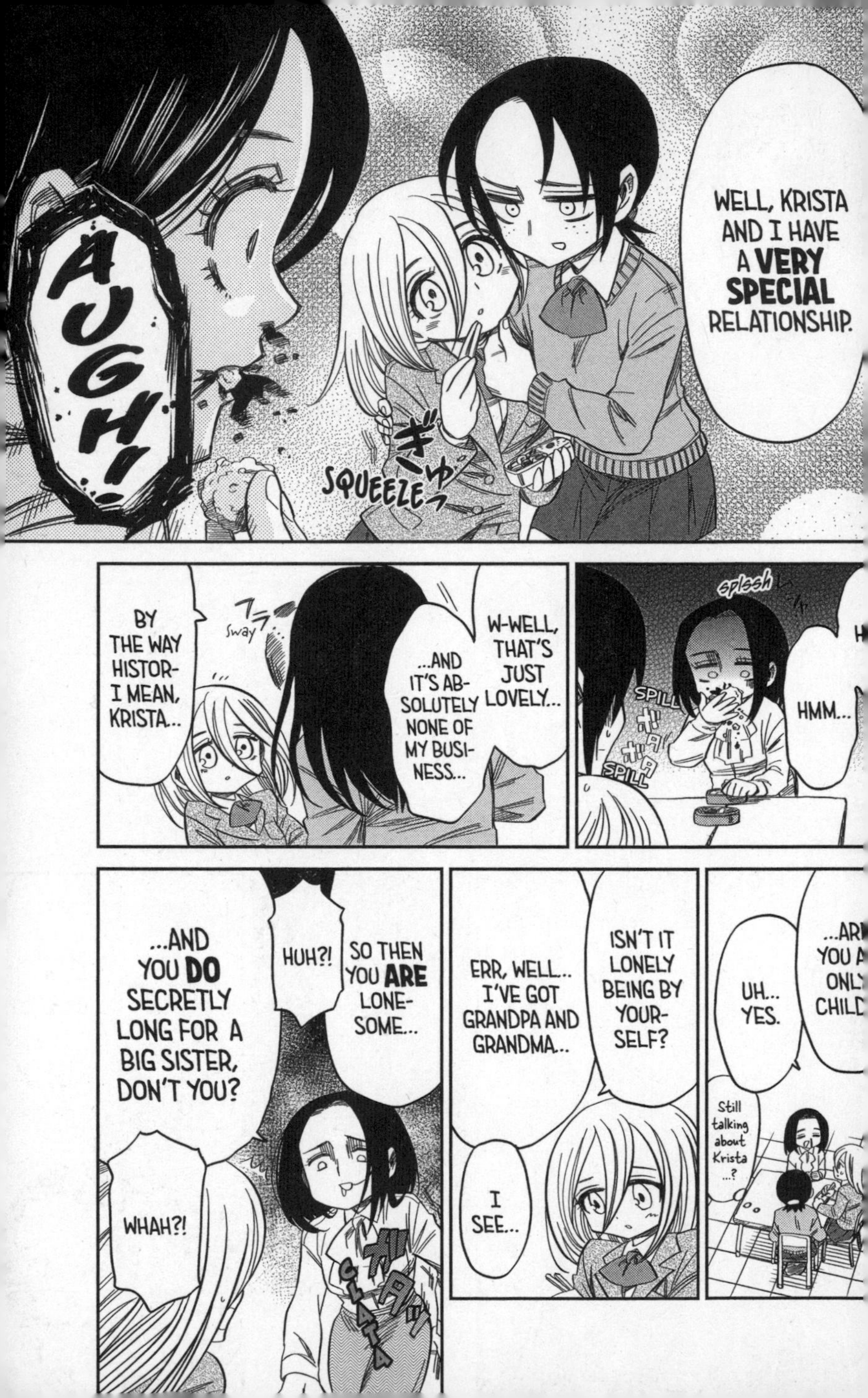

WELL, KRISTA AND I HAVE A VERY SPECIAL RELATIONSHIP.
SQUEEZE
AUGH!
HMM...
splssh
SPILL SPILL
W-WELL, THAT'S JUST LOVELY...
...AND IT'S ABSOLUTELY NONE OF MY BUSINESS...
sway
BY THE WAY HISTOR- I MEAN, KRISTA...
UH... YES.
Still talking about Krista ...?
ISN'T IT LONELY BEING BY YOURSELF?
ERR, WELL... I'VE GOT GRANDPA AND GRANDMA...
I SEE...
SO THEN YOU ARE LONESOME...
HUH?!
...AND YOU DO SECRETLY LONG FOR A BIG SISTER, DON'T YOU?
WHAH?!
CLATTA

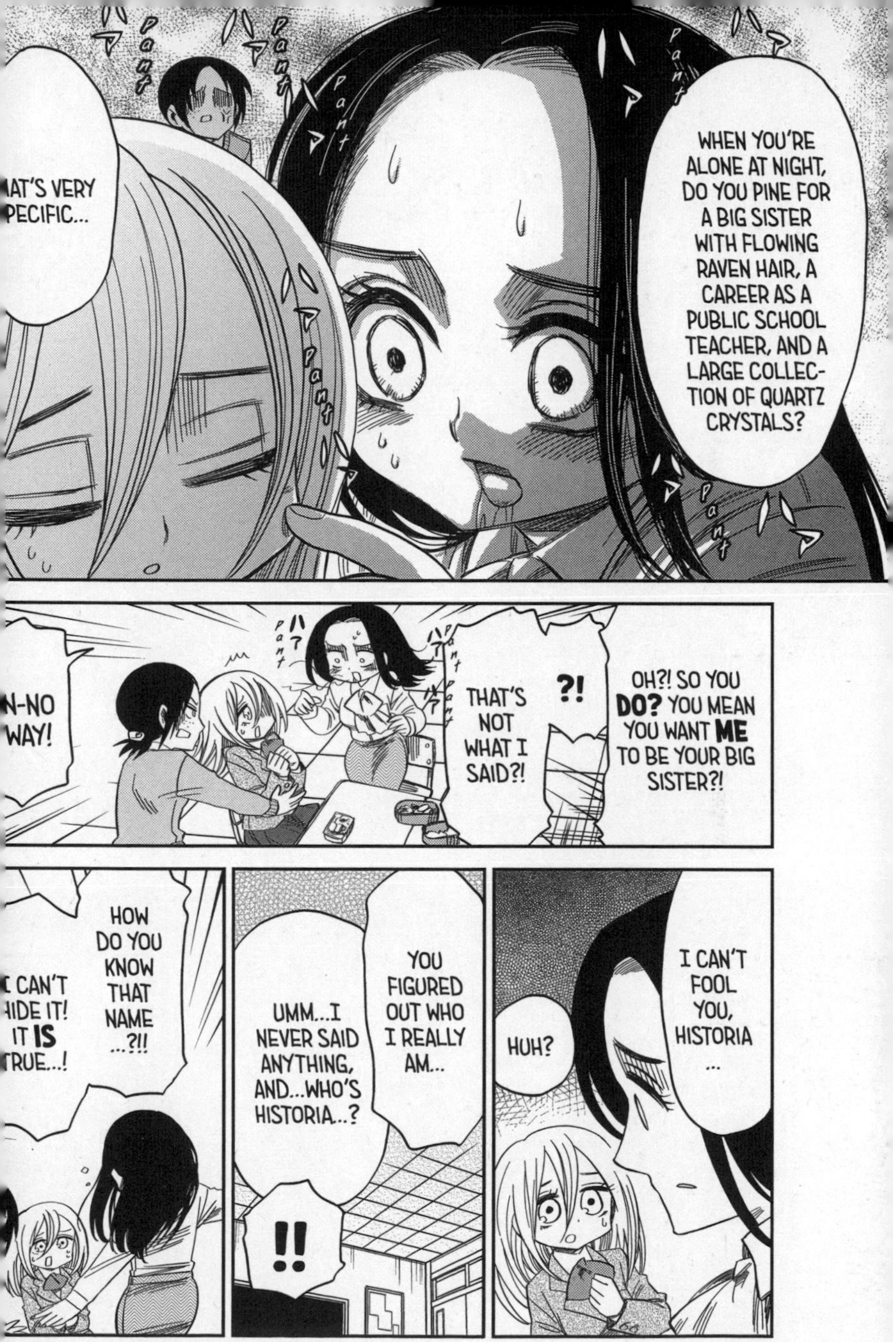
Pant Pant
WHEN YOU'RE ALONE AT NIGHT, DO YOU PINE FOR A BIG SISTER WITH FLOWING RAVEN HAIR, A CAREER AS A PUBLIC SCHOOL TEACHER, AND A LARGE COLLECTION OF QUARTZ CRYSTALS?
Pant Pant Pant Pant
AT'S VERY PECIFIC...
Pant Pant
OH?! SO YOU DO? YOU MEAN YOU WANT ME TO BE YOUR BIG SISTER?!
?!
THAT'S NOT WHAT I SAID?!
N-NO WAY!
I CAN'T FOOL YOU, HISTORIA ...
HUH?
YOU FIGURED OUT WHO I REALLY AM...
UMM...I NEVER SAID ANYTHING, AND...WHO'S HISTORIA...?
!!
HOW DO YOU KNOW THAT NAME ...?!!
CAN'T HIDE IT! IT IS RUE...!

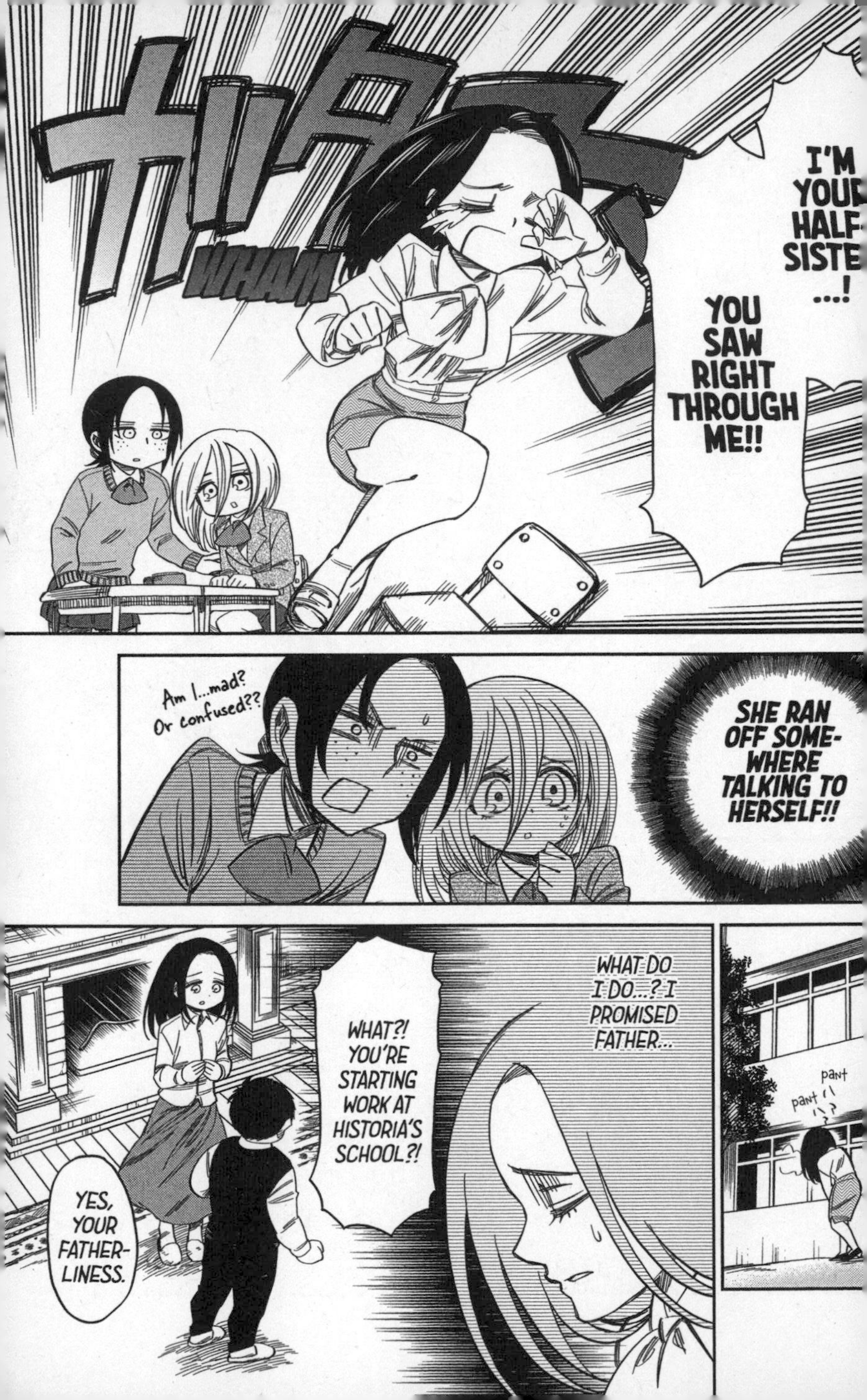
I'M YOUR HALF-SISTE ...!
YOU SAW RIGHT THROUGH ME!!
WHAM
SHE RAN OFF SOME-WHERE TALKING TO HERSELF!!
Am I...mad? Or confused??
pant pant
WHAT DO I DO...? I PROMISED FATHER...
WHAT?! YOU'RE STARTING WORK AT HISTORIA'S SCHOOL?!
YES, YOUR FATHER-LINESS.

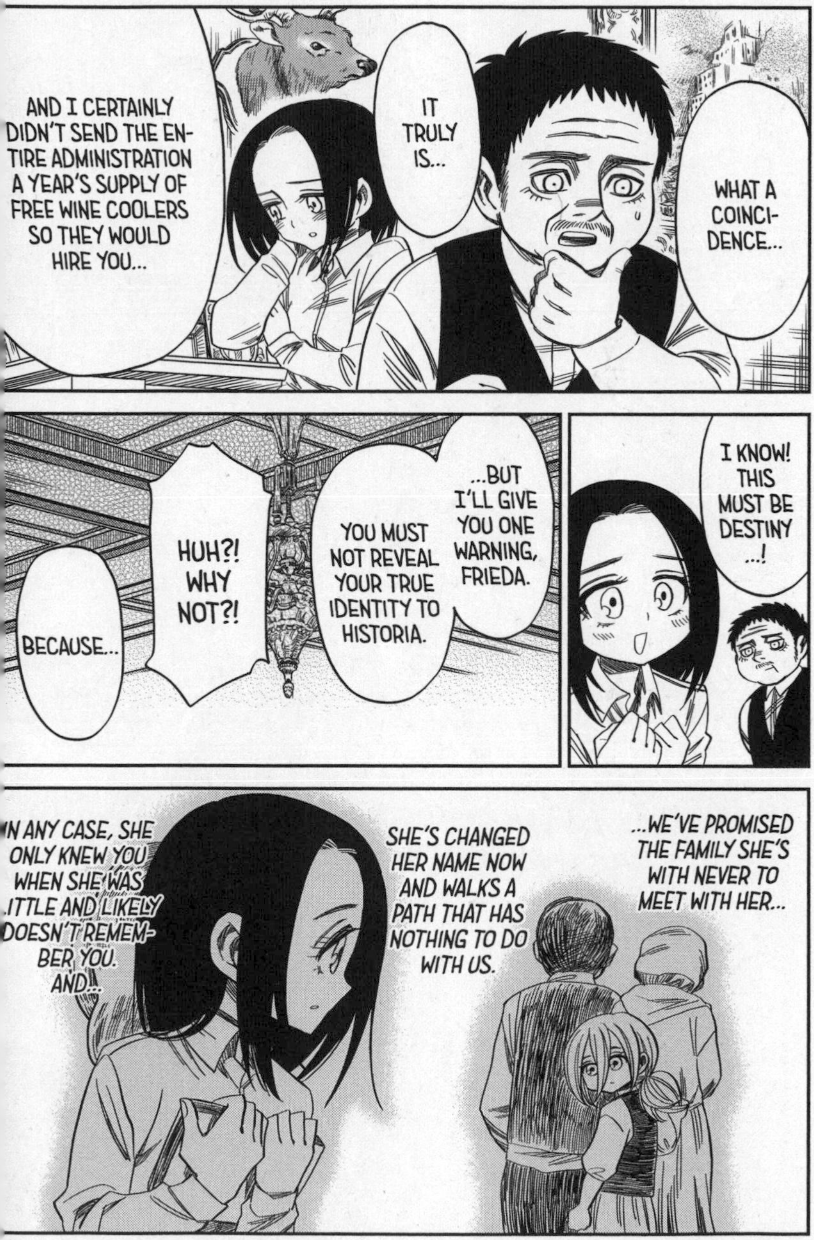
WHAT A COINCI-DENCE...
IT TRULY IS...
AND I CERTAINLY DIDN'T SEND THE EN-TIRE ADMINISTRATION A YEAR'S SUPPLY OF FREE WINE COOLERS SO THEY WOULD HIRE YOU...
I KNOW! THIS MUST BE DESTINY ...!
...BUT I'LL GIVE YOU ONE WARNING, FRIEDA.
YOU MUST NOT REVEAL YOUR TRUE IDENTITY TO HISTORIA.
HUH?! WHY NOT?!
BECAUSE...
...WE'VE PROMISED THE FAMILY SHE'S WITH NEVER TO MEET WITH HER...
SHE'S CHANGED HER NAME NOW AND WALKS A PATH THAT HAS NOTHING TO DO WITH US.
N ANY CASE, SHE ONLY KNEW YOU WHEN SHE WAS ITTLE AND LIKELY DOESN'T REMEM-BER YOU. AND...

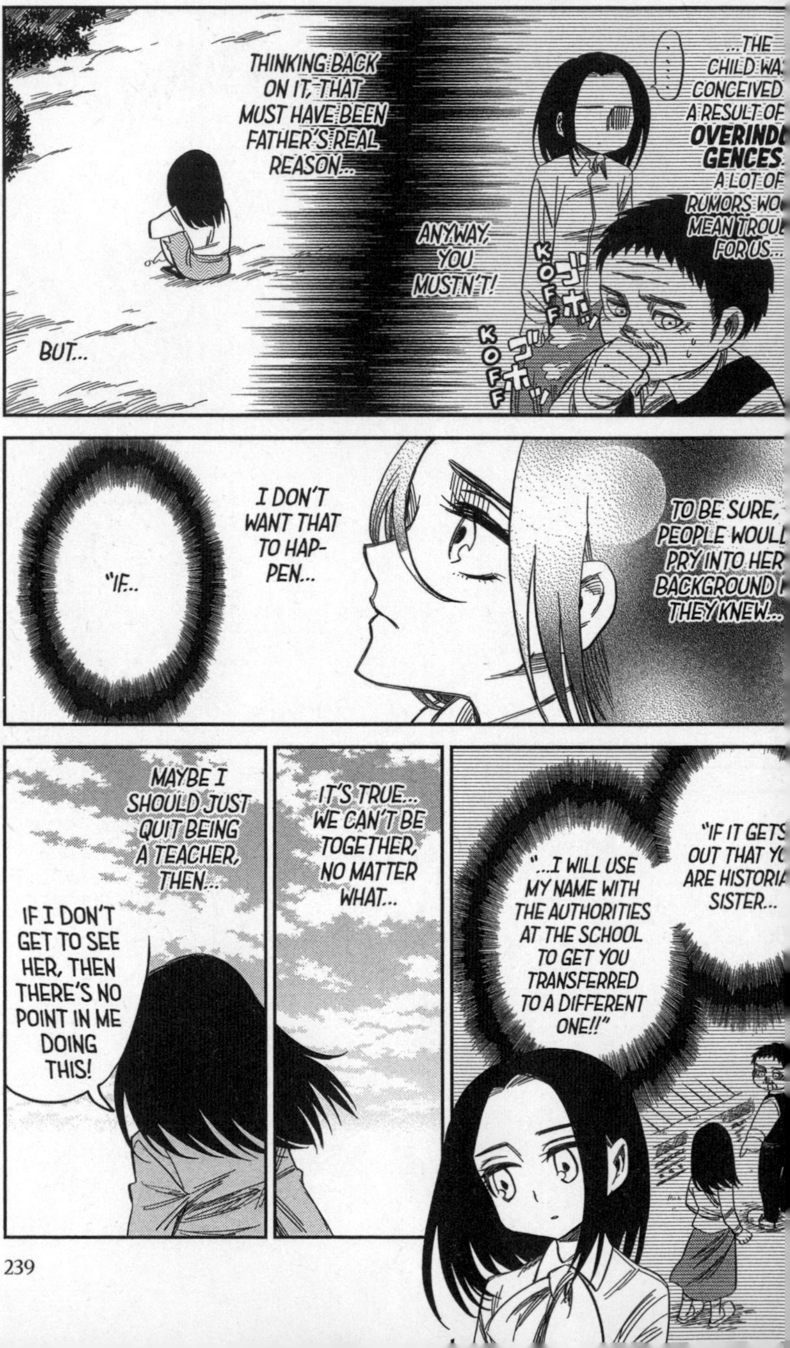
...THE CHILD WA
CONCEIVED
A RESULT OF
OVERINDU
GENCES.
A LOT OF
RUMORS WO
MEAN TROU
FOR US...
....
KOFF KOFF ゴホッ
KOFF KOFF ゴホッ
ANYWAY, YOU MUSTN'T!
THINKING BACK ON IT, THAT MUST HAVE BEEN FATHER'S REAL REASON...
BUT...
TO BE SURE, PEOPLE WOUL
PRY INTO HER
BACKGROUND
THEY KNEW...
I DON'T WANT THAT TO HAP-PEN...
"IF...
"IF IT GETS
OUT THAT YO
ARE HISTORIA
SISTER...
"...I WILL USE MY NAME WITH THE AUTHORITIES AT THE SCHOOL TO GET YOU TRANSFERRED TO A DIFFERENT ONE!!"
IT'S TRUE... WE CAN'T BE TOGETHER, NO MATTER WHAT...
MAYBE I SHOULD JUST QUIT BEING A TEACHER, THEN...
IF I DON'T GET TO SEE HER, THEN THERE'S NO POINT IN ME DOING THIS!

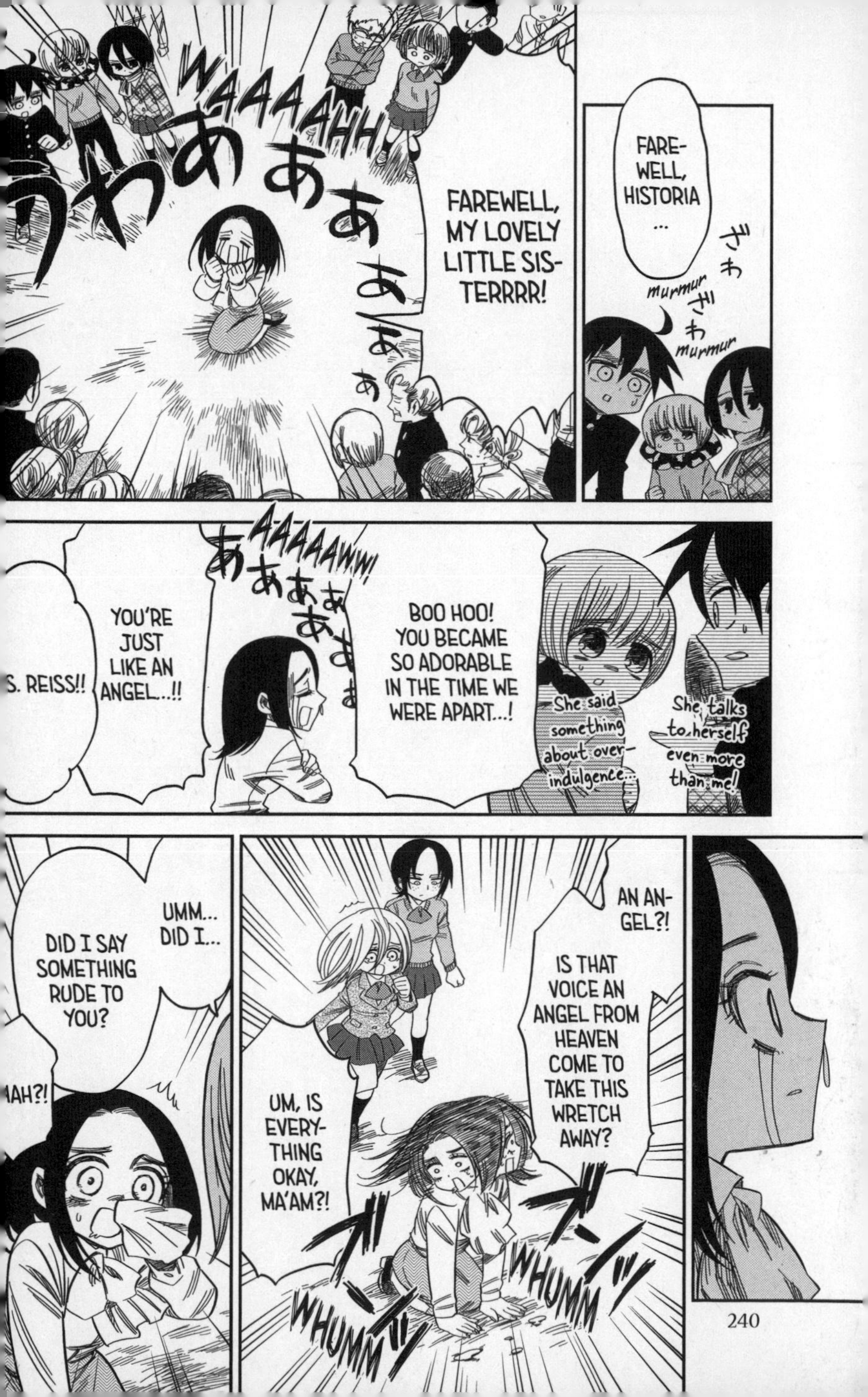
FARE-WELL, HISTORIA...
ざわ murmur
ざわ murmur
WAAAAAHH
うわああああああ
FAREWELL, MY LOVELY LITTLE SIS-TERRRR!
She talks to herself even more than me!
She said something about over-indulgence...
AAAAAWW!
あああああああ
BOO HOO! YOU BECAME SO ADORABLE IN THE TIME WE WERE APART...!
YOU'RE JUST LIKE AN ANGEL...!!
...S. REISS!!
AN AN-GEL?!
IS THAT VOICE AN ANGEL FROM HEAVEN COME TO TAKE THIS WRETCH AWAY?
UM, IS EVERY-THING OKAY, MA'AM?!
WHUMM
WHUMM
WHUMM
UMM... DID I...
DID I SAY SOMETHING RUDE TO YOU?
...AH?!

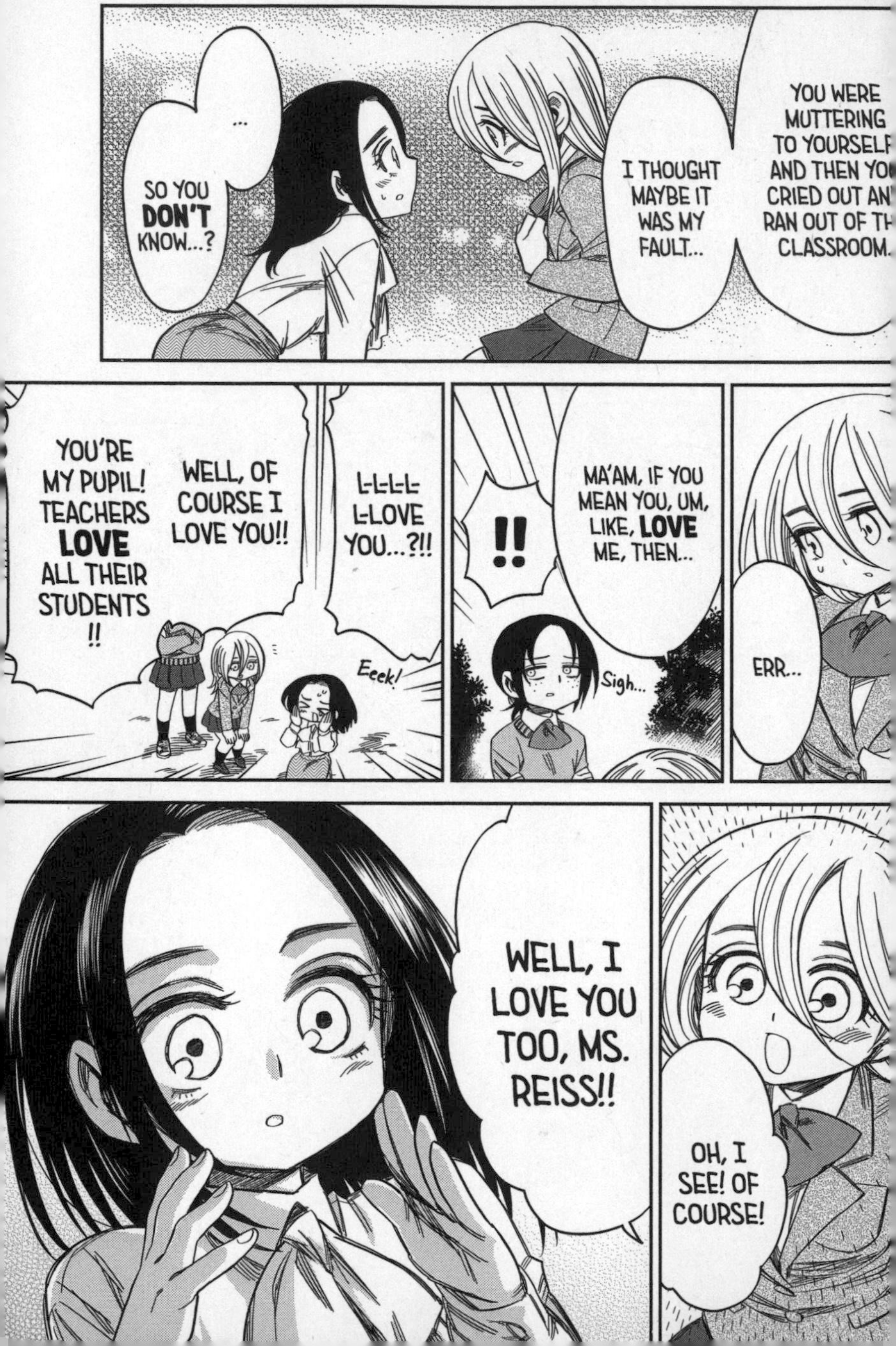
YOU WERE MUTTERING TO YOURSELF AND THEN YO CRIED OUT AN RAN OUT OF TH CLASSROOM.
I THOUGHT MAYBE IT WAS MY FAULT...
...
SO YOU **DON'T** KNOW...?
ERR...
MA'AM, IF YOU MEAN YOU, UM, LIKE, **LOVE** ME, THEN...
!!
Sigh...
L-L-L-L-L-LOVE YOU...?!!
Eeek!
WELL, OF COURSE I LOVE YOU!!
YOU'RE MY PUPIL! TEACHERS **LOVE** ALL THEIR STUDENTS!!
OH, I SEE! OF COURSE!
WELL, I LOVE YOU TOO, MS. REISS!!

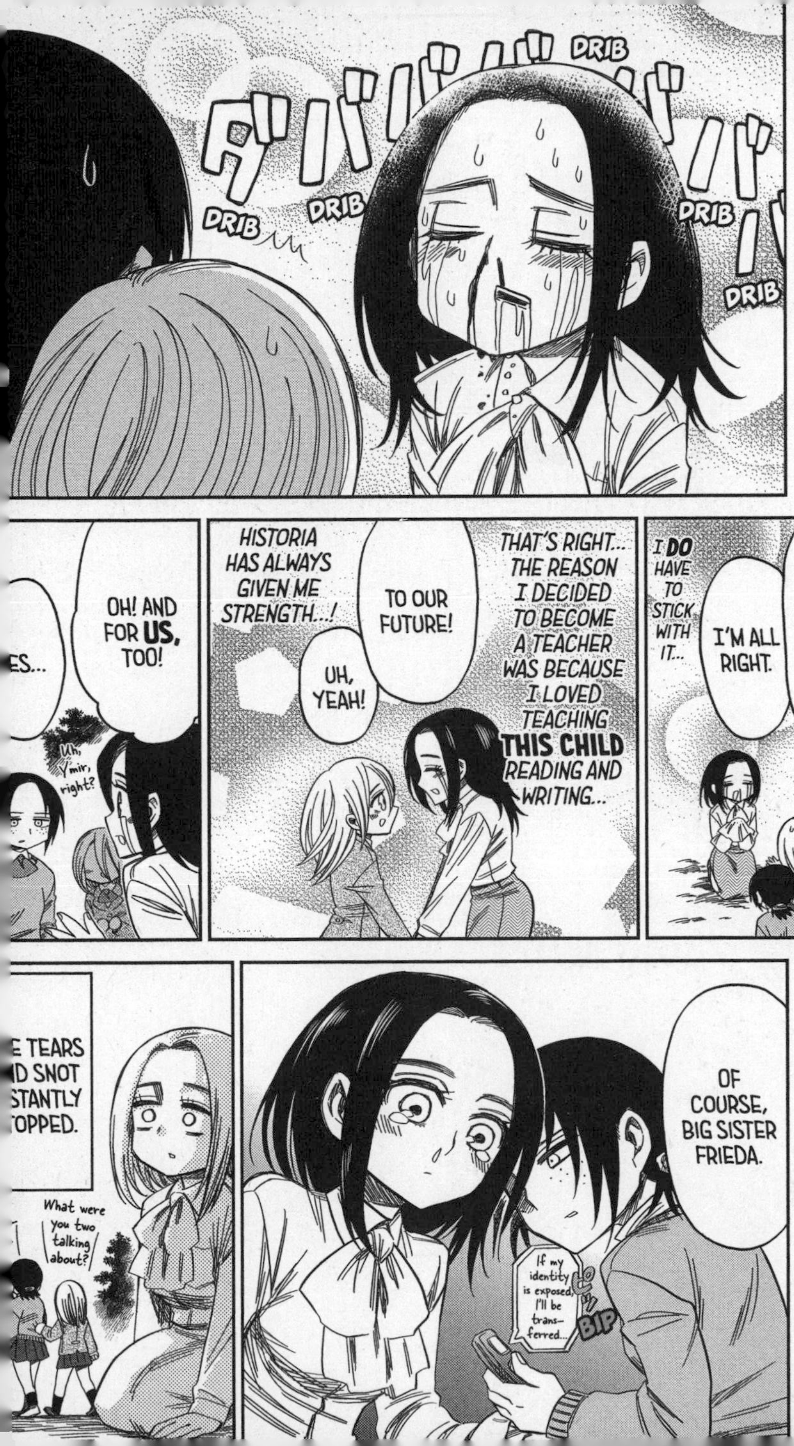
DRIB
DRIB
DRIB
DRIB
DRIB
MA'AM, UM, A VARIETY OF FLUIDS ARE DRIBBLING OFF YOUR FACE...
I'M ALL RIGHT.
I **DO** HAVE TO STICK WITH IT...
THAT'S RIGHT... THE REASON I DECIDED TO BECOME A TEACHER WAS BECAUSE I LOVED TEACHING **THIS CHILD** READING AND WRITING...
TO OUR FUTURE!
UH, YEAH!
HISTORIA HAS ALWAYS GIVEN ME STRENGTH...!
OH! AND FOR **US**, TOO!
ES...
Uh, Ymir, right?
OF COURSE, BIG SISTER FRIEDA.
If my identity is exposed, I'll be transferred...
BIP
E TEARS
ND SNOT
STANTLY
TOPPED.
What were you two talking about?

FIFTY-SIXTH PERIOD: MR. NILE'S FAMILY CIRCUMSTANCES

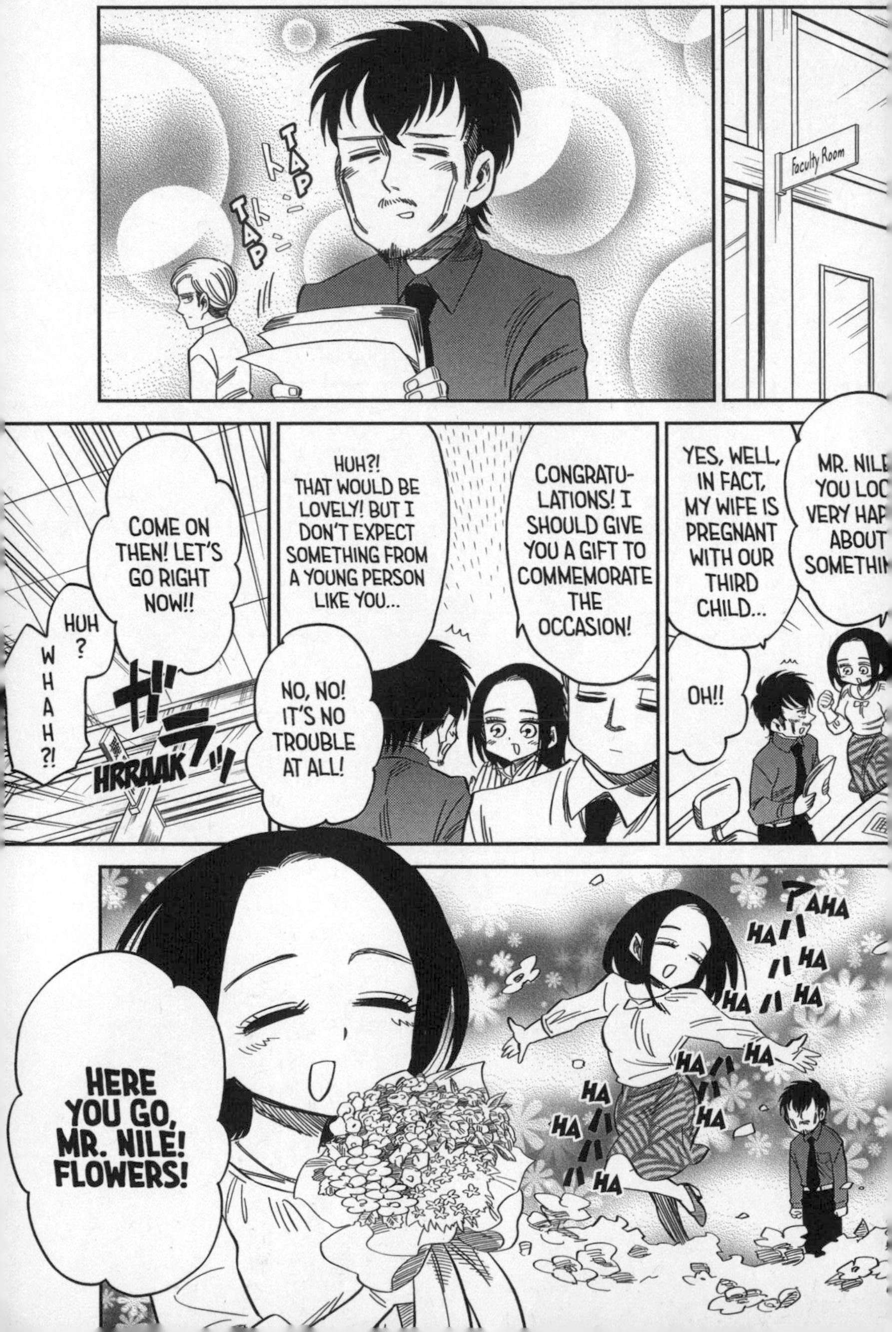
Faculty Room
TAP TAP
MR. NILE YOU LOO VERY HAP ABOUT SOMETHI
YES, WELL, IN FACT, MY WIFE IS PREGNANT WITH OUR THIRD CHILD...
OH!!
CONGRATU-LATIONS! I SHOULD GIVE YOU A GIFT TO COMMEMORATE THE OCCASION!
HUH?! THAT WOULD BE LOVELY! BUT I DON'T EXPECT SOMETHING FROM A YOUNG PERSON LIKE YOU...
NO, NO! IT'S NO TROUBLE AT ALL!
COME ON THEN! LET'S GO RIGHT NOW!!
HUH?
WHAH?!
HRRAAK
HERE YOU GO, MR. NILE! FLOWERS!
AHA HA HA HA HA HA HA HA HA HA HA HA HA

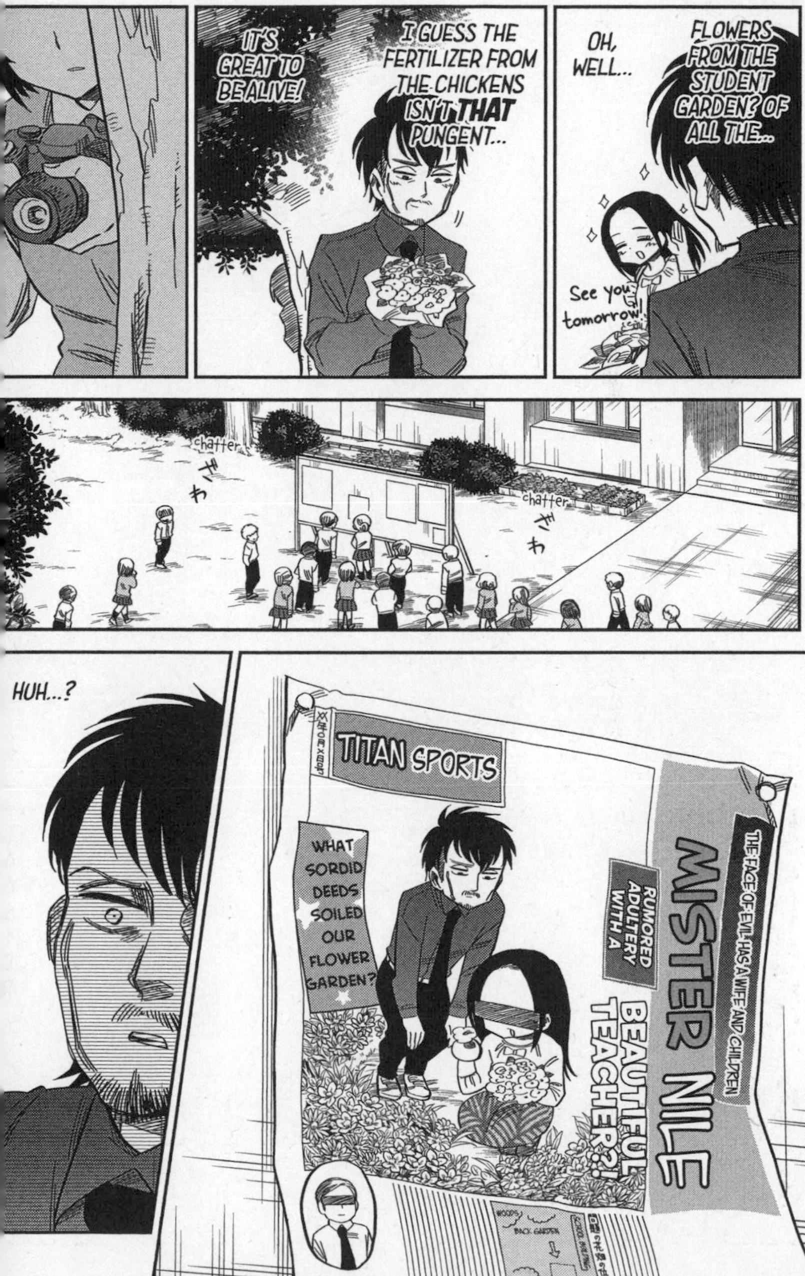
FLOWERS FROM THE STUDENT GARDEN? OF ALL THE...
OH, WELL...
See you tomorrow!
I GUESS THE FERTILIZER FROM THE CHICKENS ISN'T **THAT** PUNGENT...
IT'S GREAT TO BE ALIVE!
chatter
ざわ
chatter
ざわ
TITAN SPORTS
THE FACE OF EVIL HAS A WIFE AND CHILDREN
MISTER NILE
RUMORED ADULTERY WITH A
BEAUTIFUL TEACHER?!
WHAT SORDID DEEDS SOILED OUR FLOWER GARDEN?
WOODS
BACK GARDEN
SCHOOL BUILDING
A SAINTLY TEACHER WAS OUR ANONYMOUS TIPSTER
HUH...?

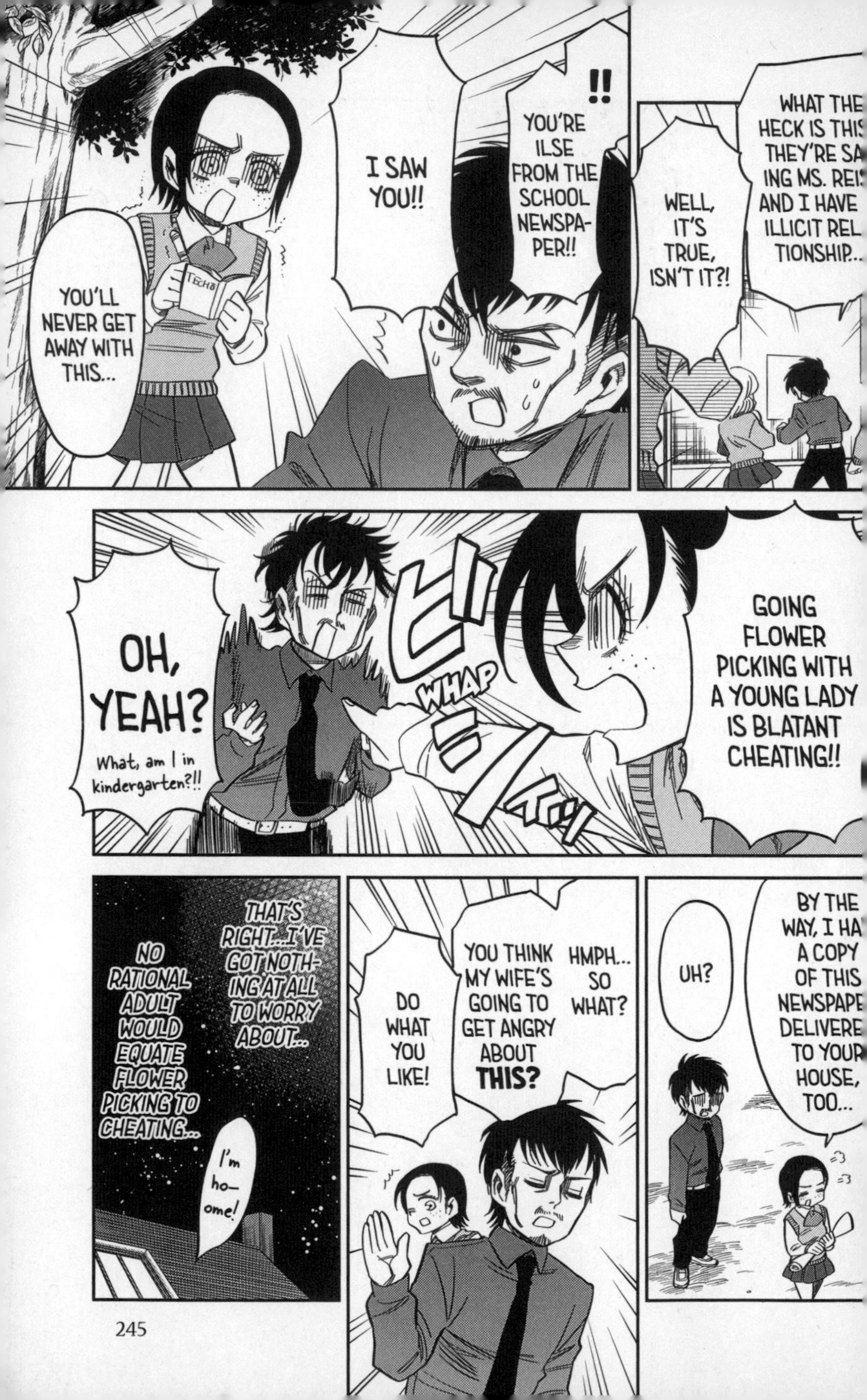
WHAT THE HECK IS THIS THEY'RE SA ING MS. REI AND I HAVE ILLICIT REL TIONSHIP...
WELL, IT'S TRUE, ISN'T IT?!
!!
YOU'RE ILSE FROM THE SCHOOL NEWSPA-PER!!
I SAW YOU!!
YOU'LL NEVER GET AWAY WITH THIS...
GOING FLOWER PICKING WITH A YOUNG LADY IS BLATANT CHEATING!!
WHAP
OH, YEAH?
What, am I in kindergarten?!!
BY THE WAY, I HA A COPY OF THIS NEWSPAPE DELIVERE TO YOUR HOUSE, TOO...
UH?
HMPH... SO WHAT?
YOU THINK MY WIFE'S GOING TO GET ANGRY ABOUT **THIS?**
DO WHAT YOU LIKE!
THAT'S RIGHT...I'VE GOT NOTHING AT ALL TO WORRY ABOUT...
NO RATIONAL ADULT WOULD EQUATE FLOWER PICKING TO CHEATING...
I'm ho-ome!

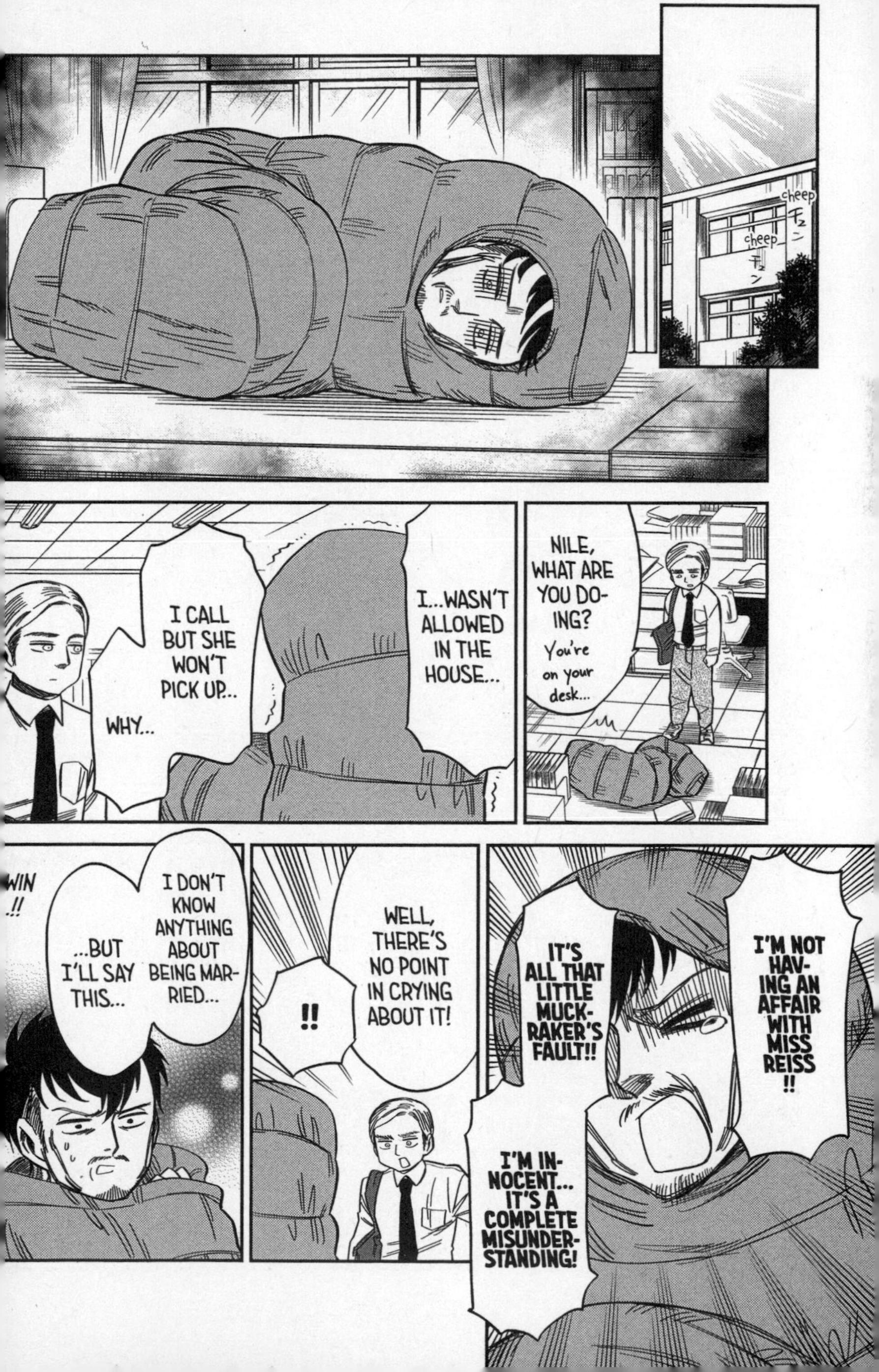
cheep
cheep
NILE, WHAT ARE YOU DOING?
You're on your desk...
I...WASN'T ALLOWED IN THE HOUSE...
I CALL BUT SHE WON'T PICK UP...
WHY...
I'M NOT HAVING AN AFFAIR WITH MISS REISS!!
IT'S ALL THAT LITTLE MUCKRAKER'S FAULT!!
I'M INNOCENT... IT'S A COMPLETE MISUNDERSTANDING!
WELL, THERE'S NO POINT IN CRYING ABOUT IT!
!!
I DON'T KNOW ANYTHING ABOUT BEING MARRIED...
...BUT I'LL SAY THIS...

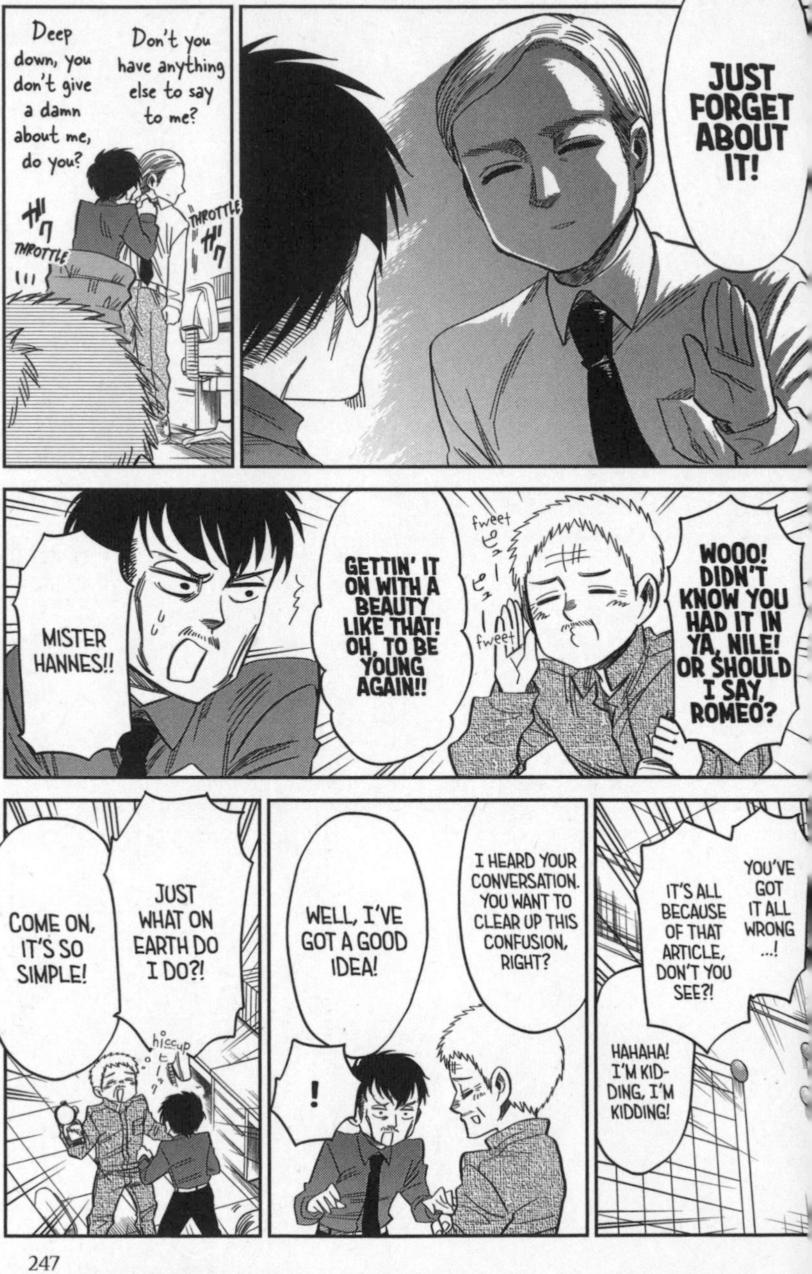
JUST FORGET ABOUT IT!
Don't you have anything else to say to me?
Deep down, you don't give a damn about me, do you?
THROTTLE
THROTTLE
WOOO! DIDN'T KNOW YOU HAD IT IN YA, NILE! OR SHOULD I SAY, ROMEO?
fweet
fweet
GETTIN' IT ON WITH A BEAUTY LIKE THAT! OH, TO BE YOUNG AGAIN!!
MISTER HANNES!!
YOU'VE GOT IT ALL WRONG ...!
IT'S ALL BECAUSE OF THAT ARTICLE, DON'T YOU SEE?!
HAHAHA! I'M KIDDING, I'M KIDDING!
I HEARD YOUR CONVERSATION. YOU WANT TO CLEAR UP THIS CONFUSION, RIGHT?
WELL, I'VE GOT A GOOD IDEA!
!
JUST WHAT ON EARTH DO I DO?!
COME ON, IT'S SO SIMPLE!
hiccup

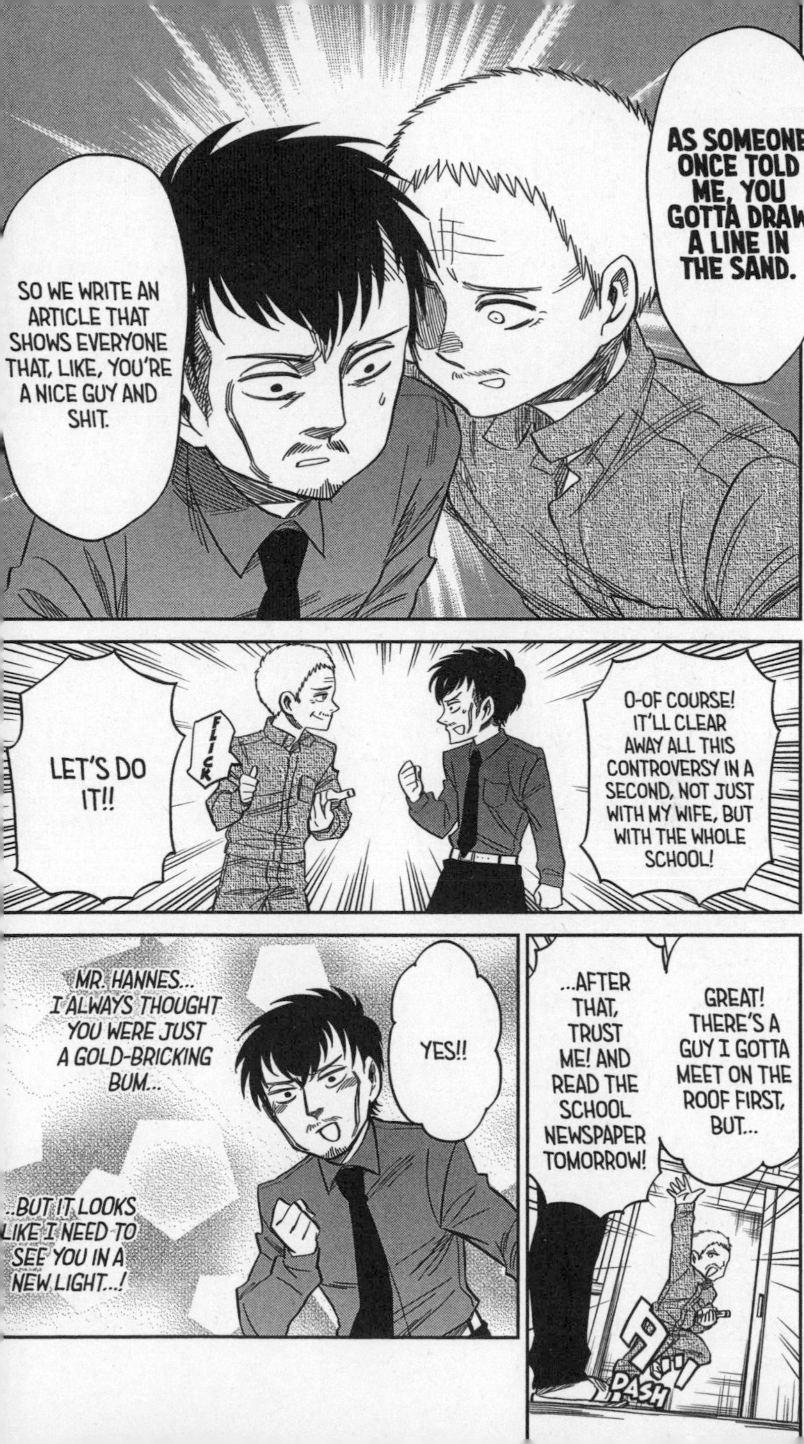
AS SOMEONE ONCE TOLD ME, YOU GOTTA DRAW A LINE IN THE SAND.
SO WE WRITE AN ARTICLE THAT SHOWS EVERYONE THAT, LIKE, YOU'RE A NICE GUY AND SHIT.
O-OF COURSE! IT'LL CLEAR AWAY ALL THIS CONTROVERSY IN A SECOND, NOT JUST WITH MY WIFE, BUT WITH THE WHOLE SCHOOL!
FLICK
LET'S DO IT!!
GREAT! THERE'S A GUY I GOTTA MEET ON THE ROOF FIRST, BUT...
...AFTER THAT, TRUST ME! AND READ THE SCHOOL NEWSPAPER TOMORROW!
DASH
YES!!
MR. HANNES... I ALWAYS THOUGHT YOU WERE JUST A GOLD-BRICKING BUM...
..BUT IT LOOKS LIKE I NEED TO SEE YOU IN A NEW LIGHT...!

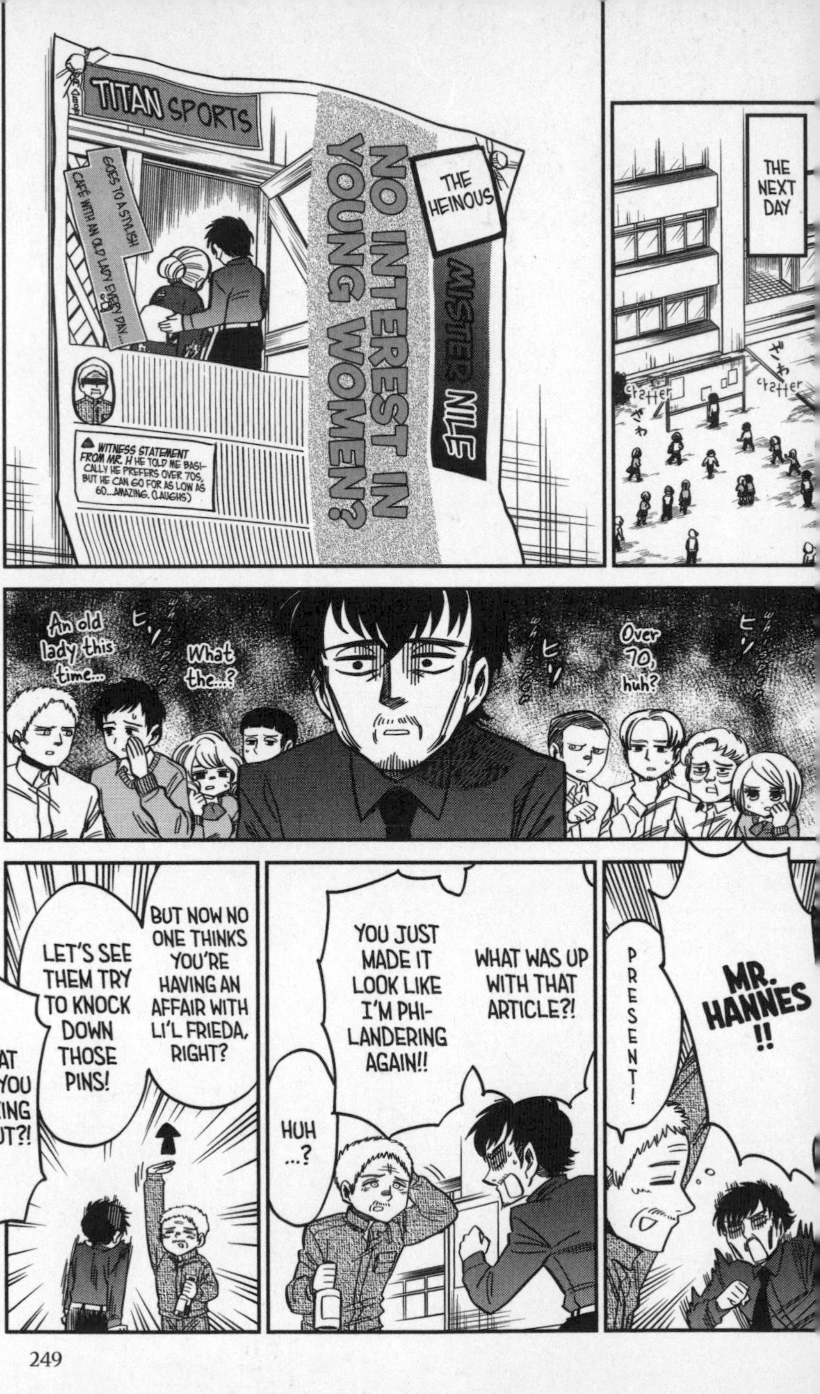
THE NEXT DAY
chatter
chatter
TITAN SPORTS
THE HEINOUS
MISTER NILE
NO INTEREST IN YOUNG WOMEN?
GOES TO A STYLISH CAFE WITH AN OLD LADY EVERY DAY...
WITNESS STATEMENT FROM MR. H HE TOLD ME BASICALLY HE PREFERS OVER 70S, BUT HE CAN GO FOR AS LOW AS 60...AMAZING. (LAUGHS)
Over 70, huh?
whisper
whisper
What the...?
whisper
An old lady this time...
MR. HANNES!!
PRESENT!
WHAT WAS UP WITH THAT ARTICLE?!
YOU JUST MADE IT LOOK LIKE I'M PHILANDERING AGAIN!!
HUH...?
BUT NOW NO ONE THINKS YOU'RE HAVING AN AFFAIR WITH LI'L FRIEDA, RIGHT?
LET'S SEE THEM TRY TO KNOCK DOWN THOSE PINS!
WHAT ARE YOU TALKING ABOUT?!

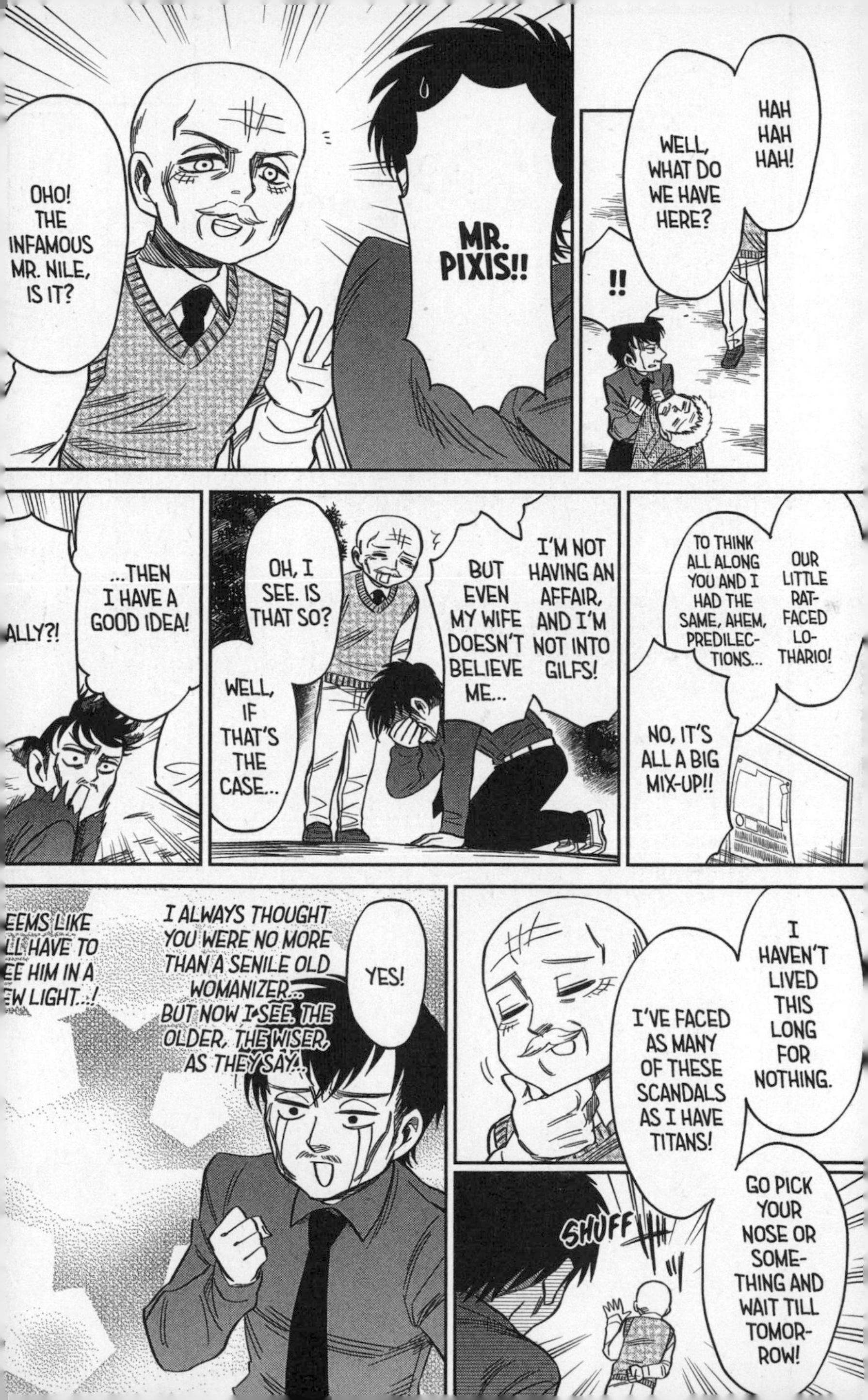
HAH HAH HAH!
WELL, WHAT DO WE HAVE HERE?
!!
MR. PIXIS!!
OHO! THE INFAMOUS MR. NILE, IS IT?
OUR LITTLE RAT-FACED LO-THARIO!
TO THINK ALL ALONG YOU AND I HAD THE SAME, AHEM, PREDILEC-TIONS...
NO, IT'S ALL A BIG MIX-UP!!
I'M NOT HAVING AN AFFAIR, AND I'M NOT INTO GILFS!
BUT EVEN MY WIFE DOESN'T BELIEVE ME...
OH, I SEE. IS THAT SO?
WELL, IF THAT'S THE CASE...
...THEN I HAVE A GOOD IDEA!
ALLY?!
I HAVEN'T LIVED THIS LONG FOR NOTHING.
I'VE FACED AS MANY OF THESE SCANDALS AS I HAVE TITANS!
GO PICK YOUR NOSE OR SOME-THING AND WAIT TILL TOMOR-ROW!
SHUFF
YES!
I ALWAYS THOUGHT YOU WERE NO MORE THAN A SENILE OLD WOMANIZER... BUT NOW I SEE. THE OLDER, THE WISER, AS THEY SAY...
EEMS LIKE LL HAVE TO EE HIM IN A EW LIGHT...!

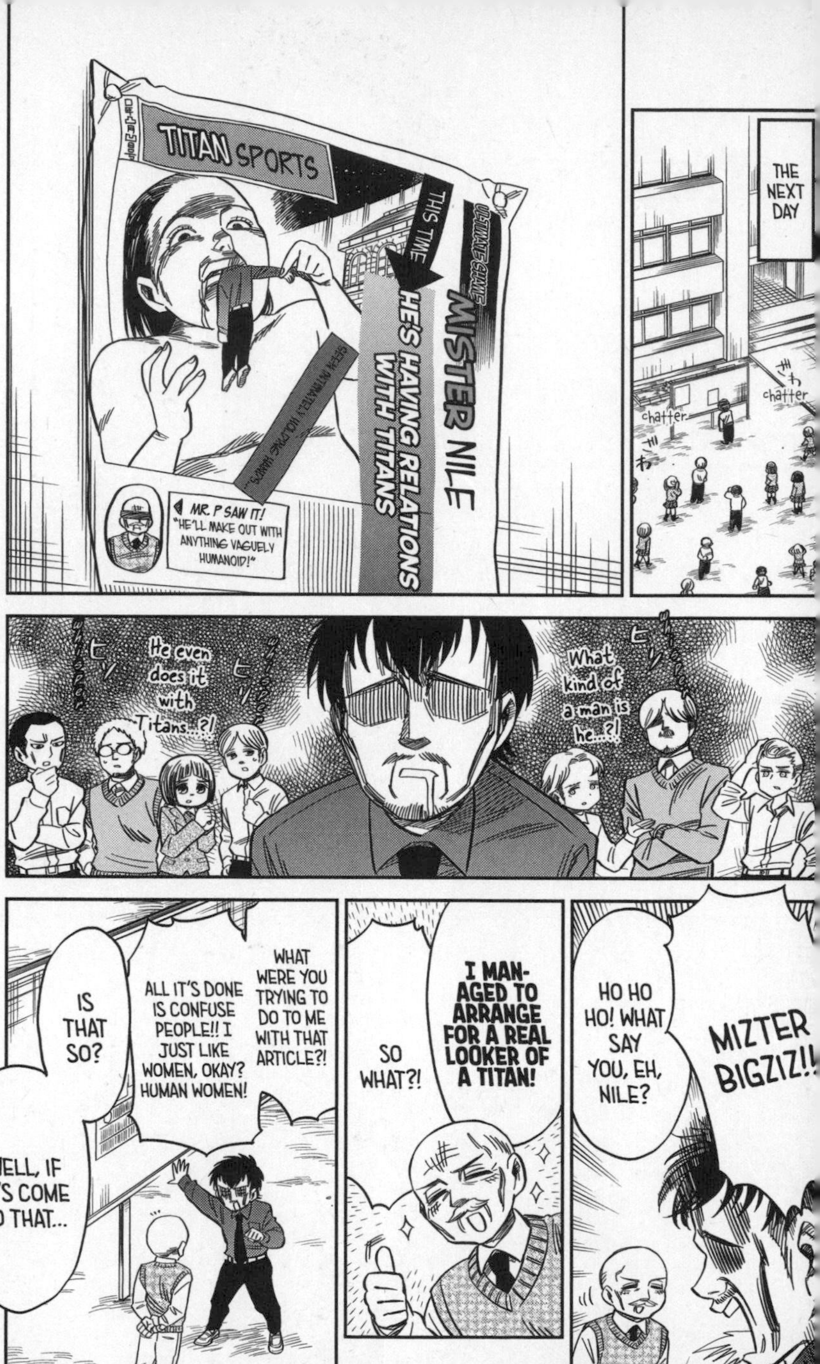
THE NEXT DAY
chatter
chatter
TITAN SPORTS
ULTIMATE SHAME
MISTER NILE
THIS TIME
HE'S HAVING RELATIONS WITH TITANS
SEEN INTIMATELY HOLDING HANDS...
MR. P SAW IT! "HE'LL MAKE OUT WITH ANYTHING VAGUELY HUMANOID!"
What kind of a man is he...?!
He even does it with Titans...?!
MIZTER BIGZIZ!!
HO HO HO! WHAT SAY YOU, EH, NILE?
I MANAGED TO ARRANGE FOR A REAL LOOKER OF A TITAN!
SO WHAT?!
WHAT WERE YOU TRYING TO DO TO ME WITH THAT ARTICLE?!
ALL IT'S DONE IS CONFUSE PEOPLE!! I JUST LIKE WOMEN, OKAY? HUMAN WOMEN!
IS THAT SO?
WELL, IF IT'S COME TO THAT...

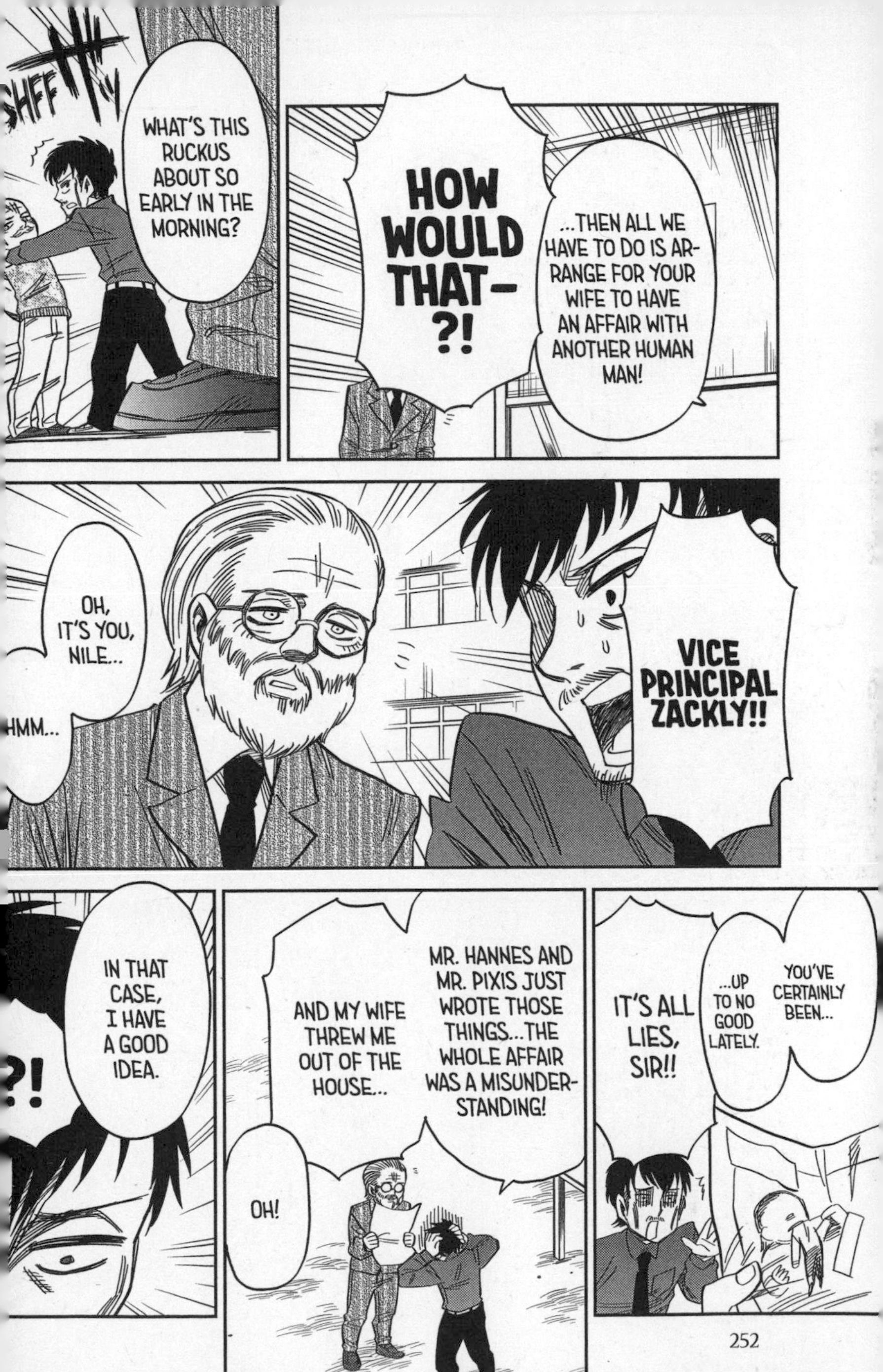
...THEN ALL WE HAVE TO DO IS ARRANGE FOR YOUR WIFE TO HAVE AN AFFAIR WITH ANOTHER HUMAN MAN!
HOW WOULD THAT-?!
SHFF
WHAT'S THIS RUCKUS ABOUT SO EARLY IN THE MORNING?
VICE PRINCIPAL ZACKLY!!
OH, IT'S YOU, NILE...
HMM...
YOU'VE CERTAINLY BEEN...
...UP TO NO GOOD LATELY.
IT'S ALL LIES, SIR!!
MR. HANNES AND MR. PIXIS JUST WROTE THOSE THINGS... THE WHOLE AFFAIR WAS A MISUNDERSTANDING!
AND MY WIFE THREW ME OUT OF THE HOUSE...
OH!
IN THAT CASE, I HAVE A GOOD IDEA.
?!

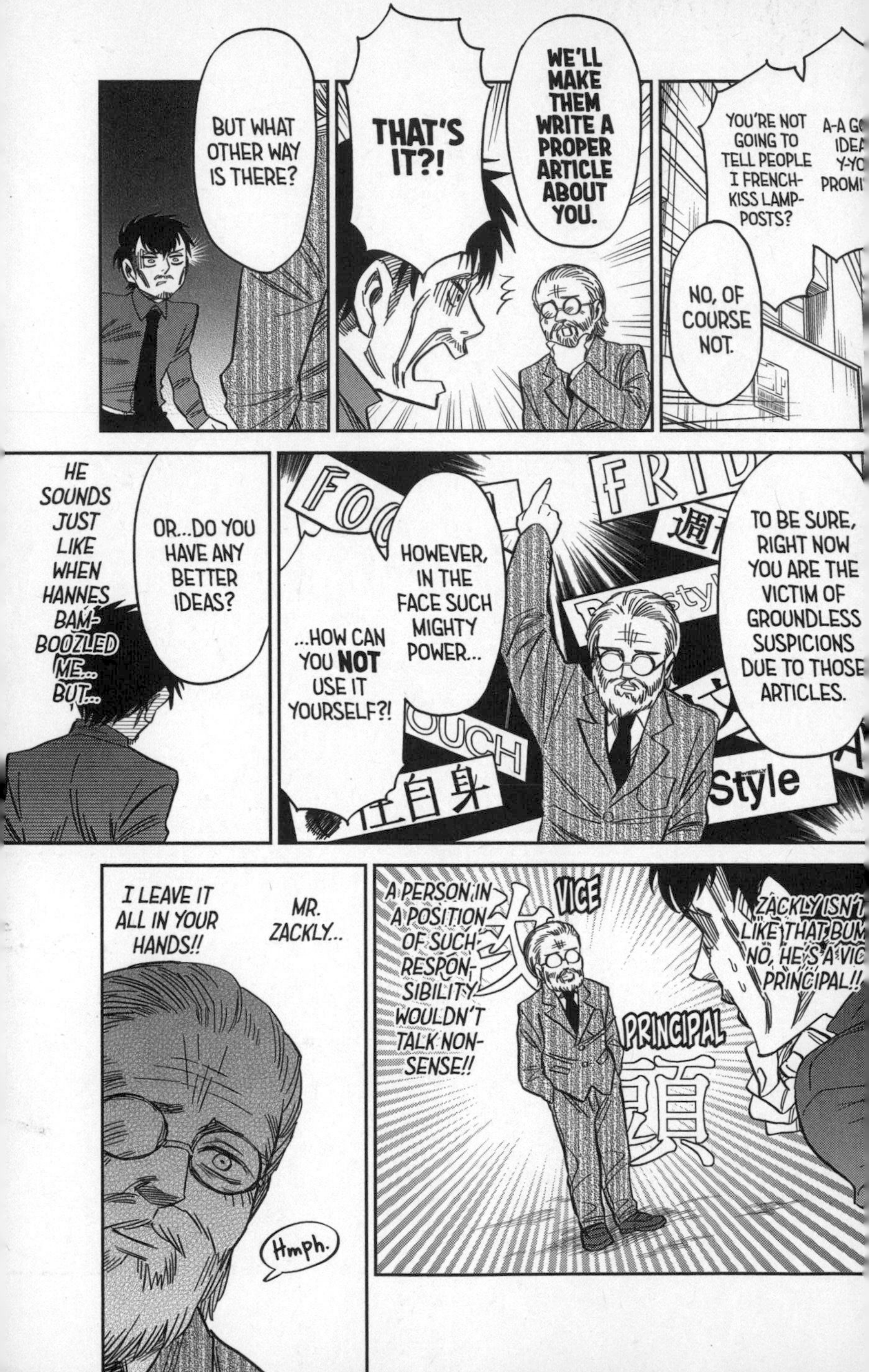
A-A G
IDEA
Y-YO
PROMI
YOU'RE NOT GOING TO TELL PEOPLE I FRENCH-KISS LAMP-POSTS?
NO, OF COURSE NOT.
WE'LL MAKE THEM WRITE A PROPER ARTICLE ABOUT YOU.
THAT'S IT?!
BUT WHAT OTHER WAY IS THERE?
TO BE SURE, RIGHT NOW YOU ARE THE VICTIM OF GROUNDLESS SUSPICIONS DUE TO THOSE ARTICLES.
Style
HOWEVER, IN THE FACE SUCH MIGHTY POWER...
...HOW CAN YOU **NOT** USE IT YOURSELF?!
OR...DO YOU HAVE ANY BETTER IDEAS?
HE SOUNDS JUST LIKE WHEN HANNES BAMBOOZLED ME... BUT...
ZACKLY ISN'T LIKE THAT BUM
NO, HE'S A VIC
PRINCIPAL!!
VICE
PRINCIPAL
A PERSON IN A POSITION OF SUCH RESPONSIBILITY WOULDN'T TALK NONSENSE!!
MR. ZACKLY...
I LEAVE IT ALL IN YOUR HANDS!!
Hmph.

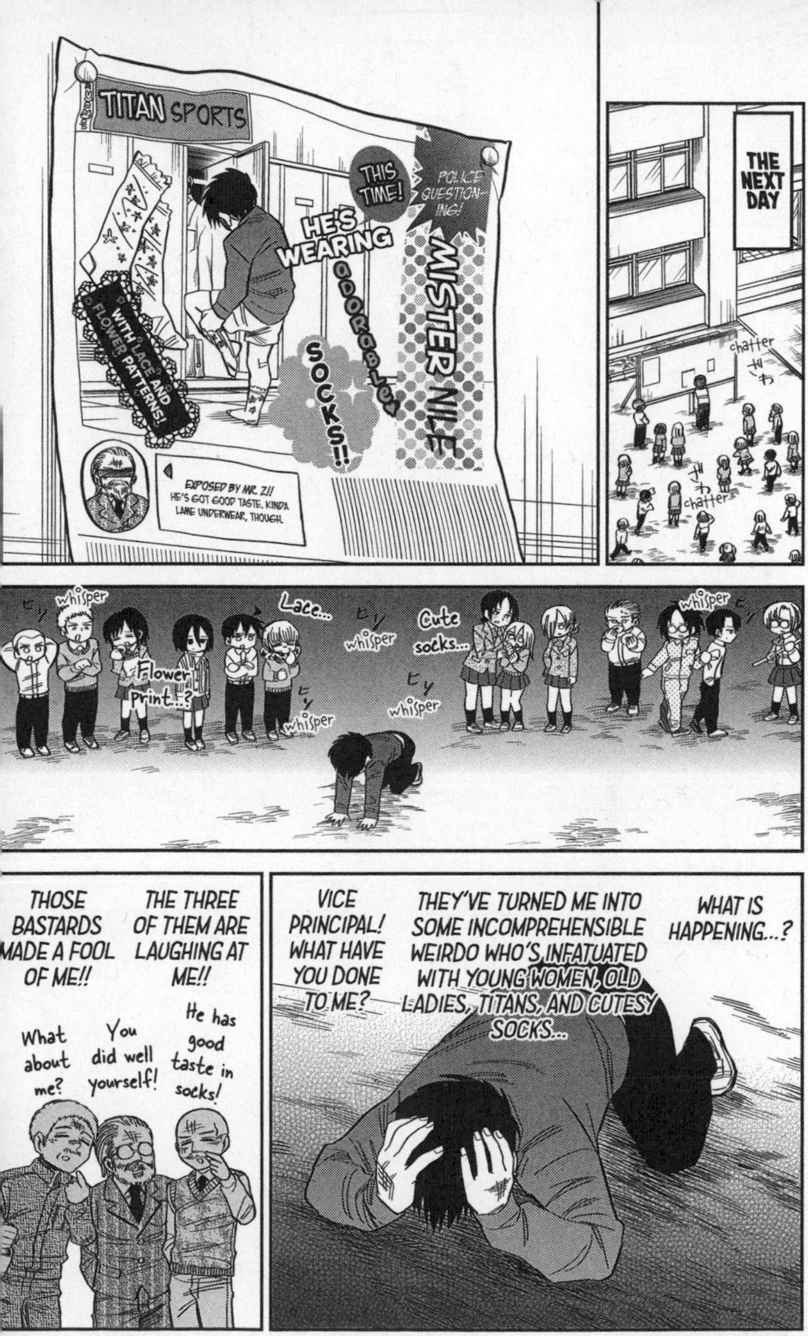
THE NEXT DAY
chatter
chatter
TITAN SPORTS
POLICE QUESTIONING!
THIS TIME!
MISTER NILE
HE'S WEARING ADORABLE SOCKS!!
WITH LACE AND FLOWER PATTERNS!
EXPOSED BY MR. Z!! HE'S GOT GOOD TASTE, KINDA LAME UNDERWEAR, THOUGH.
whisper
whisper
Cute socks...
whisper
Lace...
whisper
Flower print...?
whisper
whisper
WHAT IS HAPPENING...?
THEY'VE TURNED ME INTO SOME INCOMPREHENSIBLE WEIRDO WHO'S INFATUATED WITH YOUNG WOMEN, OLD LADIES, TITANS, AND CUTESY SOCKS...
VICE PRINCIPAL! WHAT HAVE YOU DONE TO ME?
THE THREE OF THEM ARE LAUGHING AT ME!!
THOSE BASTARDS MADE A FOOL OF ME!!
He has good taste in socks!
You did well yourself!
What about me?

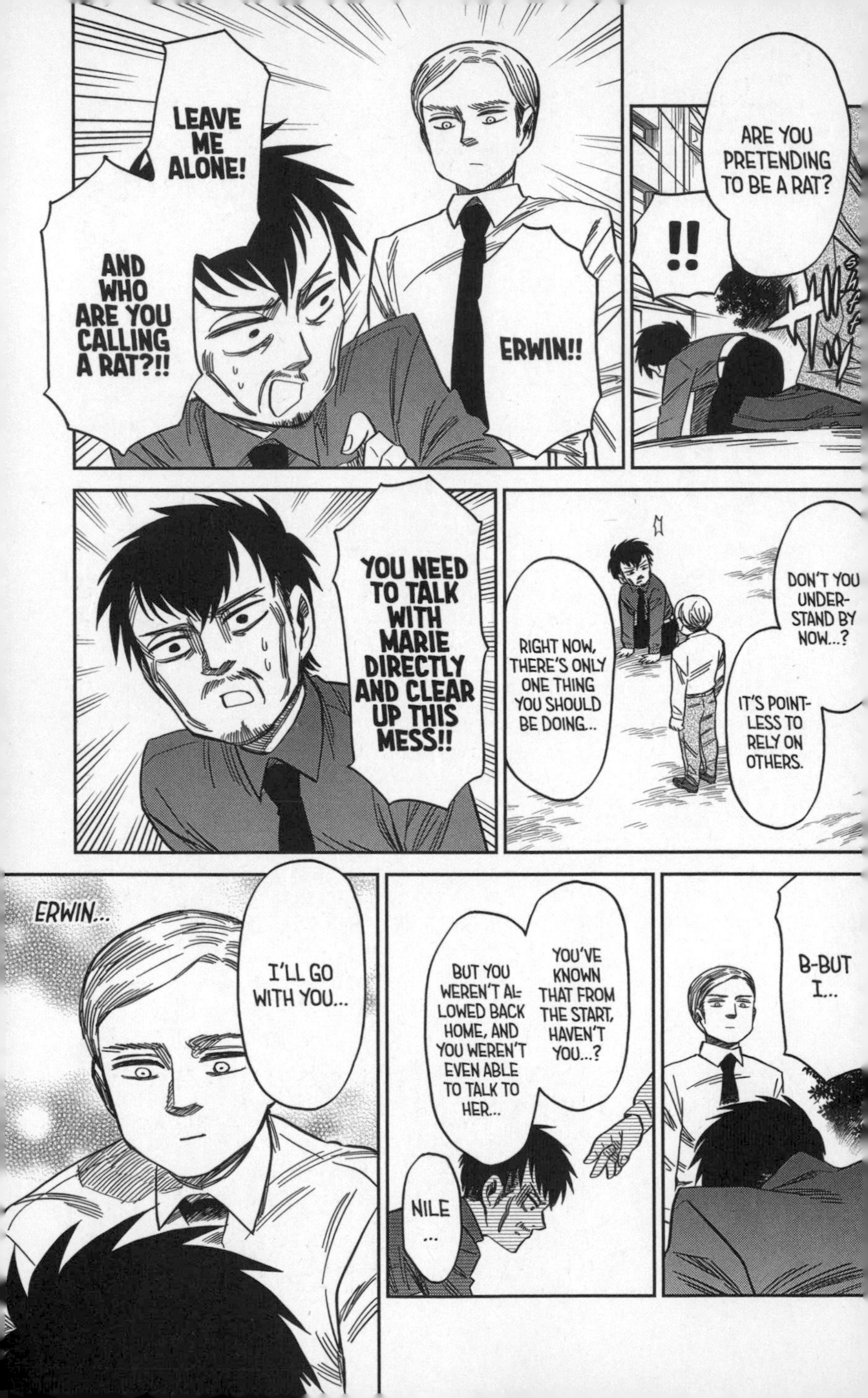
ARE YOU PRETENDING TO BE A RAT?
!!
ERWIN!!
LEAVE ME ALONE!
AND WHO ARE YOU CALLING A RAT?!!
DON'T YOU UNDER-STAND BY NOW...?
IT'S POINT-LESS TO RELY ON OTHERS.
RIGHT NOW, THERE'S ONLY ONE THING YOU SHOULD BE DOING...
YOU NEED TO TALK WITH MARIE DIRECTLY AND CLEAR UP THIS MESS!!
B-BUT I...
YOU'VE KNOWN THAT FROM THE START, HAVEN'T YOU...?
BUT YOU WEREN'T AL-LOWED BACK HOME, AND YOU WEREN'T EVEN ABLE TO TALK TO HER...
NILE ...
I'LL GO WITH YOU...
ERWIN...

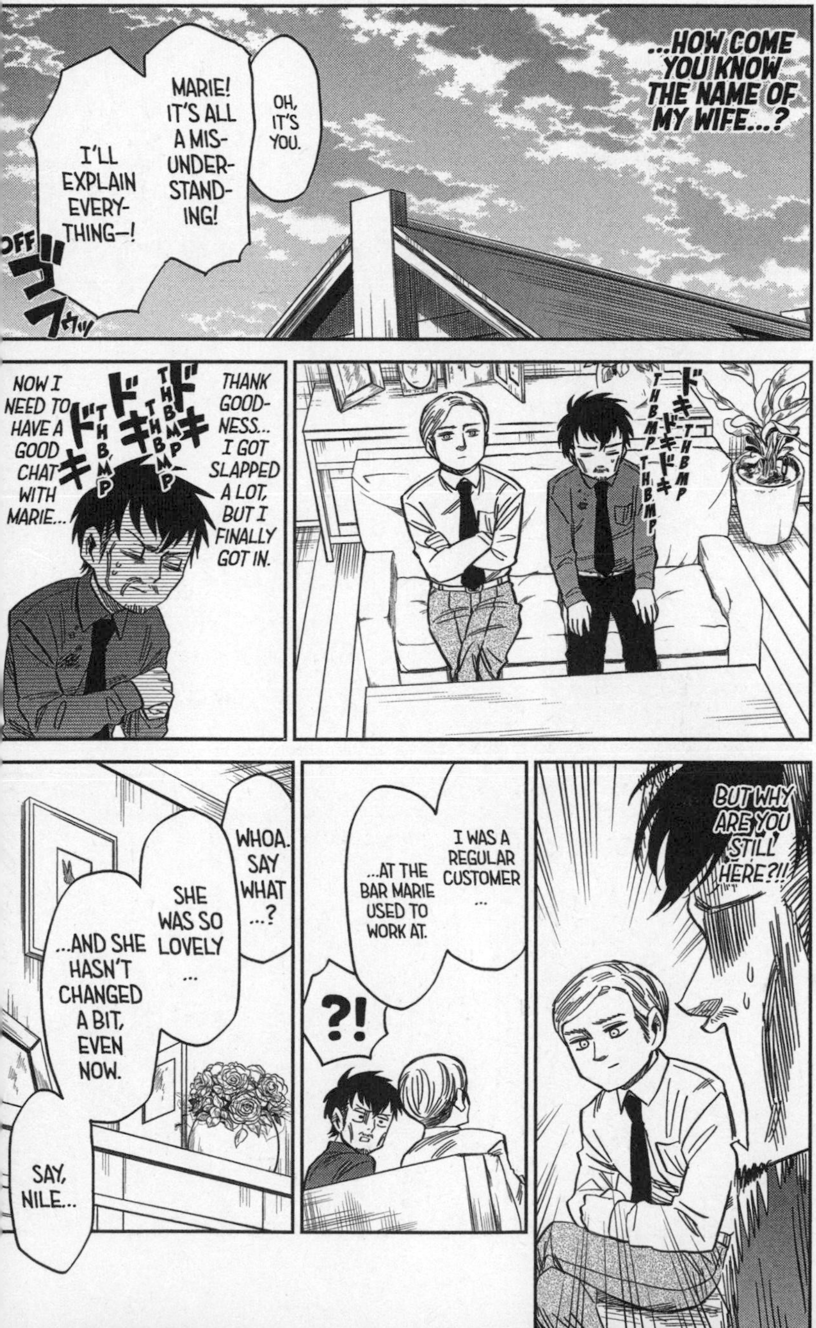
...HOW COME YOU KNOW THE NAME OF MY WIFE...?
OH, IT'S YOU.
MARIE! IT'S ALL A MIS-UNDER-STAND-ING!
I'LL EXPLAIN EVERY-THING—!
OFF ゴフッ
ドキ THBMP ドキドキ THBMP THBMP
THANK GOODNESS... I GOT SLAPPED A LOT, BUT I FINALLY GOT IN.
ドキ THBMP ドキ THBMP ドキドキ THBMP THBMP
NOW I NEED TO HAVE A GOOD CHAT WITH MARIE...
BUT WHY ARE YOU STILL HERE?!!
I WAS A REGULAR CUSTOMER ...
...AT THE BAR MARIE USED TO WORK AT.
?!
WHOA. SAY WHAT ...?
SHE WAS SO LOVELY ...
...AND SHE HASN'T CHANGED A BIT, EVEN NOW.
SAY, NILE...

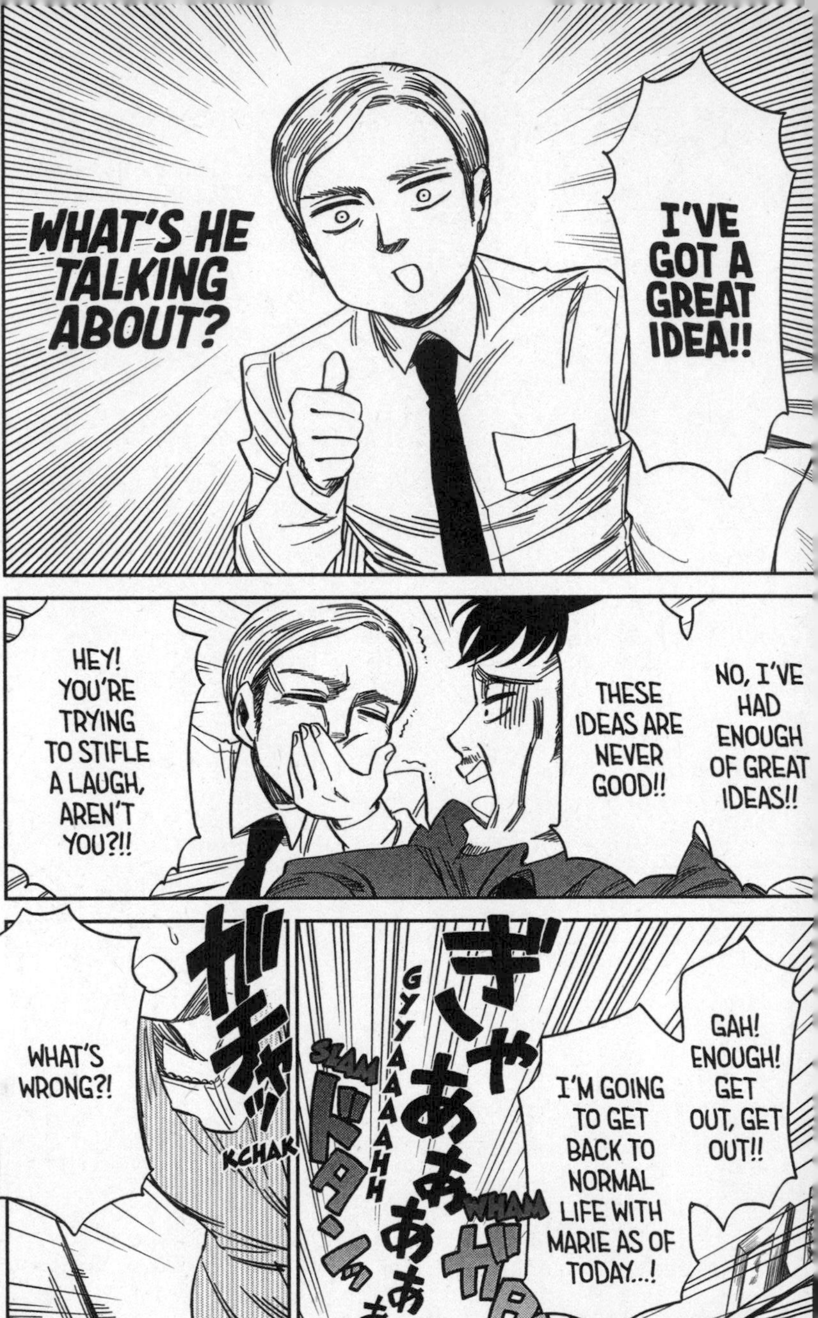
I'VE GOT A GREAT IDEA!!
WHAT'S HE TALKING ABOUT?
NO, I'VE HAD ENOUGH OF GREAT IDEAS!!
THESE IDEAS ARE NEVER GOOD!!
HEY! YOU'RE TRYING TO STIFLE A LAUGH, AREN'T YOU?!!
GAH! ENOUGH! GET OUT, GET OUT!!
I'M GOING TO GET BACK TO NORMAL LIFE WITH MARIE AS OF TODAY...!
WHAM
GYYAAAAAHH
SLAM
KCHAK
WHAT'S WRONG?!

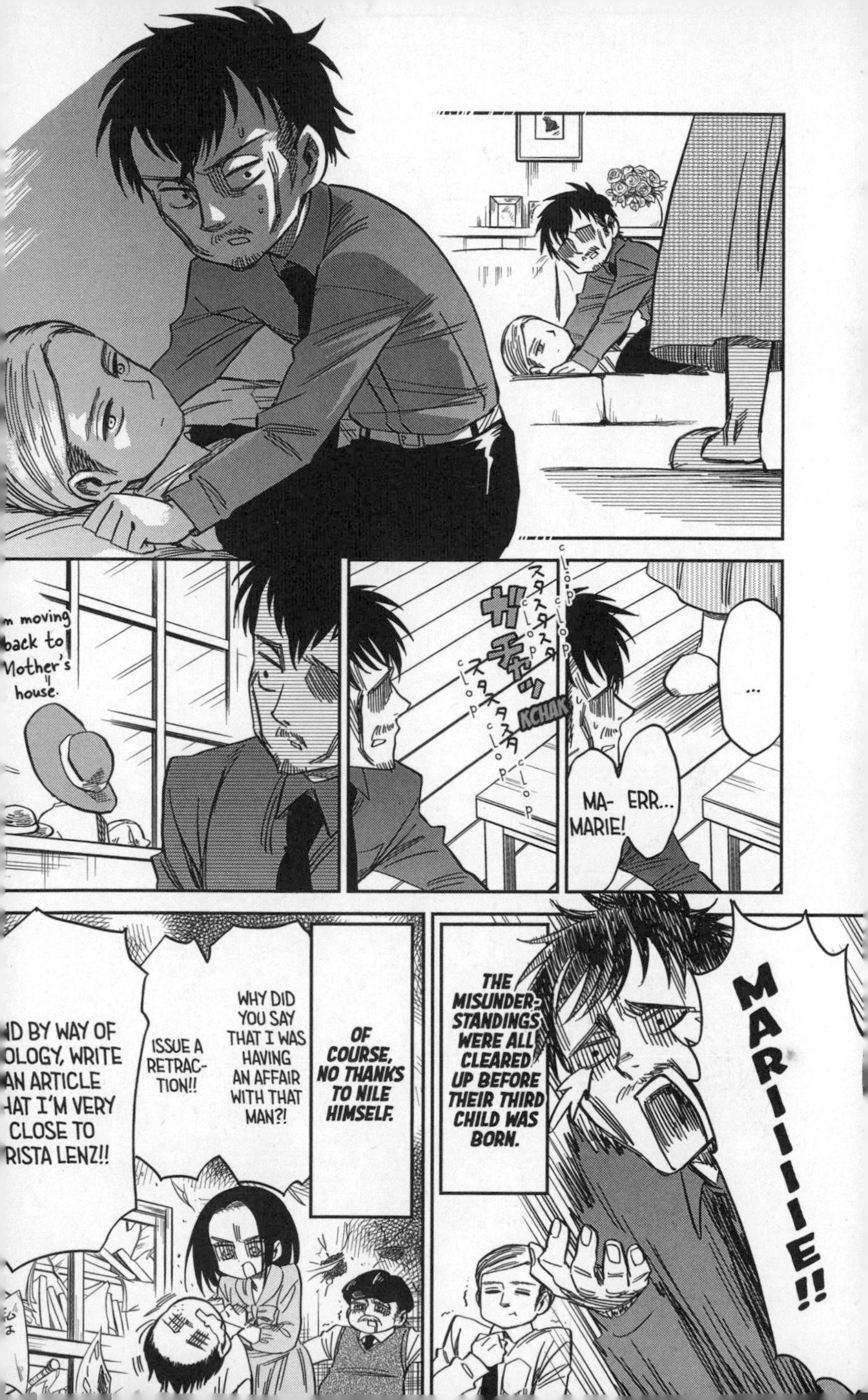

...
ERR...
MA- MARIE!
clop clop
KCHAK
m moving back to Mother's house.
MARIIIIE!!
THE MISUNDERSTANDINGS WERE ALL CLEARED UP BEFORE THEIR THIRD CHILD WAS BORN.
OF COURSE, NO THANKS TO NILE HIMSELF.
WHY DID YOU SAY THAT I WAS HAVING AN AFFAIR WITH THAT MAN?!
ISSUE A RETRACTION!!
ND BY WAY OF OLOGY, WRITE AN ARTICLE HAT I'M VERY CLOSE TO RISTA LENZ!!

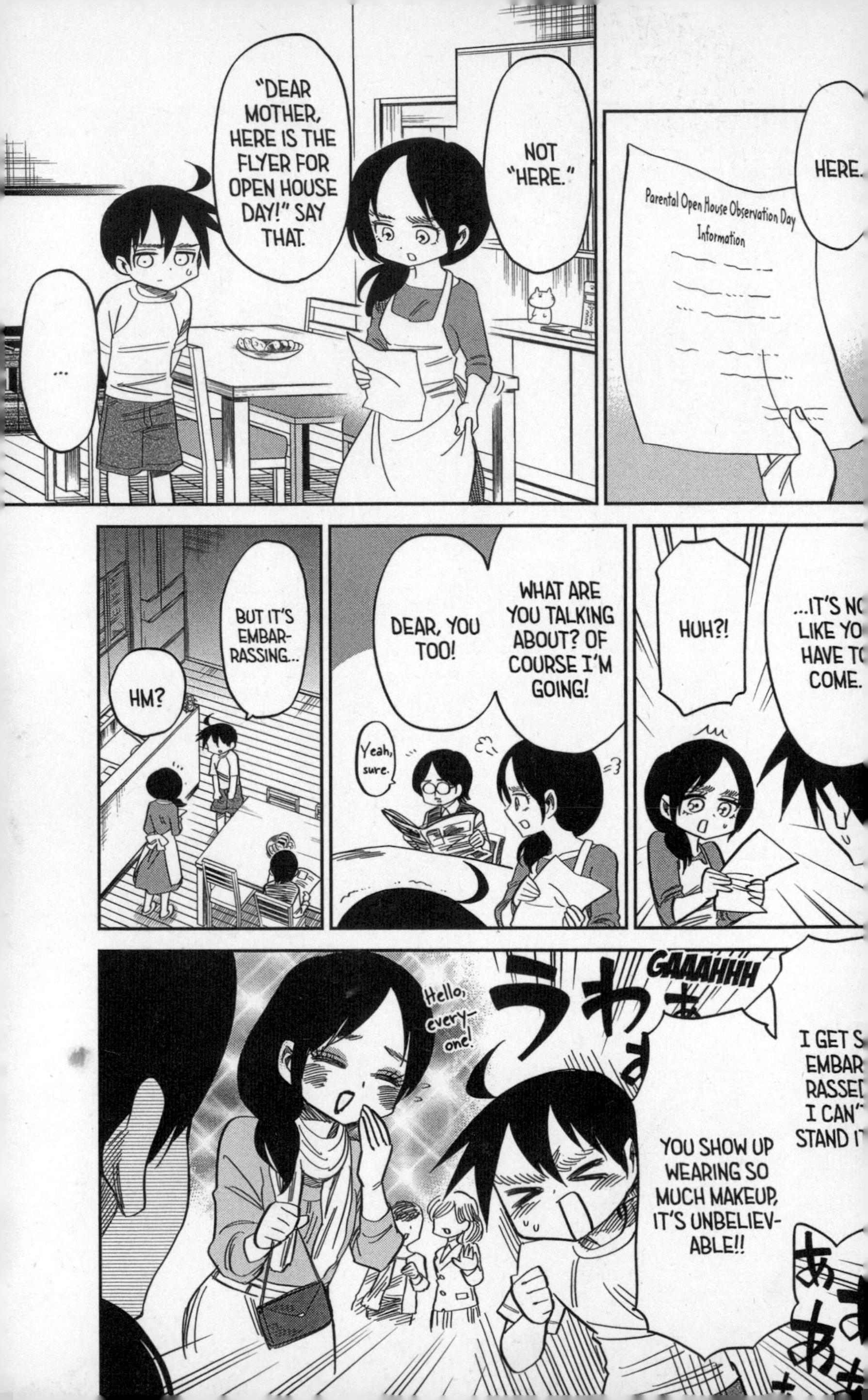
HERE.
Parental Open House Observation Day
Information
NOT "HERE."
"DEAR MOTHER, HERE IS THE FLYER FOR OPEN HOUSE DAY!" SAY THAT.
...
...IT'S NO LIKE YO HAVE T COME.
HUH?!
WHAT ARE YOU TALKING ABOUT? OF COURSE I'M GOING!
DEAR, YOU TOO!
Yeah, sure.
BUT IT'S EMBAR-RASSING...
HM?
I GET S EMBAR RASSE I CAN' STAND I
YOU SHOW UP WEARING SO MUCH MAKEUP, IT'S UNBELIEV-ABLE!!
GAAAHHH
Hello, every-one!

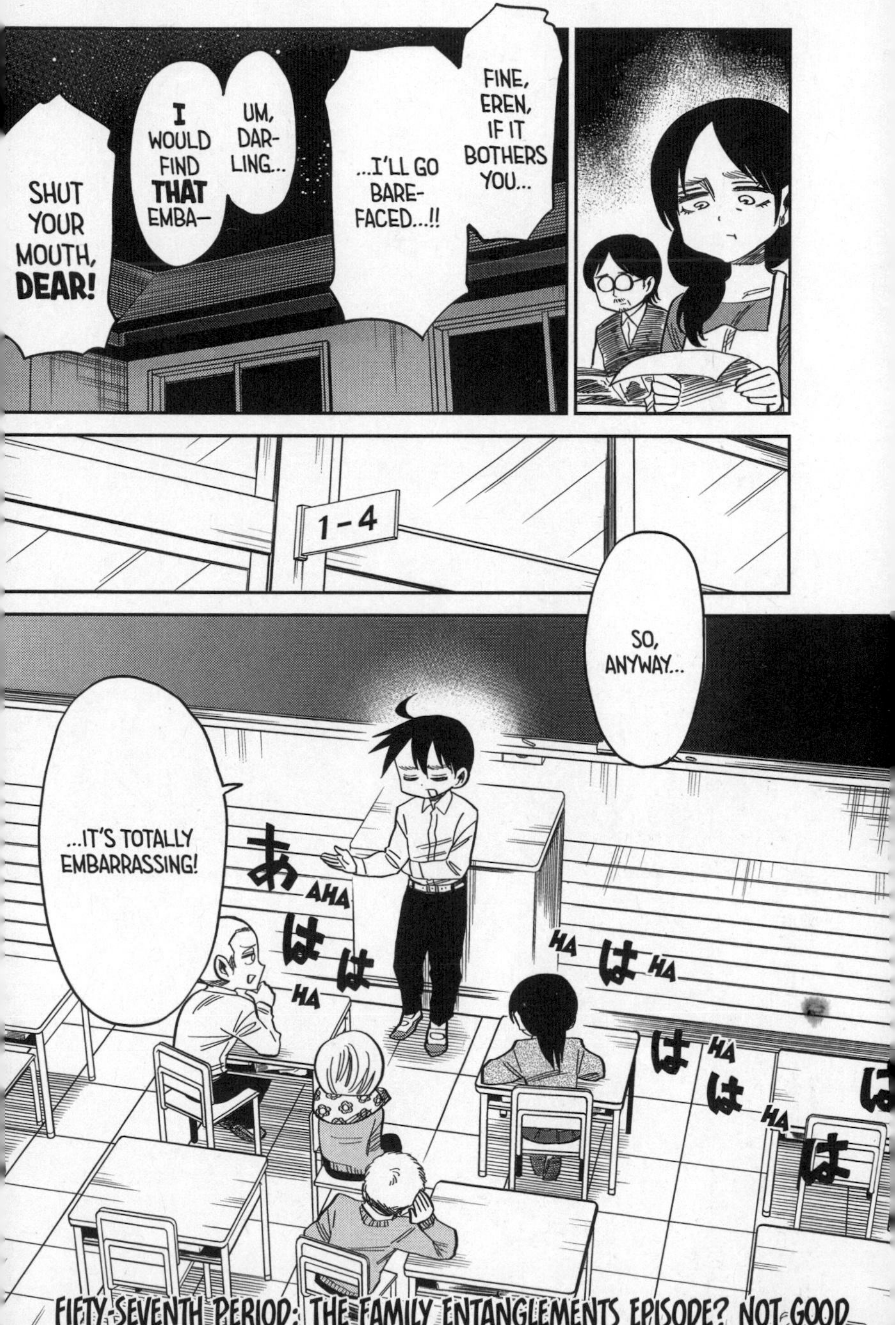
FINE, EREN, IF IT BOTHERS YOU...
...I'LL GO BARE-FACED...!!
UM, DAR-LING...
I WOULD FIND **THAT** EMBA—
SHUT YOUR MOUTH, **DEAR!**
1-4
SO, ANYWAY...
...IT'S TOTALLY EMBARRASSING!
あはは AHA HA
は HA HA
はは HA HA
はは
FIFTY-SEVENTH PERIOD: THE FAMILY ENTANGLEMENTS EPISODE? NOT GOOD

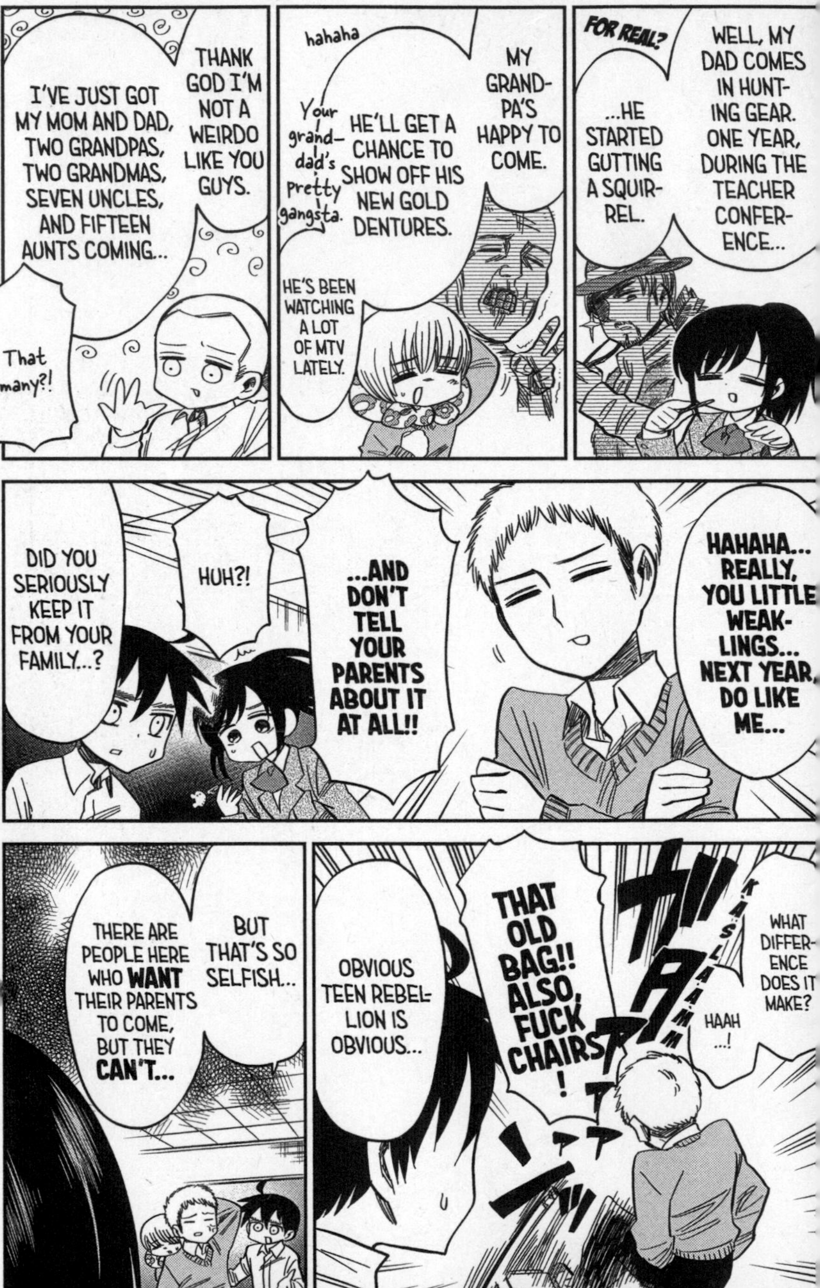

WELL, MY DAD COMES IN HUNTING GEAR. ONE YEAR, DURING THE TEACHER CONFERENCE...
...HE STARTED GUTTING A SQUIRREL.
FOR REAL?
MY GRANDPA'S HAPPY TO COME.
hahaha
HE'LL GET A CHANCE TO SHOW OFF HIS NEW GOLD DENTURES.
Your granddad's pretty gangsta.
HE'S BEEN WATCHING A LOT OF MTV LATELY.
THANK GOD I'M NOT A WEIRDO LIKE YOU GUYS.
I'VE JUST GOT MY MOM AND DAD, TWO GRANDPAS, TWO GRANDMAS, SEVEN UNCLES, AND FIFTEEN AUNTS COMING...
That many?!
HAHAHA... REALLY, YOU LITTLE WEAKLINGS... NEXT YEAR, DO LIKE ME...
...AND DON'T TELL YOUR PARENTS ABOUT IT AT ALL!!
HUH?!
DID YOU SERIOUSLY KEEP IT FROM YOUR FAMILY...?
WHAT DIFFERENCE DOES IT MAKE?
KA-SLAAMM
HAAH ...!
THAT OLD BAG!! ALSO, FUCK CHAIRS!
OBVIOUS TEEN REBELLION IS OBVIOUS...
BUT THAT'S SO SELFISH...
THERE ARE PEOPLE HERE WHO **WANT** THEIR PARENTS TO COME, BUT THEY **CAN'T**...

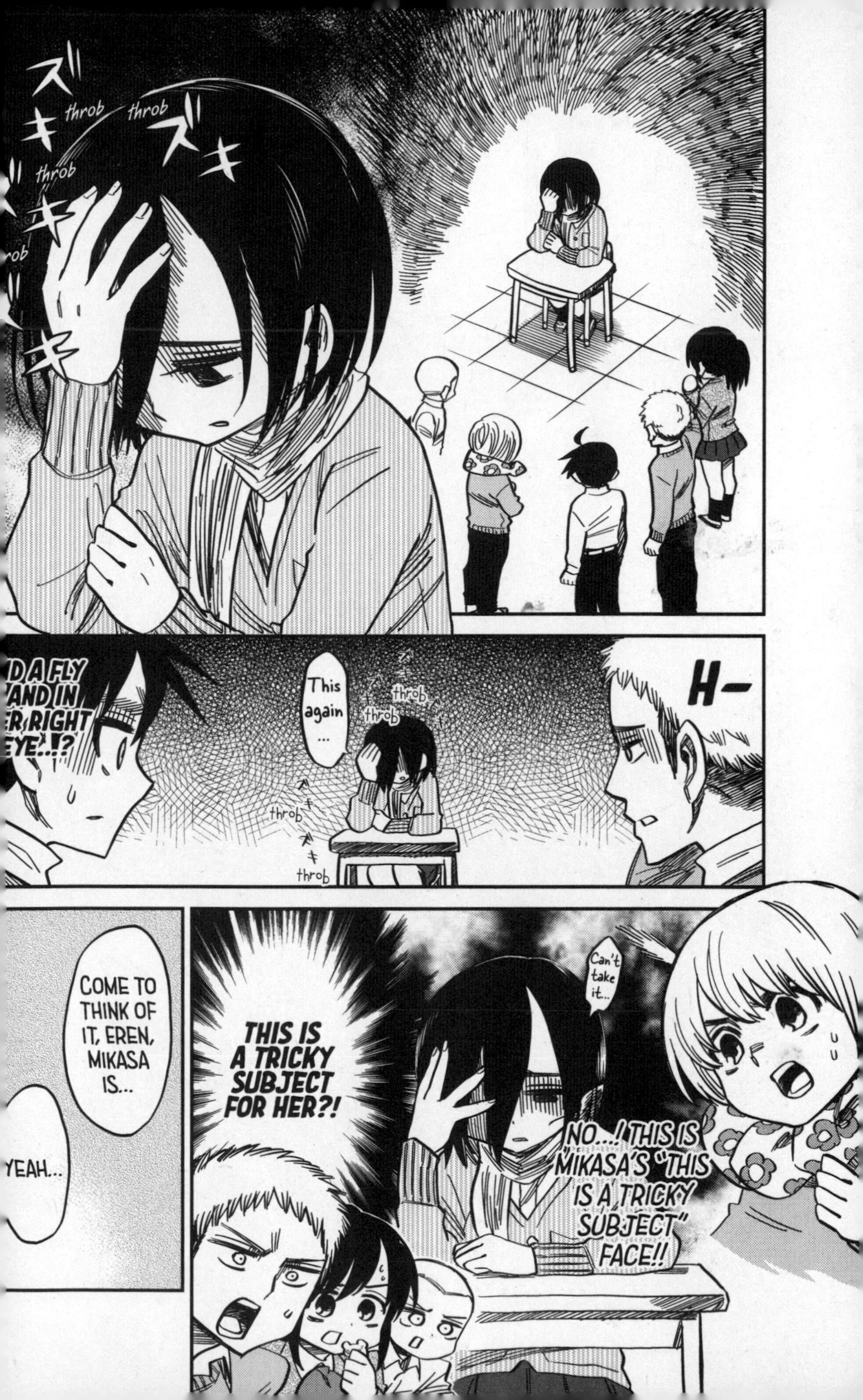

ズキ
throb
throb
ズキ
throb
キ
ob
H–
This again ...
throb
throb
throb
throb
D A FLY AND IN ER RIGHT EYE..!?
Can't take it...
THIS IS A TRICKY SUBJECT FOR HER?!
NO...! THIS IS MIKASA'S "THIS IS A TRICKY SUBJECT" FACE!!
COME TO THINK OF IT, EREN, MIKASA IS...
YEAH...

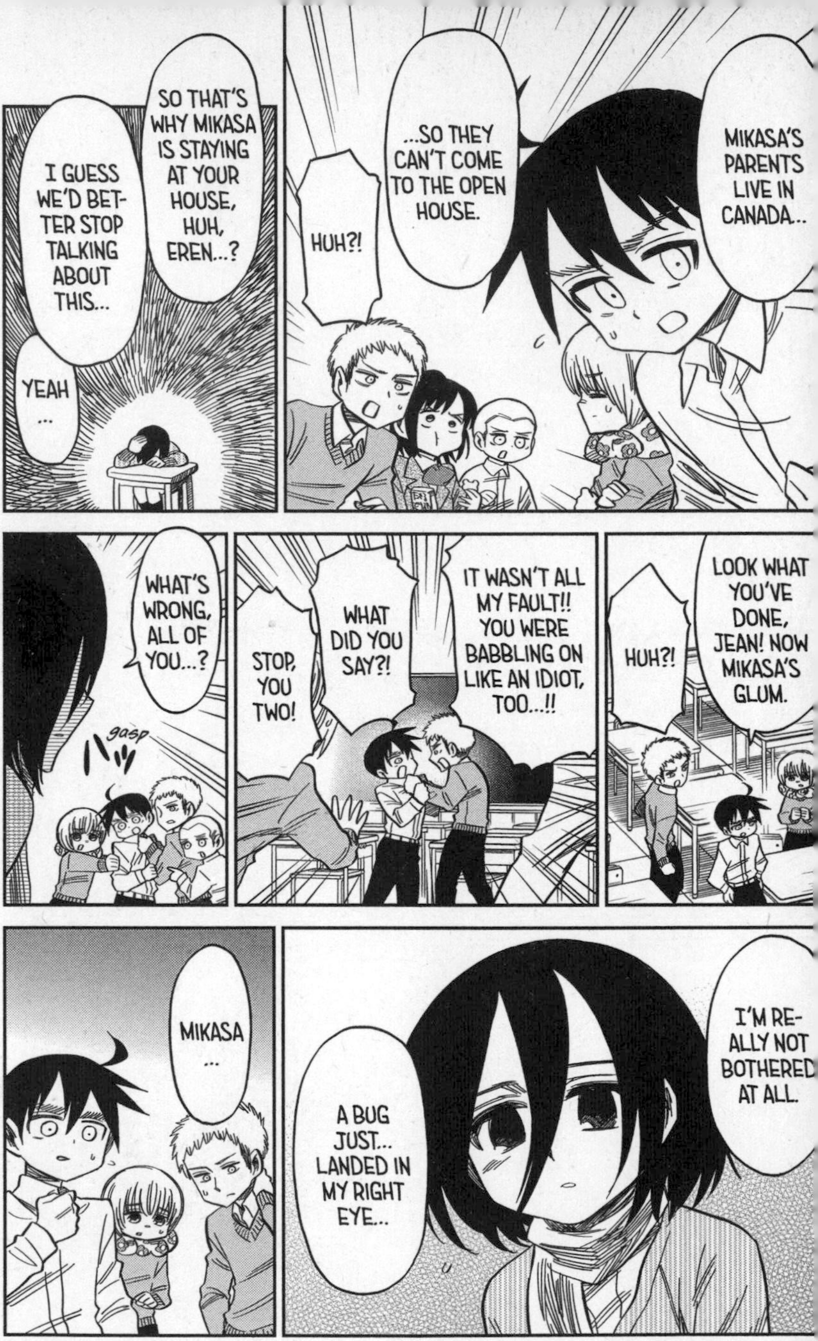
MIKASA'S PARENTS LIVE IN CANADA...
...SO THEY CAN'T COME TO THE OPEN HOUSE.
HUH?!
SO THAT'S WHY MIKASA IS STAYING AT YOUR HOUSE, HUH, EREN...?
I GUESS WE'D BETTER STOP TALKING ABOUT THIS...
YEAH...
LOOK WHAT YOU'VE DONE, JEAN! NOW MIKASA'S GLUM.
HUH?!
IT WASN'T ALL MY FAULT!! YOU WERE BABBLING ON LIKE AN IDIOT, TOO...!!
WHAT DID YOU SAY?!
STOP, YOU TWO!
WHAT'S WRONG, ALL OF YOU...?
gasp
I'M REALLY NOT BOTHERED AT ALL.
A BUG JUST... LANDED IN MY RIGHT EYE...
MIKASA...

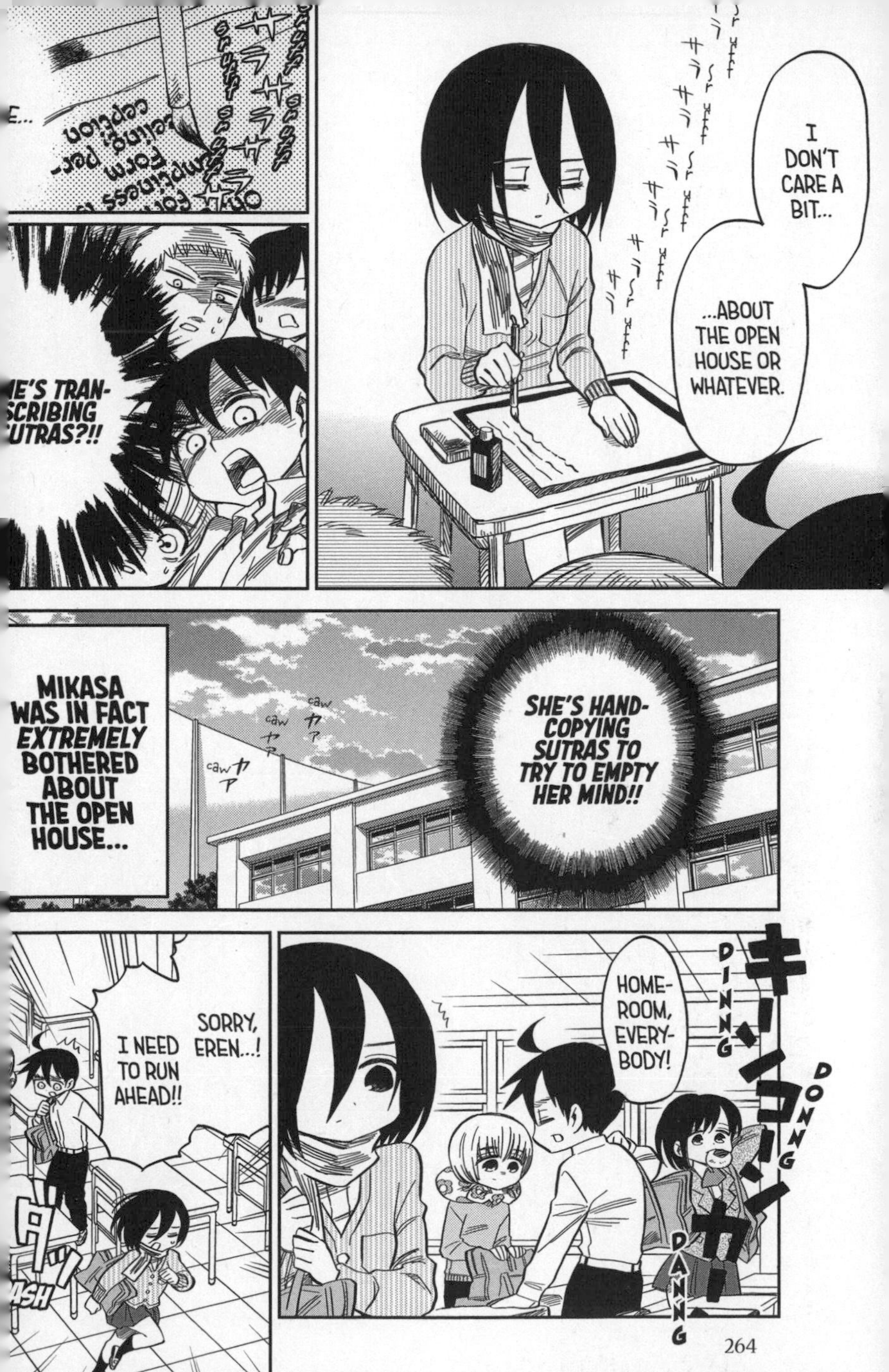
sara~r
I DON'T CARE A BIT...
...ABOUT THE OPEN HOUSE OR WHATEVER.
E...
E'S TRAN-SCRIBING UTRAS?!!
SHE'S HAND-COPYING SUTRAS TO TRY TO EMPTY HER MIND!!
caw
caw
caw
MIKASA WAS IN FACT EXTREMELY BOTHERED ABOUT THE OPEN HOUSE...
DINNG
DONNG
DANNG
HOME-ROOM, EVERY-BODY!
SORRY, EREN...!
I NEED TO RUN AHEAD!!
ASH

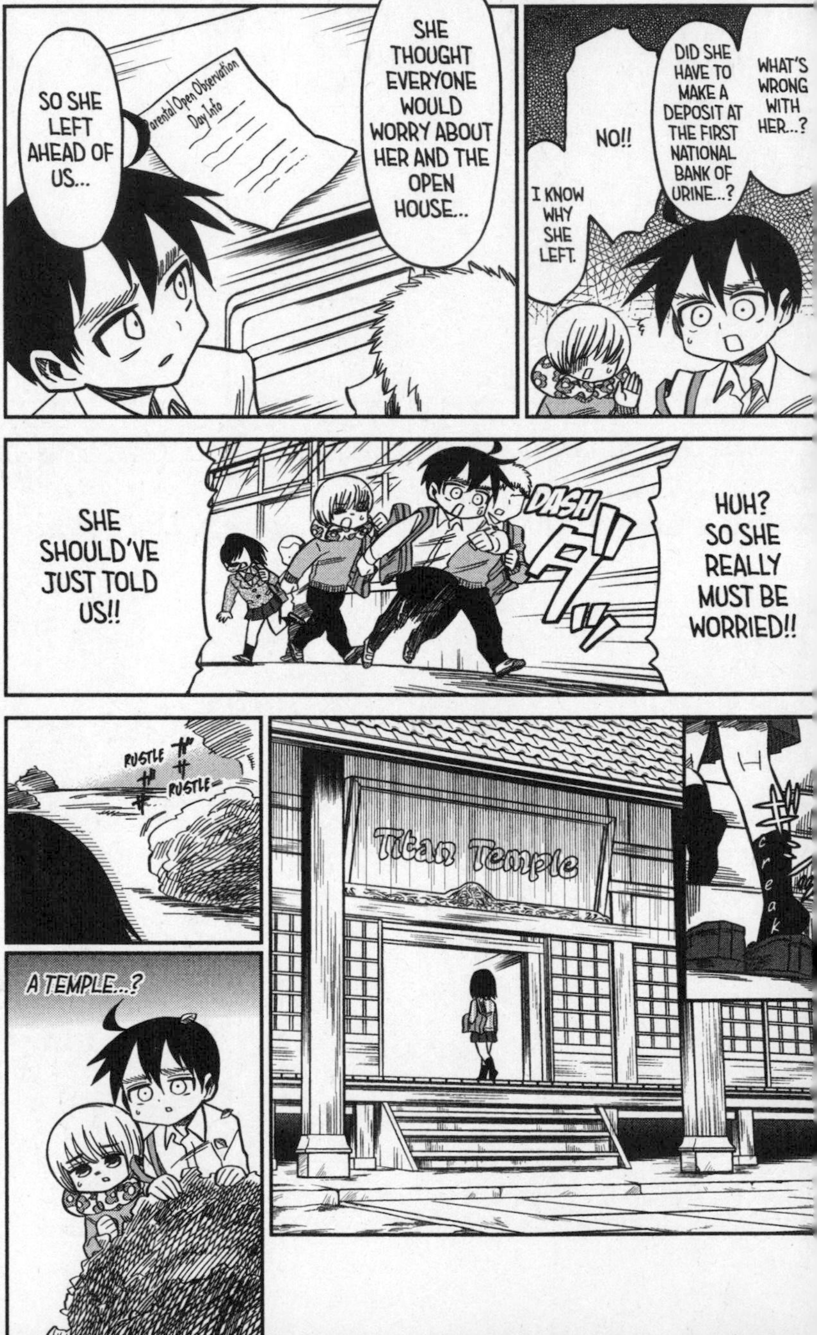
WHAT'S WRONG WITH HER...?
DID SHE HAVE TO MAKE A DEPOSIT AT THE FIRST NATIONAL BANK OF URINE...?
NO!!
I KNOW WHY SHE LEFT.
SHE THOUGHT EVERYONE WOULD WORRY ABOUT HER AND THE OPEN HOUSE...
Parental Open Observation Day Info
SO SHE LEFT AHEAD OF US...
HUH? SO SHE REALLY MUST BE WORRIED!!
DASH
SHE SHOULD'VE JUST TOLD US!!
creak
Titan Temple
RUSTLE
RUSTLE
A TEMPLE...?

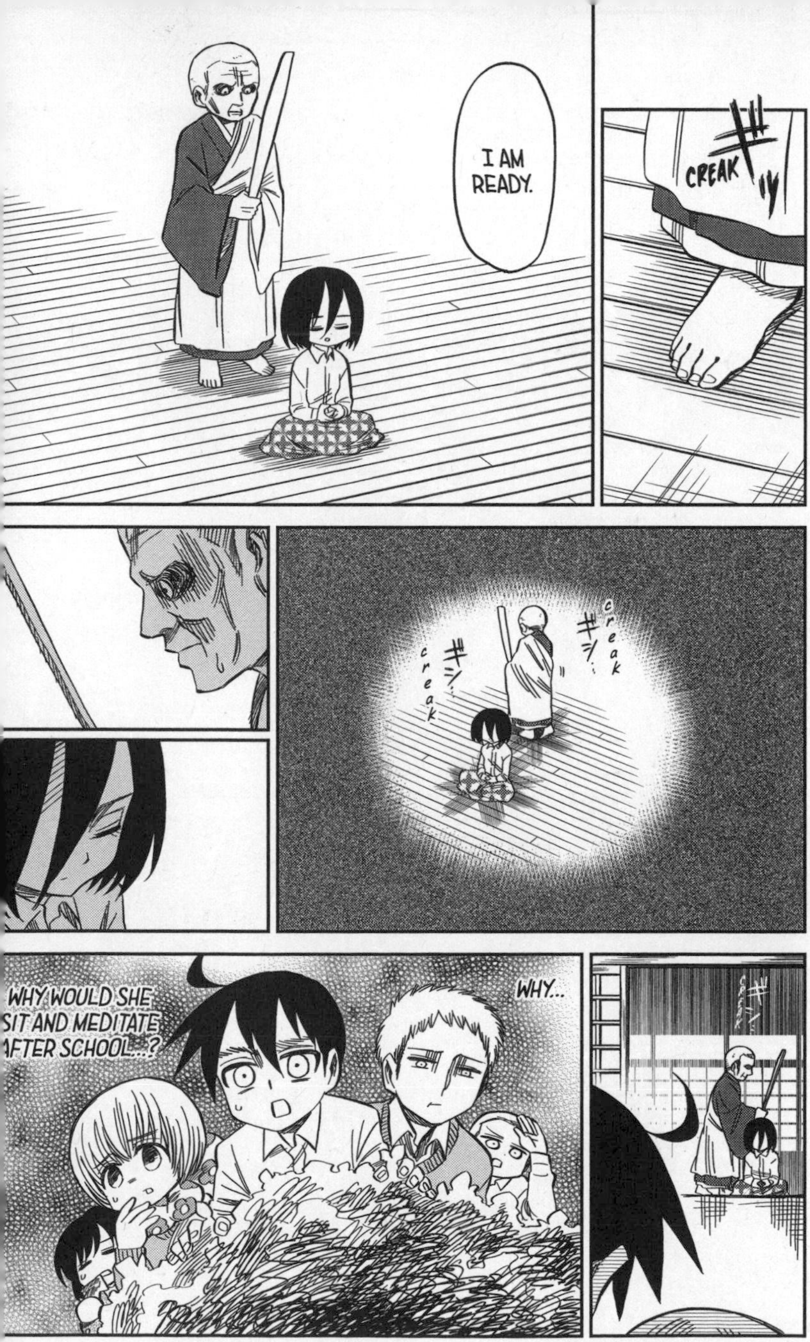
CREAK
I AM READY.
creak
creak
creak
WHY...
WHY WOULD SHE SIT AND MEDITATE AFTER SCHOOL...?

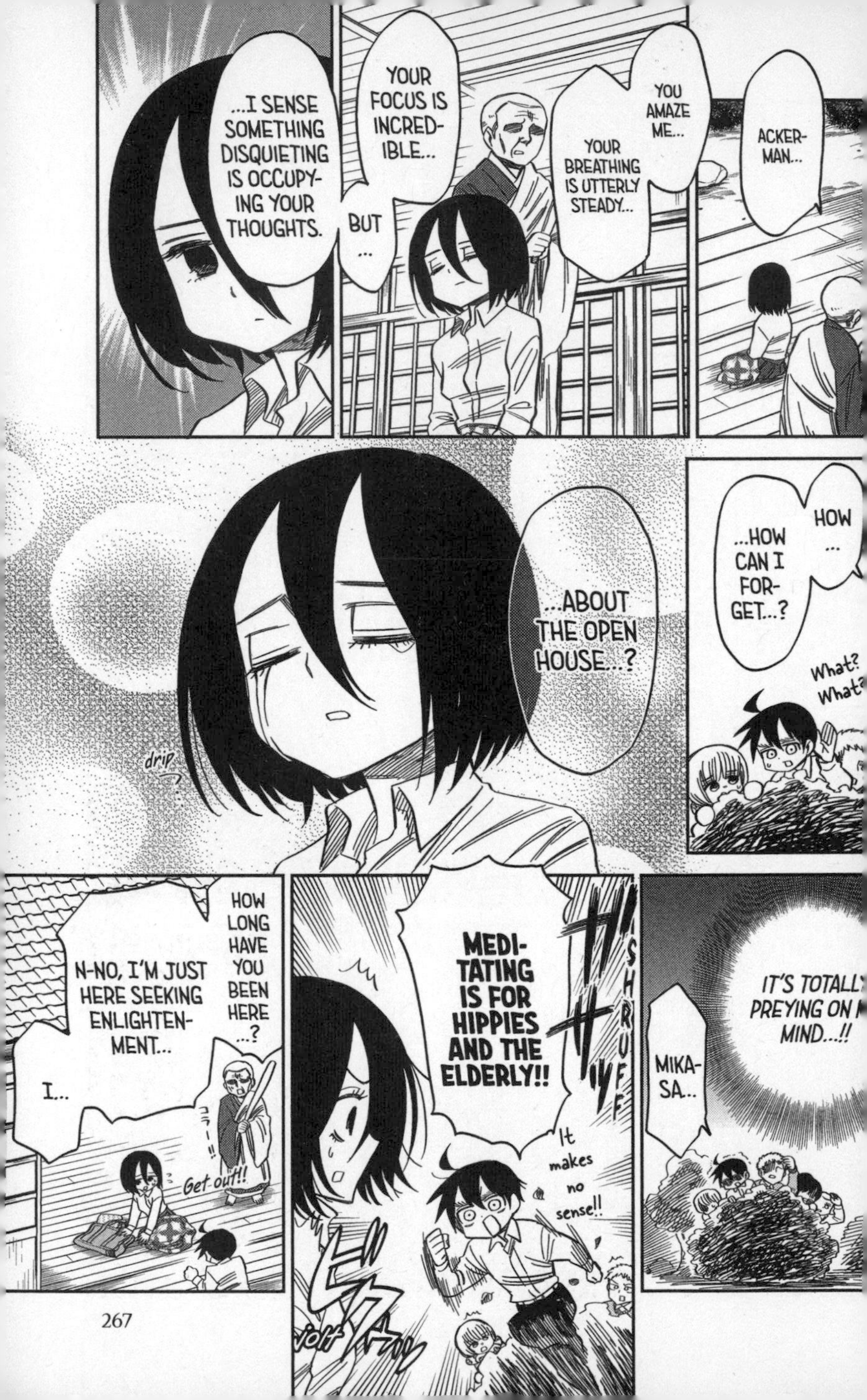
ACKER-MAN...
YOU AMAZE ME...
YOUR BREATHING IS UTTERLY STEADY...
YOUR FOCUS IS INCRED-IBLE...
BUT ...
...I SENSE SOMETHING DISQUIETING IS OCCUPY-ING YOUR THOUGHTS.
HOW ...
...HOW CAN I FOR-GET...?
What? What
...ABOUT THE OPEN HOUSE...?
drip
IT'S TOTALL PREYING ON MIND...!!
MIKA-SA...
SHRUFF
MEDI-TATING IS FOR HIPPIES AND THE ELDERLY!!
It makes no sense!!
jolt
HOW LONG HAVE YOU BEEN HERE ...?
N-NO, I'M JUST HERE SEEKING ENLIGHTEN-MENT...
I...
Get out!!

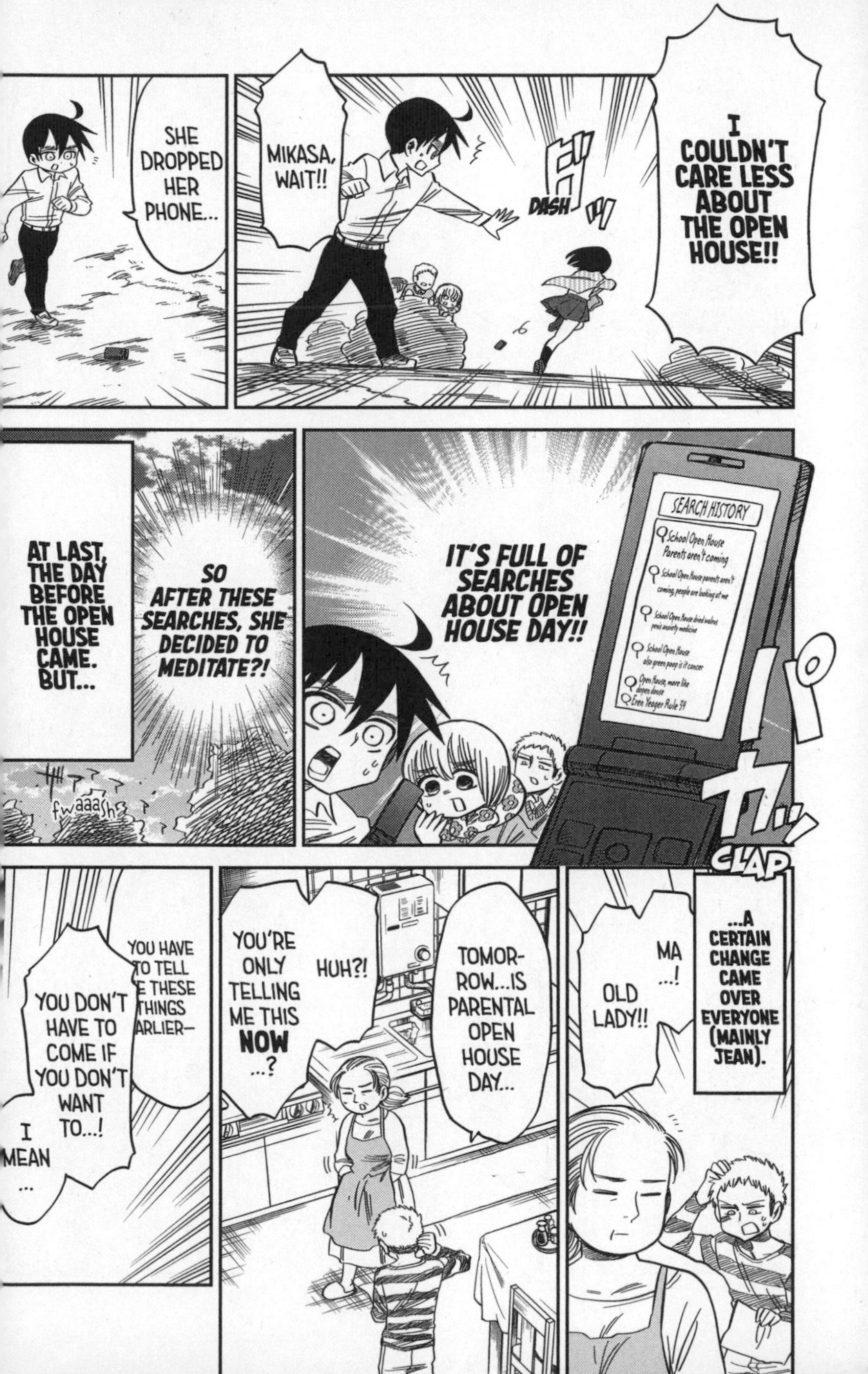
I COULDN'T CARE LESS ABOUT THE OPEN HOUSE!!
DASH
MIKASA, WAIT!!
SHE DROPPED HER PHONE...
SEARCH HISTORY
School Open House Parents aren't coming
School Open House parents aren't coming, people are looking at me
School Open House dried walrus penis anxiety medicine
School Open House also green poop is it cancer
Open House, more like dopen douse
Eren Yeager Rule 34
IT'S FULL OF SEARCHES ABOUT OPEN HOUSE DAY!!
CLAP
SO AFTER THESE SEARCHES, SHE DECIDED TO MEDITATE?!
AT LAST, THE DAY BEFORE THE OPEN HOUSE CAME. BUT...
fwaaash
...A CERTAIN CHANGE CAME OVER EVERYONE (MAINLY JEAN).
MA...!
OLD LADY!!
TOMORROW...IS PARENTAL OPEN HOUSE DAY...
HUH?!
YOU'RE ONLY TELLING ME THIS NOW...?
YOU HAVE TO TELL E THESE THINGS ARLIER—
YOU DON'T HAVE TO COME IF YOU DON'T WANT TO...!
I MEAN...

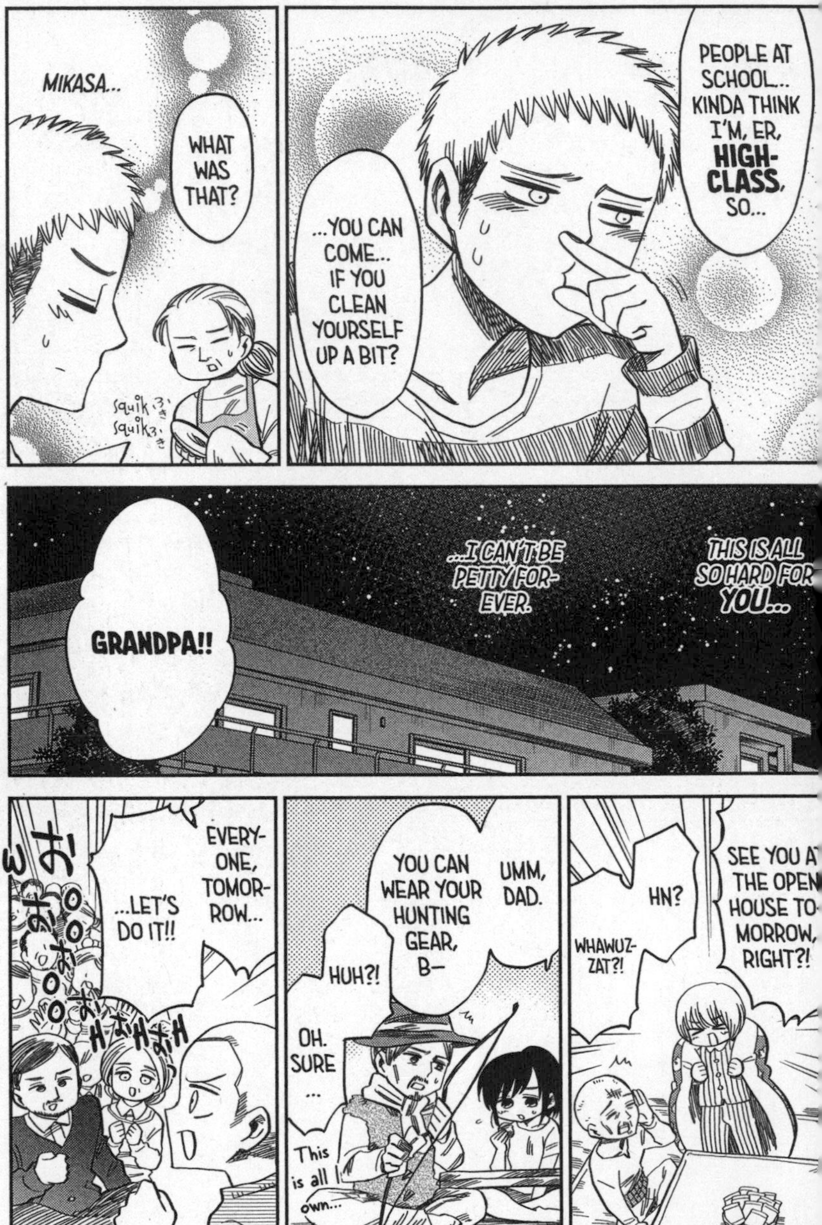
PEOPLE AT SCHOOL... KINDA THINK I'M, ER, HIGH-CLASS, SO...
...YOU CAN COME... IF YOU CLEAN YOURSELF UP A BIT?
MIKASA...
WHAT WAS THAT?
squik squik
THIS IS ALL SO HARD FOR YOU...
...I CAN'T BE PETTY FOR-EVER.
GRANDPA!!
SEE YOU AT THE OPEN HOUSE TO-MORROW, RIGHT?!
HN?
WHAWUZ-ZAT?!
UMM, DAD.
YOU CAN WEAR YOUR HUNTING GEAR, B—
HUH?!
OH. SURE ...
This is all own...
EVERY-ONE, TOMOR-ROW...
...LET'S DO IT!!

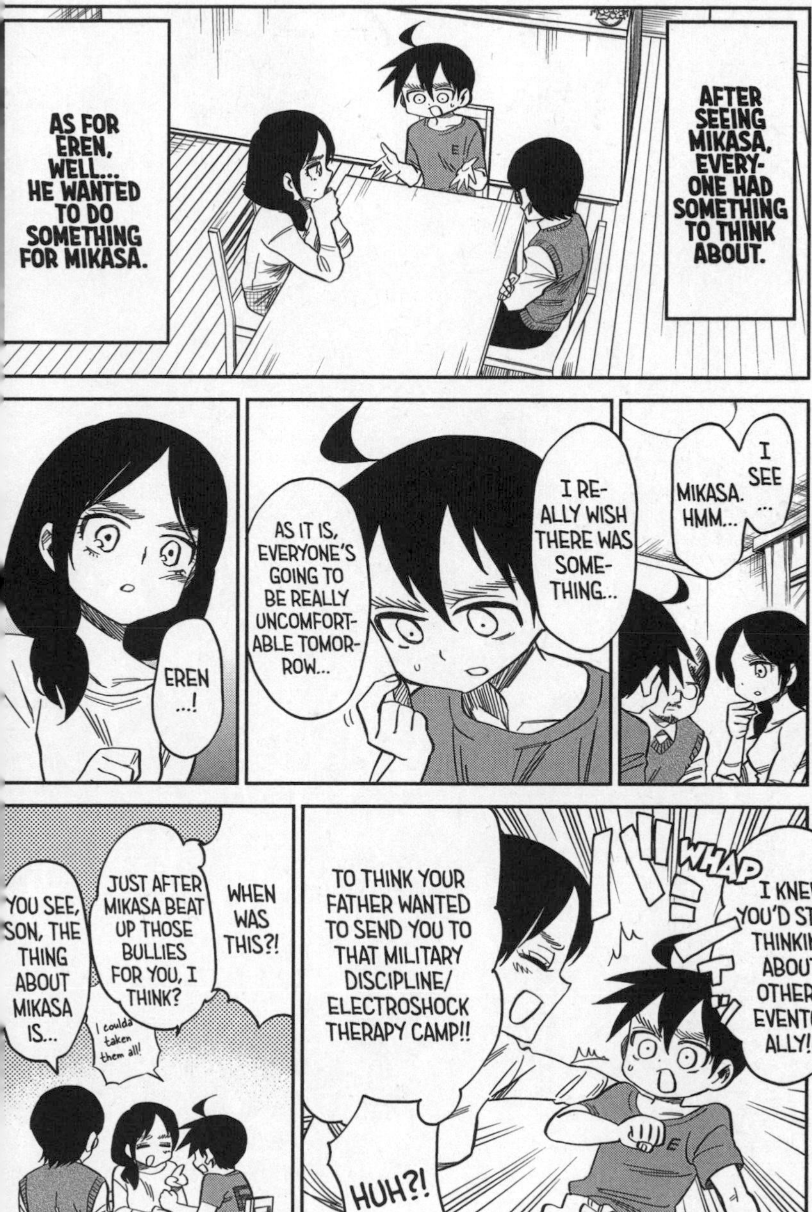
AFTER SEEING MIKASA, EVERYONE HAD SOMETHING TO THINK ABOUT.
AS FOR EREN, WELL... HE WANTED TO DO SOMETHING FOR MIKASA.
I SEE ...
MIKASA. HMM...
I REALLY WISH THERE WAS SOMETHING...
AS IT IS, EVERYONE'S GOING TO BE REALLY UNCOMFORTABLE TOMORROW...
EREN ...!
WHAP
I KNEW YOU'D START THINKING ABOUT OTHERS EVENTUALLY!!
TO THINK YOUR FATHER WANTED TO SEND YOU TO THAT MILITARY DISCIPLINE/ ELECTROSHOCK THERAPY CAMP!!
HUH?!
WHEN WAS THIS?!
JUST AFTER MIKASA BEAT UP THOSE BULLIES FOR YOU, I THINK?
YOU SEE, SON, THE THING ABOUT MIKASA IS...
I coulda taken them all!

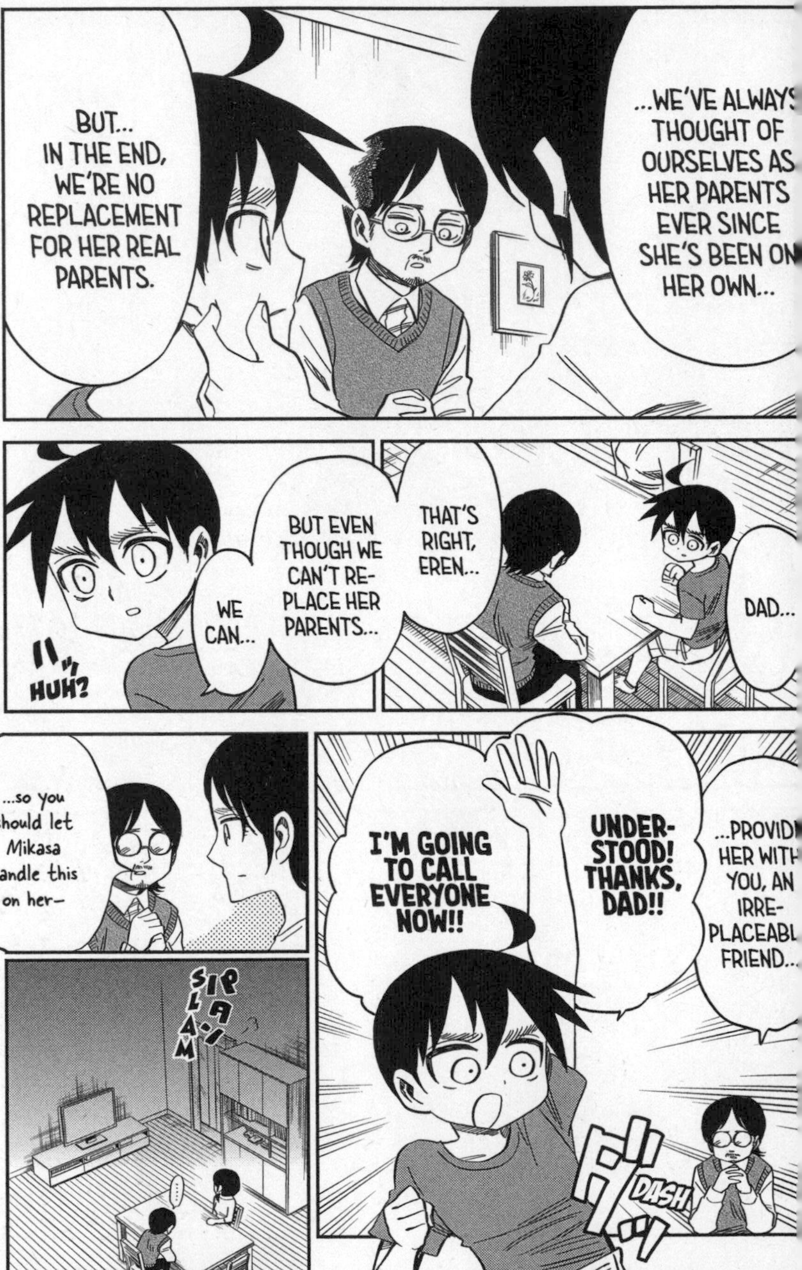
...WE'VE ALWAYS THOUGHT OF OURSELVES AS HER PARENTS EVER SINCE SHE'S BEEN ON HER OWN...
BUT... IN THE END, WE'RE NO REPLACEMENT FOR HER REAL PARENTS.
DAD...
THAT'S RIGHT, EREN...
BUT EVEN THOUGH WE CAN'T RE-PLACE HER PARENTS...
WE CAN...
HUH?
...PROVID HER WITH YOU, AN IRRE-PLACEABL FRIEND...
UNDER-STOOD! THANKS, DAD!!
I'M GOING TO CALL EVERYONE NOW!!
DASH
...so you should let Mikasa handle this on her—
KCHAK
SLAM
...

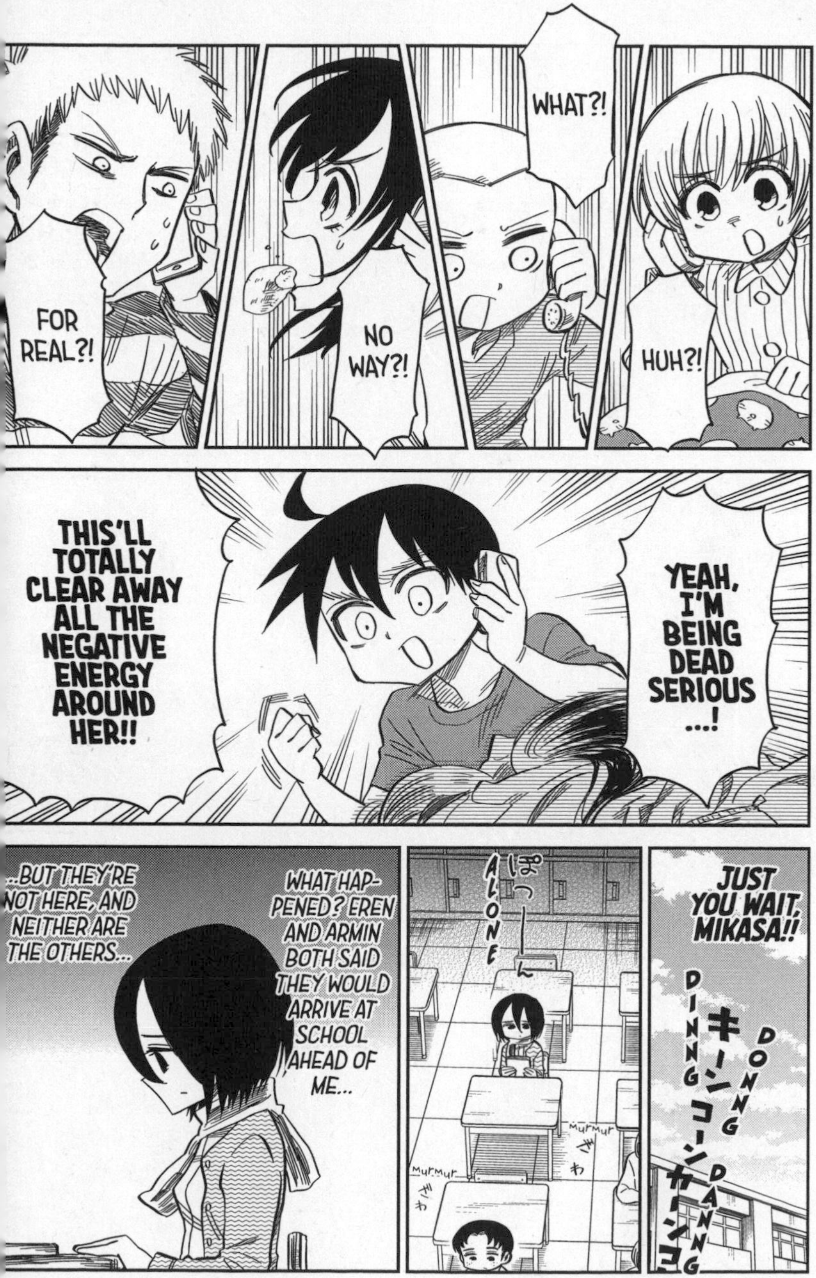
WHAT?!
HUH?!
NO WAY?!
FOR REAL?!
YEAH, I'M BEING DEAD SERIOUS...!
THIS'LL TOTALLY CLEAR AWAY ALL THE NEGATIVE ENERGY AROUND HER!!
JUST YOU WAIT, MIKASA!!
キーンコーンカーンコ
DINNG DONNG DANNG DINNG
ぽつーん
ALONE
ざわ
MurMur
ざわ
MurMur
WHAT HAP-PENED? EREN AND ARMIN BOTH SAID THEY WOULD ARRIVE AT SCHOOL AHEAD OF ME...
...BUT THEY'RE NOT HERE, AND NEITHER ARE THE OTHERS...

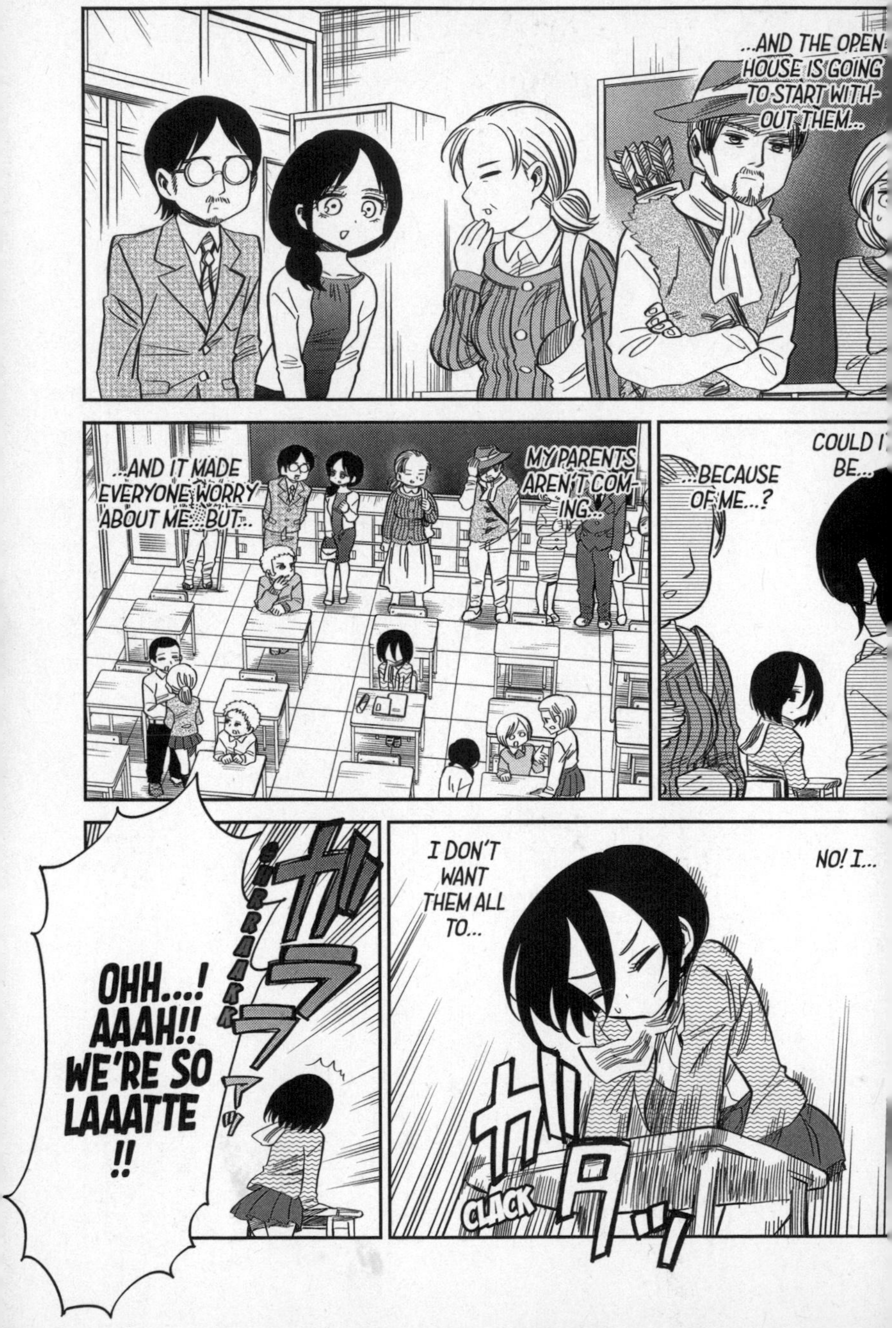
...AND THE OPEN HOUSE IS GOING TO START WITH-OUT THEM...
COULD IT BE...
...BECAUSE OF ME...?
MY PARENTS AREN'T COMING...
...AND IT MADE EVERYONE WORRY ABOUT ME... BUT...
NO! I...
I DON'T WANT THEM ALL TO...
CLACK
OHH...! AAAH!! WE'RE SO LAAATTE !!

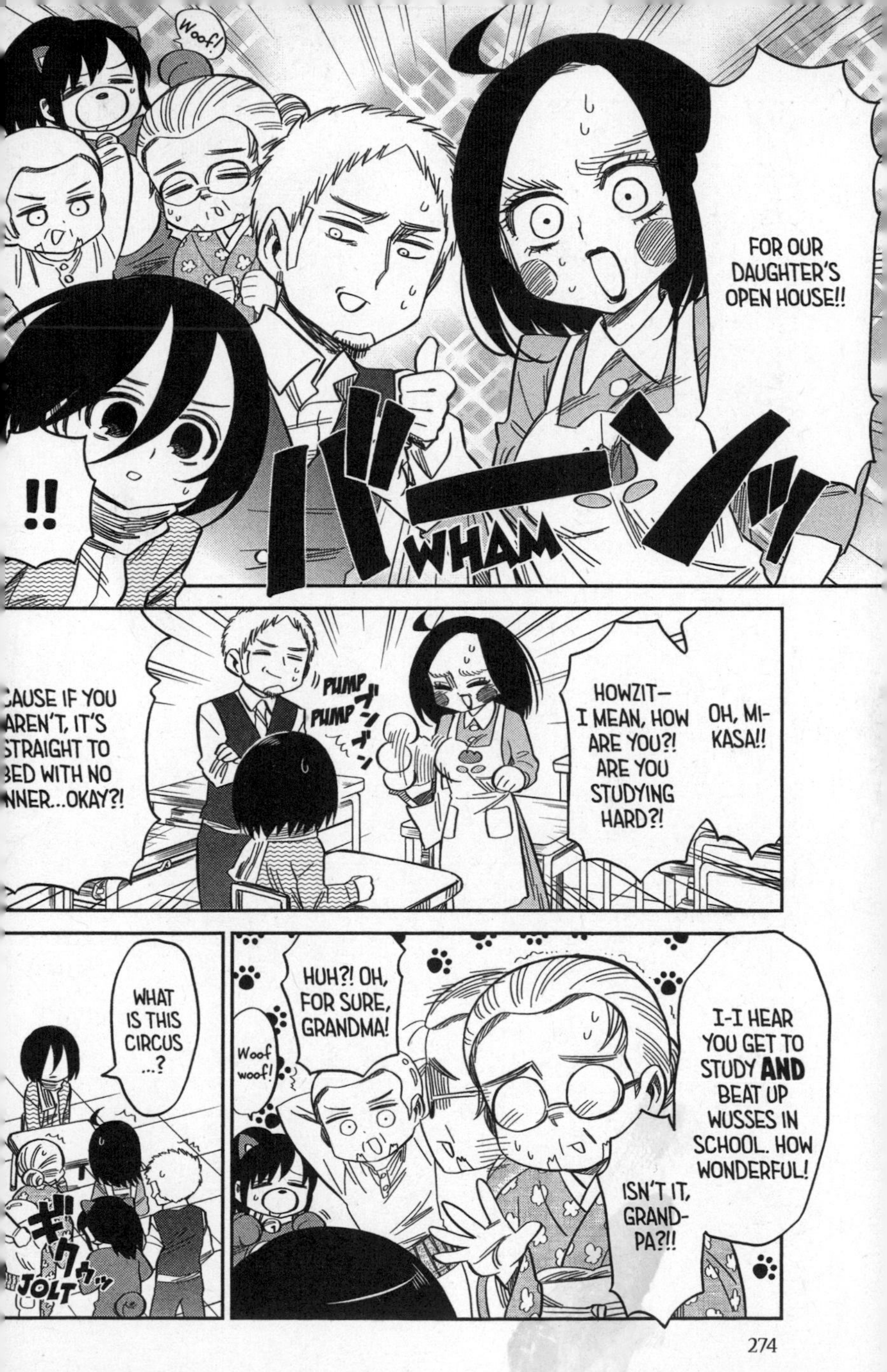
FOR OUR DAUGHTER'S OPEN HOUSE!!
Woof!
WHAM
!!
OH, MI-KASA!!
HOWZIT— I MEAN, HOW ARE YOU?! ARE YOU STUDYING HARD?!
PUMP PUMP
CAUSE IF YOU AREN'T, IT'S STRAIGHT TO BED WITH NO NNER...OKAY?!
I-I HEAR YOU GET TO STUDY **AND** BEAT UP WUSSES IN SCHOOL. HOW WONDERFUL!
ISN'T IT, GRAND-PA?!!
HUH?! OH, FOR SURE, GRANDMA!
Woof woof!
WHAT IS THIS CIRCUS ...?
JOLT

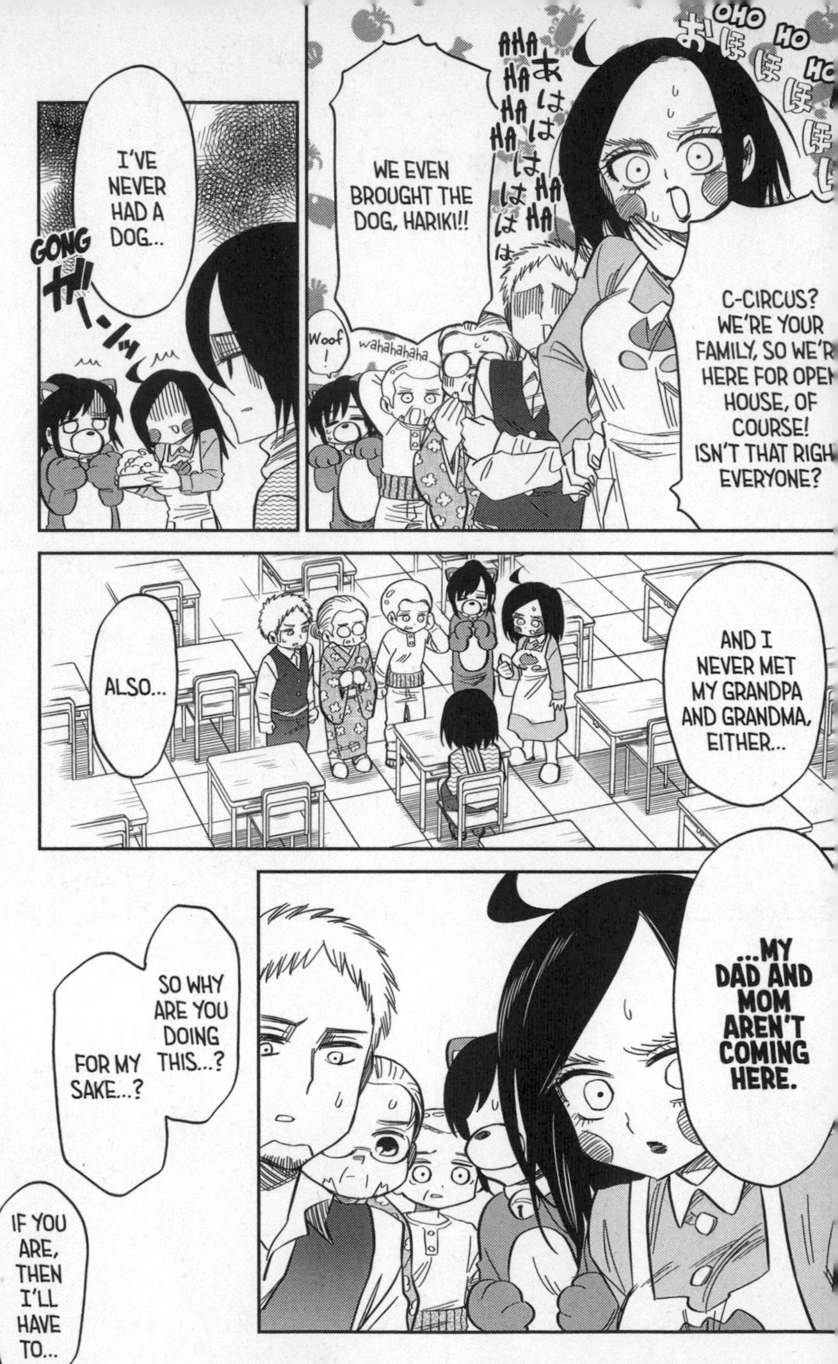
OHO HO HO
AHA HA HA HA HA HA
C-CIRCUS? WE'RE YOUR FAMILY, SO WE'R HERE FOR OPEN HOUSE, OF COURSE! ISN'T THAT RIGH EVERYONE?
WE EVEN BROUGHT THE DOG, HARIKI!!
wahahahaha
Woof!
I'VE NEVER HAD A DOG...
GONG
AND I NEVER MET MY GRANDPA AND GRANDMA, EITHER...
ALSO...
...MY DAD AND MOM AREN'T COMING HERE.
SO WHY ARE YOU DOING THIS...?
FOR MY SAKE...?
IF YOU ARE, THEN I'LL HAVE TO...

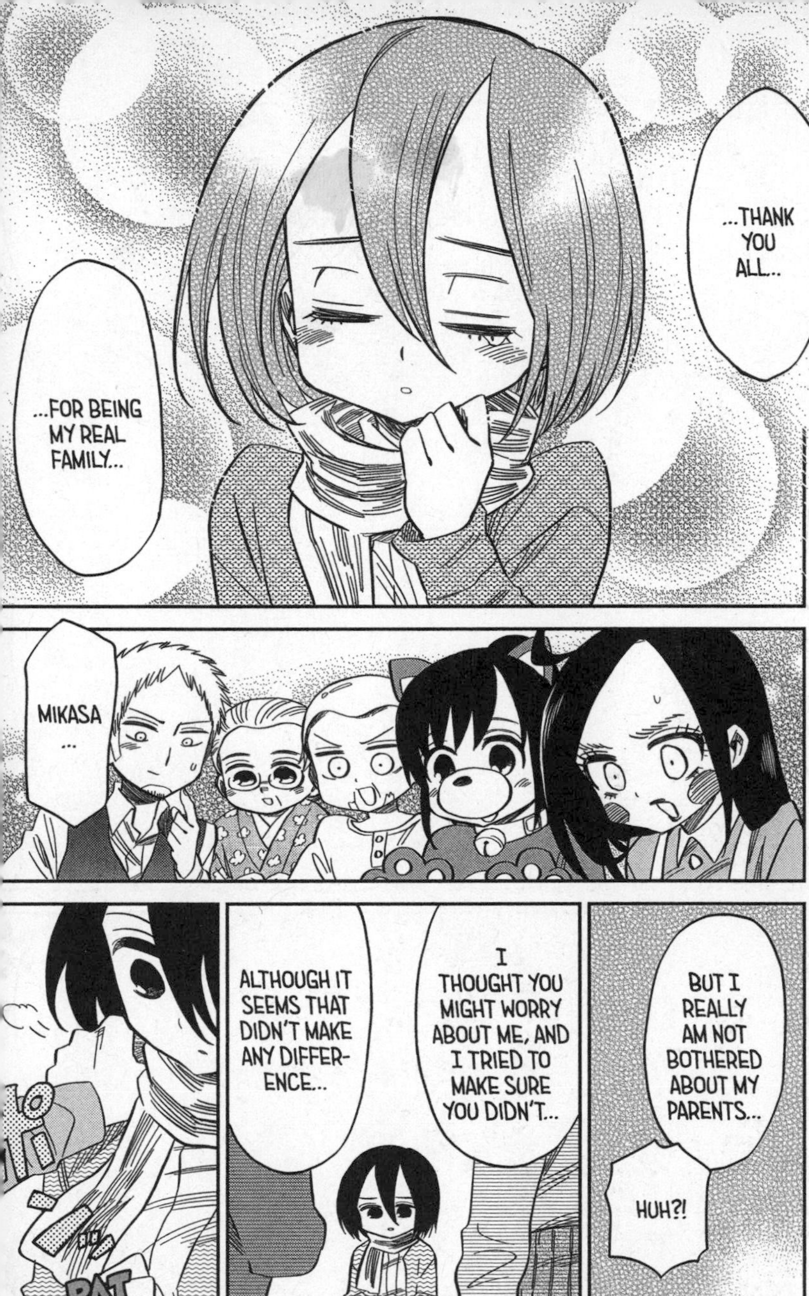
...THANK YOU ALL...
...FOR BEING MY REAL FAMILY...
MIKASA ...
BUT I REALLY AM NOT BOTHERED ABOUT MY PARENTS...
HUH?!
I THOUGHT YOU MIGHT WORRY ABOUT ME, AND I TRIED TO MAKE SURE YOU DIDN'T...
ALTHOUGH IT SEEMS THAT DIDN'T MAKE ANY DIFFERENCE...
PAT

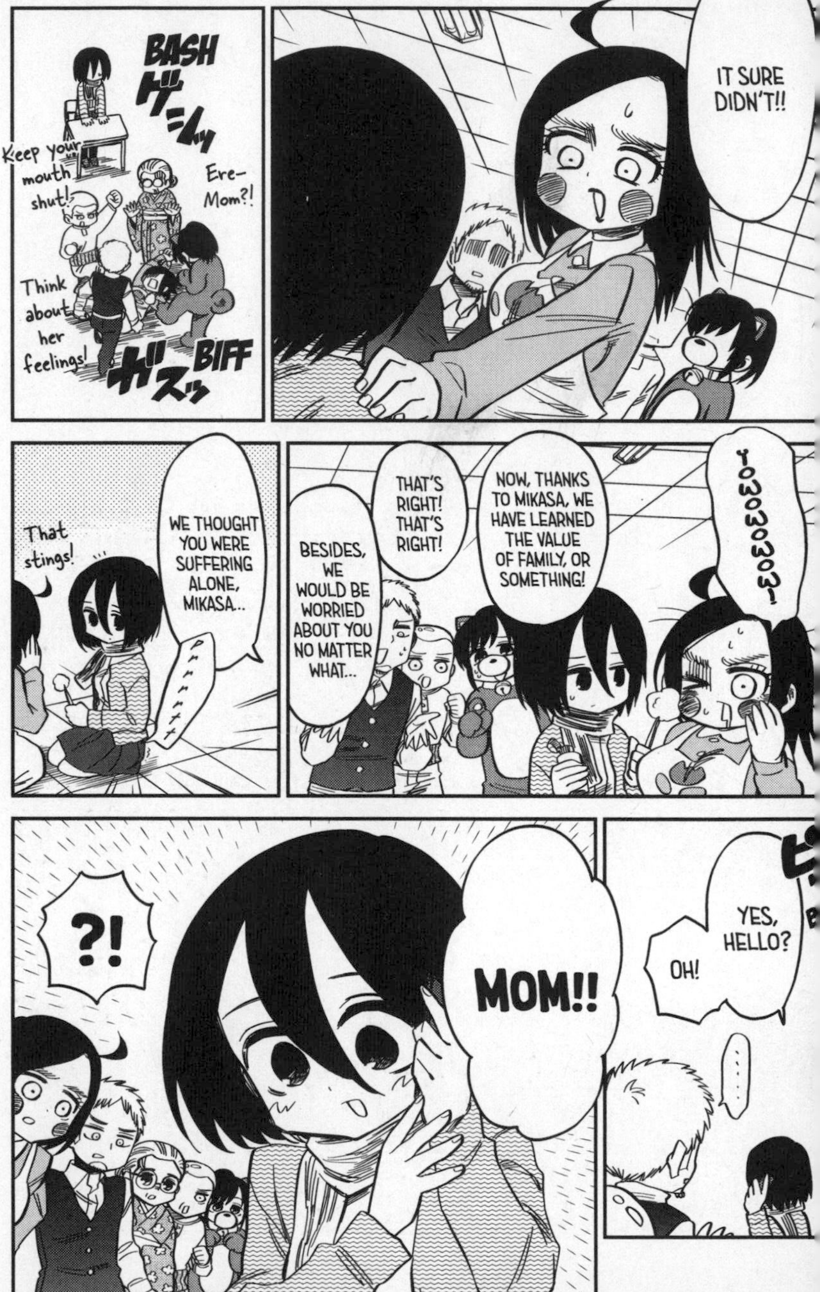
IT SURE DIDN'T!!
BASH
ゲシッ
Keep your mouth shut!
Ere-Mom?!
Think about her feelings!
ガスッ
BIFF
YOWOWOWOW!
NOW, THANKS TO MIKASA, WE HAVE LEARNED THE VALUE OF FAMILY, OR SOMETHING!
THAT'S RIGHT! THAT'S RIGHT!
BESIDES, WE WOULD BE WORRIED ABOUT YOU NO MATTER WHAT...
WE THOUGHT YOU WERE SUFFERING ALONE, MIKASA...
Prrrrrtt
That stings!
YES, HELLO?
OH!
......
MOM!!
?!

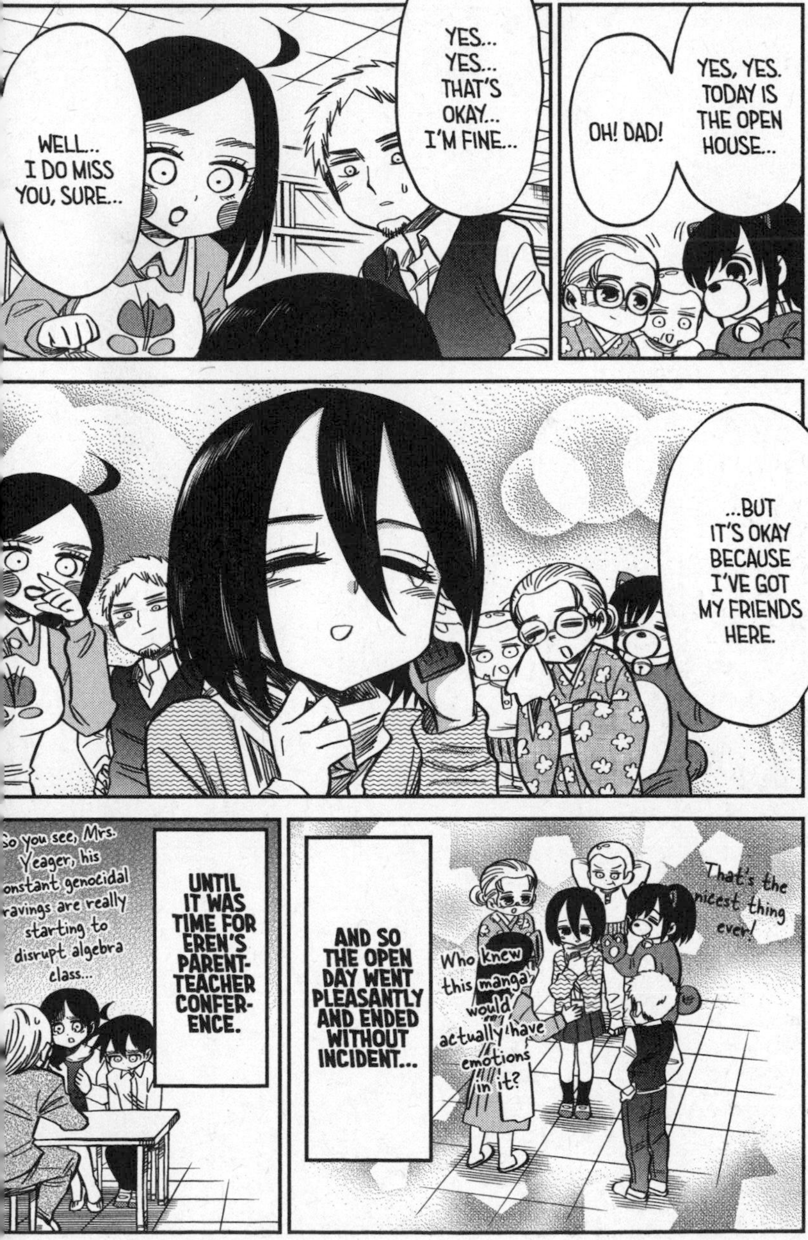
OH! DAD!
YES, YES. TODAY IS THE OPEN HOUSE...
YES... YES... THAT'S OKAY... I'M FINE...
WELL... I DO MISS YOU, SURE...
...BUT IT'S OKAY BECAUSE I'VE GOT MY FRIENDS HERE.
That's the nicest thing ever!
AND SO THE OPEN DAY WENT PLEASANTLY AND ENDED WITHOUT INCIDENT...
Who knew this manga would actually have emotions in it?
UNTIL IT WAS TIME FOR EREN'S PARENT-TEACHER CONFERENCE.
So you see, Mrs. Yeager, his onstant genocidal ravings are really starting to disrupt algebra class...

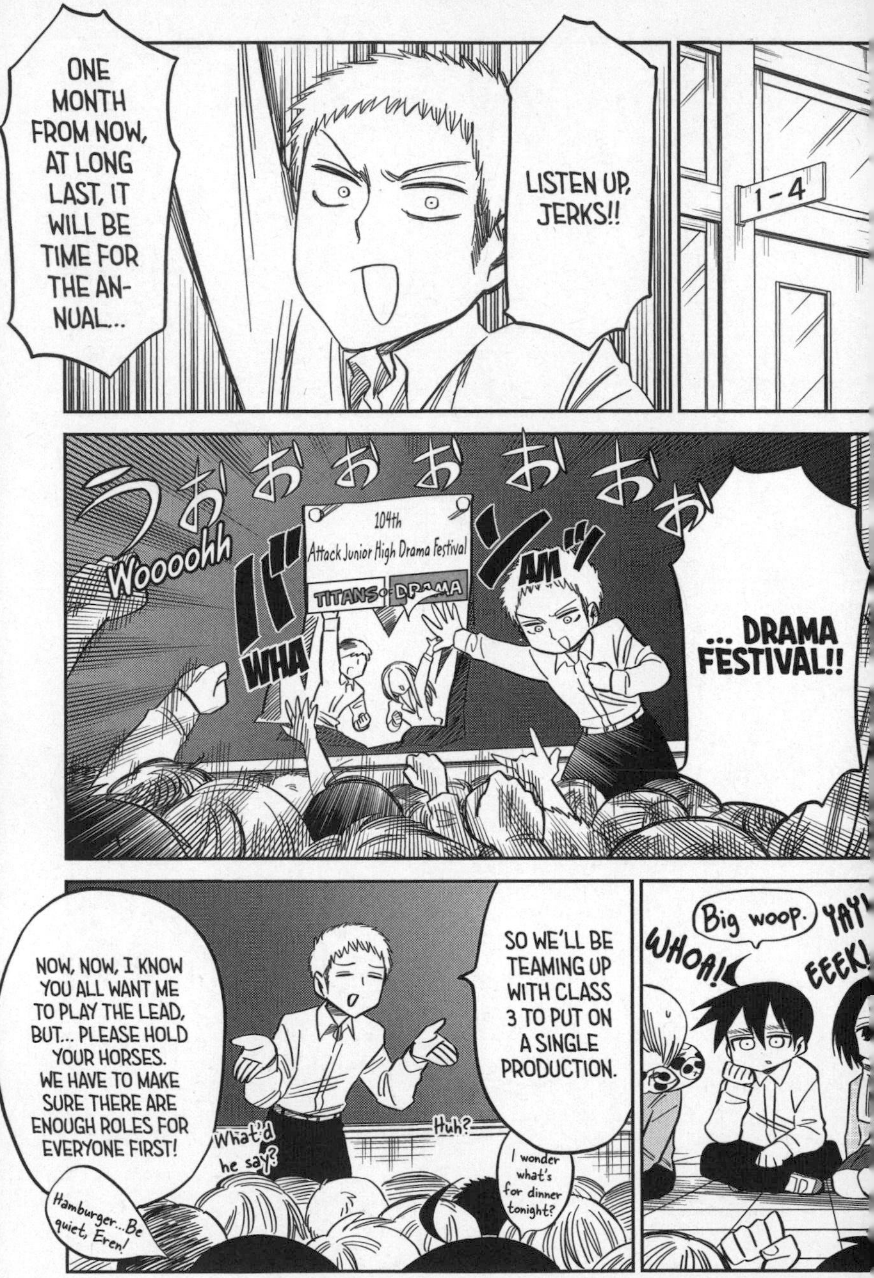
LISTEN UP, JERKS!!
ONE MONTH FROM NOW, AT LONG LAST, IT WILL BE TIME FOR THE ANNUAL...
1-4
...DRAMA FESTIVAL!!
うおおおおおおお
Wooooh
ジャン
JAM
バ
WHA
104th
Attack Junior High Drama Festival
TITANS OF DRAMA
Big woop.
YAY!
WHOA!
EEEK!
SO WE'LL BE TEAMING UP WITH CLASS 3 TO PUT ON A SINGLE PRODUCTION.
NOW, NOW, I KNOW YOU ALL WANT ME TO PLAY THE LEAD, BUT... PLEASE HOLD YOUR HORSES. WE HAVE TO MAKE SURE THERE ARE ENOUGH ROLES FOR EVERYONE FIRST!
Huh?
I wonder what's for dinner tonight?
What'd he say?
Hamburger... Be quiet, Eren!

FIFTY-EIGHTH PERIOD: EVENT-RICH JUNIOR HIGH

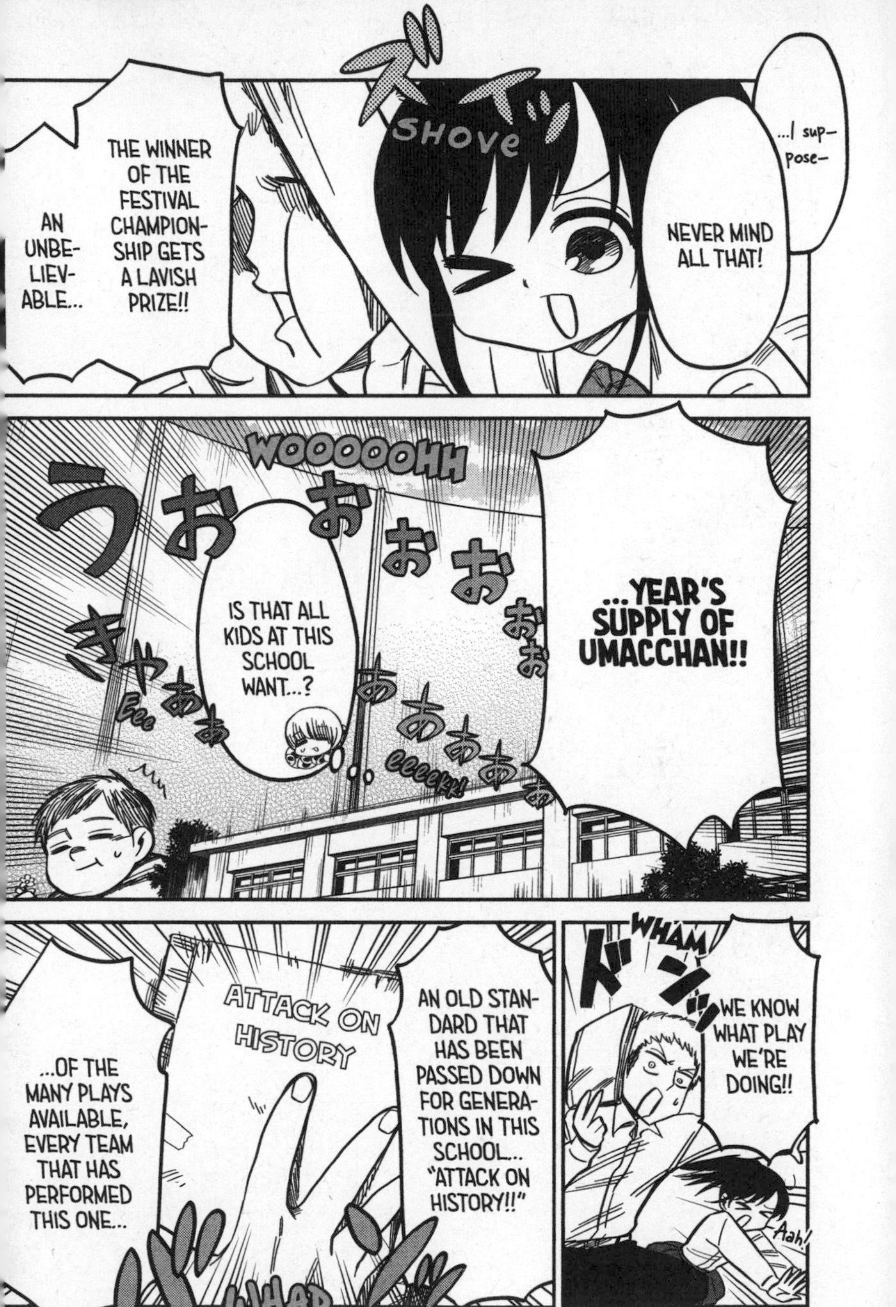
...I sup-pose—
NEVER MIND ALL THAT!
SHOVE
THE WINNER OF THE FESTIVAL CHAMPIONSHIP GETS A LAVISH PRIZE!!
AN UNBELIEVABLE...
...YEAR'S SUPPLY OF UMACCHAN!!
WOOOOOHH
eeeek!
IS THAT ALL KIDS AT THIS SCHOOL WANT...?
Eee
WHAM
WE KNOW WHAT PLAY WE'RE DOING!!
Aah!
AN OLD STANDARD THAT HAS BEEN PASSED DOWN FOR GENERATIONS IN THIS SCHOOL... "ATTACK ON HISTORY!!"
ATTACK ON HISTORY
...OF THE MANY PLAYS AVAILABLE, EVERY TEAM THAT HAS PERFORMED THIS ONE...
WHAP

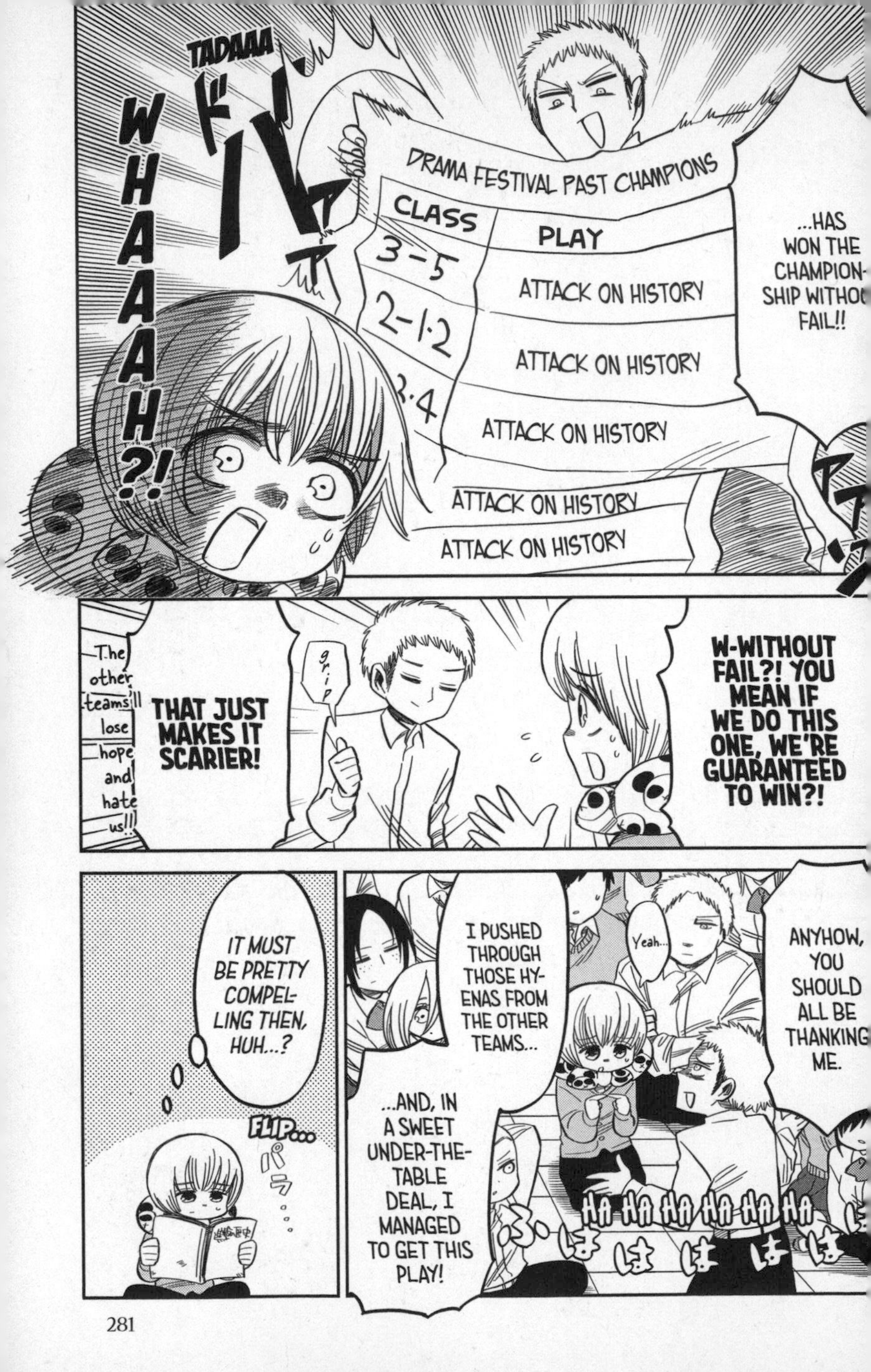
DRAMA FESTIVAL PAST CHAMPIONS
CLASS
PLAY
3-5
ATTACK ON HISTORY
2-1·2
ATTACK ON HISTORY
3·4
ATTACK ON HISTORY
ATTACK ON HISTORY
ATTACK ON HISTORY
...HAS WON THE CHAMPION-SHIP WITHOU FAIL!!
TADAAA
WHAAAAH?!
W-WITHOUT FAIL?! YOU MEAN IF WE DO THIS ONE, WE'RE GUARANTEED TO WIN?!
grip
THAT JUST MAKES IT SCARIER!
The other teams'll lose hope and hate us!!
ANYHOW, YOU SHOULD ALL BE THANKING ME.
Yeah...
I PUSHED THROUGH THOSE HY-ENAS FROM THE OTHER TEAMS...
...AND, IN A SWEET UNDER-THE-TABLE DEAL, I MANAGED TO GET THIS PLAY!
HA HA HA HA HA HA HA
IT MUST BE PRETTY COMPEL-LING THEN, HUH...?
FLIP...

Please enjoy this illustrated version of the script.

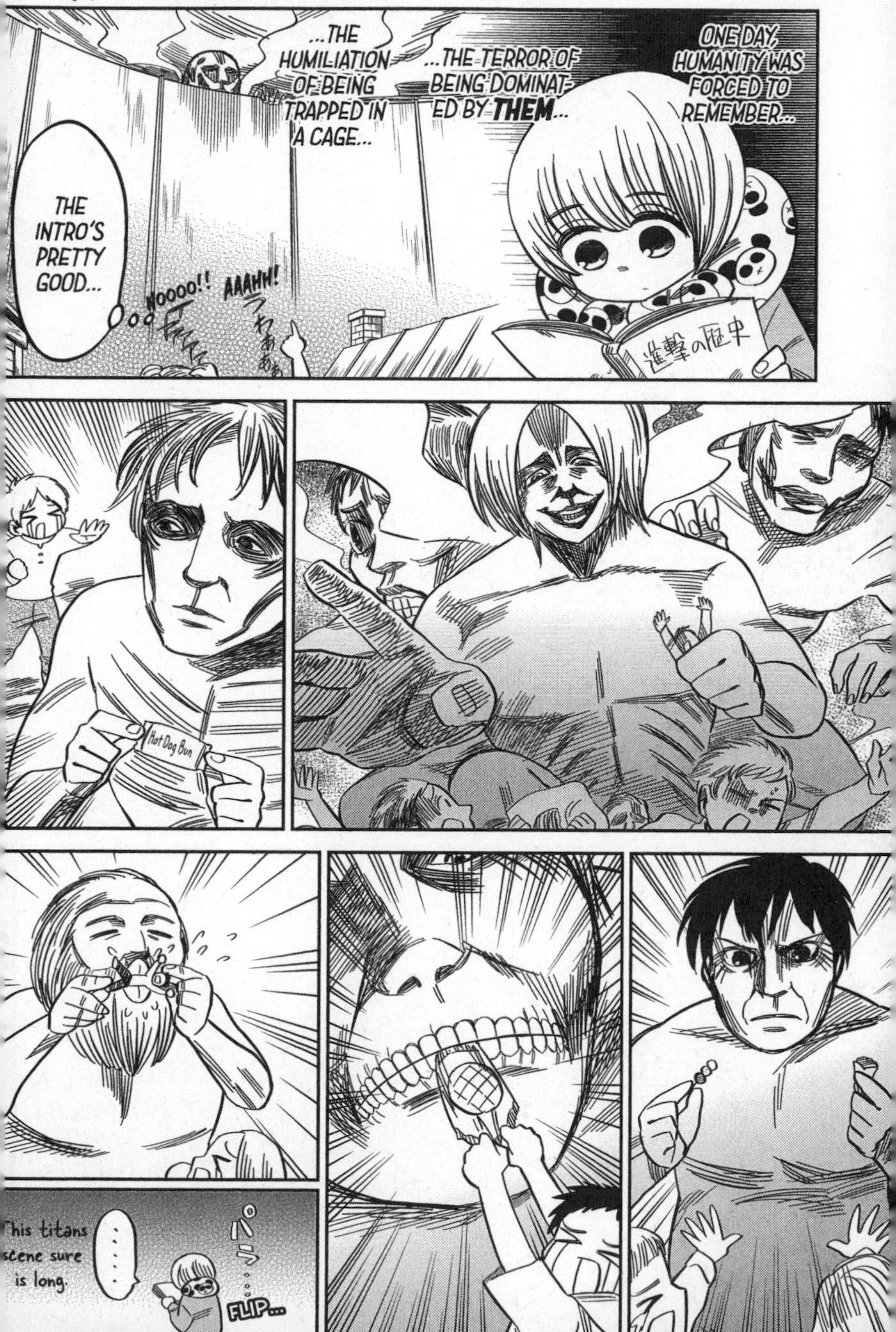
ONE DAY, HUMANITY WAS FORCED TO REMEMBER...
...THE TERROR OF BEING DOMINATED BY **THEM**...
...THE HUMILIATION OF BEING TRAPPED IN A CAGE...
進撃の歴史
AAAHH!
NOOOO!!
THE INTRO'S PRETTY GOOD...
Hot Dog Bun
FLIP...
......
This titans scene sure is long.

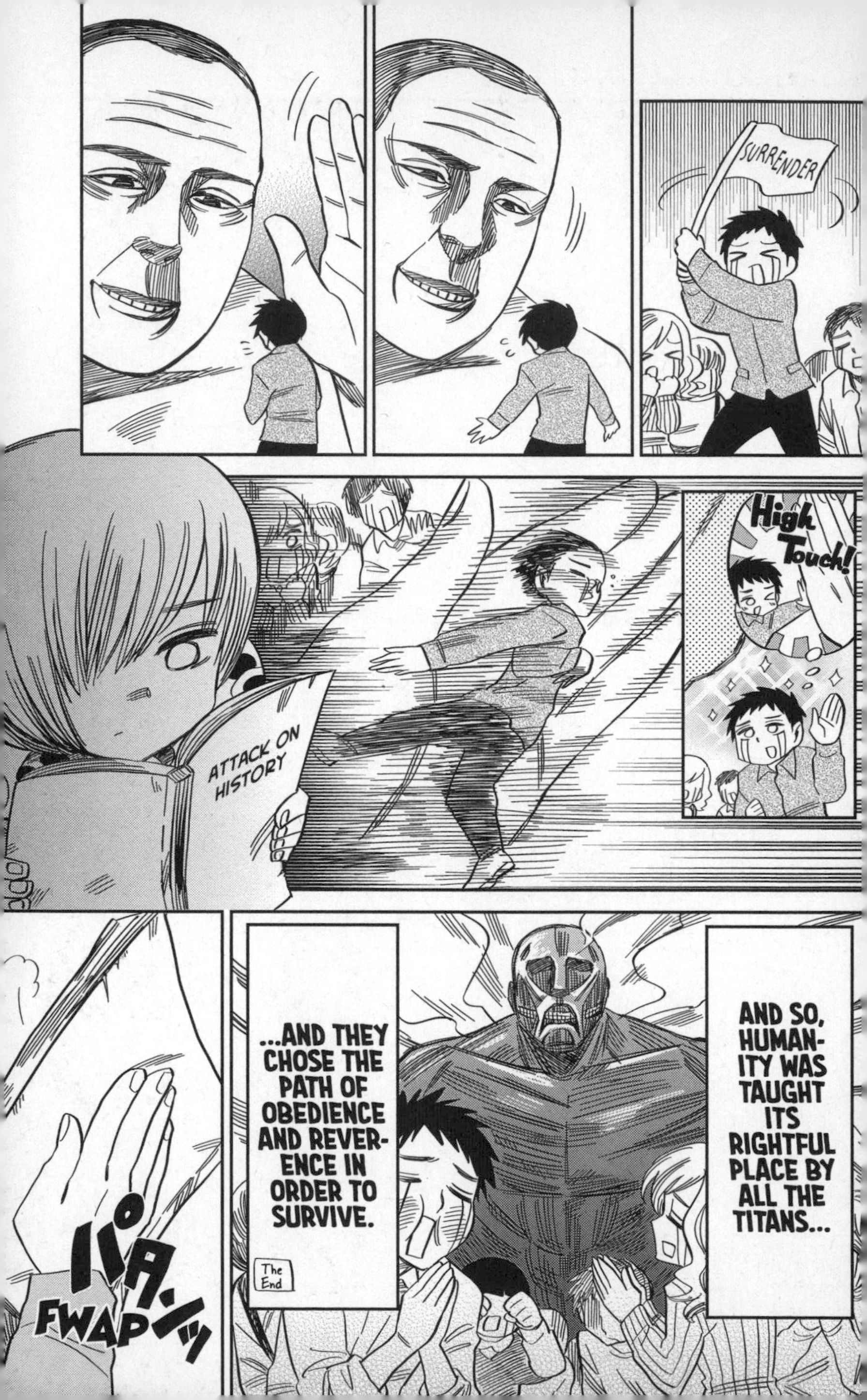
SURRENDER
High Touch!
ATTACK ON HISTORY
AND SO, HUMANITY WAS TAUGHT ITS RIGHTFUL PLACE BY ALL THE TITANS...
...AND THEY CHOSE THE PATH OF OBEDIENCE AND REVERENCE IN ORDER TO SURVIVE.
The End
FWAP

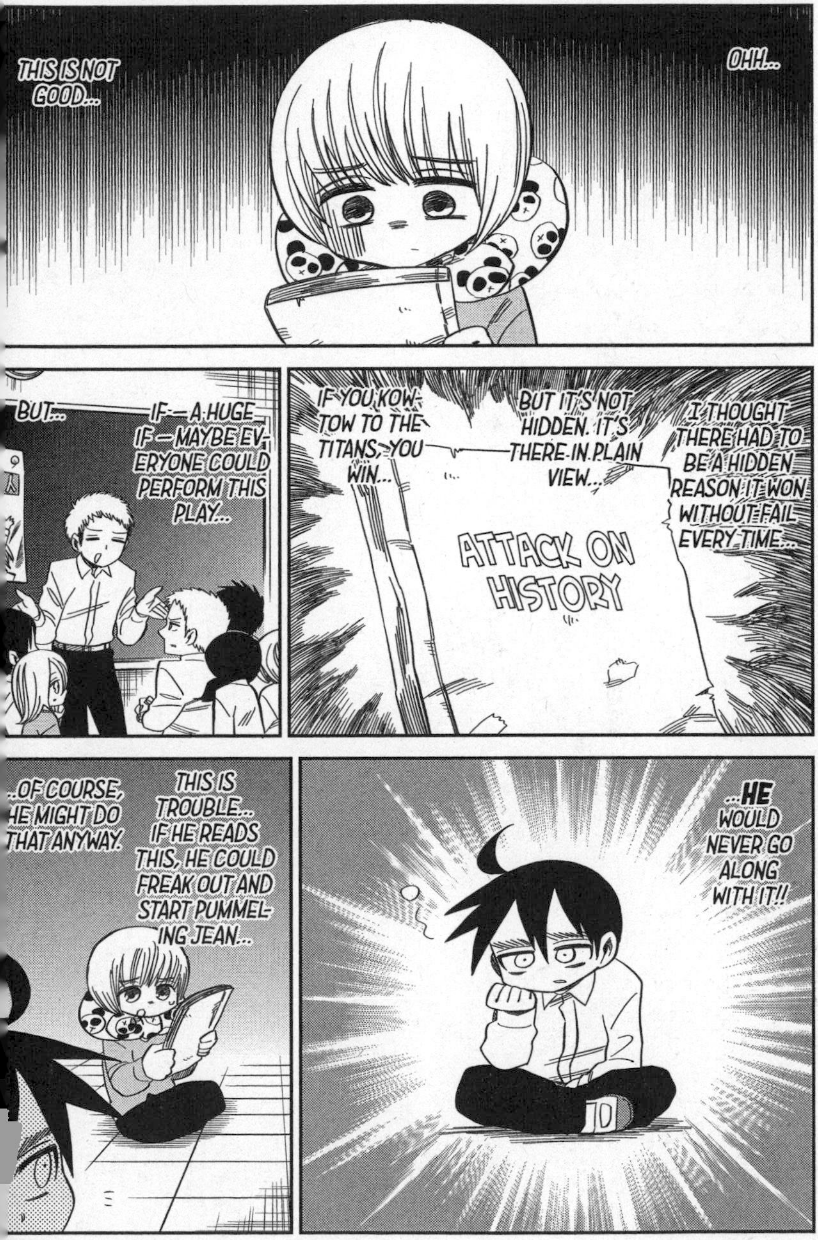
OHH...
THIS IS NOT GOOD...
I THOUGHT THERE HAD TO BE A HIDDEN REASON IT WON WITHOUT FAIL EVERY TIME...
BUT IT'S NOT HIDDEN. IT'S THERE IN PLAIN VIEW...
IF YOU KOWTOW TO THE TITANS, YOU WIN...
ATTACK ON HISTORY
IF—A HUGE IF—MAYBE EVERYONE COULD PERFORM THIS PLAY...
BUT...
...HE WOULD NEVER GO ALONG WITH IT!!
THIS IS TROUBLE... IF HE READS THIS, HE COULD FREAK OUT AND START PUMMELING JEAN...
...OF COURSE, HE MIGHT DO THAT ANYWAY.

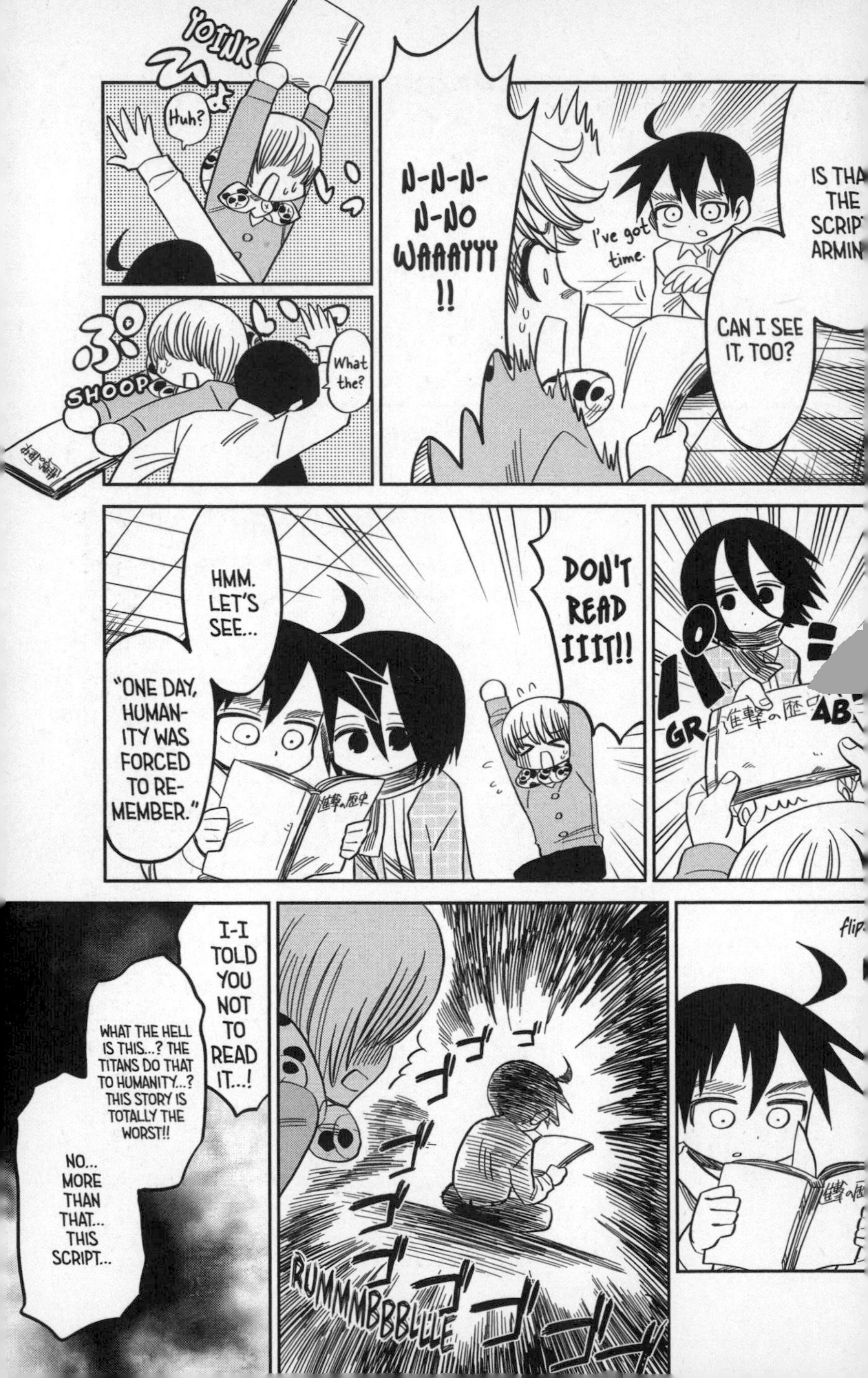
IS THA THE SCRIPT ARMIN
CAN I SEE IT, TOO?
I've got time.
N-N-N-N-NO WAAAYYY!!
YOINK
Huh?
What the?
SHOOP
GR AB
DON'T READ IIIT!!
HMM. LET'S SEE...
"ONE DAY, HUMANITY WAS FORCED TO REMEMBER."
flip...
RUMMMBBBLLLE
I-I TOLD YOU NOT TO READ IT...!
WHAT THE HELL IS THIS...? THE TITANS DO THAT TO HUMANITY...? THIS STORY IS TOTALLY THE WORST!!
NO... MORE THAN THAT... THIS SCRIPT...

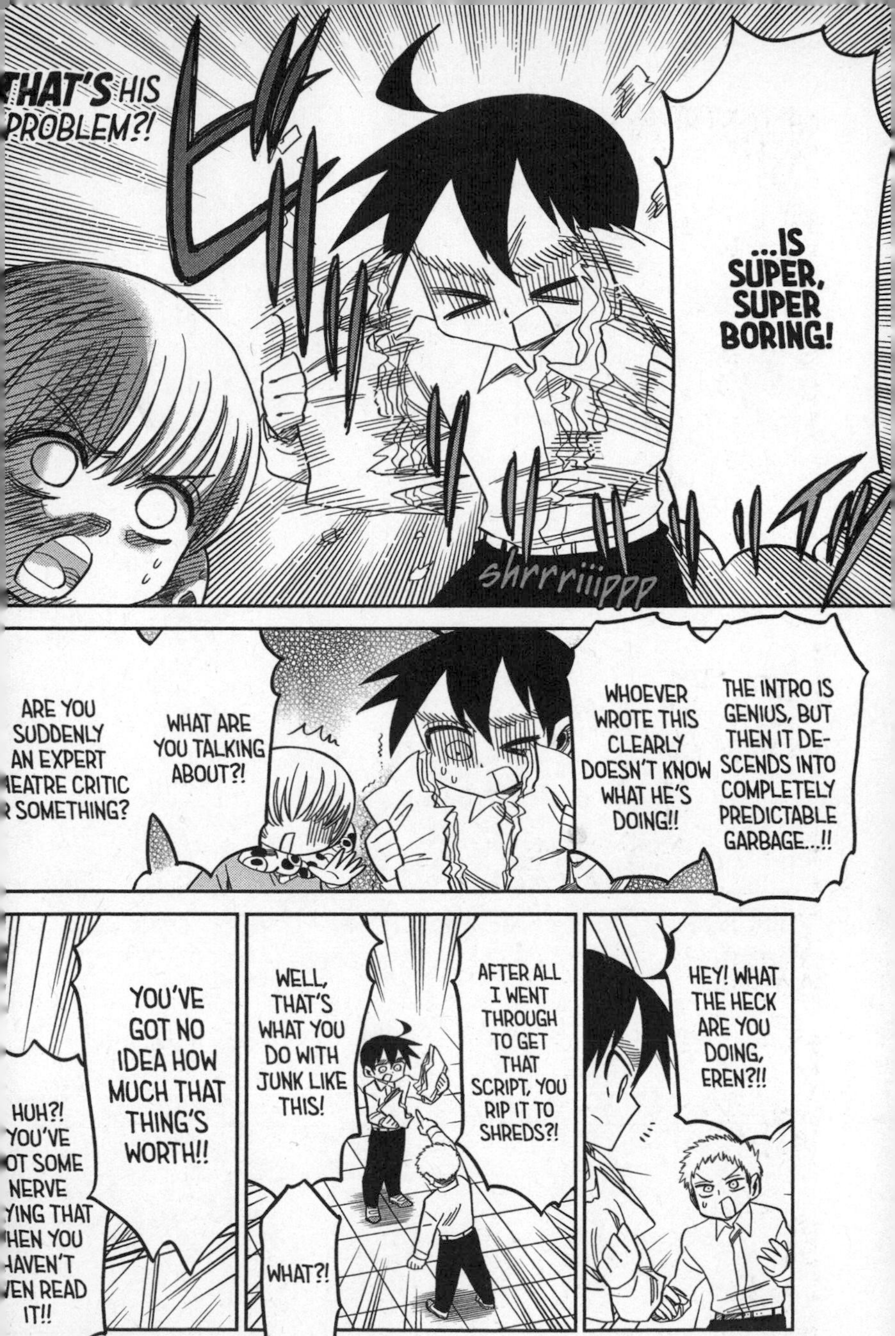
...IS SUPER, SUPER BORING!
shrrriiippp
THAT'S HIS PROBLEM?!
THE INTRO IS GENIUS, BUT THEN IT DE- SCENDS INTO COMPLETELY PREDICTABLE GARBAGE...!!
WHOEVER WROTE THIS CLEARLY DOESN'T KNOW WHAT HE'S DOING!!
WHAT ARE YOU TALKING ABOUT?!
ARE YOU SUDDENLY AN EXPERT EATRE CRITIC R SOMETHING?
HEY! WHAT THE HECK ARE YOU DOING, EREN?!!
AFTER ALL I WENT THROUGH TO GET THAT SCRIPT, YOU RIP IT TO SHREDS?!
WELL, THAT'S WHAT YOU DO WITH JUNK LIKE THIS!
WHAT?!
YOU'VE GOT NO IDEA HOW MUCH THAT THING'S WORTH!!
HUH?! YOU'VE OT SOME NERVE YING THAT HEN YOU HAVEN'T VEN READ IT!!

ビリ ZZIP
ペタ TAPE

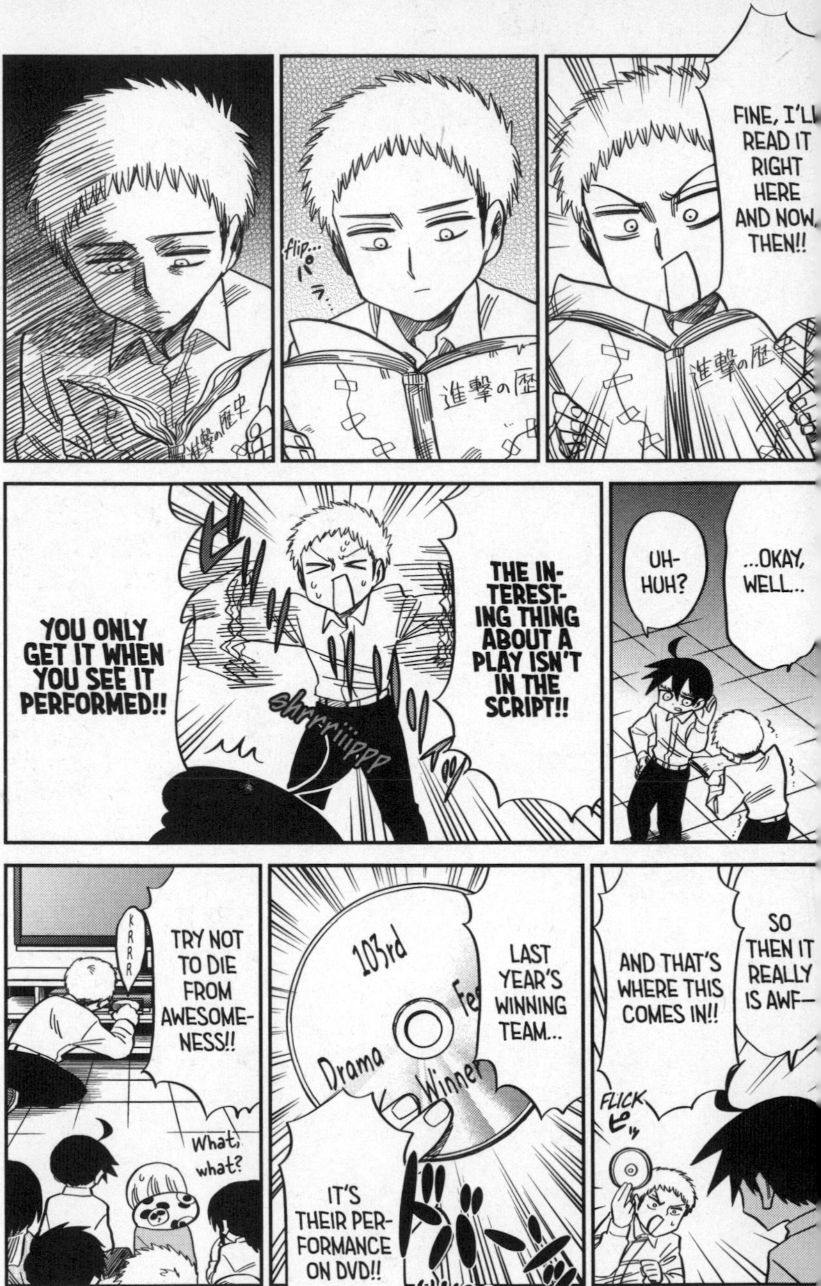
FINE, I'LL READ IT RIGHT HERE AND NOW, THEN!!
flip...
パラ…
進撃の歴史
...OKAY, WELL...
UH-HUH?
THE INTERESTING THING ABOUT A PLAY ISN'T IN THE SCRIPT!!
shrrriiippp
YOU ONLY GET IT WHEN YOU SEE IT PERFORMED!!
SO THEN IT REALLY IS AWF—
AND THAT'S WHERE THIS COMES IN!!
FLICK
ピッ
LAST YEAR'S WINNING TEAM...
103rd
Drama
Winner
IT'S THEIR PERFORMANCE ON DVD!!
WHaam
TRY NOT TO DIE FROM AWESOMENESS!!
KRRR
What, what?

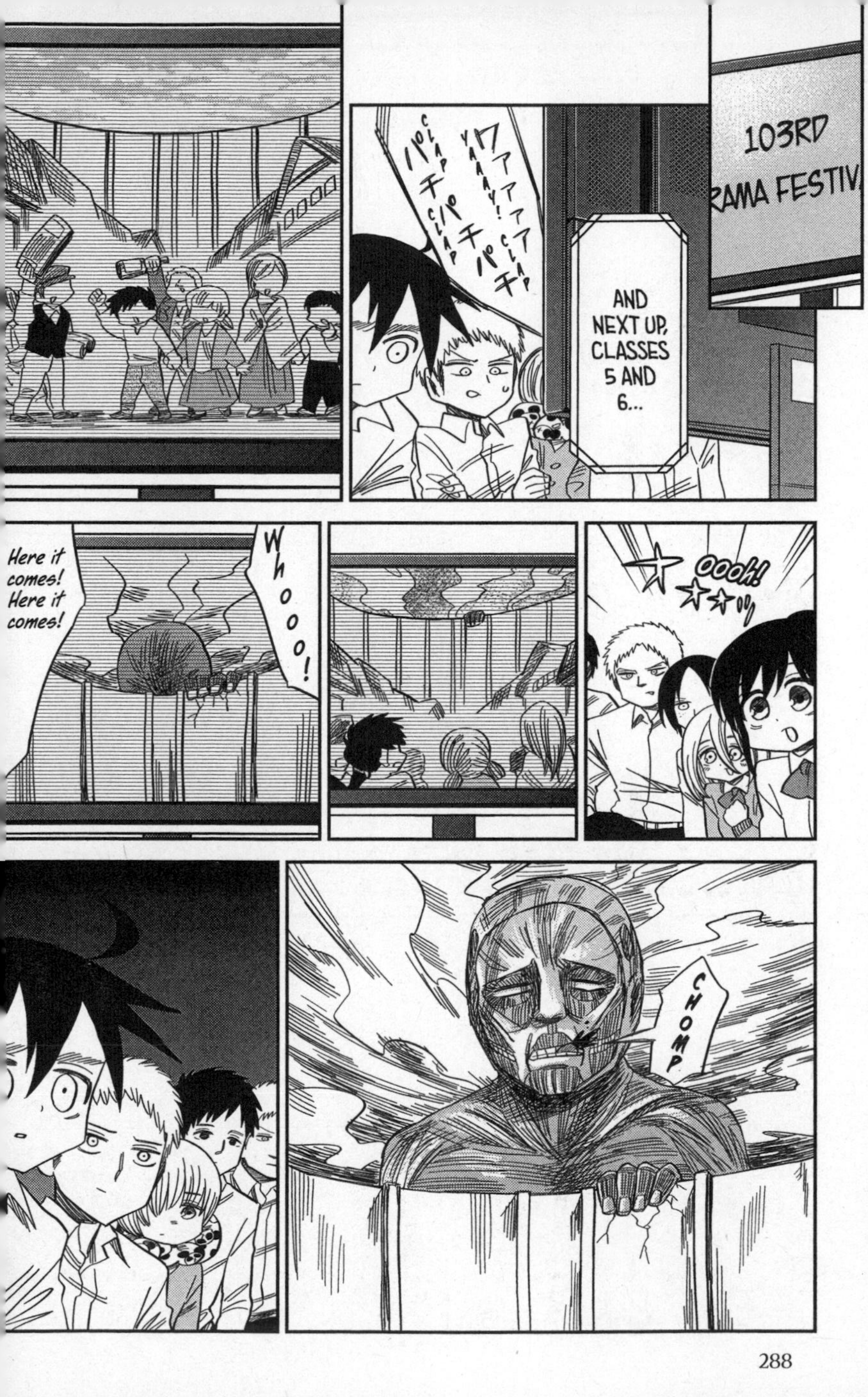
103RD
RAMA FESTIV
AND NEXT UP, CLASSES 5 AND 6...
ワァァァ YAAAAY!
パチパチパチパチ CLAP CLAP CLAP CLAP
Oooh!
Whoooo!
Here it comes! Here it comes!
CHOMP

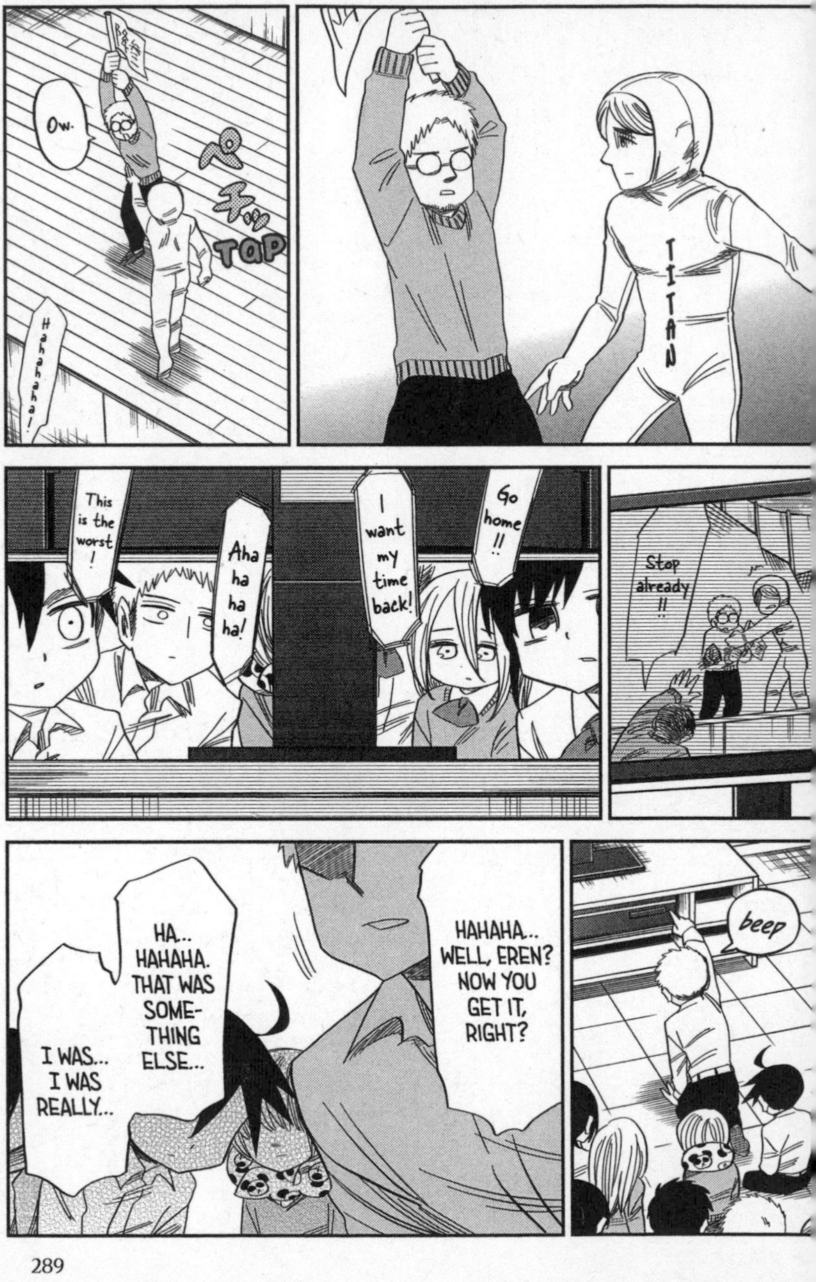
TITAN
Ow.
ペチッ
TAP
Hahahaha!
Stop already!!
Go home!!
I want my time back!
Aha ha ha ha!
This is the worst!
beep
HAHAHA.. WELL, EREN? NOW YOU GET IT, RIGHT?
HA.. HAHAHA. THAT WAS SOME-THING ELSE...
I WAS... I WAS REALLY...

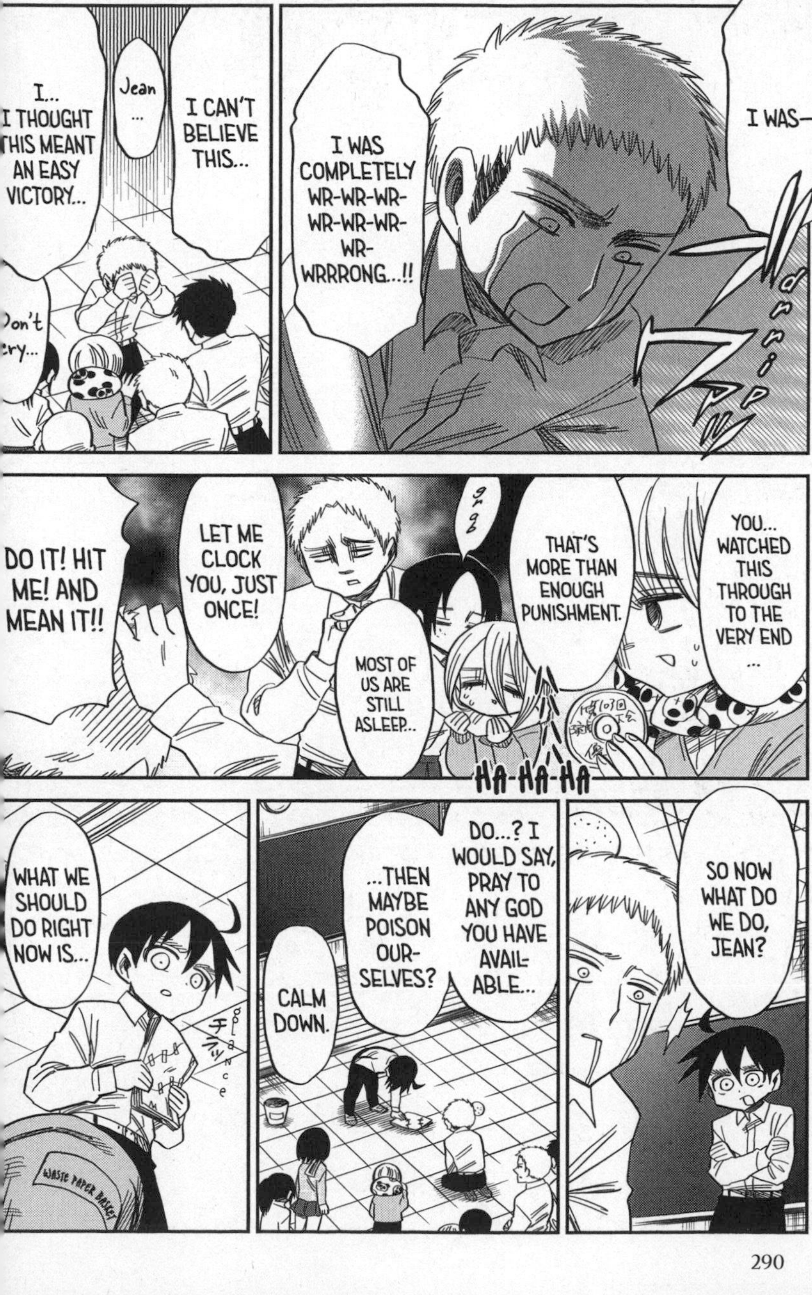
I WAS—
I WAS COMPLETELY WR-WR-WR-WR-WR-WR-WR-WRRRONG...!!
drrip
I CAN'T BELIEVE THIS...
Jean ...
I... I THOUGHT THIS MEANT AN EASY VICTORY...
YOU... WATCHED THIS THROUGH TO THE VERY END ...
THAT'S MORE THAN ENOUGH PUNISHMENT.
grab
MOST OF US ARE STILL ASLEEP...
LET ME CLOCK YOU, JUST ONCE!
DO IT! HIT ME! AND MEAN IT!!
HA-HA-HA
SO NOW WHAT DO WE DO, JEAN?
DO...? I WOULD SAY, PRAY TO ANY GOD YOU HAVE AVAIL-ABLE...
...THEN MAYBE POISON OUR-SELVES?
CALM DOWN.
WHAT WE SHOULD DO RIGHT NOW IS...
glance
WASTE PAPER BASKET

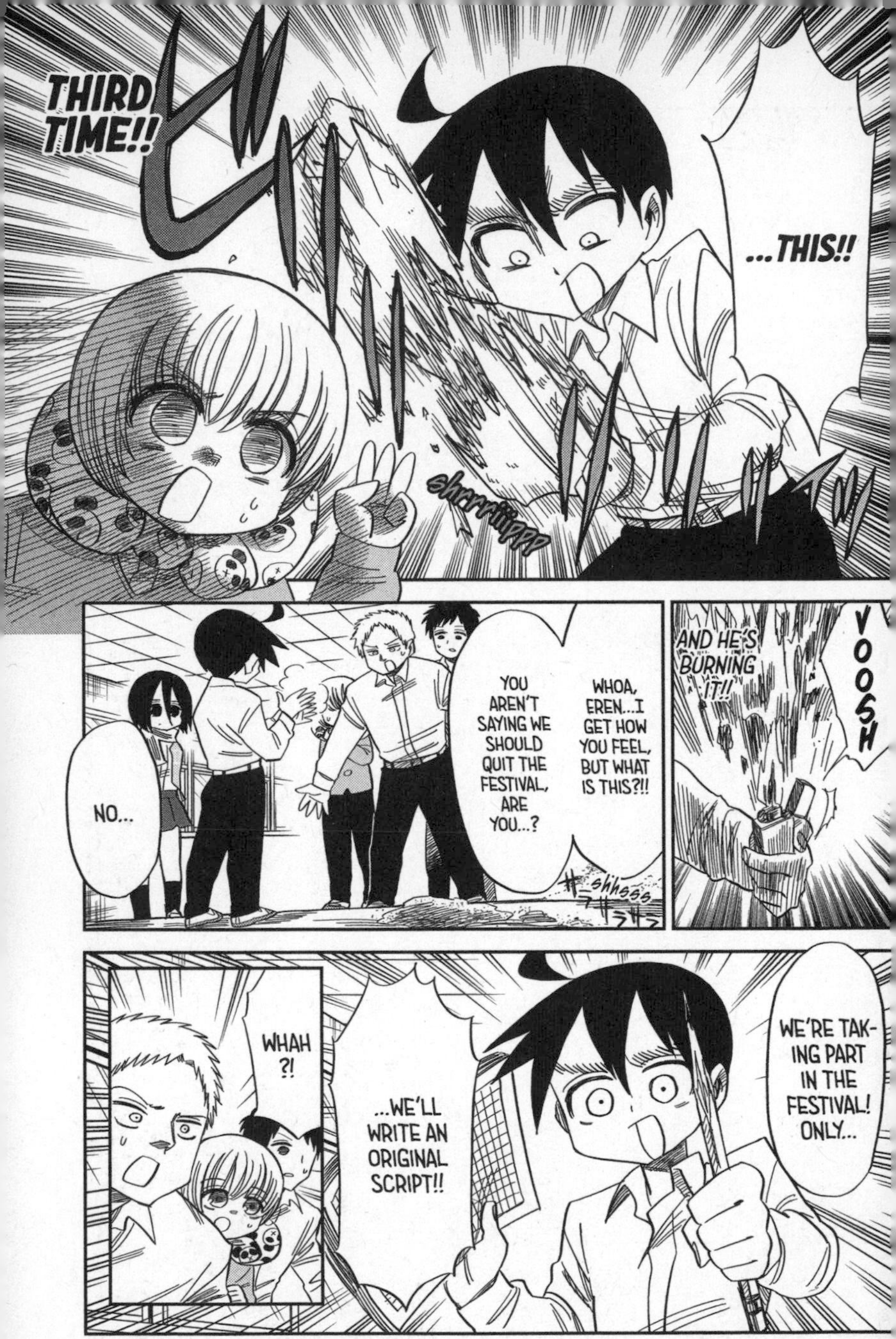
...THIS!!
shrrriiippp
THIRD TIME!!
AND HE'S BURNING IT!!
VOOSH
WHOA, EREN...I GET HOW YOU FEEL, BUT WHAT IS THIS?!!
YOU AREN'T SAYING WE SHOULD QUIT THE FESTIVAL, ARE YOU...?
shhsss
NO...
WE'RE TAKING PART IN THE FESTIVAL! ONLY...
...WE'LL WRITE AN ORIGINAL SCRIPT!!
WHAH?!

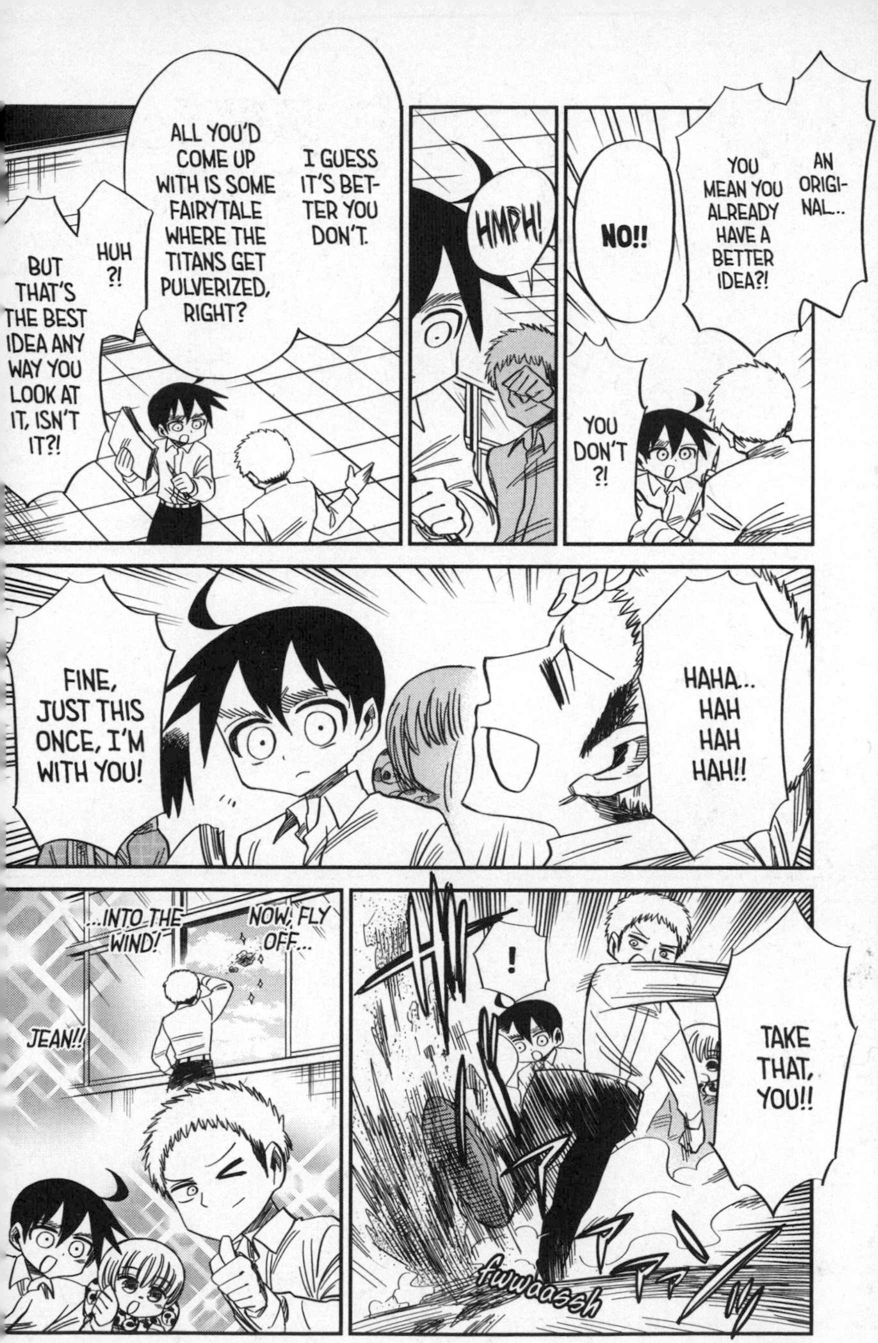
AN ORIGI-NAL...
YOU MEAN YOU ALREADY HAVE A BETTER IDEA?!
NO!!
YOU DON'T ?!
HMPH!
I GUESS IT'S BET-TER YOU DON'T.
ALL YOU'D COME UP WITH IS SOME FAIRYTALE WHERE THE TITANS GET PULVERIZED, RIGHT?
HUH ?!
BUT THAT'S THE BEST IDEA ANY WAY YOU LOOK AT IT, ISN'T IT?!
HAHA.. HAH HAH HAH!!
FINE, JUST THIS ONCE, I'M WITH YOU!
!
TAKE THAT, YOU!!
fwwaassh
NOW, FLY OFF...
...INTO THE WIND!
JEAN!!

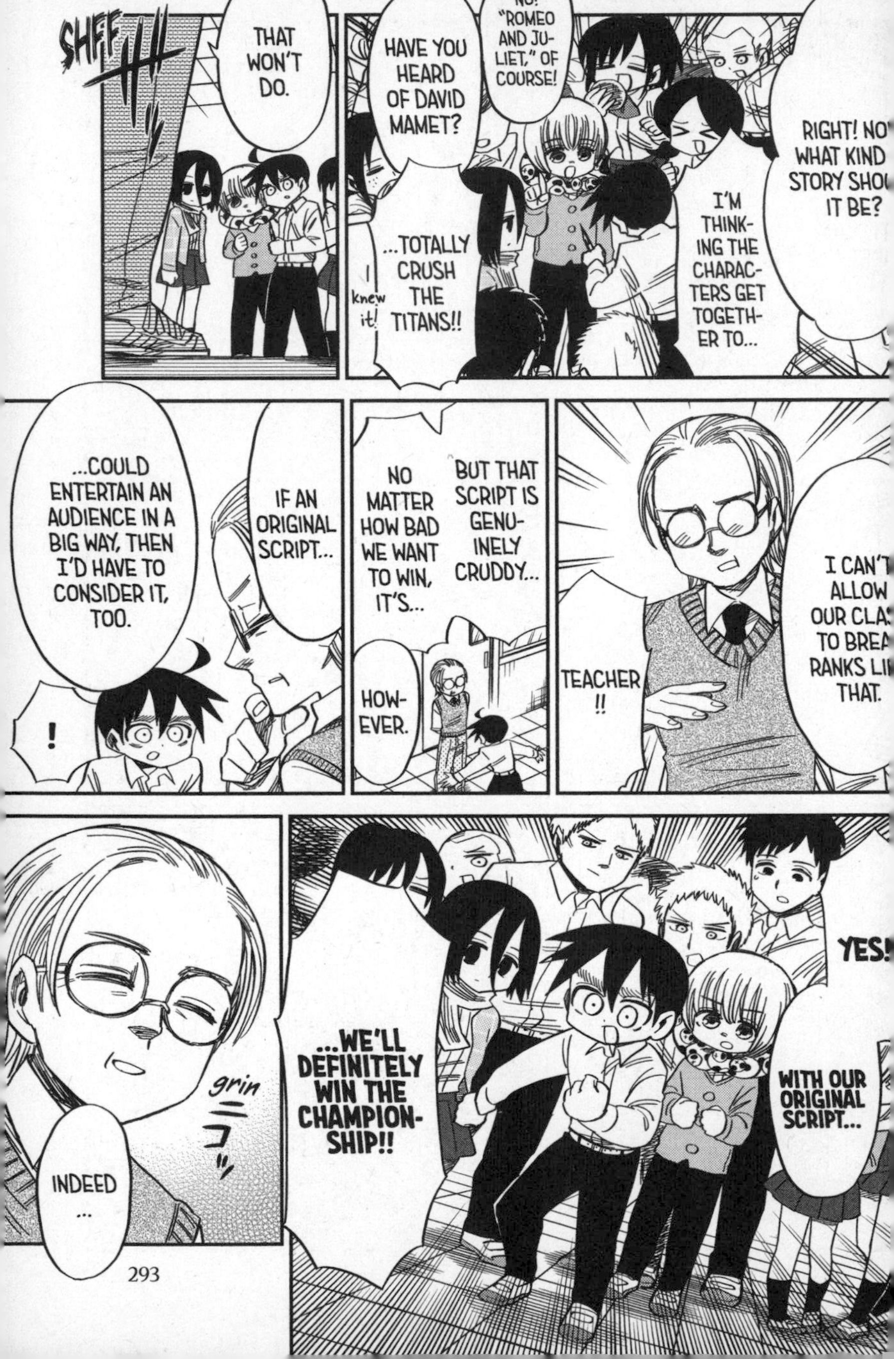

RIGHT! NO WHAT KIND STORY SHO IT BE?
I'M THINKING THE CHARACTERS GET TOGETHER TO...
NO! "ROMEO AND JULIET," OF COURSE!
HAVE YOU HEARD OF DAVID MAMET?
...TOTALLY CRUSH THE TITANS!!
I knew it!
SHFF
THAT WON'T DO.
I CAN'T ALLOW OUR CLA TO BREA RANKS LI THAT.
TEACHER!!
BUT THAT SCRIPT IS GENUINELY CRUDDY...
NO MATTER HOW BAD WE WANT TO WIN, IT'S...
HOWEVER.
IF AN ORIGINAL SCRIPT...
...COULD ENTERTAIN AN AUDIENCE IN A BIG WAY, THEN I'D HAVE TO CONSIDER IT, TOO.
!
YES!
WITH OUR ORIGINAL SCRIPT...
...WE'LL DEFINITELY WIN THE CHAMPIONSHIP!!
grin
INDEED...

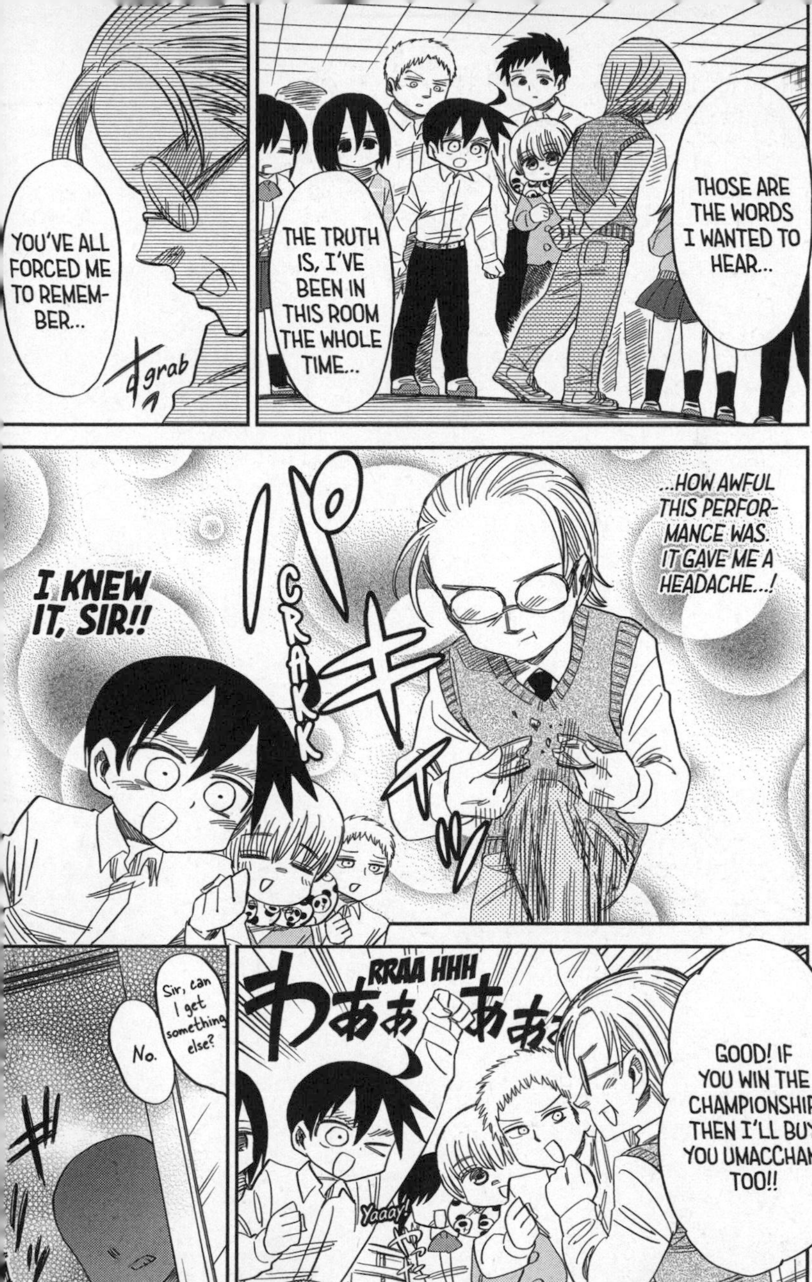
THOSE ARE THE WORDS I WANTED TO HEAR...
THE TRUTH IS, I'VE BEEN IN THIS ROOM THE WHOLE TIME...
YOU'VE ALL FORCED ME TO REMEMBER...
grab
...HOW AWFUL THIS PERFORMANCE WAS. IT GAVE ME A HEADACHE...!
CRAKK
I KNEW IT, SIR!!
RRAA HHH
GOOD! IF YOU WIN THE CHAMPIONSHIP, THEN I'LL BUY YOU UMACCHAN, TOO!!
Yaaay!
Sir, can I get something else?
No.

FIFTY-NINTH PERIOD: THE SHOW MUST GO ON

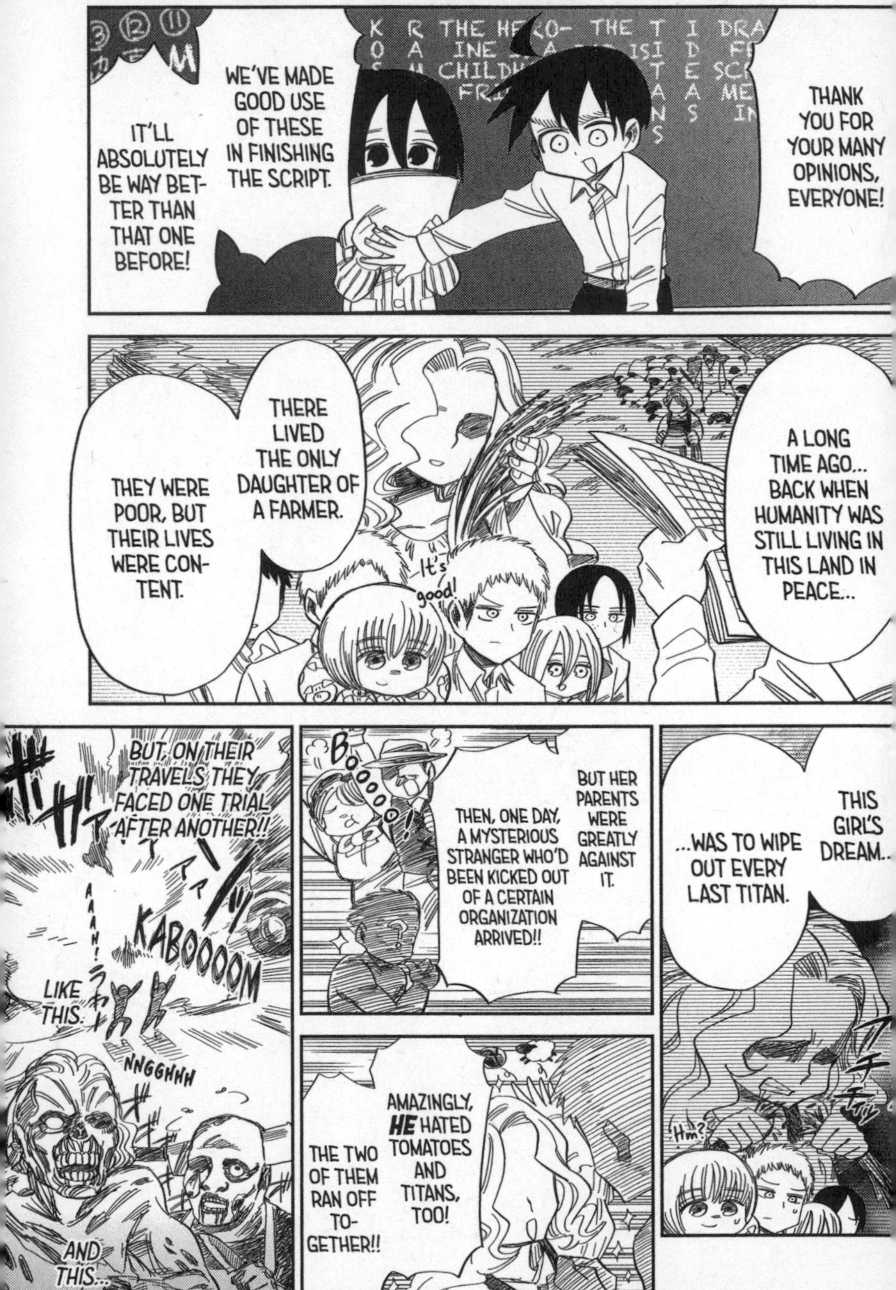
THANK YOU FOR YOUR MANY OPINIONS, EVERYONE!
WE'VE MADE GOOD USE OF THESE IN FINISHING THE SCRIPT.
IT'LL ABSOLUTELY BE WAY BETTER THAN THAT ONE BEFORE!
A LONG TIME AGO... BACK WHEN HUMANITY WAS STILL LIVING IN THIS LAND IN PEACE...
THERE LIVED THE ONLY DAUGHTER OF A FARMER.
THEY WERE POOR, BUT THEIR LIVES WERE CONTENT.
It's good!
THIS GIRL'S DREAM...
...WAS TO WIPE OUT EVERY LAST TITAN.
Hm?
BUT HER PARENTS WERE GREATLY AGAINST IT.
THEN, ONE DAY, A MYSTERIOUS STRANGER WHO'D BEEN KICKED OUT OF A CERTAIN ORGANIZATION ARRIVED!!
Booooo!
AMAZINGLY, HE HATED TOMATOES AND TITANS, TOO!
THE TWO OF THEM RAN OFF TO-GETHER!!
BUT, ON THEIR TRAVELS THEY FACED ONE TRIAL AFTER ANOTHER!!
KABOOOOM
AAAH!
LIKE THIS.
NNGGHHH
AND THIS...

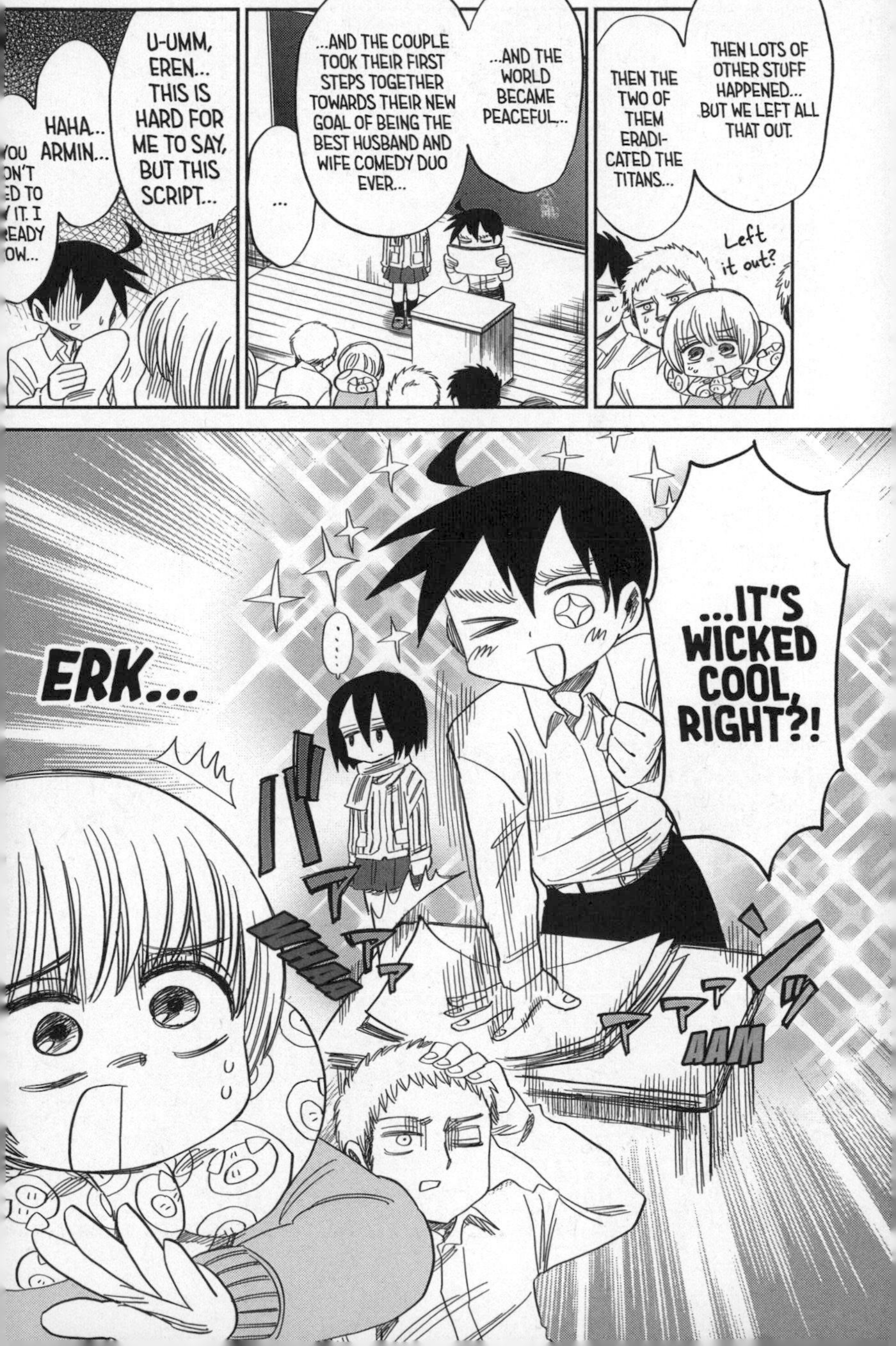
THEN LOTS OF OTHER STUFF HAPPENED... BUT WE LEFT ALL THAT OUT.
THEN THE TWO OF THEM ERADI-CATED THE TITANS...
Left it out?
...AND THE WORLD BECAME PEACEFUL...
...AND THE COUPLE TOOK THEIR FIRST STEPS TOGETHER TOWARDS THEIR NEW GOAL OF BEING THE BEST HUSBAND AND WIFE COMEDY DUO EVER...
...
U-UMM, EREN... THIS IS HARD FOR ME TO SAY, BUT THIS SCRIPT...
HAHA... ARMIN...
...IT'S WICKED COOL, RIGHT?!
ERK...
AAM

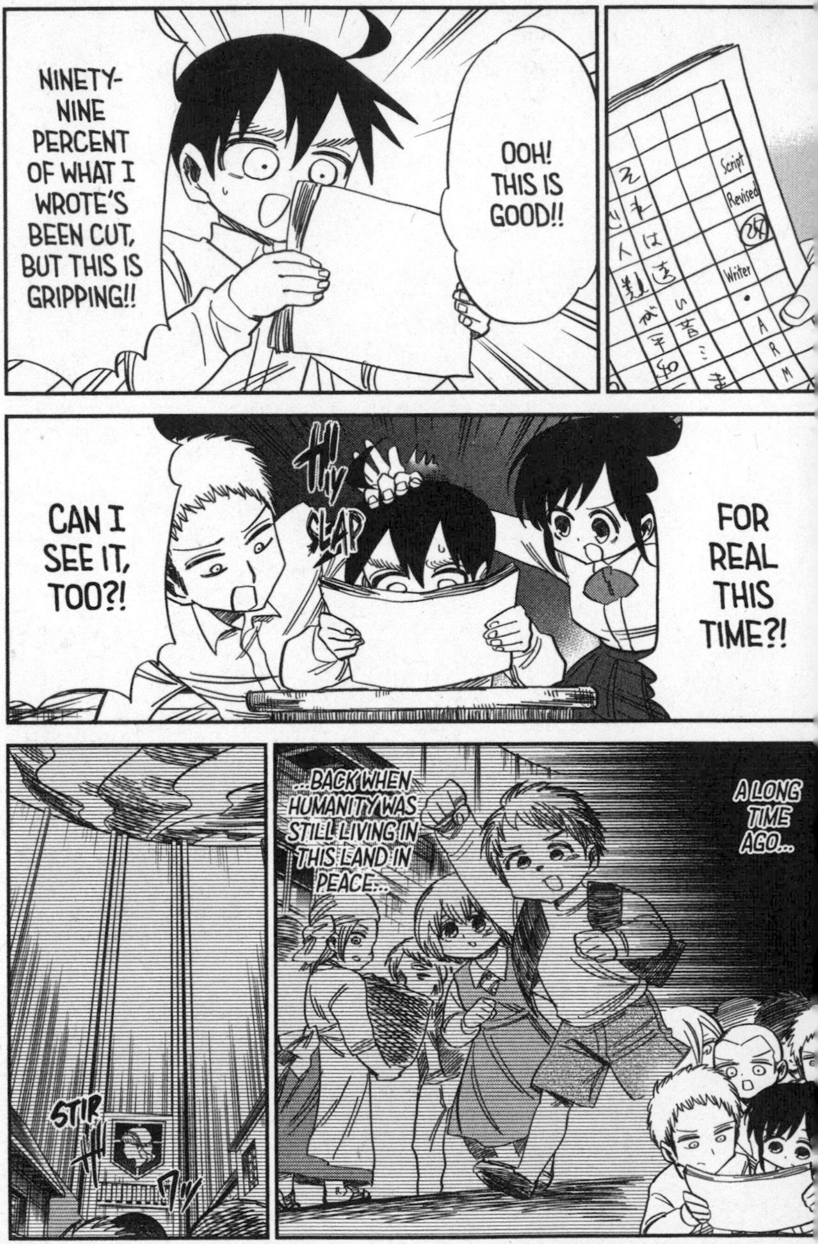
Script
Revised
Writer
OOH! THIS IS GOOD!!
NINETY-NINE PERCENT OF WHAT I WROTE'S BEEN CUT, BUT THIS IS GRIPPING!!
FOR REAL THIS TIME?!
SLAP
CAN I SEE IT, TOO?!
A LONG TIME AGO...
...BACK WHEN HUMANITY WAS STILL LIVING IN THIS LAND IN PEACE...
STIR

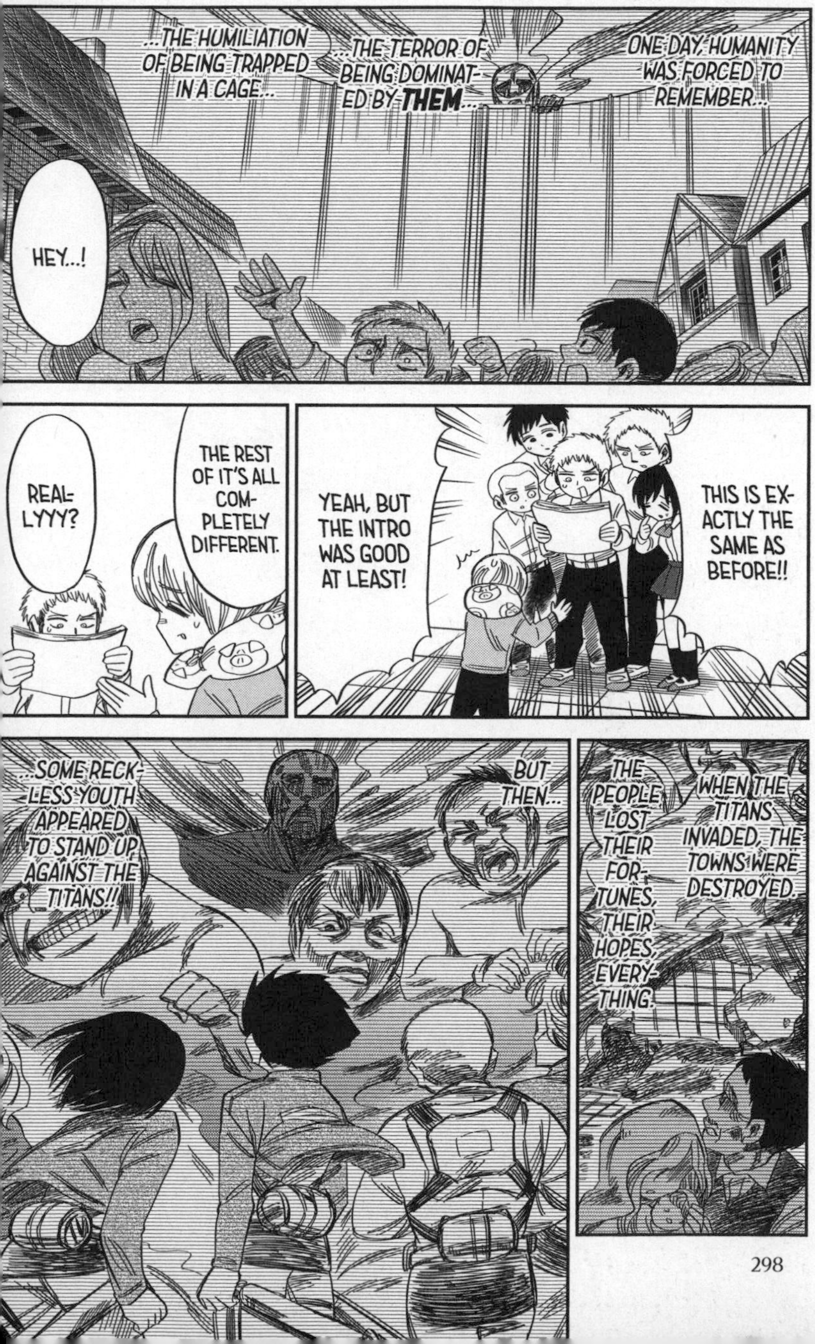
ONE DAY, HUMANITY WAS FORCED TO REMEMBER...
...THE TERROR OF BEING DOMINATED BY THEM...
...THE HUMILIATION OF BEING TRAPPED IN A CAGE...
HEY...!
THIS IS EXACTLY THE SAME AS BEFORE!!
YEAH, BUT THE INTRO WAS GOOD AT LEAST!
THE REST OF IT'S ALL COMPLETELY DIFFERENT.
REALLYYY?
WHEN THE TITANS INVADED, THE TOWNS WERE DESTROYED.
THE PEOPLE LOST THEIR FORTUNES, THEIR HOPES, EVERYTHING.
BUT THEN...
...SOME RECKLESS YOUTH APPEARED TO STAND UP AGAINST THE TITANS!!

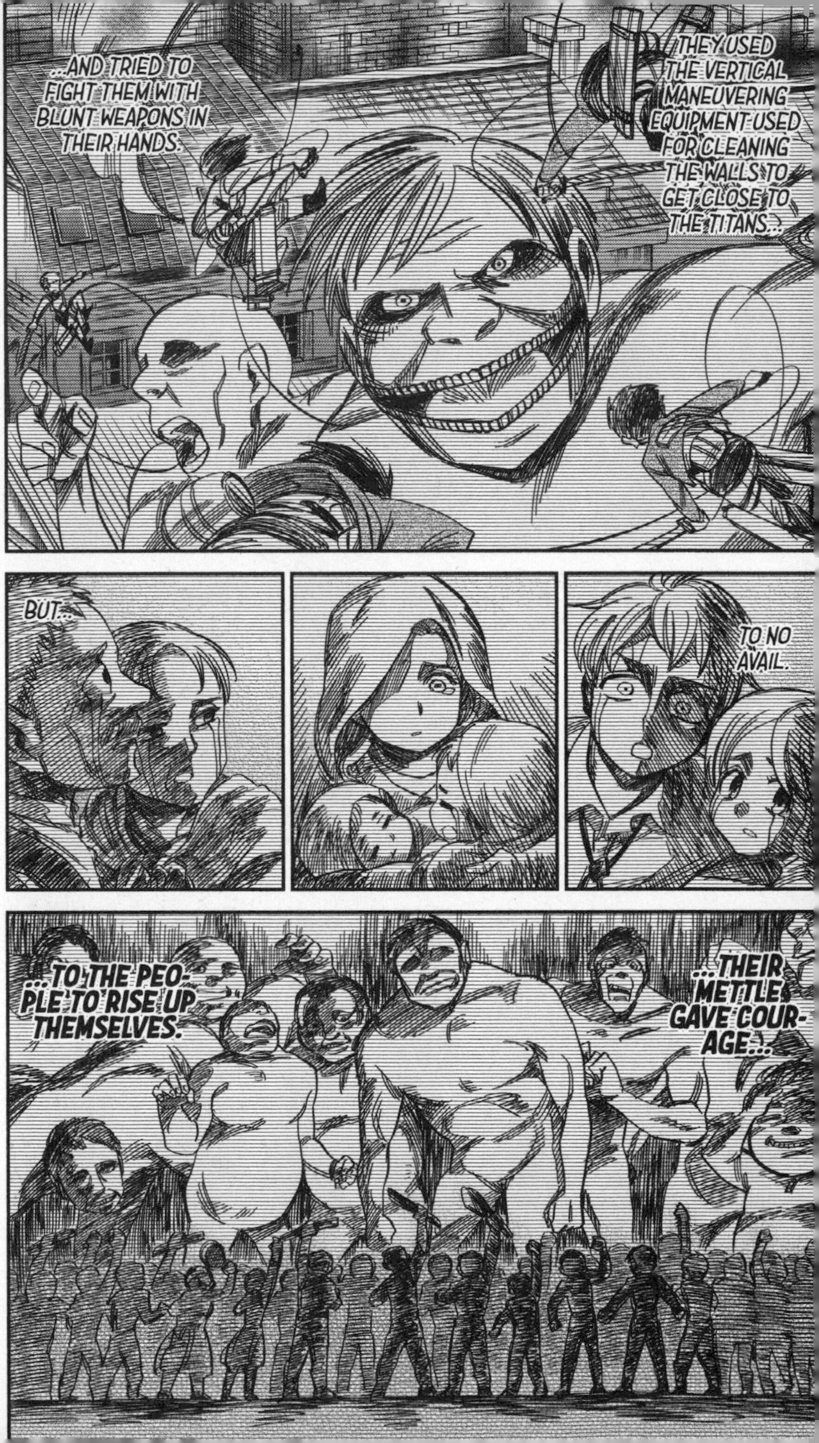
THEY USED THE VERTICAL MANEUVERING EQUIPMENT USED FOR CLEANING THE WALLS TO GET CLOSE TO THE TITANS...
...AND TRIED TO FIGHT THEM WITH BLUNT WEAPONS IN THEIR HANDS.
TO NO AVAIL.
BUT...
...THEIR METTLE GAVE COURAGE...
...TO THE PEOPLE TO RISE UP THEMSELVES.

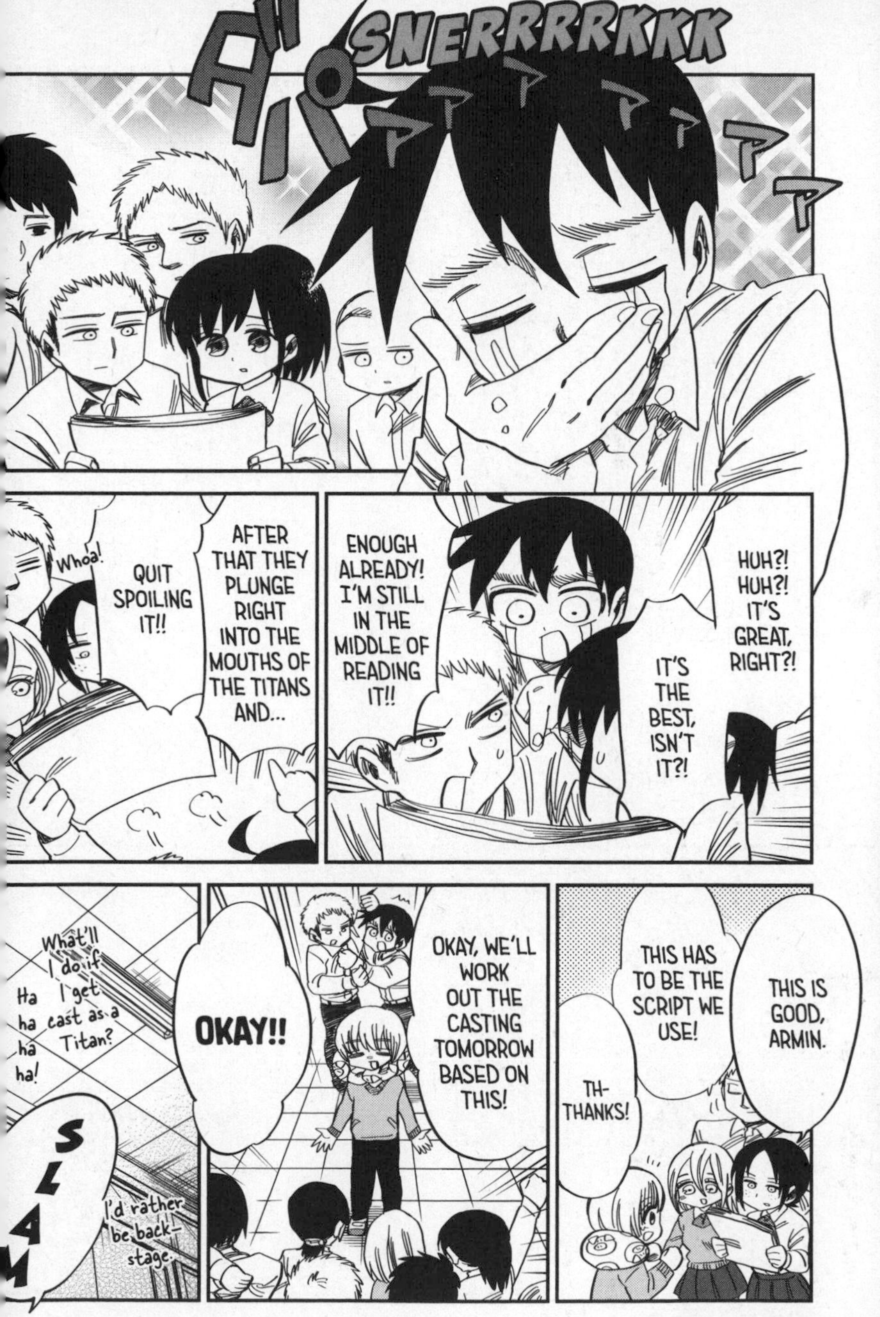
SNERRRRKKK
HUH?! HUH?! IT'S GREAT, RIGHT?!
IT'S THE BEST, ISN'T IT?!
ENOUGH ALREADY! I'M STILL IN THE MIDDLE OF READING IT!!
AFTER THAT THEY PLUNGE RIGHT INTO THE MOUTHS OF THE TITANS AND...
QUIT SPOILING IT!!
Whoa!
THIS IS GOOD, ARMIN.
THIS HAS TO BE THE SCRIPT WE USE!
TH-THANKS!
OKAY, WE'LL WORK OUT THE CASTING TOMORROW BASED ON THIS!
OKAY!!
What'll I do if I get cast as a Titan?
Ha ha ha ha!
SLAM
I'd rather be back-stage.

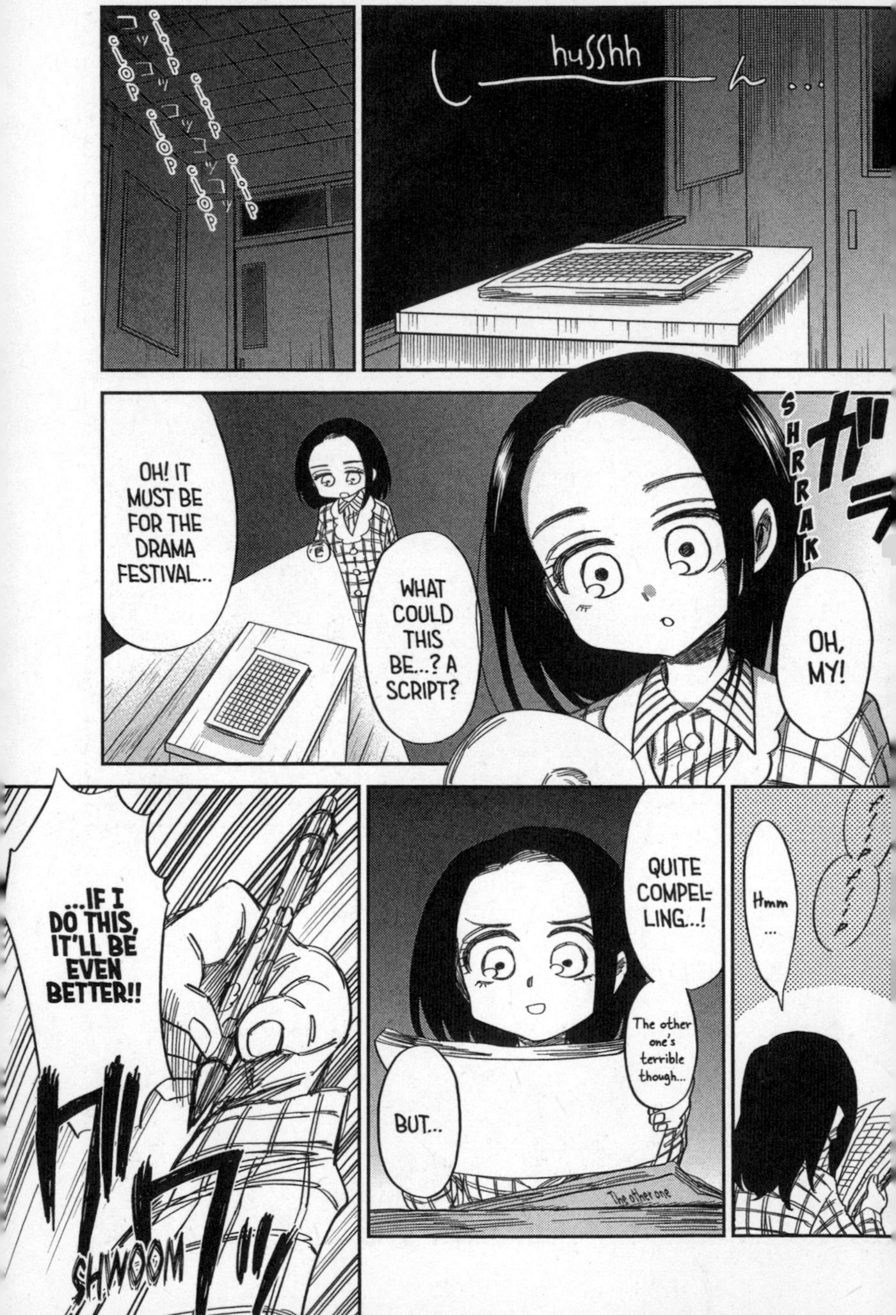

husshh
clop clop clop clop clop clop
SHRRAK
OH, MY!
WHAT COULD THIS BE...? A SCRIPT?
OH! IT MUST BE FOR THE DRAMA FESTIVAL...
Hmm ...
QUITE COMPEL-LING...!
The other one's terrible though...
BUT...
The other one
...IF I DO THIS, IT'LL BE EVEN BETTER!!
SHWOOM

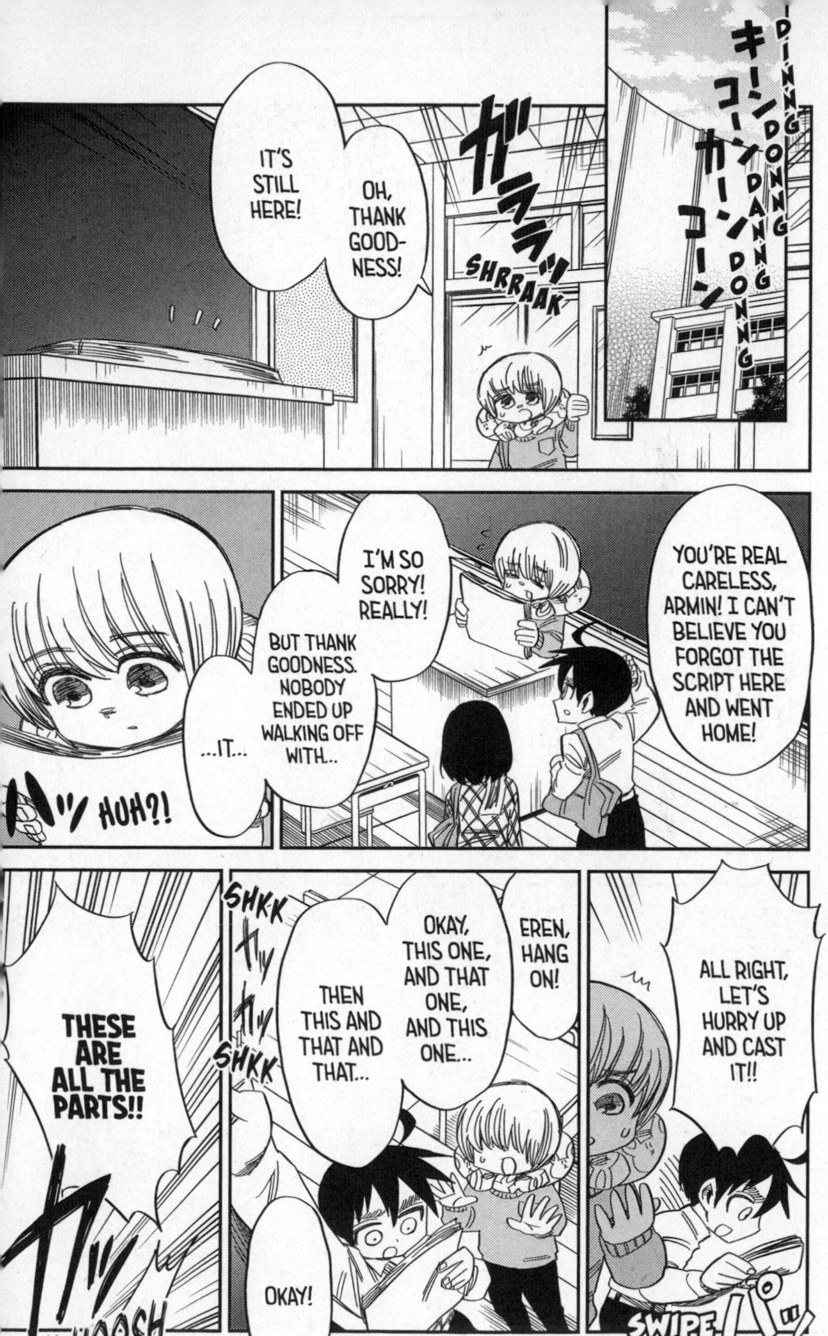
キーンコーンカーンコーン
DINNG DONNG DANG DONNG
ガラララッ
SHRRAAK
OH, THANK GOODNESS!
IT'S STILL HERE!
YOU'RE REAL CARELESS, ARMIN! I CAN'T BELIEVE YOU FORGOT THE SCRIPT HERE AND WENT HOME!
I'M SO SORRY! REALLY!
BUT THANK GOODNESS. NOBODY ENDED UP WALKING OFF WITH...
...IT...
ハッ
HUH?!
ALL RIGHT, LET'S HURRY UP AND CAST IT!!
パッ
SWIPE
EREN, HANG ON!
OKAY, THIS ONE, AND THAT ONE, AND THIS ONE...
THEN THIS AND THAT AND THAT...
SHKK
ガッ ガッ
SHKK
OKAY!
THESE ARE ALL THE PARTS!!
ガッ
WHOOSH

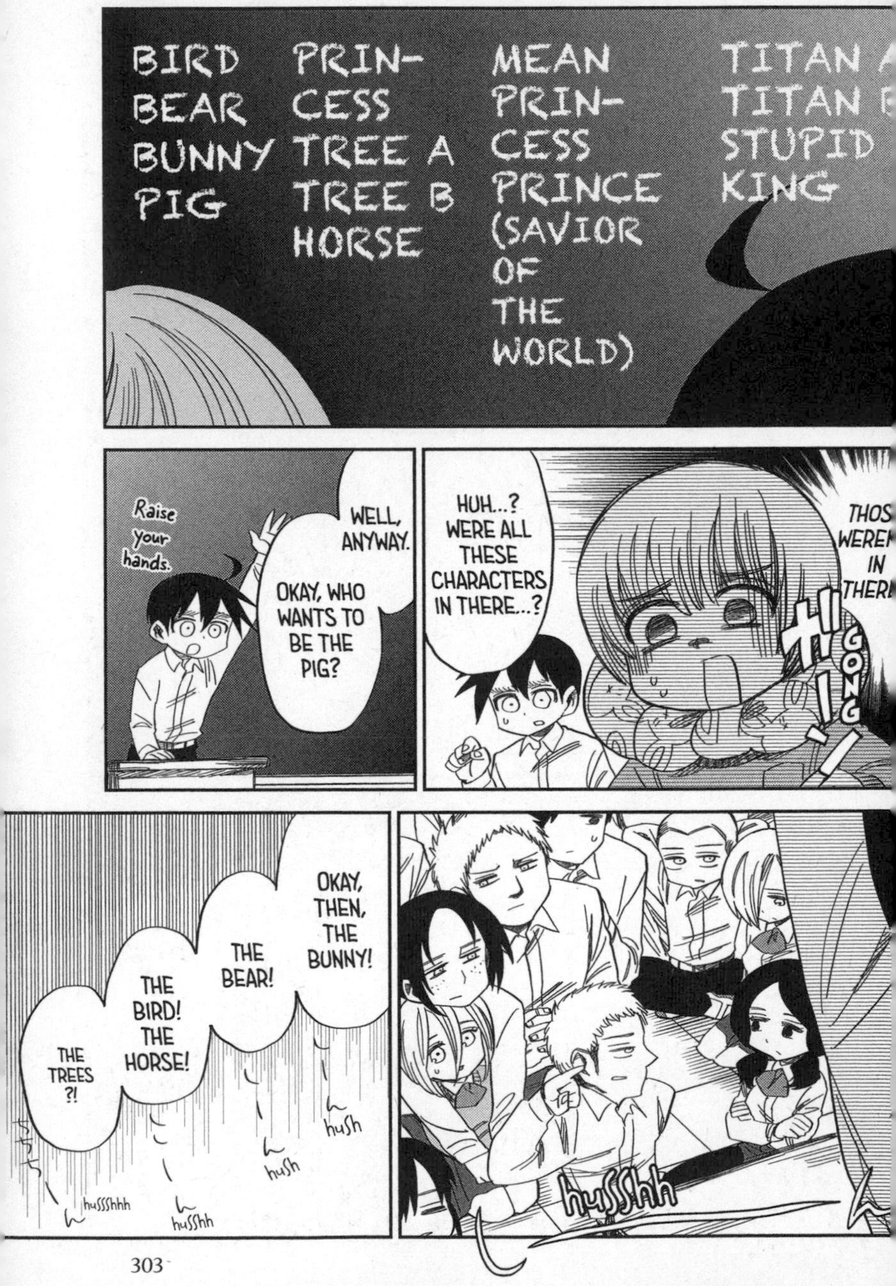

BIRD
BEAR
BUNNY
PIG
PRIN-
CESS
TREE A
TREE B
HORSE
MEAN
PRIN-
CESS
PRINCE
(SAVIOR
OF
THE
WORLD)
TITAN
TITAN
STUPID
KING
THOS
WERE
IN
THER
GONG!
HUH...? WERE ALL THESE CHARACTERS IN THERE...?
WELL, ANYWAY.
OKAY, WHO WANTS TO BE THE PIG?
Raise your hands.
hussshh
OKAY, THEN, THE BUNNY!
THE BEAR!
THE BIRD! THE HORSE!
THE TREES ?!
hush
hush
husshh
hussshhh

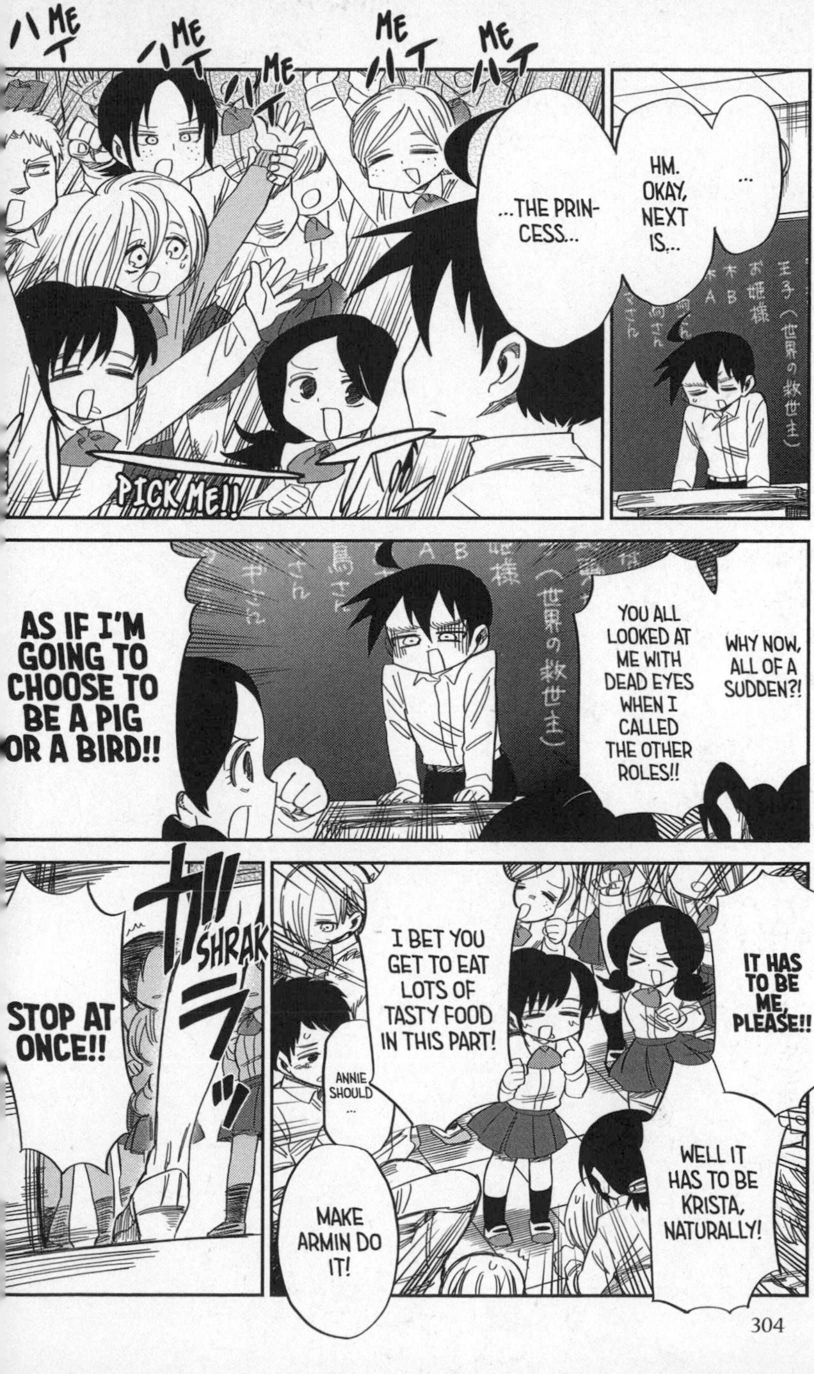
HM. OKAY, NEXT IS...
...
...THE PRIN-CESS...
ME ハイ
ME ハイ
ME ハイ
ME ハイ
ME ハイ
PICK ME!!
WHY NOW, ALL OF A SUDDEN?!
YOU ALL LOOKED AT ME WITH DEAD EYES WHEN I CALLED THE OTHER ROLES!!
AS IF I'M GOING TO CHOOSE TO BE A PIG OR A BIRD!!
IT HAS TO BE ME, PLEASE!!
I BET YOU GET TO EAT LOTS OF TASTY FOOD IN THIS PART!
WELL IT HAS TO BE KRISTA, NATURALLY!
ANNIE SHOULD ...
MAKE ARMIN DO IT!
ガラッ SHRAK
STOP AT ONCE!!

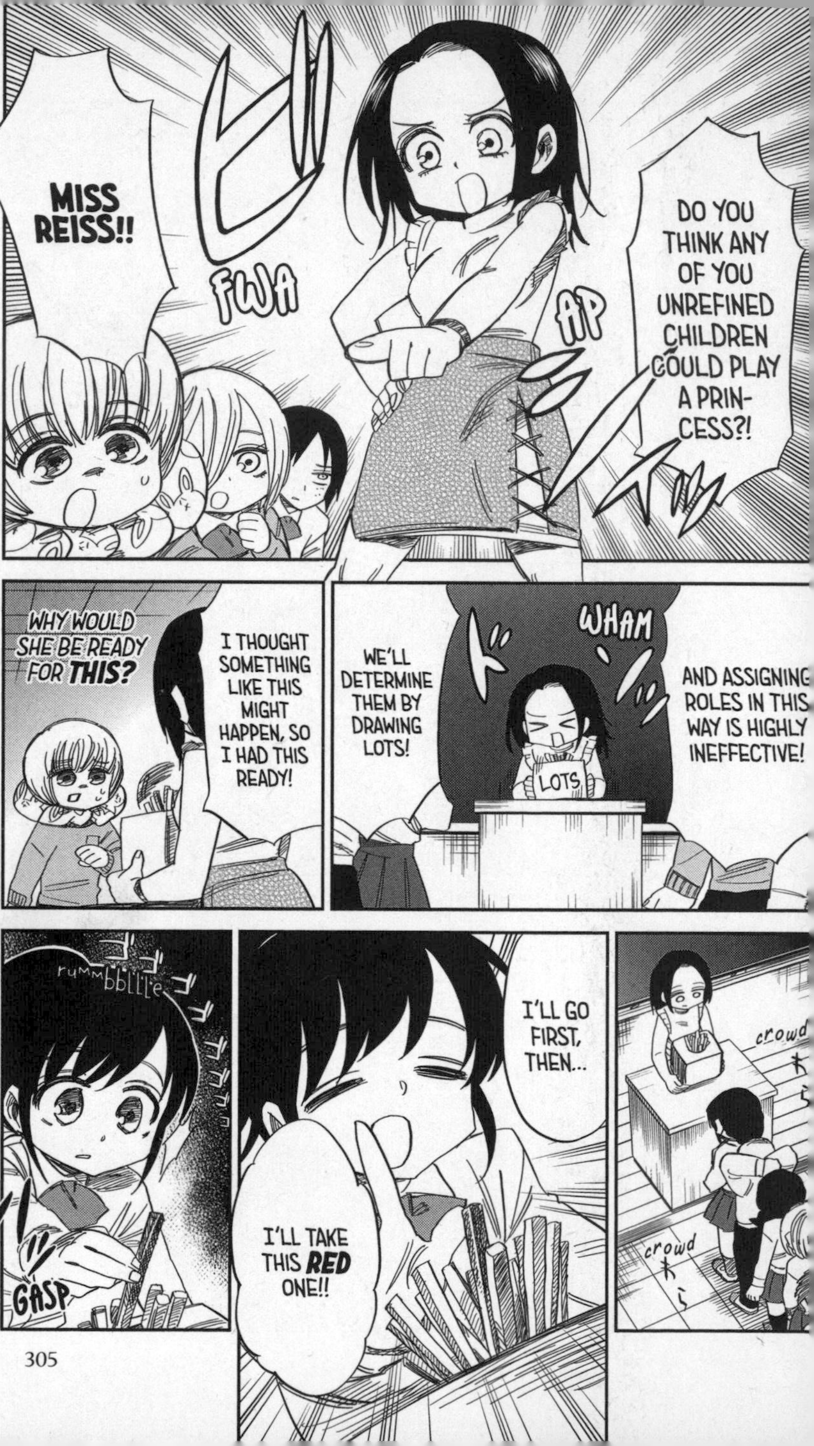
DO YOU THINK ANY OF YOU UNREFINED CHILDREN COULD PLAY A PRINCESS?!
FWA
AP
MISS REISS!!
AND ASSIGNING ROLES IN THIS WAY IS HIGHLY INEFFECTIVE!
WHAM
WE'LL DETERMINE THEM BY DRAWING LOTS!
LOTS
I THOUGHT SOMETHING LIKE THIS MIGHT HAPPEN, SO I HAD THIS READY!
WHY WOULD SHE BE READY FOR **THIS?**
crowd
crowd
I'LL GO FIRST, THEN...
I'LL TAKE THIS **RED** ONE!!
rummbbllle
GASP

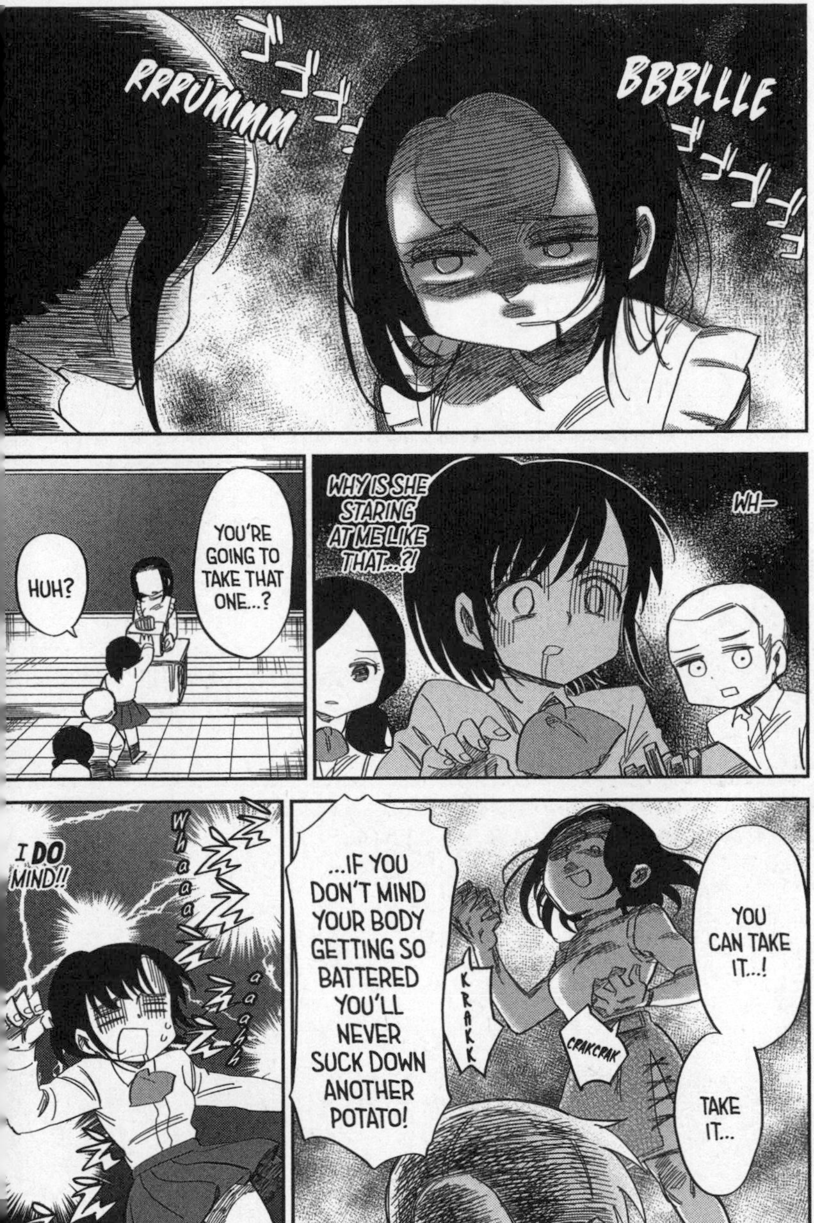
BBBLLLE
RRRUMMMM
WH—
WHY IS SHE STARING AT ME LIKE THAT...?!
YOU'RE GOING TO TAKE THAT ONE...?
HUH?
YOU CAN TAKE IT...!
TAKE IT...
CRAKCRAK
KRAKK
...IF YOU DON'T MIND YOUR BODY GETTING SO BATTERED YOU'LL NEVER SUCK DOWN ANOTHER POTATO!
Whaaaa aaahh
I DO MIND!!

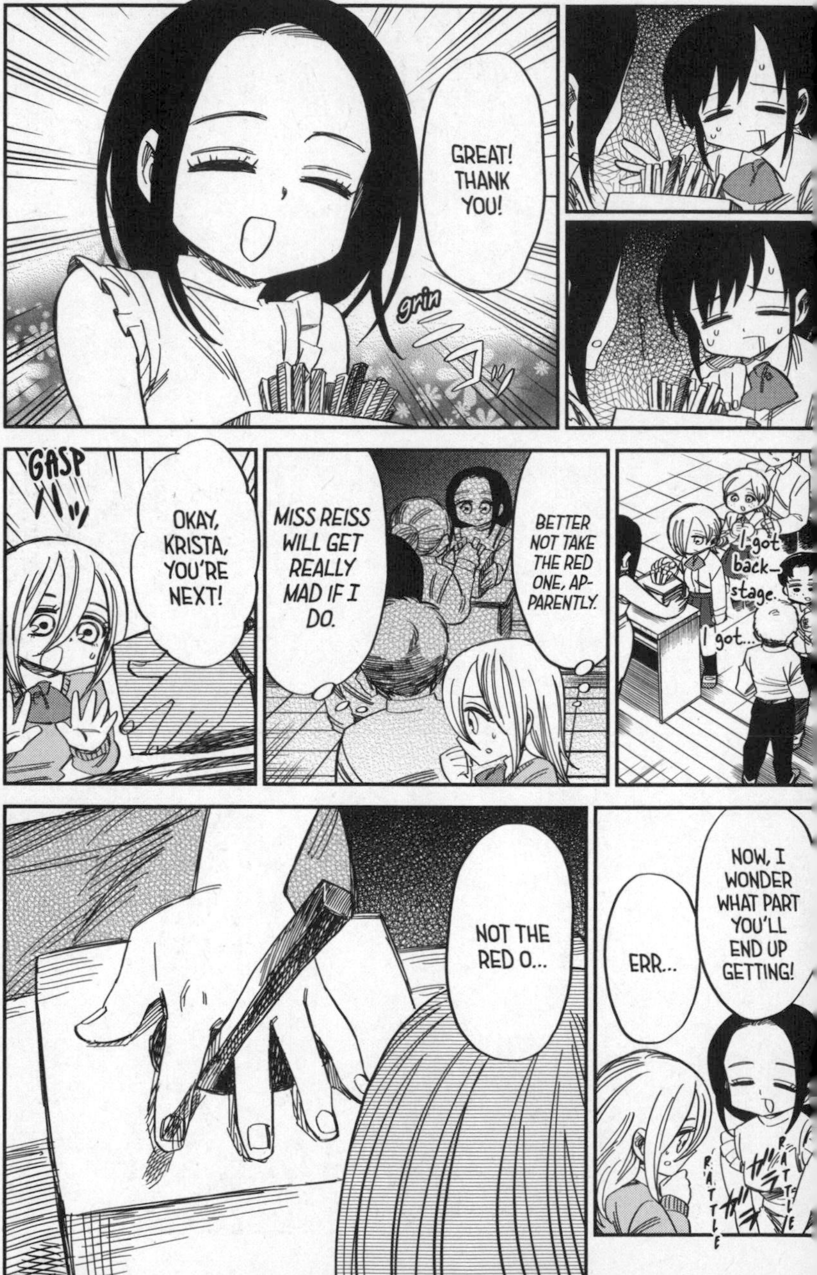
GREAT! THANK YOU!
grin
I got back-stage...
I got...
BETTER NOT TAKE THE RED ONE, APPARENTLY.
MISS REISS WILL GET REALLY MAD IF I DO.
GASP
OKAY, KRISTA, YOU'RE NEXT!
NOW, I WONDER WHAT PART YOU'LL END UP GETTING!
ERR...
RATTLE
RATTLE
NOT THE RED O...

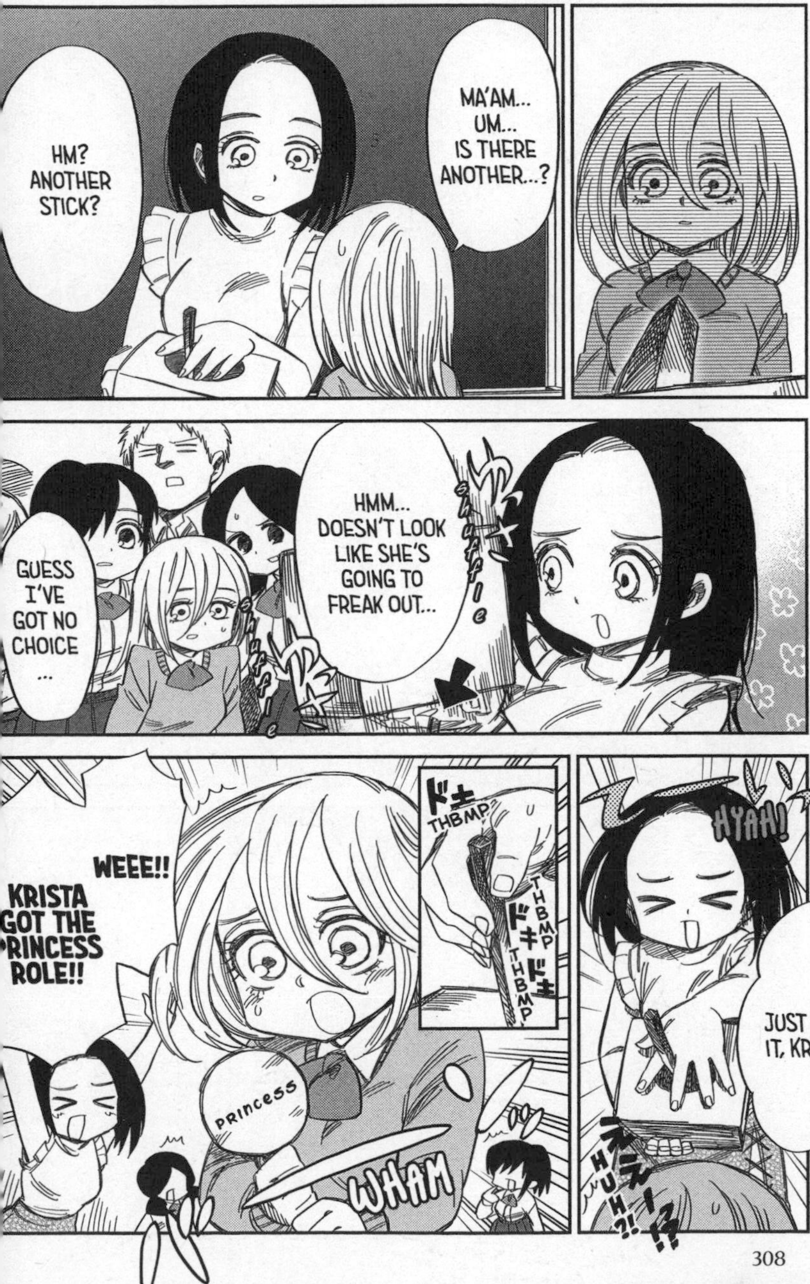
MA'AM... UM... IS THERE ANOTHER...?
HM? ANOTHER STICK?
HMM... DOESN'T LOOK LIKE SHE'S GOING TO FREAK OUT...
GUESS I'VE GOT NO CHOICE ...
HYAH!
JUST TAKE IT, KRISTA!
HUH?!!?
ドキ THBMP
ドキ THBMP
ドキ THBMP
WEEE!!
KRISTA GOT THE PRINCESS ROLE!!
Princess
WHAM

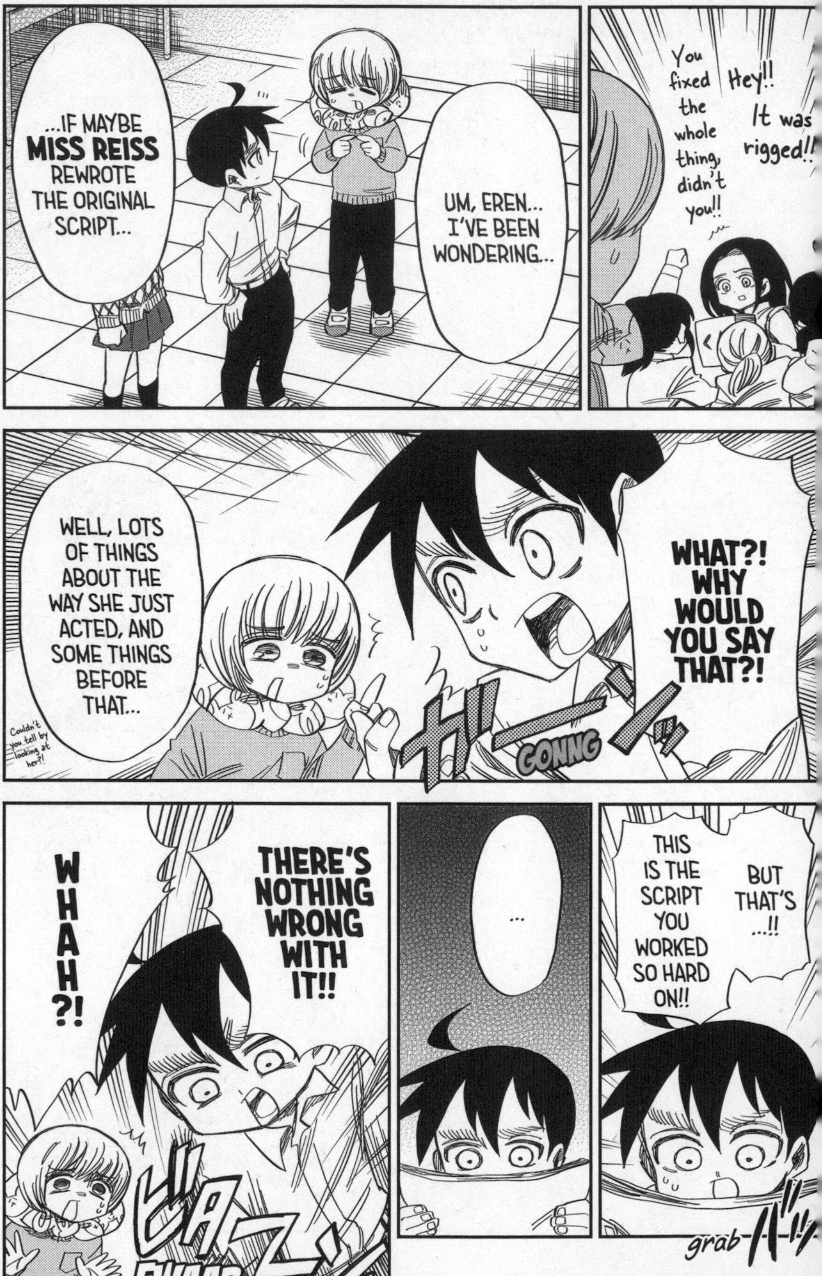
Hey!! It was rigged!!
You fixed the whole thing, didn't you!!
UM, EREN... I'VE BEEN WONDERING...
...IF MAYBE MISS REISS REWROTE THE ORIGINAL SCRIPT...
WHAT?! WHY WOULD YOU SAY THAT?!
GONNG
WELL, LOTS OF THINGS ABOUT THE WAY SHE JUST ACTED, AND SOME THINGS BEFORE THAT...
Couldn't you tell by looking at her?!
BUT THAT'S ...!!
THIS IS THE SCRIPT YOU WORKED SO HARD ON!!
grab
...
THERE'S NOTHING WRONG WITH IT!!
WHAAH?!
FWAAP

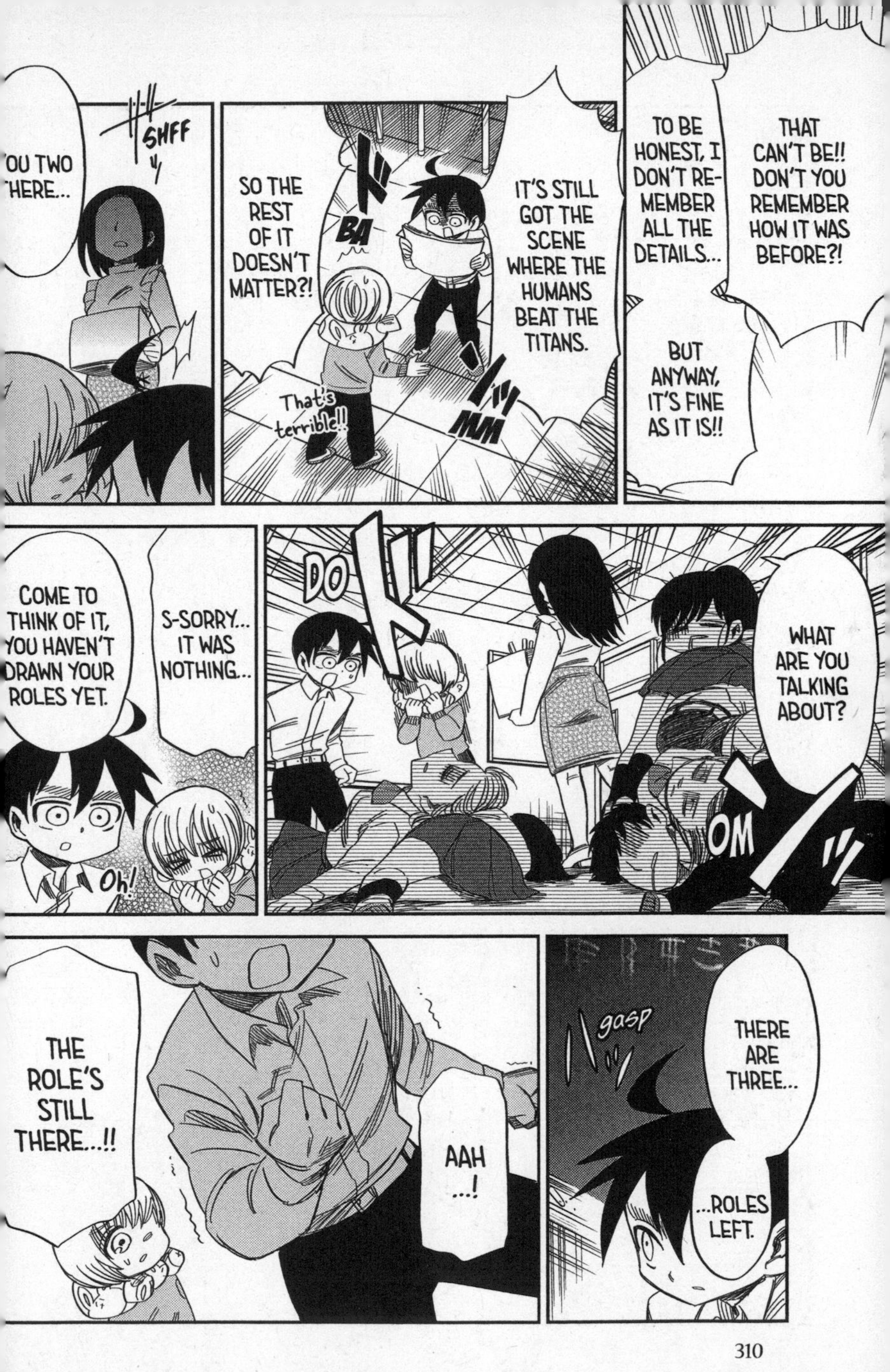
THAT CAN'T BE!! DON'T YOU REMEMBER HOW IT WAS BEFORE?!
TO BE HONEST, I DON'T RE-MEMBER ALL THE DETAILS...
BUT ANYWAY, IT'S FINE AS IT IS!!
IT'S STILL GOT THE SCENE WHERE THE HUMANS BEAT THE TITANS.
SO THE REST OF IT DOESN'T MATTER?!
BA
MM
That's terrible!!
SHFF
OU TWO HERE...
WHAT ARE YOU TALKING ABOUT?
DO
OM
S-SORRY... IT WAS NOTHING...
COME TO THINK OF IT, YOU HAVEN'T DRAWN YOUR ROLES YET.
Oh!
gasp
THERE ARE THREE...
...ROLES LEFT.
AAH ...!
THE ROLE'S STILL THERE...!!

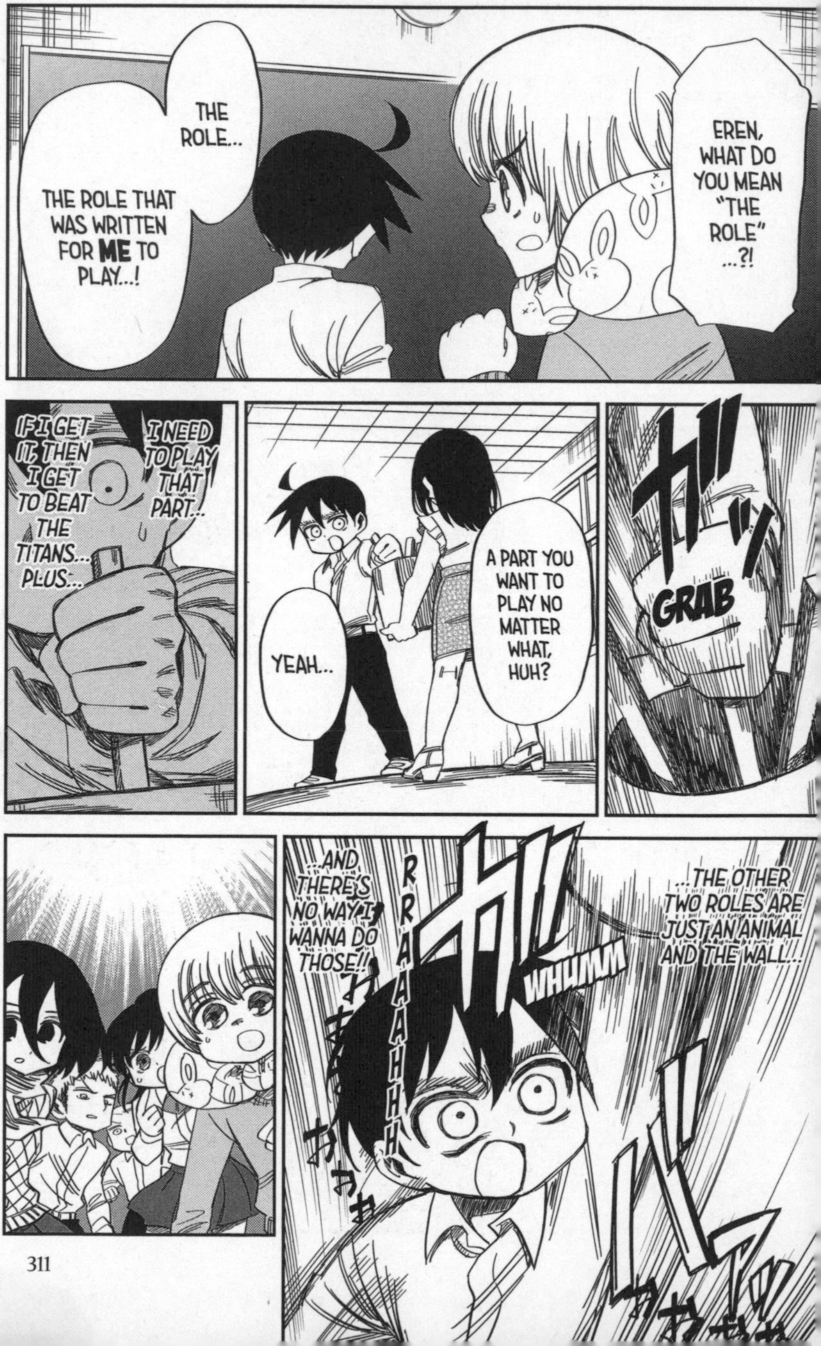
EREN, WHAT DO YOU MEAN "THE ROLE" ...?!
THE ROLE...
THE ROLE THAT WAS WRITTEN FOR **ME** TO PLAY...!
GRAB
A PART YOU WANT TO PLAY NO MATTER WHAT, HUH?
YEAH...
I NEED TO PLAY THAT PART...
IF I GET IT, THEN I GET TO BEAT THE TITANS... PLUS...
...THE OTHER TWO ROLES ARE JUST AN ANIMAL AND THE WALL...
WHUMM
...AND THERE'S NO WAY I WANNA DO THOSE!!
RRAAAAHHHH!!

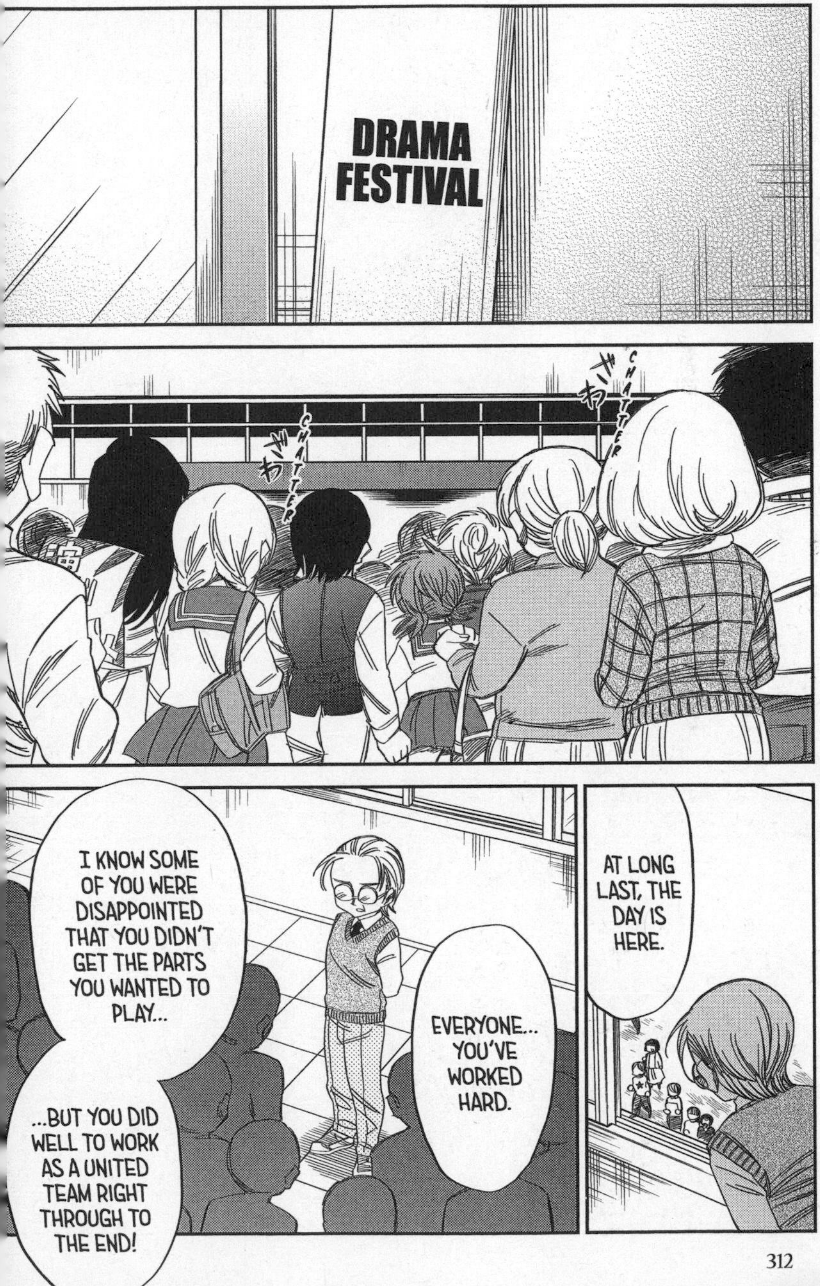
DRAMA FESTIVAL
CHATTER
CHATTER
AT LONG LAST, THE DAY IS HERE.
EVERYONE... YOU'VE WORKED HARD.
I KNOW SOME OF YOU WERE DISAPPOINTED THAT YOU DIDN'T GET THE PARTS YOU WANTED TO PLAY...
...BUT YOU DID WELL TO WORK AS A UNITED TEAM RIGHT THROUGH TO THE END!

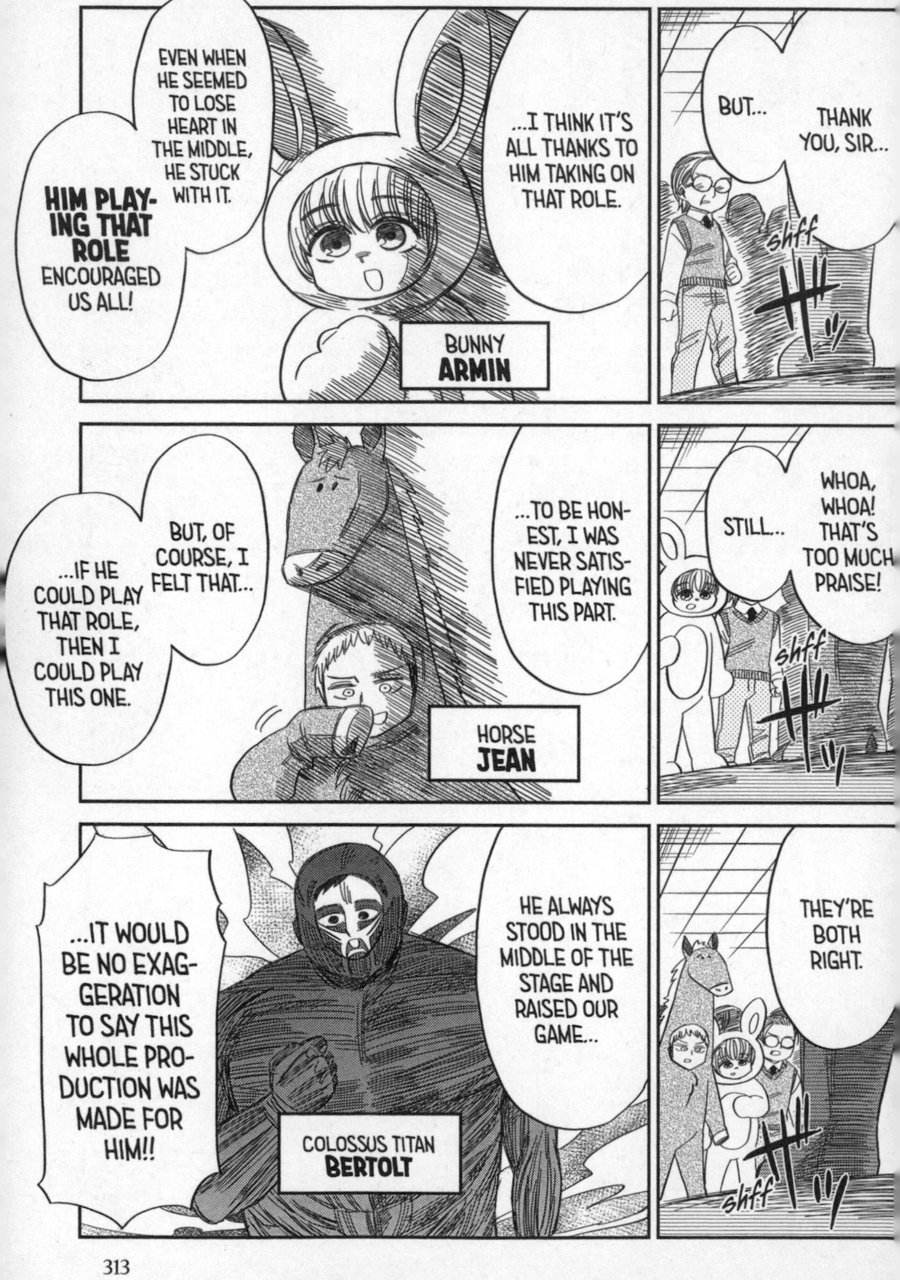
THANK YOU, SIR...
BUT...
shff
...I THINK IT'S ALL THANKS TO HIM TAKING ON THAT ROLE.
EVEN WHEN HE SEEMED TO LOSE HEART IN THE MIDDLE, HE STUCK WITH IT.
HIM PLAYING THAT ROLE ENCOURAGED US ALL!
BUNNY ARMIN
WHOA, WHOA! THAT'S TOO MUCH PRAISE!
STILL...
shff
...TO BE HONEST, I WAS NEVER SATISFIED PLAYING THIS PART.
BUT, OF COURSE, I FELT THAT...
...IF HE COULD PLAY THAT ROLE, THEN I COULD PLAY THIS ONE.
HORSE JEAN
THEY'RE BOTH RIGHT.
shff
HE ALWAYS STOOD IN THE MIDDLE OF THE STAGE AND RAISED OUR GAME...
...IT WOULD BE NO EXAGGERATION TO SAY THIS WHOLE PRODUCTION WAS MADE FOR HIM!!
COLOSSUS TITAN BERTOLT

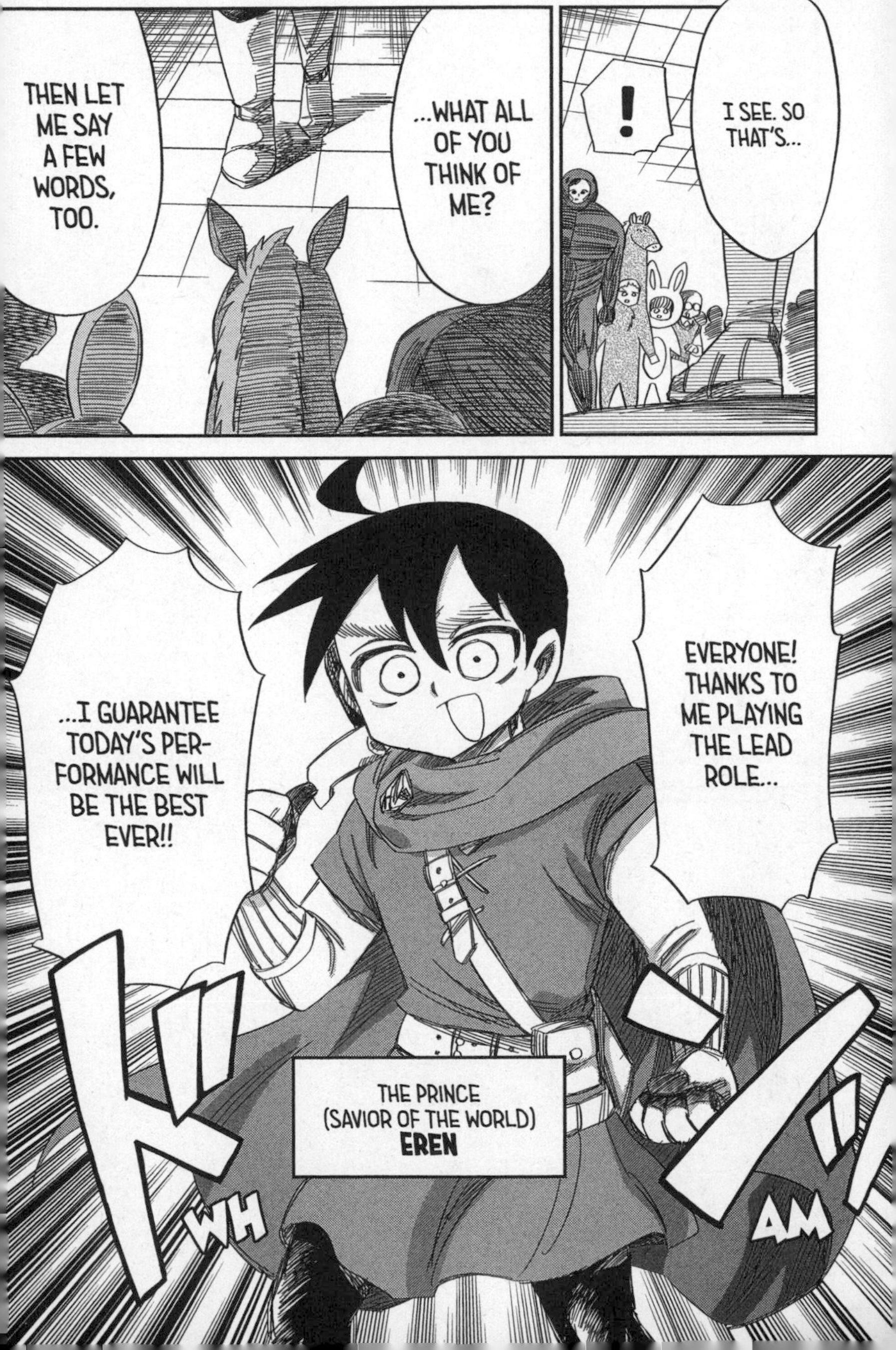
I SEE. SO THAT'S...
!
...WHAT ALL OF YOU THINK OF ME?
THEN LET ME SAY A FEW WORDS, TOO.
EVERYONE! THANKS TO ME PLAYING THE LEAD ROLE...
...I GUARANTEE TODAY'S PER-FORMANCE WILL BE THE BEST EVER!!
THE PRINCE
(SAVIOR OF THE WORLD)
EREN
WH
AM

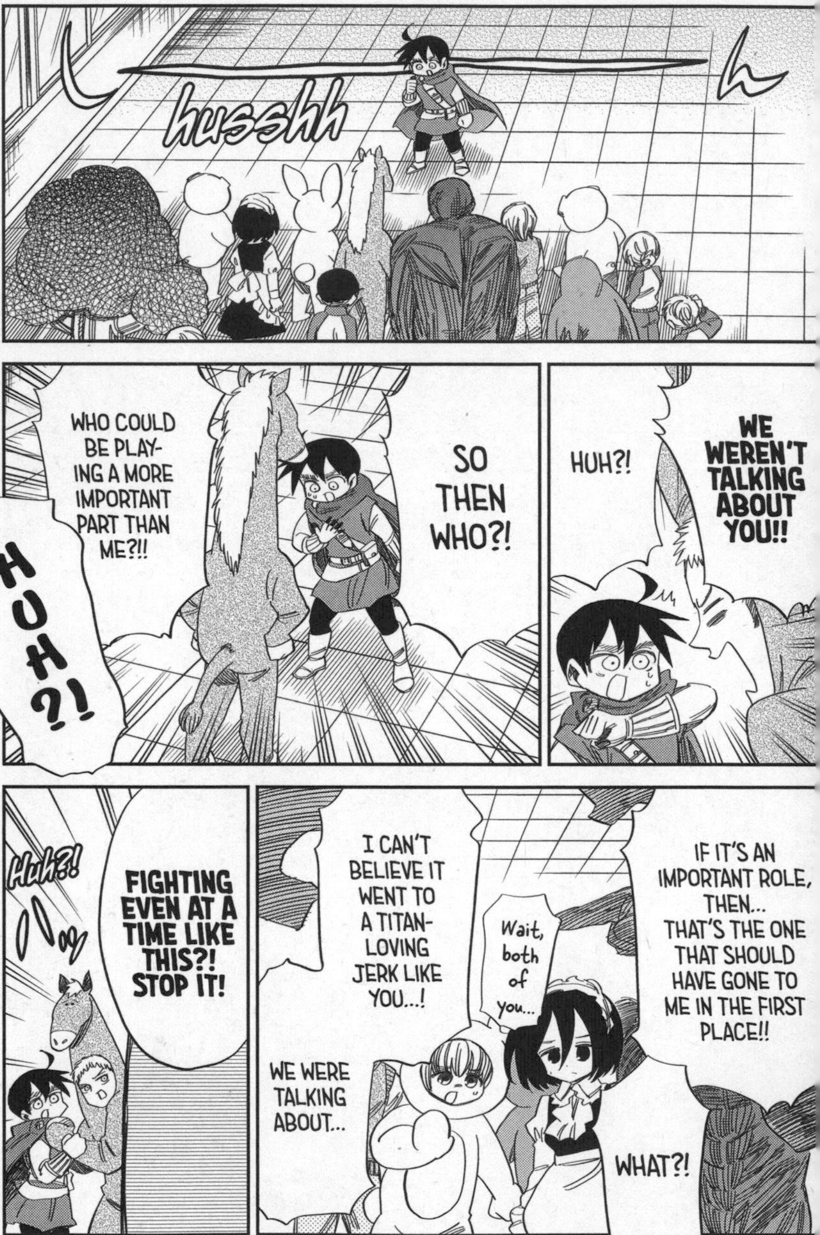
husshh
WE WEREN'T TALKING ABOUT YOU!!
HUH?!
SO THEN WHO?!
WHO COULD BE PLAY-ING A MORE IMPORTANT PART THAN ME?!!
HUH?!
IF IT'S AN IMPORTANT ROLE, THEN... THAT'S THE ONE THAT SHOULD HAVE GONE TO ME IN THE FIRST PLACE!!
I CAN'T BELIEVE IT WENT TO A TITAN-LOVING JERK LIKE YOU...!
Wait, both of you...
WE WERE TALKING ABOUT...
WHAT?!
FIGHTING EVEN AT A TIME LIKE THIS?! STOP IT!
Huh?!

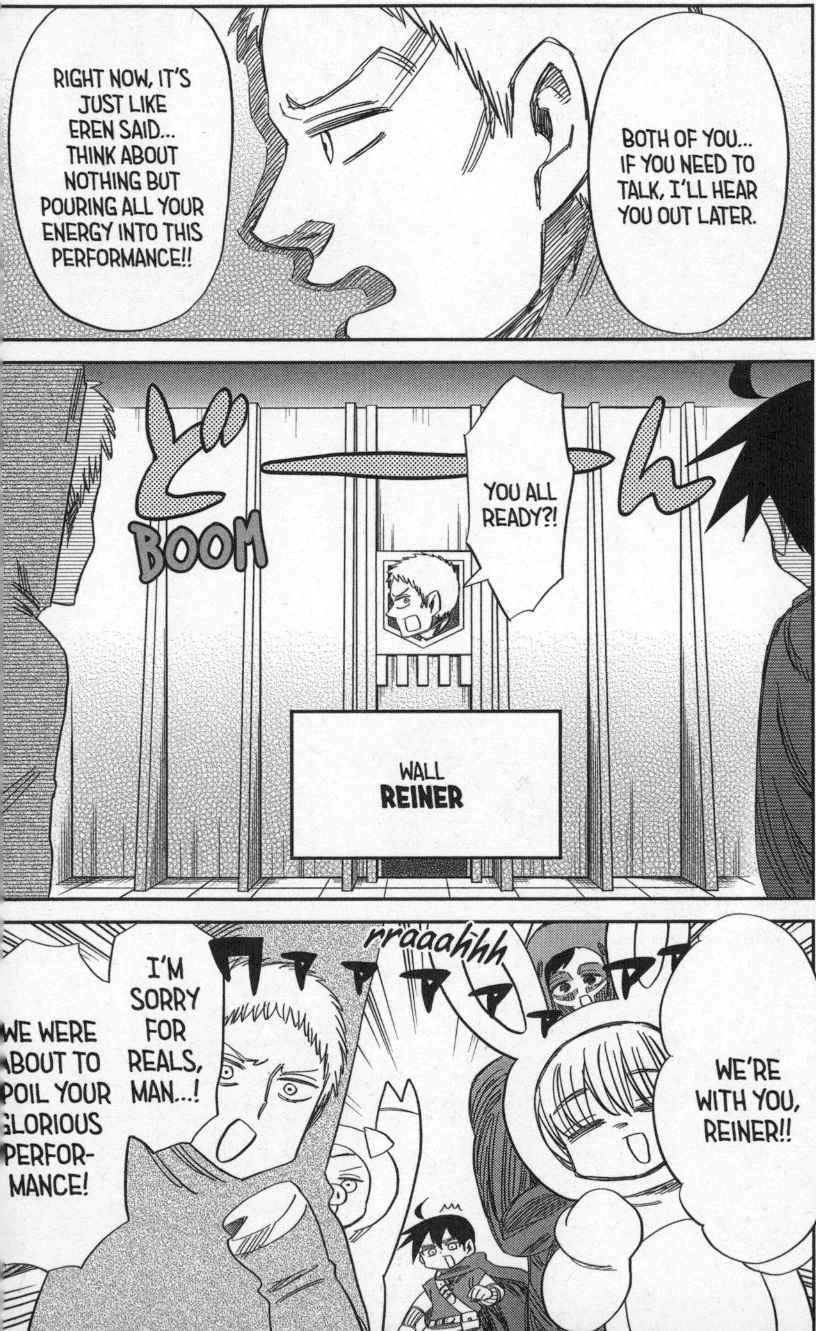

BOTH OF YOU... IF YOU NEED TO TALK, I'LL HEAR YOU OUT LATER.
RIGHT NOW, IT'S JUST LIKE EREN SAID... THINK ABOUT NOTHING BUT POURING ALL YOUR ENERGY INTO THIS PERFORMANCE!!
YOU ALL READY?!
どーん
BOOM
WALL
REINER
WE'RE WITH YOU, REINER!!
rraaahhh
I'M SORRY FOR REALS, MAN...!
WE WERE ABOUT TO SPOIL YOUR GLORIOUS PERFOR-MANCE!

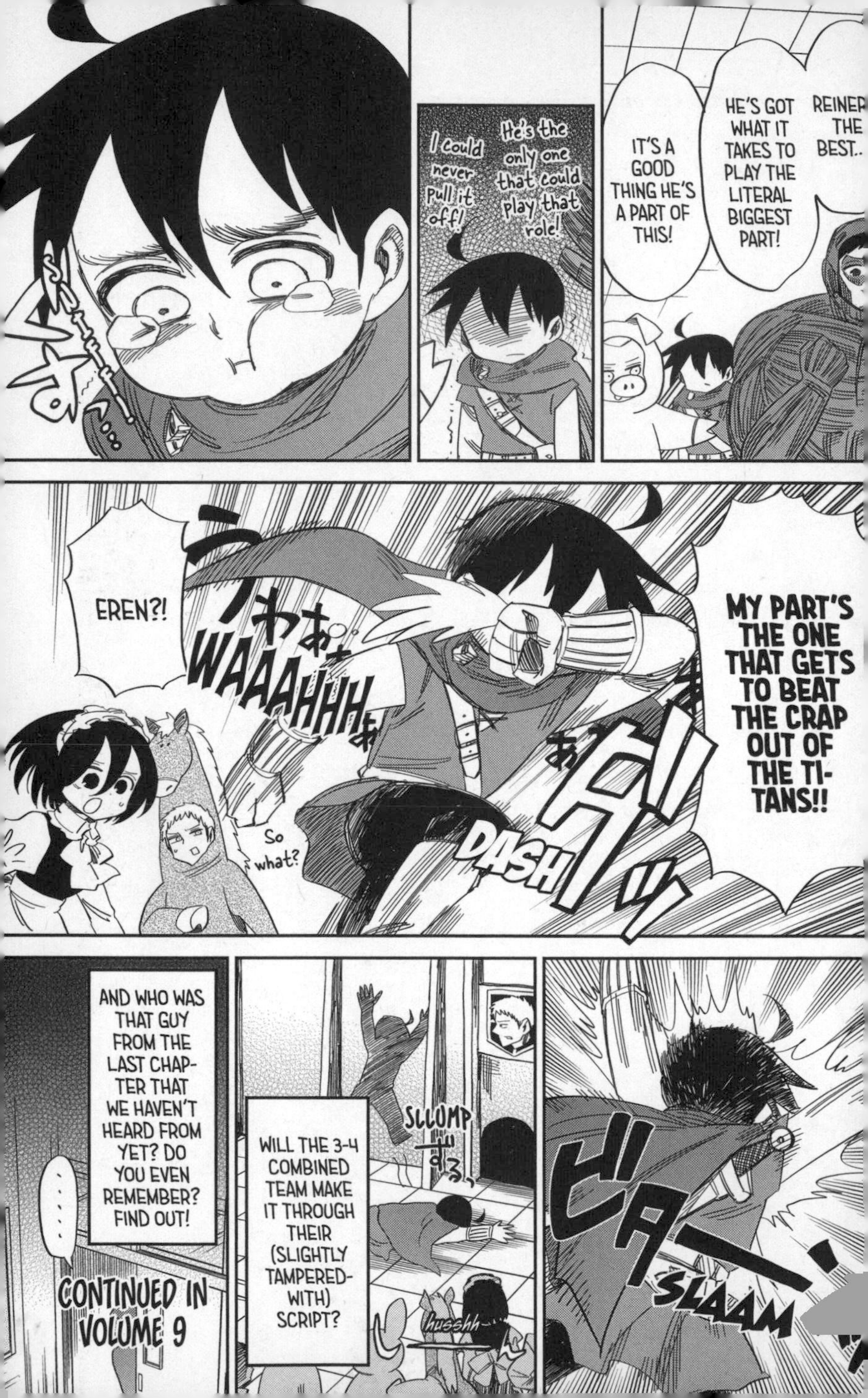
REINER THE BEST..
HE'S GOT WHAT IT TAKES TO PLAY THE LITERAL BIGGEST PART!
IT'S A GOOD THING HE'S A PART OF THIS!
He's the only one that could play that role!
I could never pull it off!
MY PART'S THE ONE THAT GETS TO BEAT THE CRAP OUT OF THE TI-TANS!!
DASH
WAAAAHHH
EREN?!
So what?
SLAAM
SLLUMP
WILL THE 3-4 COMBINED TEAM MAKE IT THROUGH THEIR (SLIGHTLY TAMPERED-WITH) SCRIPT?
husshh
AND WHO WAS THAT GUY FROM THE LAST CHAPTER THAT WE HAVEN'T HEARD FROM YET? DO YOU EVEN REMEMBER? FIND OUT!
CONTINUED IN VOLUME 9

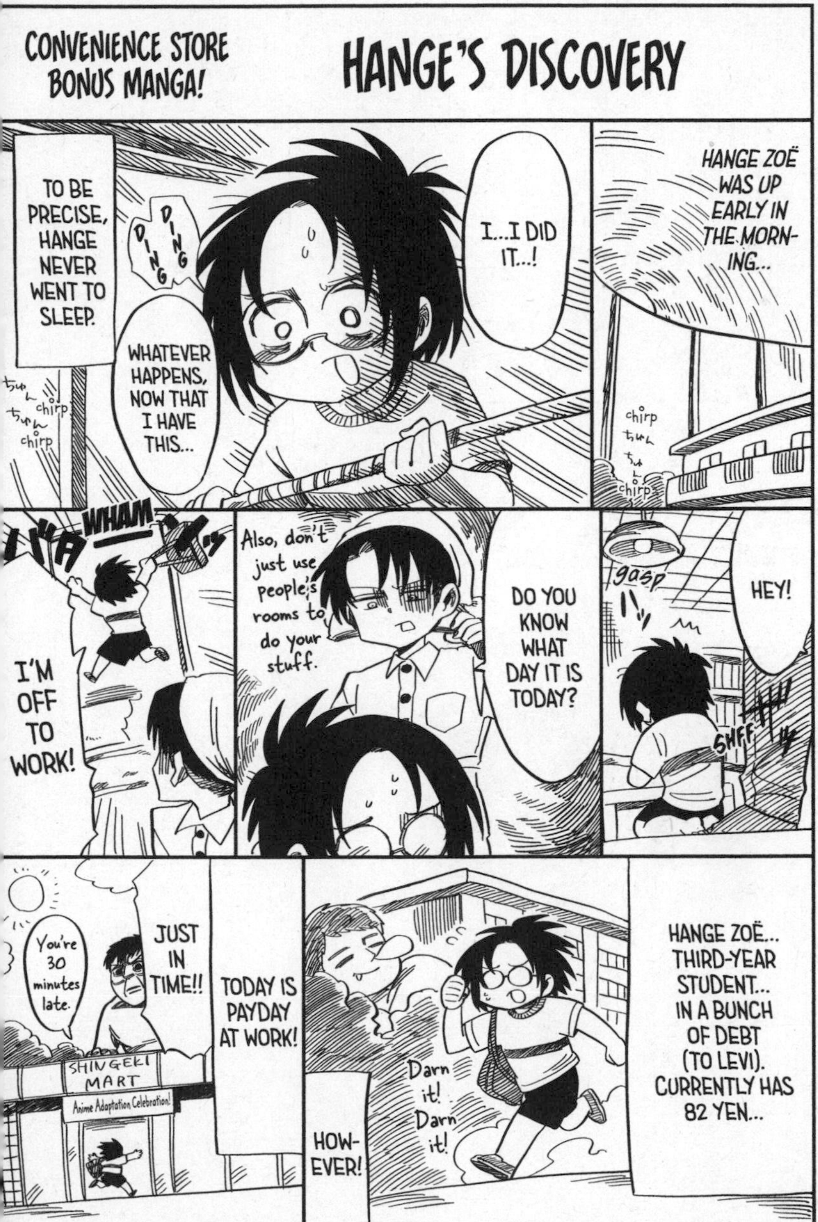
CONVENIENCE STORE BONUS MANGA!
HANGE'S DISCOVERY
HANGE ZOË WAS UP EARLY IN THE MORNING...
chirp
chirp
I...I DID IT...!
DING DING
WHATEVER HAPPENS, NOW THAT I HAVE THIS...
TO BE PRECISE, HANGE NEVER WENT TO SLEEP.
chirp
chirp
HEY!
gasp
SHFF
DO YOU KNOW WHAT DAY IT IS TODAY?
Also, don't just use people's rooms to do your stuff.
WHAM
I'M OFF TO WORK!
HANGE ZOË... THIRD-YEAR STUDENT... IN A BUNCH OF DEBT (TO LEVI). CURRENTLY HAS 82 YEN...
Darn it! Darn it!
HOW-EVER!
TODAY IS PAYDAY AT WORK!
JUST IN TIME!!
You're 30 minutes late.
SHINGEKI MART
Anime Adaptation Celebration!

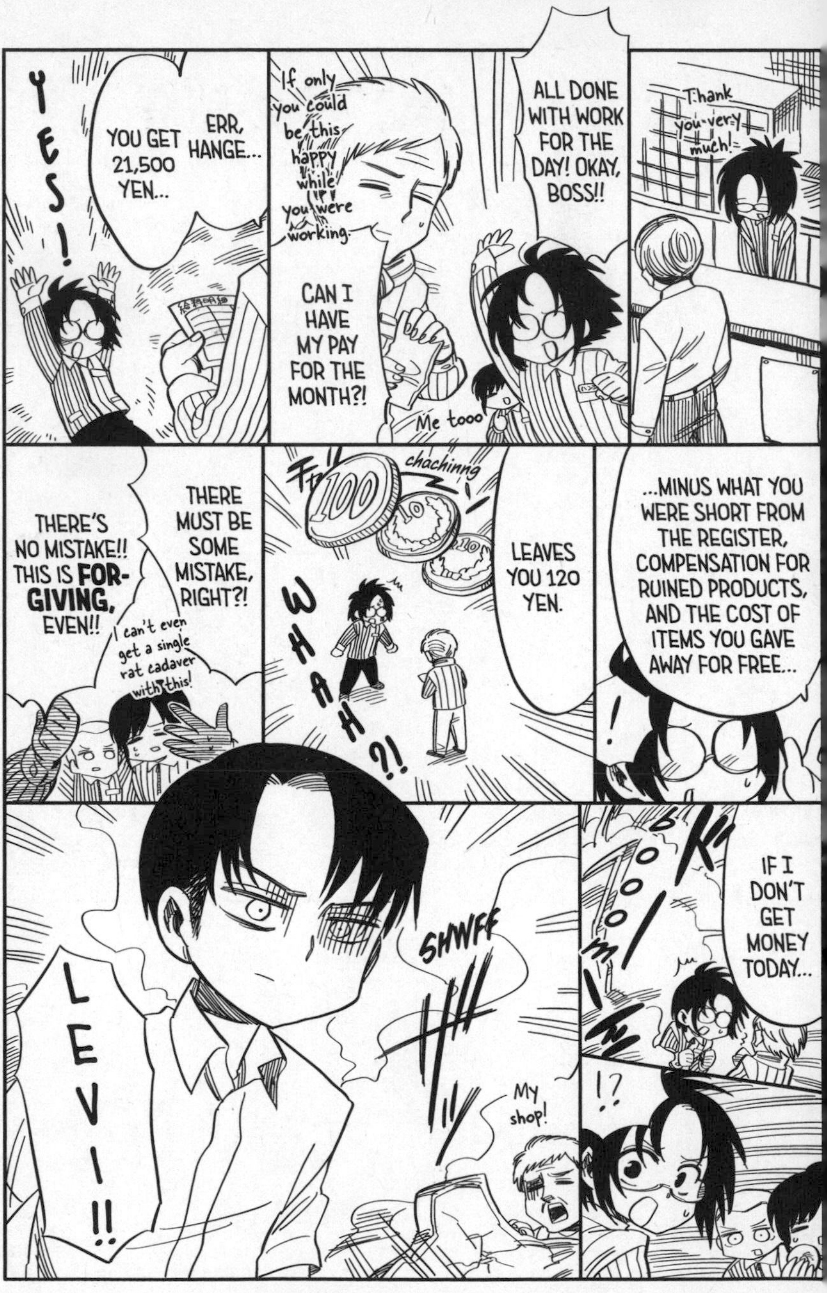
T:hank you very much!
ALL DONE WITH WORK FOR THE DAY! OKAY, BOSS!!
Me tooo
CAN I HAVE MY PAY FOR THE MONTH?!
If only you could be this happy while you were working.
ERR, HANGE...
YOU GET 21,500 YEN...
YES!
...MINUS WHAT YOU WERE SHORT FROM THE REGISTER, COMPENSATION FOR RUINED PRODUCTS, AND THE COST OF ITEMS YOU GAVE AWAY FOR FREE...
!
LEAVES YOU 120 YEN.
chachinng
WHAAAH?!
THERE MUST BE SOME MISTAKE, RIGHT?!
THERE'S NO MISTAKE!! THIS IS **FORGIVING,** EVEN!!
I can't even get a single rat cadaver with this!
IF I DON'T GET MONEY TODAY...
!?
SHWFF
My shop!
LEVI!!

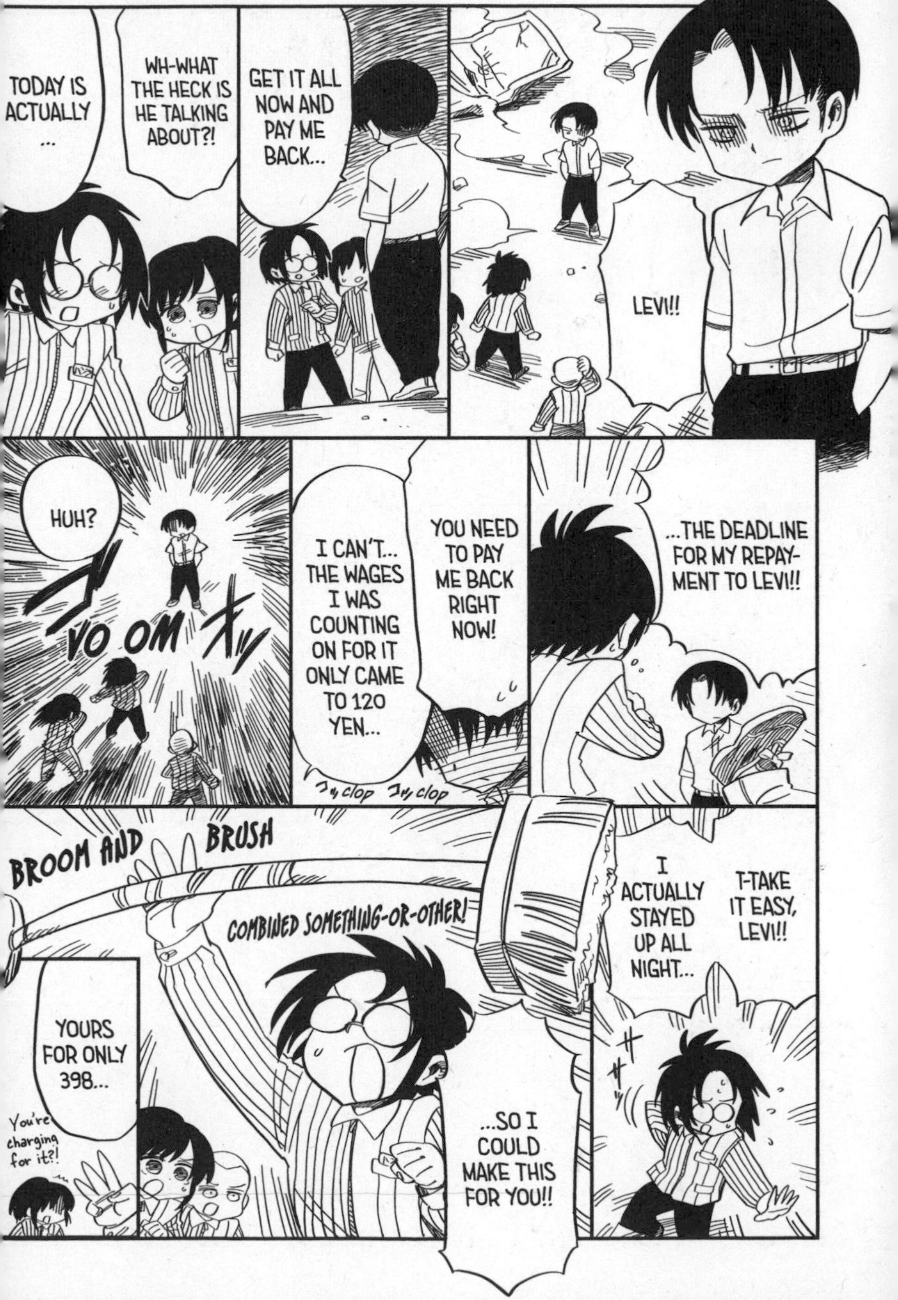
LEVI!!
GET IT ALL NOW AND PAY ME BACK...
WH-WHAT THE HECK IS HE TALKING ABOUT?!
TODAY IS ACTUALLY ...
...THE DEADLINE FOR MY REPAYMENT TO LEVI!!
YOU NEED TO PAY ME BACK RIGHT NOW!
I CAN'T... THE WAGES I WAS COUNTING ON FOR IT ONLY CAME TO 120 YEN...
clop clop
HUH?
VO OM
T-TAKE IT EASY, LEVI!!
I ACTUALLY STAYED UP ALL NIGHT...
...SO I COULD MAKE THIS FOR YOU!!
BROOM AND BRUSH
COMBINED SOMETHING-OR-OTHER!
YOURS FOR ONLY 398...
You're charging for it?!

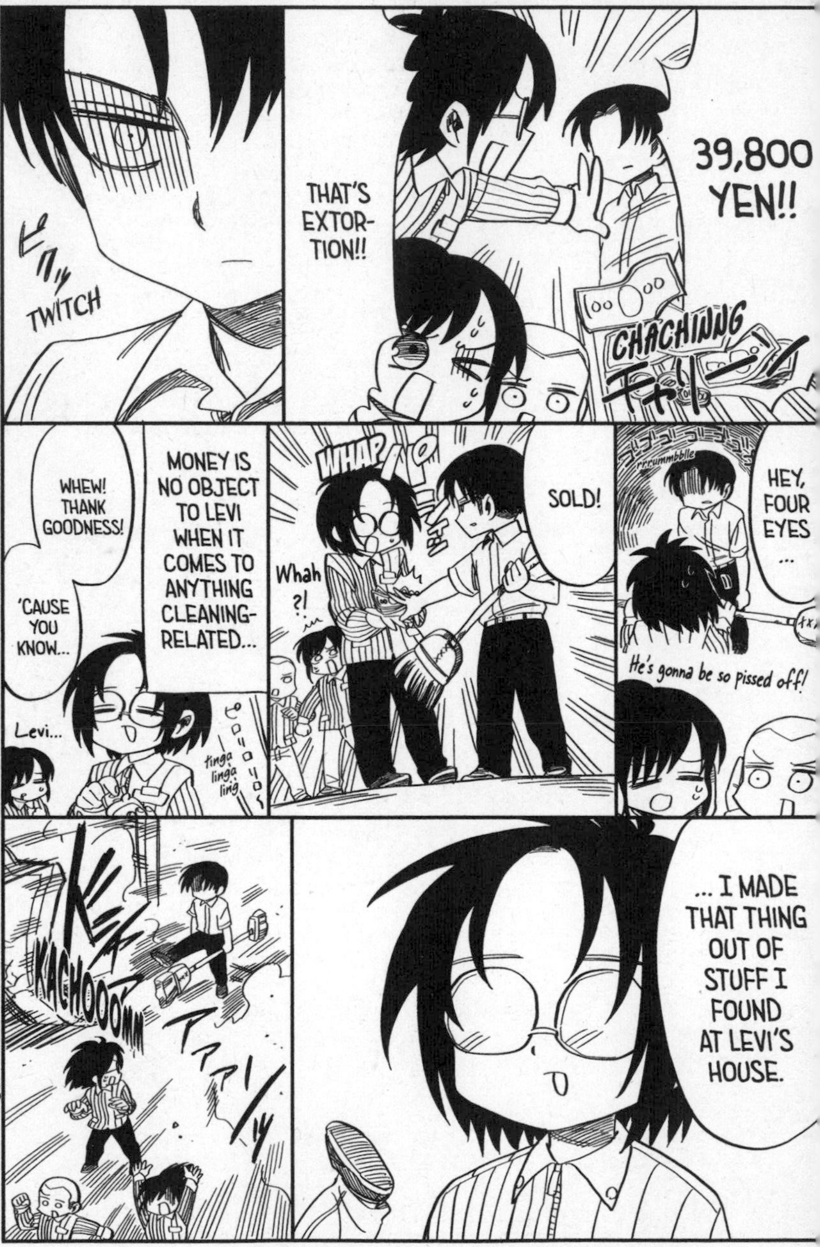
39,800 YEN!!
THAT'S EXTOR-TION!!
CHACHINNG
TWITCH
HEY, FOUR EYES ...
rrrummbbllle
He's gonna be so pissed off!
SOLD!
WHAP
Whah ?!
MONEY IS NO OBJECT TO LEVI WHEN IT COMES TO ANYTHING CLEANING-RELATED...
WHEW! THANK GOODNESS!
'CAUSE YOU KNOW...
Levi...
tinga linga ling
... I MADE THAT THING OUT OF STUFF I FOUND AT LEVI'S HOUSE.
KACHOOOMM

The End

(OF HANGE'S LIFE)

Translation Notes:

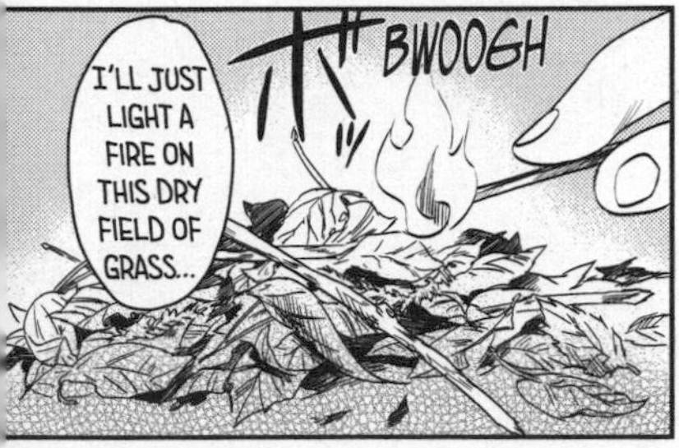
I'LL JUST LIGHT A FIRE ON THIS DRY FIELD OF GRASS...
BWOOGH

Page 5, Baked sweet potatoes

This first chapter highlights several Japanese traditions related to winter (and summer). The first of these is baking sweet potatoes over or within a campfire. Baked Japanese sweet potatoes are a treat at any time, but a steaming-hot sweet potato directly from a fire is especially welcome during the cold winter months. Still, it usually takes about an hour to cook a decently-sized sweet potato, so it would be a bit of a wait before Connie and Sasha could begin the feasting.

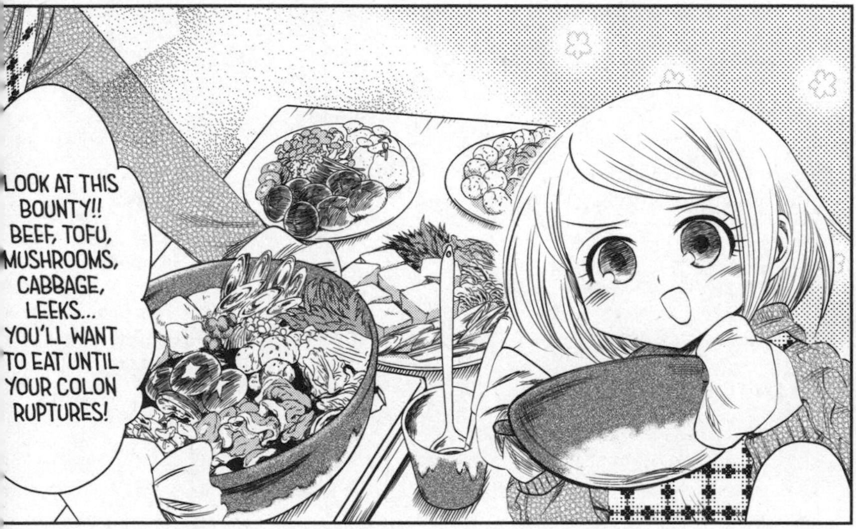
LOOK AT THIS BOUNTY!! BEEF, TOFU, MUSHROOMS, CABBAGE, LEEKS... YOU'LL WANT TO EAT UNTIL YOUR COLON RUPTURES!

Page 7, Hotpot

Another winter favorite is a main course called *nabe*. The word nabe means "pot," but when referred to as a dish, it means meats and veggies stewed in a broth and served from the pot. People then take the food directly from the pot, and either dip it in a dipping sauce or raw egg, or eat it from their rice bowl. The mix of hot veggies and meats with the cold weather makes nabe one of the things the Japanese love about winter.

Page 22, Aerobics

The calisthenics regimen that Eren is demonstrating is called *rajio taisou* in Japanese. It's basically radio-based exercises that were a staple of the Japanese people's school life (especially from the post-war period up through about the '80s). When on summer vacation, students are expected to gather on the school ground or in some other public place attended by a teacher,

and do their *rajio taisou*, getting a stamp on their stamp card for each session they attend. Sc *rajio taisou* is considered a tradition of the Japanese summer time.

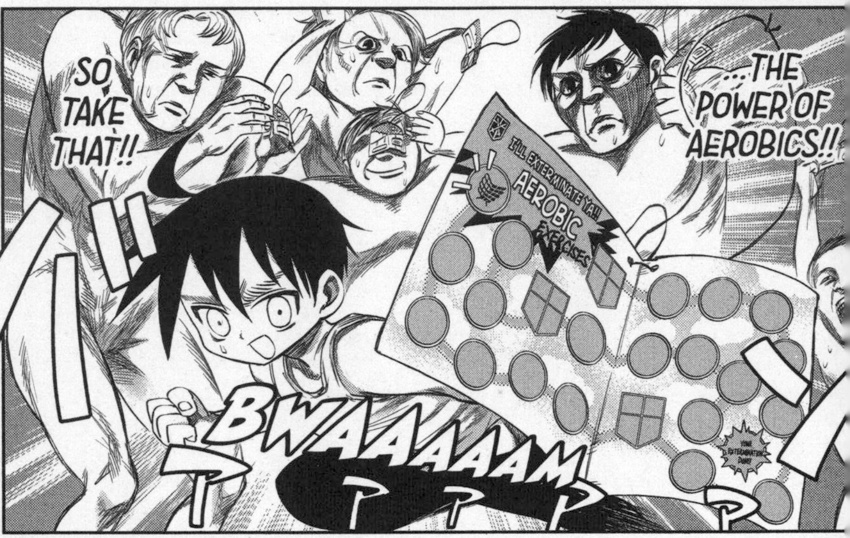
...THE POWER OF AEROBICS!!
I'LL EXTERMINATE YA!!
AEROBIC EXERCISES
BWAAAAAAM
SO, TAKE THAT!!

Page 30, No energy
One of the icons in Japanese manga, anime, and popular culture along the lines of Tezuka' Mighty Atom (Astroboy), Godzilla, and Ultraman is the children's favorite Anpanman. Since An panman is made of bread, he loses all energy when his bread is dirtied or doused with water. I this scene, Kuklo says exactly the same words when he has a full belly. It seems a full stomacl is his kryptonite.

Page 85, Sutaya
One of the largest chains of DVD rental shops (as well as selling new and used media like CDs an video games) in Japan is the chain by the name of Tsutaya. It looks like Sutaya is that chain in th Titan Junior High School universe.

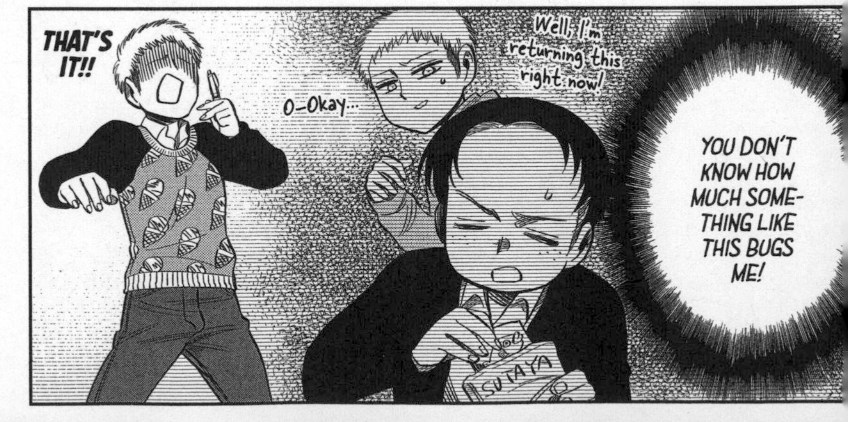
YOU DON'T KNOW HOW MUCH SOME-THING LIKE THIS BUGS ME!
Well, I'm returning this right now!
SUTAYA
O-Okay...
THAT'S IT!!

age 90, Jumping photos

 the Japanese version, they're singing a song called Yakkyuu-ken, a party song based on base-
all. At the end of each verse, everyone in the party plays rock-paper-scissors, with the loser
tripping off a piece of clothing. Reportedly, the game started in the prostitute quarters of Yo-
ohama in the late 1800s, and it later spread throughout Japan.

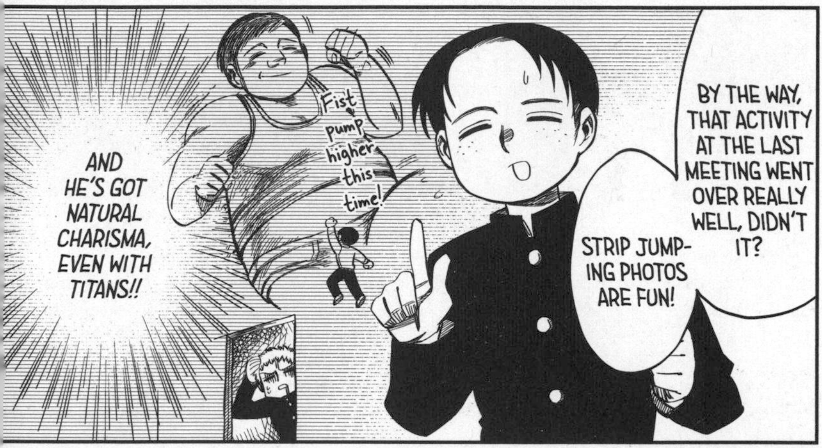
BY THE WAY, THAT ACTIVITY AT THE LAST MEETING WENT OVER REALLY WELL, DIDN'T IT?
STRIP JUMP-ING PHOTOS ARE FUN!
Fist pump higher this time!
AND HE'S GOT NATURAL CHARISMA, EVEN WITH TITANS!!

age 101, Prepaid transport card

here are several electronic systems for paying train fares throughout Japan, and generally
hese are most used by adults for commuting to and from work. So using these cards is thought
f as an adult thing to do.

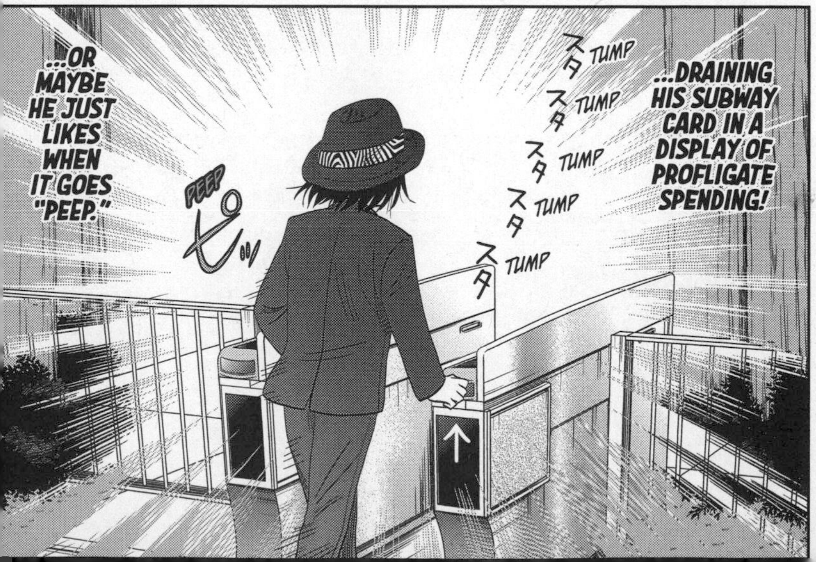
...DRAINING HIS SUBWAY CARD IN A DISPLAY OF PROFLIGATE SPENDING!
スタ TUMP
スタ TUMP
スタ TUMP
スタ TUMP
スタ TUMP
...OR MAYBE HE JUST LIKES WHEN IT GOES "PEEP."
PEEP
ピ

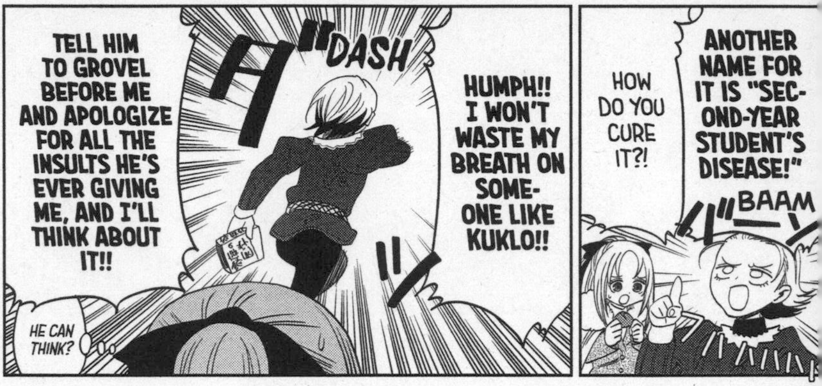
ANOTHER NAME FOR IT IS "SECOND-YEAR STUDENT'S DISEASE!"
HOW DO YOU CURE IT?!
BAAM
HUMPH!! I WON'T WASTE MY BREATH ON SOMEONE LIKE KUKLO!!
DASH
TELL HIM TO GROVEL BEFORE ME AND APOLOGIZE FOR ALL THE INSULTS HE'S EVER GIVING ME, AND I'LL THINK ABOUT IT!!
HE CAN THINK?

Page 107, Second-year student's disease
In this case, Xavi is lying to scare Kuklo. Second-year student's disease is the condition of gen eral apathy toward studies that sometimes strikes second-year students in junior high or hig school.

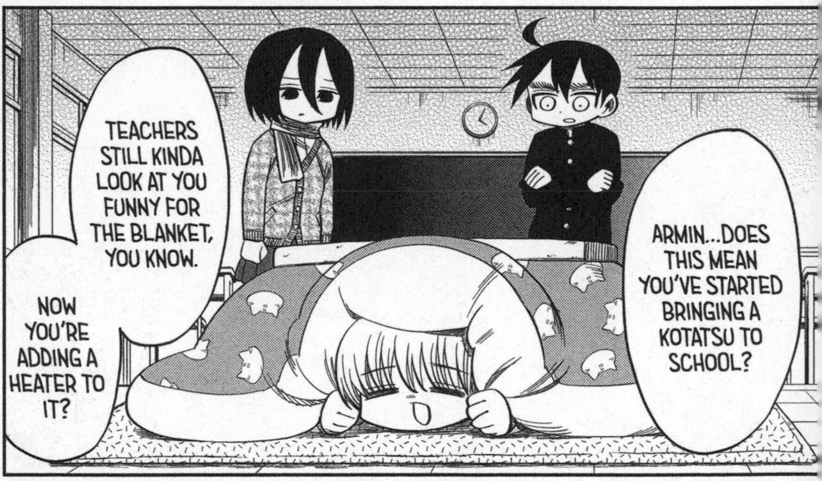
ARMIN...DOES THIS MEAN YOU'VE STARTED BRINGING A KOTATSU TO SCHOOL?
TEACHERS STILL KINDA LOOK AT YOU FUNNY FOR THE BLANKET, YOU KNOW.
NOW YOU'RE ADDING A HEATER TO IT?

Page 133, Kotatsu
A kotatsu is a low-level table with a heating element underneath and a futon comforter place between the frame and tabletop. It allows those sitting at the table to have their legs nice an warm. Since most Japanese homes lack central heating, a kotatsu makes sense. With toasty warm legs, all you really need is a thick, padded half-coat to wear while seated, and your whol body feels warm. In summertime the futon is removed for a low living-room table.

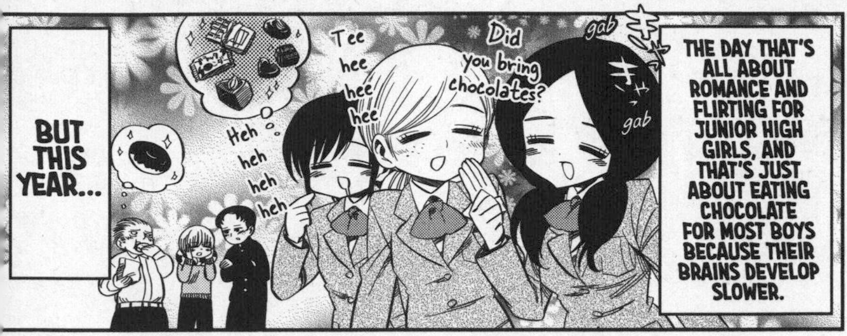
THE DAY THAT'S ALL ABOUT ROMANCE AND FLIRTING FOR JUNIOR HIGH GIRLS, AND THAT'S JUST ABOUT EATING CHOCOLATE FOR MOST BOYS BECAUSE THEIR BRAINS DEVELOP SLOWER.
gab
gab
Did you bring chocolates?
Tee hee hee hee
Heh heh heh heh
BUT THIS YEAR...

Page 171, Valentine's Day
On Valentine's Day in Japan, girls give chocolate to boys (if they're lucky), and the boys reciprocate with cookies one month later on White Day.

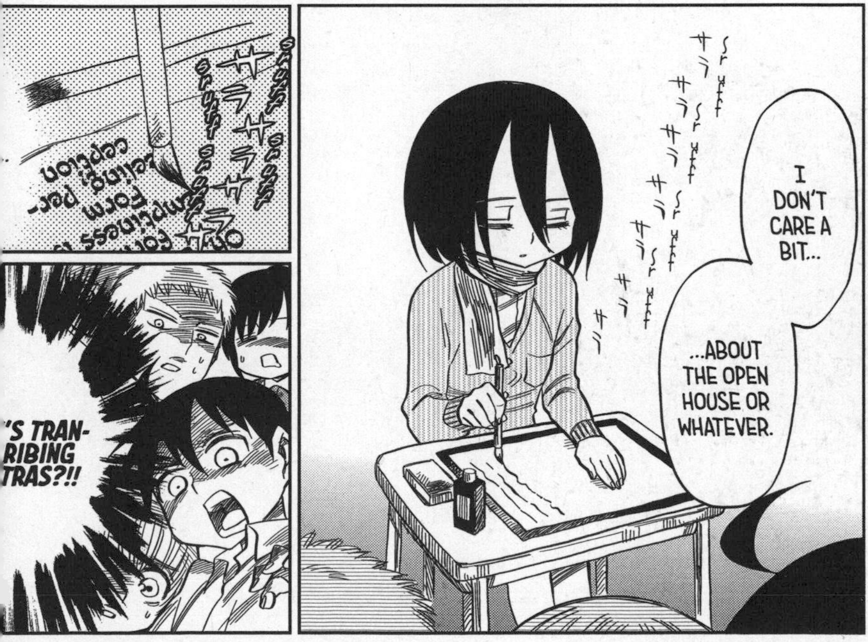
I DON'T CARE A BIT...
...ABOUT THE OPEN HOUSE OR WHATEVER.
'S TRAN-RIBING TRAS?!!

Page 264, Sutras
Mikasa is copying the "Maka hannya haramita shingyo" sutra here. A sutra is a collection of aphorisms or principles in Buddhism, and hand-copying sutras is considered an expression of piety.

Page 279, Hamburger
Mikasa actually says "oroshi hamburger," a beef patty with grated horseradish on top.

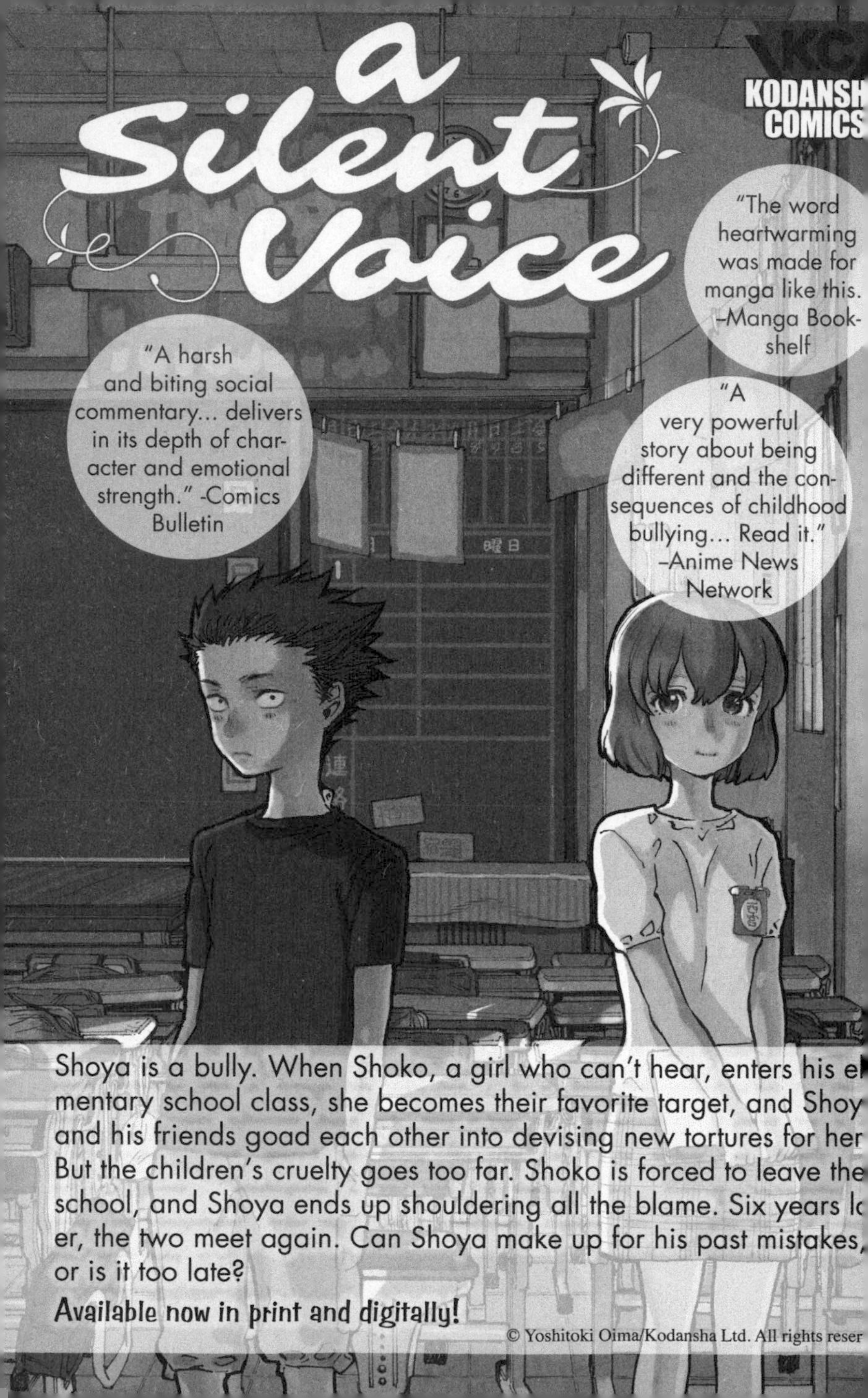
a Silent Voice
KODANSH
COMICS
"The word heartwarming was made for manga like this. –Manga Book-shelf
"A harsh and biting social commentary... delivers in its depth of char-acter and emotional strength." -Comics Bulletin
"A very powerful story about being different and the con-sequences of childhood bullying… Read it." –Anime News Network
Shoya is a bully. When Shoko, a girl who can't hear, enters his el
mentary school class, she becomes their favorite target, and Shoy
and his friends goad each other into devising new tortures for her
But the children's cruelty goes too far. Shoko is forced to leave the
school, and Shoya ends up shouldering all the blame. Six years la
er, the two meet again. Can Shoya make up for his past mistakes,
or is it too late?
Available now in print and digitally!
© Yoshitoki Oima/Kodansha Ltd. All rights reser

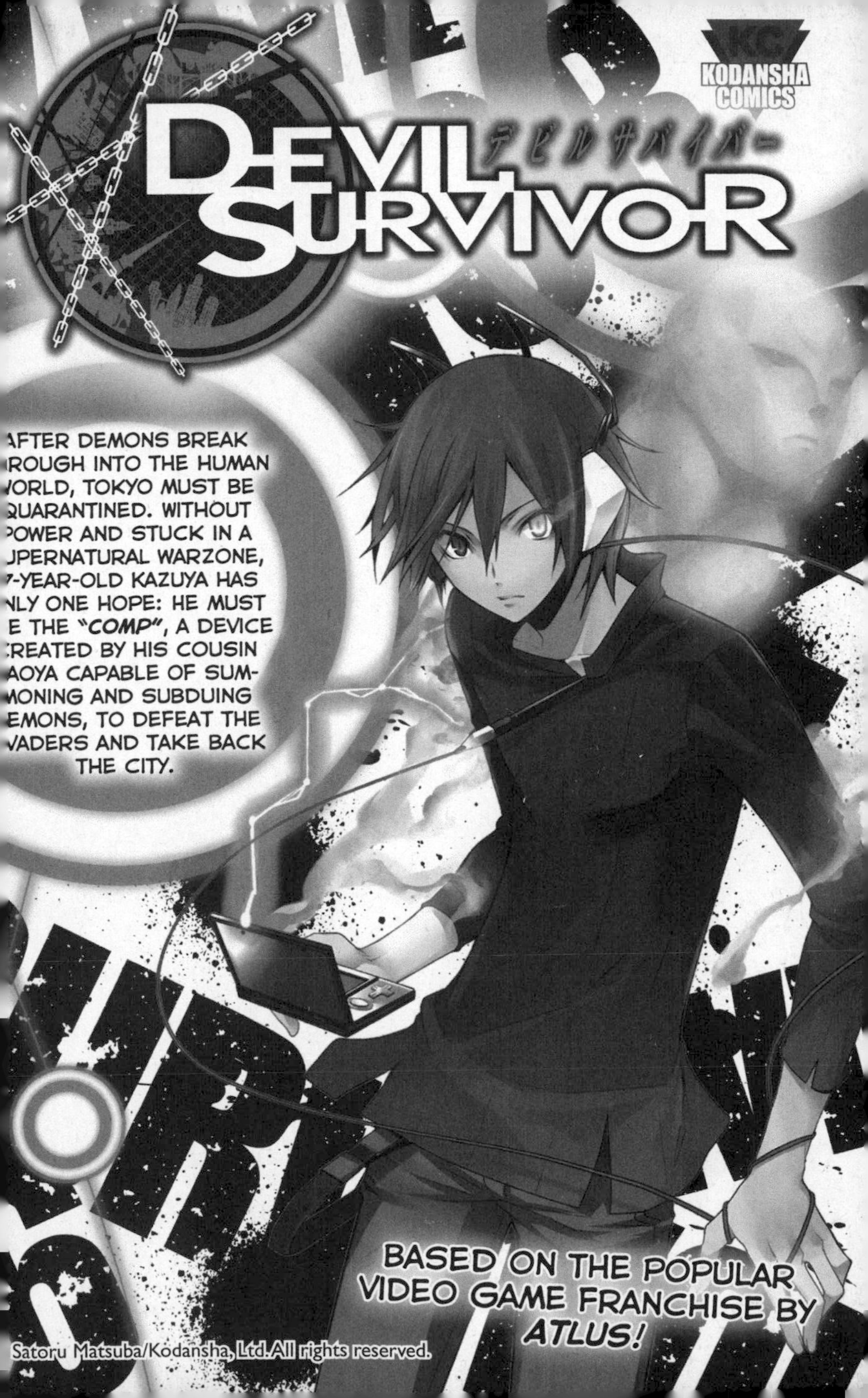
KC
KODANSHA COMICS
DEVIL SURVIVOR
デビルサバイバー
AFTER DEMONS BREAK ROUGH INTO THE HUMAN ORLD, TOKYO MUST BE QUARANTINED. WITHOUT POWER AND STUCK IN A UPERNATURAL WARZONE, 7-YEAR-OLD KAZUYA HAS NLY ONE HOPE: HE MUST E THE "COMP", A DEVICE REATED BY HIS COUSIN AOYA CAPABLE OF SUM-MONING AND SUBDUING EMONS, TO DEFEAT THE VADERS AND TAKE BACK THE CITY.
BASED ON THE POPULAR VIDEO GAME FRANCHISE BY ATLUS!
Satoru Matsuba/Kodansha, Ltd. All rights reserved.

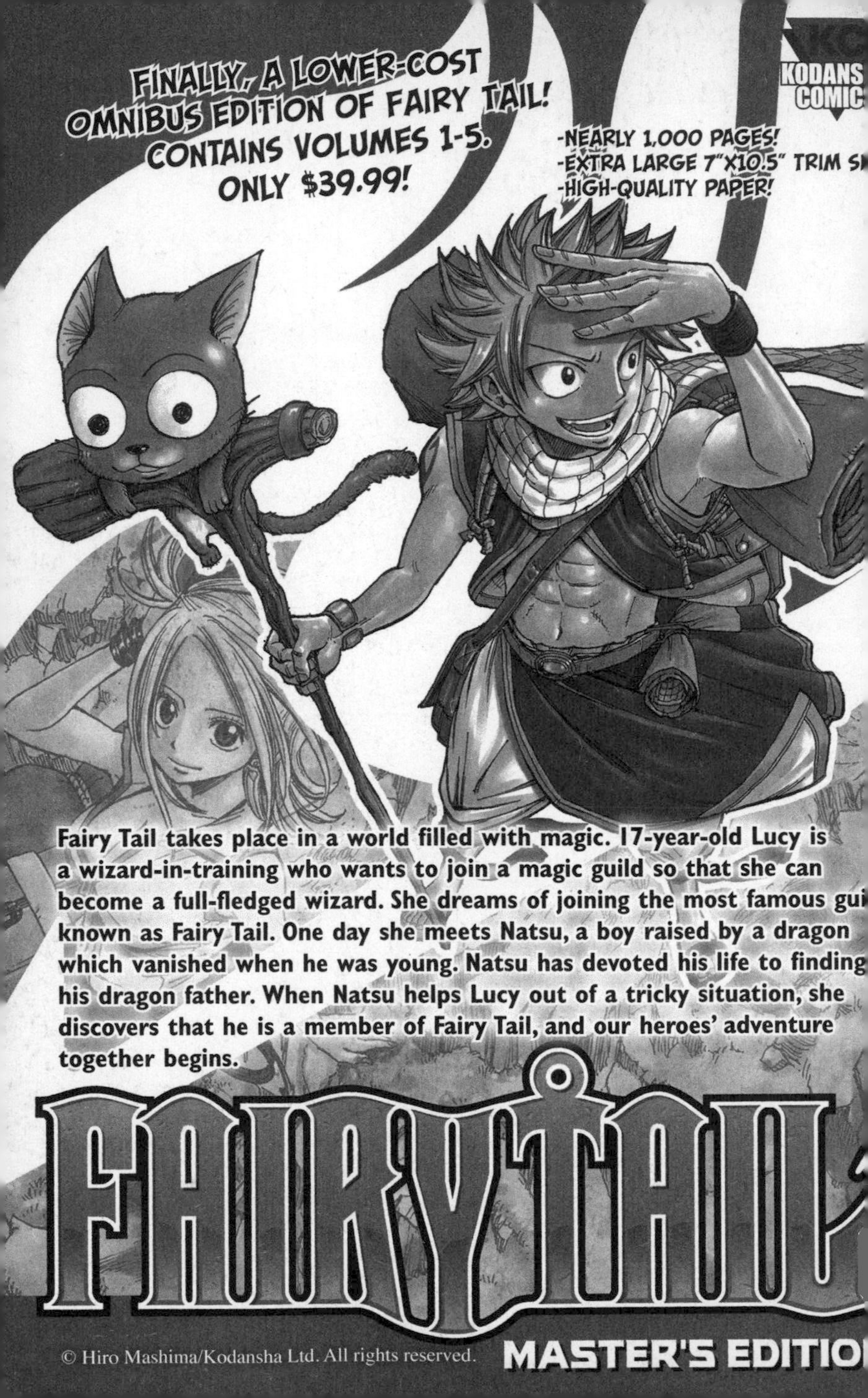
FINALLY, A LOWER-COST OMNIBUS EDITION OF FAIRY TAIL! CONTAINS VOLUMES 1-5. ONLY $39.99!
KC KODANS COMIC
-NEARLY 1,000 PAGES!
-EXTRA LARGE 7"X10.5" TRIM SI
-HIGH-QUALITY PAPER!
Fairy Tail takes place in a world filled with magic. 17-year-old Lucy is a wizard-in-training who wants to join a magic guild so that she can become a full-fledged wizard. She dreams of joining the most famous gui known as Fairy Tail. One day she meets Natsu, a boy raised by a dragon which vanished when he was young. Natsu has devoted his life to finding his dragon father. When Natsu helps Lucy out of a tricky situation, she discovers that he is a member of Fairy Tail, and our heroes' adventure together begins.
FAIRY TAIL
© Hiro Mashima/Kodansha Ltd. All rights reserved.
MASTER'S EDITIO

INUYASHIKI

A superhero like none
you've ever seen, from the
creator of "Gantz"!

Ichiro Inuyashiki is down on his luck. He looks much older than his 58 years, his children despise him, and his wife thinks he's a useless coward. So when he's diagnosed with stomach cancer and given three months to live, it seems the only one who'll miss him is his dog.

Then a blinding light fills the sky, and the old man is killed... only to wake up later in a body he almost recognizes as his own. Can it be that Ichiro Inuyashiki is no longer human?

COMES IN EXTRA-LARGE EDITIONS WITH COLOR PAGES!

Maria
THE VIRGIN WITCH

PURITY AND POWER

As a war to determine the rightful ruler of medieval France ravages the land, the witch Maria decides she will not stand idly by as men kill each other in the name of God and glory. Using her powerful magic, she summons various beasts and demons —even going as far as using a succubus to seduce soldiers into submission under the veil of night—— all to stop the needless slaughter. However, after the Archangel Michael puts an end to her meddling, he curses her to lose her powers if she ever gives up her virginity. Will she forgo the forbidden fruit of adulthood in order to bring an end to the merciless machine of war? Available now in print and digitally!

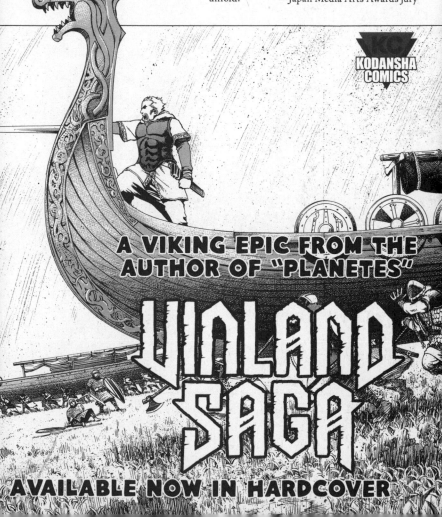

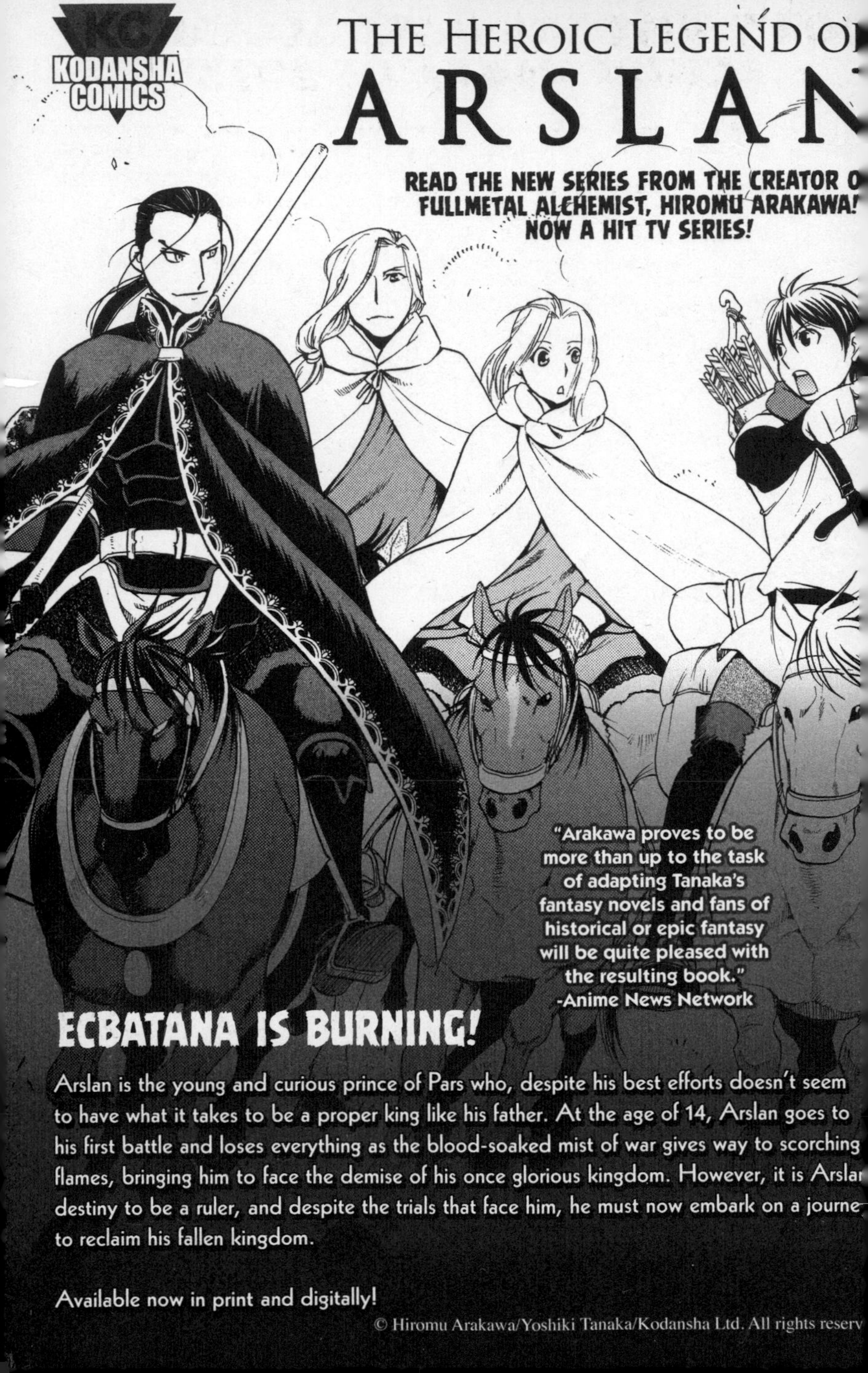
KC KODANSHA COMICS
THE HEROIC LEGEND O
ARSLAN
READ THE NEW SERIES FROM THE CREATOR O
FULLMETAL ALCHEMIST, HIROMU ARAKAWA!
NOW A HIT TV SERIES!
"Arakawa proves to be more than up to the task of adapting Tanaka's fantasy novels and fans of historical or epic fantasy will be quite pleased with the resulting book."
-Anime News Network
ECBATANA IS BURNING!
Arslan is the young and curious prince of Pars who, despite his best efforts doesn't seem to have what it takes to be a proper king like his father. At the age of 14, Arslan goes to his first battle and loses everything as the blood-soaked mist of war gives way to scorching flames, bringing him to face the demise of his once glorious kingdom. However, it is Arslar destiny to be a ruler, and despite the trials that face him, he must now embark on a journe to reclaim his fallen kingdom.
Available now in print and digitally!
© Hiromu Arakawa/Yoshiki Tanaka/Kodansha Ltd. All rights reserv

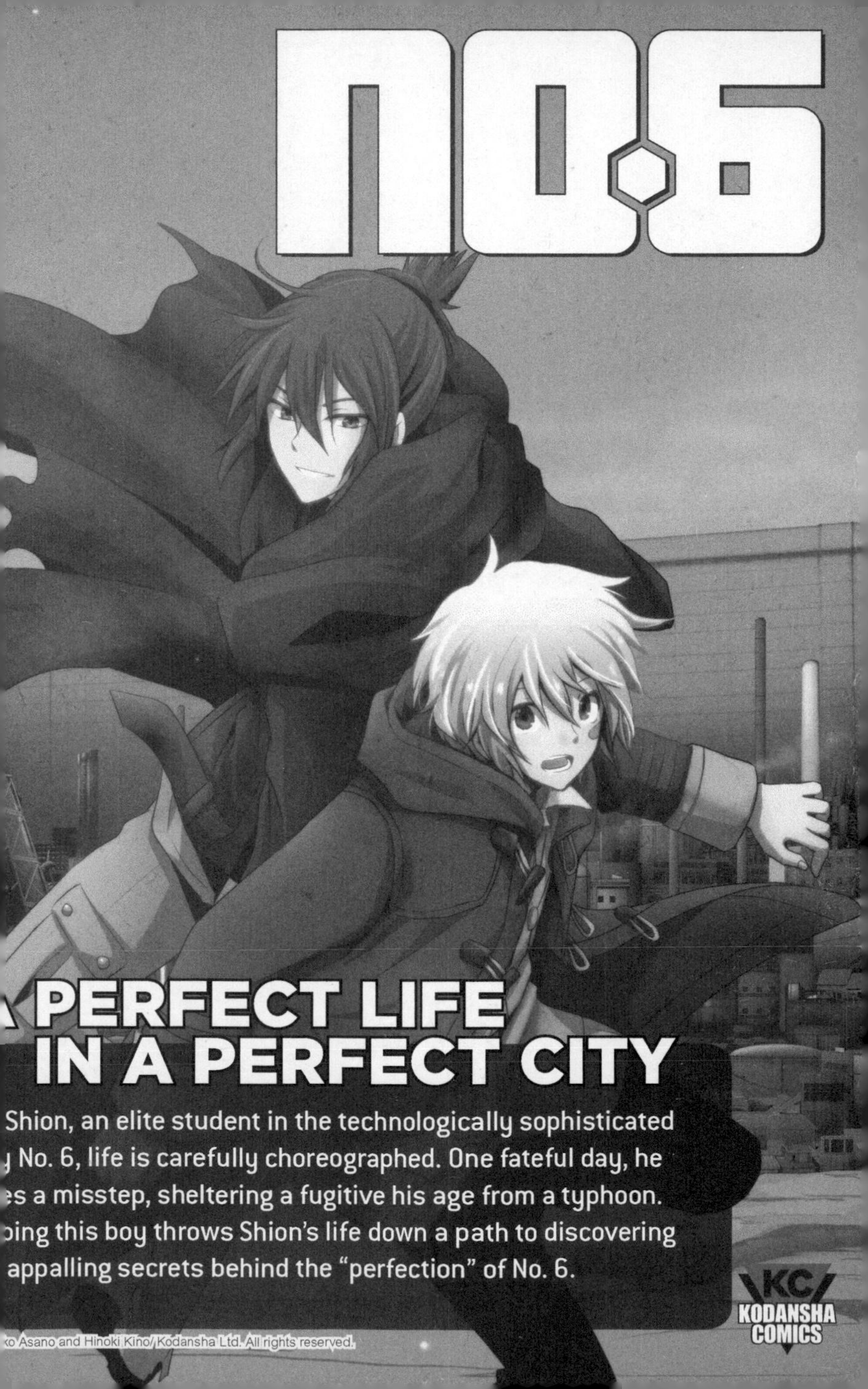NO.6
PERFECT LIFE
IN A PERFECT CITY
Shion, an elite student in the technologically sophisticated
No. 6, life is carefully choreographed. One fateful day, he
es a misstep, sheltering a fugitive his age from a typhoon.
ping this boy throws Shion's life down a path to discovering
appalling secrets behind the "perfection" of No. 6.
KC
KODANSHA COMICS
ko Asano and Hinoki Kino/ Kodansha Ltd. All rights reserved.

A Kodansha Comics Trade Paperback Original
Attack on Titan: Junior High volume 4 copyright © 2015 Saki Nakagawa/ Hajime Isayama
English translation copyright © 2015 Saki Nakagawa/Hajime Isayama

Published in the United States by Kodansha Comics, an imprint of Kodansha USA Publishing, LLC, New York.

Publication rights for this English edition arranged through Kodansha Ltd, Tokyo.

First published in Japan in 2015 by Kodansha Ltd., Tokyo as *Shingeki! Kyojin chûgakkô*, volumes 7 and 8.

ISBN 978-1-63236-113-4

Original cover design by Takashi Shimoyama/Saya Takagi (Red Rooster)

Printed in the United States of America.

www.kodanshacomics.com

9 8 7 6 5 4 3 2 1
Translation: William Flanagan and Kumar Sivasubramanian
Lettering: AndWorld Design
Editing and adaptation: Ben Applegate
Kodansha Comics edition cover design by Phil Balsman

You are going the *wrong way!*

Manga is a *completely* different type of reading experience.

To start at the *BEGINNING,* go to the *END!*

That's right! Authentic manga is read the tradition-al Japanese way--from right to left, exactly the opposite of how American books are read. It's easy to follow: just go to the other end of the book, and read each page--and each panel--from the right side to the left side, starting at the top right. Now you're experiencing manga as it was meant to be.